AN AMERICAN IN THE BASEMENT

The Betrayal of Captain Scott Speicher and the Cover-up of His Death

Amy Waters Yarsinske

Published by:
Trine Day LLC
PO Box 577
Walterville, OR 97489
1-800-556-2012
www.TrineDay.com
publisher@TrineDay.net

Library of Congress Control Number: 2013934343

Yarsinske, Amy Waters
An American in theBasement: The Betrayal of Captain Scott Speicher and the Cover-up of His Death–1st ed.
p. cm.
Includes index and references.
Epud (ISBN-13) 978-1-937584-21-4
Mobi (ISBN-13) 978-1-937584-22-1
Print (ISBN-13) 978-1-937584-20-7
1. Prisoners of war -- United States. 2. Speicher, Michael Scott. 3. Persian Gulf War, 1991 -- Aerial operations, American . 4. Fighter pilots -- United States -- Biography. I. Yarsinske, Amy Waters. II. Title

First Edition
10 9 8 7 6 5 4 3 2

Printed in the USA
Distribution to the Trade by:
Independent Publishers Group (IPG)
814 North Franklin Street
Chicago, Illinois 60610
312.337.0747
www.ipgbook.com

Publisher's Foreword

And when at length her course is run,
Her work for home and country done,
Of all the souls that in her sailed
Let not one life in thee have failed;
But hear from heaven our sailor's cry,
And grant eternal life on high!

– Author and date unknown

The law of unintended consequences pushes us ceaselessly through the years, permitting no pause for perspective.

– Richard Schickel

For he makes his sun rise on the evil and on the good, and sends rain on the just and on the unjust.

– Matthew 5:45

Over the years I have learned that there are "fail-safe" devices woven into the network of our societal synapses – archetypal dynamics that allow personal intuitions to flower, bear fruit and thereby disrupt malevolent consequences, tipping the scales towards the common good. Honor is one of these archetypes.

But in the late summer of 1969, as my father and a professor friend explained the way of the world to me, I was, to say the least, flabbergasted, if not completely nonplussed. For they told me that war was not about what I had been led to believe. That our news wasn't news, but "sway pieces," and that there were forces in the shadows, "secret societies" my father called them, which were playing huge "games" with the world. These forces were using "psychological warfare" to effect change within our Republic and body politic.

Alongside these revelations, my father told me of his intelligence career, a subject that hadn't ever been broached before. He had left the CIA ten years earlier, after a stint that had begun as an exchange student to China in 1936 and expanded in World War II with the OSS and G-2 (Military Intelligence). His last overt job, before going covert in the early fifties, was as Branch Chief, Head of East Asia Analysis Office.

My head was spinning, having been told that the war in Vietnam was being fought as a "lose scenario," so as to divide our country, engender generational conflict, and assault our Constitution. When I later mentioned some of the things my father had said, friends informed me that I was a "conspiracy theorist." So I decided to take on conspiracy theory as an intellectual discipline, which led to further investigations, and finally to this publishing venture, TrineDay, devoted to the discussion of suppressed material, and the revival of our Republic.

In Amy Waters Yarsinske's *An American in the Basement*, we get to see not only the agony that comes with the failure of honor, but through its renewal, a stark reality that presents us with an opportunity to correct the record and realize a better future for all.

Maybe even get our Republic back. That is my goal. I am tired of the lies and folderol. We, the people, can get it back when our numbers reach a critical mass. Please stand up with us. Let's fight for truth, justice, liberty and our children's future. We can take our country back from the shadows!

We all owe a huge debt of gratitude to Yarsinske's tenacity, tact and grit in gathering this story. In honoring this debt we also honor the many other patriots to whom much is owed.

Above All
Not Self but Country
This we'll defend
Semper Fi!

Onwards to the Utmost of Futures,
Peace,
Kris Millegan
Publisher
TrineDay
May 8, 2013

"The greatest successes of American intelligence have come at times when an intelligence officer was able to see what others could not, dare what others would not, and refuse to give up in the face of overwhelming odds."

– George J. Tenet, director of Central Intelligence, U.S. Central Intelligence Agency, before the Senate Select Committee on Intelligence, 6 May 1997

"We sleep safe in our beds because rough men stand ready in the night to visit violence on those who would do us harm."

– George Orwell, British novelist and essayist, 1946

"To sin by silence, when we should protest, Makes cowards out of men."

– Ella Wheeler Wilcox, American poet, "Protest," *Poems of Problems*, 1914

"For here we will follow the truth wherever it may lead so long as reason is left free to combat it."

– Thomas Jefferson to William Roscoe, 27 December 1820

"And Ye shall know the Truth and the Truth shall make you free."

– John 8:32

Table of Contents

Foreword

Since the release of my first book on Scott Speicher – *No One Left Behind*[1] – significant pieces of information that stood to change public perception and military action pertaining to his case can now be told, facts that make his the seminal case in the ongoing saga of America's prisoners of war and missing in action. *An American in the Basement* documents the incredible true story of denial, deceit and deception that cost Scott Speicher his life. This work includes information that heretofore has been kept from the American public.

After reading *An American in the Basement*, each and every military operator in any Western military, and each and every parent, family member or friend of one, should seriously question the validity of the promise made by America's leadership and the military chain of command to do everything in their power to search, locate, assist and recover all prisoners of war and those missing in action. History proves that this promise is mostly political and, worse, could mean nothing at all. When you read Scott Speicher's story you'll understand why.

But first there are some clarifications that need to be made. Many of you will want to call Scott Speicher a prisoner of war and that is completely understandable. But the fact is that the Pentagon hasn't used the term since 2000. This news came as a surprise to experts in the field who were unaware of the change. The Department of Defense has replaced prisoner of war with missing-captured. "That's very interesting," observed Simon Schorno, spokesman for the Washington office of the International Committee of the Red Cross (ICRC) when asked for comment by *Time*'s Mark Thompson in the magazine's May 17, 2012 issue. "I didn't know that."[2]

"Sometimes important things are hiding in plain sight," added Eugene R. Fidell[3], who is the Florence Rogatz visiting lecturer in law at Yale Law School, cofounder and former long-time president of the National Institute of Military Justice. "This is one. Given how the [George W.] Bush administration struggled with how to characterize the Guantanamo detainees – avoiding calling them POWs – it's not surprising that people tended not to focus as sharply on the other side of the equation, where one of our people is being detained by someone else."[4]

Department of Defense Directive 1300.18 issued on December 18, 2000, eliminated the status/designation prisoner of war (POW) for captured American service personnel, replacing it with the ambiguous designation missing-captured. The directive states:

> POW is not casualty status for reporting purposes, the casualty status and category would be missing-captured. POW is the international legal status of military and certain other personnel captured during an armed conflict between two countries and that status entitles those captured to humanitarian treatment under the Third Geneva Convention, "Geneva Convention Relative to the Treatment of Prisoners of War." The international status of POW is automatic when personnel "have fallen into the power of the enemy." There is no action required by any country in the conflict to have that status applied for their personnel and for their personnel to be entitled to the humanitarian protections of the Geneva Convention.

The Pentagon's policy sheds it of the responsibility of designating an American service member as a POW if the international community applies it automatically. But the POW moniker continues to be used extensively within the Department of Defense. Commands and offices inside and outside the Pentagon still use it as part of their naming convention, principally the Defense Prisoners of War/Missing Personnel Office (DPMO) and Joint POW/MIA Accounting Command (JPAC). Then there is the Prisoner of War Medal and the armed forces Code of Conduct (CoC), doctrine that unequivocally addresses the service member if taken as a "prisoner of war" and refers them to sections of the Uniform Code of Military Justice (UCMJ) that covers the same.

What did this policy do to the Speicher case? Secretary of the Navy Gordon R. England argued in his October 11, 2002 memorandum:

> If the government of Iraq is holding Captain Speicher, he is entitled to Prisoner of War status under international law and the Geneva Convention and would have been entitled to such status from the day he first came under Iraqi control. Although the controlling missing persons statute and directives do not use the term Prisoner of War, the facts supporting a change in Captain Speicher's category from Missing in Action to Missing/Captured would also support the conclusion that if alive, he is a Prisoner of War.

Secretary England's statement is clear that the controlling missing persons statute and directives do not specify the term prisoner of war. Had the status prisoner of war been left in the language of the missing persons statute and directives, Scott Speicher would have been listed as a prisoner of war.

Prisoner of war wasn't good enough for Scott Speicher in the fall of 2002 but it would be for Saddam Hussein less than two years later. On December 13, 2003, during the execution of Operation Red Dawn, Saddam was captured by American forces hiding in a spider hole outside a farmhouse in ad-Dawr near his hometown of Tikrit. Following his capture Saddam was transported to a U.S. base near Tikrit, and later Camp Cropper, a holding facility for security detainees operated by the U. S. Army near Baghdad International Airport. The facility was initially operated as a high-value detention (HVD) site, but subsequently increased its capacity from 163 to roughly 2,000 detainees. Almost immediately after Saddam's capture the ICRC entered discussions with U.S. Central Command (USCENTCOM) and the Coalition Provisional Authority (CPA) for access to the deposed Iraqi leader, according to the Red Cross'

Washington representative Girod Christophe. Less than a month later, on January 9, 2004, Pentagon lawyers declared Saddam a prisoner of war. With this determination the former Iraqi dictator was thereafter protected by the rules of international law and the Third Geneva Convention, which provides for the treatment of prisoners of war. What got him this designation? Saddam was a prisoner of war based on the fact that he was the former head of an enemy military force who was captured on the battlefield during a declared conflict.

Just after the United States declared Saddam a prisoner of war, the ICRC stepped up pressure on Washington to release him from custody or charge him with a crime if the United States and the new Iraqi government were to remain compliant with international law. Nada Doumani, a spokeswoman for the ICRC, informed the media that at the end of the United States' occupation all prisoners of war had to be released if they had not been charged with a crime. Doumani's comments came as the ICRC, the only independent group with access to detainees in American custody, became increasingly concerned over the legal limbo in which thousands of people were being held in the run-up to the transfer of power between Coalition and Iraqi authorities that took place June 30, 2004. Thereafter, the American military would remain in Iraq at the invitation of Baghdad's newly sovereign government.

Fast forward to the case of missing-captured army sergeant Bowe R. Bergdahl, 1st Battalion, 501st Infantry Regiment, 4th Brigade Combat Team, 25th Infantry Division, based at Fort Richardson, Alaska. During his unit's normal deployment rotation to Afghanistan, he went missing on June 30, 2009, near the town of Yahya Khel in the Paktika Province, located in southeast Afghanistan, right on the border with Pakistan's Federally Administered Tribal Areas. He was taken into custody by the Haqqani network, an insurgent group affiliated with the Taliban, probably somewhere in Pakistan.

Schorno, of the ICRC, noted that there can be no prisoners of war stemming from the Afghan conflict as far as the Red Cross is concerned. "Bergdahl's not a POW because we don't qualify Afghanistan as an international armed conflict," he stated. "We see it as an internal conflict with an international presence, which makes him [Bergdahl] a person detained in the context of a non-international armed conflict."[5] Were Bergdahl classified a POW he'd be covered by a key clause of that status: release at the end of the conflict. But as it stands, Bergdahl is being held by non-state Taliban insurgents under no obligation by the Geneva Convention to return him. He remains "missing in action," despite five Taliban videos to wit showing him in captivity.

"There are aspects of what defines a prisoner of war that is not so clearly specified in the Department of Defense and Geneva Convention definitions," wrote retired navy commander, former Central Intelligence Agency (CIA) field officer and former Defense Prisoner of War/Missing Personnel Office (DPMO) case officer William G. "Chip" Beck on August 20, 1998.[6] "Not understanding what those aspects are allows practical measures on behalf of the POWs to be minimized."

"What I mean is this: a POW is a POW, *not an MIA*." This is true, Beck iterated, even if the enemy knows that the person is a POW, "but our side does not." As long as one party, in this case the "holding party," knows that the person is alive and captive, then he is a POW and nothing else. "When and if a POW dies," Beck continued, "he does not become an MIA. He becomes a dead POW. *The accounting procedures and methodology for finding out what happened to that dead POW, as well as* ***any unrepatriated POWs still held in secret*** [bold emphasis added], *is far different from those for MIAs.*"

Beck explained that an MIA is a person who was killed, or lost and subsequently died but not while in captivity, and whose body was not recovered. "There are those in the DoD apparatus," he observed, "who will argue *all POWs and MIAs are MIAs*. One can understand the logic, but [you] should not accept it."

"*This lack of distinction serves the enemy's interest – not ours,*" Beck concluded. "It requires us to only track down those men and women who were killed in the conduct of battle, not kidnapped by the forces they confronted."

Beck concluded with a cautionary note to the families of POW/MIAs that should be kept in mind as you read this narrative:

"... do not ... comply with the MIA jargon put out on the issues. POWs are different from MIAs. So are the answers about what happened to the POWs, and so are the questions that need to be asked about them."

Endnotes

1. Yarsinske, Amy Waters. No One Left Behind: The Lt. Comdr. Michael Scott Speicher Story (Dutton/NAL, 2002, 2003; Listen and Live Audio, 2002, 2004, 2006; Topics Entertainment, 2004; Listen and Live Audio MP3, 2007; Preloaded Digital Audio Player, *Playaway*, April 2009)

2. Thompson, Mark, "Pentagon: we don't call them POWs anymore," *Time* U.S., May 17, 2012. http://nation.time.com/2012/05/17/pentagon-we-dont-call-them-pows-anymore/

3. Eugene R. Fidell is the Florence Rogatz Visiting Lecturer in Law at Yale Law School. He is a cofounder and former president of the National Institute of Military Justice and of counsel at Feldesman Tucker Leifer Fidell LLP, Washington, D.C. He is a Fellow of the American Bar Foundation, a Life Member of the American Law Institute, and a member of the Defense Legal Policy Board of the Department of Defense and the board of directors of the International Society for Military Law and the Law of War. He has also taught at Harvard Law School and the Washington College of Law, American University.

4. Ibid.

5. Ibid.

6. Beck, William G., "POW definition compared to MIA," POW/MIA E-mail Network, August 20, 1998.

Chapter 1

Iron Hand

Pilots stood around uneasily on the afternoon of January 16, 1991, anxious about mass preflight briefings aboard the *Saratoga*. The carrier's aircrew was on edge; no one was comfortable with what was about to happen. This was not a routine mission. As they waited to hear from the *Saratoga*'s battle group commander, some of them prayed quietly, others talked nervously in small groups. Others, still, could think of nothing else but families and friends back home. All of them knew their mission down to the last detail.

Iraq had let the January 15 deadline to withdraw from Kuwait expire. America was going to war. While no one knew what to expect that night, they were ready as they could ever be. The few combat-seasoned aviators aboard the carrier felt the same roiling emotions as nugget pilots (trainees) on their first cruise. In eight hours or less, they'd all be flying into combat. Then Rear Admiral George N. "Nick" Gee started to speak. They listened somberly.

"Gentlemen," Gee brought them to attention, "George Bush has called on us to do our duty, to liberate Kuwait, and that liberation is going to start tonight. There are several types of people back in the United States right now who will be watching as your bombs start dropping over Baghdad. It's going to be just about time for the evening news back home," he told them. "There's going to be a guy sitting in the bar with long hair and a beard, an old hippie type, who is drinking beer and watching TV, and he's going to go, 'Fucking A, those are my boys, god damned U.S.' There are going to be moms out there that are crying and saying, 'That's my boy.' They are going to be watching you. You need to do this well. This will be with you for the rest of your lives. You will remember this night forever, so you want to do the best job you possibly can because if you don't, you will regret it until you die." Everyone listened. No one was reassured.

Lieutenant Barry W. "Skull" Hull felt his mouth go bone dry. The Strike Fighter Squadron Eighty-One (VFA-81) Sunliner pilot wasn't alone. "The very first thing we did was get a time hack so we'd all be on exact time," Hull recalled later. "We're synchronized. In thirty seconds it's going to be twenty-four after the hour, then ten, nine, eight and then Gee called 'Hack!'" The atmosphere remained somber until the mass briefing ended. Then the squadrons went to their own ready rooms for individual mission briefs.

Hull was joined in the VFA-81 Sunliners ready room by Lieutenant Commanders Scott "Spike" Speicher and Tony "Bano" Albano, Commander Michael T. "Spock" Anderson, and Lieutenant Philip "Chauncey" Gardner, all of them preparing to climb into their F/A-18 Hornets and roar off the carrier *Saratoga* in the Red Sea, across Saudi Arabia toward Baghdad. Thus began Operation Desert Storm. They would be joined by scores of other navy pilots from the *Saratoga* and other aircraft carriers poised to launch aircraft at Iraq on the first strike of a new kind of air war. In the planning room, the Sunliners reviewed the timing of the attack, their flight paths, and targets.

Speicher wasn't originally scheduled to fly that night. Squadron commander Spock Anderson tapped him as the airborne spare. He would fly in and take over if any of the other Hornets were forced back to the *Saratoga*'s flight deck with a mechanical failure. The spare had to know everybody's mission. But the role was not enough for Speicher. He went to Anderson and told him he didn't want to be the spare, to be the one who'd have to turn around and come back to the ship without firing a shot. His argument was convincing. Anderson relented and put Speicher on the first strike.

The spare position then went to Hull, but he balked, too. "I go, 'Wait a minute, I don't want to be the spare either.' It's not like I was some sort of big hero and the truth is, it's not like Spike was being a hero," said Hull. "I wanted to be in there with my buddies." The truth is, so did Scott Speicher. To resolve the predicament with Anderson, Hull went looking for Spike. "The skipper didn't like me very much," Hull confessed later, so he figured if he got Spike's help smoothing it over, he might get put on the first strike, too. "I said, 'Look, what you did for yourself, you gotta do it for me, too.' Spike goes, 'Yeah, sure.'" To ensure Spike's success with Anderson, Hull told him that he'd get Lieutenant (junior grade) Conrad "Banker" Caldwell to fill in as the spare, "and I guarantee you," he told Spike, "Banker will know every single mission." And he did. Hull was back on the mission. Later, he thanked Spike.

Emotions ran high before the first strike launched from the deck of the *Saratoga*. In a letter home, written just days before the mission, Barry Hull told his family that Saddam didn't appear to have his bags packed for his trip back to Iraq. The dictator wasn't leaving Kuwait willingly. "I suppose it could be arranged to send him [Saddam] back, maybe inside his own personal bag," he quipped. The Sunliners, without question, were ready to go into harm's way. Hull was confident that the big picture was understood and that they'd be able to focus on the details he and his fellow Sunliners would soon encounter in combat. "Occasionally we have the luxury to sit back and think, 'The plans are ready, now what else do I need to do?'"

He ran down the list of tasks all the Sunliners had to accomplish as Saddam's deadline to withdraw from Kuwait drew closer. "We've sanitized our flight suits. That means all nametags and patches are removed. We wear our dog tags. Personal weapons are carried."

His survival gear was so full of water that, "You guessed it," he exclaimed, "my Oreos got smushed and I had to eat them and restock. Oh, well." Wallets contained only the pilots' military identification cards, family pictures, cash and credit cards. "The SAR [search and rescue] guys tell us if we go down, we might be able to rent a car and drive out. Weird, huh?" Hull also carried sunscreen, Chapstick and, of course, his Vuarnets. "Would you rather be seen in the desert in Ray-Bans or Vuarnets?" he asked his sister. "One of our maintenance troops gave me a raghead hat, the turban thing, in case I need to go incognito."

Captain Dean M. "Milo" Hendrickson, Speicher's carrier air wing commander, was one of only a few pilots on board *Saratoga* who'd been around long enough to have seen sustained combat. "You're going to come back," he warned pilots on the first strike, "Then you're going to look around ... and one of you won't be here." Most of the Sunliners had no idea that this warning might actually come true.

The Sunliners' ready room was six decks down on the *Saratoga,* so the Hornet pilots used the escalator to get topside with the sixty pounds of flight gear each carried. In the same letter, Hull described the feeling of seeing the hatch leading outside. "A few deep breaths are taken at this point," he wrote home, "because I'm about to enter another world. It's dark and dangerous, and if you're not careful it will kill you." The hatch to the flight deck was always pitch dark and seemed to suck the light out of Hull's flashlight. The hatch led to a catwalk, down a small flight of steps below the flight deck. Past the catwalk pilots stepped among fueling hoses, extra catapult wires and chocks and chains and yellow gear. Looking into the lights, only the shadowy outline of men moving quickly back and forth to aircraft could be made out. Looking away from the lights, there was the reflection off goggles and more darkness.

During a combat dry-run just a couple of days before the big show, there had been several hundred men topside. Hull had to find a man with a Sunliner patch to tell him where his Hornet was on the flight deck. "He knows what I want," Hull wrote home, "and just points without my asking." The twenty- to thirty-knot wind bent over pilots and deck crew as they worked to get planes on and off the deck. "Your flashlight gives you a small tunnel vision to see clearly," he continued, "and all the rest is noise and shadows. No faces, just helmets and goggles." Hull had once before gone through an entire night launch and not known who his plane captain was; it was too dark on the flight deck to identify anyone and too loud to talk.

Before Hull could reach his jet, a Hornet slammed onto the deck fifty feet to his left and startled him. Maybe the Hornet's pilot had boltered; he gave everyone a fantastic light show as his tailhook dragged down the deck at 150 knots spewing sparks and lighting up the night before pulling up and coming around again. All over the deck ordnancemen loaded and unloaded carts stacked with air-to-air and air-to-ground missiles and smart bombs. Steam from the carrier's catapults blew by, sometimes completely enveloping the men standing in it. As the steam cleared, Hull shone his light onto the Hornet he was looking for, and it was then he spotted his plane captain, who would get him ready and off the deck.

A half-hour before launch, the air boss came up on the loud-speaker: "Gentlemen, it's time to get into the proper flight deck uniform, sleeves rolled down, helmets on and buckled, goggles pulled down, life vests on and securely fastened. Let's check around the go birds for FOD [foreign object debris]. Whenever you're ready, gentlemen, let's crank 'em up, crank the go birds." No matter how many times a navy pilot hears those words, he still gets goose bumps.

Mounting his Hornet and settling in, Hull looked back on the ladder to see his nineteen-year-old plane captain close behind, ready to strap him in. With a quick word or two, Hull's plane captain wished him a safe flight and scampered down to do one last preflight check of the Hornet. From his cockpit perch, Hull could just make out the outline of the plane captain and the unmistakable glow of the blue wands in his hands. As the Hornet's engines fired up, the canopy came down with a thud, then slid smoothly forward and locked into place.

Fifteen minutes passed before Hull was ready to give a thumb's up. The chocks and chains were removed from his Hornet, nose wheel steering engaged, and he armed his ejection seat. Taxi directors in yellow shirts came out to guide Hull's Hornet to the catapult, while he ran down takeoff checks and rogered the weight board, a process that calculates the gross weight of the Hornet, including ordnance, fuel, gear, and pilot weight so the correct thrust can be applied to the catapult launch. Hull spread the wings of the Hornet and made certain they locked into place. One last big turn and the jet was on the catapult. Hull described the rhythm and cadence of the men on the deck. Ten men moved swiftly under the Hornet to do final checks and hook up the launch bar; the taxi director's small, precise signals kept everyone in check. Ordnancemen armed the Hornet's weapons, then passed the plane back. All stations checked "go."

Hull's heart was pounding. The yellow shirt checked with the catapult officer, and Hull got the signal to run up the Hornet's engines. As he released the brakes, the hold-back keeping him stationary on the catapult, Hull added full power. His head tilted back and the lights came on – the nighttime salute. The catapult officer touched the deck, signaling launch, and five seconds later Hull's Hornet lurched forward. Within two seconds Hull was doing over 180 miles per hour, pinned to the seat. Hurtled off the end of the flight deck into the air, Hull said, "You better believe most of us tap afterburner." A few nights later he and his squadron mates would roar off the *Saratoga*'s deck for the first air strike of the Persian Gulf War.

In the planning room, Scott Speicher and Tony Albano learned that they'd take off well after midnight and return around dawn. Hearing that news, they decided they'd better get some sleep and walked back to their stateroom. Speicher crawled into the top bunk, Albano into the bottom. They lay still for forty-five minutes, hearts pounding, minds racing. So many thoughts were going through their heads.

"I can't sleep," Albano finally said softly.

"I can't either," said Speicher.

Around 1 o'clock in the morning local time they put on their flight suits, boots and gear, and walked through the mess deck and up to the flight deck. Speicher, Albano, and fellow Sunliners slapped hands. "See you back on deck in a couple of hours," Albano told Speicher.

Scott Speicher had come to the Sunliners as a very junior department head. He didn't become a lieutenant commander until the squadron was underway on the Operation Desert Shield deployment. Speicher arrived at Aviation Officers' Candidate School (AOCS) in Pensacola, Florida, in July 1980. After completing AOCS at the top of his class, he was commissioned an ensign in the U.S. Navy on October 24 of that year. After he finished his flight training, Speicher reported to the Attack Squadron 174 (VA-174) Hellrazors for initial A-7E Corsair II replacement pilot instruction before moving on to the VA-105 Gunslingers, where he made deployments aboard the USS *Carl Vinson* (CVN-70), USS *Forrestal* (CV-59), and from a base in Iwakuni, Japan. Over the next three years he transitioned from the A-7E Corsair II to the F/A-18 Hornet and qualified as a flight instructor on the VFA-106 Gladiators. His tenure as a flight instructor was followed by a rotation back to a fleet squadron. Scott's students later described him as a patient and thorough flight instructor.

Speicher and Albano met long before they shared a stateroom aboard *Saratoga*. "We developed a close working and then a close personal friendship," Albano said later. "We had similar personalities." They were also in a tightly knit squadron environment where pilots ended up living together in close quarters for six to nine month stretches. "We work together and rely on each other to save one another's life and provide both mutual support on liberty as well as in the air and in combat," he continued. Albano had just rolled off Carrier Air Wing 17 staff, where he'd been senior landing signal officer (LSO), to join the Sunliners. By chance he ended up filling a slot with the Sunliners that had been occupied by Scott's roommate, who'd left for his next assignment. "We became roommates and fellow department heads." But Bano had also just spent time with Scott and some of the other Sunliners at Fallon, Nevada, where the squadron had gone for pre-deployment workups.

"Everyone goes to Lake Tahoe," he recounted, recalling a funny incident that happened while the squadron was there. "It's nice in the wintertime because you can go skiing. Everyone goes and gets a chalet," Bano explained. "I remember Scott being passed out. I don't know if he passed out or just got tired of being in the bar we had gone to, but he went out to the van and it was freezing out there." Scott had bundled up and climbed under all the coats piled in the backseat. "He's out there," he continued, "and everyone's getting in the car." Speicher was under all the coats, but no one knew it yet. "Where the hell is Spike?" they thought. Then someone jumped in the backseat, on top of the coats, and Spike started rising up like a hamster out of pile of sawdust. "He just laid in the back of the van and went to sleep," recalled Bano. "I said, 'Spike, I gotta get you back. You're going to freeze out here. I'm going back to the bar, but I'm going to put you to bed, buddy.'"

"Thanks, Dad," Spike murmured.

Later, during the Christmas holiday, the *Saratoga* pulled into Haifa harbor and put off liberty boats for the crew and air wing personnel to go into Israel to see the sights. Sunliner pilots were relaxing in a hotel in Haifa where they'd set up a squadron admin, a stopping off point, sometimes one, usually several, hotel rooms to hang out and have a good time. Several floors up on a balcony, the Sunliners set up a cookout. Spike noticed construction going on across the street. "Twenty bucks I can hit the bulldozer with this kielbasa," Spike said, smiling broadly. "You're on," his friends replied. So Spike grabbed a whole kielbasa, ducked into the room to line up his shot, then quick-stepped to the railing and flung it up and out across the street, smack into the top of the bulldozer. The operator looked over and started yelling, and the pilots cackled: "Direct hit! Direct hit!"

On Christmas Eve Scott went ashore with Sunliner executive officer Commander Bill "Maggot" McKee, Bano, and Lieutenant Craig "Bert" Bertolett. "We toured around Jerusalem," Bano remembered warmly, "and then we went around Bethlehem that night." Several days later they toured the area around the Sea of Galilee and tried to find the location of the Sermon on the Mount and other sacred biblical events. Scott read the Bible regularly for two reasons: his faith and historical perspective. "He read the Bible a lot prior to us going to Israel," Bano said. "That's the kind of guy he was – very studious when he wanted to be, very passionate about learning things that he didn't have a clear understanding of … he wanted to learn more about a place we were going to go to."

But the Sunliners' liberty did not last long. Around lunchtime on January 16, the squadron got sudden word they'd be going into combat. Adrenaline started flowing as the pilots went up to the strike planning rooms to look over the mission. Before they knew it, they'd be up on the flight deck, manning their Hornets. The hours flew past.

They were all anxious. Barry Hull knew he must be more uptight than he thought because his mouth was so dry. "I need a drink of water," he kept thinking as he stood in the paraloft, the room used to fix and store parachute gear, suiting up in his flight gear before heading up to the flight deck on the escalator. "I must be more nervous than I think I am." Then he remembered the Diet Coke and apple he'd packed in his pockets for the flight. "These missions are so long."

Though he'd high-fived his best friend, Tony Albano, Scott was quiet, introspective. No one was doing a lot of talking. It was time to concentrate; they had a mission to fly. It was a pitch-black night with just a sliver of twinkling moon. But at least it was clear. Once on the flight deck the Sunliners sensed the seriousness of what they were about to do. "None of us had ever been in combat before," Hull said.

"We had aircraft turned up and launch safe," Chief Aviation Structural Mechanic (AMSC) Chief Terryl Chandler later remembered. Chandler was a Sunliner flight deck coordinator. "That night was an emotional period of time for everyone on the roof [the flight deck]. Everybody was ready." Despite the whine and roar of aircraft engines tuning up, the *Saratoga*'s crew could still hear the snapping and popping of the carrier's battle flags going up as they prepared their aircraft for launch.

The Sunliners were lined up on the aft port side of the *Saratoga*'s flight deck. Squadron leader Spock Anderson was up first in Hornet AA401 – the jet he preferred – then came AA406, -402, -404, and -403, Scott Speicher's plane. Banker Caldwell, the spare, sat in AA410. Phil "Chauncey" Gardner, Albano and Hull sat in-between, each finishing up final flight checks and thinking intently of the mission ahead. "We ran the lineups and I shook each pilot's hand and told them we'd be there when we got back," Chandler said. "But by the time I got Speicher, he'd already climbed into his Hornet and the engines were turned up. I told his plane captain to shut down his port engine. Mr. Speicher looked at me, but he trusted my judgment and knew there wasn't anything wrong. I let the boarding ladder down, climbed up and shook his hand like I'd done the others. I wanted him to know that we'd be waiting for him when he got back aboard."

They all took off without any problems. "He was in one of our best jets that night," said Chandler. "AA403 was ready to go."

The *Saratoga*'s crew launched forty-six aircraft off the catapults in twenty-five minutes, including the Sunliners' Hornets. That meant roughly every thirty seconds an aircraft was shot off the deck into the darkness. The pilots headed for their rendezvous point, an aircraft refueling tanker flying over Saudi Arabia. The tankers flew a big circle in the sky to fill up inbound Coalition aircraft, *Saratoga*'s Hornets among them. But the tankers were on a tight schedule. Up on Vulture's Row, an observation deck above the ship's bridge, Lieutenant Commander Mark I. "MRT" Fox watched Scott Speicher take off. Spike tapped the blowers as he lifted off the deck into the darkness, headed for his tanking point.

The first night's mission was going to be about five hours long. Most of the action was at least a fourteen-hundred-mile round trip from where the *Saratoga* floated in the Red Sea, so success at the tanker was critical. Though nervous that night, *Saratoga*'s pilots would eventually get used to tanking off the KC-135 Stratotankers, capable of carrying upwards of 200,000 pounds of fuel, nearly ten tons of gas per jet, per mission, if needed. But the KC-135 could be very unforgiving, especially at night in bad weather, "the goo" as pilots liked to call it. Designed largely for air force use, the KC-135 was adapted to the navy's drogue refueling method, a process where a fueling basket was fitted to the end of a six-foot, barely flexible hose stuck on the end of the tanker's boom. There was a lengthy learning curve for aircrew on both sides. For this process to go well, especially at night, took patience. Tanking at night was no cakewalk. Failing to get enough fuel the first go-around wasn't good either.

When Barry Hull wrote his folks back home in South Carolina that previous October during the battle group's simulated air strikes over Saudi Arabia, he'd gotten a taste of tanking off the KC-135 under poor conditions. With most of the *Saratoga*'s jets going for the tankers, there was only one problem: There were over fifty aircraft in a small piece of sky, and conditions were hazy and very gusty with thick cloud cover. "Our tanker track took us directly through a thunderstorm." It was the first time he'd tried to tank off a KC-135 in the middle of the night in cloud cover with five of his squadron mates trying to do the same, all flying tight formation so they didn't lose one another in the goo. "Everyone seemed to keep their cool though," he continued, "and we did the whole thing comm out – not one word – except, of course, for some chatter from the F-14 [Tomcat] guys, but you have to expect that from them." The memory of that trial by fire months earlier stuck with Hull.

One by one, bound for Baghdad, a succession of fighter jets rotated into position to stick a probe into the tanker's refueling basket and fuel up. Since he had a long track yet to go on his mission, Hull pulled his jet away and slipped to the back of the formation. As he did, he looked down into another pilot's cockpit. "We were at the left side of the tanker moving in," he recalled. "I came off the basket and to the right side of the tanker. I pulled my plane up twenty or thirty feet and looked down at this guy below me tanking." He didn't know who it was and couldn't ask; they were flying comm out. Piecing it together later back on the ship, he realized he had been looking down into Scott Speicher's cockpit.

Hull marveled at what he saw below: the glow of the instrument panel and the green formation lights of the F/A-18 Hornet. "Man, this is so cool," Hull said to himself. "Think of the power."

Designed for both air-to-air combat and bombing ground targets, the F/A-18 sported a sophisticated electronic identification system and packed two AIM-7M Sparrow and two AIM-9M-2/-4 Sidewinder missiles for taking on enemy fighters. Near the target, the pilot could flip a switch, go from air-to-air to ground attack mode, and drop a bomb. On this night Speicher and his squadron mates were each loaded with three high-speed anti-radiation missiles, also called HARMs. "The HARM missile is an extremely sophisticated, deadly weapon. I love those things; they're about a million bucks a pop," Hull said. The HARM was racked on the F/A-18s that night to take out Iraqi radar, command and control centers, and surface-to-air missile sites. The Sunliners and their sister squadron, the VFA-83 Rampagers, ten Hornets in all, would roll in on their assigned targets just seconds following a volley of cruise missiles from American warships. The Iraqis were expected to detect the cruise missiles, flip on their radar, and man up their surface-to-air missile (SAM) sites. Just then the Hornets would launch their radar-seeking HARMs and slam Iraqi defenses. "The ten of us were like spokes on a wheel," Rampager pilot lieutenant commander David G. "Frenchy" Renaud described later, "all [of us] coming toward this target, shooting off our missiles." Then a third wave of bombers would come through and hammer the targets.

The *Saratoga*'s Hornets mission was suppression of enemy air defenses and ground targets. The pilots called them "Iron Hand" missions and they were intended to deal the Iraqis a devastating blow that first night of the air war. It was an intricately devised plan, relying on precise flight paths and accurate information from U.S. Air Force E-3 AWACS airborne radar and communications aircraft that circled high overhead monitoring the hundreds of aircraft and missions being flown into the wee hours of January 17, 1991.

Coalition pilots needed every warning that technology might provide as they pressed for Baghdad straight into one of the most sophisticated integrated air defenses ever encountered, with about 500 radar installations located at nearly 100 sites across Iraq. Air force lieutenant general Charles A. "Chuck" Horner, in charge of the Gulf War air campaign, told allied commander army general H. Norman Schwarzkopf that one of every five of his aircraft might get shot down that night. Horner's prediction would have added up to hundreds of possible losses.

Within minutes of leaving the tanker Speicher and other Hornet pilots got a close look at what worried Horner. They crossed rugged terrain along the Saudi border, and as soon as they entered Iraq, antiaircraft fire streamed up at them. Mission leader and Rampager executive officer commander Bob "Ripper" Stumpf, the element leader, was already anxious. "We proceeded solo and then rendezvoused with the tankers in western Saudi," he remembered later. "They dragged us across the drop off point, about fifty miles south of the Iraqi border." Stumpf was behind an A-6E Intruder pilot at the KC-135 Stratotanker, and the pilot must have had the jitters. The Intruder crew took such a long time to get fuel that Stumpf broke off the tanker run and headed for the target without a full tank. This troubled him the further into the mission he got, but there wasn't anything he could do about it. The refueling tanker wouldn't have gotten to him anyway; it broke off its position with the Hornets and headed for its next scheduled tanking assignment.

As he moved closer to his target track, Stumpf's radar warning devices filled his cockpit with warbles and whistles and deedle-deedles. He looked toward the horizon and saw something glowing. It pulsated toward the horizon as though alive. In the clear night sky he couldn't tell how far away it was. It could have been five miles or fifty. "We didn't really expect this but pretty much as soon as we entered Iraqi airspace there was antiaircraft fire, missiles and triple A [antiaircraft artillery]." Stumpf had flown in the navy's 1986 raid on Benghazi, Libya, but that was routine by comparison to the first night of Desert Storm. Orange balls of antiaircraft fire shot up at him. "Holy shit," he thought, "I think I'm going to die."

Each of the *Saratoga*'s Hornet pilots was assigned an altitude in the twenty-five to thirty-thousand-foot range to prevent mid-air mishaps, but Stumpf started flying up and down quickly to become a tougher target. "That was a violation of the plan because there were so many planes over Iraq that night that each person was assigned a certain route and a certain altitude. You were supposed to stick to it," he said. "If everybody did what I did, they would deconflict, kind of like the FAA does. But I figured the chances of getting hit by a missile were much greater than getting hit by some other airplane I couldn't see." Stumpf and other Hornet pilots would have to rely on the eyes and ears of Cougar, the air force AWACS circling the western Iraqi skies that night.

Cougar was not their normal airborne controller. It was there to drop tracks[1] because the navy had no Joint Tactical Information Distribution System (JTIDS)[2] capability, and the Tactical Digital Information Link-Airborne (TADIL-A)/Link 11[3] was saturated. The E-3 could bury the navy with tracks; high frequency (HF) bands were problematic over the Gulf region. The E-3s all had JTIDS and their radar net covered Israel to Iran, and could maintain the TADIL-A/Link 11 with the Turkish E-3 and the air force RC-135 Rivet Joint. Normally, the navy's E-2C Hawkeye carrier-based tactical battle management airborne early warning, command and control aircraft was the Sunliners' eye in the sky, but on this night, headed into Iraqi airspace, the AWACS ran the show. Even so, two of the *Saratoga*'s VAW-125 Tigertails E-2C Hawkeyes – AA600 and AA603 – were on the strike and positioned at a midway and return point to watch out for the navy strike package.

The Sunliners' and Rampagers' mission profile meant that each man flew alone without a wingman. To make matters more complicated, the rules of engagement were strict regarding beyond visual range (BVR) friend or foe identification. With hundreds of jets in the sky, the possibility of blue-on-blue – a friendly fire kill – was extremely high. Hornet pilots, by the rules of engagement, had to confirm an enemy fighter at least two ways before firing a missile. They had to see it with the naked eye, nearly impossible at night unless the opposing aircraft got extremely close to one another, and they could identify it electronically and the controller had to thus declare it hostile. But they had to have the approval of the AWACS controller to shoot down the bandit, an enemy aircraft. That night aboard the AWACS the air force tactics officer tracking the *Saratoga*'s Hornets was Captain Jimmy Patterson. The AWACS surveillance radar, in theory, should've been able to distinguish friend or foe right away, but that wasn't the case as Stumpf's Hornets pressed into Iraqi airspace.

Hull saw the same pulsing glow that had caught Stumpf's eye. At first he thought it must be an optical illusion. Then he thought the Middle East must have its own version of the Northern Lights. Soon he was in it. What he'd seen from what seemed a great distance was suddenly in front of him, behind him, to both sides. "I just remember being terrified," he said later. The whole landscape was lit up with an intense glow that only intensified the closer he got. Iraqi antiaircraft fire shot up like Fourth of July sparklers, illuminating the night and blanketing the ground. Then the realization of what it was hit Hull like a gut punch. The glowing vat turned out to be Baghdad. Hull's warning gear began chirping and wouldn't stop, distracting him the longer it continued sounding off. He remembered what Vietnam-era fighter pilots often did; he reached over and turned it off. "Screw it," he said, and started using his own eyes to look for missiles. Looking into the darkness around him, Hull pondered the old-timers' advice, occasionally glancing anxiously at his Hornet's radar homing and warning gear that he'd just switched off. "I'm going to die looking at this gauge," he thought.

Just then the controller aboard Cougar called out: "I've got a pop-up SA-6."

"You do not want to fly through the envelope of an SA-6. It'll shoot you down," Hull said. The SA-6 was one of Iraq's most feared surface-to-air missiles. A pop-up meant that the satellites hadn't picked it up. The eighteen-foot SA-6, mounted on a half-track, could reach a jet at thirty thousand feet and explode when it detected the metal of the aircraft. Hull waited for someone to ask for the missile's location, but no one did. "Damn it," he said. "Give me the coordinates!" Finally the controller rattled them off. Hull jotted the location on his kneeboard and compared it with where he was. But then he got this overwhelming sinking feeling. "Oh God, no! I'm dead over the top of an SA-6." He pushed on and never saw the missile.

The *Saratoga*'s pilots glanced outside their cockpits for immediate threats and down at their radars, sweeping for enemy fighters. Cougar's controllers updated the air picture as the Hornets pushed toward Baghdad, but a little over two hours into the mission, bearing north-northeast, Sunliner pilots were startled to hear their strike leader and commanding officer, Spock Anderson, break into the radio frequency using his air tasking order (ATO) call sign Quicksand 01. He didn't call Cougar. He first called one of the *Saratoga*'s Hawkeyes, the Sunliners' usual airborne controller, that was set up between the navy strike package and the Jordanian border to watch for bad guys trying to sneak down Iraq's border and break into the navy attack line. This Hawkeye was in communication range; the other wasn't.

"Tigertail 603 ... Sunliner 402[4]. I've got a fast mover (he splits out the range) on my nose; he's hot," Anderson called out. The range was so close it made the hair on Hull's neck stand up. "This is Quicksand 01. Confirm bandit. Request permission to fire."

Anderson needed Tigertail 603's mission commander to call the fast mover a bandit instead of a bogey, an unknown. Tigertail wouldn't do it – and couldn't. That was the AWACS operator's call. At least it was supposed to be. Anderson later estimated that he was about forty miles from his target when he picked up a MiG-25PDS Foxbat E, a Soviet-made interceptor fighter that could fly at nearly three times the speed of sound, approaching about 1,000 feet above him. "He was going very fast," Anderson recounted later. "He was headed west-southwest and trying to get around me." Then Anderson and the MiG started turning into each other, and Anderson got a good look at the Iraqi-marked aircraft. "I got a radar contact on him first, and then I had a visual contact on him. I was very positive it was a MiG-25."[5] There was also no mistaking the identification of a MiG-25 with the onboard computer library Anderson and the other Hornet pilots were flying with during the war. There was no computer anomaly where the MiG-25 was concerned, no mistaking it for the equivalent of a friendly aircraft.

The hair on the back of Barry Hull's neck shot up. He had been so concerned with shooting his HARMs that he had his Hornet in a bombing mode rather than sweeping for enemy fighters. "Oh my God! What was I thinking?" Hull flipped the switch and started scanning for air threats. And then he saw the MiG. "Oh my God, oh jeez – oh shit!" Hull had always wanted to be a fighter pilot. "I just thought it would be cool." Now there were real bad guys out there, and they wanted to kill him. With the MiG on radar, Hull called Cougar, the air force AWACS. "Confirm bandit?"

But the response from Cougar came back, "Negative. Negative bandit. Confirm bogey."

The call from Anderson had also jolted other Sunliner pilots. Albano, flying a few miles behind Anderson, knew what "hot" meant. The Iraqi fighter's nose was pointed almost directly at the nose of Anderson's Hornet. A few pilots thought they heard Anderson identify the enemy, but the MiG-25 concealed another surprise that night that none of the Sunliners, Rampagers or other Coalition pilots that night could have expected: its pilot.

Russian instructor pilots rotated in and out of Iraq at the invitation of the Hussein regime before and during the Gulf War, their primary purpose to train Iraqi pilots in the MiG aircraft Saddam purchased from the former Soviet Union. When it became clear that war with the United States and its Coalition allies loomed large, Moscow saw opportunity, a chance to observe the skills of America's latest crop of aviators, especially those flying the nascent F/A-18 Hornet. Wars are large-scale experimental laboratories to learn what works and what doesn't; the Persian Gulf War did not disappoint. American pilots were flying against pilots using Soviet-style air combat tactics, some with sharper skills than others.

The Russian Air Force later published a broadly read comment in the August 7, 1991 *Komsomolskaya Pravda* by Lieutenant Colonel Vladimir Vysotsky that became early confirmation of a problem that was not fully appreciated for years to come. A Russian reporter asked Vysotsky whether the outcome of the Gulf War would have been different if Russian pilots had flown Saddam's MiGs into combat. Vysotsky's answer was "Hardly" – it would be about the same. After all, experienced Russian pilots had trained Saddam's pilots and they weren't that bad, right? Vysotsky's reply was unexpected. "Every pilot with a rational head on his shoulders knows that in case of war, the role reserved for him is that of cannon fodder. He also knows," said Vysotsky, "that the situation worries very few people in the highest command echelons." Vysotsky seemed unconcerned that he'd made overtly strong statements to which Moscow might take strong exception. Instead he offered up the view that he "knew what would happen to his attack aircraft in the first days of the war."

That night, high over the pulsating glow on the fringe of Baghdad, Spock Anderson was facing down a Russian-trained pilot in an Iraqi MiG-25 who had come off an Iraqi airfield directly below the Hornets' attack line, flushed out by U.S. Air Force F-15s sweeping for MiGs over Al Taqqadum Air Base, thirty-five miles west of Baghdad.

The MiG pilot flew right over Phil "Chauncey" Gardner's cockpit to get to Spock. "I was feeling some heat," Gardner would recall later. "We had the timing of our shots about a minute to two-and-a-half minutes apart. We were on the west side of the strike package." But the Hornets still had a respectable distance between them, estimated later to have been a five-mile combat spread. They were also flying altitude splits so that the Hornets could operate as a formation of single ships. This way each Hornet pilot could focus on getting his HARMs on target, which was critical to the protection of bombers following over the target, and not be concerned with collision avoidance. Hull called the Sunliners' five-mile combat spread "a relatively small piece of sky." A huge "however" is that HARM shooters operating as single ships have zero mutual support, particularly at the distance apart they were flying that night. A relatively small piece of sky to a fighter pilot traveling at eight miles a minute is not so small when the bad guys show up.

Chauncey was in the middle of the pack, behind Spock Anderson, to the left in the 10 o'clock position, when all hell broke loose and the MiG started to converge on Spock. He heard Spock repeatedly ask Cougar for permission to fire. The AWACS kept declaring a merge plot, meaning Spock and the MiG-25 were too close to one another to distinguish the two aircraft on radar. Chauncey flipped to Choctaw, one of the Sunliners' assigned frequencies. Then he realized there were more MiG-25s in the air around them. "Flying with lights off, the sky was so filled with planes it was the equivalent of doing it blindfolded," he later said of that night.

Meanwhile, Albano looked around frantically for the MiG Spock was chasing on his radar. "He was either out of my radar's field of view or in what I would call a beaming maneuver, which wouldn't negate my radar but it makes it [the MiG] harder to find." By the time it was all over, the only chatter Bano heard on the radio was Spock and the AWACS. The only one who seemed oblivious to the MiG was Scott Speicher, who was flying without any enemy radar warning because of a system malfunction that did not become known until later. Much later.

Anderson kept asking Cougar for permission to fire as he and the MiG pilot roared through the dark sky at each other. Anderson didn't want to shoot down one of his own. No stain clung to an aviator more than a blue-on-blue kill, a friendly fire incident that would never go away. Fellow pilots would talk behind the pilot's back, ask what was wrong with him, get uneasy about flying with him. Anderson wanted someone else to see what he saw. They'd be told dozens of times: Better to let the bad guy go than shoot down a good guy.

But how could the AWACS not see the MiG? There were several possibilities, but the most likely one was a phenomenon called a Doppler notch. Pilots call it beaming. When two aircraft are flying at or near the same speed and headed in the same direction, both aircraft can vanish from the AWACS' radar screens. The MiG-25 slipped into the notch and disappeared from Cougar's screens. Thus Jimmy Patterson couldn't see what Spock saw; he couldn't give permission to fire. But Spock couldn't know, not just then, that Cougar was as blind as Scott Speicher to the threat bearing down on him.

"Confirm bandit," Anderson said again, not quite yelling but emphasizing the words strongly.

"Negative bandit," the controller said. "Declare bogey."

Now sweeping, Hull spotted the enemy jet on his radar, but it wasn't coming toward him. Albano and the others desperately looked for the MiG-25 but couldn't find it. The AWACS controller came back at Anderson and said, "Standby, looking…"

Anderson asked a third time, even more firmly, "Confirm bandit."

"Negative… bogey. Negative… bogey."

Denied again, Spock Anderson had one last heated verbal exchange with Cougar followed by something about his intention with the MiG that no one up that night is willing to confirm. He then went off the AWACS frequency and back to the navy E-2C Hawkeye – to Tigertail 603 - to get a bandit call. And just as he did so, Cougar called back, now seeing the MiG-25, and said: "Confirm bandit! Confirm bandit!" But it was already too late. Setting up for their HARM runs, Hull and Gardner heard Anderson get permission to fire from the air force E-3. But an air force AWACS operator heard – and saw – something else. Tigertail 603 had put a hostile track on Speicher's Hornet. Just then Cougar came back at the Hawkeye to remove the hostile track – the plane was friendly – but Tigertail 603 didn't do it fast enough. An F-14 Tomcat had been cleared to fire beyond visual range (BVR). The next thing the AWACS heard was the splash call by the F-14.

The Iraqi MiG and Anderson's Hornet zoomed past each other one last time at a combined speed of better than Mach 2. The MiG pilot never fired an air-to-air missile that night and, according to the Sunliners' end of deployment ordnance report, Spock didn't either.[6] After three turns with Anderson, the MiG broke away and headed east. Anderson returned to his target track. "I'm pretty sure I saw Spock's HARM missiles being launched as I was approaching the axis at a perpendicular aspect. But this was after he had already broken off the engagement with the MiG-25," said Albano. The *Saratoga*'s other Hornet pilots figured the MiG-25 had bugged out, just kept flying away from them knowing they didn't have the power to catch him. Some A-6E Intruder aircrew saw the unmistakable exhaust trail, nearly three-hundred-feet long, of the MiG right over their heads. A few minutes later, at 3:49 in the morning local time, an intense flash startled Anderson. He noticed that it came from the east, where Scott Speicher had been headed on his HARM mission. In all the confusion that followed, no one paid attention to who said it, but one A-6E aircrew heard a navy pilot cry out:

"Fireball! Fireball! Somebody just got hit!"

There were four navy Intruders in the area where Scott Speicher was last spotted. With their night vision goggles (NVGs), they could see airborne threats no one else could. One of them did a left 360-degree turn looking for the MiG that had flown over their formation. The Iraqi interceptor was gone, but they could see flaming wreckage careening toward the desert below.

"Who would have guessed that a MiG-25 would circle back behind us?" Hull observed. "I mean, you just think about it, when you meet in the merge, when you've got over seventeen hundred knots of closure and somebody goes *whhhhhhhewwww* past you…" Seeing the MiG-25 so close was unnerving.

Dave "Frenchy" Renaud, close by, heard Anderson say the MiG had turned "cold," meaning it was out of firing range. "When a fighter turns away like that," said Renaud, "he takes himself out of the head-on envelope of the Sparrow missile. He's not in range anymore." He was right. The MiG-25 was gone. A few minutes later Renaud saw a big explosion off to his right. It seemed close, maybe five or ten miles away. He didn't see the missile, just the flash, and the bright light mesmerized him. He watched it sparkle and glow all the way to the desert floor. "Must be an Iraqi jet getting knocked out by an F-15," he thought. That made sense. Air force F-15 Eagles had launched ahead of the other jets and were set out to sweep for Iraqi interceptors. The radio frequency was still buzzing, so Renaud didn't report the explosion. But there was a lot of unnecessary chatter that night. He also didn't mark his latitude and longitude at the time he spotted the flash. Just in case, though, he did talk into a tape recorder running in his cockpit. He remembers saying into his HUD [head-up display], "I see a big explosion off to my right. There's a secondary explosion."

Scott Speicher had also heard Spock Anderson's calls to Cougar about the MiG-25, but it never occurred to him that the enemy interceptor had turned east in his direction. He was still on autopilot and locked on his HUD when the Foxbat blew past him, creating what the AWACS controller later called another merge plot. Though there was more than one MiG-25 in the area that night, the one that Spock chased was subsequently determined to be the most likely guilty party in events that surround the loss of Speicher's F/A-18. Inexplicably, though, that Foxbat kept going and cleared the area. Then a missile fired beyond visual range detonated in proximity to Spike's Hornet.

Stumpf saw the explosion, too. The blast lit up his Hornet like a strobe. There was a pale yellow flash that some of the pilots who saw it described as the exhaust of a missile; others said it was a rocket plume. "You knew something was there," said Stumpf, "but I didn't see a fireball. I wasn't looking directly at the flash." Pay attention, Stumpf told himself, and don't do anything stupid. He and Renaud pushed on, firing HARMs at their targets, and, as planned, turned south for the tankers.

Stumpf had never fired a HARM before. As his HARMs released, one by one, they made a *whoosh* sound so loud he could hear it. The Hornet shook with each one coming off the rail. "It takes off and it's real bright … white exhaust … big exhaust plume coming out of this rocket, real fast and these actually start climbing. They go out in front of the airplane and start this steep climb," he described later. The HARM's proportional guidance system causes the missile to arc as it homes in on the selected target, making appropriate inflight corrections. "At that point you're thinking about getting out of Dodge without getting bagged, so you're going fast and changing altitudes, navigating so you hit the proper exit points, which were all defined earlier, so you look like a good guy, not a bad guy." Stumpf wanted to haul out of there, but instead had to chug back to conserve fuel. It seemed to take forever to reach the Saudi border.

Renaud got worried after firing his HARMs. "I think I got most scared," he said, "when I shot my third HARM and I had to do a one-eighty... from the target area. It took me a longer time when I wanted to make the turn, and I can remember getting a little bit slow in the turn so I lit up the afterburners to get more power." Then he thought to himself, "Now I'm going to get myself seen."

Hull also lit his afterburners to blaze home, then remembered that doing so would make him an easy mark for a heat-seeking missile, and he backed off. The Hornets all converged at the refueling tankers, where they had to pass through a gateway, a specific location and altitude that would let Coalition air and ground forces know they were not enemy aircraft trying to slip through. On the way back, the *Saratoga*'s Hornets turned on their identify friend or foe (IFF) so friendly aircraft could distinguish them from the enemy. About twenty miles from the Saudi border they started checking in with Cougar. Speicher, whose ATO call sign was Indian 502, should have reported to Cougar ahead of Albano, but didn't. Anderson asked Albano to try to reach Speicher, so Albano tried a tactical frequency used only by VFA-81.

"Spike... Bano... You up?"

Nothing.

"Spike... Bano."

He switched to another frequency. "Spike... Bano... You up?"

Silence.

Albano radioed Hull and asked him to try. "Skull, can you talk to Spike?"

"Spike... ? Skull."

"Spike, have you got me?"

"Spike, come in! Spike, everything okay?"

"Spike! How copy?"

No response.

Hull radioed Albano and said he couldn't raise Speicher. "Bano, I haven't got him. I'm heading south. Everything's fine with me, but I can't raise him." Albano relayed the message to Spock.

"Bano's back up."

"Any word?" Anderson asked.

"No, sir."

As they rolled off the tanker and headed back to the ship, Dave Renaud heard Albano talking to Hull: "I wish Spike would check in."

Tony Albano knew it was not a good sign that Speicher hadn't answered. He ran all the possible scenarios in his head as they headed back to the *Saratoga*. First he figured Spike had had a mechanical failure, turned around and gone back to the ship. Or maybe he flew to one of several divert airfields for an emergency landing. Bano never considered, not then, that the MiG-25 had gotten Speicher. "From what I heard," he said, "the MiG just started running toward the east, toward Baghdad, and I don't know if anyone else saw [the MiG] or anything like that. There were no reports of him [the MiG] later." Whatever happened, Bano never thought for a moment that Spike was dead. Speicher could have ejected and been rescued by a special operations team or, in the worst case, ejected and started evading capture. That possibility sobered Albano, and he flew in silence back to the *Saratoga*.

As the Sunliners and Rampagers made the Saudi border, waiting for them was the other E-2C Hawkeye Tigertail AA600. It had been "in the box" all night, flying a tight elliptical pattern over the northeast corner of Saudi Arabia. The Hawkeye crew wasn't comfortable being separated from their air wing strike package and out of the lead controller's role, but they were lucky, in the end, to be there at all. Their participation in the first strike was not part of the original plan. "At the last minute, with everybody wanting a piece of the action that night, they were given a role," recalled Tony Albano. The Hawkeye crew was assigned to cover friendlies egressing Iraq and to guard against the possibility of an Iraqi jet trying to make a break for a sneak attack on the fleet in the Red Sea. But they were well within communication and control range. Anderson knew it.

Lieutenant Commander Mark E. "Shark" Cantrell, the Hawkeye's mission commander, was tasked that night to keep up with the navy's combined strike package off the aircraft carriers *Saratoga* and *John F. Kennedy*. He had help from his air control officer (ACO), Lieutenant Richard "Rick" English, and radar officer (RO), Lieutenant David "Wavy Davey" Adams, seated to his left and right. "Our sole job [on that mission] was to try to keep air force fighters under AWACS control from shooting down our guys. But there were just too many planes up that night for us to get a clear picture of anything, and we were out of range once we parted ways with the F/A-18s and A-6Es at the crossover point on the border, where we stayed back and the AWACS took over control of the strike. We did stay," he said later, "in contact with the AWACS, and every time we called them up they were there."

As the *Saratoga*'s F/A-18s began crossing back over the Iraq-Saudi border, Cantrell, English and Adams counted noses coming out of Iraq, checking to make sure they all made it. "I remember all of us saying at the same time, 'Where's Spike?'" said Cantrell. "We checked a couple of times, tried different frequencies and got nothing. We called the AWACS to see if they had him. Nothing. I got on the radio with the JRCC [Joint Rescue Coordination Center] in Riyadh via the AWACS and told them we were missing an airplane." Cantrell's call should have been enough to initiate a check of divert airfields where Speicher might have landed his jet if it was damaged, but also to alert Special Operations Component, U.S. Central Command (SOCCENT) that there was a pilot down. It wasn't. Back on deck, the E-2C crews headed immediately for the carrier's intelligence center to debrief the flight. Cantrell told intelligence officers Speicher hadn't checked in and that he'd notified JRCC in Riyadh. But the JRCC later claimed no record of that communication from the Tigertail's Hawkeye. Worse than that, no one knew just then what had happened to Scott Speicher.

Endnotes

1. Remove the contact designated from all parts of the tactical picture/stores.

2. The Joint Tactical Information Distribution System (JTIDS) is a high-capacity communications system that provides secure jam-resistant transfer of digital voice or data information, position determination, and unit identification to suitably equipped terminals.

3. Tactical Digital Information Link-Airborne (TADIL-A)/Link-11 employs netted communication techniques and a standard message format for exchanging digital information among airborne (TADIL-A) tactical data systems. Link-11 data communications must be capable of operation in either the high frequency (HF) or ultra-high frequency (UHF) bands. TADIL-A is used by a number of intelligence platforms such as the air force RC-135 Rivet Joint that conducts signal intelligence (SIGINT) data collection, including communications intelligence (COMINT) and electronic intelligence (ELINT).

LInk 11 provides high speed computer-to-computer digital radio communications in the high frequency (HF) and ultra-high frequency (UHF) bands among Tactical Data System (TDS) equipped ships, aircraft and shore sites.

4. Pilots do not always fly the aircraft with their names painted on them. Sunliner 400 was the CAG aircraft, which typically displayed the color paint scheme. Sunliner aircraft were numbered by chain of command, from CAG, the commanding officer, executive officer, and so forth. In fact, the Hornet flown by Scott Speicher – Sunliner 403 – had LT Barry "Skull" Hull stenciled below the cockpit. "Sunliner" is the navy's tactical call sign for VFA-81. But the ATO compliant lexicon for the squadron during Operation Desert Storm was "Quicksand." Anderson is Quicksand 01 but also – according to the navy standard – Sunliner and whatever aircraft number he flew per mission.

5. Miller, Mark Crispin, "Death of a fighter pilot," *New York Times*, September 15, 1992.

6. The VFA-81 ordnance log indicates that only three air-to-air missiles were fired by the Sunliners during the war: two AIM-7M Sparrows and one AIM-9M Sidewinder. The Sparrows and Sidewinder were fired during a later mission on January 17, 1991, by Lieutenant Commander Mark Irby "MRT" Fox and Lieutenant Nicholas "Mongo" Mongillo against two Iraqi MiG-21F-13 Fishbeds. The Fishbeds had not engaged the Sunliner strike package; they were running from *Saratoga* F-14 Tomcats on a MiG sweep about twenty miles ahead of their F/A-18s. The Tomcats had turned to chase down the Fishbeds, which, as fortune would have it, turned right into the Sunliner strike package, and actually about 1,000 feet below them. Erring on the side of caution, the Tomcats did not fire on the MiGs because they were at risk of hitting the F/A-18 strike package. A *Saratoga* VAW-125 Tigertail E-2C Hawkeye vectored Fox and Mongillo toward the MiGs. Fox set his switches to heat and pulled the trigger, which launched his Sidewinder; he had intended to set up for the Sparrow and realizing what he'd done, reset when he didn't see the AIM-7M's signature smoke trail. Fox fired again, this time with the Sparrow. By the time the Sparrow got to the target, the MiG had been destroyed by the AIM-9M. Mongillo fired a Sparrow and destroyed the second Fishbed as it flew well below and under his wing. The MiG pilots had been so

focused on being shot down by the Tomcats that they flew right toward the Sunliner flight and the outcome was just the same.

Chapter 2

Where's Spike?

There was a four-hour cycle between preparing to receive the first strike and prepping for the next one. "We'd gotten the first group back and were counting noses when we realized that there was one missing. The moment the rest of them got on deck," said flight deck coordinator chief Terryl Chandler, "they bolted for the ready room, except for Spock. He came over to me and said, 'Chief, I think we lost Speicher.'" Chandler took four of his plane handlers and staged up on the bow for the next two hours waiting and hoping that Scott Speicher would come back. They stayed there until the wing's air boss, Captain James R. "Jet" O'Hora, came over the radio on the roof and said, "Sunliners, break the deck."

"We knew then that he wasn't coming home," Chandler said, emotion breaking his voice. "We waited for him as long as they'd let us stay up there. When I shook his hand, it meant something to me. It meant we'd be there for him when he came back. I promised him."

Dave Renaud strode through the *Saratoga*'s passageways in a state of shock, his mind replaying that night's strike over and over trying to sort the radio calls about the MiG-25, the fireball he'd seen and the pilots he'd heard trying to reach Spike on the radio. He couldn't believe that of all the pilots in the sky, he'd had the best view of the explosion. The flash was so big he couldn't imagine anyone flying over Iraq at that time could have missed it. He chastised himself for not marking his position, and for not breaking into the AWACS frequency to report what he saw. But the radio was busy, and he had missiles to fire. Everything had been so confusing. Worse, it had happened so fast.

The air wing intelligence officer asked Renaud if he'd seen anything out of the ordinary. He told him about the fireball, how big and bright it was and how he watched it fall to the desert below. "It didn't look to me like that was a survivable explosion," Renaud said. "You know," the intelligence officer told him, "Speicher did not come back. Go straight to Spock Anderson and tell him what you know."

Renaud found Anderson in one of the ready rooms. Since he always flew with a tape running in his head-up display to record the action in front of the Hornet and in the cockpit, he offered it up. On a night mission the video would be worthless, but he'd still have the sound, including radio communications and anything he said in the cockpit. They listened to the tape a couple of times and were able to determine where Renaud was when he spoke into the microphone about the explosion. They matched that against other Hornet data which had tracked Renaud's flight minute by minute.

If a surface-to-air missile or an enemy fighter had knocked Speicher out of the sky, Anderson would have to know precisely where to direct special operations forces to search. They pulled out Renaud's flight chart. Renaud scribbled a circle where he thought he'd seen the explosion. Next to it he wrote "Spike."

In the meantime, Bob Stumpf headed to the carrier's intelligence center for his post-mission debrief. As he wound his way through the ship, he ran into a Sunliner pilot; he doesn't recall who it was. "Hey, how'd it go?" Stumpf asked. "Speicher didn't come back," said the pilot. "Oh my gosh," said Stumpf. "I guess I thought he was probably on the ground, evading, or that there was a rescue mission in process and we'd see him in the morning." There were two likely scenarios going through Stumpf's mind: ejected and rescued, or ejected and captured. He never considered that Speicher was dead. Stumpf based this belief on the fact that in an air-to-air situation, the missiles have smaller warheads than ground-to-air missiles. Air-to-air missiles are designed to render the aircraft unflyable, not kill the pilot or totally destroy the aircraft.

"As I recall," said Stumpf in a July 2001 interview, "Spock Anderson started a personal movement ... I mean he took it upon himself to figure this out." He remembered Anderson saying, "I got to figure out what happened to Spike. I need to make sure things are happening." Anderson stopped by Stumpf's stateroom and asked for all the data from his flight. "We went to the airplane and dumped all the information out of the computer. I gave him a big stack of printouts that defined my flight pattern. He did a very detailed analysis trying to figure out when [Spike] went down, what happened, and I know I asked Frenchy [Renaud] from our squadron to be Spock's assistant if he needed any help."

Meanwhile, Albano wondered if Speicher had his survival radio, and, if so, was he simply going by what they'd all been told briefing the mission: Don't turn on your radio and monitor it because the Iraqis will use direction finders to locate you. "They had that capability." If he'd done everything right, Albano thought, he felt sure Spike was alive. Albano wondered where he'd landed. With the winds the way they were, he could have landed up to two-and-a-half miles from where his Hornet was believed to have impacted the desert floor. Then Bano inevitably came back to the thought, one he couldn't get out of his head: "Could I have done more about the MiG-25?"

Anderson's initial push to figure out where Scott had gone down didn't get a great deal of support from the air wing chain of command. The *Saratoga* started recovering aircraft from the first air strike at 5:38 A.M. local time. By 7:04 A.M. the ship had finished recovery of its planes, minus one. The petty officer of the watch wrote in the ship's deck log: "Completed recovery of aircraft with the exception of F/A-18 side #403 – Pilot LCDR Speicher of VFA-81." Shortly before launching the second wave of aircraft at 11:12 that morning, the *Saratoga*'s commanding officer, Captain Joseph S. Mobley, came up on the 1MC, the shipboard address system, to announce that Speicher had not come back from the first strike. But still, no one had notified Naval Forces Central Command (NAVCENT) that they had a pilot missing.

The delay by Speicher's air wing, Carrier Air Wing 17, in reporting his loss was critical. As a rule, the first four to five hours after a shoot down is the best window of opportunity for combat search and rescue (CSAR) success. This time frame was exceeded twice over before Lieutenant General Chuck Horner received Speicher's status information and told General H. Norman Schwarzkopf that the navy had lost an airplane.

Back in Riyadh, General Schwarzkopf had no reason to believe the first air strike had been anything less than a complete success. No one had said anything about a lost pilot. "My air force component commander, Chuck Horner, had told me," he said in an August 21, 2001 interview, "we could expect as high as twenty percent casualties, which would have been literally in the hundreds of aircraft shot down, so I was very anxious for the first report back." He received it from the navy at 5:50 a.m. local time. In his combat diary, it reads: "All 56 aircraft from the first strike are back." At 6:55 a.m. General Horner called Schwarzkopf to say, "All aircraft back." Still no mention that the *Saratoga* was shy a Hornet pilot.

"Again," Schwarzkopf reiterated, "I just assumed he was talking about all aircraft that were used in the first strike. They were going to be flying through the worst of it." Schwarzkopf didn't get his first indication that he had any downed aircraft until 12:55 local time the afternoon of January 17, "and that report stated at that time there had been two losses: Speicher and the British GR-1 Tornado crew of Flight Lieutenants John Nichol and John Peters. My God," he exclaimed, "that is an order of magnitude better than what we expected."

"I know [Anderson] was terribly frustrated," said Stumpf. "He was not happy. I got the sense that he wasn't getting the help that he needed from the hierarchy." From combat reports the assumption was made that Scott Speicher had gone down in a ball of flame. Adding to that perception was the fact no one had heard a call from Speicher on any emergency frequencies. But in all the confusion, had they just been missed? The other possibility was that Scott had experienced total electrical failure, in which case he didn't have the chance prior to ejection to make a radio call from the cockpit. The deputy air wing commander (DCAG) on *Saratoga,* Captain David V. Park, had flown in A-6E Intruder on the first strike, and while he didn't know for sure about Spike until he got back on deck, he was concerned enough to initiate checks for him before going to bed. "I asked them to check divert fields before I got some sleep. We were all tired, exhausted from the mission," he said later. "I got up four hours later and no one had done it. I made them do it when I found out." By then nearly eight hours had slipped by and Scott Speicher was still out there. "We on the *Saratoga*," said Park later, "never confirmed he went down."

Dave Park and Captain Dean M. "Milo" Hendrickson, Carrier Air Wing 17 commander, also called the CAG, a legacy term from the earlier Commander, Air Group term for the air wing, were in key positions to save Spike. "As DCAG," said Sunliner pilot Craig "Bert" Bertolett later, "Park was in the prime role to be responsible for communicating between what the squadron and air wing knew. For example, the oversized radios for vest pockets, disabled seat locators, [where] Frenchy's estimated crash site [for Speicher was], and what CENTCOM or [Vice Admiral Stanley A.] Arthur's staff should have known to execute smart decisions about CSAR." Bertolett was not alone making this point. "I've often blamed the faceless 'somebody' in the organization who failed to act, communicate and decide," Bertolett said.

Hendrickson and Park had issued the order to air wing squadron maintenance officers to turn off the electronic transponders (ELTs) in the ejection seats of all jet aircraft. They were not alone in this order. Some of the other air wing commanders on aircraft carriers in the Red Sea and Persian Gulf had done the same. This singular act helped seal Scott Speicher's fate that night. Another, of course, was reportedly the Motorola AN/PRC-112 radio. The new radios arrived on the ship January 16, just hours before the first air strike launched. Rushed into service, the Motorola AN/PRC-112 never went through the battery of operational testing that normally takes place before a new product is introduced to the fleet. The AN/PRC-112s, since improved and sold to more than thirty countries, have worked fine, according to Motorola. Yet the navy had to issue a directive that the AN/PRC-112 had to be placed in a Ziploc bag because it would short out if exposed to too much moisture. The radio was not meant for carrier aviation. Further, it was not configured to fit in the vest pockets of naval aviators' flight gear. PR1 Ted Phagan, the Sunliners' paraloft chief, told Scott and the others on the first strike: "There's a real good chance if you eject, this thing's not staying in your pocket." Though Phagan jury-rigged a flap to hold the radio in place for aviators on later strikes, it was too late to help Scott Speicher. So he thought. Scott Speicher didn't try to pack the AN/PRC-112 into his flight vest. He'd strapped the radio good and tight to his leg. Tony Albano did the same thing. The worse that could have happened, Albano said later, was that he'd landed on it when he parachuted out of the Hornet to the desert floor below. Not surprisingly, some navy aircrews insisted on keeping their old radios, GTE-Sylvania AN/PRC-90s, when they found out the new ones were too awkward, and risky, to carry. Plus, the AN/PRC-90-1 and -2 models were improved over the version carried by aircrew over Vietnam. The AN/PRC-90 operated on 121.5, 243 and 282.8 MHz AM, and it also included a beacon mode, and a tone generator to allow the sending of Morse Code. After the AN/PRC-112 began to show its shortcomings, the AN/PRC-90 became a navy pilot's prize possession.

The media seemed to know more about one missing aviator than the entire chain of command aboard the *Saratoga* in the hours immediately following his shoot down. Less than twelve hours after Scott was shot down, Paris Antenne-2 Television Network, broadcast in French, ran a news spot at one o'clock in the afternoon Paris local time that included an Islamic Republic News Agency (IRNA) report that an American jet was downed and the pilot ejected. Less than six hours later, back in Washington, the Joint Chiefs of Staff (JCS) sent a message traffic that included a printed transcript of the Paris Antenne-2 broadcast. Scrawled in the margin someone wrote: "Only U.S. plane lost was a navy F-18; pilot never heard from." But no one ran down the source of the information run by the Paris network nor did anyone pass it to CSAR forces in Riyadh that a pilot ejected and was now on the ground.

Speicher's initial loss report was not filed until twelve hours after his aircraft was first went missing. This report was forwarded from

Rear Admiral Gee to Rear Admiral Riley D. Mixon, senior commander in Red Sea. "Riley," wrote Gee, "the loss of AA403 during our initial Baghdad strike is most unfortunate." Gee's report included facts culled from aircrew debriefs and observations and investigation done by Spock Anderson. Anderson reported that Speicher was headed to Al Taqqadum, his target, some forty miles west of Baghdad. His time on target (TOT) was estimated to be 3:50 in the morning Baghdad time. Speicher never made his assigned tanking point along the Raisin tanker track at 4:40 A.M. local time. A radar cut gave Speicher's last position as 29°15'N 041°00' 30"E. The time was 3:20 A.M. and Spike was headed 015 degrees true. His launch point was 015 degrees, 268 nautical miles from his refueling point.

At 7:30 A.M. the following day, January 18, Anderson filled out the requisite paperwork for the Defense Intelligence Agency (DIA) that provided critical information on Scott's last mission. He was still listed as Duty Status, Whereabouts Unknown (DUSTWUN). Anderson cited the message traffic he'd sent reporting Speicher's loss, around first light on January 17, then added, "No firm info as to where and when the aircraft was lost or the fate of pilot. Search initiated." There were two problems with the report: no search for the pilot had been initiated at first light on January 17 and under the blank for "location of loss" Anderson scribbled CLASSIFIED. Why not DUSTWUN? After all, in truth, Anderson had no idea where Speicher was, not exactly, not then – right? But he marked his pilot's whereabouts a secret and no one could understand why. In the meantime, shipboard, air wing and squadron log books, including maintenance and ordnance records, that pertained to Speicher's flight, his jet and the mission; information from Sunliner and Rampager HUD tapes; voice tapes made from the pilots' hell hole recorders located behind the pilot's seat, and aircrew debriefs were pulled together in the Combat Data Information Center (CDIC) and turned over to the CAG before being sent forward for evaluation.

Bob Stumpf thought that Anderson had compiled enough information to go look for Spike. He'd provided a good approximate location. More importantly there was no evidence that Scott Speicher was dead, "so it seems to me that with all our massive array of airpower and rescue forces available, [much of it] exercised just a couple of days later that I know of firsthand," said Stumpf, "it was all there, it was in place and we should have gone in and looked." But Stumpf realized, too, that the *Saratoga* was a long way from CSAR forces in Riyadh. "We were seven hundred miles away from where Spike went down. We couldn't just pick up the phone and call Riyadh and say, 'Hey, go ahead. Launch the rescue.'"

What Stumpf and the other pilots on *Saratoga* didn't know was that when the coordinates for Scott Speicher's probable crash site were reported as 32°45'N 044°45'E, which would turn out to be far from where he actually went down. By then the damage was done. The wrong set of coordinates stuck to Speicher's file for more than a year after he went missing. But so did something else.

Twelve hours after Scott was shot down and thousands of miles away, Secretary of Defense Dick Cheney and Chairman of the Joint Chiefs of Staff General Colin Powell briefed the media about the first air strike of the Persian Gulf War. The picture they drew for the public was largely true. Coalition pilots had struck Baghdad hard, delivering a series of highly successful air strikes against the Iraqi capital. But then Cheney's demeanor noticeably changed. "There's been a single American aircraft lost," Cheney told reporters. "It involves a single casualty. I don't know that we want to identify the aircraft, do we?"

Cheney looked at Powell.

"It was an F-18," Powell said.

"Was that a wounding or a death?" a reporter asked.

"A . . . ," Cheney hesitated, "a death."

Cheney didn't name Speicher, but the *Saratoga*'s pilots knew who he was talking about. As soon as the squadrons returned that morning, Speicher's fate became the buzz of the ship. Cheney's statement assumed the blast Renaud saw was Speicher's jet and that he couldn't have survived the explosion. Cheney's presumptive statement would fuel the assumption that Speicher died for years to come. "How do you say something like that," said Albano later, "without knowing all the facts?"

Bob Stumpf heard that Speicher hadn't tried to contact anyone with his survival radio, but he also heard that the Sunliners' new radios wouldn't fit in their vest pockets. Maybe Speicher lost his radio when he ejected and couldn't contact anyone. He knew that Renaud hadn't seen a parachute after the explosion, but it was the middle of the night and a parachute could not have been seen. Stumpf thought they would declare Speicher killed so quickly only if someone had found his body. "Killed in action, that's bullshit," said Stumpf. "They had no business saying that because there was no evidence he was dead. So he's missing in action at that point, but they said 'killed' so I'm thinking, 'Well, shit, they know something we don't know.' To me, that was very decisive, absolute, to say that he was KIA [killed in action]."

If Speicher wasn't dead, the pilots knew that what Cheney had said could doom him. If the Iraqis captured Speicher and if President Saddam Hussein knew U.S. leaders thought he was dead, perhaps Saddam would keep him. An American pilot would be a trophy prisoner. Fellow pilots hadn't assumed Speicher was dead. If a missile impacted Speicher's Hornet, he likely ejected, they thought. "So, you know, it was premature," said Stumpf, of Cheney declaring Speicher killed in action. But what none of the *Saratoga*'s pilots, and much of Speicher's chain of command, didn't realize was that Cheney's public pronouncement of death was nothing more than that – a snap judgment in front of a room full of reporters. The navy's official status for Scott Speicher was still MIA.

Why had Cheney declared Scott dead? When NAVCENT vice admiral Arthur requested information about the loss incident, Milo Hendrickson told him that Scott's Hornet had been blown out of the sky with no chance of survival, no ejection. Arthur called Vice Admiral Jeremy "Mike" Boorda, then chief of naval personnel back in Washington, and repeated what he'd heard from Scott's air wing commander. When Cheney came in the next morning to give his now-famous press briefing, he stuck his head first in Boorda's door and asked where they stood on the F/A-18 loss. "Hey, it doesn't look good," said Boorda. Cheney replied, "He's dead?" "Yes, sir, pretty much he's dead," Boorda told him.

In a war involving pilots launching bombing raids from carriers in two different seas and coordination between military leaders in Washington and Riyadh, it might take days to thoroughly search for a downed pilot. Later that day, Anderson called a meeting of his officers. Barry Hull remembers Anderson giving the news straight. "Guys, you know Spike didn't make it back last night," he told them, "and he didn't divert either."

"That's when it hit us," said Hull. "What the hell happened? Where's Spike?" He remembered what he and others kept thinking, "Well, he must be pissed off 'cause he's walking around in the desert and he's got sand in his boots. We just never let ourselves think that he was dead."

That afternoon in Jacksonville, Florida, navy wives, relatives, friends and colleagues anxiously wondered which Hornet pilot had been killed. A middle-class neighborhood had sprouted under the flight path of Cecil Field Naval Air Station. There was no ignoring the jets when they roared overhead. Many of the pilots' teen-agers went to Nathan Bedford Forrest High School, Speicher's alma mater, where his wife, Joanne, had briefly taught home economics before quitting to have Meghan, then three, and Scott's namesake, Michael, not quite two.

Scott met Joanne at Florida State University (FSU) in 1977. She was a public relations and marketing major; he was a business major one year ahead of her. She would never forget the time he went to his first job interview, in his senior year at Florida State. It was for a typical nine-to-five desk job. He couldn't see himself pinned down behind a desk every day and told her so. "I want to fly," he confessed.[1] Though he'd never flown an airplane before, years of listening to his father, Wallace, a World War II fighter pilot, tell stories about his missions hooked Scott on the idea. The career path seemed perfectly suited to Scott, the risk-taker with the impish grin, the kid from Missouri who moved to Florida and loved to sunbathe. "You're living in Florida, man, you gotta have a tan," he'd say.

Scott Speicher loved the thrill of life on the edge. He was the guy who one-upped his Florida State buddies on the rite of passage of diving from a thirty-foot cliff into Big Dismal Sink, a sinkhole about fifteen to twenty miles south of Tallahassee. "When you got there," said David Rowe, his friend from Nathan Bedford Forrest and Florida State, "depending on the water level, it's anywhere from a thirty- to sixty-foot sheer drop to the water." They all took turns jumping feet first off the edge of the cliff. To get out, they'd grab a rope and pull themselves out of the mud and slime at the edge of the water below. Speicher watched his friends jump in, one after another, then stood at the edge of the cliff and grinned. "C'mon, Spike," they hollered up. "Is that the best you can do? That's baby lotion!" he yelled down. "That's baby lotion" was Spike's way of saying, "That ain't nothing." Speicher climbed an oak tree on the western edge of the sinkhole and soared headfirst about sixty feet into the water. "Headfirst," his friend recalled, "then a back flip. I can see him now with his arms flying, head back, looking to spot the water." Rowe thought right then that Spike was destined to get catapulted from aircraft carriers for a living. "Way to go, Spike! You're the man!" There was no doubt that Scott was okay. "You had to know Spike," said Rowe.

Soon after graduation from Florida State in 1980, Scott headed for Aviation Officers' Candidate School (AOCS) in Pensacola. He was an excellent pilot from the start. Two-and-a-half years later Scott had completed flight training and married Joanne, who was working as an assistant department store buyer, in a navy wedding ceremony at Cecil Field in December 1983. From the beginning, the couple understood the dangers associated with Scott's flying. He made sure she knew what to do if anything happened to him. He'd make her recite it to him every time he left for workups and lengthier deployments. "If anything happens to me, you know what to do?" Scott asked her. She'd always reply yes.[2] Joanne never imagined she'd actually have to put into action any of the contingency plans they discussed.

The car that wound its way down the street, past the yellow ribbons and red, white and blue streamers that had been tied to lampposts five months earlier when carrier battle groups first deployed for Desert Shield could have stopped at many homes in that neighborhood, but they knocked on the door of Joanne Speicher's battleship-gray ranch house. Joanne had heard what Secretary Cheney said, but she didn't know who'd been killed. They told her. The Boy Scout, the kid who had balanced on the end of the diving board for a shot in the high school yearbook, the husband who sat on the floor with the four- and five-year-olds in his Sunday school class coloring and pasting pictures, would not be coming home when the war was over. Now, as navy officers in crisp dress blues stood in Joanne's doorway to give her the news, suddenly the past worries, the fears that she'd hesitated to share with Scott, came flooding back.

Joanne's mind raced back to the day he left on the deployment, to August 7, 1990. She remembered that the morning was not especially remarkable, other than the fact Scott was heading off to the air station to leave for six months or more. She told Kathryn Casey of *Ladies Home Journal* that she kissed him good-bye at the front door and off he went. The children waved. "This was part of our lives," she told Casey of the deployment. "It was like a regular day."

Joanne kept to her routine, taking Meghan to her preschool three times a week and Michael to a Mothers' Day Out babysitting program held at a nearby church on Wednesdays. Casey reported in her June 1991 article, "Ten days after Scott left, his letters began arriving. They were scrawled on yellow legal paper, and he often signed them 'Spike.'" Though Joanne had not been in the habit of keeping Scott's letters in the past, she started to tuck them away in her top dresser drawer. She told Casey that she'd not wanted to burden Scott with disappointing news, but when she realized their attempt to conceive a third child hadn't worked, she had to write and tell him that it hadn't happened. "I was disappointed. He was, too. Later I felt like there was a reason it hadn't happened." He wrote back, "Don't worry about it. We'll do it. There's time."

Joanne didn't get scared until around Christmas, when tensions in the Middle East ratcheted up with passage of the United Nations (UN) Security Council resolution permitting the use of troops against Iraq if it didn't vacate Kuwait by January 15. With that resolution President George H.W. Bush had been given the green light to go after Saddam Hussein for his fall invasion of Kuwait. In letters she and Scott exchanged during the holidays, Joanne began to share her fears with Scott, to tell him that what was happening in the Persian Gulf scared her. "You know that I am completely proficient in this airplane," he tried to assure her. "I'll be home. I guarantee it."[3]

When the deadline for Iraq's withdrawal from Kuwait got closer, Joanne was glued to her television set like the rest of America. When the January 15 deadline came and went, she knew fireworks were going to follow. She'd been almost euphoric about Scott's participation in the first strike. She woke up the following morning and turned on the television to find out what was going on. Then she heard a reporter talking about a downed F/A-18. Suddenly a dose of hard reality snapped Joanne out of her euphoria. But since no one had called to tell her anything had happened to Scott, she went about her daily routine. There didn't seem to be any reason to worry. Not yet.

Joanne later recalled that all she heard when the car pulled up in front the house was the door closing. "She looked out the screen door," Casey wrote, "toward the driveway and saw the admiral of Cecil Field, the local base, the commodore, the commodore's wife, and the chaplain. The men were in their dress blues." "They didn't have to say a thing," Joanne remembered of that terrible day. "The first thing I asked was 'How did it happen?'" What followed after she uttered those words was a blur. The Speicher house soon filled with family, friends, officials from Cecil Field, and well-meaning squadron wives. They came and went. Joanne sat slumped on a couch talking to them, one at a time, sometimes in small groups. She was in shock. She was overwhelmed. Then she thought of Meghan and Michael. Meghan was old enough to understand, but Michael wasn't. He played on the floor with his toys just like any other day, except for the crush of visitors in his house. When Michael's two-year-old curiosity got the best of him, he stopped playing to visit among familiar faces and complete strangers, but he had no idea why they were there.

Meghan was a different story. Joanne took Meghan into her daintily decorated little girl's bedroom to tell her about her father.

As they sat there together, Joanne asked her if she knew why all the people were in the house. "No," she said. "It's because they have something to tell me about Daddy," Joanne explained. "Something happened to Daddy's airplane." They were quiet for a few minutes, then Meghan said in her little voice, "My daddy?" Joanne nodded and said, "Yup."[4] Sensing her mother's grief, Meghan knew that whatever had happened to her father, it was bad. Joanne didn't have to say another word.

She didn't know for certain what had happened to her husband, but Joanne's thoughts drifted to what he might have been thinking in his last moments in the airplane. The torment brought on by these thoughts was nearly unbearable. But the children kept her focused. She drove Meghan to preschool the next morning.[5] All she could think about was what could have gone wrong. Where was Scott? She wouldn't know the answer to that question for many years to come.

Casey wrote that on Joanne's thirty-second birthday, the first Sunday following Scott's loss, she had a friend send President Bush a telegram. She didn't want the president to think she was angry about what might have happened to Scott. Her support for U.S. action in the Persian Gulf remained unwavering and she wanted him to know how she felt. The president got the message and replied a couple of weeks later. "I am proud of your wonderful husband, and I will never forget him," President Bush wrote. "Sometimes God acts in strange ways – ways we do not understand right away."[6]

The president's letter wasn't the only one to arrive at Joanne's door. For several weeks to come, letters Scott had mailed in the days preceding his disappearance were brought by a tearful mail carrier. Folded inside each envelope were several pages of yellow legal paper filled with Scott's thoughts. He always assured Joanne he'd come home.[7] She was numbed by each word, still unsure what had happened to her husband. Maybe he'd make it. Maybe he would come home. After all, the *Saratoga*'s captain, Joe Mobley, kept personally communicating with her. "Every effort," he said, "continues to be made to locate Scott." Spock Anderson told her the same. "All, repeat all, theater combat search and rescue efforts were mobilized." She couldn't know that this was far from the truth. She was terrified and hopeful at the same time. But it was taking its toll.

Two weeks after she'd learned of Scott's loss, Joanne finally came to grips with the feelings of loss she'd kept pent up inside her. It was late, perhaps half past two in the morning, and she'd talked for hours with friend Albert "Buddy" Harris, who'd decided it was time for Joanne to let out the emotions she'd hidden so well from everyone, but most especially the children. She confessed her deepest thoughts, the fears she had for Scott but didn't want to hear herself say. "I didn't want Scott to know. I didn't want him to be scared for one second. I didn't want him to think, "Oh, no, I'm going down,'" Joanne told Kathryn Casey. "And I couldn't bear the thought of having a service and having nothing to bury."

Several days later Joanne received a large brown envelope that contained Scott Speicher's personal effects, including a red nylon wallet with his Florida driver's license, credit card and pictures of the children, his gold wings, a gold wedding ring – and one last letter, written January 16, 1991, the day before he disappeared. "All along I knew that there would be one more letter," Joanne said.[8] The content of the last letter Scott placed in his personal effects speaks for itself.

"As I sit down to write this letter," he explained, "things in this part of the world seem to grow more intense every hour. I am more certain," he continued, "that our air wing will be called upon…If you are reading this letter, it will be for one of two reasons: 1) I have decided I need to personally share these thoughts with you instead of holding them inside, or 2) something has happened to me. I hope it is number one."[9]

He penned separate sections to Joanne, Meghan and Michael, each beginning with "I love you." To his children, he offered his heartfelt wishes for what he wanted them to do with their lives. He told them to set goals and pursue a good education. Be kind to one another, he said. Put God first in your lives. To Joanne he said, "You are the centerpiece of my life. I have lived with you in complete satisfaction. If I am gone, learn to love again." Joanne, wrote Casey, was quieted by Scott's words. But just then she believed Scott was dead. She was ready to move on. The children would move on. "I'm at peace. I feel like it's over, and he is in a better place. I would have been angry if he died in a car crash. This was his life, and Scott wouldn't have wanted it any other way."[10] Asked what she would say to Meghan and Michael about their father when they wanted to know what kind of person he was, she told Casey, "I'll tell them he was a good man. That he loved them very much and he didn't like to leave. That he loved his job, he loved to fly, he loved his country and he loved God. That he was doing what he had to do. That they should be very proud of him, because he's a hero."

News of Scott's loss rippled through all who knew and loved him. Reactions were personal and professional. Anyone who'd known him was affected in some way by the news. Wallace Speicher didn't accept the news that his son was shot down and might never get back. He kept telling everyone, "Scotty's coming home."

David Rowe, Scott's friend since high school, had just finished a day of deer hunting in Eustis, Florida, when he turned on the television. A day after the air strikes started, Americans craved news coverage and television networks obliged. Rowe knew many navy pilots from living in Jacksonville, but also through his job at the naval aviation depot there. From what he heard coming out of his television set, the United States had lost its first pilot of Operation Desert Storm. CBS News' Dan Rather's voice came up as the photograph of a smiling pilot in a flight suit flashed on the screen. It was Scott Speicher. When Rowe saw the picture on television, nausea swept over him. He slid off the couch onto his knees, slapped the floor and cried. "God, no!"

Marine F/A-18 pilots at Sheikh Isa Air Base in Bahrain heard the news about Scott Speicher almost immediately. Among them was a young captain with VMFA-333 Fighting Shamrocks, Patrick R. "Roller" Rink, who first met Speicher as a Hornet instructor pilot. Rink was his student. He'd never forgotten him since. "He was a great teacher."

The Marine airfield at Sheikh Isa was supposed to be a secret, but everyone knew about it. The fourteen-thousand-foot airfield was new, thus no Bahraini airport personnel were attached to base when the Marines flew their Hornets into the break over the control tower and landed on Sheikh Isa's pristine airstrip. "The potential for at least one of the gaggle of about one hundred fifty fighters to swap paint at the ninety, or to meet in the middle of the runway after doing simultaneous approaches from opposite positions, was averted by adopting a calm and organized, though completely spontaneous, cadence of radio calls between flights," Rink said later. "Thank God there was no Fresnel lens at the end of the runway," he continued, referring to the series of lights that help pilots land on the deck of an aircraft carrier by projecting a landing "ball" that pilots use to guide them onto the flight deck. "I don't think any of us jarheads, and especially the air force Wild Weasel Phantom drivers, remembered what the ball looked like."

The hangars were modern structures with detached office buildings that reminded Rink of his dentist's office back in Florida. Two miles north of the airfield were barracks, brand-new and empty. To get there they drove down a newly paved, sand dune-lined road along the west side of the airstrip. Or they could take public transportation. That consisted of dilapidated buses three-quarter the size of ones in the United States. "They were driven by Pakistanis and Jordanians who secretly dreamed of NASCAR careers when the war was over," Rink explained. "They didn't dig the fact that we all carried our nine-millimeter Berettas in shoulder holsters everywhere we went. I know of at least one occasion in which one of those Berettas was used to persuade the madman driver to slow his Pakistani butt down."

Sheikh Isa was a tense place to be. Spaced along the airfield road, roughly several hundred meters apart, were twenty-foot cement guard towers. They were rarely manned, and when they were, the Bahraini troops manning them had their machine guns pointed at the Marines on their way to the field instead of outward, toward the potential threat. "Those pistols of ours," Rink said, "were feeling pretty comfy [wherever] this occurred." At the north end of the runway were fuel pits, and beside it was a Bahraini Roland mobile SAM. For a while the crew inside the Roland chassis thought it was amusing to track the Hornets with their targeting radar as they took off. "That nonsense stopped when we locked them up with our ground attack radar returning from missions. I'm sure they saw the HARMs draped under our wings."

The barracks looked like two-story dormitories, with living areas twice the size of normal college dorm rooms. But there were too few buildings to accommodate all the American pilots. A tent city was set up to house the troops and aircraft maintenance personnel. Ground officers and pilots, those going directly into combat, stayed in the barracks. It sounded like a good deal to everybody until they did the math. There were eight men to a room, but at least they had air conditioning.

Close quarters made for better stories, especially after the shooting started and nightmares kicked in. Hearing one of the boys scream "Pull up!" or "Break right" in the middle of a deep sleep put a damper on rolling over and going back to sleep. Even more remarkable, it was amazing to Rink how fast some of the pilots learned to don a gas mask while still asleep, and just as sheepishly tear it off. "We even had one guy draw his pistol, drop into a shooter's stance and do a John Belushi dance like the actor did in *Animal House*." He didn't remember any of it the next morning.

When the Marines at Sheikh Isa heard about Spike, Roller, his squadron mates and other Hornet pilots were gathered in the lobby of the barracks. They'd shoved an ottoman against one of the walls, and on top of it was their primary source of wartime intelligence: a little twelve-inch television. Cable News Network (CNN) was playing ninety-nine percent of the time. Every day they'd swing through the lobby for the latest news. "It was not a morale booster to see our intelligence people huddled there also getting updated," observed Rink, slightly amused at the sight. "As you can imagine, the lobby became quite popular when the shooting started. Most of us couldn't sleep very well from the moment we knew the shit was about to hit the fan, which was the night prior to the commencement of festivities."

Roller was standing in the lobby watching CNN along with a dozen or so other pilots when the news broke that a Hornet had been shot down. It was dark outside, and he was still trying to wake himself up for the mission brief that was about to get started. Later that morning, he was scheduled to fly a bombing sortie on the Az Zubayr rail yards in the slot between Iran and Kuwait, north of the mouth of the Tigris and Euphrates Rivers. In a telling comment tied to this mission, Rink described what missile fire looked like. That mission was the first time he'd ever encountered a SAM missile. "Huge explosion. I actually heard the *Whumpf!* and remember thinking for sure one of us had been hit. Being new to getting shot at, I wasn't so sure it wasn't me." But the giant orange and white ball he saw was only the missile's warhead. Everybody was okay. "I can see how someone without combat experience might have thought Spike's jet was blown to bits," he said.

In that lobby in the wee hours of the morning the news of a Hornet shoot down sucked the air out of the room like a giant fist to the gut. Hearing about the first casualty of the air war was not what any of them needed before stepping into the cockpit for a trip north. Yet the Marines' attitude quickly changed to anger. "Though we didn't know who the pilot was, we were pissed and someone was going to pay. While wondering who the unlucky pilot was," said Rink, "we also wondered how the SAR [search and rescue] would react. Any one of us would have fought the first jerk who even suggested that we wouldn't go in to get the downed pilot.

"I don't think we found out the downed pilot was Spike until later that day. That was another blow. Spike had been my instructor during initial training in the Hornet," Rink recalled. "Now here I was, still wet behind the ears with a license to carry enough ordnance to wipe out a small town, and not nearly as much knowledge and skill to effectively employ those weapons as the man who had just been shot down. You can imagine," he continued, "where my seat cushion quickly ended up the next time I got in the cockpit to face the SAMs and triple A." Still, he didn't really have the luxury of time to dwell on Spike, other than thinking the usual "Why haven't they found him?" Not only was he busy trying to keep his own backside from sitting in an interrogation room in downtown Baghdad, but he was also upgrading to flight lead – under combat conditions.

Back on the *Saratoga*, Speicher's squadron mates were in much the same position as the Marines at Sheikh Isa. They had missions to fly and little time to dwell on what happened to their friend. The United States had not yet claimed air superiority over Iraqi skies. But that would come soon enough. Sunliner pilot lieutenant Craig Bertolett wrote his family and friends near the end of the war that he'd been confident all along that "we would own the skies within three days." The night after Speicher went down, the *Saratoga* lost an A-6E Intruder and a few days after that, an F-14 Tomcat. "We've had some losses as I'm sure you've heard," he told them. "LCDR Speicher did not return from his mission the first night. He was an instructor of mine when I was learning to fly the Hornet and joined our squadron just over a year ago. He was an excellent pilot and a great person."

It took several days for Speicher's loss to feel real to the other Sunliners. Dying on a mission became a real possibility. "Spike, he's better than me and he got it," Hull kept thinking. "That means I can get it." Lieutenant Douglas "Coop" Cooper was as shocked as the rest of his squadron mates that Spike hadn't returned. No one could've imagined that he wouldn't make it. They figured he'd be found and later returned to the ship. "I'll never forget the night that I had the duty with the senior chief, just a few days before the shooting started. There was nobody else in the ready room and senior chief and I were sitting behind the desk doing nothing particular. Must have been close to midnight," he remembered, "when in walks Spike. He looks around, makes sure no one else is nearby. You could tell he wanted privacy. Next thing you know, he pops a tape in the VCR and gets comfortable in one of the ready room chairs, thinking we're not going to notice. The chief and I just smiled at each other." Spike had put in a tape of his children that Joanne had sent out to the ship. "He was quiet, then you'd hear him just having the best laugh."

For Stumpf, a seventeen-year veteran pilot, climbing back in cockpit of his Hornet for a second mission was the toughest thing he had ever done. Stumpf, Hull and the others tried to block out what happened to Speicher on that first strike and bear down on knocking out Iraqi air defenses. "There was much more running through my mind," wrote Barry Hull of that first night, "but the main emotion was fear." He also realized that all the practicing the Sunliners had done before the war had paid off. Pilots were conditioned to keep their eyes open, their heads on a swivel, for threats around them, especially those from behind, what pilots call their "six." "Someone told us way back if we didn't check six in practice, we wouldn't do it in combat. Everyone on that mission came back with a sore neck from jerking our heads back and forth, checking six. The instinct of survival, I've felt it pretty good now, I think."

Anderson released the findings of his investigation on January 25, eight days after Scott Speicher went down. He recommended that Speicher's status stay MIA. This status was predicated both on the positively confirmed reports that Speicher's aircraft had been shot down, so word was put out for the consumption of the *Saratoga* air wing, crew, Speicher's family and friends, of an identifiable crash site. He also reported that "theater strike rescue forces have reported no visual signals or radio communications from LCDR Speicher. Strike rescue efforts will continue."

Yet a signal had been sent. One of the many tragedies associated with the Speicher case is the dismissal of a report by a former Joint Rescue Coordination Center (JRCC) commanding officer, information that was not presented until April 21, 1994, as part of the investigation conducted after Speicher's wreckage was located. Two clicks were picked up on January 18, 1991, by an air force RC-135 collection platform and a navy E-2C Hawkeye. The communication, heard about 8:21 p.m. local time, came in on the "404" emergency guard frequency. Department of Defense Prisoner of War/Missing Personnel Office (DPMO) analysts subsequently dismissed the incident, correlating it to the A-6E Intruder lost off *Saratoga* on the night of January 17. But it could not have been the Intruder crew. One of them dropped his radio on the way down in the parachute, and the other, who'd broken his collarbone, removed his flight vest with his radio in it after getting help from his bombardier-navigator to do so. As they moved to evade potential captors, the A-6E crew left the pilot's vest behind, with the radio inside. They didn't have a radio to make any calls or make any clicks on 404 guard frequency.

Further, Anderson's statement that strike rescue forces were looking for Scott Speicher was misleading. No rescues were planned or mounted. That wasn't Anderson's call. But all of this paled in comparison to what was actually known about Speicher's jet. No one knew just yet that a decision had already been made – far removed from the *Saratoga* – that Spike would be left behind.

Endnotes

1. Casey, Kathryn, "The wings of love," *Ladies' Home Journal*, June 1991, p. 197. *The Ladies' Home Journal* interview was the first and only interview Joanne L. Speicher gave after Scott Speicher's loss. The Office of Naval Intelligence, which kept track of most media associated with Speicher's loss and eventual investigation, forwarded this article with several others to the author.

2. Ibid., p. 197.

3. Ibid.

4. Ibid., p. 198.

5. Ibid., p. 199.

6. Ibid.

7. Ibid.

8. Ibid.

9. Ibid.

10. Ibid.

Chapter 3

The Day After

"The day after he got shot down," said Rear Admiral J. Michael "Carlos" Johnson, "I told the people down at Cecil Field how he got shot down." As the director of the Office of Naval Intelligence's Strike Projection Evaluation and Anti-Air Warfare Research (SPEAR) group during Desert Storm, then-Captain Johnson provided critical analyses to support combat operations in the Persian Gulf. But he also got involved in sorting out each American air loss. SPEAR analysts culled data and imagery from highly classified collection platforms and AWACS aircraft, searching for information that might tell them what happened to Scott Speicher. Airborne collection platforms in Speicher's sector that night went far beyond the AWACS, and included the navy EP-3 Aries II, several air force RC-135 Rivet Joints and EC-130H Rivet Fire/Compass Calls, and the J-STARS, which was making its combat debut over Iraq. The J-STARS was a Grumman Boeing E-8 aircraft used to provide ground surveillance of the enemy from the air.

Information gleaned from the air force's collection platforms provided critical data and infrared nighttime imagery of the aircraft that engaged Scott Speicher's F/A-18 Hornet in the wee hours of January 17, 1991. Going back over these images immediately after his loss, analysts saw, frame by frame, the heat spikes of the MiG-25PDS Foxbat E's engines as the aircraft turned east and was on the run; it wasn't the shooter. Then they saw an air-to-air missile come off the rail of the assaulting aircraft – the jet that fired the weapon that really took down Speicher's Hornet – and just then they saw it strike Speicher's Hornet. Then they caught the rocket motor of Speicher's ejection seat fire off. All saw clearly what happened when the missile struck Speicher's F/A-18 and none dispute that the Hornet's ejection seat separated from the aircraft. In the darkness over Iraq, Scott Speicher was headed to the desert floor.

"We knew at the time that it was an attack from another aircraft," said Johnson. "We also know that nothing catastrophic had happened to Speicher's aircraft," meaning that the jet hadn't blown apart in midair. They looked at infrared overheads and scanned for Speicher using electronic intelligence platforms. Infrared could pick up the magnesium fire from the tires on Speicher's jet. But they could also go back to the air force collection platforms and acquired Speicher's track right away. This is what made Johnson so confident of what had taken down Speicher's jet. He could eliminate any missiles launched from the ground. An SA-6 couldn't have gotten him; none were under his flight path. And it couldn't have been an SA-2 or -3. Those weren't close enough to where Scott was last seen. Then they checked pilot reports, particularly those submitted by A-6E Intruder pilots and bombardier-navigators because they wore night vision goggles. No one saw any SAM trails. SPEAR covered all the possibilities and then Johnson immediately briefed the chain of command.

To anyone who'd not seen what Johnson and others had, all the evidence, at first, pointed to the MiG-25 and the Bisnovat R-40/NATO AA-6 Acrid missile it carried. The MiG-25 in question came from the Iraqi air base at Al Taqqadum, where Saddam's air force quartered its MiG-25s and Sukhoi Su-25 Frogfoots. Later, in his widely publicized August 5, 2003 press briefing, then Defense Secretary Donald H. Rumsfeld talked more about the Iraqi airfield. "We'd heard," he told reporters, "a great many things had been buried, but we had not known where they were, and we'd been operating in that immediate vicinity for weeks and weeks and weeks [after the March 20, 2003 invasion] [perhaps] 12, 13 weeks, and didn't know they were [there]. He wasn't sure how many aircraft had been found but continued, "It wasn't one or two." This was a classic example, he iterated, of the challenges that the Iraq Survey Group (ISG) faced locating weapons of mass destruction in Iraq. "Something as big as an airplane that's within," he paused, "a stone's throw of where you're functioning, and you don't know it's there because you don't run around digging into everything on a discovery process." He ended the exchange with well worn advice that fits the Speicher case as much as any other when he cautioned "the absence of evidence is not evidence of absence." As it turned out, American investigators found thirty to forty MiG-25s and Su-25 ground attack jets buried at Al Taqqadum.

On the first *Saratoga*/Carrier Air Wing 17 strike of Operation Desert Storm, supported by dual carrier and U.S. Air Force suppression of enemy air defense (SEAD) operations, the carrier's A-6E Intruders hit Al Taqqadum airfield, located just then in the most heavily defended Iraqi area west of the capital. Despite heavy flack, numerous surface-to-air missile attacks on their aircraft, and the preponderance of enemy fighters coming up into the navy attack line, the Intruders destroyed key buildings and heavily damaged the airfield's ramp and taxiways. High above the airfield, the F-15 MiG sweepers applied the heat.

What we know about the MiG-25 that engaged Spock Anderson is this: it had been in afterburner two-thirds of the time it flew hit-and-miss through the navy's strike package. Expertly threading his Foxbat through Spock Anderson's Hornets, the MiG's pilot knew he was running in a crowd, a crowd with enough friendlies to shoot one another down that his chances of being shot at were unlikely and his escape assured. The rules of engagement, in fact, kept American pilots from firing on an enemy aircraft until the bandit was in the clear.

"We realized that the MiG-25 pilot [Lieutenant Zuhair Dawood of the 84th squadron of the Iraqi Air Force[1]] hadn't communicated with his handler that night either," said Johnson. The problem with the MiG-25 story is twofold: Johnson pointed out both. No enemy fighters fired on Coalition aircraft that night despite an after action report filed by the Central Intelligence Agency (CIA) that attributed Speicher's loss to the MiG-25's AA-6 Acrid missile. Further, no Iraqi media made a hero out of a MiG pilot for shooting down a first-line U.S. Navy fighter. In the days that followed: nothing from Iraqi propagandists and, importantly, no chatter from Iraqi intelligence indicating its air force had picked off a navy pilot. "If an Iraqi pilot shot down an American F/A-18," Johnson iterated, "it would've been in the Iraqi media by morning. It wasn't." Later information confirmed what Johnson said. The MiG-25 pilot scrambled from an Iraqi airfield below the American attack. To reiterate, the MiG-25 had been flushed out by U.S. Air Force F-15 Eagles hunting enemy aircraft and was trying to get away from them when the MiG pilot found himself weaving through the navy's strike package. The F-15s hung back after Anderson engaged the MiG. But they hadn't gone away.

So who got Scott Speicher? "I personally thought it might have been a midair between Speicher and the MiG-25," Johnson speculated when he first got word of the incident and hadn't yet evaluated the collection platform imagery. The two aircraft were, as the AWACS controller documented, merged "on top of one another" for a few seconds, observed Johnson, so the MiG-25 wasn't able to fire on him. Certainly, the AWACS saw this, too. After-action analysis suggested rightly that the MiG-25 had passed by Scott Speicher at breakneck speed. He was running east. Further, when Speicher's wreckage was discovered later, crash investigators saw no evidence of a midair collision. The evidence did show missile damage. This begged the question that no one wanted to ask and answer publicly, not then, not now.

"I heard that an Eagle pilot claimed he bagged a MiG-25 just after, so maybe he got him," said Tony Albano. "We were on air force AWACS strike frequency that night and the F-15s were on a different CAP [combat air patrol] fighter control frequency, which is where I think the confusion occurred trying to identify the MiG so Spock could shoot."

Despite Johnson's analysis of Speicher's shoot down, despite the fact that it was an air-to-air attack on his Hornet, and despite the lack of physical evidence that Scott perished with his aircraft, then-Secretary of Defense Dick Cheney told the press that a surface-to-air missile had taken down Speicher's F/A-18. "There seemed to be a great deal of resistance," observed Johnson, "to admit an air-to-air loss." No one wanted to talk about anything but "total victory," a flawless performance by U.S. pilots. "We've destroyed twenty-nine Iraqi aircraft, with not one air-to-air loss on the part of the Coalition," claimed General H. Norman Schwarzkopf at a briefing held in Riyadh on January 30. "The score is totally one-sided," said President George H.W. Bush to the media pool six days later. "In fact," he continued, "in every engagement in the air, the Iraqi planes and pilots have gone down."[2] Had they?

The air war was not, as Mark Crispin Miller observed in his *New York Times* article "Conduct of the Persian Gulf War," "quite the shutout that the U.S. propagandists kept extolling." The thought of a Soviet-made MiG-25 taking out a U.S. Navy F/A-18 could ruin the pretty picture the Pentagon wanted to paint at war's end. In its final report to Congress the Pentagon claimed, "Fortunately, all but one plane (an F/A-18 from the USS *Saratoga*) returned safely." Miller wrote that the Speicher episode was further obfuscated by an upbeat description of his loss to an Iraqi MiG. "Our relief," states the report, "in having successfully completed the strike without loss to ourselves was overwhelming."

A naval officer confided to Miller that it was primarily an ego issue that no one wanted to come clean publicly about the MiG-25. "That refusal," wrote Miller, "to acknowledge any loss, was surely hardened by the American perception of Iraqi 'backwardness' – much as in Vietnam, where U.S. officers likewise deemed the enemy too primitive to thwart our gleaming weaponry."[3] But little did Miller or anyone else realize just then that no one with access to highly classified intelligence, including Carlos Johnson himself, believed that a MiG-25 shot down Scott Speicher. His squadron mates, knowing none of this, believed that the official version was nothing more than a convenient means of subverting the truth of who took down Speicher's Hornet that night. Who fired the missile beyond visual range and then didn't own up?

Interdepartmental confusion provides prequel. Back at the beginning, before the war started, targets for the air campaign had been crafted by the U.S. Air Force, whose planners dominated Schwarzkopf's staff at Riyadh. General Chuck Horner, Central Command Air Force Commander (CENTAF) and Joint Force Air

Component Commander (JFACC), and his predominantly air force staff, maintained strict beyond-visual-range rules of engagement, concerned that anything less would result in possible blue-on-blue kills. Friendly fire was clearly on Horner's mind when the rules of engagement were posted for all air assets in the Red Sea and Persian Gulf. While there were no confirmed cases of air-to-air friendly fire incidents during the Persian Gulf War, it doesn't mean they didn't happen. Of the 148 American combat deaths, twenty-four percent were killed by fratricide, a total of 35 troops. Eleven others died in detonations of allied munitions. Nine British service personnel were also killed in an air-to-ground friendly fire attack when a U.S. Air Force A-10A Thunderbolt II attacked a group of Warrior infantry fighting vehicles (IFVs).

Air force colonel John A. Warden III crafted the original Instant Thunder air campaign that morphed into Operation Desert Storm. Daily missions were broken into air tasking orders (ATOs). These orders scheduled and coordinated all daily Coalition air activity that took place over Iraq and Saudi Arabia. Warden's planning didn't cover navy fleet defense sorties because he couldn't know what navy assets would be available to him when he was writing it on August 6, 1990. Warden planned around air force, and only air force, participation. "We were told to build an air option," he wrote later, "and we did it from an air force perspective because of the expertise that we had and what our tasking was."[4]

Warden attended a brief with General Schwarzkopf at MacDill Air Force Base in Florida on August 10. Schwarzkopf told his planning staff to prepare appropriately for integration of Special Forces, army helicopters, Marine Corps ground and aviation assets, and planning proffered from the navy, among others. Horner brought in air force brigadier general Buster C. Glosson to rewrite Warden's original strategy, concerned that Warden's plan would not integrate assets beyond the air force nor strike the decisive blow against Iraq that Washington wanted. Glosson's planning team, nicknamed Checkmate and located in a Pentagon subbasement, quickly expanded the plan from eighty-four targets and a seven-day air campaign to one far greater. As December arrived and more aviation assets arrived in-theater, it was clear that even with the direction Horner had given Glosson, the plan still leaned toward the air force. To Glosson's credit he tried wherever possible to accommodate the other services, but his was not the only hand on the planning process. The team grew exponentially as war drew near, eventually including Special Forces and intelligence. But many others were missing from the table.

The daily air tasking orders, which took their cue from the overall air campaign plan, provided each sortie with ATO call signs, airspace deconfliction, friendly air defense coordination, electronic warfare, suppression of enemy air defenses (SEAD), and combat search and rescue (CSAR). The document also divvied out target assignments, weapons required to effectively take out the target, and escort and tanker rendezvous schedules. A completed ATO looked like a three-hundred-page telephone book.

Horner's chief air plans officer, Lieutenant Colonel John A. Corder, took his boss' lead and established stringent rules of engagement to avoid shooting down friendly aircraft. These rules required friendly fighters to make two types of independent verification before a bogey became a bandit and air-to-air missiles were fired. But the Navy didn't have one aircraft with the sophistication Corder required. The F-14 Tomcat could identify friend or foe transponders in opposition aircraft, but did not possess more sophisticated electronic identification features found in the air force's F-15 and F-16 aircraft. The F/A-18 Hornet had advanced electronic features but was hobbled by its inability to clearly distinguish friend from foe. One Marine Corps pilot told a postwar House Armed Services Committee, "We need to start buying airplanes more like the air force, with the full set of gear. Instead, we buy Cadillacs with rollup windows, like the F/A-18 with unsatisfactory radar warning receivers, expendables such as chaff and flares, and missile and bomb racks. I would give up one of the twelve aircraft in my squadron," he said, "in order to fully equip the other eleven." Corder made the comment: "My perception was the navy thought the reason we were insisting on two independent means of verification was because we were going to take the opportunity to wrest the Top Gun medal away from these guys. It was a manhood thing."[5] But it had nothing to do with manhood, not really, and everything to do with an unyielding policy that hamstrung the F-14 Tomcat for the entire war.

In his analysis of joint air operations in the Persian Gulf War air campaign, then air force major P. Mason Carpenter observed that the navy F-14 with the AIM-54C Phoenix missile could fire at targets fifty-five to sixty miles away, and the navy wanted to be able to employ it. "The navy," he wrote, "wanted to use AWACS to distinguish enemy aircraft from friendly, but, again, the USAF commanders were reluctant. AWACS, by itself, was unsatisfactory because AWACS-identified positions," he continued, "can be off by as much as five or six miles." None of this considered the biggest problem of all: the difference between the air force and navy employment of fighter aircraft. Carpenter added that the air force developed its tactics from "air saturated" Central European environments in which enemy fighters were harder to identify, thus the air force sculpted and procured its extensive identification systems to avoid or reduce fratricides. The navy planned air operations for a blue water, controlled environment.

Desert Storm more closely resembled the air force's experience in Central Europe, and though NAVCENT vice admiral Stanley Arthur understood it, he knew his carrier battle group commanders were frustrated by the restrictions put on use of the Phoenix missile. Though the degree of displeasure varied widely from one aircraft carrier to another, the unhappiness was generally shared all around. Arthur's commanders weren't happy. Carpenter noted that frustrated naval officers believed the strict rules of engagement were designed "to optimize USAF air-to-air capabilities at the expense of the navy." He quoted navy officers sent to the Joint Force Air Component Commander's special planning cell: "This war was utilized by the USAF to prove 'USAF Air Power,' not prove that combined forces or even joint forces could force multiply and more effectively conduct the war. For example," they cited, "the F-14 was originally restricted from forward combat air patrol (CAP) position because CAP aircraft were required to have the ability to electronically identify (EID) and interrogate IFF, friendly and foe."

Horner later recalled a visit from Arthur that ended in stalemate. "Stan Arthur came to me because the F-14 guys wanted to use the Phoenix. I understood exactly where he was coming from," Horner said. But he asked Arthur to take his case to Schwarzkopf and let him adjudicate it. "This is one area where we have an honest difference of opinion," Horner confessed then and later. Arthur went to Schwarzkopf, but the general didn't understand the argument so he referred it back to Horner. "I understand where you are coming from," Horner wrote Arthur, "but the trouble is, the risk is higher than the benefit."[6]

Lieutenant Commander Eddie "Fast Eddie" Smith planned the mission Scott Speicher flew the night he went down. Fast Eddie was one of the navy staff on the JFACC at Riyadh. He was also an F/A-18 pilot. "It should have been a benign and relatively safe sortie for all involved," he said. He was intimately familiar with the big picture over western Iraq that night. The possibility of friendly fire and a missed MiG-25 drew pointed comment from Smith. "There should have been no air force aircraft in the vicinity, or at least closer than the AWACS." But according to Fast Eddie other friendlies could have been on the edge of the HARM shooters' range, perhaps air force F-4 Wild Weasels, "although," he said, "nothing else friendly [was out there] that could have reached out and touched Scott, at least not air force-wise." Then he qualified that statement. Smith stated that while several issues divided the navy and air force during the war, the air force F-15 pilots' practice of flipping to the navy's part of the ATO to check out where the navy's MiG sweepers' were going to be to get in on the action was among the most problematic. The Eagle drivers knew, he said, that navy pilots were forbidden from firing on enemy aircraft without proper identification beyond visual range, and they took advantage of it. That night F-15 pilots weren't supposed to be anywhere close to the navy Hornet strike package, but they were.

A House Armed Services Committee report released on March 30, 1992, over a year after the war ended, documented what frustrated navy pilots already knew: that the air tasking orders often hindered their ability to respond to real-time battlefield developments, and air force pilots opportunistically lay in wait to jump on a designated navy target when the navy had the situation well in hand. The report cited the example of two brothers, one a navy pilot, the other an air force pilot. During the air campaign the Persian Gulf Carrier Task Force came across reliable intelligence that several MiGs were parked at an Iraqi airfield. The navy passed the information, marked urgent, to Riyadh several times, asking for a tasking in the ATO to attack the target. The next few ATOs arrived without a tasking to the navy to attack the airfield. Carrier air wing commanders again contacted Riyadh to say, according to recorded statements in the House document, "Hey guys, this is a great juicy target. Let us take it out." Again the ATO arrived without the tasking. Eventually the navy pilot called his air force brother at Al Kharj Air Base through the commercial satellite hookup and told him about the target. The next day the navy pilot got a message from his brother: "Mission accomplished. Thanks for the DFC!" The DFC is a Distinguished Flying Cross.

Eagle pilot captain Brent A. Beecham of the 71st Tactical Fighter Squadron, 1st Tactical Fighter Wing, didn't fly the first night of the air war, but he was briefed before his mission the next day to listen for any message from a downed navy pilot. Though he didn't have a name to go with the request, that pilot turned out to be Scott Speicher. "I do have a friend, Steve "Tater" Tate, who was in the area the first night and shot down a [Iraqi] Mirage F-1," said Beecham. "I have talked with other air force pilots, all of who believe that an F-14 shot down Scott." While they may believe this, he also emphasized the confusion that existed in the opening days of the air war. There was an incident in which a pilot from Beecham's squadron was given permission to shoot down a target that had been made a bandit. But the pilot wasn't so sure the target was an enemy fighter and held his fire. The aircraft he might have shot down, had he followed the AWACS guidance, was a U.S. Air Force F-111 Aardvark.

Marine Corps Hornet pilot Patrick Rink shared a similar story: "I know of at least two occasions where the Marines were cleared by the AWACS and our EID display to fire on MiGs. But they turned out to be friendlies. Thank God we didn't shoot." The F/A-18 EID software used during the Persian Gulf War would, almost without fail, identify Marine Corps AV-8 Harriers and air force F-4 Wild Weasels as MiG-21s. The Hornet software could also paint the French Mirage aircraft as a foe. "Bottom line," said Rink, "That was an eye opener for everyone, and I'm really surprised we didn't have some blue-on-blue those first few missions."

The navy strike package that flew into Iraq that first night of the air campaign was accompanied by navy F-14 Tomcats, which provided forward combat air patrol, and EA-6B Prowlers to jam enemy radar and communications. Fast Eddie Smith observed that the Prowlers wreaked havoc with aircraft radars, too. That night Tomcats and Prowlers vectored between the HARM shooters. The navy and Marine Corps were accustomed to working together, thus the presence of the EA-6B aircraft would not have caused problems. "We would have been," said Smith, "on the correct [directional] axis to avoid [interference from the Prowlers' jamming equipment]. The air force AWACS, though," he continued, "might not have been. We just weren't that well coordinated." He'd heard that the AWACS missed the MiG-25, the one everyone assumed got Scott, because of the Prowlers. When he asked around, Smith located two separate and credible sources who confirmed what he'd heard about the AWACS missing the Foxbat until it was too late. In other words," he said later, "that might be what's so secret and the reason the air force won't cooperate" with queries into Scott Speicher's loss that night.

The air force's reluctance to cooperate could well be as Smith suggests. The AWACS operator's misstep ultimately started a cascade of mistakes "in the flying of it" that took down Speicher's jet. Though infrared nighttime footage remains under the tight control of the air force, it did permit limited access to the tape during the Speicher investigation. There were eight kills officially recorded the first day of the air war over Iraq, six of them, all beyond visual range, credited to the air force, and two by the navy, both within visual range. Only in more recent years has a record surfaced that might clarify who shot the missile that inadvertently got Speicher.

Fighter Squadron Thirty-Two (VF-32) Swordsmen F-14A from the USS *John F. Kennedy* (CV-67) air wing – no aircrew named – claimed to have killed an Iraqi Air Force F-1EQ Mirage with an AIM-54C Phoenix but this couldn't be confirmed. Then there was the report of a VF-32 F-14A that claimed to have damaged/had a close encounter with the MiG-25PDS Foxbat E – it fired an AIM-7M Sparrow at the fleeing Iraqi jet. This incident isn't mentioned in any official record of what was shot that night and it wasn't talked about either. But it was remembered by an air force controller who recalled the navy pilot's concern about friendlies and the "Fox 1" – the call out when a pilot fires the Sparrow – and he, like two other air force operators up that night, heard the splash call loud and clear. The controller, when asked about that night in early February 2002, stated that ever since the war he felt like the navy was hiding something.

"If [Speicher] was shot down west of Baghdad [and he was]," wrote Beecham on December 9, 2009, it was more likely the 58th Squadron in the area where Speicher's Hornet went down. He recalled that his squadron, the 71st, had a run in with the 58th on January 17: "We were about to intercept a MiG-29 over Al Taqqadum Air Base when the 58th came out of nowhere, shot down the MiG and then blew right through the middle of our sixty-plus-aircraft formation. My squadron commander called theirs [Colonel Rick Parsons]," he continued, "and told them he would shoot them down if they got near him again. He was pissed."

The 58th belonged to the 33rd Tactical Fighter Wing based at Eglin Air Force Base, Florida, and flew out of King Faisal Air Base, Saudi Arabia, during Desert Storm. As the war progressed, the 58th flew 1,689 combat sorties and destroyed fifteen other enemy aircraft. Despite the great air victory experienced by the 58th and Coalition air power in the war, it is that first day's statistics that are the most important: three Mirage F-1EQs, one Mirage F-1EQ probable (later determined to be a maneuvering suicide), five MiG-29 Fulcrums, and the most important of all, the loss of one U.S. Navy

F/A-18 Hornet. Officially, the 58th got four of the six air force kills that night; the 71st and an EF-111A from the 48th Tactical Fighter Wing are credited with the other two. The time frame and circumstance of the air force's January 17 kills do not line up with Speicher's loss. But patterns of behavior offer insight into what was going on that night and how it might have happened. Repeated air force after-action systems and operational reports collectively mention too much noise and confusion in the cockpit and not taking the time to properly identify the target.

We know now, given the preponderance of evidence provided by the infrared imagery and investigators' findings that it was a combination of an American fighter pilot's actions and AWACS controller mistakes that led to Speicher's shoot down. A serviceman who became privy to events on board *LaSalle observed,* "I truly hate that [it was a] blue-on-blue shoot [down], [and] regardless of who fired ... it's really a matter of what happened next that makes this all FUBAR [fucked up beyond all recognition] in the first place ... considering all of our weapons are designed to kill the bird [aircraft] and not the pilots. We both know it's what happened in the following hours [after the shoot-down] that ultimately killed Scott anyway it went down."

In all the years since Speicher's blue-on-blue shoot down on January 17, 1991, it is the cover stories and lies told many times over, with a different flourish each time intended to deceive and further mislead the public, that has muddied his fate and cast doubt over his initial survival. The absence of open and constructive dialogue, of honesty and the pursuit of truth on the ground robbed Scott Speicher of his life and did nothing to better the standards of training, discipline and cooperation between the United States' armed services and its allies, a point certainly not lost on one of the Persian Gulf War's key participants.

General Sir Peter de la Billière KCB, KBE, DSO, MC, DL, in charge of the British Special Air Service (SAS) forces during the Persian Gulf War, was asked directly about the fratricide issue in a March 30, 2003 interview with the BBC's David Frost. Referring to Desert Storm, General de la Billière's replied:

> Well I'd rather call it blue on blue, I don't like friendly fire, it doesn't describe it all aptly. Yes, it's, I've fought in many campaigns and there's never been a campaign where there hasn't been blue on blue situations and they're most regrettable - the most regrettable type of casualties you can have. And they are a reflection of the standard of training and pre-operational cooperation between the forces involved. And I think that in my view we've had too many situations in this war [Desert Storm] and one has to ask whether the services, whether they be British or American, have been given enough time to train together, when things are peaceful and quiet, as opposed to being diverted on to other commitments, which of course leads on then into a peacetime situation where you ask whether the army is strong enough, or the services are strong enough, numerically, or whether in fact they've got too many commitments to do their training.[7]

Scott and Joanne Speicher's friend Albert "Buddy" Harris was a navy F/A-18 pilot who'd met Scott in Pensacola in 1980 when both were in Aviation Officers' Candidate School training to be fighter pilots. Harris went to his first fleet squadron and left for deployment soon after. Ten days before his scheduled return home Harris' house in Jacksonville caught fire. The only clothes he had were the ones he'd taken on deployment. Speicher heard what happened and showed up at the ship when Harris got back. Scott handed Buddy a suitcase of his own clothes. "Here you go," Speicher said. "You need these worse than I do."

Harris was now working at the Pentagon compiling a report that documented the navy's role in Operation Desert Storm's air campaign. Comments he made later, in the fall of 2001, certainly added fuel to the blue-on-blue debate that has long shrouded the Speicher case. Harris was frustrated, for good reason, by everyone involved denying responsibility. "It kept getting me angry because these people kept saying: 'It's not our fault, it's not our fault.' And it absolutely was their fault. And unfortunately, those are some of the same people now who are in a position to go forward and try to resolve...," he hesitated, "to get Scott repatriated." Asked about the air force and navy roles in Scott's shoot-down, whether it was a fighter pilot or AWACS controller who made the mistake, Harris interjected quickly, not faltering in his response. "Fighter jet. That guy didn't really…it really wasn't his fault. It was the navy's fault. The [AWACS] controller gave clearance to fire to Anderson… [who'd gone back to the E-2C Hawkeye to get his permission]. Pretty much nobody disputes that. But Spock is the only one who disputes it. Everyone else goes, 'Yeah, I heard it,' [in reference to Anderson getting permission to fire from the AWACS controller] but Spock says, 'I didn't hear it.'" Spock Anderson didn't hear the permission to fire call from the AWACS because he had gone off his assigned tactical frequencies, aggravated with the controller's repeated response "Negative bandit. Declare bogey."

Once off his assigned frequencies, Anderson missed the critical call from the AWACS to take out the MiG-25, a call air force assets heard clearly. "But Spock had just switched frequencies," Harris said, "and went back to his squadron frequency," which was also not right, because it is possible to listen to both. "So, he was off frequency. That's why he didn't hear it. The strike leader ended up not being on the same frequency as the whole pack, which is a very unusual circumstance." Certainly, it is this confusion that started the shoot-down finger pointing between the air force and navy in the wake of Speicher's loss. Speicher's F/A-18 brethren were sure it had to be an air force F-15 that jumped the navy ATO and killed "a MiG" mixing it up with a Coalition aircraft that was probably Speicher. The only problem with that thinking is the timing of air force kills that night – they weren't in sync with the time-frame in which Speicher's jet was hit. Air force fighter pilots and AWACS operators have never wavered in their statements that it was the F-14 was responsible for the loss of Scott Speicher's Hornet.

Others would disagree. Craig Bertolett, speaking of Anderson later, defended his commanding officer's knowledge of the ATO that night. "Spock knew the ATO cold," said Bertolett, "so if there was a way to solve the MiG-25 problem, I'm sure he attempted it." He cited examples of Anderson's problem-solving in the air. "During workups back off the east coast of Florida he'd carry a cellular phone in the cockpit. He'd call the shore detachment and supplement the comms regarding maintenance and parts. Also, during Desert Storm," he continued, "he'd take NVGs [night vision goggles] into the cockpit; he'd let us do it also. These were the binocular type used by ship's company to defend against small boats at night, and not the aviation, helmet-mounted kind. We wouldn't take them into bad guy country… [just] on combat air patrols." The bottom line, said Bertolett, is that "he was a technology guy, loved gadgets, and kept looking for ways to apply them." He also wouldn't have let Scott Speicher get shot down if he could do something about it.

The AWACS controllers on board Cougar that night bear part of the blame for Scott Speicher's loss. When Anderson and the MiG pilot merged the last time, hurtling toward each other at a closure rate of one thousand seven hundred knots, Anderson performed a maneuver called "the bug."

"We call it a bug out," said Barry Hull. "You point your nose directly at somebody and you merge. You try to merge at 180 degrees out with no angles on either one of you and you unload and you go." For an enemy fighter to turn around and chase you down once a pilot has "unloaded" or given the jet full power is nearly impossible at that point. "But who would have guessed," he said, "that the MiG-25 could blow through the formation like that?" The question asked later: Where was the AWACS in all this? The AWACS should have been all over the merge, vectoring fighters into position for a successful bug, and giving frequent situational reports (SITREPS) on the position and aspect of the MiG. "If this isn't what happened," said former Marine fighter pilot Patrick Rink, "the AWACS definitely dropped the ball. The MiG was pushed to the back burner when he should have been priority one."

Barry Hull had part of the answer to what happened, if only he'd kept his HUD tape from that night. He replayed it for himself so many times he can recite the radio calls nearly verbatim. "I remember listening to the audio later. I wish I hadn't done this. It embarrassed me because my breathing is, you know… I sounded scared. So I erased it. Now I wish I hadn't." At the time, Hull explained, "I was in the middle of this war. I can't sound scared." No other Hornet pilots on Anderson's strike saved copies of their HUD tapes from that night either. Should they? In hindsight many of them would answer yes, most especially given what they'd later find out happened to Speicher. With a Hornet from the *Saratoga*'s strike package unaccounted for, shipboard intelligence officers collected the HUD tapes from every Hornet on the mission.

On his tape Hull said it was possible to hear all the radio transmissions. "It recorded everything I could hear in my headset." He added later that much of what he knew, and he didn't know if it was still classified or not, had been top secret. "I will tell you on the other side I was pounding my hand against the canopy and saying, 'Pull the fucking trigger.' But God, you know, things happen."

"There's some other points in there I can't go into right now," Harris said, pointedly putting off questions about the way everybody's mission was flown that night. "I've agreed not to with the secretary of the navy. Some mistakes were made in the flying aspect of it. People felt very guilty about their mission and how [the MiG-25] got past [strike combat air patrol]. There were some people up there who were supposed to be supporting him [Scott Speicher] and they failed miserably."

No one person was at fault, not the way Harris sees it. A series of mistakes led to Scott Speicher's shoot down. Still, Harris observed, with tensions high that night, any flash would have seemed like an immense explosion, especially with darkness as the backdrop. "They did see a secondary explosion, but they thought it was large pieces of the aircraft impacting the ground," he said. "Turns out it appears to have been Scott's ejection."

Neither Hull nor any of the Hornet pilots with him that night fault Spock Anderson for what happened to Scott. "We all live with our demons," said Hull in retrospect, "and there's nothing that can be done about it, and that's not the point."

"He's so right," added Rink. "It's easy to Monday-morning quarterback, but having experienced the chaos with every mission, I can tell you there doesn't seem to be anything negligent here, until the government decided to try and let what happened to Spike blow away in the wind as if one life doesn't matter in the big scheme of things."

The night that Scott went down has been analyzed over and over by Department of Defense analysts, contractors and field investigators who turned up much information that later formed a better picture of what might have happened. While two decades have passed since that first air strike against Baghdad, one wonders whether it matters how he got shot down. In the big scheme of things to which Rink refers, now more than twenty years later, probably not. But perspective is everything. Does knowing who and what took down Speicher's Hornet matter to investigators looking at survivability of the pilot? Yes. Should we care what may have contributed to the loss of Scott Speicher to stop a repeat of the same in the future? Yes. Should we care what may have contributed, short- and long-term, to his death? Yes, absolutely. Finger pointing between the navy and air force certainly colored the search for ground truth in the Speicher shoot down from day one. Add the Iraqi MiG-25 to the mix and what happened over the skies of Iraq that night just gets even harder to follow. But was it?

If Scott was the victim of fratricide, how could it have happened? Was this "the mistake in the flying of it" to which Buddy Harris refers? Fratricide is never just about who pulls the trigger. In a situation such as Carlos Johnson described, in which Speicher's Hornet and the Iraqi MiG-25 are "on top of one another" in a merge plot, a missile fired in their direction could make a split-second choice of its target. The MiG-25, at two-thirds afterburner and hauling east, passed too quickly by Speicher to get caught. The missile chose Scott Speicher, just then focused on his mission. He had bunted the nose of his Hornet, lowering his jet to get into position at the right altitude for his HARM run. Being radar dead, he never saw what was coming.

In a world of highly sophisticated weaponry, human error has been greatly lessened. Yet a string of missteps, mistakes and near misses marked the first night of a new kind of war and led directly to Scott Speicher's loss. The day after marked the beginning of the so-called mystery of what happened to one man and a search that enveloped the lives of all who tried to find him. But those who bought into the "mystery" bought a lie – a well-crafted and executed deception, a slight of hand that would take over the lives of all who knew the truth, men whose collective conscience could no longer keep quiet about what they knew – from day one. But mostly they had lived with a secret that left them conflicted, traumatized and, in more than one case, completely shattered. They couldn't make sense of it.

Back on the USS *America* (CV-66) Red Sea battle force and air wing commanders, Central Intelligence Agency officers, senior military intelligence officers, and a crash and salvage team had assembled; they would subsequently convene aboard the Red Sea command ship USS *LaSalle* (AGF-3), responsible for controlling and coordinating the Maritime Intercept Force and serving concurrently as flagship for NAVCENT vice admiral Stanley A. Arthur, to go over U-2 spy plane photos of Speicher's downed Hornet and 360-degree photos of the crash site taken by the Central Intelligence Agency's covert operative on the ground, the first man to arrive on the scene of the smoldering wreck, the first to see AA103 pancaked on the desert floor, and the magnesium from the Hornet's wheels burning so hot and for so long after the crash that it made them easy to spot on infrared imagery from the air. The CIA officer had arrived on the scene within a day of Speicher's loss whereby he made his observations of the scene, took his pictures and rode away.

The choice to first assemble on board *America* and not *Saratoga* was made for two reasons – the first practical – and the second necessity. The *America*, with Captain John J. Mazach in command, had been fitted out with the combined Command, Control, Communication, Cryptology, and Intelligence (C4I) package that included systems such as the Navy Tactical Command System Afloat (NTCSA), the Contingency Tactical Action Planning System (CTAPS) and Advance Tracking Prototype. Although these systems were not unique to the fleet, it was the first time they had been integrated into one comprehensive package and this was significant. Coupled with the disseminated capabilities of the Naval Tactical

Data System (NTDS), *America*'s C4I package allowed intelligence and operations information to be integrated into one single tactical picture. Utilizing digital data links between other ships, *America* had intelligence processing capabilities unparalleled by any other ship in the fleet.

Pictures of the Hornet indicated it landed upright. But they also showed the original position of the ejected canopy and ejection seat – two important pieces of physical evidence, one subsequently moved by the Bedouins as a navigation marker (the canopy), and the other (the ejection seat) disappeared entirely. From the ground photos of the jet it was clear that the nose cone was sheared off. Ordnance was strewn on the desert floor. Spock Anderson saw the pictures, too. He was there.

Everyone was uneasy about what they saw. The F/A-18C Hornet Lot 10 carried an avionics package that was loaded with gear that navy commanders and intelligence officers not only want protected from the Iraqis, Iranians, Russians and Chinese, but also the United States' allies in the region, including Saudi Arabia, Egypt, Jordan, Kuwait, and the emirates. Inside the cockpit were Speicher's black boxes, the command-launch computer that controls and monitors the high-speed anti-radiation missile (HARM) load he was carrying to his target; the KY-58 secure encrypted radio, his head-up display (HUD) and Hornet's data storage unit (DSU) that included information programmed specifically for Speicher's mission and detailed information that pertained to aircraft performance, much of it highly classified.

No one – friend or enemy – was going to get the avionics package off Speicher's Hornet. Finding the aircraft was never in question – it was located the same day Speicher went down. This discovery was quickly followed by a plan to get back the avionics package and cover up the circumstances that led to the blue-on-blue shoot-down. The avionics package and the cover-up were now more important to the team assembled on the *LaSalle* than finding the pilot who'd successfully ejected from his stricken jet.

When the pictures flashed up on the screen, some insisted "Where's the pilot?" "Why aren't you going after the pilot?" There had been – evidenced by the pictures – a good ejection and the pilot, according to one observer present on *LaSalle,* had "hauled ass" away from the crash site to avoid being picked up by the Iraqis. The magnesium can burn a very long time, remarked another participant, and having it burn was like sending up smoke signals to the enemy to come inspect the source of the "fire." Speicher followed his training and moved away from the aircraft to avoid detection. Most certainly by January 22, 1991, iterated one of the evaluation team members, the navy was not only knowledgeable of the position of the crash site of Speicher's Hornet but had already deployed a joint military team to the site that performed an inspection of the wreckage, observed and recorded the ejection seat and retrieved the avionics package from the jet. They'd also collected evidence of something else – something that later crash investigators would never get – evidence of the missile from the shooter who'd brought down Speicher's Hornet.

The damage to Speicher's Hornet was consistent with damage from an AIM-7M Sparrow missile. The AIM-7M has an 88-pound high explosive blast fragmentary warhead and was, at the time, the principal beyond visual range (BVR) air-to-air missile used by the West's air forces. The Sparrow featured a new inverse monopulse seeker (matching the capabilities of Skyflash), active radar fuse, digital controls, improved electronic countermeasure (ECM) resistance, and better low-altitude performance; it was used to good advantage in Operation Desert Storm, where it scored many U.S. Air Force air-to-air kills. Of note, the AIM-7M's overall kill probability is still less than forty percent.

Luckily for Scott Speicher it knocked out the aircraft and didn't kill the pilot. The Sparrow's damage to the Hornet was like a fingerprint to the men who stood in the desert looking at what it had done to Speicher's jet. What the crash site didn't give them was the Hornet's data storage unit (DSU), which was not recovered until nearly four years.

Returning to what Carlos Johnson said: "The day after he [Speicher] got shot down I told the people down at Cecil Field how he got shot down." For Johnson to know that Speicher's Hornet was shot down by an assault from another aircraft, for him to eliminate the MiG-25PDS Foxbat E as the firing aircraft and for Johnson to be confident enough of this information to convey it to the air wing at Cecil Field [and the officers and CIA on board *LaSalle*] on January 18 is significant, because SPEAR not only had the air force infrared nighttime imagery showing the firing aircraft and Speicher's Hornet but also all-source intelligence[8] collected up and evaluated on the same day that Speicher was shot down.

With all of this information in hand, SPEAR also knew the identity of the real shooter and precise circumstance that led to Speicher being blown out of the sky. When he was hit, observed an AWACS operator orbiting during the first strike, if someone had seen Speicher hit, they would have known where he was right away. "We had to review radar tapes to locate where the kill occurred."

Evidence found at the scene was immediately reported back to *LaSalle* and just as quickly disregarded – especially after examination of the ejection seat indicated a good pilot ejection and no sign of the pilot. Rather than go search for the pilot, the team got an order – tersely communicated – to return to base. They also got a warning, the same warning conveyed to the chain of command on *LaSalle* and the men on the evaluation team: under penalty of imprisonment they were instructed to maintain strict confidence at what they had seen, collected, and recorded. No one was ever to know that they knew where Speicher's Hornet had gone down. No one was ever to find out that a joint military team had been to the crash site and what they'd taken from his jet. "Remember," they were told, "talk and you're going to jail." This was enough warning for most of them. They didn't want any trouble. They had families of their own. They had careers. At that moment they didn't think there was a choice either. But it didn't make them feel any better about what they'd just done to Scott Speicher. They'd have to live with that for the rest of their lives.

Why disregard clear evidence of an ejection and a pilot on the run? To those who had insisted the focus needed to be on finding the pilot they were told by the "men in clothes" [civilians] and scruffy beards – CIA officers – "there is no pilot; nothing you see is real." But what they had seen was very real and Scott Speicher was very real and very alive. Still, when asked during the briefing what Anderson believed happened to his pilot, the reply was uncomfortably brief and on cue: he'd seen a fireball engulf Speicher's jet and it was unsurvivable. The tension in the room was palpable. Many present were quietly incredulous. There was no disputing the facts collected from the crash site – there was a pilot and he had ejected cleanly from his stricken jet. He'd even tried to communicate. No one denied those facts either. But when they deliberated whether to go get him or not it was still a no go. He was stranded … left alive to die.

According to a member of the evaluation team, a rescue of Speicher was possible even as late as January 22. But the CSAR planners had nothing to go on for more than four days by the time the *LaSalle* team brought them into the discussion, so they reasoned why risk a rescue and a Special Operations team, when you have been told he and his jet were destroyed at altitude. With this attitude and SOCCENT commander colonel Jesse L. Johnson not in favor of attempting a CSAR, Speicher's luck ran out. Johnson hadn't gone out to *LaSalle* to be part of the discussion. He'd stayed at his headquarters at King Fahd International Airport (KFIA), northwest of Dammam, Saudi Arabia.

Speaking of the decision to forgo extracting Speicher immediately following his shoot-down, the same *LaSalle* participant added that "when truths [of what had actually happened to Speicher – he'd ejected and evaded away from a smoldering aircraft] worked their way up the chain [of command], it [a rescue] wasn't going to happen. [At that point it was] still a better than 60 percent recovery rate, well worth the effort to any rescue trained personnel."

A primary participant in the events that took place on the *LaSalle* revealed that it all came down to the circumstances surrounding how Speicher got shot down – the confusion during the engagement with the lone MiG and Spock Anderson – and that, if found out, would jeopardize not only Speicher's squadron mate but his squadron commanding officer and those above him in the chain of command. These were "the mistakes in the flying of it" to which

Buddy Harris would refer and to which a number of participants on the first strike have further confirmed, a series of mistakes and missteps that ultimately started in motion a cover up that was a betrayal of Scott Speicher, a betrayal made more complete when the evaluation team, a group of men that included flag and general officers, captains and colonels, and commanders and lieutenant colonels – most of them aviators, some of them attached to Special Operations Component Central – went along with the "men in clothes" who guaranteed no one would ever know what happened to Scott Speicher. Anderson gave little fight. He was caught up in the circumstance of the shoot down. Everyone else did as they were told. No one said anything. No one questioned it. A room made up of men in uniform and "men in clothes" fell silent.

"How would you like to be him [Speicher] knowing, hoping in his heart they'd come get him. What a fucking let down," observed one of the men privy to what happened just then, "What a fucking let down when they didn't come [get him]."[9]

Endnotes

1. Sadik, A., and D. Zampini, "Tretij Den' (i posledujuschie...)"["The Third Day (and beyond...)""] Aviacija i vremja (Aviation and Time) No. 6 (2005). The first part of an article about actions of Iraqi Air Defense during the war in 1991 written by direct participant of the event.

2. Miller, *New York Times*, September 15, 1992.

3. Ibid.

4. Mann, Edward C., III. *Thunder and Lightning: Desert Storm and the Airpower Debates*. Maxwell Air Force Base, Alabama: Air University Press, 1995, from the second chapter.

5. Carpenter, P. Mason, *Joint Operations in the Gulf War: An Allison Analysis, Thesis*, School of Advanced Air Power Studies, Air University, Maxwell Air Force Base, June 1994.

6. Ibid.

7. *BBC Breakfast with Frost interview*: General Sir Peter de la Billière, commander, Desert Storm British troops and professor Paul Rogers, Bradford University, March 30, 2003.

8. Intelligence products and/or organizations and activities that incorporate all sources of information, most frequently including human resources intelligence, imagery intelligence, measurement and signature intelligence, signals intelligence, and open-source data in the production of finished intelligence. In intelligence collection, a phrase that indicates that in the satisfaction of in-

telligence requirements, all collection, processing, exploitation, and reporting systems and resources are identified for possible use and those most capable are tasked.

9. Interview with confidential source, July 16, 2012.

Chapter 4

Going Home Minus One

"The war keeps on keeping on," Barry Hull wrote home in early February 1991. The world saw televised pictures of Kuwaiti oil fields on fire; Hull saw them up close and they were horrifying. The destruction in Iraq was unimaginable. The Sunliners reached the point they'd radio in targets based on fires, sometimes smoke, rising up from previous bomb hits. "Coop," Hull called over to squadron mate Lieutenant Doug Cooper, "I've got a line of trucks two miles northeast of the big black smoke just north of the original target."

The worst part of the war for pilots was fear of combat itself. "After doing it a month, I can now take it further before it kicks in, but once it throws itself in your face," wrote Hull in mid February, "there is no stopping the terror that sweeps through your body." That first night over Iraq "anything and everything sent me into a state of terror." As the air war wore on, that reaction lessened, but it didn't go away entirely. "One night recently," he continued, "one of our strikers had a system malfunction just before Miller time, aviator lingo for release of bombs on target, which is very unusual for a Hornet, but anyway, he dropped his bombs a couple of miles off target." Looking out from his cockpit, Hull saw one of the explosions made by the other Hornet. The ordnance caused a huge flash and for a split second Hull thought a SAM had reached out and touched him. He was terrified until he realized what it was. That first night, when Scott went down, the missile that detonated under his Hornet seemed large enough to make everyone think the entire plane had exploded. By February Hull and the others knew that any missile going off at night was going to look bigger than it would in the daytime.

The longer the war dragged, being cool under pressure came readily to mind far faster than being scared. "I forgot about it, [that] first night over Iraq," he wrote later, "but it's back with me now. The fear is there, but so is the calm." The Sunliners were wrought with emotion that ran the gamut from Hull's "When is this war going to end so we can go home?" to "Yeah! We were studs today! Did you see that ammo dump go up in flames? Secondaries for twenty minutes! What a light show!" And then there was the ubiquitous, "Listen, I'm beat. Don't call me unless you need me to brief. I'm going to sleep." One of Skull's personal favorites was "Gosh, Skull, you got another big pile of mail, and more cookies! Oh, they're from your sister Nora? Well, uh ... I just ate, thanks anyway." Then he'd go feed them to the maintenance crew. Another common one: "Hey, Oscar, looks like my mom baked another batch of brownies. I'll throw a few toward the duty desk to create a diversion. Then you open the door and I'll see if I can get the rest up to our room." Now that he'd seen combat, Hull knew, like the others, the importance of creating a diversion. His favorite mood, he wrote, was "Hey, I'm just going to sit here and read these letters and do a little daydreaming. Unless the war breaks out, don't call me. Oh yeah, the war did break out. Well, it can wait."

Close to the end of February, missions off the *Saratoga* continued into Iraq, sometimes Kuwait, depending on the target. After crossing the border, adrenaline pumping, they'd head for their targets, continuously talking to the controller. The AWACS, far away from the strike group, eventually smoothed their working relationship with navy pilots and watched over them more closely on missions. "They have some female controllers," wrote Hull. "They are great at controlling. You know why? It's not because they do a better job, although they do just as good a job. It's because of their voice. When you hear a female voice, you instinctively listen up." The navy loaded a female voice, in fact, in the F/A-18's computer alert system. Pilots called the female computer voice "Bitchin' Betty." "When Betty talks," Hull wrote home, "we listen. Also, it has to do with a study of fighter pilots. They found we are abnormally sensitive and caring, tender, romantic, sweet thangs and thought it would be appropriate to have a female voice, since we just hate those male chauvinist stereotypes. Shucks."

When tasked to hit more difficult targets, the Sunliners proved the versatility and strength of the Hornet, qualities largely dismissed in postwar air war analyses. They fired sophisticated ordnance, performed in a matter of seconds or they'd miss the target. Combine that job with personal fears and apprehensions and the pucker factor went up tenfold. They had become, through loss, through fear, through shared experience combat seasoned fighter pilots.

A cease-fire was called on February 27. The war was over. The *Saratoga*'s pilots had hit targets all over Iraq, from Baghdad to Iraq's borders with Syria and Jordan and back to Kuwait. "There were a few occasions of blue-on-blue," wrote Hull on March 2, but he didn't think at the time there were any from the *Saratoga*. He was thinking mostly of the ordnance dropped perilously close to ground troops, some of whom were killed. "We briefed in detail. Not even counting the grief of the families, but from the pilot's point of view, it would be hard to live with yourself knowing you dropped on blue troops."

With the war over and an occasional no-fly day, footballs, joggers and sunbathers replaced the hundreds of plane handlers on the flight deck. But war had done something else to the Sunliners; it made them family. Though some would soon be leaving the squadron for another assignment, the bond was there. "There is an unspoken commitment to each other," wrote Hull. "We sit around and complain, but if an outsider badmouths one of us, look out. I guess I can criticize family, but no one else can." He'd miss his friends and the flight time. But one thing he wouldn't miss at all was the fear of combat. "I sure won't miss living on this boat, trying to sleep through cat shots, trying to deal with the idiots in the post office, standing alerts at all hours of the night, spending month after month away from home, and taking showers where not only the hot water runs out, but the water runs out!"

Navy officers called Scott Speicher's roommate, Tony Albano, on March 4 and told him to go to Riyadh, Saudi Arabia. Iraq had released American and Coalition prisoners of war (POWs), and Albano was sent to see if Speicher was among them. He wasn't overly optimistic, but there was a chance. That hope died quickly. By the time the plane touched down in Riyadh with twenty-one American prisoners of war, Albano was told Speicher wasn't among them. He flew back to the *Saratoga*. "I didn't even get to stay long enough to see my other shipmates," he mused later.

In another letter home, Barry Hull observed that they'd heard the POWs were released. "That's good news." But the pervasive feeling aboard *Saratoga* was not elation for freed shipmates; they just wanted to go home. "There's nothing more they can do to us," he concluded. "I think we've been through the worst. Now we wait and listen. Every time the captain, Smokin' Joe Mobley, gets on the horn, we hope it's to tell us we're headed west. He hasn't told us yet, but that's okay. Now that the shooting has stopped, waiting is easy."

By mid-March the *Saratoga* was headed home. Despite the anticipation and excitement they felt as the ship drew closer to Jacksonville, to reuniting them with missed family, friends and colleagues, the Sunliners were still short one of their own. "The one thing that will stick with the VFA-81 pilots when all else has faded is the loss of Scott Speicher," Hull wrote on March 15. "The twenty-four-hours-a-day closeness we have out here makes for such tight friendships, and that adds to our sadness. Some people you feel when they are around. With Scott, we feel him not being around. We came to expect a certain sense of humor and response out of each individual that made up our team, and we feel his loss." This was the next-to-last letter Hull wrote on the Desert Storm deployment. His last was a note to himself that he never intended to mail. It was written March 27, the day of the traditional fly-off of air wing aircraft to their respective home airfields. Though he'd been scheduled to go, Hull gave his jet up to a married friend. He relished instead the moment he'd walk off the boat into a sea of well-wishers, a postwar homecoming that filled him with wide ranging emotion that went from nervous excitement to great sadness.

"I'm sad," Hull confessed, "that the closeness the junior pilots developed will start to fade. I feel sad for the loss of Scott. I feel sad knowing I will probably never see another time like this again." What's important, he decided, is what you take with you when it's all over. For Barry Hull, these were the main things: "First of all, we lost a good friend in Scott Speicher. What a great guy he was. I still can't believe it happened to him. Second, I love my country. It used to get on my nerves to hear some old geezer preaching about how good we have it in the United States. Now," he decided, "I think there is a little of that in me. I won't go around being a pain about it, but it will be there in me from now on. There is one more thing" he wanted to remember and it was, by far, the most important thing he'd learned during the cruise, "and that is how much I love my family."

Longtime friend David Rowe, joined by several of Scott Speicher's other college friends, decided to hold a golf tournament in his honor. Even before the Sunliners got home, Rowe and John Webb, who everyone called "Webby," were grieving deeply for Scott. Webb had been in Scott and Joanne's wedding. The golf tournament seemed like a good idea, especially if they could help Joanne with money for Meghan and Michael's education. "At first," said Rowe, "Joanne said, 'Look, I'm going to take care of the kids. I don't need any help.'" Then Webb's wife Linda explained to her, "Look, these guys are grieving and all they're trying to do is something." Then Joanne gave her blessing.

The golf tournament wasn't scheduled to take place until the squadron returned from deployment. The fly-off was March 27, and the *Saratoga* pulled into Mayport the next day. Rowe went over to Spock Anderson's house one night after the squadron's return. They talked about the golf outing and swapped Spike stories. Rowe told Anderson about the time Spike jumped from the cliff, and Anderson told Rowe about Scott's hitting the bulldozer with a kielbasa.

Rowe had a good laugh with Anderson. The relationship warmed. Then Rowe asked if Anderson didn't mind telling him what happened to his friend. "It was a SAM that got him?" Rowe asked. Anderson's eyes filled with tears. "It was no SAM that got

Spike," he said. "Let me tell you what happened." So Anderson told Rowe about how Spike came to him begging to go on the mission, and Anderson said no. But Spike came back a second time and Anderson changed his mind. "So we launched, we'd just refueled and we split to our targets," Anderson told Rowe. "Right after we split to the targets, I got a tone. I was locked." Then he told Rowe about the MiG, and how the rules of engagement leaned toward letting an enemy fighter go if you weren't sure. "So I locked him," Spock continued, "but problem was I couldn't keep up with him because I was loaded down with weapons." When Anderson locked up the MiG, he bugged out. Rowe was surprised, because for months the Pentagon stuck to the story that Speicher had been downed by a surface-to-air missile. "I'm telling you right now, don't believe what you're being told," he told Rowe. "It was that MiG that shot Spike down. I had him, Dave, and I could have taken him out."

The day of the golf tournament John Webb and two of Spike's other college roommates flew in from Texas and South Florida. "Commander," asked Rowe, "if you wouldn't mind, please, would you tell these guys, these are some of Scott's best friends, would you mind telling them what you told me?" "I don't have any problem with that at all," replied Anderson. They staked out a large shade tree and with it, some privacy. Spock told them what happened to their friend.

Meanwhile, John "JR" Stevenson, an A-7E Corsair II driver assigned to squadron on board the *Kennedy*, got back from his deployment at the end of March. The *Kennedy* sent its air wing home the same day as the *Saratoga*, and the ship berthed the following day in Norfolk. Two weeks later Stevenson ran into Joanne Speicher outside the Rocket 17, the Cecil Field officers' club, and told her about the MiG-25. Joanne had never been told about the MiG and she would've not known about it then had Stevenson not said something. He told her they should've been able to find some sign of Scott's wreckage because the MiG's flight path was recorded not only by surveillance aircraft but also seen by any number of *Saratoga* and *Kennedy* pilots who got electronic and visual identification on the MiG. Many of them had seen the MiG-25's distinctive afterburner trail. The MiG-25 lit up the *Kennedy*'s strike leader, Commander Mark "Lobster" Fitzgerald, commanding officer of the VA-46 Clansmen. From the cockpit of his A-7E, Fitzgerald got a good look at the MiG as it streaked off to the east.

Joanne thought about what JR said and soon after she made the decision to go see Dean "Milo" Hendrickson, Scott's CAG. She wanted to know about the MiG. But he told her to go home and stop asking about it. Angered by Joanne's visit, Hendrickson's office called Stevenson. Milo wanted JR front and center. He hadn't cooled down. When JR got there Hendrickson closed the door and proceeded to chew him out for telling Joanne about the Foxbat. Hendrickson made it abundantly clear that he was never to bring up the MiG again. "I wasn't even in Milo's air wing, so I had no idea what he wanted when I got there," Stevenson said later. "It was unsettling." With that, the official story of what happened to Scott Speicher started to come unhinged.

At the end of Scott Speicher's May 22 memorial service two buglers, one echoing the other, played "Taps" as a low-altitude missing man formation roared over Cecil Field's chapel. His service, packed with his family, friends and squadron mates, had been emotionally charged from the start. Lieutenant Ron Craddock, Light Attack Wing One chaplain, began with a reading from Psalms 104:33-34. "I will sing to the Lord all my life; I will sing praise to my God while I live," he read somberly. "Pleasing to him be my theme; I will be glad in the Lord." That passage suited Scott. He held God close to him every day, and like many of his friends on the ship, he'd read the Bible more frequently as war loomed large. After Tony Albano eulogized Scott, Spock Anderson gave his remarks. As he steadied himself to speak, tears filled his eyes and he began to sob. "The man was devastated," said Dave Rowe. "When you look in a man's eyes, especially a warrior, and you see the tears, the pain in their eyes... These guys compartmentalize. They put it away."

After the presentation of awards by Vice Admiral John K. Ready, commander in chief, Naval Air Force Atlantic Fleet, Commander Bill McKee, Scott's executive officer, read from Deuteronomy 6:6-9: "Take to heart those words which I enjoin on you today. Drill them into your children. Speak to them at home and abroad, whether you are busy or at rest. Bind them at your wrist as a sign and let them be as a pendant on your forehead. Write them on the doorposts of your houses and on your gates." He also read from the much-used passage about the strength and endurance of love from 1 Corinthians 13:4-8a. Aviators sobbed quietly in the pews.

After Chaplain Craddock's reflections, the chapel filled with choked voices singing "Eternal Father Strong to Save": "Lord, guard and guide the men who fly/Thro' the great spaces of the sky/ Be with them traversing the air/In darkening storms or sunshine fair/O God, protect the men who fly/Thro' lonely ways beneath the sky."

Scott Speicher, husband, father, brother, son and friend was mourned deeply for the good man that he was and the pilot who'd sacrificed the full measure of devotion to his country. But little did his family, friends and fellow Sunliners know – Scott Speicher had survived his shoot down. He was alive and stranded in the Iraqi desert and no one had looked for him and no one was going to, not for years to come. Truth was obfuscated by military and civilian bureaucrats increasingly engaged in covering up what had gone wrong.

CHAPTER 5

LEFT ALIVE TO DIE

The war had been over a few days when Marine Corps Captains Patrick "Roller" Rink and Frederick W. "CJ" Sturckow hopped into one of Sheikh Isa's Toyota pickup trucks and made the forty-minute drive to Manama, on the north end of the island. "We went to the port and finagled our way on board the USNS *Mercy* (T-AH 19), where recently repatriated American POWs were marshaling before going home. CJ was looking for Lieutenant Robert "Smilin' Bob" Wetzel, pilot of the A-6E Intruder from the *Saratoga* shot down January 18, 1991. Bob and his bombardier-navigator, Lieutenant Jeffrey N. Zaun, were returned to American forces on March 4. CJ had been Bob Wetzel's best man in his wedding. While CJ talked to Bob, Roller started talking to many of the other POWs. He noticed that Scott Speicher wasn't one of them and asked the pilots and Major Rhonda L. Cornum, the U.S. Army flight surgeon captured after her helicopter was shot down en route to pick up a downed F-16 pilot, if they'd heard anything about Spike. "All but one of them hadn't. But remember," cautioned Rink, "at the time we thought Spike was dead." Everyone echoed Tony Albano's disappointment that Scott was still unaccounted for, still missing somewhere in Iraq.

What Albano and Rink didn't know was that Scott Speicher's name had not been put on the International Committee of the Red Cross (ICRC) list of Coalition prisoners of war and missing in action (POW/MIA) personnel the United States and its close allies expected the Iraqis to release at war's end. How could this happen?

Postwar evaluation of United States Central Command (CENTCOM) problems revealed many shortcomings. Relevant to prisoners of war and missing in action, evaluators took umbrage with Riyadh's way of reporting casualties and took the command to task over it in their final report. The problem was this: casualty information came to the Joint Chiefs of Staff (JCS) by CENTCOM but also individual armed services. Although this parallel reporting system had existed for many years, by Desert Storm its efficacy had fallen apart. Data requirements and submission times of critical information varied, often dramatically. Thus, the JCS received inconsistent reports, which it kicked back to CENTCOM to resolve; this distracted CENTCOM from its myriad wartime responsibilities. But what this dual reporting system also did was set up the JCS and major component and combatant commanders for major failure, catastrophic failure if you happened to be the missing man and no one had you in their system because the reporting streams never crossed. No one compared notes.

Casualty reporting was hamstrung, too, by time, level of effort required, and the degree of importance the chain of command put on POW/MIA accountability. CENTCOM headquarters wasn't prepared to handle requests for detailed information about men who had become prisoners of war, or gone missing in action, nor were they ready to answer questions about noncombatant troops classified DUSTWUN, those whose status could not be determined and yet remained at highest risk of never being returned because no one had figured out if they had gone absent without leave (AWOL) or been captured.

Prior to Operation Desert Storm, CENTCOM's priority had been reporting noncombat-related deaths and accidents. When the shooting kicked into high gear, its priority shifted uneasily to service members categorized as missing in action. But as a result of constant requests for detailed information on other-than-missing-in-action, CENTCOM was forced by circumstance to refocus its reporting response, leaning toward greater emphasis on fratricide-related casualties. Missing in action went to the back burner. Whether the request pertained to an MIA, soldier killed or wounded by fratricide, or someone who went AWOL, it didn't matter. Any of the innumerable information requests attached to a casualty exceeded CENTCOM's ability to answer it. Less than a week into the war, CENTCOM was already passing off responsibility for casualty accountability to the individual armed services. Speicher, among others, fell through the cracks.

The POW/MIA issue was high on General Schwarzkopf's agenda when he met with his Iraqi counterparts at Safwan Airfield in occupied Iraq on March 3 to negotiate terms of the cease-fire. He and Joint Forces Commander General Prince Khalid bin Sultan bin Abdul Aziz met with seven Iraqi military officials led to the negotiation table by Deputy Chief of Staff Lieutenant General Sultan Hashim Ahmad Al Jabburi Al Tay. After a two-hour meeting, the Iraqi military formally accepted all demands for a permanent cease-fire. "When I went to the tables with the Iraqis to negotiate the continuation of the cease-fire," Schwarzkopf said later, "one of the first questions I put to them is that I wanted all of our POWs returned, and in addition to that, I wanted all the bodies of anybody who had been killed returned to us. That was one of the first conditions that I put on the Iraqis for the continuation of the cease-fire." General Ahmad agreed to the immediate release of a small number of prisoners of war as a show of good faith from an undefeated enemy. The Iraqis did not, after all, consider themselves losers.

The next day, on March 4, the Iraqis released ten prisoners of war, six of them American. They were turned over to U.S. officials by the International Committee of the Red Cross near the Jordanian border station of Ruwayshid, then transferred to the *Mercy* for medical evaluation and treatment. The following day Iraqi authorities released another thirty-five prisoners, fifteen of them American, to the Red Cross. "At the end of the war," continued Schwarzkopf, "I was assured one hundred percent that everyone was fully accounted for and that there was no MIA situation." He had been lied to.

Several American aviators were still missing. The Red Cross later concluded that many names had been left off the list they received *from* the Iraqi government, names the U.S. military had not accounted for nor asked for at war's end. But by then it was too late to go back and deal with Baghdad for men's lives, men who were now left behind. "If he wasn't a POW," said Schwarzkopf of

Speicher, "he wouldn't be on the list. Again, it doesn't make sense that the Iraqis would have listed everybody except one person on a POW list that they give to the Red Cross. Why, if they're going to withhold one name, why that specific name, and the only logical explanation if he was alive, is the fact that they didn't know that he was captured. But that," he rationalized, "doesn't make any sense either, because knowing how centralized the Iraqi military was, they would certainly know something like that."

But the truth is that the United States hadn't accounted for all of its missing in action and had no plans to do anything about it, not then and not later. While true that Baghdad presented a list of Coalition prisoners in its custody via the Red Cross, it also received at least two lists back from the Red Cross with the names of Coalition personnel, by nationality, that their respective countries wanted returned immediately. Upon receipt of each list the Iraqis waited to see whose names appeared on the list. Thus, if an American service member was not asked for, Saddam was handed a trophy prisoner by omission. In a reply to a message sent to the Iraqi government on October 21, 2001, specifically about Scott Speicher, Dr. Fahmi El Qaisy, legal affairs chief of the Iraqi Ministry of Foreign Affairs, wrote back on November 6 that "the American authorities did not claim for him within the lists of the POWs in 1991, nor did it include his name as missing."

The U.S. government didn't report any pilots or ground troops falling into Iraqi hands in the opening days of the war, even though Iraq's minister of information, Latif Nassif Jasim declared on CNN that American and British airmen had been captured. The Pentagon issued a blanket denial. Lieutenant General Thomas W. Kelly[1], then director of operations to the JCS, stood before a packed press room and told reporters that no Americans had been taken prisoner by Iraqi forces. His exact words were "We know of no American prisoners of war." Kelly and others in the Pentagon didn't back off from their denial until Iraq went public with tapes of American and British POWs it had captured and provided them to major media. Among the most memorable of the videos was navy lieutenant Jeff Zaun, the bruised and battered A-6E Intruder bombardier-navigator off the *Saratoga*, picked up by the Iraqis along with his pilot, Lieutenant Bob Wetzel.

But it was another Desert Storm case that brought American captives in Iraqi custody full circle, and it was arguably the most bizarre of the war. Had one of the soldiers' parents not gone public, out of fear his daughter wouldn't be returned if he didn't act, she and her partner might never have made it home. Army specialists Melissa Rathbun-Nealy and David Lockett were drivers of a heavy equipment transport (HET) captured by Iraqi soldiers after their vehicle and another became separated from a supply convoy on January 30, 1991. As the two vehicles proceeded north, they came under enemy fire. The second HET managed to escape, but Rathbun-Nealy and Lockett were surrounded and captured.

After their capture, Rathbun-Nealy and Lockett were never listed as MIA by the 233rd Transportation Company nor the company's chain of command up to the Department of the Army in the Pentagon. Nor did the pair ever receive the designation POW. Why? "The reason lies with United States Army regulation," explained Colonel Millard A. Peck, then chief of the Defense Intelligence Agency (DIA) Special Office for Prisoners of War and Missing in Action. "Missing" by U.S. Army definition is very distinct from MIA. "Missing" is reserved for personnel unaccounted for in noncombatant operations. From the U.S. Army's point of view, the convoy was a noncombatant operation, even though it came under enemy fire. Thus, Rathbun-Nealy and Lockett were never listed as MIA or POW, even though the army had information that they had been captured under fire. "This distinction," concluded Peck, "is an important illustration of how the Department of Defense uses technical distinctions to avoid a finding of POW/MIA."

In his letter to Melissa Rathbun-Nealy's parents, Lieutenant Colonel J. G. Cole, chief of POW/MIA Affairs, demonstrated for Senate investigators that the Department of Defense knew a great deal about what had happened to their daughter and her fellow soldier, Specialist Lockett, but had failed to follow up obvious leads or ask obvious questions. "There were no signs of fighting or blood," wrote Cole, "but personal gear had been scattered around the area, and weapons were missing. As the Marines searched around the vehicle shouting for the soldiers, they were confronted by several Iraqi foot soldiers at the HET and an armored personnel carrier [APC] approximately fifty meters north, headed in their direction. No shots were exchanged by the Marines. They backed off and called in attack helicopter support, which destroyed the APC within thirty meters of the HET. The Marines returned to the area the following morning, where they collected some of the personal equipment and found the vehicle running but no trace of Rathbun-Nealy or SPC Lockett. During the battle in and around Khafji several Iraqi soldiers were captured." Presumably, these captured soldiers could positively identify Rathbun-Nealy and Lockett by looking at photographs, but they were not shown any.

Iraqi soldiers did give witness statements. "Following interrogation of enemy prisoners of war by Saudi forces," according to Peck's report, "two reports were received. One concerned information provided by an Iraqi lieutenant who witnessed the capture of an American male and female. He further stated that both had been injured and that the white female had sustained an injury to her arm. The second report received from Saudi forces concerned two other Iraqi prisoners of war from a captured patrol who indicated they had seen a white female and a black male near the city of Al Basrah, Kuwait," not far from where their HET was abandoned. To the lay observer like Leo Rathbun, sightings of a white female and black male soldier in Iraqi custody sounded like a good "live-sighting" report, based on circumstances that almost exactly dovetail with the circumstances of the missing soldiers off the HET.

When Leo Rathbun asked Lieutenant Colonel Cole why his daughter was not listed as an MIA with these sightings on record, Cole replied that the Iraqi lieutenant had not made "a positive identification" – as though, stated the Senate report, "there were hundreds of pairs of white female and black male soldiers captured in the area." Cole went on to state that U.S. interrogators had no picture of SPC Rathbun-Nealy to show the Iraqi officer – even though her photograph was by then showing up in every newspaper in the Western Hemisphere. (The same was true of Lieutenant

Commander Michael Scott Speicher, whose picture appeared for days on the front pages of newspapers and in weekly and monthly magazines.)

Without positive identification, Rathbun-Nealy and Lockett could not be listed as POW/MIA – and never were. "Had there been an extended war and extended negotiations to secure the return of prisoners, the name of neither one," wrote Peck, "would have appeared on any list of POW/MIAs being sought. They were listed only as 'missing,' that is, unaccounted for but not known to be in enemy hands. Had a difficult negotiation been required to secure a return of listed POW/MIAs, Iraq need never have returned Rathbun-Nealy and Lockett because they were not on the list." This is what Colonel Millard Peck reported as a "vivid illustration" to remember when pondering "the bureaucratic mindset that refused to go outside of artificial restrictions in order to find real people. If the case had been prolonged, if the report had come months or even years later, if the vivid memories of the event had gathered dust in DoD files, the same facts would have rung true."

The Rathbun-Nealy case was only part of it. Scott Speicher was only part it. The "it" was the dark, unsettling side of America's prisoners of war and missing in action issue that Colonel Millard Peck underscored in his February 12, 1991 letter of resignation, a document that resonated with this investigator and which, even today, cannot be dismissed. Peck originally accepted his post as chief of POW/MIA Office based on two primary motives: first, he had heard that the job was so contentious and frustrating, because of its complex political nature, no one would volunteer for it. This, of course, made the job appear challenging. Secondly, since the end of the Vietnam Conflict, he had heard the persistent rumors of American servicemen having been abandoned in Indochina, and that the government was conducting a "cover up" so as not to be embarrassed. "I was curious about this," he wrote, "and thought that serving as the chief of POW/MIA would be an opportunity to satisfy my own interest and help clear the government's name." Peck had also found it interesting that his previous exposure to the POW/MIA Office, while assigned to the Defense Intelligence

Agency (DIA), both as a duty director of intelligence (DDI) and as the chief of the Asia division for current intelligence (JSI-3), was negative. "DIA personnel who worked for me," he observed, "when dealing with or mentioning the Office, always spoke about it in deprecating tones, alluding to the fact that any report which found its way there would quickly disappear into a 'black hole.'" But Peck also looked into the general attitude of active duty military personnel as to what they thought about the POW/MIA issue. Surveys of active duty military personnel indicated that time eighty-three percent believed there were still live American prisoners in Vietnam. This idea was further promulgated in a number of legitimate veterans' periodicals and professional journals, as well as in the print and broadcast media, which convinced Peck that where there was so much smoke, there must be fire. He lasted only eight months in the job.

Particularly disturbing to Peck were persistent rumors of a government conspiracy that alleged U.S. military personnel had been left behind to become fodder for victorious communist governments in Vietnam, Laos and Cambodia, and that for "political reasons," or running the risk of a second Vietnam, the existence of American prisoners of war was officially denied. "Worse yet," wrote Colonel Peck, "was the implication that DIA's Special Office for POW/MIA was an integral part of this effort to cover up the entire affair so as not to embarrass the government nor the Defense establishment. As a Vietnam veteran with a certain amount of experience in Indochina," he continued, "I was interested in the entire POW/MIA question, and willingly volunteered for the job, viewing it as sort of a holy crusade."

But what Peck called "the harsh reality" was that heading up the DIA Special Office for POW/MIA was not a pleasant experience. His plan had been to be totally honest and forthcoming on the entire issue and aggressively pursue innovative actions and concepts toward clearing up "the live-sighting business," thereby refurbishing the image and honor of DIA. "I became painfully aware, however, that I was not really in charge of my own office, but was merely a figurehead or whipping boy for a larger and totally Machiavellian group of players outside of DIA. What I witnessed during my tenure as the cardboard cut-out 'chief' of POW/MIA could be euphemistically labeled as disillusioning," he penned in his resignation letter. "That national leaders continue to address the prisoner of war and missing in action issue as the 'highest national priority' is a travesty."

From Peck's vantage point, he observed that the principal government players were interested primarily in conducting a "damage limitation exercise," and appeared to knowingly and deliberately generate an endless succession of manufactured crises and busy work. Worst of all, a "mindset to debunk" was alive and well – in fact, flourishing. "It is held at all levels, and continues to pervade the POW/MIA Office," he wrote, "which is not necessarily the fault of DIA. Practically all analysis is directed at finding fault with the source. Rarely has there been any effective, active follow through on any of the sightings, nor is there a responsive 'action arm' to routinely and aggressively pursue leads."

The latter was a "moot point" since the POW/MIA Office was continuously buried in an avalanche of ad hoc tasking from every quarter, all of which required an immediate response. It was impossible to plan ahead or prioritize courses of action. "Any real effort to pursue live-sighting reports or exercise initiatives was diminished by the plethora of 'busy work' projects directed by higher authority outside of DIA. A number of these grandiose endeavors bordered on the ridiculous, and – quite significantly – there was never an audit trail." None of the tasking assigned to Peck's office was ever requested formally. There was, and still is, he would say later, a refusal by any of the players to follow normal intelligence channels in dealing with the POW/MIA Office.

Under the header "duty, honor and integrity," Colonel Peck wrote: "It appears that the entire [POW/MIA] issue is being manipulated by unscrupulous people in the government, or associated with the government. Some are using the issue for personal or political advantage and others use it as a forum to perform and feel important, or worse. The sad fact, however, is that this issue is being controlled and a cover up may be in progress. The entire charade does not appear to be an honest effort, and may never have been." When Peck assumed his position as chief in the POW/MIA Office he was somewhat amazed and greatly disturbed by the fact that he was the only military officer in an organization of more than 40 people. Since combatants of all services were lost in Vietnam, he noted for the record that there should have at least been a representative from each Service for a matter that was, after all, of the "highest national priority."

Since the normal mix of officers from all Services was not found in the POW/MIA Office, "it would appear the issue, at least at the working level, has, in fact, been abandoned. Also, the horror stories of the succession of military officers at the O-5 and O-6 level who have in some manner 'rocked the boat' and quickly come to grief at the hands of the government policymakers who direct the issue, lead one to the conclusion that we are all quite expendable," Peck added. Thus, by extrapolation one could conclude that the same bureaucrats who would sacrifice anyone who was what he called "troublesome" or contentious, would do the same to prisoners of war and missing in action. "Not a comforting thought," Peck stated for the record. "Any military officer expected to survive in this environment would have to be myopic, an accomplished sycophant, or totally insouciant." From what he had witnessed, Colonel Millard Peck concluded, "it appears that any soldier left in Vietnam, even inadvertently, was, in fact, abandoned years ago, and that the farce that is being played is nothing more than political legerdemain done with 'smoke and mirrors,' to stall the issue until it dies a natural death."

Colonel Peck's exposure of America's lackluster performance on the prisoner of war and missing in action issue was a red flag. The U.S. government's failure to account for its own is a chilling reminder that the nation's civilian and military leadership has not heeded innumerable lessons learned since the founding of the republic. As a nation, the United States continues to bear the burden of the missing, haunted by the specter of the fading faces of men – and women – who have clung to life in the hope of one day returning home. If but one prisoner of war remains detained alive in Southeast Asia, no resources of the U.S. government should be spared to locate that individual and effect his or her return to the United States; it is the least America owes them for their service. The same can be said of those missing and held captive from the Korean Conflict, Persian Gulf War and America's most recent engagements in Iraq and Afghanistan. Peck exposed the troubling pattern of denial, deceit and deception that would cripple accountability for Speicher from day one.

Throughout this narrative you will be introduced to men, in some cases, whose cases closely mirror the experience and the outcome of Scott Speicher's; these are men who had been largely forgotten by the time Speicher went missing in January 1991. One them was that of captive American John H. Noble. Though what happened to Noble took place over four decades before Speicher's disappearance, the circumstances remain relevant today.

At the very least his experience is instructive to the American media, which questioned the validity of the slaveholder mentality in the wake of Speicher's lengthy captivity and eventual death. Noble's story tells us there was prequel to what had happened in the Gulf over twenty years ago, that the game played by a captor is always for keeps, and that without the American public being made aware, the United States government would have had just as soon let Americans be held as prisoners of war and let action slip away than make a real effort to get them back.

On July 18, 1955, U.S. Secretary of State John Foster Dulles wrote Soviet President Nikita Khrushchev that the American people shared with other peoples of the world a real concern about the imprisonment of some of their countrymen in the Soviet Union. "Most of these people," observed Dulles, "have been held since World War II. It is time," he cajoled the Soviet leader, "to liquidate problems rising out of that War so that we may proceed with greater mutual trust to the solution of major issues facing the world today."

One of the men to whom Dulles referred was John Noble, a Detroit native and co-owner of a precision camera factory in Germany who had been taken into custody in Dresden by the Soviet Narodnyy Komissariat Vnutrennikh Del (NKVD) in July 1945.

(The NKVD was both the public and secret police of the Soviet Union better known for its gulag involvement.) Noble was shuttled from prison to prison, starting in Dresden, but eventually Muhlberg, Buchenwald, Erfurt, Weimer, and Lichtenberg in Germany, and Orsha, the first stop inside the Soviet Union before ending up at Vorkuta, 50 miles from the Arctic Circle. His initial detention at Dresden was the beginning of a *nine*-year ordeal. By the time Noble reached Weimer, he wrote: "There almost seemed to be no life. No one spoke." News was tapped from cell to cell. "I heard there were Americans, British and Frenchmen here," and he wondered who they were, why were they there and could anyone to whom he tapped a message get word of his imprisonment if they were freed. No one at Weimer could answer his last question. Four years after his stay at Weimer, Noble learned the names of two of the Americans held there with him: William Verdine and Homer Cox. Verdine tried to escape but was caught before he reached the last Soviet outpost. Cox would later help Noble get home.

Weimer was a place where sentences were passed on its unwilling victims. Noble recalled his own sentencing vividly, in all its symbolism, complete with red flags, red drapes and secret police officials sitting stoically behind a red-covered table. The girl at the table asked him the inevitable, routine questions of identity and then shoved a printed form at him for signature. Then there was a space with the figure "15" written in it.

"What is this?" he asked, pointing to the figure.

"You have been tried in Moscow and sentenced to fifteen years of slave labor," was the reply.

Noble described later the feeling of dread that chilled him. Back in his cell, he discovered that his blanket and belongings had already been wrapped into a bundle and tossed into a pile of about forty other prisoners' bundles who had been sentenced within the same hour.

Though Weimer was a place of silent despair, Noble found Lichtenberg "a bedlam of terrible and tortured noises." From there, he and the men in his group were moved further east, to Brest-Litovsk, where they were herded from mail cars across a plank and into regular prison cars bound for the Soviet Union. The train ride was hell. There were wire cages on the side of a narrow corridor for the guards to walk. In each cage there were three horizontal wooden shelves about six to seven feet wide, like large tables extending from the wall of the car to the wire of the cage. Five prisoners were packed on each shelf, fifteen prisoners per cage, 120 per car. "The prisoners were placed on the shelves with feet toward the wall of the car, heads against the wire of the cages. Some lay on their backs, some on their stomachs, depending on how they squirmed when ordered onto the shelf. My position was stomach down," he wrote. None of the men could move once they laid down in the cage. Guards came twice a day to let the men go to the bathroom. The trip lasted six weeks.

Making his way into the prison at Orsha, Noble observed whitewashed walls nearly black from the patchwork of names scratched, penciled, some even written in blood, from floor-to-ceiling. He remembered one name on the wall at Orsha, which he saw accidentally. Though it was partly obscured, the name was either Roberts, Robertson, or Robinson. Behind the name was a date put there a few days earlier, from mid-August 1950, and after it was another identification, an important one, "Maj. U.S.A." "Here was another far-from-comforting reminder that the power of the Soviet was great enough," Noble later observed, "to snatch other Americans from freedom and into the night of the prison world."

The man whose name stuck with Noble for the rest of this life could have been Major Frank A. Roberts, a U.S. Army Air Force officer assigned to the 882nd Bomber Squadron, 500th Bomber Group, Very Heavy, which flew the B-29 Superfortress from Saipan to attack mainland Japanese targets. Roberts' status was missing in action until January 23, 1945, when the War Department issued a presumptive finding of death.

From the Orsha prison, Noble and his group were entrained to Moscow, perhaps following the same path to the gulag at Vorkuta, in Komi, an Autonomous Soviet Socialist Republic (ASSR), that took Roberts, too. "The idea of being in the capital of the land that had imprisoned us was a stilling thing," he wrote of the experience.

On the outskirts of Moscow was the "Red Press" prison, what Noble called the "largest of the transit stops in the busy Soviet jail world." Officials at the Red Press sent them to Vologda, 300 miles north of Moscow. In the silence of the stops, as the train made its way into the barren tundra of the Ural Mountains, the largest center of gulag camps in European Russia, Noble realized the most desolate thing a human can know, "that no one cared about us and that no one could do anything about our plight. It was as though the Soviets had made time stand still," he continued, "and paralyzed history itself. In the silence, once, a man suddenly shrieked and buried his head in his arms, overcome with despair." When the shriek died away, "only the cold Russian wind was left."

Noble's life at Vorkuta was the closest thing possible to living death. He never expected to live through the winter of 1950-51. Besides the odd Canadian, he was the only American in Camp 3, a place where 4,500 men worked three of forty coal pits. Noble's camp was not the largest. There were an estimated 235,000 men and women at Vorkuta while Noble was there, some 12,000 of them guards, technicians and officials, roughly 105,000 of them prisoners, and another 120,000 of them prisoners freed from the camps but not allowed to leave the area. Vorkuta supplied about six percent of the Soviet Union's coal production. In addition to the coal mines, slave laborers worked in brick factories, power plants and hospitals, and on railroad lines, streets, city and village construction, food transport; others provided prison help. From information Noble gathered, he estimated that by mid-1954 there were 25 to 28 million people in Soviet slave labor, concentration, prisoner of war, secret and repatriation camps, Ministries of Internal Affairs (MVD) and State Security (MGB) prisons, investigation centers, and juvenile labor and detention camps.

"Vorkuta was a league of nations," Noble told the world after returning to the United States in January 1955. There were Greeks, Spaniards, Yugoslavians, Lithuanians, Hungarians, Germans, British, Dutch, and French, in addition to the Americans Noble met and whom he knew were spread throughout Vorkuta. Ten of the Greeks he met had been taken by the communists during their civil war, which followed closely on the heels of World War II. "Many other Americans are still in the Soviet," he told American officials later. While he did not get to meet all of them, he did come in direct contact with Privates William Marchuk and William Verdine and two other Americans, Homer Cox and a man he knew as "Towers." This was Leland Lorch Towers, returned to the United States in 1954 with Cox. There were also a few men who claimed American citizenship. In Camp 10, where Noble lived from 1953 to 1954, there was William Vlasilefsky, an English-speaking, Russian-born prisoner who claimed he was an American citizen. Vlasilefsky told Noble that he had spent his early life in the western states and part of his family still lived in Seattle, Washington. He also let Noble know that he had been in the U.S. Army in the early 1930s, and then migrated to China, where he began a successful business. In 1949, Vlasilefsky's life changed dramatically – and not for the better – when communist Chinese authorities summoned him to Peiping [Beijing]. When he arrived, Vlasilefsky was immediately arrested and sent to a Soviet slave labor camp. He was just one of those who Noble reported about to American authorities when he got home.

Prisoners were funneled to Vorkuta from camps in Tadzhik and Irkutsk in Soviet Asia; Omsk in Siberia, and Magadan in the Far East, where transferred slave laborers told Noble there were many Americans, including, by then, veterans of the Korean Conflict, both officers and enlisted men, in their camps. From what Noble heard, they were prisoners of war captured by the communist Chinese and North Koreans who had been shipped to the Soviet Union for safekeeping.

Days passed into weeks and weeks into months at Vorkuta. As time marched by, Noble worried what all America's missing worried: "I wondered whether the U.S. government knew where I was. Were they doing anything?" He was not allowed to write his mother or brother George in Detroit, or his father, who he believed was still in a Russian prison in East Germany. He did not know that the Soviets had released his father in 1952 and he was back in Michigan.

"There were times when I hoped for some official sign that they [the U.S. government] knew of my existence," Noble confided later. "God knows, I might become one of the 'forgotten' men I had heard about, living out my life in slave camps, lost in the morass of Soviet 'bureaucracy.'" He had just one glimmer of hope, a postcard the Russians never allowed him to personally send out of Vorkuta. Only a select few prisoners were granted the privilege of sending cards through the Red Cross to their relatives. Noble was not one of them, but as he observed, too, "America was on its way to becoming world enemy number one, according to Soviet propagandists." He bided his time, waiting for the moment that might create an opportunity for him to get a postcard out under another prisoner's name. The time came in May 1954 when the censor was replaced by a successor who cared far less about Noble and the rest of the men in the camp.

Noble smuggled a card out of Vorkuta in the name of his friend, Rudi Rohrig, sending it to a distant relative in West Germany. But Noble wondered whether its recipient would interpret the words "noble nephew" and send the card on to Detroit. The relative did. It was six months before Noble realized the postcard had made it to his parents in Detroit. Noble's father took the postcard to Washington, where he asked the State Department to get his son back. In June 1954 Noble was unexpectedly called to the Vorkuta camp commander's office and told, to his surprise, that he was Moscow bound and, then going home to the United States. These were words he did not expect to hear. Homer Cox, who Noble had first met at Weimer, was also going home.

Before he left Camp 3, Noble was taken to Camp 15. Outside the gate another slave was working to repair a fence. The man asked Noble if he was an American, to which he nodded yes. "We have two of your countrymen here who are also going away," the man replied. A few minutes later he met U.S. Army Privates Marchuk and Verdine. They rode together to the train station. Marchuk explained that he had been picked up by the Russians after having too much to drink in a Berlin bar and wandered across the line into the Soviet zone; Verdine was kidnapped on duty at the demarcation line between the United States and Soviet zones. After boarding a passenger train from Vorkuta to Moscow, Noble and the others were transferred to Potma, a repatriation camp. From there he sent a postcard to his aunt in Berlin; this might be an unremarkable event if not for the fact that on September 26, 1954, he received a reply, the first word Noble had from the outside world in more than nine years. Noble was confined at Potma for over four months; the Russians wanted him to put on weight before he reached the West.

On December 30, 1954, Noble was told he was ready for transport back to Moscow, and three days later he and Marchuk were on a train to Berlin, where American authorities were prepared for their turnover. Verdine was supposed to have been on the train, too, but had been separated from Noble and Marchuk. "I couldn't imagine," Noble wondered afterwards, "they kept Verdine at Potma. The Soviets knew we would report his whereabouts as soon as we were free." Verdine did make it home, but Noble and Marchuk did not know it, not just then.

There was much that Noble did not know until he got home. While Noble's postcard certainly helped, it was word brought to American authorities by Homer Cox after his release in July 1954 that left no doubt Noble was held captive in Vorkuta. Secretary Dulles sent a note to the Kremlin requesting Moscow account for John Noble. There was no guarantee of a reply. From the end of World War II when Noble was taken through the summer of 1954 the Soviet Ministry of Foreign Affairs answered all diplomatic notes with the statement that the Soviet Union had no knowledge of Noble. Once evidence of his captivity became known through Cox, the State Department stepped up the pressure.

On February 5, 1954, Secretary Dulles demarched Soviet Deputy Minister of Foreign Affairs Valerin Alexandrovich Zorin, asking the Soviet Union to account not only for Noble, but Marchuk and Verdine, too. The United States insisted it had absolute knowledge of their location, specifically noting that Ambassador Bohlen had conveyed the same information to the Russian ministry regarding Noble's general whereabouts in demarches number 200, dated August 29, 1953; number 446, dated November 14, 1953; and number 567, dated December 30, 1953. "At this time it has been established that he [Noble] was confined by Soviet authorities in a correction camp near Vorkuta, Komi ASSR. His last address was reported in the embassy's demarche number 446." But Moscow ignored the February 5 aide-memoire and all prior demarches from Washington requesting information on Noble and, ultimately, Washington's repeated demands for his immediate return.

Secretly, Moscow knew it had been caught in a lie. On February 18, 1954, Minister of Foreign Affairs Viacheslav Ivanovich Molotov directed the Minister of Internal Affairs (MVD) Sergei Nikiforovich Kruglov to launch a thorough inquiry into all three cases, with the mindset that the Soviet Union would be left at its conclusion with no choice but to return the men to American authorities. "Keeping in mind that the U.S. government published the text of the [February 5] aide-memoire, apparently striving to cause a sensation surrounding this matter, I request that the MVD USSR take measures in order to speed up the review of the cases of Marchuk and Verdin [*sic*], and also report what response, in the MVD USSR's opinion, should be given to the Americans' requests on the location of Noubl [*sic*] and the status of his case."

Molotov sent the chairman for State Security [the first chairman of the KGB], Ivan Aleksandrovich Serov, a message on March 23, "in connection with the new appeal from the U.S. embassy on the Americans Verdin [*sic*], Marchuk, and Noubl [*sic*], who are imprisoned in the USSR, I request that you speed up the reply to the letter from the Minister of Internal Affairs dated 18 February on this matter." A week later, on March 30, First Deputy Foreign Minister Andrei Andreyevich Gromyko was sent a Top Secret note, presumably from Serov: "As per your request, the investigative material in regards to the convicted American citizens Verdin [*sic*], Marchuk, and Noubl [*sic*] was reviewed by us. An examination of the material shows that Verdin [*sic*], Marchuk, and Noubl [*sic*] were sentenced to long terms without sufficient basis. Therefore, we have presented appropriate sentences to the USSR Procuracy with a request to repeal the sentences." The message from Serov concluded that Gromyko would be able to respond to Bohlen after a decision by the Soviet Supreme Court to repeal their sentences had been carried out. The Soviet Supreme Court voted to expel Verdine, Marchuk and Noble on May 19, 1954. But there was a catch. The Americans would not be released to U.S. authorities without special instructions, which took months to craft, approve and execute. Moscow, as always, expected Washington to pay a high price for the return of three Americans at Vorkuta.

A Top Secret Russian directive to Molotov and Kruglov from the Communist Party of the Soviet Union Central Committee dated December 31, 1954, granted Kruglov permission to return Marchuk and Noble to American authorities in Berlin, holding back Verdine for two to three weeks longer, presumably to make certain his chronic bronchitis was under control before the trip to West Germany. In return, Moscow wanted back eleven children of Soviet citizens and one of their diplomats, Yuri Rastvorov, who the Russians described as "detained" by American authorities. Zorin was instructed to tell Bohlen during upcoming talks that the United States was likely to get a positive response to its request for information regarding Marchuk, Verdine and Noble if it responded quickly to the Soviet Union's February 15, 1954 demarche on Rastvorov. Washington did not give up Rastvorov, a Soviet defector granted political asylum in the United States. Rastvorov was a valuable asset to U.S. intelligence. A few weeks after Noble and Marchuk returned to the United States, Rastvorov informed Eisenhower administration officials in a private January 28, 1955 meeting that American and United Nations prisoners of war were held in Siberia during and after the 1950 to 1953 Korean Conflict.

The diplomatic game of cat-and-mouse that eventually freed Noble took place in the shadows. From Michigan Congressman Alvin Bentley's perspective, lacking the diplomatic backstory, it was not moving fast enough. Bentley personally discussed Noble's case with President Dwight Eisenhower in December 1954 and it was only after this meeting that the President sent a diplomatic note to Ambassador Bohlen in Moscow informing him that the United States government had absolute proof Noble was a prisoner and thus guaranteed leverage with Moscow to get him back. Bohlen took up the matter directly with the Kremlin with greater urgency, to which Moscow caved quickly. In truth, Molotov had already conceded defeat. The Soviet Union was never going to get Rastvorov and all his secrets bottled up and back to Moscow, where a firing squad awaited him. Marchuk, Verdine and Noble were thus returned to American custody. Countless other Americans were not so lucky.

At Vorkuta Noble was so close to the North Pole, it was too cold for bacteria to survive there, yet *he* did. He labored in mines, pushing two-ton coal cars, even after his body weight plummeted from 155 to 95 pounds. He was kept totally incommunicado. The Russians kept his name out of their files and refused to acknowledge his existence for more than seven years. If not for a postcard sent through his trusted friend in the Vorkuta prison system and details of his ordeal provided by Homer Cox, the State Department stood a lowly chance of securing his release. John Noble would never have made it back. While it was obvious that the Russians could have gotten rid of any evidence that Noble was alive, they did not, perhaps comfortable that the MVD could hide his existence from American authorities indefinitely.

Noble's first words to the American press on his return to the United States were indicative of the wealth of information he would provide Washington regarding men still missing in the depths of the Soviet Union: "I have much to tell," as he stepped from behind the Iron Curtain. And he did. "I heard that an American engineer, seized while working for the Reds in Vladivostok, is still in Lubianka Prison in Moscow," he wrote, aware that his making their existence known might help the U.S. government leverage the man's release. Noble reported many Americans left behind in the Soviet Union. Most of them, eventually known to be in the thousands, never came home. They were unsuspecting servicemen, soldiers, sailors and aviators who'd served their country in World Wars I and II, some from the cold war, and they were also hapless American citizens. None of them ever saw their families again.

One of the unlucky Americans oft cited in congressional reporting is Massachusetts textbook salesman Newcomb Mott. He'd traveled to Scandinavia in late summer 1965 and took a walk across the Russian border with Norway to get a Soviet "red" stamp in his passport. It was a walk from which he never returned. Five months later Mott endured a violent death at Boris Gleb, a Russian village not far from where he went missing. The State Department handled his case poorly and was never able to deliver a strong enough argument nor muster the resources to effect Mott's release.

Another case, one with a better ending, was that of Commander Columbus Darwin "CD" Smith, a naval officer the Japanese couldn't seem to capture and keep. Though he'd been caught and locked away in an "escape-proof" facility at Shanghai, Smith did escape and began to evade for over six hundred miles behind enemy lines. He had help from Chinese resistance, but also the U.S. government, which intentionally declared Smith "officially dead" to get the Japanese thinking American forces weren't looking for him. This bought Smith time. After making his contact point hundreds of miles from Shanghai, Smith made it home. His worst problem, comically, was getting his status changed back to "living."

These precedents, thousands of them from World War II, including Noble and Smith, and, in later years, Mott, are a necessary backdrop to understanding our present problems and were of high interest to sorting out the particulars of how Scott Speicher was able to evade for so long and, after capture, what happened to him.

While there were historically far more cases going back to World War I, they'd fallen off the radar. Collectively, all point to the fact there was a mindset, a method and a pattern of behavior and action that colored events before the United States engaged in Desert Storm. Doubters, observed North Carolina Senator Jesse Helms, should examine more compelling evidence cited in the report published by the U.S. Senate Foreign Relations Committee Republican Minority Staff in October 1990 and released publicly in the spring of 1991, ironically the day after Scott Speicher's memorial service was held in Jacksonville, Florida. The information contained in the report points to Washington's significant problems in handling the POW/MIA issue from policy to action. America's leadership had forgotten that missing men could, and should, have a bearing on our national policy and honor among nations. Off the record, away from the headlines, the U.S. government had lost its way on the issue. The priority to act vanished decades before, replaced by other considerations that remain today: grand visions of a foreign policy of peace and reconciliation; desire for a new economic order of trade and investment; ideological imperatives to downplay the hostility of antagonistic foreign governments; and the natural tendency of America's vast bureaucracy to eliminate its workload by filing cases marked "closed" instead of finding the missing soldier, sailor or airman.

At the time Helms' committee staff looked at POW/MIA files, the intent was to cull Washington's handling and evaluation of live-sighting reports, firsthand narratives by witnesses who believed they had seen American military personnel alive in various locations in Southeast Asia, the Korean Peninsula, Communist China and the Soviet Union. These live-sighting reports provide tantalizing glimpses of prisoners of war and missing in action who have since vanished into the bureaucracy of the Department of Defense. The staff found – and further research for this volume supported – many illustrative cases to make the point that legitimate, proven sightings and information was being regularly dismissed. American prisoners of war and missing in action from the Korean Conflict were reportedly seen alive as late as 1982, according to a redacted CIA document dated 1988 obtained under a Freedom of Information Act (FOIA) request. "There is no reason to believe that this is the last report on U.S. prisoners of war and missing in action held in North Korea," stated the Senate Republican Minority Staff in its summation of that document. More recent information puts American prisoners of war, identified by name and location, alive in North Korea today.

For Vietnam, the U.S. government had at least 1,400 such reports that had been received up to the publication of the minority staff's final report in May 1991. They've since received many more firsthand sighting reports and compiled stronger information via overhead imagery, signals intelligence, and audiotape, videotape and photographs of Americans in captivity in Southeast Asia that continues to be suppressed within the Pentagon and U.S. intelligence agencies and hidden from the American public. Additionally, the U.S. government has received – and still receives – thousands of secondhand reports – accounts often full of vivid detail, such as "my brother told me he saw 11 American prisoners of war being transported in a truck at such and such a place." Yet, amazingly, the U.S. government has not judged a single one of these thousands of reports to be credible. Instead, the policy enunciated by an official statement of the U.S. government in 1973 was that "there are no more prisoners in Southeast Asia. They are all dead." This policy – in the face of extensive evidence that all U.S. prisoners of war in Southeast Asia were not dead – thus evolved into the U.S. government's policy that there is no credible evidence of any U.S. prisoners of war still alive in all of Indochina. This, too, is the policy – a "mindset" as it were – that was in place when the Persian Gulf War began in January 1991.

The American public knew little of the numbers game being played concerning the fate of the nation's prisoners of war and missing in action nor organized attempts to cover up the actual number of men the United States government thus wrote off, leaving them in foreign prisons. There is no way of knowing how many from the past are still alive today alongside new prisoners of war taken by the United States' worst enemies. Destruction of Senate Select Committee on Prisoners of War and Missing in Action classified documents pertaining to "the numbers game" and credible live sighting reports were subsequently revealed in a series of damning memorandums written by a high ranking Defense Intelligence Agency analyst assigned to the Senate committee, Virginia attorney John F. McCreary, in the spring of 1992. But it was a series of memorandums, most addressed to attention of Senate Select Committee on POW/MIA Affairs Staff Director Frances Zwenig[2] by select committee Investigator Sedgwick D. Tourison Jr. that sent diehard Washington insiders ducking for cover. Tourison's – and other investigators' statements – exposed a dark chapter in American history, one that would have permanently ended the careers of anyone tainted with it if they got caught. There's something a bit ironic, too, that just as the Senate select committee opened its investigation of America's missing in Southeast Asia, the cases of those lost over the Gulf in 1991 were fomenting, but had not been fully revealed to the American public.

Tourison's December 17, 1991 memorandum to the select committee indicated that it was the Department of Defense, responsible for all official American prisoner of war and missing in action information, that provided details to him on the history of its casualty reporting. Tourison got more information from his meeting with the DIA's Special Office for POW/MIA Affairs (now the DPMO). By the time he'd begun to coalesce information from the Defense Department and POW/MIA Affairs, Tourison had already established a detailed baseline of what the military services and intelligence agencies did and, importantly, did not know, of the fate of America's missing. Tourison quickly figured out that for Zwenig there was no single and reliable U.S. government record of all Americans who may have been captured during the war in Southeast Asia. Tourison couldn't speak to what had just happened in the Persian Gulf earlier that year; his task had been to look for evidence of live Americans in Southeast Asia, specifically Vietnam. He informed Zwenig that there "are two 'lists' of unaccounted-for American military missing in action, only one of which is official."

Information provided to the Select Committee by the DIA, Tourison's employer, didn't come from the official list of American military missing. Tourison provided information about the eight U.S. Air Force officers and enlisted men on board an EC-47Q aircraft – call sign Baron 52 – lost while on a signals intelligence mission over Laos on February 5, 1973, and who'd been reported as killed in action by the air force just three weeks after their loss. The death declaration was issued in the absence of any compelling evidence of death and, importantly, in a manner inconsistent with the normal casualty investigation procedures. "Furthermore," wrote Tourison, "U.S. military intelligence resources in Laos and Thailand which could have been employed to help determine the fate of such personnel may have been actively prevented from doing so by the Central Intelligence Agency station in Vientiane, Laos."

Tourison's preliminary analysis of the "two sets of books" documented that during the first week of public hearings conducted by the Senate Select Committee on POW/MIA Affairs, the select committee heard from a broad sampling of Defense and State Department witnesses who stated that the total number of Americans unaccounted for in Southeast Asia was only 2,273 men. This figure was later couched as 2,271 men after the return of the two unaccounted-for Americans' purported remains; however, a preliminary investigation subsequently disclosed that the Defense Department's own "official" list of U.S. military casualties only listed 2,239 American military personnel missing in action. But that wasn't what was so remarkable. What proved troubling was the fact that 2,238 of these servicemen had their files marked with a presumptive finding of death, all, but air force colonel Charles E. Shelton, still carried as missing in action and presumed alive.

While the select committee hadn't yet received the DIA's latest breakdown of the 2,271 men listed as missing in action, there was an obvious discrepancy, Tourison wrote, between the "official" Defense Department figures and the figures provided to the select committee by government witnesses. Based on witness statements, the 2,271 missing in action included all American military personnel and civilians just then unaccounted for in Southeast Asia. But there was already mounting anecdotal evidence that the 2,271 of America's missing didn't include any military deserters. This would suggest that the total number of missing in action ultimately presented by the committee "must be a minimum figure."

Tourison's examination of the Department of Defense's "official" records for the period January 1973 to September 1977, showed that at least one American serviceman previously classified as a deserter during the war and not reported to the Pentagon because deserters were excluded from casualty reporting – Robert R. Garwood – later returned alive from captivity. Garwood, accused of being absent without leave (AWOL), came home from Vietnam in 1979. The AWOL category was left out of the Pentagon's statistics during time of war. Still, Garwood's Marine Corps headquarter considered him missing in action as late as September 1977. Post Operation Homecoming intelligence revealed that several individuals believed to have died in a non-hostile situation had actually been captured alive and died in captivity.

Further, Tourison discovered mounting anecdotal evidence of lack of accountability for and reporting of American civilians who were missing in action and who'd never been reported to American consular officials; this finding indicated the possibility that the total number of civilians who could have become missing might be larger than first believed. Tourison's work came on the heels of Washington's first hearings on America's prisoners of war and missing in action. He'd find even more anecdotal evidence that false wartime casualty reporting from the military services for casualties attributed to Laos. "Several hundred were initially reported as missing in South Vietnam and only perhaps four years after the Paris Peace Accords," he observed, "did the military services submit corrected casualty reports reflecting their country of loss to be Laos." Of these men, Tourison noted that all were subsequently reclassified as dead based on a presumptive finding of death. "Such false reporting," he continued, "has clearly raised the specter of other flaws within the minds of some next-of-kin."

Based on a preliminary examination of the available official data from the Department of Defense and the total number of missing in action provided by the government's witnesses as 2,271 missing in action, Tourison documented that it was possible to tentatively conclude that the Pentagon, blessed by the White House, had been maintaining two active and totally distinct "sets of MIA books," neither of which, he observed, "can be assumed to be a totally reliable source of information concerning the total number of Americans who did, or may have become, unaccounted for in Southeast Asia. The preliminary investigation revealed that the Defense Department was aware soon after the January 1973 Paris Peace Accords that the number of prisoners of war and missing in action whose names appeared on the "official" Defense Department casualty lists was at significant variance with the list of prisoners of war and missing in action maintained by the DIA and the Joint Casualty Resolution Center/Central Identification Laboratory, Hawaii (JCRC/CILHI).

While both DIA and JCRC were aware their respective figures were at variance with the "official" figures, no action was taken until mid 1977 when a Defense Department official visited Hawaii to conduct an audit of the missing in action totals maintained by the JCRC. That visit arguably ended with an agreed upon list but only as of mid 1977. The DIA and JCRC continued to maintain a list that included American civilians, but not deserters, which the "official" Defense Department records also excluded.

In point of fact, Tourison reported "the 'set of books' presented by the DIA to the select committee didn't represent the Defense Department's own official total of American military personnel missing in action. Tourison added that "while the military services are authorized to provide their own individual military service missing in action totals, only the Defense Department's Directorate for Management Information Operations and Control, not the Defense Intelligence Agency, has been specifically appointed by the Secretary of Defense to present the official Defense Department military casualty figures." This convoluted authority over missing men's status, one that had begun per Defense Department Instruction 7730.22, effective March 20, 1973, established one point within the department for all statistical data on American casualties in combat areas. This applied not only to the casualty reporting from Southeast Asia but to all past and future conflicts. The Directorate for Information Operations was quartered in the Office of the Assistant Secretary of Defense (Comptroller) and specified as the sole agency for all official casualty statistics.

The definition of casualties published in the Joint Chiefs of Staff official dictionary dated 1969 defined the various categories of casualties used in all official reporting through Vietnam. A companion Department of Defense Instruction 1300.09, dated March 23, 1973, updated next-of-kin notification procedures and established Defense Department Form 1300 as the document used to record and report all active duty dead and missing casualties. During the late 1970s the Defense Department comptroller's office reorganized and the Washington Headquarters Services (WHS) was thus established. The combat casualty reporting function thus transferred from the comptroller to the WHS. Defense Department Instruction 7730.60, published and effective on September 27, 1979, established the Directorate for Information Operations and Reports (DIOR), Washington Headquarters Services, as the sole point for all official noncombat casualty data. This move effectively placed all U.S. military active duty casualty statistical reporting to one single office; it was not until August 26, 1982, that the Defense Department issued Instruction 7730.63, which superseded Instruction 7730.22 and authorized the military services to provide official statistics and make technical adjustments to reporting formats and data items. This instruction was still in effect when the U.S. reported casualties from Operation Desert Storm.

While the DIA was preparing to provide the chronology of their casualty figures for the select committee, Tourison's examination of available official data revealed major discrepancies that came back again to the "two sets of books." The Department of Defense's "official" U.S. military casualty figures specifically excluded any category and reporting of "deserters" within official U.S. military casualty totals, thus the Department's might be considered less than "all inclusive." Official U.S. military personnel casualty figures from the time of the Paris Peace Accords through September 1977 represent more than numbers: each is an unaccounted for, deceased or returned American soldier, sailor or airman.

A day prior to the official implementation of the Paris Peace Accords – January 27, 1973 – the Defense Department's official record of American casualties in Southeast Asia, other than wounded, and based on reports to the Defense Department from the individual military services, included 45, 941 dead as the result of hostile action; 10,303 dead due to non-hostile action; 1,929 unaccounted for; and 84 returned to U.S. military control. Men returned to military control included two categories: those who'd been released by hostile forces during the war and those who'd been initially declared "missing" and later located and recovered by American forces, generally within three days of having been declared missing.

The 1,929 American military listed as unaccounted for were divided into three categories. These were categories consistent with the Defense Department's definition of casualties and were predicated on reports submitted to the Pentagon by the individual military services. Missing and prisoner categories officially reported by the Defense Department as of January 1973 included 1,220 missing in action; 118 missing due to non-hostile activity; and 591 prisoners of war. Five months after Operation Homecoming, the Defense Department was constantly updating casualty figures, which took into account whatever information the military services had about their missing man and further included intelligence shoehorned into America's known prisoner of war dossiers – and the Pentagon and intelligence services did know who was still in captivity. But mostly these updates were not used to the benefit of the missing. Rather, they were used to reduce the total number of unaccounted for, in a less than accurate fashion.

What Tourison found should have been instructive for what would happen in the Persian Gulf less than twenty years later. But it wasn't. The Defense Department moved 11 men from prisoner of war to died while captured; 9 men from missing in action to died while captured; 59 men from missing in action to died while missing; 2 men from missing due to non-hostile circumstances to died while captured; and 3 men from missing due to non-hostile activity to died by the same as of June 2, 1973. Overall, Defense also published further adjustments to its wartime casualty statistics: 46,040 dead due to hostile action; 10,304 dead due to non-hostile circumstances; 1,283 unaccounted for; 67 prisoners of war; and 650 returned to military control.

The numbers just kept changing. More information would come in and it seemed to shift the numbers downward each time. None of the information coming in – even intelligence that clearly indicated American servicemen still alive and in enemy captivity – drew much attention. Four years after Operation Homecoming, 50 American servicemen previously carried as prisoners of war were reclassified to have died while captured; 13 previously carried as missing in action were reclassified as having died while captured, and 513 missing in action were declared dead while missing, most of these based on a presumptive finding of death.

The cumulative total of presumptive findings of death were first made a matter of formal entry in the Defense Department's casualty statistics in August 1975, and the term "body not recovered" was first used in the department's March 31, 1976 casualty statistics report. Noteworthy, too, is that total deaths attributed to hostile and non-hostile circumstances included only the following: those who died and their remains were recovered; those reported as died based on a presumptive finding of death; those active duty military personnel who died prior to January 28, 1973, and up until the American-flagged merchant ship *Mayaguez* incident[3] in May 1975, within the Southeast Asia area; and those who died after departing Southeast Asia of wounds and injuries sustained in-theater. Just as Tourison filed his report in December 1991, the Pentagon's instruction as it pertained to the nation's military casualties didn't report on, compile nor provide casualty data for American civilians and any U.S. government civilian employees, including Defense contractors. Tourison argued that additional investigation was needed to verify the authority given the DIA and JCRC to compile, maintain and provide the casualty figures it had provided to the select committee.

The select committee raised the possibility that many men listed as missing in action were declared dead based on an expeditious presumptive finding of death. At the time of Tourison's investigation, he discovered limited anecdotal data that the military services may have relied on intelligence evaluations or judgments coming out of American returnees and intelligence available to some within the Defense Department who'd met to review missing in action files just after Operation Homecoming. There was further anecdotal evidence that the DIA didn't have a firm understanding, at that time, of the prison system – and the movement of prisoners – inside Vietnam, Laos and Cambodia. This lack of understanding carried over to the Iraqi prison system and the use of extraterritorial prisons to maintain Baghdad's plausible deniability when asked if it held American and other coalition prisoners of war.

Documentary evidence provided via human intelligence (HUMINT) collection in Thailand was specifically authorized in

1972 to glean prisoner of war and missing in action information vis-à-vis clandestine operations in Laos. Intelligence sources were tapped to materially assist the DIA headquarters in its effort to adequately address post 1975 reporting. But this collection effort was stymied by at least two, and possibly three, CIA stations in Southeast Asia and a general malaise that erupted in the U.S. intelligence community. The cumulative problem terminated nearly all known American military HUMINT operations from 1974 to 1975; the residual and largely unstaffed effort ended by 1977. If any American prisoners of war remained alive and in Southeast Asia as of 1975, there is solid evidence that the Department of Defense didn't reasonably and properly exercise all its options, observed Tourison, to meet its statutory responsibilities to account for all missing in action and relied more heavily on analysis that could not be supported by reasonably accurate and objective judgment.

Tourison ultimately observed that, of those "two sets of books," neither set could be considered accurate, which contributed to the continued lack of confidence in the U.S. intelligence system to accurately assist in documenting the fate of Americans missing in action. More than a lack of confidence, this flawed system spelled dire consequences for America's missing servicemen and also those civilians who'd gone into harm's way in the service of the nation. The numbers game, as it played out in government documents, statements and media reports and argued in open and closed select committee hearings, angered and frustrated the families of the missing and, above all, called into question the national will to account for these men and women who are the nation's blood and treasure.

Rather than giving the benefit of the doubt to the service member that he is alive, the Department of Defense made a presumptive finding of death. The latter determination spelled a life in purgatory for thousands of Americans held by communist forces against their will, but also those held today by enemy nation states and terrorist organizations worldwide. The minority staff found that in spite of 1,400 reports of firsthand live-sightings in Southeast Asia, the Department of Defense, remarkably, still believes it has "no credible evidence." No one working personnel recovery just then and in the years to follow could understand how the Department of Defense dismissed those reports and the many more that have come in since the staff published its report in 1991.

The Republican minority staff conducted hundreds of interviews and reviewed raw intelligence data secreted within the files of the Defense Department. The interim report published in October 1990 suggested that the Department of Defense was more interested in manipulation and managing the issue than in finding living prisoners of war listed as missing. But as the investigation proceeded, the weight of the evidence of failure, a failure of the United States government to meet its sacred trust, became overwhelming. The staff's investigators pondered the possibilities. Was it really possible that officials in the Executive Branch charged to resolve solution of prisoner of war and missing in action issues failed so miserably to respond to the needs of the American people? Was it simply that the emotions of the prisoner of war/missing in action activist community had made an objective appraisal of the Department of Defense's work impossible? Had the staff read too much into all those files secreted away at the Pentagon? Hardly.

In reviewing hundreds of raw intelligence files on the 1,400 reports, Republican minority staff investigators found a predisposition by Department of Defense evaluators to ignore corroborative evidence, and found little interest on the part of those evaluators to follow up what a good police detective would consider good leads. In many cases, the chilling fact was that the Department of Defense quietly disposed of most of its corroborative evidence, intent on upholding the validity of the department's "no credible evidence" policy. "It is contrary to common sense," wrote the minority staff in its final report, "that all of these reports – all 1,400 – are spurious, especially in the light of such obvious contradictions as the actual return of the unfortunate Private Robert Garwood in 1979."

The minority staff observed that Garwood was a battle casualty taken into custody by the North Vietnamese under fire. At Garwood's subsequent court martial, in which he was charged as a collaborator and deserter, the Department of Defense solved two problems by taking him to trial: by bringing the charges, the

Defense Department sought to redefine his case as a voluntary expatriate and thus not technically a prisoner of war, which enabled the Department of Defense's evaluators to dismiss fully sixty-four percent of the live-sighting reports as sightings of Garwood. Since Garwood reported that he had been moved from prison to prison, the faulty logic of the Defense Department seemed to demand that any report from the prisons he cited must have been sightings of Garwood. The policy that there was "no credible evidence" of living prisoners made it necessary to assume that other U.S. prisoners in those prisons could not and did not exist.

Garwood was convicted of one count of simple assault on a fellow prisoner of war, one count of aiding the enemy by acting as a translator, interpreter and interrogator, one count of wearing black pajamas, the enemy uniform, and one count of transporting a Kalashnikov AK-47 (unloaded) during a patrol. Whether these convictions added up to meaningful collaboration with the enemy or not, it was never proven that he was a voluntary deserter. The bottom line was that the "no credible evidence" policy was incorrect: discredited on the sole basis of having gotten back Private Robert Garwood, a man who was not supposed to exist. Garwood and other American prisoners of war in Southeast Asia were supposed to be "all dead."

Reports of Garwood had obviously proven true. Since Garwood was alive in Indochina from 1973 to 1979, Department of Defense policy was salvaged to some degree by his court martial. As a "collaborator" he may have been in North Vietnamese custody in 1973, but he no longer fit the definition of "prisoner." Nonetheless, Garwood, on his return, reported seeing another presumed deserter, Earl C. Weatherman, alive in 1977. He stated also that a third presumed deserter, McKinley Nolan, was also alive after 1973. It may be assumed that Garwood was not reporting a live-sighting of himself in these cases.

The Defense Department would have the public believe that sixty-four percent of the men sighted had to be Garwood. In the hope of proving its point, the Defense Department circulated a document among prisoner of war and missing in action families that claimed to show twenty U.S. personnel listed as deserters or absent without leave (AWOL) had been left in North Vietnamese custody after Operation Homecoming, the 1973 prisoner exchange, because of their unlucky status. Four others are listed as disappearing under unexplained or unusual circumstances. The Republican minority staff took no position on the validity of this list, but it did note that almost all of the individuals cited appear on a Defense Intelligence Agency (DIA) alphabetic list entitled "U.S. Casualties in Southeast Asia" dated February 26, 1980, but are conspicuously absent from a similar DIA list dated August 22, 1984. Interestingly, Garwood stated publicly on his return to the United States as well as to U.S. Senate investigators under follow-up questioning that he had, indeed, seen at least thirty U.S. prisoners of war offloading from a box car in Vietnam in the late 1970s.

The Senate Republican minority staff had just announced it was about to publish its findings when Hanoi announced that it was willing to open its territory to relatives to search for any prisoners of war and missing in action, alive or dead. While that was viewed as an encouraging development, the Department of Defense had still not opened "its territory," file storage spilling over with live-sighting and secondhand reports. These were not being made available to families of prisoners of war and missing in action or to any qualified investigator, particularly to United States senators, members of Congress and their staffs. This lack of openness characterized the operations of the Department of Defense Special Office of Prisoner of War/Missing in Action (POW/MIA) Affairs, and colored the atmosphere, even after it made the transition to Defense Prisoners of War/Missing Personnel Office (DPMO).

Colonel Millard A. Peck's resignation offered unexpected and extraordinary confirmation of the Republican minority staff's interim report. Observers described Colonel Peck as a man who had accepted the position with high motives and a deep sense of dedication to the prisoners of war and missing in action who were his primary concern. "Colonel Millard A. Peck felt that he could no longer fulfill the demands of duty, honor, and integrity under the policies which he was asked to implement," wrote Jesse Helms. "In a detailed and forthright letter, which did not become public until May [1991], Colonel Peck confirmed that a 'cover up' has been in progress. He spoke of a 'mindset to debunk.' He said that there was no effort to pursue 'live sightings.'" Helms attached Peck's entire report to the letter and forwarded it to committee members and staff. "The fact," observed Helms, "that Colonel Peck's conclusions were so similar to the conclusions of the minority staff is a matter of regret, rather than vindication. I had hoped that the minority staff investigators would be able to alter their preliminary findings, because the implications of a deliberate effort by the United States government to deceive the American people is a matter that all of us would prefer to believe unthinkable." Senator Helms further made clear to whoever would read the staff report that Colonel Peck's statements should be evaluated in light of the colonel's long career of faithful service in the United States Army, including three combat tours in Vietnam, for which he was awarded numerous medals for gallantry, including the nation's second highest award, the Distinguished Service Cross. At that time he was also one of the few men with intimate knowledge of the way in which the United States government had carried out its prisoner of war and missing in action policy.

When Scott Speicher was omitted from the Red Cross list, it was because the Pentagon assumed, without proof, that he was dead. But this assumption was nothing more than pabulum for the public. Among the second group of Coalition prisoners returned by Iraq were two probable killed in action (PKIAs). Marine Corps captain Craig Berryman and air force captain Dale Storr were put on the list even though the Pentagon was pretty certain they were dead. So American officials were floored when they saw Berryman and Storr among repatriated prisoners of war.

Navy lieutenant Bob Wetzel's story had a different twist. Carlos Johnson went up to Bob after a post-Gulf War Tailhook Association symposium and told him that the Office of Naval Intelligence (ONI) knew he was alive and captured within an hour of his shootdown. But they couldn't publicly declare him a POW without giving away how they knew. Bob was lucky. At least his name ended up on the Red Cross list and he had a fighting chance of coming home.

The Department of Defense revised its casualty data on March 6 to twenty-six missing in action and no prisoners of war, believing the Iraqis had returned all captives. Schwarzkopf insisted, "I can tell you absolutely without qualification that by the time the war was over, and certainly before we ever came home, that I had been told that one hundred percent had been accounted for. That was the report that was given to me because I asked over and over again. I'm absolutely convinced," he said, "that there was no neglect on the part of anybody in my command with regard to the sensitivity of this matter or effort we made to recover bodies or prisoners of war."

To the best of his knowledge, General Schwarzkopf was right. He'd been guaranteed by his staff that they'd done their jobs and accounted properly for all U.S. service members. But they were anxious to get everything over with. At war's end it was far easier to declare missing men killed in action, body not recovered (KIA-BNR) than to resolve the thornier issue of their precise whereabouts.

"From day one," insisted Carlos Johnson, "he [Speicher] should never have been anything but an MIA. We didn't have a game plan for pilots like Scott Speicher." Back in Riyadh, CENTCOM didn't have the names of half-dozen unaccounted-for navy aviators on the Red Cross list. Names conspicuously absent, in addition to Speicher, were Lieutenants Patrick K. Connor, Robert J. Dwyer, William T. Costen and Charles J. Turner, and Lieutenant Commander Barry T. Cooke. Their cases hung in limbo for the simple reason no one had put their names on the list. As it turned out later, nobody did much to look for them either.

The remains of Turner, Costen and Connor purportedly turned up weeks later. Connor's remains, according to reports, washed up in the mud of Faylaka Island on March 31. His VA-36 Roadrunner A-6E Intruder had taken a shoulder-fired SAM missile up the tailpipe on February 2. Connor and his bombardier-navigator, Barry Cooke, were on the Department of Defense's MIA list but not on the ICRC's list. Nine days later, the navy retrieved the tail section of their aircraft. Barry Cooke is unaccounted for today, a distinction he continues to share with Robert J. Dwyer.

Without the names of unaccounted-for aviators on the ICRC list, most especially Speicher, "we lost leverage with Iraq and support in the international community for getting him back," said Carlos Johnson. "The political cowardice was unconscionable. We had the mentality that had there been some glimmer that he survived, we would've gone to find him, but we didn't look at it close enough to make that determination." Johnson made the observation that Speicher's whole case went back to the argument, "Do you risk hundreds for one? We'd crossed the line to say no, you don't. We had policies of convenience, not conviction."

Ambassador Richard Butler, former executive chairman of the United Nations Special Commission (UNSCOM) for Iraq, offered his expert opinion of Scott Speicher's situation. "There is a tendency on their [the Iraqis'] part to lie, hector and play games. This reached its height on biological weapons. You'll probably recall," said Butler, "my big showdown meeting on August 3, 1998, in which the Iraqis asked me to declare them biological/chemical and arms free. I refused. They had four tons of VX. We could tell them this, prove it with pictures and documentation." When they lie, he observed, they lie big. The Iraqis had already accused former Marine Corps intelligence officer Scott Ritter, one of Butler's weapons inspectors, of spying for the Central Intelligence Agency. "When the Iraqis say you're a spy, that you've been seeking one of your aviators, they are vociferously covering up. When they cover up loudly, they are most guilty and diabolical. This means Speicher is probably," Butler indicated in a 2001 interview, "still alive. Otherwise, why accuse us of searching for him?"

Butler believed that some of the blame for Speicher's circumstance lay with CNN and their blanket coverage of the war. "I have personally seen [Foreign Minister] Tariq Aziz watching CNN," said Butler. "I walked into his office during one of the inspection meetings and when he saw I noticed, he immediately turned off the television set." CNN, in Butler's opinion, bears "a heavy responsibility in all this. I have been to the network's top executives to tell them just that, and to caution them about how heavily CNN is patronized by the Iraqis." Saddam liked the coverage he got from

CNN. All the Iraqis initially learned about Speicher from CNN the night of his initial loss was that the United States was missing a pilot and his name was Michael Scott Speicher.

Vice Admiral Thomas R. Wilson, then director of the Defense Intelligence Agency (DIA), concurred that the cable network CNN bore some of the blame. "We created the circumstance for [the Iraqis] to keep him when we declared him gone so quickly after the shoot down and didn't ask for him after the war," said Wilson in 2001. "There was a public perception of Scott's loss via CNN that preempted an official death declaration on May 20, 1991, but even that declaration of death was without clear evidence that a death had occurred. We should never have classified him anything but MIA based on what we knew at that time," Wilson concluded. But the White House was interested in tying up loose ends and that meant there couldn't be any unaccounted-for service members from Desert Storm. This position is articulated best by the rush to close missing men's files. "As you know, all POWs have been returned by Iraq and we have resolved the last two MIA cases [one of which was Speicher's and the other was Barry Cooke] from Operation Desert Storm," wrote Vice President Dick Cheney to Ann Mills Griffiths, then-executive director of the National Alliance of POW/MIA Families, on June 14, 1991. "The lessons Vietnam taught us," he continued, "were used in the Gulf War, and the country is well aware of the success we had in resolving the fates of American POWs and MIAs in that war." The vice president painted a pretty picture. But it was diametrically at odds with the findings of Helms' Republican minority staff report and, importantly, the truth. Washington had learned from its experience with Vietnam how to debunk any evidence of any live POW/MIAs in Southeast Asia and move on quickly. This is the "lesson Vietnam taught us." Washington learned to leave men behind "better" than the last time.

Why hold Scott? Butler offered a view that was made moot after the United States stormed into Iraq in March 2003 and Saddam Hussein's sons, Uday and Qusay, never got the chance to use Speicher the way that he suggested. Both were killed by U.S. forces on July 22, 2003. Saddam, on the run, was captured on December 12. But what Butler had to say then provided insight into the Iraqi regime that once held him. "The Iraqis would exact a terrible price for him. They have a ten-year-investment in keeping him. If he's still alive," observed Butler, "and they would keep him going to use him, it means they've kept him against a rainy day, for a tremendous thunderstorm." This meant that when the time came, they'd put it all on the line for something of enormous value. Saddam and his sons likely did not expect the United States to pursue them all the way to Baghdad in 2003, believing that the son of the same president who had pressed an attack in 1991 would follow his father's footsteps. They were wrong. While true that the Iraqis could have used Scott Speicher to stop bombings, sanctions or as leverage in a regional dispute, they hadn't done so, at least not publicly. Butler suggested that none of those reasons presented "a tremendous thunderstorm." None were pressing enough to cause Saddam to reveal his captive to the world. He pointed to thousands of Iranian prisoners in Iraqi jails from Saddam's eight-year war with his next-door neighbor between 1980 and 1988. He pointed to the hundreds of Kuwaiti prisoners in Saddam's custody, prisoners never seen again. "When I observed that there were hundreds or thousands involved in this respect," said Butler, "what I've continued to hear from other diplomatic sources in this: 'The Iraqis know for the United States, it only takes one.'"

Everything seemed to lead to the same question: Why didn't anyone ever go look for Scott Speicher? A January 19, 1999 memorandum from Deputy Assistant Secretary of Defense for POW/Missing Personnel Affairs Robert L. Jones stated eight years after the fact, "Search and rescue forces were alerted and possible divert airfields were contacted with negative results." Jones' memo made another statement: "LCDR Speicher's crash site was not located prior to termination of Operation Desert Storm." Neither of these statements is true. No rescue forces were ever contacted to search for Scott Speicher. While the chain of command from the JCS to CENTCOM to Speicher's commanders aboard *Saratoga* knew Speicher was down, information that he ejected purportedly never made it to the SOCCENT intelligence (SOCCENT J2) staff, in charge just then for dispatching search and rescue. But there was also another mistake, one that would have put rescuers in the wrong place had they ever looked: coordinates for Speicher's crash site were inaccurately reported. Further, though SOCCENT got the message about the radio clicks reported on January 18, nothing was done to run it down.

According to Bob Stumpf, within twenty-four hours of Speicher shoot down, pilots on *Saratoga* calculated exactly where they had last seen his "fireball" by comparing notes and reviewing data recorded by aircraft and HUD recorders. During their intelligence debriefings on the ship, Lieutenant David Renaud, who for a long time was believed to be the closest pilot to Speicher at the time he was hit, reported seeing explosions five miles away, in Spike's direction, at the same time Stumpf witnessed a blast in the sky. Renaud even drew a little circle on his map where he calculated he had last seen the fireball. "This information," said Stumpf, "was relayed up the chain of command. Years later, when the wreckage was actually located, it was in the precise spot they had identified."[4] This didn't matter in January 1991. The wrong set of coordinates was run up the chain of command. "His commanding officer [Mike "Spock" Anderson] and his CAG [Dean M. "Milo" Hendrickson] should have been more involved and they should have grabbed the torch and run with it," said Buddy Harris of the lack of search for Speicher, "and they just didn't do that."

Vice Admiral Stanley Arthur, the commander of all allied naval forces in the Persian Gulf region, went on record to say, "The first report was 'airplane disintegrated on impact; no contact with the pilot; we really don't believe that anyone was able to survive the impact.'" Yet when it comes to combat, time and again the amazing and unexpected have happened. During Operation Homecoming in 1973, Major Douglas B. "Pete" Peterson, shot down in September 1966, was debriefed. A few weeks before he went down, Peterson had been engaged in air combat over North Vietnam. He returned from the mission to report his wingman was dead. A missile hit him, Peterson reported, and the aircraft was engulfed in a huge explosion. He saw no parachute, no beepers were heard and hundreds of pieces of the aircraft had flown through the air. He'd seen all this with his own eyes. A funeral was held shortly thereafter for his friend. When Peterson was shot down not long after and captured by the North Vietnamese, he was taken to Hanoi, where the first American he saw in prison was his "dead" wingman. How could that be? But there he was. Peterson's story is hardly the only one like this.

Certainly one of the reasons no one looked for Speicher was fear of losing his search teams to the same fate. The Jesse Johnson backstory has everything to do with his refusal to go get Speicher just after his shoot down. During Desert Storm General Schwarzkopf put army colonel Jesse Johnson in charge of search and rescue. Johnson thereafter instituted strict guidelines before any search was launched. Teams would have to hear from a downed pilot, find his location and assess the risk before going into Iraq. "We had a very, very sophisticated search and rescue plan made up, so that in the event that anybody went down," said Schwarzkopf, "we could dispatch search and rescue if they were alive on the ground. We could hopefully rescue them, a very dangerous mission, I'm sure you can understand."

All reported downed aircrew were considered, at least technically, actionable search and rescue events. But not all of them could be carried out due to shoot down location, lack of precise coordinates (such as Scott Speicher's) and lack of confirmation the aircrew was still alive. Timothy G. Connolly, the former army Ranger and later principal undersecretary of defense for special operations and low-intensity conflict, said in 2001 of the low number of rescue missions executed during the war, where he was assigned as part of a group working with Iraqi resistance, "We did virtually no SAR for anyone. Jesse Johnson, head of special operations for Central Command, was responsible for combat SAR forces. His rule was, we're not launching unless there's somebody on the ground waving their arms for us. He didn't want to risk casualties." That was a drastic policy change from Vietnam, where teams would head out and search immediately when word came down that a pilot was shot down. Although seventy-one search and rescue team members were killed, air force CSAR saved more than four thousand Americans' lives and the navy picked up hundreds of others.

During Desert Storm thirty-seven fixed-wing aircraft were lost in combat, but Johnson launched search teams for only seven of them. CSAR rescued only three pilots. Kuwaiti resistance made at least three attempts, possibly more, to rescue downed aviators in their territory. But either the pilot got picked up or the rescue route was so saturated with Iraqi troops that the Kuwaitis weren't able to get to them.

General Schwarzkopf was taken aback when informed in 2001 that no search and rescue was done for Scott Speicher. "I would be very surprised at that," he said, "unless the reports were so specific as to say that there could not have been life or that he could not have survived the crash." Then he said something more that raises the question of how well informed he'd been of Johnson's CSAR activities, or lack thereof. "I do know we did run many search and rescue missions," Schwarzkopf insisted. "If there was any chance at all that there would have been survivor, they would have gone out and attempted to recover him." Yet the math is simple: seven searches out of thirty-seven, three recoveries, none of them inside the four- to five-hour window CSAR likes to work with, and the lives of thirty aircrews hanging in the balance, including Scott Speicher's.

Communication between CENTCOM and SOCCENT J2 fell apart before the first shot was fired. A September 1990 article in Saudi Arab's English-daily the *Arab News* reported that the Jordanian-based tribal leader of the Shammar tribe supported Coalition efforts against Saddam Hussein. The SOCCENT J2's Kuwaiti contacts confirmed this. The Shammar tribe is one of the largest in Arabia, with over one million members in Saudi Arabia, concentrated today around Hail; an estimated one-and-a-half million in Iraq; about 100,000 centered in Aljahra, Kuwait; over one-and-a-half million in Syria; and an unknown number in Jordan and Egypt. Sources state that in the Shammar tribe's golden era, about 1850, it ruled much of central and northern Arabia from Riyadh all the way to Syria, and on to the Aljazeera area of northern Iraq. The Shammar tribe, specifically the Shammar Jarba, made a strong ally, especially due to its members' routine travels, not unlike many of Iraq's native tribal groups, passing easily over national borders between Jordan, Syria, Saudi Arabia, Kuwait, Iran and Iraq, most of them unnoticed by Saddam's border guards.

Major James Gregory Eanes[5], an air force escape and evasion officer assigned to SOCCENT J2 staff, submitted a memorandum to army lieutenant colonel John P. Grace, his SOCCENT J2 boss. In the memo, submitted at the beginning of Operation Desert Shield, Eanes suggested that SOCCENT J2 initiate a campaign to solicit tribal support and to establish direct communication with tribal leadership to establish an escape and evasion network. Grace nixed the idea. He told his staff that escape and evasion networks were a CIA operation and not his responsibility. Grace wasn't well informed. Seven years earlier, at a personnel recovery conference, the CIA stated that it was out of the business of setting up escape and evasion networks. The CIA's only interest in indigenous tribal groups was cultivation of political and paramilitary organizations to supplant Saddam. Grace indicated almost indignantly that it was SOCCENT J2's job to wait for orders, not initiate operational concepts. Eanes gasped and wondered what the hell they were doing there. "I was really steamed at the time," he said later, "feeling our job was to prepare for the coming conflict. But Grace and others somehow thought we were strictly there as a deterrent rather than a liberation force."

John Grace was a by-product of the Vietnam era, a veteran who survived the politics of the post-war period by not taking a proactive stand on any issue that fell under the category of career buster. Though no one on his staff knew it then, he also suffered from severe asthma and remained heavily medicated during his SOCCENT J2 tenure. Lieutenant Commander Michael Williams, his deputy, once found Grace on the floor of his room comatose. A second time Grace nearly died, and this eventually led to CENTCOM sending him home in late September to early October 1990. Eanes' memo never made it beyond Grace's desk, despite the fact it was flagged to the attention of SOCCENT Operations (SOCCENT

J3) chief army colonel James Fletcher. That November Fletcher told Eanes he was never shown the memo.

By the time Fletcher told Eanes he'd never seen his plan for an escape and evasion network, Saddam Hussein had initiated a reward program of his own in anticipation of a Coalition attack: cash rewards for downed aircrew captured by any Bedouin, Bidun or Iraqi civilian. Saddam's cash offer was $35,000 for each airman taken prisoner and turned over to Baghdad authorities. SOCCENT J2 policy was to stay out of bidding wars with America's enemies, thus there was, and is, no price tag put on friendly assistance. Each airman carried a blood chit, a written notice, in several languages, into combat. If shot down, the notice identifies the airman as an American and encourages the local population to assist him. The concept of the blood chit is over two hundred years old, but was reprised by the United States during World War II and has been issued to airmen flying combat over hostile territory ever since. Blood chits have been carried by airmen for operations in Panama, Grenada, Somalia, Bosnia, and the Persian Gulf War. Since 1991 the use of blood chits has continued, including recent operations over Southwest Asia since 2003. The difference today is that the Operation Desert Storm blood chit package includes money and, depending on the theater of operation, a point-and-talk pictorial display. The bottom line is that during Desert Storm the Department of Defense preferred the offer of a reward to the assistor, whatever that person wanted in return, including livestock, camels and horses. In the past, this worked. During Desert Storm, it didn't. Shortly after the first Coalition air strike in January 1991, it was readily apparent Saddam was winning the reward game. Sheep and goats weren't as tempting as cold, hard cash. SOCCENT J2 had a chance to establish an indigenous escape and evasion network but missed the chance. The chance never came again.

Eanes and others back in Riyadh found that the navy offered up little information about its downed aircrews. Naval Forces Central Command (NAVCENT) rescue coordination center (NRCC) was collocated with Vice Admiral Arthur's command on USS *Blue Ridge* (LCC-19). The NRCC was responsible for all over-the-water CSAR for the Persian Gulf and Red Sea. NAVCENT divided responsibility between regional controllers: Combined Task Force 151 (CTF 151) in the Persian Gulf and Combined Task Force 155 (CTF 155) in the Red Sea. CTF 151 assigned units and developed plans to support CSAR operations and coordinate with SOCCENT and multinational forces in the region. But neither task force was set up to handle over-land losses, often hundreds of miles away from carrier battle groups in their area of responsibility.

"NAVCENT could have tried its own recovery operation," said Eanes. "Each service component was responsible for its own SAR. Technically, SOCCENT was only to be called for denied areas [inaccessible areas behind enemy lines] because we had the specialized assets to get into the denied areas." The navy has a file with Scott's name on it marked NRCC N001, the first navy case that went to its rescue coordination center on the *Blue Ridge,* Arthur's Persian Gulf flagship. The file contains messages tied to Scott Speicher's loss, including whatever intelligence was gleaned for the rest of the war. Absent from the file is documentation of a physical search. Absent is any reference to what happened on board *LaSalle.* Included are two sets of crash coordinates, one of them wrong. The reality then and later is that the navy was highly unlikely to launch a CSAR from the Red Sea, over seven hundred miles from where Scott Speicher went down, a fact that Arthur confirms in a communication on July 10, 2010.

As for SOCCENT, its policy was simple, observed Eanes: "If we could not verify a man on the ground, we weren't going after him. The risk posed to the assets and special operations force crew did not outweigh the gain. With our limited assets and guidelines [set up] to avoid casualties," he iterated, "we could not take a chance on a recovery without verifiable contact." If SOCCENT rejected the mission, it went back to the Joint Rescue Coordination Center (JRCC) to tap anyone else who might take it on, perhaps the Kuwaiti resistance or British Special Air Service (SAS). SOCCENT turned down at least one rescue mission because the enemy threat was too great, said Eanes. "An army team picked up that mission, was predictably shot down and lost its helicopter."

This was flight surgeon major Rhonda Cornum's flight. Her commander dispatched Cornum and her crew to pick up downed F-16 pilot major William R. Andrews. Due to where Andrews had gone down, in the thick of Iraqi forces, it was a risky rescue. They did no pre-mission analysis before launch and the CSAR ended badly, both for Cornum's team and Andrews, who was captured the moment his boots touched the desert floor. Yet under equally challenging circumstances, SOCCENT repeatedly tried to rescue helicopter crews, even when, in one particularly difficult case, the attempt failed but CSAR continued to maintain radio contact for two days with the downed airmen. This baffled knowledgeable observers. Why try so hard in some very risky cases, yet make no attempt whatsoever for so many others?

SOCCENT never received any communication from the NRCC the night that Scott Speicher went down. Thus Eanes never dispatched a CSAR for him. The tragedy is compounded, according to Eanes, by the CSAR assets standing by, who could have gotten to Speicher within forty-five minutes. Rescue forces were on high alert in the event of heavy air losses. The first shots of the war were fired at 2:38 A.M. on January 17 by 101st Airborne Division Air Assault pilots who destroyed two key early warning radar sites in western Iraq. Code named Normandy, their mission was one of the evening's most dangerous. Two Iraqi Tall King long-range radar sites, roughly thirty-five miles apart, were hit by a two U.S. Special Forces MH-53J Pave Low and four AH-64A Apache helicopters that infiltrated and exfiltrated from a forward airfield at Al Jouf, Saudi Arabia. A total of twenty-seven Hellfire missiles were fired on these sites. The attack was over in four-and-a-half minutes. Another Apache and a UH-60 Blackhawk helicopter waited south of the border, ready to execute a CSAR if needed. But no air force or army aircraft was lost along the corridor opened up by the Pave Lows and Apaches that night. "We owned the airspace," said Eanes. "The 101st Airborne's assets remained on the border, and I could've contacted them on the ground for assistance. I didn't know Scott Speicher was down." The navy hadn't reported his loss.

"Schwarzkopf and Horner had a war to run," said Eanes. "One downed pilot is just part of the breaks of the game and was not something that could have or should have consumed their thoughts at that time. They had more important things to focus on," he said later, "and they had staffs and commanders responsible for taking appropriate actions. A commander has to depend on those staffs and the people at the commands to do their jobs correctly and, if an error is made, to be mature and responsible enough to admit the mistake so corrective actions could be initiated." What Eanes didn't know until much later is that he'd coordinated the drop of British SAS teams on Speicher's correct loss coordinates as soon as the night of January 20.

To better explain his point, Eanes spread out the evasion chart Scott would've carried with him on his mission. As he smoothed the edges of it down on his kitchen table, Eanes was visibly upset. It was painfully obvious that as an operator on the ground he still felt responsible for Scott Speicher, who had needed his help. He put his finger on the intersect point for 33°00' N 042°00'E on the map, and said affirmatively, "I had a British SAS team here." Bravo One Zero and Bravo Three Zero were dropped in the area to hunt SCUD missiles and disrupt enemy movement. Chris Ryan, of the SAS, later wrote a detailed narrative of his team's operations behind enemy lines from January 22 until the time they were caught. Ryan observed that he and his team, Bravo Two Zero, should've paid closer attention to their cover story for the mission: a search and rescue team sent to recover downed airmen.[6] SAS Bravo teams all operated under the same cover story; ironic, since a downed airman was in the very area in which Eanes had inserted them.

Bravo Two Zero's experience could not have been all that different from Scott Speicher's own as he unfastened his parachute harness and assessed his surroundings. The landscape was not what they expected it to be; all around them was hard-packed dirt and rock. The desert landscape looked like the surface of Mars. There was no sand to fill bags for machine gun nests. Goat herders' dogs barked incessantly. They could hear a young Bedouin boy calling out to quiet them. But the dogs kept barking, sounding repeated warnings to their masters that someone was out there in the night who didn't belong. Voices carried far in the vastness of the wadi.

Had they been heard? The men on Ryan's team watched and listened for the enemy. "It was so cold," Ryan wrote later, "that several of them struggled into their NBC [nuclear, biological and chemical] suits and lay around in them." During the winter months in Iraq, nighttime temperatures dip well below freezing. Scott Speicher wasn't equipped to stave off the cold.

The loss of a *Saratoga* VF-103 F-14A-plus Tomcat on January 21 illustrates just what happens to an aircrew forced to eject over the same terrain that swallowed up Speicher and tested the staying power of an unprepared SAS team. During his descent from the Tomcat, Lieutenant Devon "Boots" Jones, the Tomcat's pilot, saw his backseater, Lieutenant Lawrence R. "Rat" Slade, in his parachute roughly four hundred feet away, but received no response when he shouted out to get Slade's attention. In the predawn darkness Jones sighted the exploding wreckage of his F-14 below the cloud layer about five nautical miles away, but lost visual contact with Larry Slade. Jones suffered loss of manual dexterity during his descent, due to the extreme cold at high altitude. After reaching the ground, Jones' initial communication was somewhat garbled due to difficulty operating his survival radio. Jones' estimate of the crash site location was also inaccurate, thus delaying the response time of CSAR. Jones also found the desert hardpan so packed he was unable to dig a hole large enough to bury his parachute and seat pan. At dawn Jones regained his bearings and moved about two nautical miles to the pickup site, an area in which he was able to use his survival knife to dig a hole deep enough to hide in until the rescue team arrived. He was recovered in a daring daytime extraction. Jones was lucky. There would be no daring rescue for Scott Speicher.

Years after Speicher went missing, in late 2001, retired vice admiral Michael L. Bowman, former commander of Naval Air Forces, Pacific Fleet, stated that a classified message made its way around the Red Sea carrier air wings that a special operations team had possibly located the wreckage of Scott Speicher's Hornet. The war was not over yet. Bowman remembered the message well because he was the air wing commander on the USS *America*, also in the

Red Sea, at that time. Though he couldn't recall many specifics of the message, the one detail he did remember well was that a special operations team had picked up a flight helmet and a few items of pilot gear near smoldering wreckage. The team purportedly, he said, could not get close enough to the aircraft to positively identify it by bureau number. No one knows for certain, if it was an SAS team who grabbed up the gear, but at the time this sighting and gear recovery was supposed to have occurred, SAS had teams on the ground in that part of Iraq and SOCCENT did not. "I can state without reservation," said Greg Eanes, "that no SOCCENT-associated Special Forces teams found pilot gear immediately after the event. My recollection is that we didn't even have any teams in Iraq at that point, though the British had several."

But Bowman and Eanes weren't the only ones to recall this information. General Schwarzkopf also recollected the information to which Bowman specifically referred. "As I recall at the time," he added, "I was asking Chuck Horner the status of search and rescue on the two pilots that were down." As Schwarzkopf remembered it, he heard that a combination of information sent back through "a fellow pilot" who'd witnessed the explosion was part of the reason no one looked. But the rest hinged on the fact that "search and rescue people went out and reported back no visible life at the scene of the crash. Again, that's my recollection, but I can't be specific."

A March 10, 1991 message from Captain Bernie Smith, assigned to NAVCENT, to Rear Admiral S. Frank Gallo, deputy chief of naval personnel, on March 10, 1991, detailed a March 9 conversation between Captain Stephen R. Loeffler and Smith's office. Though not the message Bowman read, Smith similarly wrote that information to that date was "the best we can obtain from aircrew debriefs and radio communications relayed up the chain. We have intentionally made this a classified message in order to give you as much detail as possible." Listed as MIA, in addition to Scott Speicher, were Lieutenants Connor, Costen, and Turner; Lieutenant Commander Cooke, and Captain Reginald C. Underwood, a Marine. The message Smith sent to Gallo indicated that Speicher's wreckage had been located in the area the *Saratoga*'s Hornet pilots calculated it would be in their own investigation. Despite this information, Smith's evaluated it thusly: "It was not possible to determine if the aircraft was Speicher's, but no other aircraft were lost. There were no communications or beacons reported." Smith wrote at the end of the message that he "hopes this information will assist in dealing with the families. A concern is that we raise no false hopes."

Scott Speicher's death was smoke and mirrors. He was dead by perception. Defense Secretary Dick Cheney's misstatement to the press was not the military's official determination of Speicher's status. The navy and Department of Defense (DoD) determined that Speicher was MIA. But on May 22, 1991, in part due to actions taken by Chief of Naval Personnel Vice Admiral Mike Boorda, the navy changed him to killed in action, body not recovered (KIA-BNR). Despite this administrative designation, the case remains open until a body is recovered. "You never give up looking for a KIA-BNR any more than you would an MIA," said Buddy Harris. But it was easier for Joanne Speicher to get on with her life if Scott was declared killed. She was told Scott's fate was obvious: no ejection, no radio contact, and, most damning of all, an unsurvivable fireball. Though no one was ever put on the ground to look for him, in the minds of Scott's chain of command, he went down with his jet.

Harris recalled, "Joanne said, 'He's dead, he's gone' and she put it behind her as best she could. She tried to steer her children's lives in the most normal way possible. That was her goal from day five or so after he was shot down. Harris also remembered her saying. "Hey, you know, I'm freaking here, but these children need me. They need a normal life." She put off the media, with the exception of the *Ladies' Home Journal* feature published in June 1991. Soon after what happened to Scott Speicher faded from the front page and the chances of anyone pressing for his return faded with every day that passed.

Endnotes

1. Army lieutenant general Thomas W. Kelly, known best for his daily Pentagon briefings of the press and public during the Persian Gulf War, died of cancer at his home in Clifton, Virginia, on June 6, 2000. During the war, Kelly was the operations director for the Joint Chiefs of Staff.

2. After spending her congressional tenure working to debunk the left behind American POW/MIAs in Southeast Asia, Frances Zwenig is the Counselor at the US ASEAN Business Council responsible for the ASEAN countries on the mainland, including Thailand, Vietnam, Laos, Cambodia and Myanmar. Zwenig's long association with the region began with being a Peace Corps Volunteer in Thailand. Just to review further, Zwenig's experience on Capitol Hill includes the following: administrative assistant to Massachusetts Democrat Senator John Kerry; staff director for the Senate Select Committee on POW/MIA Affairs; chief of staff to then Ambassador Madeleine Albright, U.S. Mission to the United Nations; vice president and counsel, U.S.-Vietnam Trade Council; and executive director, Burma-Myanmar Forum. She graduated from College of William and Mary, with an A.B. degree, The Fletcher School of Law and Diplomacy, with an M.A. and Duke University School of Law, with a J.D. degree.

3. On May 8, 1975, the U.S.-flagged merchant ship *Mayaguez* left Hong Kong bound for Thailand; it was a bad time to be in the South China Sea waters off Vietnam, Thailand and Cambodia. The Khmer Rouge government of Cambodia was in a dispute with Thailand over watery boundary lines, and in Vietnam, Saigon had fallen and American troops and personnel were evacuating. A few days later, on May 12, a Cambodian gunboat crew, claiming the *Mayaguez* entered Cambodian territorial waters, boarded the ship and took her captain and crew prisoner. It was an act that set off a tragic chain of events that proved deadly to both Cambodians and Americans. Within hours of the ship's capture, the United States began positioning forces in the region. The day after its seizure, the *Mayaguez* was taken to Koh Tang Island, approximately 30 miles from the Cambodian mainland, while her crew was taken to nearby Koh Rong Island. In an ongoing effort to rescue the ship's crew, eighteen Americans – 15 Marines, two navy corpsmen and an air force helicopter pilot – were killed in the raid on Koh Tang, according to the Pentagon, of which eight remain unaccounted for.

4. Stumpf, Robert E., "Scott Speicher, prisoner of war," *National Review Online,* guest comment, March 19, 2002.

5. Eanes retired from the U.S. Air Force as a colonel after over 25 years of service in August 2011. He was formerly leader of the DIA Iraq Survey Group (ISG) Speicher Investigation; deputy to the Intelligence Community POW/MIA Analytic Cell (DIA/JWS6), senior staff officer to DIA Office of Operations and senior military advisor to DIA/MIO (now DRI); former reserve director for ISR at Air Force Special Operations Command (AFSOC) and chief of E & E [Escape and Evasion] Operations Branch, Joint Services SERE Agency. Extensive experience in training, leading, managing personnel in all-source collection and analysis in support of tactical, operational and Strategic National Intelligence requirements, in both peacetime and wartime environments.

6. Ryan, Chris. *The One That Got Away*. London: Brassey's, 1998, p. 30.

Chapter 6

The Falcon Hunter

A little over two years after Scott Speicher was officially declared KIA-BNR, in 1993, Robert G. Dussault, then deputy director of the Joint Services Survival, Evasion, Resistance, and Escape (SERE) Agency (JSSA), got a call that took him completely by surprise. A friend in the Office of Naval Intelligence (ONI) called to say that he had reliable indicators that Scott Speicher was alive and had been discovered and held by friendly Bedouins. Dussault's ONI contact, a navy SEAL and HUMINT handler, a case officer whose clandestine indigenous source operated in Iraq whenever needed. The handler was very concerned, according to Dussault's recollection and his notes, because of his certainty that the information was accurate. Up to that point, the Department of Defense Prisoner of War/Missing in Action Office, which became Defense Prisoner of War/Missing Personnel Office (DPMO) the following year, held the staunch opinion that Speicher was KIA-BNR. Armed with the handler's new information, Dussault's JSSA found itself in the tenuous position of challenging DPMO's position, thus Speicher's KIA-BNR status. This was a status that only grew more complicated.

Almost a year into President William J. Clinton's presidency, on November 19, 1993, the International Committee of the Red Cross (ICRC) passed a note from an Iraqi delegation dated October 14 that declared "no additional information is available" concerning Lieutenant Commander Speicher. The note read thusly: "Regarding the Lt. Commander (Captain Pilot?) Michael S. Speicher. His name was reported by his colleague pilot Robert James who repatriated home through your esteemed delegation on March 5, 1991. No additional information is available about him in spite of [our] investigation and tracing." First Lieutenant Robert James Sweet was a U.S. Air Force A-10 pilot captured on February 2, 1991, and released on March 5. But Sweet never told his Operation Yellow Ribbon debriefer that he informed the Iraqis about Scott Speicher.

"[The U.S.] played some games with Iraq from the political aspect to try to find out if they would acknowledge information [about Scott]," said Buddy Harris, who ended up investigating his friend's shoot-down while assigned to the Pentagon after the war. The State Department had provided some teasers to the Iraqis, but they didn't jump at any of them. Because Baghdad held fast and didn't appear responsive, Harris observed that State concluded, "There's no way Iraq has any knowledge of him. He's definitely dead. They were pretty well convinced he blew up in his plane because nothing was found." The Iraqis continued to put off American officials who communicated with Saddam's representatives through the ICRC.

Lieutenant Jeffrey D. Brown remembered the debate over Speicher's status from the start of the Clinton presidency. Brown was an A-6E Intruder pilot assigned to a military internship in the Office of the Secretary of Defense when he came across the Speicher case. "I was there from 1992 to 1994," said Brown, Virginia commissioner of Labor and Industry, in 2001. "We were starting the transition between the departing Bush administration and the Clinton inauguration that January. The push in late 1992 from President Bush's staff was to get out of the White House and out of Washington ahead of the Clinton team." This was problematic for the Speicher investigation because the Bush national security team had collected data about the war, including his case. "Unfortunately," said Brown, "most of the data that might have helped Scott wasn't pouring in until after Bush lost the White House in the November presidential election." After that happened no one stepped in to continue the full court press on Speicher, who'd already fallen off everybody's radar screen. Intelligence gathered since the end of the war was set aside.

After Bill Clinton officially took office in January, Les Aspin was named his defense secretary. Aspin had served as Clinton's defense advisor since the start of his presidential campaign, and because of his leadership position in the U.S. House of Representatives, Aspin's views on defense issues were well known. Shortly after taking over the Defense Department, Aspin openly discussed the dangers that had emerged after the cold war; the uncertainty that sweeping reform would take in the former Soviet Union and Soviet bloc states; the enhanced possibility that terrorists or terrorist states could acquire nuclear weapons; the likely proliferation of regional conflicts, and the failure to take adequate account of the impact on the American economy of its national security interests at home and abroad. Given these potential problems and the end of the cold war, it seemed clear that the Pentagon was about to enter a period of profound change.

"It was clear from day one we weren't supposed to ask questions about Scott Speicher," Brown recalled. Aspin's agenda was clear and Scott Speicher wasn't on it. "Les Aspin told us all we had were three issues to deal with: gays in the military, force drawdowns from a six hundred-ship navy, and base closures. He didn't want to deal with Scott Speicher," Brown iterated. "There were, of course, all political issues between OSD [Office of the Secretary of Defense] and the joint services." The schism within the military, particularly between joint service and OSD, was a political morass. "It was not an accidental breach of the warrior's code where Scott Speicher was concerned," according to Brown. "Speicher was ignored." While Brown didn't know if it was a conscious, directed act to ignore Scott, the attitude was clear: there were more important fish to fry and Speicher wasn't one of them. "The lack of respect for the military during the Clinton administration was exemplified by the Scott Speicher case," said Brown.

The Joint Services SERE Agency was the DoD's lead for Operation Yellow Ribbon, the individual debriefing of all repatriated prisoners of war. Bob Dussault was the senior member of the team that set up and later culled through the debriefs and also published the captivity summary for the Department of Defense. Some of these cases got Dussault's attention when the circumstances of the loss didn't marry up to what was being reported through intelligence channels. "During Desert Storm my people had to provide briefings and their assessments to generals in the Pentagon on a regular basis," Dussault explained, "and for these we were getting intelligence from all sources. But just in my short and quick exposure to these cases, certain things that did not fit sort of stuck in my head. I do recall [intelligence] reports of guys going down and being treated a certain way in [the] reporting that did not happen to match any of the handling received by the returnees." Information gleaned from repatriated POW/MIAs at war's end told one story; intelligence reports often told another. "Either the reporting was bad or we did not get everyone back who was captured," he concluded.

One of those Operation Yellow Ribbon reports caught Dussault's attention right away. It belonged to navy lieutenant Larry Slade, the Tomcat radar intercept officer (RIO) shot down January 21 on a mission near Al Asad Airfield, and held as a prisoner of war. His pilot, Lieutenant Devon Jones, evaded and was picked up by CSAR. The Iraqis repatriated Slade in the first group of aviators sent back, in good faith, through the ICRC on March 4. An April 2, 1991 message traffic from the Joint Chiefs of Staff to the intelligence community via Combined Task Group 168 (CTG 168) reported statements made by an Iraqi interrogator concerning the status of a U.S. Navy F/A-18 pilot, Scott Speicher, during Slade's questioning. At one of Slade's interrogations he was told by his captors that an F/A-18 pilot off the *Saratoga* was dead. The statement seemed to have been made to elicit information on American air wing personnel. Slade was asked if he knew the pilot of the F/A-18. He said no. The interrogator became visibly agitated. He believed that the air wing was a tight-knit family and that Slade would know the pilot. Aggravated by Slade's negative response, he said, "Well, he's dead." But Slade was provided no information to suggest how or when Speicher might have died.

The field comment attached to Slade's debrief noted, "This may correlate to Lieutenant Commander Speicher, USN. The source [Slade] does not recall which interrogator nor at which site and session this comment was made." Additionally, Lieutenant Commander Henry Corscadden and Lieutenant Raymond Lagamasino, Slade's debriefers, noted in hindsight, based on the interrogation's "superficiality" and widespread publication of Speicher's status, "Slade believes the interrogator obtained the information from the press." The Iraqis were on a fishing expedition with Slade. They didn't seem to have Scott Speicher at the time of Slade's interrogation sessions. They didn't know where he was. Was he dead? No one knew exactly, not even the Iraqis. "I got information daily and helped make the debriefs more comprehensive," said Dussault. "However, there were some things that fell through the cracks until questions about Scott came up a couple of years later." These questions started with telephone calls from a navy case officer who handled an asset known as the Falcon Hunter.

In the fall of 1993 a local Bedouin tribe purportedly found the wreckage of Scott Speicher's Hornet and began picking up broken pieces that had fallen away from the fuselage to sell them in the black market souk. Soon CIA agents were tipped off that parts of an American jet were being sold. The source of that information was the Falcon Hunter, a Qatari sheikh with strong ties to the Iraqis. The Falcon Hunter came upon locals bartering parts in a marketplace and asked the sellers if they knew where the crash site was located. It was December 1993 and the sheikh had reportedly come to the western Iraqi desert to hunt bustard with his falcons. But what he really wanted to see was the aircraft wreckage. Bedouin shepherds took him to the plane and he knew what they had found was a U.S. Navy jet off the *Saratoga*, lost during the Persian Gulf War. This was a stunning, almost miraculous find. Or so everyone thought.

The Falcon Hunter reported his discovery to ONI, said Dussault, who then reportedly asked that he return to the site to take photographs and collect a serial number from some part of the aircraft that might facilitate its proper identification. By this time the CIA was fully involved in the investigation, arranging the second visit with Qatari officials to the wreckage. The Falcon Hunter entered the Iraqi desert again under the cover of a hunting party to investigate the site as anxious American officials waited to see what he turned up. They didn't have to wait long. On December

19, 1993, during a meeting with a U.S. liaison officer in Doha, the Falcon Hunter, accompanied by Qatar's assistant chief of staff of operations, training and planning to Iraq, turned over a stack of photographs and a piece of the wreckage. His pictures included shots of the Hornet's canopy and large sections of the aircraft, including its relatively intact engines, the cockpit and part of the tail with the word "Saratoga" clearly visible. The ejection seat lay nearby. More importantly, the Falcon Hunter had secured a metal plate stamped with identification numbers. Those numbers came back to a Hornet flown in the Persian Gulf War, identified a by Bureau No. 163470. The last man to fly that jet was Michael Scott Speicher. Or so they thought.

The navy assigns each of its aircraft a specific, unique bureau number (BuNo). Scott Speicher was lost in AA403 BuNo 163484, which was stricken from the inventory on January 17, 1991. Bureau No. 163470, the aircraft number recorded on Speicher's incident reports after the Falcon Hunter's December 1993 discovery, is wrong. Though this aircraft did fly with VFA-81 and was side number AA400 on January 17, 1991 (and was still with them as late as July 1994), it was later observed flying at China Lake, assigned to a Naval Weapons Test Squadron, by the time investigators began deconstructing what happened to Speicher's jet. The Falcon Hunter had retrieved a shard of metal from the radar mount pulled out of a cannibalized Sunliner aircraft, Bureau No. 163470, and placed in Speicher's Hornet, Bureau No. 163484, before he launched on the first air strike of the war. To compensate for malfunctioning parts on sophisticated, multi-million dollar jet aircraft, a "can bird" was set aside to supply repair parts, particularly on aircraft carriers far removed from available new plane parts. Thus, any operational jet on an aircraft carrier might have parts from many different planes of the same type. This explained what the Falcon Hunter had found. Lieutenant Commander Fast Eddie Smith later confirmed the radar mount came from an F/A-18C.

Since his tenure on the ATO planning staff at Riyadh during the war, Fast Eddie Smith became the Pentagon's resident expert on the F/A-18 Hornet. But he wasn't asked to run down the parts trail from one bureau number to another. He was only asked to confirm that the part came from an -18C. And Scott's Hornet was the only –C lost during the war. The part swap never made it into the navy maintenance system register, so the last aircraft attached to that component was Bureau No. 163470, which was not the aircraft Speicher flew that night. The error was also never caught by crash investigators.

The Falcon Hunter had turned over a stack of three-by-five photographs. There were two sets, one for each of his visits to the crash site, each showing that the aircraft was totally intact and now inverted. The cockpit was still with the aircraft and the engines were still encased within the body of the aircraft. Fast Eddie only saw the first set of pictures, not the second. He saw no ejection seat in his set, but from what he could tell, there was a canopy, separated some distance from the Hornet. He also noted that shortly after he got the pictures, he received a cryptic telephone call telling him that the photographs "don't exist." Disturbed by this, he gave the pictures back to intelligence. Shortly after finishing his analysis of the photographs and radar mount, Fast Eddie was pushed out of the loop. Scott Speicher's case remained closed.

Though Scott had dropped off the public's radar screen, he was a matter of intense concern within the Office of Naval Intelligence (ONI), whose covert operative, the Falcon Hunter, reported his crash site, and to the Central Intelligence Agency. But Scott also had the attention of Lieutenant Commander Jeffrey S. Manor, then special assistant for POW/MIA Affairs at the Bureau of Naval Personnel and a naval aviator. Late one Friday afternoon in 1994, Manor recalled, he got a secure telephone call from a lieutenant in the ONI. The caller sounded troubled by what he was reading on his end. The subject was Scott Speicher and numerous loss reports attached to his casualty file. Manor and his assistant, Lieutenant Geoffrey G. Stothard, a P-3C Orion pilot, got to work, researching what they'd thought was a closed case. Both knew that there were still three naval aviators in their files whose remains were not returned from Desert Storm: Speicher, Lieutenant Commander Barry Cooke and Lieutenant Robert J. Dwyer. Several years had passed since the end of the war. In truth much of Manor's and Stothard's efforts had turned back to Vietnam-era case files. The Persian Gulf War was "case closed." So they thought.

Manor didn't have to dig far before he saw what the lieutenant in ONI did. He started to see the same set of unsettling facts concerning Scott Speicher's case and he also saw something else. "I haven't seen anyone make a big deal that public law was violated by having Scott declared deceased early," said Manor. "To me, it's one of the key elements to him being 'forgotten.'" Public law is clear. Title 37 of the United States Code (USC) Section 535 Chapter 10, Payments to Missing Persons Act, requires that a person carried in a missing status cannot be declared deceased until one year and one day after his loss. Speicher was lost January 17, 1991. He was declared deceased on May 22, 1991.

"This is a clear violation of the public law to which I'm referring," said Manor. "Scott's case is not the only one in which public law was violated. The Desert Storm missing individual [LCDR Barry Cooke] was an A-6E aviator whose case is not as controversial as Scott's, who should have been carried in a missing status for at least a year also." Manor's right. Cooke should have been MIA. So should Dwyer. Neither Dwyer nor his F/A-18A Hornet were ever located. Manor and Stothard found it extremely odd that these and other cases were closed as KIA-BNR so quickly, since public law was so clear in how they should have been handled. "There are no gray areas," Manor iterated.

As Manor's investigation continued on behalf of the Office of the Chief of Naval Operations, he discovered even more unsettling information. The Missing Persons Act, which applied to noncombatant and combat cases, required that only the secretary of the navy or his designee could declare a sailor or Marine deceased. "It was clear from paperwork in LCDR Speicher's file that [Vice] Admiral [Jeremy M. "Mike"] Boorda (then chief of naval personnel) was the driving force behind both aviators [Speicher and Cooke] being declared deceased. We discovered a memo from Admiral Boorda to the secretary of the navy announcing his 'decision' to declare LCDR Speicher and his fellow missing aviator deceased. The memo," said Manor, "predates the so-called missing person boards that were held to determine [the dispensation of] the cases. I say 'so-called' because we interviewed two of the three members of the boards, and despite it being less than three years after they were held, neither member could tell us much about how they came to their decision."

Neither board member Manor and Stothard interviewed was briefed on the requirements of the Missing Person Act, which would clearly have resonated with both men, as it did after the fact, when told there was a year-and-a-day requirement before a finding of death could be made. But beyond this lapse in understanding the law, none of the three officers who sat in on Speicher's determination hearing had clearance for special compartmentalized information (SCI) to hear or read information that might have raised reasonable doubt that Scott was not dead.

The more Manor and Stothard continued to work on Speicher's file, the angrier they became. Speicher's case had been poorly handled back in 1991. They could see it. "I'll never forget my assistant [Stothard] saying, 'That SOB, he just left him behind.' That 'SOB' referred to the CNO at that time, Admiral Boorda." Boorda had become chief of naval operations on April 23, 1994.

Manor still believes that Scott Speicher's case was closed so quickly and no one touched his file for so long because of Admiral Boorda's direct involvement. The evidence is compelling: Boorda's May 1991 memorandum to Chief of Naval Operations Admiral Frank B. Kelso II and Secretary of the Navy H. Lawrence Garrett III declaring Scott Speicher KIA-BNR; Manor's discussions with his predecessor, and his interview of Admiral Boorda's personal envoy to Joanne Speicher, Captain Dale V. Raebel.

"Our review of the file itself revealed Admiral Boorda's own personal touch on everything [having] to do with the [Speicher] case," Manor said. Boorda's propensity was to do the unusual, to do what he thought was right for the family versus what was right for the missing service member. "I don't believe that he was being pressured from above, not from what I saw," observed Manor, "because there was no communiqué from the top down [in Speicher's casualty file, not just then], only Admiral Boorda's memos discussing how he was controlling the case." From Manor's observation, shared by others in his department, it was clear Boorda believed that it was best for the family to put the loss behind them. "This meant convincing Mrs. Speicher that there was no hope."

Boorda's plan to convince Joanne Speicher that her husband was dead was executed quickly. On April 29, 1991, he notified Joanne's casualty assistance calls officer (CACO), Lieutenant Commander Tony Salazar, an F/A-18 pilot at Cecil Field, that the navy was ready to change Scott Speicher's status to KIA. Shortly thereafter he amended this to a request for KIA-BNR. Boorda sent Raebel down to Jacksonville to talk to Joanne about the navy's efforts to date, and to discuss an already planned May memorial service at Arlington National Cemetery. Raebel made a sympathetic choice to visit with Joanne. He'd been shot down while flying off the *Saratoga* in August 1972. He was captured and spent roughly seven months as a prisoner of war in Hanoi. Raebel's trip to Jacksonville turned out to be unnecessary after Captain John W. Curtin, commander of the light attack wing, intervened and personally visited with her instead. The next day, April 30, Salazar called to confirm with Boorda's office that there was definitely no need for Captain Raebel to come down. Everything was taken care of, he was told. Joanne Speicher had signed off on Scott's change of status to KIA-BNR.

"Apparently they gave her the option of leaving him MIA or declaring him officially dead. She chose to move on with her life," said John Webb, one of Scott's best friends from college. "That's my understanding."

Soon after Joanne's decision, a quick board was convened on May 20, 1991, and Scott's status was changed to KIA-BNR. Manor and Stothard were disquieted by what happened to Speicher. "We just couldn't believe that making the family feel good came before finding out exactly what happened to one of our aviators," said Manor. "It would have been so easy to find his wreckage. We could have demanded anything we wanted. Iraq would have had to acquiesce and the American public would have supported the effort 100 percent."

Everything Manor flipped in Speicher's file had Boorda's fingerprints all over it. "From the Boorda memo and the other memos [in Speicher's casualty file], it is apparent," concluded Manor, "that it was Boorda's idea to wrap this up in some nice 'Gulf War Heroes' package with no loose ends like missing aviators." Note the *plural* "aviators." He'd predetermined Speicher's final status to the date of his memorial service, hastily arranged to take advantage of burying remains he believed to be Speicher's. On March 20, 1991, the Iraqis turned over to the ICRC remains they claimed belonged to a "U.S. pilot by the name of Mickel." They even supplied a death certificate along with these remains, which amounted to a pound-and-a-half of desiccated flesh. The remains arrived at Dover Air Force Base, Delaware, on March 23, and shortly thereafter were assigned a case number: DS1-256. Five days later, on March 28, the Iraqi delegation to the third session of the postwar Tripartite Commission agreed to provide a witness statement regarding their questionable identification of these partial remains. Though in poor condition, the remains consisted of decomposed upper torso tissue, mostly skin, and nothing else. Despite this request, there was no additional information forthcoming from Baghdad that might explain why they thought the remains were Speicher's. They probably hoped the unidentified remains would satisfy Washington.

We do know that one of the military policemen who'd escorted the remains was skeptical of the Iraqis' motives from the start. "After the cease fire," he recalled nearly nine years later, "my [military police] team, along with a full-bird colonel, were ordered to Iraq to escort the remains of a U.S. pilot shot down over Iraq. I always wondered," he opined, "who the name of the pilot [was] we escorted back to Kuwait. I know now that these remains were supposedly Michael Speicher." He remembered that on entering Kuwait again, the colonel stopped the ambulance so they could open the coffin and make sure it contained remains. No one wanted to do that while still inside Iraq's border. "I was standing outside the ambulance," he continued, "and he told me that the coffin contained remains but that's as far as it went." Nothing felt right about it – not then and not later.

Dr. Victor W. Weedn, a major in the army medical corps who'd set up the Armed Forces Institute of Pathology (AFIP) DNA typing capabilities and remained the program's director, was called in to examine the remains the Iraqis claimed belonged to Speicher. "So here is this pound of tissue or so, two major fragments," he observed when first shown what he was asked to examine. "I think it was really less than a pound. It was clear that you could see that it was skin with some hair on it." But, he continued, "the skin was olive colored. It was Caucasian, but it was dark. There was some subcutaneous fat and it was old, and it was dried out. This is not like somebody who died and the remains quickly recovered and sent to us." There was also a metal fragment, originally believed to have been bone.

"We did a Western Blot test on site at Dover Air Force Base mortuary," Weedn explained. The Western Blot analysis was the first of three types of tests performed on the remains to determine identity and is standard procedure when the AFIP receives remains through its Dover facility. The Western Blot test is a serum electrophoretic analysis used to identify proteins. Forensic pathologists reverse dot blots where polymerase chain reaction (PCR) products are hybridized with allele-specific oligonucleotides for the purpose of detecting RNA, cancer and pathogens in a specimen. It's a game opener in a greater repertoire of genetic testing. But Weedn's tissue sample didn't give him enough to get anything conclusive. He went to outside laboratories with more sophisticated equipment and capabilities to obtain the results he needed to determine identity of the remains tagged DS1-256.

Running the PCR helped Weedn amplify a specific region of DNA to identify genetic traits of the person whose remains were on his table. The regions amplified are normally between 150 and 3,000 base pairs in length. The DNA result obtained by Weedn later enabled him to exclude Speicher as the origin of DS1-256.

Weedn needed to complete his DNA testing quickly, thus he arranged corroboration from colleagues with credible capability to provide independent verification of his results. "In this case, I basically sent it to the contract laboratory we used," he explained. "It was LabCorp [LabCorp/Roche Biomedical Laboratories, located in Research Triangle Park, North Carolina]. Dr. Marcia Eisenberg did the testing." But it was taking too long to get results from Eisenberg, so Weedn performed his own mitochondrial DNA (mtDNA) test to see what turned up. "We really pioneered that kind of testing. We worked with some people at the National Institutes of Health. I think it was Lloyd Mitchell[1]." Weedn determined it was possible to extract mtDNA from DS1-256. Though he didn't have much to work with, mtDNA can be done on bone, muscle tissue, skin, hair, blood and other body fluids, even if environmental factors have degraded the sample. But the remains must have enough material for testing, despite all that, to supply conclusive results. Additionally, mtDNA is inherited from the mother only, thus in situations where the mother is not available for a comparison sample, any maternally related person will do. "Essentially," said Weedn, "this is a reverse parentage test, so we looked at the wife and two children and we asked the question: could the tissue that's returned to us from the Iraqis be the father?" Weedn was hoping to compare DS1-256's DNA against Speicher's mother, Barbara Louise[2], who at that time was still alive. But Barbara was in a long-term care facility in Jacksonville suffering from progressive Alzheimer's disease. She died on October 14, 1991.

Weedn went to plan B and contacted Joanne Speicher to ask if he might get DNA samples from her and from the children. "The first thing she said was, 'You can have my blood, but you can't have it from my children because they're only one and two years of age and I'm not going to let you stick them for blood.'" Though surprised, Weedn relented. He tried other avenues to get samples of Speicher's DNA, "like [from a] toothbrush. We got to where we would ask for various things trying to get at real samples," he explained. Real samples sufficient to test DNA eventually turned up among Scott's personal effects on the ship, but in the first attempt with Joanne, Weedn clearly remembers that he was told, "No, we don't have anything [with his DNA]." Weedn observed that there often difficult questions you have to ask as an investigator to make accurate determinations. “There are issues of parentage,” he said. “Is the person really the father of the children? That’s what led me to eventually call for a [DNA] sample on all service members and that’s what we do now, just for these kinds of [situations]. It’s used far more than what people realize, for what I consider to be a very humanitarian purpose, the return of remains to their families. This case alone tells you how important that function is.”

After being told he couldn’t have blood from the Speicher children, Weedn said, “Well, not a problem. We can use oral swabs and that’s what was done. We got our first set of swabs and they were absolutely clean. I mean it,” he iterated, “it looked like somebody gave us the wrong swabs. It looked like they were fresh out of a package without anything on them, without saliva, without cells.” There was nothing. Undeterred, Weedn asked for a second set and his laboratory took the extra step of dispatching a military jet to Jacksonville to get them back to Weedn as quickly as possible. The navy took this very seriously, he recalled later. “That day I asked for the second set, I had them. So it was a big deal and I think that shows the seriousness of the military [on this issue].”

After all the samples were taken, comparison DNA tests were run on tissue from DS1-256 against Lieutenant Commander Speicher’s sera drawn in July 1990 and stored in the Department of Defense HIV repository. Comparison tests were also made using hair clippings from his electric razor and hair from a deodorant bar, obtained from among Speicher’s shipboard possessions. The results of these tests were compared with the DNA test run on oral swabs and plucked hairs from Joanne Speicher and the couple’s children, Meghan and Michael Jr. Speicher’s stored sera wasn’t helpful. When the HIV serum test is performed, it removes all the white blood cells that have to be present for the DNA test. After analysis of the second set of oral swabs from Scott’s wife and children Weedn compared DNA to the remains of DS1-256. “We showed that the sample we had [from Speicher’s children] was inconsistent with [DS1-256] being the father of those children, so we wrote it up that way in the report. Based on that information, assuming he was the biological father, this tissue, states our report, was not that of LCDR Speicher."

Then came a surprise Weedn didn't see coming: Scott Speicher's DNA didn't match his mother's. When the results came back inconclusive Wallace Speicher[3], Scott's father, finally told investigators what he'd been holding back, that Scott was not their biological son. They had adopted Scott as an infant directly from his biological parents soon after his July 12, 1957 birth. Scott's biological parents were described as "a nice, young college couple" who'd personally delivered Scott to the Speichers' Kansas City, Missouri house that July; it was a private adoption so Scott's biological parents were able to meet the Speichers. Born in Wyandotte County[4], Kansas, adjacent to Kansas City, Missouri, his name at birth was Gregory and whether this is a first or last name is unknown. The Speichers changed it to Michael Scott on a delayed birth certificate filed in October 1957; this certificate is today held in the state archive in Jefferson City, Missouri. Somewhere in the same archive is his original birth certificate naming his biological parents.

Since mtDNA comes from the biological mother, this meant the samples from Barbara were useless. That's when hair from the electric razor and deodorant bar became so important. Though the DNA sequence was very poor, it was enough to conclude that DS1-256 wasn't Speicher. But to be certain Weedn also performed a genomic test, a genetic typing test. Though it was difficult to get genomic DNA results from DS1-256 because of its degradation, hair pulled from the tissue proved enough for limited testing. With this test, Weedn was able to absolutely conclude that "the remains identified as DS1-256 are conclusively not LCDR Speicher. They are a negative match with strong conviction. A positive result would not be easy to state so strongly," he wrote.

The Armed Forces Institute of Pathology Office of the Armed Forces Medical Examiner issued a memorandum to the Department of the Navy, Bureau of Medicine and Surgery on May 6, 1991, that read, "Results confirm that those remains are not those of LCDR Michael Scott Speicher." Boorda's note at the bottom of page read: "They are running results for more evidence, but he

[Weedn] doesn't really need them. It's just good lab practice and helps demonstrate the conclusion to other people." Dr. Richard C. Froede[5], the armed forces medical examiner, signed off on Weedn's findings and forwarded them up the navy chain of command. Weedn's results were passed to Captain Curtin and Lieutenant Commander Salazar.

Manor was tasked by the Office of the Chief of Naval Operations to determine whether CENTCOM and the navy front office knew for certain that Speicher's remains were not returned. "It was clear from the file that everyone from the CNP [chief of naval personnel] up to the SECNAV [secretary of the navy] knew [that his remains had not been returned]," he said, "and I believed that the anecdotal evidence made it irrefutable that CENTCOM knew [before DS1-256 ever made it to Dover]." Though he never found the answer he was looking for in Speicher's casualty file as to why Washington didn't pursue his case further with Baghdad, Manor did speak to a reserve lieutenant working in the navy casualty office during Desert Storm who explained everything as he knew it. "He told me that he relayed to CENTCOM... a Major Bagley, I seem to recall was the CENTCOM POC [point of contact]... he [Bagley] was involved in the Speicher case from day one... [he knew] that the remains that the Iraqis turned over as being Speicher's were determined not to be his. Major Bagley told the lieutenant, 'Those son of a bitches, they sat across the table and swore up and down that they were Speicher's remains.'"

Manor briefed his boss, Timothy Trant, a GS-13 department head. "He ordered me not to relay the conversation I had with the reserve lieutenant. When I strenuously objected, my boss made the decision to accompany me to brief the CNO's office." As Manor entered Boorda's office suite with Trant in tow, Manor knew he'd not be allowed to pass the information he had on the remains the Iraqis claimed were Speicher. But he later had the chance to update one of Vice Chief of Naval Operations Admiral Stanley Arthur's captains who worked in operations. Manor told him what he knew. Trant never knew he did it, not then. "It was not right," that he could not provide the same information to the CNO's office. Trant covered his error in judgment by casting fault with CENTCOM for believing the Iraqis in the first place and failing to find out if the remains were Speicher's before they were shipped to Dover. The implication was that CENTCOM didn't press the Iraqis hard enough and let the matter drop. When Manor tried again to tell Trant that CENTCOM did know that the remains weren't Speicher's, Trant blocked Manor from entering the information in Speicher's casualty file. This information would have led to a paper trail, confirmation between the Bureau of Naval Personnel and CENTCOM that all knew the pound-and-a-half of flesh was not Speicher's before the board met to declare him KIA-BNR. "I felt this information was critical to their [staff] briefing to Admirals Boorda and Arthur and was worth the risk of [my] being disciplined," Manor explained. Had navy leadership known what he did, Manor is convinced Speicher's case would have remained open. The board that convened May 20 was under the impression that CENTCOM wasn't aware the remains weren't Speicher's, but CENTCOM did know and did nothing to dispel bad information provided to those deciding Speicher's fate. "I'm not sure why Admiral Boorda was not opposed vigorously," said Manor. "The personnel dynamics were certainly a factor."

Speicher's case was the first time DNA was used for something other than reassembling human body parts. "We did a fair number of cases where we attached this arm to that body based on DNA," said Weedn, but Speicher's case was the first in which DNA was used to establish a person's identity from almost nothing. After Speicher was declared KIA-BNR, Weedn was perplexed. The navy's attitude was, said Weedn, "Well, we're declaring him KIA and he's dead." It wasn't Weedn's job to sort out Speicher's status. He made the assumption that because there was no body, the navy must have held out the hope his remains would be found. But Weedn had no idea about the politics of Speicher's status that had set Washington on its ear. He was just as surprised as everyone else when the decision was made to declare a pilot dead without conclusive evidence, and to his knowledge, no crash site.

DS1-256 also raised troubling questions. While Weedn evaluated it as "Caucasian, but very dark," a conclusive evaluation of the remains was never done. But Weedn had his suspicions. From the beginning, Weedn and his staff were convinced that the remains belonged to an Iraqi soldier. "This may be the difference," Weedn observed, "between a missing in action and killed in action [determination]. What I'm implying when I say that is that maybe the Iraqis are trying to cover up the fact that they are holding someone hostage."

Later, when it was Manor's job to investigate the actions and determinations of those involved early in Speicher's case, he read Victor Weedn's DNA finding in Scott's file. "To me," Manor said, "the fact that the Iraqis turned over remains trying to palm them off as Speicher's was important. They knew they had to do something. [Doing] nothing would have aroused more suspicion and caused more intensive investigation. However, given my experience with Southeast Asia [Vietnam-era POW/MIA cases], turning over remains that weren't even Caucasian would have caused me some pause if I was on the board." Manor was disturbed by the plethora of missed opportunities that dotted Speicher's casualty file. His predecessor, who'd handled Scott Speicher's case from the beginning, was capable, but she wasn't a carrier aviator. Nor had she flown ejection seat aircraft. Perhaps more telling than that, she was brand new in her job when Scott's particularly complicated case came across her desk. Mistakes were made. "As you are well aware," said Manor, "the Missing Persons Act can be somewhat complicated, although very clear on the declaration of death requirements."

There was enough clear evidence in Speicher's casualty file by the time he took it over for the previous casualty officer to oppose the navy declaring Scott dead, even if the officer's complaint was entered into Speicher's casualty file for board members to see it at a later date. "We had a more formal board for a navy lieutenant who committed suicide by jumping out of a Cessna north of San Diego," observed Manor, "than we conducted for Lieutenant Commander Speicher." Without a challenge to Boorda's determination, Secretary Garrett changed Scott Speicher's casualty status from MIA to KIA-BNR for administrative purposes on May 22, 1991, with a date of death of January 17, 1991.

Scott Speicher's casualty file contained little classified information, at least between his loss date in January 1991 and Manor's investigation through 1994. Most of what was in Speicher's file that was releasable during Manor's tenure in the navy POW/MIA office is now inaccessible. "I spent three years at the Defense Intelligence Agency and am fully aware of the requirement of sources and methods to be protected long after the information is gathered," Manor wrote to this investigator later. "However, the classified information from 1994 and prior is none of that. It pertains primarily to the operational nature of the war at the time it was being fought."

But information in Speicher's casualty file also revealed Boorda's behind-the-scenes decisions both as chief of naval personnel and CNO, the status review board's results, and the lack of involvement of the people who really knew public law or should have, said Manor. To avoid blame, access to Speicher's casualty file was closely guarded. "Hopefully," he continued, "you'll be able to impress upon the navy leadership that politics, whether well intentioned or not, should never supersede the goal of obtaining a reasonable accounting of our lost servicemen and servicewomen." In an effort to keep information in Speicher's file out of the news, the navy stamped much of it classified. "I was afraid that you were going to make some people nervous by asking for the casualty file," Manor said. "It's pretty damning to the navy leadership."

Timothy G. Connolly had only been in his Pentagon job for a few months as the principal deputy assistant secretary of defense for special operations and low-intensity conflict when in 1994 a staffer came back from a meeting with a curious question: "Do you know anything about a downed pilot from Desert Storm?" Connolly quickly jumped on the case. As a former army Ranger, he knew that if Speicher had been left behind, it might have been a fog-of-war mistake. But the war was long over. He contacted the Department of Defense POW/MIA Office for a briefing on Scott Speicher. After listening to what they had to say, Connolly said to them, "Let me tell you the story I've got."

Connolly's story started with a Kuwaiti secret police colonel who claimed to have been in a military hospital with an American pilot during the last days of the war. "I was with a special operations unit that was attached to the 83rd Brigade of the 82nd Airborne Division," said Connolly. "We ended up spending the thirty-day ceasefire interval in March outside a town in Iraq called An Nasiriyah. It's on the Euphrates. In fact," he continued, "it was the 82nd Airborne Brigade that blew up what turned out to be the nerve gas complexes up there." But one of the brigade's other roles was to liaise with Iraqi resistance and, more importantly, people the resistance had freed from Iraqi prisons, from Iraqi Shi'as to as many as 2,000 Kuwaiti nationals forcibly removed from their country during Iraqi occupation. Their number included Egyptians, Palestinians and Omanis living in the wrong place at the wrong time. Many of them worked for wealthy Kuwaiti employers and had no stake in the war.

"I got called over to where my unit was," recalled Connolly, "and we had an individual who identified himself as a colonel in the Kuwait Ministry of the Interior." The colonel, among many others, had escaped a prison in nearby An Nasiriyah after an insurrection against their Iraqi jailers. With so many refugees anxious to get out of Iraq, makeshift camps were set up by resistance leaders to house and feed those who'd managed to get away. Camp Mercy was one of them. This residential tent city was filled with people whose pain and misery was palpable; its sights and sounds unforgettable.

"When the Iraqis took prisoners in Kuwait," said army sergeant major John Thomas, who'd been with Connolly during the war, "they took not only the person they were after but the whole family, old people and children, too." Camp Mercy had a four-lane highway leading up to it. "I'll never forget this father who brought his little girl over to a medic from the 82nd Airborne treating refugees out of the back of a little white Toyota pickup truck," said Thomas. The little girl's eyes were big brown, empty pools. Her arm was badly burned. She'd been standing near a round that went off. "I watched as the medic started to cut away dead, burned flesh. While it must have been extremely painful, there was no emotion on her face, no expression of her agony. Her brown eyes just stared." These people had seen Hell.

But getting home wasn't going to be easy. Lieutenant Colonel King Davis, commanding officer of the 450th Civil Affairs Brigade, responded to a call from the G5, their civil affairs headquarter. While he had the G5 on the line, King wanted to know Army Central Command (ARCENT) policy on the transport of refugees and general dislocated civilians liberated in Iraq. He learned that his unit was authorized to use Iraqi military vehicles to move Kuwaitis toward home as soon as possible. "The American embassy in Kuwait City didn't want to deal with refugees or help us," said Thomas. "We wouldn't have been able to get those people back into the city from Camp Mercy if Mr. Connolly hadn't known how to navigate narrow back roads and shortcuts. His Ranger training, his ability to follow the maps, got us there before the deadline [to return Kuwaiti citizens to their country and] to cross the border into Kuwait."

Thomas and another sergeant commandeered a couple of Iraqi trucks at gunpoint to transport the wounded, disabled and sick. "You remember the move *Three Kings*?" asked Thomas. "The scene at the end with the refugees trying to get through the fence, that was us." Lieutenant Colonel Davis was, in fact, a technical advisor and script consultant on the 1999 movie starring George Clooney. "The story is loosely based on our mission to Iraq during the war," said Connolly, "minus the gold, unfortunately."

More pressing to Major Kenneth H. Pritchard, a U.S. Army reservist, and Captain Connolly was information conveyed by the Kuwaiti secret police colonel Abdullah Al Jairan. They told G2, army intelligence, what he said about being with a U.S. pilot in a military hospital in the vicinity of An Nasiriyah in mid-February. The colonel wanted to help the U.S. Army in any way he could, including looking at photographs to identify the pilot. "G2 suggested we inform CW2 Sullens [a chief warrant officer attached to military intelligence] to [do the] interview since Captain Smith [another intelligence officer], who was to come that day, did not show up." Pritchard recorded this exchange in the log kept by a special detachment of the 450th Civil Affairs Brigade attached for combat operations to the 3rd Brigade of the 82nd Airborne Division, on March 4, 1991. "[The Kuwaiti colonel] told us that he had been in An Nasiriyah, in a hospital, like three days prior to this, next to an American pilot," said Connolly. Connolly's unit found this very interesting because the time frame was so crucial: it occurred right after the prisoner of war exchange. The colonel was still offering to look at pictures when Connolly last had contact with him. He wanted nothing in return for his help. He had already received respectful treatment. "We radioed back to the 18th Airborne Corps headquarters in Saudi Arabia," Connolly continued, "our higher headquarters, and said to the G2, the intel people, 'Here's what we got.'" The response Connolly received was one he'll never forget. "The prisoner exchange has taken place. We're not missing anybody. We have one hundred percent accountability, therefore this guy is blowing smoke at you. It can't be true." The Kuwaiti colonel was sent back to Kuwait City. Connolly would never hear from him again.

Odds are that even if Connolly's civil affairs group had succeeded in getting the Kuwaiti colonel in front of American authorities, the army would have been absent the linguists to make sense of what he was trying to tell them. The G2 backstory during Operation Desert Storm, written by Brigadier General John F. Stewart Jr., intelligence chief of the U.S. Third Army and published in April 1991, documented the insufficient number of Arabic linguists with understanding, in particular, of Iraqi dialect in units intended for intelligence collection work. "Arabic," he observed, "is one of the most difficult languages for Americans to learn. Defense Language Institute statistics prove that." Prior to Operation Desert Shield, U.S. Army requirements for Arabic were significantly less than other languages, such as Russian. These two factors, language difficulty and priority, added up to less Arabic linguists available than were needed for intelligence, let alone for civil affairs and basic interpretation purposes.

Working through the Kuwaiti embassy in Washington, U.S. Army intelligence on the ground in Kuwait and Iraq was augmented in January 1991 by about 300 hastily trained Kuwaiti volunteer linguists, most of whom went to work as signal intelligence (SIGINT) operators; a few them also helped with document exploitation and did some interpretative work. It was this absence of adequately trained U.S. Army Arabic linguists deployed with field intelligence assets, most especially those able to interpret Iraqi dialects, that was the more significant problem. How they might have been used was another. There were not enough Arabic speakers with operational intelligence training to gather human intelligence (HUMINT) information among the indigenous population. This impaired HUMINT collection on Scott Speicher and other airmen missing in action. Operation Desert Storm was, Stewart concluded, "critically short on clandestine HUMINT."

While Manor met with increasing resistance to convey and record information in Speicher's casualty file, Tim Connolly couldn't get what the Kuwaiti colonel had said out of his mind. Knowing now that the wreckage of an F/A-18 Hornet had been discovered in the Iraqi desert, the what-ifs began to race through Connolly's head. The DoD POW/MIA Office had brought him up to date on what they knew about pieces of a Hornet for sale in a black market souk. What about that American pilot? Working through the Defense Intelligence Agency, JSSA, Bob Dussault's command, tasked a satellite to search for Speicher's wreckage and pinpoint its exact location. But they ran into a problem. "When the Qataris pointed out the location on the map and we sent the imagery overhead to look at it, there wasn't anything there," said Connolly. "These guys were 150 kilometers [93.2 miles] from where they actually thought they were. So rather than say, 'Okay, these guys don't know shit,' the DoD POW/MIA guys came up with the idea of going back through the infrared imagery and the archives to identify every single instance in which there was an IR [infrared] event, meaning there was some heat source that had suddenly appeared on the desert floor. They correlated those heat flashes against what they identified as SCUD launches and discovered that there was one heat flash that didn't correspond to a SCUD." And when they imaged that latitude/longitude, they found Speicher's jet. The imagery to which Connolly referred was shot January 17, 1991, by a U.S. Air Force U-2 aircraft – a fact that further corroborated the U-2 imagery available to the evaluation team on board *LaSalle* that used the same imagery along with a stack of 360-degree photographs shot on the ground. That team had left Speicher behind. What would happen this time?

The wreckage on the U-2 film was confirmed for the second time as Speicher's in April 1994. Fresh satellite imagery clearly showed investigators the scope of the crash site. There were shots of something that looked like the ejection seat the Falcon Hunter had already photographed, and, near that, a manmade object. From overhead imagery the F/A-18 site looked largely undisturbed. To the surprise of those who originally analyzed the imagery, the Hornet had landed right side up. Intelligence analysts were certain that it landed inverted. They were wrong. The DoD POW/MIA Office said they'd look into it. "They looked back at all the after action interviews of every POW who was brought back, including the Special Air Service [SAS] guys from the UK, to see if anyone had any stories about anyone else who was unaccounted for," said Connolly. "They also traced where they were found and how they got to Baghdad, to see if there was any evidence any of them had been taken on a circuitous route." They sent an investigator overseas to talk to somebody, and Connolly wished they could have talked to the Kuwaiti colonel. But the colonel could not be found. Colonel Abdullah Al Jairan had disappeared. Despite the DoD POW/MIA Office's attempts to confirm or refute Connolly's information tied to the colonel's claims, in Connolly's words, "the bottom line was . . . they didn't think it was true."

Albert "Buddy" Harris was in the Pentagon working for an assistant chief of naval operations. Still in uniform, he was helping compile a report of all the navy's Gulf War missions, every strike flown, every bomb dropped. One day in late 1993 he came across a CIA report that stated Speicher had been shot down by a surface-to-air missile (SAM). He called the CIA to straighten that out.

Harris told the CIA that the Department of Defense changed the finding about Speicher being shot down by a SAM. The DoD determined that Speicher had been taken down by an aircraft, though arguably it was not known if it was friend or foe. Carlos Johnson was certain that it was not the MiG-25PDS Foxbat E; no enemy aircraft fired on Coalition aircraft that night. But the rest of the story hinges on personal responsibility and how the mission was flown by the navy and the air force. Harris' conversation with the CIA shifted to the story about Speicher's Hornet being found. The Qatari's photographs had just come in. Harris' assignment had made him one of the navy's experts on Desert Storm and he was asked to help. When Harris noticed the pictures of the Hornet and the canopy made it look like Speicher ejected, he spoke up. He was told to find out what information originally led the navy to conclude Speicher didn't eject from his stricken jet.

Harris remained close to Scott's family after he disappeared. He was angered to see so much evidence that he knew firsthand had not been shared with Joanne Speicher. "The family wasn't told anything," he said. They received one letter after another from admirals and captains saying no stone would be left unturned. The navy claimed it would search until they had conclusive evidence that Scott was either dead or alive. They told Joanne, and Scott's father and sister, not to give up on him after Defense Secretary Cheney's press conference gaff. "'We haven't given up on him,' they told the Speicher family repeatedly. 'Everything available will be used to get Scott back.'" But these were hollow claims and hardly truthful. "Cheney jumped the gun," Harris said. "That wasn't Boorda's intention; that wasn't Colin Powell's intention. Basically, he just misspoke. Basically, everybody just assumed, 'Okay, [Cheney has] got more information than I do. He's gone. Let's press on.'" But as information came in, it pointed to a pilot who ejected. It pointed to a pilot who landed safely in the vast Iraqi desert. It pointed to a pilot who waited, looking to the horizon, for rescuers to pick him up. It pointed to a pilot who was left behind.

Like all pilots who flew in Operation Desert Storm, Scott had gone through survival training. Before his mission that night he'd filled out a DD Form 1833, an authentication card, which contained various information that he'd later use to identify himself, and that the DoD could use for verification purposes. Pilots also received command codes, usually letters, and short words to be used by them for identification if they became evaders, escapees or prisoners of war. The letters and words provide the pilot's chain of command a time frame of when the pilot was lost. The procedure for this process can be found in two unclassified joint service manuals: one on combat search and rescue and the other on survival.

The clearest evidence of Speicher's survival came from a ground-to-air signal evaluated by JSSA in 1994, although there would be evidence later that was not only stronger but more compelling. Evaders understand that they will have to persevere to survive and get themselves the help they need to get out of extremis circumstances. They know that ground-to-air signals may be the only means to get the message out, to tell their searchers they survived and want to come home. They also know that weather has a tremendous impact on the arranged signal put down on the ground, including shifting sands and storms prevalent in the Iraqi desert. Some signals, if made with rocks and timbers, and even some constructed of more permanent landmarks for parts of the signal, can still be affected by the elements. Some, if in depressions in the ground, can become much better signals if the depressions fill with water. None of these particular circumstances apply directly to Scott's case, but illustrate the complexities of ground-to-air signals.

Scott, like all evaders on the ground, appreciated what could be seen from different collection platforms. This knowledge helped him decide how large to make a signal in order for it to be seen. Some signals in sand and dirt do not require much to be seen effectively from the air. Camera angle and shadows are critical. This means that a shot taken from directly above the signal may not be best, but it also depends on where the sun is at the time the satellite, aircraft or drone is overhead. If the sun and the collection platform are directly overhead at the same time, the signal can become invisible.

In Scott's case, once all the overhead imagery was assessed, there was absolutely no doubt that he had built his signal many times, almost to the be point where he had to question whether anyone was looking for the signal or that he was possibly not using the right one. He'd put down strong Roman crosses and directional arrows clearly seen in more than a dozen images shot from oblique angles in the vicinity of his crash site, each marked for *his* case file. He also tried his letter of the day and short word of the week. Scott made all his signals from a combination of readily available rock, natural landmarks and depressions in the desert floor. These images, irrefutable evidence of his survival, remain classified.

In addition to JSSA's imagery analysis, the National Imagery and Mapping Agency (NIMA), in response to a FOIA request, stated that it had imagery for three different dates between 1993 and 1995 at the crash site and a ten-mile radius around it, including the area of the first detected ground-to-air signal. These date parameters match up to the more than a dozen pictures referenced above. Tonnette K. Fleming, the NIMA FOIA specialist, also emphasized that debriefs from pilots from the night Scott Speicher was lost "would have been useful to planning an imagery search for LCDR Speicher in January 1991. However, no such information [the pilot's reports] was provided to the imagery community in either 1991 nor at any other date. Information of this type," wrote Fleming, "would reside with the U.S. Navy, possibly USCENTCOM, the Joint Personnel Recovery Agency, DPMO or the flying squadrons' or ships' records."

Scott had two signals to use: the letter of the day and the short word for the week. Both of these were based on his special instructions (SPINS) before leaving the *Saratoga* the night of the first air strike. Using his letter of the day for an evasion signal, which he clearly did, many times over without a response, may have made Scott wonder why no one came. Did no one see it? Was it not clear enough? Was he using the wrong letter? To avoid this problem, Scott varied his signals, using Roman crosses and directional arrows that were part of his training, his instruction to searchers that he was *here* or going *there*. At other times it looks like he tried spelling out his short word of the week. The signal detected by a satellite and recorded on film for analysis by JSSA in 1994 was not his letter of the day, but the first letter of his word for the week – the letter *M*. The letter was seen very clearly by JSSA Director Colonel Robert C. Bonn Jr. on film in the possession of DPMO. Bonn certified his analysis that either the letter of the day or any part of Scott's word for the week was acceptable as strong evidence in light of all else that Scott was alive. Bonn also included in his memorandum a statement to his chain of command in the Pentagon that everything in the U.S. intelligence inventory should be used to affirm Scott Speicher being alive.

In his January 27, 1998 memorandum to the director of Central Intelligence, NIMA Director Rear Admiral John J. "Jack" Dantone Jr., explained that during the week of December 15-19, 1997, a member of his staff provided a series of briefings to Senators Robert Smith and Rod Grams, Representative Steve Buyer and staff of the House National Security Committee and the Senate Select Committee on Intelligence regarding Speicher's ground-to-air signals, located about 900 meters, roughly 981 yards or a little over a half mile, from his downed Hornet. In the memo's margin, he'd jotted down that the letters were an *E* or *M*. Bonn had already certified the letter as an *M*. This important piece of information hadn't been conveyed to NIMA. "A continuing review," wrote Dantone, "revealed a possible second marking. This development was briefed to staff of the House Permanent Select Committee on Intelligence and the Senate Select Committee on Intelligence on January 9, 1998." In the margin, he'd made a note of the letter that was identified as a second marking – an *S*.

These ground-to-air signals were irrefutably Scott Speicher's. Bob Dussault, then JSSA deputy director and a recognized expert in signals interpretation, saw the Speicher ground-to-air signal that Bonn certified. He also affirmed that it was Scott's marker. "I scrounged a quality print," said Dussault. "There [were] more than one potential manmade marks" that could have been made by Speicher. With his level of frustration growing, Scott began to try anything. Looking at the situation from his perspective, he was desperate and unable to draw attention to himself. His modified and varied approach was intended to draw a clearer picture for collection platforms. He had nothing to lose and everything to gain by boldly sculpting his signals on the ground. JSSA was fully aware that Scott was putting down one particular ground signal consistent with his mission, thus Bonn went on record thusly, certifying his finding and sending it up the chain of command. But JSSA had no knowledge of any signals being in the vicinity of the crash site before they requested coverage in 1993-94. Once they did, evidence located on the ground was very clear. When asked if the symbol on the ground belonged to Scott, Buddy Harris said, "It was in an area away from the crash site and the best they could determine it was a symbol to communicate."

Bonn was absolutely positive about what he'd seen, Dussault recalled later. But curiously, about two months after certifying Speicher's signal, Bonn came back to Dussault and ordered him not to find any more signals on the imagery they'd received from DPMO. "He had gone uptown to see some generals and came back shaking like a leaf. He shortly thereafter wrote and sealed a document marked to be opened only upon his death. He kept it in his safe." Bonn, who left JSSA on August 4, 1994, was also reprimanded by Assistant Secretary of Defense for Command, Control, Communications and Intelligence (C3I) Duane P. Andrews' special assistant, Ronald J. Knecht, who also worked closely with Acting Deputy Assistant Secretary of Defense for Prisoner of War/Missing in Action Affairs Edward W. Ross, who between January 1993 and May 1994 was also serving collateral duty as acting director of the Defense Prisoner of War/Missing Personnel Office (DPMO). Andrews, Ross and Knecht, said Dussault, had worked hard to persuade Pentagon leadership that none of what they were seeing on overhead imagery were legitimate ground-to-air signals, from those shot over Southeast Asia to those belonging to Scott Speicher. "I was rather down," said Dussault. If they wouldn't do anything for thousands of missing in action in DPMO and JSSA files, why would they bother with one?

Behind the scenes and far from public scrutiny credible evidence that Scott Speicher was still alive and wanted to come home was buried, overcome by two events beyond the control of investigators looking into his case: the movement of POW/MIA intelligence analysts from DIA to DPMO, and ongoing Senate Select Committee on POW/MIA Affairs. Within the Department of Defense the DIA and DPMO were convinced Speicher was dead, but the JSSA, with its resources in the field and at Fort Belvoir, without question, gave Speicher the benefit of the doubt. This internal conflict, which started in late 1993 with the discovery of Scott's Hornet, dramatically affected what was and wasn't done for the navy's best-known missing pilot from the Persian Gulf War. He thus became the centerpiece of a tug of war between those who strongly believed, based on evidence and science, that he was still alive and those who had him prematurely buried under his jet. Unfortunately, the camp that vehemently argued he was dead was also the one in the best position to help him. Strongly entrenched in the latter camp at that time were Frederick C. Smith, principal deputy assistant secretary of defense for international security affairs; J. Alan Liotta, DPMO deputy director, and Franklin Kramer, assistant secretary of defense for international security affairs. They did nothing to help Scott Speicher. More than that, it appeared increasingly obvious that it mattered more to them that they be proven right, largely to avoid admitting they'd made mistakes, than to save the life of one man. Scott had to be dead because they said so.

JSSA's information was dismissed during high-level discussions within the Department of Defense. Smith, Liotta, Kramer and others called it unreliable, improbable, impossible, but it wasn't. To make certain that none of the evidence uncovered in Scott Speicher's case gained traction within DoD, JSSA got orders from the Joint Chiefs of Staff to leave the Speicher case alone. "[The JCS] wanted State and CIA to handle it," said Dussault, "and that is what we did." Dussault's assessment was confirmed by Buddy Harris, who stated that in 1995 and 1996 most especially, a great deal of information was released on Scott. The information that came out, said Harris, always pointed to the fact that "they wanted him to be dead."

Mitigating the fact that Scott's ground-to-air marker, confirmed by JSSA in 1994, was discounted by the DIA and CIA's joint imagery command, the National Photographic Interpretation Center (NPIC) at the Washington Navy Yard, is those agencies' particularly poor track record in photographic and satellite analysis. When tested by JSSA's Dussault in 1994, they failed. Dussault put out twenty-four good ground-to-air signals in West Virginia and went so far as to provide them with the outside coordinates for all the signals. "Go find them," he said.

Of the twenty-four ground-to-air signals, they found four. Then they came back to Dussault and asked him to describe the others they hadn't found. JSSA provided descriptions of each one; they eventually found six more. "That's a total of ten out of twenty-four," Dussault explained. "Real sad. I lost faith in photo interpreters at that point and had solid evidence for my position and they all knew it. Empirical evidence is a matter of record." JSSA had put out big, obvious symbols and signals, the same ones a downed aviator is trained to do. Dussault's SERE personnel meticulously recorded and photographed their signals and took the coordinates of each one. "We knew the ground truth," said Dussault. Then JSSA instructed the DIA and CIA to take satellite shots of the area in which the ground-to-air signals were laid down and to provide JSSA the photos under the belief that these would be used to build a training package for all new photographic interpreters in both intelligence agencies, a tool to help them locate evader and prisoner of war symbols in the future.

When they failed to pass the JSSA test, it should have been further confirmation for the Senate Select Committee on POW/MIA Affairs that photo interpretation testimony offered by the DIA, CIA and NPIC ought to be called into question. After all, the Senate Select Committee was already disturbed by the DIA and CIA's collective inability to read evader symbols. In its January 13, 1993 report, published well before JSSA tested the agencies' ability in West Virginia and they failed, the Senate Select Committee was surprised to find that neither the DIA nor CIA imagery analysts were familiar with Vietnam-era pilot distress symbols. They also discovered that neither the DIA nor CIA imagery analysts had a requirement to look for possible evader and prisoner of war ground-to-air signals prior to the committee's inquiry. Imagery analysts from both agencies confirmed their failings under oath.

Chuck Knapper, a DIA imagery analyst, stated he was unfamiliar with distress symbols before committee investigators interviewed him about them in April 1992. Knapper was DIA's principal imagery analyst – one of only two – dedicated to the DIA's prisoner of war imagery task. The Senate Select Committee brought Knapper and his CIA counterpart in front of the panel to find out why pilot distress symbols were still getting short shrift. During his deposition he was asked:

"So for the first six to seven months that you were working POW imagery analysis you were not familiar with evader symbols?"

Knapper replied, "That's correct."

In response to the question whether he had been looking for evader symbols in the photography before he met with Dussault's analysts at Fort Belvoir he answered, "I was not."

When asked if his predecessor had ever given him the indication that evader symbols were something DIA was looking for in prior years, Knapper indicated he had not. Knapper also stated under oath that although committee investigators suggested he contact JSSA to become educated in the distress symbol program, he did not arrange for such a briefing until June. He'd put it off.

The committee found a similar lack of knowledge on pilot distress symbols at the CIA, both in interviews and depositions. Roger Eggert, a CIA imagery analyst, also had no knowledge of pilot distress symbols. When a senator asked him, "Were pilot distress symbols something that you had ever studied before spring of this year [1992]? Eggert answered, "No."

The dispute over Scott Speicher's ground-to-air signal had repercussions. The schism between JSSA and DPMO grew wider. JSSA sought information, as it became available, from the Joint Chiefs of Staff and other DoD agencies, but nothing came over from DPMO. But using its friendly contacts elsewhere, JSSA kept tabs on the Speicher case. It was through alternative outlets of information that JSSA began to build a credible case that after repeated attempts to signal U.S. forces failed, Speicher remained in the protection of the Bedouins who'd first come to his aid the night he was shot down. The JSSA had also gained access to the one person who could corroborate this fact: our Qatari sheikh code named the Falcon Hunter. The Falcon Hunter's handler met with JSSA between 1994 and 1998 to discuss changes in Scott Speicher's circumstance. "I was told at the time," said Dussault, "that the Falcon Hunter could go into the area almost anytime and meet with the

Bedouins. He was the first to give us word that Scott was okay. We never talked about [Scott's] treatment because they [the Bedouins] were assisting him, keeping him alive, and would soon want to turn him over to the U.S. in a manner secure for Scott and for them. They did not want Saddam to learn about their efforts."

The CIA was asked more than once to set up a meeting to get Scott Speicher turned over to American control. This went on for more than a year after the Falcon Hunter reported Speicher's location. They were afraid Saddam would find out, come after Scott and kill them all if he was convinced they'd protected an American pilot for even a day. Joint Staff and CIA were all aware of what the Bedouins were asking. Photographs taken by the Falcon Hunter, which remain classified even today, bore witness to their story and Scott's survival: he was in the pictures. When asked to return to the desert for another look at the aircraft, the Falcon Hunter was also tasked to look for the pilot who'd flown it; his handler's later meetings with JSSA were prompted by ONI's concern that Scott Speicher's whereabouts had changed. Something inexplicable had happened.

Of the myriad pieces of the Speicher puzzle, Bedouin interaction with him in the desert of Iraq for a protracted, and what seemed like too long a period of time after he was shot down, was the hardest for investigators to get their heads around, harder still for Speicher's family, friends and the American public. Some called it improbable. Others said it was impossible. Still others disparaged the possibility altogether, saying it lacked credibility. But this goes directly to a lack of understanding and appreciation for the Iraqi tribal culture and, in more general terms, the Iraqi people, what binds them together, supplants their sense of being Iraqi and sustains their nationalism, no matter who rules the country. Those who believed it improbable that Speicher ended up in their care and protection discounted centuries of tribal honor, custom and obligation to a wayward stranger, even one fighting in their country, who is disoriented, perhaps injured, and certainly unprotected from the inhospitable cold of an Iraqi winter night. Iraqi Arabs are generally hospitable and generous. Giving a warm reception to strangers stems from the nomad culture of the desert, where travelers depend on others to survive. Iraqis have continued this custom in modern times, demonstrating courtesy and consideration to strangers. This expression of friendliness, generosity and hospitality is considered a matter of personal honor.

Iraq's twenty-four million people are largely urbanized, but roughly a quarter of the population still lives in a desert-bound, rural setting like their ancestors did for centuries before them. Amatzia Baram, a senior fellow at the U.S. Institute of Peace in Washington and a professor of Middle Eastern history at the University of Haifa in Israel, is one of the world's leading experts on Iraqi tribal culture. (Modern Iraq hasn't had been through thorough anthropological research in decades.) "Tribes have grown and divided for centuries," says Baram. "Certainly there are hundreds, and likely more than one thousand, tribal organizations now in Iraq." Of these, Baram has said that there are likely twenty to thirty large tribes, also called federations, with 100,000 or more descendants.[6] Arab tribal society is traditionally ordered in multiple levels by confederation, tribe, clan, house and extended family.

The word "tribe" is often misleading when used without context. The most important basis for tribal organization is the extended family: the khams, which consist of all male children who share the same great-great-grandfather, thus five generations of men in a single family. In the khams, every man owes allegiance to the other.[7] Members of an Arab tribe, no matter its loyalty to Baghdad, could have Sunni, Shi'a and Kurd members, often broken out into sub-tribal groups within the larger tribe.

The most significant tribal confederations within Iraq today, remain the Muntafiq, Anaiza, Dulaym, Shammar, Zubayd, Ubayd, Bani Lam and Al-bu Muhammed. During Iraq's eight-year war with Iran Saddam increased his hold over Sunni and Shi'a tribes. The majority of Iraq's ruling elite came from Saddam's tribe, Al-bu Nasir, and its allied tribal groups in Tikrit. During the Iran-Iraq War the Dulaym, Jubbur, Ukaplat, Mulla, Sa'idat, and Shammar, all Sunni tribes, and the Al Ahbab, a Tikrit Shi'a tribe, sided closely with Saddam.

Baghdad relied heavily on tribal loyalty to stave off its Persian next-door neighbor. Though many were settled in urban areas, they remained Bedouin and thus the most genuine Arabs. Saddam saw their lineage as a strength; it made them trustworthy and loyal. Saddam also believed that Iraq's Bedouin population had retained core tribal values: communal spirit, honor and valor. There were rewards for their support. Those without adequate means of support, whether Sunni or Shi'a, joined the military or worked for the Iraqi government. Outlying tribesmen were rewarded with roads, electricity and water systems if they cooperated. But just as Saddam could dole out perks, he could just as swiftly dole out punishment, even death. He was known, even during Iraq's protracted war with Iran, to replace uncooperative tribal chiefs with those he favored. He'd split tribes to make control easier. He killed to settle scores. He killed to kill. The Kurds knew his brutality. So did the Shi'as.

"Baghdad through the 1990s encouraged the reconstruction of clans and tribal extended families where they existed," wrote Dr. Judith S. Yaphe, senior research fellow at the National Defense University, Institute for National Strategic Studies, specialist in Middle East policy, and former CIA analyst. "In other areas, the government allowed the manufacture of new 'tribal' groups based on economic ties or greed. Where the initiative was weak, Baghdad apparently encouraged prominent citizens to take the initiative or permitted non-leading families to manufacture an entity in order to gain power and wealth." "This," she continued, "has created a new symbiosis: the state advances the favored tribes and the favored tribes protect the state. The state benefits from its absorption of the tribes and the tribes use the state to enrich themselves."[8] But by the time Saddam went to war with the United States and its allies in January 1991, the Shammar confederation had already distanced itself from Baghdad. The feeling was mutual. With the rivalry between Saudi Arabia and Saddam Hussein at its worst, they'd lost favor in Iraq due to their close family ties to Riyadh. Made up of Sunnis and Shi'as, this was the tribe that SOCCENT J2 didn't cultivate fast enough for an escape and evasion network during Desert Shield, the ramp up to Desert Storm. This is the tribe that claims, even today, to be the largest tribal confederation in Iraq. The Shammar confederation spans central Iraq, south of Baghdad to the Syrian border in the northwest. But where Speicher went down, Anbar Province, he would have been hard pressed to avoid Sunnis from the Dulaym Tribal Confederation, the majority of the nearly one-and-a-half million living in what was Saddam's largest governorate.

Other major tribes unrelated to the Anbar Dulaymis, in addition to the Shammar Jarbas, are the Zobas and the Anaizas. The Shammar Jarbas are primarily located in the Aljazeera region in western Iraq between the Euphrates and Tigris Rivers along the border with Syria and the Anaiza along the border with Saudi Arabia. The sheikh general of the Anaiza is Miteb Anaiza, but he is also the sheikh general of the family that includes the House of Saud, the royal family of Saudi Arabia and families related to the royal family of Kuwait. The bottom line is even if they didn't get to Speicher first, Dulaym tribesmen moved among the other tribes, including sparsely populated areas of Anbar. So did Saddam's intelligence collectors.

In the complex hierarchy of Iraq's desert tribes, the nomadic Bedouin tribesmen who came upon Scott Speicher were herders, their sheep and goats providing the material for the cloth of their black tents, a type of highly adaptable shelter used by tribes throughout Southwest Asia. In the desert the black tent is flattened and lowered to shield tribesmen from sun, sandstorms and extreme heat. In the cold, it is completely enclosed. The women of the tribe are weavers, fashioning not only the roof, walls and flooring of their homes, but many of the furnishings, blankets and clothing, all rich in color, texture and design. These tribesmen have established patterns of behavior, largely defined by geography and the change of seasons. As livestock herders, they have a tradition of *dira,* territory that is worked during the time of year that best suits the survival of the herders, their families and the livestock. The *dira* can encompass an area that averages 120 miles by 180 miles. During the course of a calendar year a tribe of herders migrates on a circular tour that covers their entire territory. Since most of these nomadic tribesmen don't recognize national borders, crossing into Jordan, Kuwait, Syria and Saudi Arabia is not uncommon. This is a transhumant way of life. The movement of nomadic tribal groups, some of them small, are particularly hard to track. Such was the case of the group that protected Scott Speicher.

But why would they risk everything to harbor an American pilot? Arab thought processes are often much more independent of thought and self determined than that of Westerners. While the tribal elders who confronted Scott were afraid, the instinct to offer aid far outweighed concern that they might be discovered hiding him. They would have been well aware of the risk, if not directly, then by word of mouth. Many members of the Dulaym tribes were purged, jailed and murdered by Saddam's security forces due to suspicion of coup plots and disloyalty. No one was spared. Men, women and children were butchered just the same. Saddam warned any tribe that if they helped American or British airmen, they'd meet the same fate.

To protect him, to protect themselves, they would have dressed Scott in their clothing, the traditional Arab *dishdasha,* and taught him how to blend into the camp, especially if visitors appeared. They kept him in the tents, hidden from view. But as he traveled the western Iraqi desert with them, he also left clues for ground searchers. He didn't pass up any chance that someone might see them and send help, even after he was captured. An I-beam in a remote maintenance shack bore Speicher's initials MSS, and "9-15-94" bookends the period when he was first taken into custody by Saddam's mukhabarat, the intelligence service. But the same initials – always MSS – usually accompanied by a date, were later found throughout Iraq and follow his travel with nomadic Bedouins across the western Iraqi desert; he was with them *that* long. He left clues everywhere he went with his Bedouin protectors, careful not to leave signs too obvious if Iraqi forces were one step behind him. From these clues and his numerous and varied ground-to-air signals, American intelligence should eventually have been able to reconstruct Speicher's movements from the time he was shot down to the time he was placed in Iraqi custody.

So what could Scott Speicher offer the Bedouins in return? What could he give them to repay the favor of their protection?

Speicher carried, like all Desert Storm airmen, a blood chit issued by CENTCOM that he would use to communicate to indigenous tribesmen, and perhaps use as enticement for them to return him to friendly forces when the right time came. Speicher's blood chit carried a serial number that was reported to JSSA, now Joint Personnel Recovery Agency (JPRA), which can today account for every blood chit issued since World War II. Scott's SERE training told him what to do if ever in this situation, Dussault explained. "Do whatever they say, following their instruction because their lives are at stake as well. Do not offend them. Stay away from their women. The latter will offend them more than almost anything else."

The Falcon Hunter notified his handler, who called JSSA, notifying them as the Defense Department's executive agent for operational prisoner of war and missing in action that Bedouin tribesmen were ready to return Scott Speicher to U.S. control. For more than three years, lacking affirmative response, they tried to repatriate Speicher. But the Clinton administration and U.S. intelligence operating in the region didn't answer. Saddam began to suspect that an American pilot was alive and with one of the western Iraqi tribes. As the tribesmen tried again to communicate their desire to turn him over, their pleas grew increasingly urgent. They eventually knew Saddam's agents were out looking for the pilot in their protection. This was especially true after Washington notified Baghdad through the ICRC that a team wanted to come search the crash site. JSSA took the Bedouin reports seriously. They'd been corroborated by the JCS J3 and two JCS sources, including the CIA and ONI, who shockingly revealed that Speicher remained with tribesmen into late 1994.

The Bedouin tribe who'd protected Speicher since his shootdown repeatedly asked for a time and place to give him back. The Falcon Hunter's statements were corroborated by a second, independent CIA source, and still another corroborating witness, a member of his "hunting" party, who'd seen what he had. The Saudi prince[9] who went searching with the Falcon Hunter knew the Shammar and several of the other tribes well. Better yet, he was a major in the U.S. Army reserves and thought he understood the mindset of the American military. He'd made frequent trips over the Iraqi border into their camps, offering to get Speicher out if the Americans could guarantee safe passage. He waited for instructions. When they finally came the prince was incredulous. The Joint Chiefs were told it was a no-go. All of this occurred after U-2 spy plane imagery confirmed the wreckage site for the second time and the Falcon Hunter turned over his photographs. With all of this in hand, Admiral Arthur wanted to send a covert mission to the site in April 1994. Classified documents indicate that the chance of success, contrary to the administration's reservations, was high. The area was very sparsely populated. But at a Pentagon meeting held on December 23, 1994, Secretary of Defense William J. Perry and Chairman of the Joint Chiefs of Staff General John M. Shalikashvili told everyone to stand down.

"I do not want to have to write the parents and tell them that their son or daughter died looking for old bones," General Shalikashvili later explained of the decision to leave Scott Speicher in the desert. "To send America's sons and daughters into harm's way is the most serious recommendation a military leader can make. This is a sacred trust," he said. "I concluded that there was no overwhelming need to put our soldiers at risk to covertly search a three-year-old crash site when the Red Cross option was available. I stand by that decision."

There was silence. No one could believe what they were hearing. What the Clinton team didn't say, was that bringing Scott Speicher home would unquestionably reveal that they'd known he was there and wanted to come home since taking office. Scott made a good witness to his own demise. So did the Falcon Hunter. So did the prince of Saudi Arabia. So did the CIA agent who'd also visited the camps. All began to get the picture. Rather than a good-news story of a missing Desert Storm pilot coming home to his family, Speicher was a political liability.

The administration didn't want another liability, after the October 3, 1993 carnage that had taken place at Mogadishu, Somalia, involving a force of U.S. Army Rangers but also America's elite Delta Force. U.S. soldiers paid a high price to extract two of Somali warlord Mohamed Farrah Aidid's top lieutenants. The mission thrust the world's most sophisticated military power against a mob of civilians and Somalian irregulars. Americans got a rare glimpse of dead and wounded American soldiers being dragged through the streets. U.S. commanders thought it highly unlikely that Aidid's rag-tag force could shoot down American Blackhawk helicopters. They did that and more. A simple mission had turned into the biggest firefight in which American troops were involved since Vietnam. Weighing the loss of life and what the president considered a massive public relations setback, it should have come as no surprise that the administration backed off going after Speicher. The decision had irrevocable consequences.

Scott Speicher's blood chit was never recovered. The blood chit, logically, should have been shown and turned over, as required, to the tribal elders to convey to American military forces, and lacking the availability of a U.S. military command in the area, CIA and ONI assets on-scene. The blood chit represents a reward for the safe return of American aviators. This was true of Speicher's blood chit as much as any other. The reward didn't have to be of great monetary value. "To poor people," said Dussault, "even a few camels, a few dogs and water bags are valuable. Better to get something than have Scott Speicher walk away scot-free." But no one could know for certain what the tribal elders were thinking, what they might do. No one would ever get the chance to find out either.

Saddam's complex network of security and intelligence agencies that protected him and his regime from internal and external enemies, had tagged Speicher as a threat. With sights set on finding Speicher, Saddam's intelligence network made queries with tribesmen throughout the western Iraqi territory, focusing particular attention on those in Anbar, where it was believed a small group had picked Scott up the night of January 17, 1991. Backtracking and persistence paid off. He'd found his prize.

On March 1, 1995, Saddam Hussein agreed to allow an American search team led by the ICRC to visit the crash site. But citing "unforeseen bureaucratic delays," Baghdad stonewalled entry to the Americans for nine months. Saddam was buying the time he needed to pinpoint Speicher and the Bedouin family group that had him. There was expansive territory to cover to find one pilot.

Still, it took Saddam more time than he thought to find them. What followed was a bloodbath. Scott Speicher was beaten and taken into custody. His Bedouin protectors were machine-gunned, the price they paid for holding an American pilot. Two sources first reported the deaths: the driver who delivered Scott Speicher to Baghdad and the Falcon Hunter. Overhead imagery confirmed the rest, bodies sprawled around black tents, lying motionless, women covering children, old and young men who died trying to defend them dead all the same. Some had tried to flee. They didn't get far.

Endnotes

1. Dr. Lloyd G. Mitchell, who aided Dr. Victor Weedn in 1991 is today best known as the founder, president, and chief scientific officer of Intronn LLP, which is actively engaged in the research and development of Splicesome Mediated RNA Trans-splicing (SMaRT) Gene Therapy. This technology has applications to gene therapy, RNA repair, regulation of gene expression, genomics (identification of splice sites and introns), and gene knock out. Prior to starting Intronn, Dr. Mitchell was affiliated with the George Washington University Medical Center, University of South Florida Medical Center, and the National Institutes of Health, where he was when Weedn sought out his assistance on the Speicher case.

2. Barbara Louise Beattie Speicher was born January 14, 1926, in Hutchinson, Reno, Kansas, and died in Jacksonville, Duval, Florida, on October 14, 1991. She was the daughter of Robert Gail and Ione Mary Naile Beattie.

3. Wallace Leroy Speicher, Scott Speicher's adoptive father, was born October 2, 1920, in Grant, Kossuth, Iowa, and he died on June 30, 1995, in Saint Johns, Florida. He was married to Scott's adoptive mother, Barbara, until they divorced on September 17, 1979. Wallace was the son of William Walter and Fannie L. Jennings Speicher, and one of eight children and the oldest son; his siblings were Wilma, Gladys, Gerald, Naomi, Dean, Daryl and Robert.

Wallace's father and Scott's adoptive grandfather, William Walter Speicher, was born on March 20, 1895 to John and Sarah Cornell Speicher; he died in 1989 in Grant, Kossuth, Iowa. Wallace's mother and Scott's adoptive grandmother, Fannie Jennings Speicher, was born September 15, 1899, in Grant, Kossuth, Iowa, and she died there on June 25, 1992, at the age of 93. Wallace was in the container supply business in North Kansas City, Missouri, from April 17, 1959, to January 1, 1974.

Wallace Speicher was also a prolific inventor and held several U.S. Patents, including Pat. No. 3174661 issued March 23, 1965, for designing a dispenser cap having a sliding closure; Pat. No. 3484013 issued December 16, 1969, for a container having suspension means; and Pat. No. D199591 issued 1964 for a new jug design.

Of note, a liquid dispensing jug having a vented handle is disclosed in U.S. Pat. No. 3251514 issued on May 17, 1966, to Wallace L. Speicher. The jug has a lower portion, an upper, tapered portion, an outlet spout, and a tubular handle. There is a shoulder in the outlet spout proximate to the point where the tubular handle communicates with it. This shoulder causes liquid, when being poured, to move away from the entrance of the handle portion, allowing air to continuously flow therein, thus preventing pulsation and splashing.

4. Wyandotte County is adjacent to Kansas City, Missouri, and forms part of the Kansas City Metropolitan Area. Wyandotte's county seat and most populous city is Kansas City with which it shares a unified government.

5. Dr. Richard C. Froede was the first armed forces medical examiner and a key figure in the formation of the Armed Forces DNA Identification Laboratory (AFDIL) and DNA repository. He died on February 9, 2011.

6. Otterman, Sharon, "Iraq: the role of tribes," Council on Foreign Relations, backgrounder, November 14, 2003.

7. Ibid.

8. Yaphe, Judith S., "Tribalism in Iraq, the old and new," *Middle East Policy*, June 1, 2000.

9. While it is common practice for America's allies to send members of their military through U.S. military service schools, war and staff colleges, Saudi law specifically forbids the country's citizens from belonging to other nations' military services. According to Saudi law it was illegal for the prince to belong to the U.S. Army reserves. Such transgressions are a capital offense in Saudi Arabia. His participation in the hunting party is evaluated and credible intelligence. The Saudi prince's name is not revealed for obvious reasons.

Chapter 7

Promise Kept

Back at Fort Belvoir Joint Service SERE Agency director air force colonel John Chapman and his deputy, Bob Dussault, received word of what happened in the Iraqi desert. Both were taken aback by the news, but hardly surprised. Chapman, Colonel Bonn's replacement, was fully aware of what had taken place in the months immediately leading up to Scott's capture. His and Dussault's dealings with the JCS Joint Special Operations Center (JSOC) were less than fruitful. They'd hoped to get approval for a rescue mission. None came. After discussions began with the International Committee of the Red Cross (ICRC) and Iraq for a visit to the crash site, both of them knew they'd lost Scott Speicher. But they still had the crash site. The Falcon Hunter's visits to Speicher's downed Hornet started a cascade of information that arguably provided investigators with more information than they needed to prove Scott had survived his shoot down. Pieces of the puzzle, the backstory before his capture, started to come together. So did Iraqi deception operations on his crash site.

"[The Iraqis] have significant historical experience [with denial and deception operations]," Dr. John Yurechko, DIA officer for information operations and denial and deception operations and an expert in the strategy and methods used by different countries to deceive and hide their weapons of mass destruction (WMD) programs, told reporters at an October 11, 2002 foreign press briefing. "I mean, the denial and deception efforts started long before Desert Storm. They used it in their war with Iran, both on the battlefield and on a strategic level." He pointed out that the Iraqi denial and deception program under Saddam involved not just a specific government organization. On the contrary, said Yurechko, "it involved inculcating down to the lowest worker level the whole concept of denial and deception." Prefacing his comments, Yurechko told the press that his job was much like theirs, the job of a reporter. "I try to find answers to a lot of very difficult questions." This includes not relying on a single source to make a judgment. While his briefing that day was unclassified, he cautioned that there would be subjects touched upon by reporters in the room that he couldn't address. "I have to protect my sources," he said, "like you do." But what he had to say about Iraq's intentions couldn't have been clearer.

Yurechko's message was simple. "Denial and deception are interrelated. Denial is the basis for successful deception. You can't blur the truth, or lie convincingly, unless the truth is first concealed." He pointed to the challenge the West, most especially the United States, would face trying to separate truth from Iraq's sophisticated denial and deception machine. He pointed to the obvious: that after Desert Storm the Iraqis directed a massive, well-organized denial and deception effort to defeat the UNSCOM inspection system. "A number of foreign inspectors, senior UNSCOM officials and Iraqi defectors have described this effort in considerable detail," Yurechko told them. He cited inspector David A. Kay's article on denial and deception practices of WMD proliferators, published in the winter 1995 *Washington Quarterly*; British inspector Tim Trevan's 1999 book, *Saddam's Secrets*; several insightful articles and reports by former U.S. inspector David Albright, and former UNSCOM Chairman Richard Butler's 2000 book, *The Greatest Threat*. "And if these Western sources don't suffice," he iterated, "there [was then] a small but growing body of accounts by knowledgeable Iraqi defectors." Further citations included a February 23, 2000 State Department study "Saddam Hussein's Iraq," the October 2002 CIA document "Iraq's Weapons of Mass Destruction Programs," and the British government's 2002 assessment "Iraq's Weapons of Mass Destruction."

What does all of this have to do with Speicher? Many of these denial and deception activities were targeted against the UN and UNSCOM inspectors. Some were directed against the United States and Western intelligence. WMD wasn't the only area in which it was practiced. The same concealment and sanitization exercised over its WMD facilities was used to hide Speicher from U.S. authorities. Such sophistication relied on high mobility and good command, control and communications. The example Yurechko used was placing WMD facilities in residential areas to conceal them from inspectors. "There is a famous aphorism I can think of by the late Amron Katz, he was a specialist in arms control," Yurechko said, "He said, quote, 'We have never found anything that our enemies have successfully concealed,' unquote." Speicher was no different.

The JCS didn't get the result of a feasibility study on a covert military operation at the Speicher crash site until May 1994. It took a few months before a planning order made its way down to Special Operations Command at Fort Bragg, North Carolina. The July 5, 1994 order started the planning process for this operation. The original order read:

> When directed by the NCA, USCINCCENT [United States Commander in Chief Central] will conduct military operations to investigate a Desert Storm F/A-18 crash site in western Iraq to retrieve information and/or recover designated pieces of wreckage to assist in determining the fact of the pilot whose remains are unaccounted for.

The National Command Authority (NCA), defined by law, is the president of the United States and the secretary of defense. Both are required to make decisions, including the release of nuclear weapons on a target or the initiation of covert operations inside another country's sovereign borders. Immediately on receipt of the message, special operations planners started mapping out a feasible insertion of Special Forces onto the crash site.

But the message received by CENTCOM army general J. H. Binford Peay III changed before it reached him. The message Peay passed to his staff included significant changes to the original body of the order:

> When directed, COMSOCCENT [Commander, Special Operations Command Central] deploys a JSOTF [Joint Special Op-

> erations Task Force] to USCENTCOM AOR [area of responsibility] and conducts intrusive military operations in conjunction with JTF-SWA [Joint Task Force-Southwest Asia] assets to investigate a Desert Storm F/A-18 crash site in western Iraq. Mission is to retrieve information and/or recover designated pieces of wreckage to assist in determining the fate of the pilot, and if possible recover his remains.

The JTF-SWA were already in theater to support U.S. enforcement of the no-fly zone over Iraq. The change of wording from "whose remains are unaccounted for" to "if possible recover his remains" suggested there was more at stake than aircraft parts. The first statement suggested that Speicher's fate was unknown; the second made it clear planners believed Speicher already dead.

Four covert teams assembled at Hurlburt Air Force Base, Florida, to execute the order that had come down from the JCS to JSOC. They were Delta Force, familiarly known as "snakeaters." They were experts from the army's Central Identification Laboratory in Hawaii (CILHI). They were investigators from the Naval Air Warfare Center Weapons Division (NAWCWD), also called China Lake. And there was one investigator from Naval Safety Center Norfolk (NAVSAFECEN), Lieutenant Michael Buran, an experienced aircraft mishap expert and navy helicopter pilot. Buran wasn't originally part of the team. But then neither was anyone from the safety center, not until China Lake's parachute expert Bruce W. Trenholm insisted someone from Norfolk needed to go. Buran became the only active duty navy member of the ICRC team to enter Iraq in search of what remained of Speicher's Hornet and perhaps its pilot.

Soon after the prospective team was chosen, General Shalikashvili called them together. The JSOTF now consisted of seventy-four Deltas and army Special Forces, forty-two navy field investigators and active duty personnel, and ten DIA analysts and field officers. Investigators went through weeks of commando training, taught by their Delta mirror, assigned to each civilian member of the team and responsible for their training and action in the field. Some of the Delta Force assigned to this mission had been at Mogadishu in

1993. Others had been behind enemy lines during Desert Storm. "When they handed you a Colt AR-15 automatic rifle, these guys told us, even with a laser scope, not to fire unless they were standing right in front of us," said Buran. Delta Force, the serious shooters, did all the planning. It was their responsibility to get everyone in and out of Iraq without incident.

Buran made a few calls and got an F/A-18 airframe shipped from San Diego to the JSOTF desert training ground at Fort Bliss, Texas. They practiced taking apart the cockpit for its vital components before blowing it up. The Pentagon got Lieutenant Commander James Otto Stutz Jr. to provide investigators all possible F/A-18 background information. He didn't go with the team to the desert. The team was still getting read up on the aircraft as August 1994 came and went. This included a call for information by Naval Air Systems Command in Washington to an aerospace engineer at Naval Aviation Depot Norfolk, Michael E. Brock, for photographic, dimensional and operational specifications for the Hornet's Martin-Baker SJU-5A ejection seat. Brock was told to reply directly to J. Alan Liotta, DPMO deputy director. Brock wrote Liotta in early September that he presumed the information involved a mishap of some sort. He cautioned that since he'd not spoken to Liotta directly, "I cannot ascertain exactly what type of information you truly need." Brock attached basic information on the Martin-Baker's ejection sequence. After discussion with Peter Yost, a colleague at the Naval Air Warfare Center, Warminster, Pennsylvania, Brock went back to Liotta, informing him that Yost could supply basic ejection seat dimensions.

Brock and Yost provided all they had on the ejection seat. But back at China Lake, Trenholm got word that the JSOC needed preliminary ejection event analysis. He was told only, just then, that it pertained to an F/A-18 mishap. Covert planners wanted to know where to look and what to expect when they reached the crash site. Trenholm's September 7, 1994 report included the projected descent path an ejected seat would follow to the desert floor below. He told JSOC Major J. Pryor to evaluate such an ejection, he used three factors: location of the aircraft canopy, type of aircraft ejection seat, and the pilot's size. "The location of the aircraft impact site is less critical," he wrote, "since the aircraft lift surfaces may divert its flight path away from the original course and heading after the ejection event. The canopy, on the other hand, has a more predictable trajectory based on the ejection airspeed, and it generally maintains the original aircraft heading at the point of ejection." To be more responsive to the JSOC request, Trenholm loaded test data on the canopy travel distance versus airspeed. He conducted tests at the Supersonic Naval Ordnance Research Track (SNORT), where the trajectory of an ejected seat was measured using film analysis. His final document walked the JSOC through the entire ejection analysis and modeling and simulation.

Liotta asked JSSA to provide further ejection seat information. But this had taken place much earlier than fall 1994. That June, just two months after Colonel Bonn ordered him to stop analysis of Speicher's ground-to-air signal, Bob Dussault got a call from DPMO. "They asked if I could scrounge an F/A-18 ejection seat. I knew what they were up to," he said later, "but they wouldn't tell me. They learned that they couldn't find something they hadn't seen before. It was quite clear that I was persona non grata for any old stuff, but new, they were interesting to learn all they could. I was getting images and new tests with simple phone calls." Clearly, recovery of the ejection seat was the major thrust of JSOC planners. For whatever secrets it held, the seat had to be located, no matter the cost.

The location of Speicher's aircraft canopy was calculated based on ejection altitude and windage that was then confirmed by the JCS and JSSA from overhead imagery. The canopy's discovery in the exact location it should have been, shown on the film, indicated a successful ejection. "This sign alone," said Dussault, "even before the ICRC trip, convinced us he had ejected successfully." Based on his background and decades' long experience with SERE training and recovery operations, Dussault believed that Speicher should always have been considered alive until his death could be conclusively proven, not the other way around. But DPMO continued to look for Shalikashvili's "old bones." Speicher would get no help until he could prove he wasn't dead.

"Like I told General [Harry E.] Soyster and international security affairs [in the Pentagon]," Dussault recalled of his conversation with the general in September 1991, "if John Noble's case depended on them, he would still be in Russia." DPMO has been rightly accused of focusing on the wrong end of POW/MIA operations, waiting until Shalikashvili's self-fulfilling prophecy of old bones makes the mission a hunt for the dead, not the living. Recovery of downed airmen is about getting them back, not DPMO running complex analyses to determine whether they are alive or dead in advance of any effort to help them. "That rests with the CINC [commander in chief] who lost the guy," said Dussault. "But is this how it happened? Nope. DPMO decided on the case. Scott was dead. Drop it, CINC." DPMO spent an excessive amount of time, much of it wasted, doing nothing for Scott Speicher. This was in spite of growing evidence that demanded they take a closer look.

Overhead U-2 imagery again confirmed that Speicher's Hornet pancaked onto the desert floor about one hundred miles northeast of the Saudi border town of Ar Ar. This made a convenient point from which to insert a covert team. MH-6J Little Bird Special Operations helicopters could fly to the crash site from Ar Ar with a team of experts to examine the wreckage. There would also be specialists from China Lake, Norfolk and Hawaii. Each man would be heavily armed in case the team came under attack from the Iraqis. But no one wanted to think about it. Not then. They rehearsed the mission over and over at Bliss, memorizing the tasks that they would have to do quickly once on the wreckage. Still, sneaking across the Iraqi border would be tight. The Iraqis already suspected the Americans were after a pilot.

After the Persian Gulf War, Saddam ordered the construction of a string of radar towers along Iraq's border with Saudi Arabia. American intelligence observed the sites to learn which ones were occupied and which ones weren't. It wasn't hard to figure out when the towers were occupied. Iraqi soldiers tossed their gear at the base of the towers when they went on duty, thus the tower was operational and high risk. JSOC planners determined the manning status of each tower at different times of day down to the last detail. They found a corridor near Ar Ar that made the town the best possible option for the team's ingress and egress to the crash site. With the wreckage an hour away, they'd be on the site overnight and return to Saudi Arabia in the morning. The mission profile was low risk. Demolition experts assigned to each team carried fuses, plastique and a posthole digger to place charges and blow up what remained of Speicher's cockpit after they'd gone over it for anything useful. If the Iraqis discovered them, they could get out in a hurry and be back in Ar Ar in forty-five minutes.

But the covert mission wasn't a sure thing. Back at the Pentagon, Tim Connolly thought time was wasting. The Iraqis could happen on the site any day. Questions were being raised about Speicher's wreckage on both sides. But the Iraqis were far more interested in the pilot. They wondered where the pilot must be for the Americans to be so anxious to examine the wreckage. Washington hadn't asked to see any other crash site? And there were others. In fact, there were others from which no remains had been recovered. What made this one unique? Was it the gear on board the jet? Probably not. What about the pilot? Probably so.

A second camp in the Pentagon suggested the diplomatic route. They suggested Washington approach the ICRC and ask it to contact Baghdad. The ICRC would tell the Iraqis about the crash site and ask for permission to take a team to investigate it. The diplomatic proposal posed no risk of lives, and many political and military leaders were still shaken by what happened at Mogadishu just a year earlier. The ICRC option offered the added benefit of showing the Iraqis that the United States was playing by the rules.

When military planners heard that the diplomatic option was on the table, they thought it must be a ghost option, a backup for appearance's sake. It couldn't be real. Connolly didn't like it. If the United States went in undercover, intelligence could guarantee that the information gathered was untainted and used to investigate further. He also didn't want to tell Iraq exactly where the site was, if they didn't already know, which is what the diplomatic notification would have to do to gain access to the wreckage. Even if they only gave Iraq the general vicinity, Saddam would move quickly to get ahead of them and find Speicher. Connolly was worried, too, over how much time had already passed. He tried to speed up the process, warning those involved: "If it were to become known that we had identified the potential remains of a service member who had potentially died in combat and we were not immediately going in there to assure they wouldn't fall into the hands of the enemy, we would be crucified politically."

Buddy Harris and a small number of investigators examined the first set of the Falcon Hunter's pictures and the overhead imagery of the wreckage. The F/A-18's canopy appeared to be about two miles, maybe a bit less, from the crash site. When a pilot ejects, small explosives ignite and blast off the canopy. It appeared as if that's exactly what happened to Speicher's jet. Those who looked into Speicher's disappearance early on didn't have wreckage to examine, but they determined he hadn't ejected because no one heard his emergency locator transmitter (ELT). A downed pilot's ELT normally emits a distinct whooping signal that surveilling aircraft and other pilots would hear on a UHF frequency.

Being a pilot, Harris knew that some aviators liked to have their ELT disconnected when they flew over hostile territory. They thought the signals made it easy for the enemy to find them if shot down. Harris asked a couple of people from Speicher's squadron, VFA-81, about a disconnected ELT in Speicher's seat, but they claimed they hadn't disconnected any ELT devices that night. Maybe the ELT malfunctioned, he thought. When he checked into that possibility he learned that the beacons have several electronic backups that make them extremely reliable. But then he found VFA-81's maintenance officer, Lieutenant Commander Steve "Ammo" Minnis. If the ELTs were disconnected, he would know about it. Yes, Minnis said, the beacons had been disconnected. Harris had been misled. "Did you know they didn't go after Scott and look for him because they didn't know this and got no signal?" Harris told Minnis. Minnis was stunned. The higher-ups knew that the ELTs were turned off, he told Harris. The ELT message should have been conveyed to CSAR. "There's just no way," Minnis said. That piece of information had to have been known by his superiors.

Investigators were shocked, too. They'd already been told about the incompatible Motorola survival radios, the AN/PRC-112s, that were too large to fit into the pilots' vest pockets. Since controlling aircraft and CSAR would be monitoring radio traffic for a signal to come get him, they assumed he couldn't communicate. Perhaps he lost the survival radio on the way down. Maybe it malfunctioned. But they didn't know his ELT was disconnected. Certainly, if the squadron's maintenance logs up to January 17, 1991, were available, this would have been an easy question to answer. But they weren't. Those log books had been sent over to *LaSalle* and from there no one will say where they ended up. There are some good guesses but no one knows for certain. Given the lack of CSAR for Speicher, his potential radio problems and the disconnected ELT, military planners could make a near-perfect case for the covert mission. Or could they?

Connolly left his office and walked through the Pentagon to the secretary of defense's conference room in the E-ring. This briefing, which would decide whether to go in as a covert operation or under the banner of the ICRC, was a long time coming. It was now December 23, 1994, a year since Speicher's F/A-18 had been found in the Iraqi desert. General Shalikashvili took a seat at the head of the table. To his left sat his top planner, the director of operations for the Joint Chiefs of Staff, air force lieutenant general Howell M. Estes III. Beside Estes was the deputy principal secretary of defense for international security affairs, Frederick C. Smith. Secretary of Defense William Perry sat to Shalikashvili's right with Perry's undersecretary of defense for policy, Walter B. "Walt" Slocombe. Down the table was Colonel William G. "Jerry" Boykin, head of Special Operations Division J33. Boykin was later outed by Attorney General Janet Reno as one of two Delta Force officers the Federal Bureau of Investigation (FBI) asked for, by name, for their expertise when the Bureau stormed the Branch Davidian compound in Waco, Texas. Aides holding briefing packets, transparencies and flip charts stood uncomfortably along the walls. There was no one from Connolly's office, though but him, and many from international security affairs. Connolly thought this was odd as he took his seat.

There was no way to know what direction Perry and Shalikashvili would take. At no time was Connolly's boss, the assistant secretary of defense for special operations and low-intensity conflict, Henry Allen Holmes[1], involved in any of the planning. If the secretary of defense or chairman raised a question, it was Pentagon protocol that only someone directly involved in the mission's planning could answer it. But none of the planners who worked out the details of the covert mission were in the room. "This thing's been preloaded," Connolly thought. As staffers threw up the presentation on the wall, page by page, Connolly followed his handout. His counterpart, Fred Smith, talked about the diplomatic mission. Then one of Shalikashvili's staff laid out the military option. They had done a threat analysis of the covert mission, breaking it down into its critical components: infiltration, actions on objective, and exfiltration. In each case they rated chances for success as high and threats low.

Though Shalikashvili's staffer made the covert operation look flawless and controlled, start to finish, Connolly knew it wouldn't be that easy. When he was an army Ranger, a dozen men, including his battalion commander, died just while training for a special operation. Military missions, covert or not, carry some level of danger. But the odds for this one looked as promising as any other. So he thought. The longer the meeting wore on the more Connolly felt support for the covert option slipping away. Finally, having heard enough, Connolly addressed Perry and Shalikashvili directly. "This country has an obligation to go in and find out what happened to this pilot," he said. Then he quoted the fifth stanza of the army Ranger creed: "I shall never leave a fallen comrade to fall into the hands of the enemy." He paused. Still sensing the group's hesitation to send Special Forces into harm's way so soon after Somalia, he took one more shot.

"Mr. Secretary," Connolly said, "I will go out the door of this conference room. I will stand in the hallway and I will stop the first five people who walk by in military uniform, regardless of their gender. I will explain to them what the mission is. I will ask them if they will volunteer to get on the helicopters, and I guarantee you that all five of them will volunteer."

Secretary Perry thanked him for his impassioned statement, then turned to Shalikashvili. "Mr. Chairman, what do you think?" It was just then that Shalikashvili made his "looking for old bones" statement. He wasn't necessarily speaking for the majority, but his opinion pulled more weight. "Sorry thing," said Dussault, "was [that] all the Joint Staff wanted to do something. [They'd] made plans, encouraged others to make plans. And in the end it was all called off by the famous Shalikashvili speech, thus turning it all over State and the CIA." Though he wasn't there for the briefing, Dussault knew Shalikashvili had made the claim that one soldier wasn't important enough to authorize military action. "I don't know if he said it because that is how he felt or because he was told by higher ups that was the case and he and DoD were going to have to live with it."

Perry wanted some time to think about all that was said in the meeting. In the meantime he directed the military to keep the covert option on the table. But Connolly knew Shalikashvili's feelings, expressed at the meeting's end, had already derailed a Special Forces entry into Iraq. Neither Perry nor Shalikashvili had the mettle for putting any forces in jeopardy for this mission, Connolly observed. Two weeks later, on January 4, 1995, Perry told Secretary of State Warren M. Christopher that the United States needed the ICRC to approach the Iraqi government for a humanitarian mission to the Speicher crash site.

A month after their late December meeting, Connolly got a letter from the deputy secretary of defense. Perry had chosen the diplomatic route. This was largely at the insistence of Fred Smith, whose office believed that Speicher was dead and that his remains were under the jet. But not everyone shared this view, most especially the Iraqis. Baghdad knew something was going on from the ICRC's first communication, a request to send an emissary to Iraq to discuss an American team that wanted entry into the country to search a crash site. If Scott Speicher was purportedly dead, recalling Secretary Cheney's pronouncement on January 18, 1991, and if

Baghdad had returned remains it said were his, what was the United States trying to discover now? Maybe, just maybe, the Americans didn't think he was dead. Maybe they knew the remains weren't his. Perhaps there was something of value to America's national security buried among the jet's debris? Neither the U.S. Department of State, the Pentagon nor CENTCOM ever went back to the Iraqis to demand answers after DNA analysis proved the remains they returned, certified as Speicher's, weren't his. The Pentagon made a presumptive finding of death where there wasn't proof of one. But Scott Speicher was very much alive and in assisted evasion mode.

More than a month passed before the ICRC signed off on the plan to accommodate an American team's visit to the crash site. Michel Cageneaux, ICRC director of Middle East operations, was dispatched to Baghdad to negotiate the deal. Their February 14 meeting went smoothly, but Fred Smith said afterward that the Iraqis took detailed notes and hung on everything said. While they weren't provided coordinates for the crash site, alerted to the missing aircraft by the ICRC on behalf of the United States, it was clear the Americans were in search of more than the aircraft. Scott Speicher was now the hunted.

On the face of it the meeting in Baghdad had gone well. But that assessment was short-sighted and naïve. Saddam just wanted time to think it over. Back at Fort Bliss, covert teams went through a complete dry run of the mission, code named Isolated Ivory, a veiled reference to Shalikashvili's jibe about looking for Speicher's "old bones." Washington was notified through diplomatic channels on March 1, 1995, that the Iraqis agreed to the plan but the team had to have Iraqi officials escort them in. March is a cold month in the desert clime, and inhospitable for a search team. The desert hardpan was still frozen solid, a fact learned the hard way by downed Coalition airmen and Special Forces over the winter of 1991. The ICRC mission was on, though no one knew exactly when the Iraqis would let the mission into the country to search. In the meantime Isolated Ivory was still active at Fort Bliss.

Despite all that was said in Secretary Perry's conference room, a covert plan crept forward. Their objective was retrieval of the cockpit and ejection seat, both of which held great value to some around the table that December day. They didn't want Iraqis to get either. Of the four covert teams formed in the summer of 1994, one secretly broke away to train at the Naval Strike Warfare Center, Fallon, Nevada.

"I was out there [Fallon, Nevada] in late spring, early summer 1995," explained a navy commander who spoke only on condition of anonymity. The commander engaged a Delta Force member in conversation off and on. "They had been out here for a short time when one day he said, 'Yeah, man, we're going out to the desert to get some guy's cockpit and bring it back.' One day they were gone. But a few days later they'd returned from the mission." The commander's recollection is confirmed by Lieutenant Commander Allen "Zoomie" Baker, halfway around the world in Riyadh just then. Baker had been on the Joint Staff between 1994 and 1995 and was a new arrival in Saudi Arabia when Delta Force snakeaters went to investigate Speicher's crash site. They checked in, he observed, with operations and moved out to the site using the planned insertion point at Ar Ar. They knew what they were looking for. The Falcon Hunter's photographs had already shown JSOC planners that Scott's cockpit looked intact. But they'd have to go check it out to know for sure. Planners were keenly interested to find out if the distinct outline of a chair resting on the desert floor – visible on the U-2 imagery – was actually the hundred-pound shell of Speicher's Martin-Baker ejection seat. They also wanted the jet's avionics package back, unaware that all of it had already been removed. The ICRC convoy rolled out of Baghdad headed for the crash site the morning of December 10, 1995. Nine months had gone by since Iraq initially agreed to the search. From overhead imagery shot at intervals right before the ICRC team's departure from the Iraqi capital, Pentagon officials confirmed the presence of truck trails leading to and from the site, raising concerns about the integrity of the Hornet's wreckage.

This team knew nothing of the covert visit to the site. And also knew nothing of Iraqi deception operations there. Two classified documents, one dated May 28, 2003, subject line Iraqi deception operations involving the Speicher crash site discovery, and the other, IIR [intelligence information report] 7 739 0377 03, address this clearly. From information contained in the subject line of these reports, unclassified information found in others, investigators' statements and a confidential source at NSWC Fallon, there is proof enough that there were at least three disturbances of the Speicher crash site immediately prior to the ICRC's December 10 arrival. One was American – the second American visit after careful documentation of the site and retrieval of sensitive avionics from the aircraft immediately post-shoot down – and the other Iraqi. It is also abundantly clear that the site of Scott Speicher's crashed Hornet continued to be an object of interest for Saddam for years to come.

The ICRC team was cautious with the crash site coordinates. They waited until the night before leaving Baghdad to convey the latitude and longitude of the site to their Iraqi escorts: 33°00'125"N 042°15'28"E. This was the coordinate military planners attached to the crash site. They were wrong – by a mile. The distance between where they believed the crash site to be and where it was actually found would turn out to be 1.756 kilometers or 1.09 miles. When the team arrived at the coordinates originally provided they saw nothing but desert. Bedouin herders stood nearby on a sandy path waving their arms at the lead vehicle. They knew what they were looking for. With the help of simple herders the team ultimately located Scott Speicher's wreckage at 33°00'114"N 042°15'28E, a full 150 statute miles from the coordinates originally reported when Spock Anderson recorded his last known coordinates back in January 1991 and filed them in a series of reports.

There were only four ICRC representatives on the team, code named Operation Promise Kept. The rest were Deltas and military investigators. CILHI sent its chief anthropologist, Dr. Thomas D. Holland, to examine any human remains Smith's office strongly believed were buried under the Hornet. Experts from China Lake and Norfolk were on the team. There was also a medic, explosive disposal expert and three linguists. Baghdad attached two aircraft investigators to the team roster and ordered Republican Guard to encircle the site's perimeter for "their protection." "Each person on the mission had his own agenda, his own reasons for being there," said Mike Buran later. Some of those agendas had been determined by a boss back in Washington, some had been assigned tasks outside their expertise and understanding. "I knew that the agenda of the ICRC was to find the body," said Bob Dussault. "My guys trained everyone [all the Americans] who went on the trip... on two different occasions. I know what went into preparing the team. Liotta," Dussault recalled, "was also much involved. But the focus was not to gather all the possible evidence [of Speicher's fate], just [information] which supported his [Speicher's] death." The investigation had two possible outcomes: the truth or the truth fashioned in advance by the Pentagon that had already concluded Scott Speicher was "old bones."

Buran was among the few investigators on the crash site in December 1995 who believed that Speicher shouldn't have been declared dead before there was proof to support that conclusion. But he was at a disadvantage to argue the point. He took orders like everybody else. Within three hours of leaving Baghdad he and the others stood on a moonlike surface southwest of a city in the vicinity of Tulul ad al-Dulaym, Wadi Thumayl. They were 1,080 feet above sea level, in the desert, less than thirty kilometers – 18.64 miles – to the south of a major east-west highway. There were no remarkable landmarks in the area. The Saudi border was about two hundred kilometers – roughly 124 miles – to the northeast. Several Bedouin camps were pitched in the desert to the north and northwest of the crash site. While visible to the team, they kept their distance. Dirt trails radiated out from the camps to nearby paved roads. Other than those few noticeable ripples in the terrain, there was nothing but light brown sand made up of weathered rock particles less than half a millimeter in diameter, larger scattered rock and a few clumps of grass, shrubs and vines.

As they climbed out of their Land Rovers and trucks, the team could see Speicher's wreckage and knew exactly what had happened without shoveling the first spade of dirt or examining one piece of his jet. Speicher's Hornet was now right side up. Big chunks of it, easily recognizable parts like the engines, lay in a circle no more than sixty feet in diameter. There was no significant crash crater and the wreckage showed minimal fragmentation, all consistent with terminal velocity, high angle and low-power impact. Team experts knew what that meant. The jet lost power and dropped like a falling leaf straight to the desert floor. Speicher's jet had not, as first believed, been blown to bits midair. Investigators quickly noticed something else: the cockpit was missing. The entire cockpit and instrument bay section, from forward of the wings to just aft of the gun, had been sheared cleanly from the rest of the fuselage. Someone else had gotten to the crash site ahead of them.

"It was like a car in the junkyard that you'd decided you wanted just the part from the front windshield to the bumper and cut it off," said Buran. "The Iraqis couldn't afford *batteries* in that country because of the embargo. We brought our own. Yet the cockpit of the aircraft was cut off clean and quickly." He was incredulous. The precision of the cut wasn't the work of the Iraqis, he thought. They didn't have the equipment nor adequate remote power source to do what had been done to Scott Speicher's Hornet.

Whoever had been to the site first would have had to sidestep gingerly around Speicher's ordnance, much of which was scattered about the axis of the aircraft. Bedouins, although normally anxious to take down an aircraft for salable parts and scrap, wouldn't have breached the Hornet's perimeter with missiles half-buried in the sand. Past experience proves this true. They'd scavenge pieces thrown clear of the main debris field. Anyone unfamiliar with aircraft ordnance would have stayed away from the fuselage. Then who had gotten there first?

Tim Connolly got it right – at least as much as he knew at that point. Connolly wasn't privy to the Joint team that got to Speicher's jet just after his shoot down. "I would not be surprised," he said, "if it turned out the U.S. government went in covertly at some point." Buran's February 15, 1996 report called it "another force." "From the evidence of the crash site before the ICRC team arrived, it is likely that another force… examined the wreckage and removed major portions of the cockpit and instrument bay section." Then they all noticed that the ejection seat, obvious on overhead imagery about two miles from the aircraft wreckage, had been removed. Another critical piece of evidence had vanished. Other members of ICRC team would comment on the missing parts of Speicher's jet, too. They used the words "professional" to describe the manner in which the cockpit was removed. Some of them speculated that whoever had done it was looking for Speicher's body under the aircraft. They realized just then that not only was it "professional" but "calculated." Missing were two major evidential parts of the aircraft. Two pieces that might lead investigators to unequivocally conclude that Scott Speicher had survived his shoot down. The ICRC team just then had no knowledge of the joint military team that exploited Speicher's Hornet immediately after his shoot-down.

The ICRC team recovered whatever else it could find. There was nose gear and the twenty-millimeter M61A1 Vulcan cannon. There were wings, engines, tail rudders and stabilizers. The radar antenna was gone. They assumed Bedouins, maybe the bustard hunters who they were told found the site, took it. Ordnance included everything Scott Speicher's Hornet was carrying on his mission minus one HARM. He had three. He'd also been carrying two Sparrow and two Sidewinder missiles. "Can't remember if we had two drop tanks [vice] one," said Tony Albano. "We always carried the ubiquitous centerline drop tank. Except, of course, Banker, who had only two HARMs so he could recover with both still on." Banker Caldwell was the airborne spare on the Sunliners' first mission of Desert Storm. Albano explained that if a three-HARM Hornet had problems that recovery required he jettison one or find a divert field to land. Ordnance was carefully removed from Speicher's wreckage and roped off. "We had people familiar with armament to take care of this," said Bruce Trenholm. Armament specialists dug a pit to bury it before the team left the desert. But not before members of the team removed the fins from Speicher's HARM missiles as souvenirs.

The team recovered major parts of the Hornet outside the main debris field, including the wing fuel drop tank, found 4,000 meters (about 2.5 miles) north; the centerline fuel drop tank, located

2,500 meters (1.5 miles) north, and the canopy, which had come down 670 meters (.42 miles) northeast. A long-burning post-crash magnesium burn from the Hornet's tires, coupled with erosion from the wreckage sitting in the desert exposed to the elements, contributed to the breakdown and disintegration of the composite components of the aircraft that they recovered. The wings were in bad shape.

Investigators started at the F/A-18's nose and roped off an excavation area. As they started their work they realized that whoever had beat them to the site knew what they were doing. A pile of backfill, sand dug from elsewhere, was heaped near where the cockpit should have been. Popped rivets lay on the ground nearby. The backfill, they thought, looked like it'd been there less than a month. It was clear, too, that parts of the Hornet's computer had been removed. Given all this, they decided to start digging in the same spot as whoever had been there first: the cockpit. Dirt under the cockpit showed signs of recent manual digging. They excavated it further, taking it down fifty centimeters (1.64 feet) to culturally sterile soil. This information was reported to the ICRC's Michel Cageneaux in a 1997 memo prepared by Lieutenant Commander Kevin J. Wilson, who worked in the office of the assistant secretary of defense for international security affairs/DPMO. Investigators continued to excavate down the midline of Speicher's fuselage finding no significant cockpit debris and pilot-related material. They also found no pilot's remains.

Post-crash analysis concluded the Hornet's engines shut down in flight. Both were in relatively good condition. Absent the cockpit and ejection seat, key evidence of missile damage was missing. But there was just enough to tell that the warhead that detonated under Speicher's jet was packed with high explosive. The Hornet's fuel lines were cut and its starboard wing flaps blown off, enough to kill the airplane but not the pilot. "The damage," claimed one investigator, who asked for anonymity, "was consistent with an AIM-54C Phoenix missile," a fact he wasn't allowed to include in his final report. The controversial Phoenix, the missile that F-14 Tomcat pilots were told they weren't allowed to fire, has a 135-pound blast fragmentation warhead designed to bring down enemy aircraft. With a range of over one hundred nautical miles, it was the Tomcat's longest-range missile. But the Phoenix missile's official history doesn't mention employment during Operation Desert Storm nor the Phoenix shot at the F-1EQ. Despite the Phoenix missile's much touted capabilities, it is on record as having only been fired twice in combat by the U.S. Navy, both over Iraq in 1999 and, even then, there were no confirmed targets destroyed.

The investigators' declassified reports also offer no mention of the possibility that it might have been the AIM-7M Sparrow. The Sparrow has an 88-pound high explosive blast fragmentation warhead while a guidance and control section (GCS) tracks the target; directs and stabilizes the missile on a lead-angle navigation course to the target; and starts warhead detonation by use of an active radar proximity fuze or a backup contact fuze. The guidance system uses energy reflected from the target and data received from the missile fire-control system to track the target. A comparison of these signals allows the guidance section to sense changes in target position and create signals used by the control section to control movement of the wings and thus maintain course to target intercept. The fact that more than one air force controller, one of them "a tactics guy" can confirm the Sparrow would appear to rule out the Phoenix.

The wing and centerline drop tanks of Speicher's Hornet, found north of the main debris field, still had their pylons attached. This indicated to investigators that the pylons were torn from the fuselage in flight, subject to excessive aerodynamic forces over a short period of time. This is consistent with an aircraft that has come down in a flat spin or falling leaf mode.

As work continued near the jet, members of the team formed skirmish lines, spreading out and walking slowly to look for less obvious evidence, perhaps something small that provided another piece of the puzzle. Buran was paired with an Iraqi Air Force investigator, a man who went by the pseudonym Mohammed. He'd been a MiG pilot during the Iran-Iraq War. Shot down twice, Mohammed had a bad back from parachuting out of his aircraft a second time. He no longer flew. With his flying days over, he was sent to Great Britain to learn the business of aircraft mishap investigation. Out in the middle of the western Iraqi desert he and Buran talked frequently. At one point he stopped Buran as they walked the site looking for clues and asked if aircraft mishap investigators were needed in other countries. "Are there jobs for people like us?" he asked. "Oh, yes," said Buran. "Lots of them." Mohammed smiled broadly. He later gave Buran a set of his Iraqi pilot's wings, a gesture between two pilots. Buran still has them.

Baghdad limited the search area. But during their recovery effort, team members surveyed a circular area about ten kilometers in diameter (about 6.2 miles) centered on the aircraft crash site. About thirty meters north (.0186 miles), east and south of the site, the team noticed several low, rectangular rock piles. Dr. Holland shovel-tested rock piles closest to the wreckage assuming they might indicate a gravesite. But none had been subject to subsurface disturbance within ten years prior to their site visit. Holland found no remains. They also found no personal pilot gear either. The only item tied to the cockpit that they found on the site, excluding the DSU, were two switches and one warning light indicator. Nothing else.

Two thousand feet (.378 miles) to the north they noticed something manmade propped upright on a sandy knoll. As team members got closer, they saw it was the canopy frame, what was left of it. Bedouins stood it on end, perhaps as a landmark. No one knew for sure. A Bedouin boy had scrawled in Arabic across the bottom of the canopy frame how much he hated it there. The canopy-jettison rocket motors had been fired. Investigators could tell this was the case just looking at the even and complete burn marks on the frame. As they picked through evidence on the ground, the team got a clearer picture of what Scott Speicher had and hadn't done. He'd initiated the canopy jettison. This finding favored his survival. He'd ejected from the aircraft. To the south they found his missing HARM missile. This didn't indicate Scott released it to regain control of his stricken Hornet, said Albano. The missile, like the others found, had been ripped from the aircraft as it hurtled toward the desert below.

A couple of days into the site visit, navy flight mishap investigator Bruce Trenholm got a call on his radio that left him unable to believe what he was hearing. Iraqi officials at the site had just notified the team that a young Bedouin boy claimed to have come across a flight suit herding his sheep. The flight suit was roughly three-and-a-half kilometers northeast of the wreckage. Trenholm drove over to it. Members of the team were already there, standing around it in a circle. Standing nearby was the boy's "uncle," a robe-clad, impeccably dressed man wearing polished wing-tip shoes, hardly the attire of a shepherd. The boy complained the flight suit smelled bad. He hadn't touched it. Odd, thought Trenholm. Something was wrong with the story. But he wasn't allowed to interview the boy. The flight suit wasn't on the ground when found. "It had been handed to us," said Buran. "That's a big difference."

Trenholm could see for himself that it was an American Nomex flight suit, standard aviator coveralls resistant to fires exceeding several hundred degrees. He could also see that it had faded from its usual olive green color to a greenish yellow. "I was told that it was Michael's flight suit," said Trenholm. "But all I said at the time was 'Well, all I can tell you is it's a flight suit. I don't know whose it is.'" He'd have to run tests to make sure it was Speicher's. Out there in the desert, standing there holding a flight suit, there were more questions than answers. "I mean, you know, the deal was we were looking for Michael Speicher. That was our task. You know there's a flight suit, but it's just like an Easter egg hunt basically, and here's his flight suit. 'This is his.'" Trenholm was suspicious from the start. The sudden and dramatic appearance of a key piece of forensic evidence suggested that Baghdad's deception had swung into high gear. "I can't verify whose it is," he said. "If I don't see anybody wearing it, then I'm not really sure it's yours." During repeated prior visits by the Falcon Hunter and American CIA field agents who'd "gone native" to report from the desert between 1991 and 1994, no U.S. Nomex flight suit was found lying around on the desert floor or splayed across a rock waiting to be picked up. Thus the "discovery," begged serious questions. Where had it been all this time? Where was the pilot who'd worn it? Was he Scott Speicher?

Near the place where investigators were handed the flight suit a cluster of pilot aviation life support system (ALSS) equipment was discovered: a fragment of ejection seat upper-leg garter, three fragments from a survival raft, pieces of a parachute strap, an inflatable raft, a twenty-millimeter shell from the Hornet's nose cannon, and six pieces of an anti-G suit that a pilot wears to lessen aerodynamic forces. They also found a signaling flare. Someone had tried to light both ends of the flare, one used for daytime, the other for night. The bottom line was this: the flight suit and all ALSS equipment recovered by the team had been cut with a sharp object. Though much of it had what looked like bloodstains, none suggested massive external bleeding.

"The flight suit was cut up the back not including the collar," explained Trenholm. The cuts up the back included the legs and the crotch, where the suit was notched or cut around the straps and fasteners of Speicher's torso harness, leaving a diamond-shaped cut by the groin area of each leg. The flight suit, if it was Speicher's, had been places other than the desert, Trenholm remarked later. This finding was predicated on the presence of foreign trace evidence on the flight suit, including carpet fibers and dog hair. Perhaps from a Bedouin herder's black tent? Carpet fibers and dog hair would both be present there. Still, no one could say just then how long Scott Speicher had worn his flight suit. No one knew how long he might have kept it either. These were questions that investigators hoped they'd eventually be able to answer. Baghdad's restrictive search area made it harder to get to ground truth. Admiral Arthur observed later, on July 10, 2010, that "if he had ejected immediately upon being hit, the chances of the canopy or he being anywhere in the vicinity of the crash site are about a million to one." The search area, unrestricted, would clearly have been more fruitful for the ICRC team.

American investigators were further denied access to Bedouins they could see just outside their circular search area. "The Bedouins in that area out there, they're nomadic tribes and they go from point A to point B to point C," said Trenholm. "They do this all year round. They are like gypsies. They just travel. There was a small

Bedouin tribe not too far away, but we never had any dealings with them at all. The Iraqis were there. I think the whole Iraqi army was there." Trenholm wasn't exaggerating by much. Iraqi Air Force general Khaldoun Khattab was there. So was the Republican Guard. So were Saddam's best intelligence operatives. "Every time the Bedouins tried to tell us something or even looked like they wanted to tell us something," said Mike Buran, "one of these intelligence guys intervened." They ran interference for days. But they had their reasons. Saddam's intelligence was rapidly working through those small tribal groups. They needed to know if any of them knew about Scott Speicher and the family group that had protected him.

The Bedouins moving in and around the area of Speicher's downed Hornet had to know Saddam's men were looking for something or someone to have sent such a large force into this desolate patch of desert. Time was growing short for those who'd protected and at the very least known about Speicher. As soon as the ICRC left the area, the Iraqi troops who'd ringed the Americans' camp would quickly turn on them. Speicher's Bedouin protectors were prepared to go down fighting. They knew Saddam wasn't coming to send them to jail. He would be coming to kill them. Even if Speicher had still been with them, he couldn't just run up to the ICRC camp. Though most of the ICRC team were Deltas, neither he nor the Bedouins who'd protected him knew that and it really wouldn't have helped any of them to force the team into an unwinnable standoff with Khattab's men. The Iraqis had overwhelming firepower ringing the site and the team. Saddam's mukhabarat, the Iraqi Intelligence Service (IIS), made sure that the Bedouins who might tell the team about Speicher never got the chance.

Saddam's IIS found Speicher. Their job wasn't hard. Neither the Americans nor the ICRC had asked for the Iraqis' help locating the crash site. This told Saddam that the Americans had to have been monitoring the crash site a long time to know where it was and what they were going to find. He could judge for himself that whatever and whoever the ICRC was there to find had to be close by. Saddam delayed the ICRC team's entry into Iraq long enough to locate the man who went with the Hornet wreckage. Saddam had to assume that Speicher would be back in the area if still with the same Bedouin family group. They migrated, predictably and circuitously, in and out of the same grazing areas with the change of season. It was nearly mid-December and thus if Speicher were still with the group, he'd be making his way into Anbar Province to the place where he'd first made contact with them. Saddam couldn't be certain, but he could be ready. His search area soon narrowed to the tribal groups in the vicinity of Tulul ad al-Dulaym, Wadi Thumayl. Since the site was being watched Saddam had to know that his best chance to get to Speicher was before the ICRC team got to the area. Baghdad couldn't afford an international incident with an ICRC team caught in the middle. After Baghdad gave the ICRC mission the green light, it was too late. Saddam had his prize. Khattab, the Republican Guard and the IIS were sent out to make certain the Bedouin group present around the site didn't talk.

Baghdad held the team to the search area negotiated prior to their arrival. At its widest point the circular search area was eighteen to twenty meters. Anything outside the prescribed coordinates was off limits. "Bruce [Trenholm] had taken some wind drift calculations that he thought we should've looked at," said Buran. "But the Iraqis didn't want us going outside the predetermined search perimeter. We thought that perhaps given the winds that night, he [Speicher] might have ended up slightly beyond where we initially thought." Buran and Trenholm had been hamstrung, in truth, by both sides from searching the area where Speicher's ground-to-air signal was detected by overhead imagery. Baghdad didn't want them to see it. Washington didn't either. They could see the area but couldn't walk into it. "Our hands were tied," said Buran. "The Iraqis said no." But so had the American chain of command.

DPMO later published its analysis of Speicher's ground-to-air signal (GTAS), the same one Colonel Bonn and Bob Dussault certified was the navy's missing pilot's marker. DPMO's statement, undated and eventually forwarded to ONI in March 2002, read that the ICRC team "searched the entire vicinity and noted nothing they considered to be any type of survival symbol." The ugly truth was that the team had never been allowed to search there at all. They'd lied. But worse, they'd fabricated information received from the team. "Iraqi military units routinely draw designs in the desert sand during training exercises," wrote DPMO of their December 1995 findings. "The site of the unidentified marking is in the general vicinity of an Iraqi military training area." The facts are altogether different.

"There's nothing out there, nothing but sand, dirt and rocks," said Trenholm. "Nobody goes through there but the native people." Buran iterated that the only population in that part of the western Iraqi desert were the Bedouin sheep herders and "lots of sheep. We're talking a lot of them," he said. "The entire crash area was covered with sheep droppings everywhere you looked."

DPMO debunked itself further trying to sell the story about "tracks radiating out from the crash site" when it stated "the marking [the tracks] could not be associated with any known Iraqi military unit." Further, the ICRC team never claimed to have seen evidence of motorized vehicles in the area, despite the fact DPMO reported "analysts believe the ground marking may have been caused by tire tracks left by some unidentifiable vehicle. Motorized vehicles have been noted in this area." This, too, was a fabrication. "The site was in the middle of nowhere and I mean nowhere," said Trenholm. No one went willingly into the harsh environment of Iraq's winter desert clime except the herders who'd learned to cope with extreme drops in temperature. But it troubled Trenholm to think of Speicher out there in the freezing cold. This was December he thought. Speicher was shot down in January. If it was cold for the ICRC team in a tent with plenty of layers of blankets and thick sleeping bags, he knew it would have been bone-chilling for Speicher.

The team's investigation wound down after their fourth full day in the desert. As they drew closer to their tents, Buran, Trenholm and several other team members noticed something that took them aback. Next to the team's tents, piled high, were artifacts from the aircraft and crash site that they hadn't mapped in the debris field. When they asked where it'd come from, the Iraqis pleaded ignorance. But it really wasn't ignorance; it was a sign. Among the items was the one aircraft component they'd hoped to find, barring the absence of the cockpit and ejection seat: the DSU. If there was one piece of equipment that could tell investigators what happened to Speicher, barring recovery of the cockpit section and ejection seat, this was it. But its sudden appearance had them wondering where exactly it had come from and who'd had it. Why retrieve it and not other, equally important pieces of the wreckage? Were the Bedouins who took money from Buran for the DSU the same ones who'd protected Speicher?

The DSU had been blown out of its case and shut down immediately. Buran and the rest of the team later learned that this happened while the Hornet was still airborne, when Speicher ejected. There is no mention in the team's findings of it, but the DSU is located in the F/A-18C Lot 10s behind the pilot's left hip. The top [faceplate] of the DSU is exposed directly to the flame of the ejection seat when the pilot departs the aircraft. "There would be scorch marks present to the top of the unit from this exposure," observed Sunliner AMSC Terryl Chandler later. "The Hornet is a tough jet," Chandler continued. The front faceplate of Speicher's DSU was gone.

The DSU fell away from the Hornet before the jet impacted the desert floor. The bottom plate of the memory unit had a midline fissure roughly half its length. The edges of the fissure were jagged and displaced outward from the center of the unit. The front faceplate, with its handle and motherboard, was missing. If information could be recovered from the damaged DSU, it would reveal a minute-by-minute mechanical picture of Speicher's last flight. The DSU could also provide insight from its cordoned-off secure files. But for Buran, at that moment, there was only one problem: getting it out of Iraq. Buran downplayed its importance in front of Iraqi officials. They already seemed surprised that it was found. He offered the Bedouins money for it. They accepted. He quickly stowed it in his personal gear. It was the only way he was going to get it out of the country without raising further suspicion among the team's Iraqi hosts.

Before he left the crash site Mike Buran had one more thing he wanted to do. He cut the tailhook off Speicher's Hornet and brought it back for Michael Scott Speicher Jr., who was eighteen months old the last time he saw his father. He turned it over to Scott's former commanding officer, Spock Anderson, to clean up and present to Speicher's son. The "hook" is a cherished symbol of a naval aviator's flying career. At least Scott Speicher's son, he thought, would have something from his father's aircraft to remember him by.

The team pulled out of Iraq on December 16, 1995. They'd collected physical evidence and preliminary findings that once fully evaluated called into question the Pentagon's presumptive finding of death in the case of Michael Scott Speicher. But what they missed altogether was the man who'd flown the jet they'd come to investigate. They'd missed Scott Speicher. Just as the Bedouins predicted, General Khaldoun Khattab and "the whole Iraqi army" moved in and it was over.

The Pentagon would have to tell Joanne Speicher what the ICRC team found in the western Iraqi desert. Details of the mission were bound to become public and the Defense Department didn't want her reading about it in the newspaper. There was already much that she hadn't been told. The ICRC had intermittently asked Baghdad to account for Scott Speicher and Barry Cooke since the war. But Joanne wasn't notified of these inquiries. Whether Buddy Harris, then working in the Pentagon, mentioned the information to her as it became known to him is speculative. But his proximity to the Speicher family was closer than his Pentagon chain of command knew. When Washington engaged the ICRC to get Baghdad's permission to visit the crash site, the navy decided it was time to contact Joanne. As plans were made and next-of-kin considerations discussed, Harris knew he had to come forward with one more piece of information for his bosses in the Pentagon.

Over two years before, on July 4, 1992, Harris had married Joanne Speicher. He'd not mentioned the marriage to his colleagues. He'd not told his superiors. But he kept investigating the case. A few investigators who worked with Harris purportedly knew he'd married her, but most didn't. Jeff Manor recalled later how forthcoming a navy captain from the Chief of Naval Operations' special operations group had been with him during a meeting to discuss Speicher's status. "He told me right away about the mess with Buddy Harris. I think it was then that I informed him that things were even worse because Joanne was not the primary next-of-kin. It was a wrinkle," Manor explained, "that I don't think they initially considered. I'm not sure what I would have done in Buddy Harris' place. I know that Admiral Arthur secured a promise from him that he wouldn't release anything to Joanne until the navy decided to do so. I'm not sure why all this stuff was not code word since it involved possible special ops."

Code word, a level of classification above top secret, would have required members of the Speicher investigation team, including Harris, sign a secrecy agreement that prohibited them from disclosing classified information about the case. The one exception to this rule of law is when a witness has been served a notice of deposition by a U.S. Marshal. That person is then required under oath and sworn to tell the truth under penalty of perjury before the U.S. Senate Select Committee on Intelligence in closed session. But code word wasn't used among the team, so there was no way to keep Harris from discussing the case with Joanne then or others later. To those who didn't know, finding out about Harris' marriage to the wife of the man he was investigating was a clear case of conflict of interest, no matter how well intentioned, no matter how much he believed his work as part of the team boosted Scott Speicher's case in front of his boss. Harris was in a tough position. Despite what anyone thought of him, he knew deep down that what he'd done to help Scott was the right decision.

Admiral Arthur pulled Harris into his office after he found out about the marriage to Joanne Speicher. They talked for about an hour. Arthur told Harris he wouldn't have been assigned to Scott's investigation if he'd known the truth. But it was just as well. "Basically he said he's sorry," Harris said. Arthur took full responsibility for what happened to Scott. During the war, he'd been in charge of Desert Storm naval operations. He thought his staff had made serious mistakes. Now, Arthur confided to Harris, he was going to do everything he could to make it right, to get answers to all the questions that had been asked since Speicher's jet went down. It was a heartfelt promise, but Admiral Arthur was hamstrung by the same bureaucracy that said Scott Speicher was "old bones." His chances of being able to get Speicher back under those circumstances was moot.

William G. "Chip" Beck worked closely with Admiral Arthur during Desert Storm. Beck had been pulled from his job at the CIA, where he'd been a station chief. The navy needed him back. Commander Beck was the navy's official combat artist for the duration of the war. But he was also a naval intelligence officer. "I was on the USS *Ranger* [CV-61] the night that the air war commenced," he said later, "the night that Scott Speicher was shot down. I believe from the comments I heard at the time the navy, and certainly Admiral Arthur, believed the initial reports that Speicher was killed in the shoot down of his aircraft. Exactly why a SAR bird wasn't sent into the area, I don't know." Beck thought he'd gotten to know Arthur enough to characterize him as a caring and competent leader and a human being "who wouldn't knowingly leave one of his men in the lurch. Like most people at his level," he explained, "he accepted the professional assessments of his subordinates, and had too much else going on to probably focus on the details that might have [otherwise] caused him to question the analysis [he'd received]. After all," Beck concluded, "that is what his subordinate staffs and DPMO were supposed to do at their stages of the action [and] post action investigations."

After his meeting with Arthur, Harris would have to watch the Speicher investigation from the sidelines. "Instead of being part of the group and listening to what everybody else had to say, my tasks became more menial," he said later. Rather than uncover, evaluate and present information up the chain of command, Harris was relegated to gathering information that was passed to a navy captain to present in group sessions. "The group tended to always have meetings when I was not there or they wouldn't have any time to notify me. I was slowly put on the outside," Harris explained. It had become clear he was no longer part of the team. He understood. But he wasn't sure he'd have done anything differently. "So at that point I had to tell Joanne."

Harris' marriage to Joanne Speicher hadn't really gone unnoticed. It wasn't the forthcoming comments of a navy captain that tipped Manor to Speicher's next-of-kin rights issue. He already knew about it. "Technically," he explained, "Joanne was no longer the next-of-kin since she was remarried. [Speicher's] father was." But his office had difficulty tracking down Wallace Speicher at the time DNA testing was performed on DS1-256. "Nobody knew if he was dead or alive." Manor found him in a Jacksonville nursing home, but Wallace was at the end stages of dementia. He died on June 30, 1995. Before his health sharply declined, Wallace was outspoken on Scott's case. He wanted his son back. "I think," Manor explained, "[one reason concerned] money because of Scott's loss. Add to that, he was not Scott's natural father." Scott's adoption complicated the next-of-kin issue. While he had a sister, Sheryl Speicher Long, she, too, had been adopted by Wallace and Barbara Speicher.

At the time of his loss, Scott Speicher's children were minors ineligible to become next-of-kin until they reached the age of eighteen. The Defense Department played with the semantic between "primary next-of-kin" and "member of the immediate family," thus setting up problems the navy hadn't dealt with to date: what to do if he were ever declared missing again. "We didn't know what we were going to do," said Manor. "All that retroactive pay had to go to someone." Primary next-of-kin, in reference to a missing person at the time Scott Speicher was lost, was defined as an individual authorized to direct disposition of the person's remains. But a member of the immediate family was considered, as Manor explained, altogether different. A member of the immediate family of the missing person meant the spouse, if they hadn't remarried or divorced the service member; a natural, adopted or recognized illegitimate child, but only if that child had reached the age of eighteen or, if not eighteen, a surviving parent could speak for them; a biological parent, unless the law revoked custody by court decree and it was never restored; or a brother or sister of the service member, if they were at least eighteen years of age.

Under the aforementioned guidelines, had they been strictly interpreted, Joanne Speicher-Harris was no longer Scott Speicher's primary next-of-kin nor a member of his immediate family. Had the navy followed legal guidelines, the primary next-of-kin qualified to make decisions for Scott Speicher and receive his retroactive pay after July 4, 1992, was his father, Wallace. But by the time Manor found Wallace he was far too sick to assume the role of primary next-of-kin. The only person left to fulfill that role was his sister. No one in Manor's position had ever encountered such a complicated and sensitive family situation. After Speicher's fate was called into question and he was moved to missing and, later, missing-captured status, Joanne Speicher-Harris was paid two lump sums of Scott's back pay, one installment in 1996 and another in 2001.

Buddy Harris couldn't have been pushed aside from the Speicher investigation at a worse time. Word from the ICRC team was beginning to reach the Pentagon. Everyone hoped that they'd found answers that would clear up the mystery of what happened to Scott Speicher once and for all. But what they didn't know just then was that the Hornet's wreckage would only make them feel worse.

Back in the Pentagon, Secretary of Defense William Perry wanted to know how long it would take to resolve the issues in the case. "I told him it'd be thirty to forty days," said Bruce Trenholm later. Yet despite this, on January 17, 1996, J. Alan Liotta, DPMO deputy director, briefed New Hampshire Republican senator Robert C. "Bob" Smith, a ranking member of the Senate Armed Services Committee, to tell him what the ICRC team had found. Smith had tracked Speicher's case since the Falcon Hunter visited the wreckage three years before. What Smith heard from Liotta was grave news: the Red Cross team had found nothing to suggest that Scott Speicher survived his shoot-down. But that wasn't the truth. The truth took years to work its way to the surface.

Endnotes

1. Holmes was born in Bucharest, Romania, to American parents. He earned his bachelor's degree in 1954 at Princeton University, where he was a classmate of Donald Rumsfeld. Holmes then joined the United States Marine Corps, leaving as an infantry captain in 1957 to study at the University of Paris, where he graduated with a certificate in 1958 and was hired as an intelligence research analyst for the United States Department of State that same year. Holmes began his

diplomatic career by joining the Foreign Service in 1959; his first posting was as a consular and political officer in Yaoundé, Cameroon. He continued to advance through various State Department positions for the next two decades, including posts in Rome and Paris, until his appointment as ambassador to Portugal in 1982. From 1985 to 1989 Holmes served as United States assistant secretary of state for politico-military affairs. In 1989 he was appointed ambassador at large for Burdensharing in which he ensured balanced security responsibility among NATO members, Japan, and other American allies. Following this he was nominated by President Clinton to be assistant secretary of defense for Special Operations and low-intensity conflict. During this time his office generated a plan for the Department of Defense to launch new national counterterrorism strategy to respond to "the gauntlet the international terrorists have thrown at our feet," but as referenced in the 9/11 report, the paper never went beyond the Office of the Principal Deputy Under Secretary of Defense for Policy.

Chapter 8

Dead or Alive?

A few weeks after the ICRC team wrapped up its inquiry, aircraft investigators, life support experts, aviation engineers and forensic anthropologists filed their reports. Their findings drew a fairly clear picture of what had happened to Scott Speicher on his last flight. That picture differed sharply from what New Hampshire Senator Bob Smith had been told by J. Alan Liotta. Five days before Liotta briefed Smith a McDonnell Douglas investigative team extracted the information from Speicher's DSU. Each member of the team – Jeff Edwards, an aircraft mishap investigator; Scott Reynolds, an F/A-18 product safety analyst; Kevin Schmitz and Jeff Staudacher, DSU data retrieval, and Glen Patterson from Hamilton Standard, the DSU's manufacturer – played a key role in pulling off about 93 percent of the data, despite significant damage to the memory unit. Data fed into the DSU is recorded onto the memory unit from a low chip to a high chip. Power loss to Speicher's DSU was abrupt and occurred between the time data was being written from the low chip to the high chip.

The McDonnell Douglas team's final report gave lead investigators a detailed time line of events involving Speicher's Hornet, from the time he launched to the moment he was hit. Data started recording to Speicher's DSU at 1:35:29.25 A.M. Baghdad local time. The Hornet's throttles were set to 98 percent, full military power. Weight off wheels occurred at 1:36:18.44 as Speicher left the deck of the *Saratoga*. Everything in his flight appeared normal during the climb out to cruise altitude, which varied between 21,000 and 23,000 feet. But then his problems started. Eight minutes after takeoff his jet recorded a lengthy series of maintenance status panel

(MSP) code and built-in test (BIT) code failures. Several of these would play a significant role in what happened to him that night.

At 1:43:30.65 Speicher got a warning that indicated he had a HARM command launch computer (HARM CLC) failure (MSP Code 375). One, two or all three of his HARM missiles might have been inoperative. Seconds later he got a HARM to radar warning receiver (HARM/RWR) interface failure (MSP Code 377). The HARM CLC failure would either have degraded or eliminated the HARM to RWR interface that enabled the HARM to characterize threats. As he neared his first target at 3:46:25.95, two hours and ten minutes into the flight, the jet's computer recorded another failure. This one was to the ALR 67 radar warning receiver analyzer failure (MSP Code 111), the device that detected threats to the aircraft from air or land. It was this failure that corresponded to the BIT Code 94 failure of the Hornet's countermeasures weapon system. The read-only memory (ROM) on the second of two processors was declared failed, which thus caused the analyzer to declare a failure. The severity of this failure can vary from minor degradation to complete loss of displayed threat information, explained crash investigator Mike Buran, but in his opinion "he was totally blind" to air-to-air threats. The severity of the degradation Buran described would have been displayed to the pilot on the azimuth indicator to the right side of the cockpit instrument panel, so Speicher could have looked over at another gauge to notice how well – or not – the device was working.

The DSU recorded multiple, significant avionic BIT code failures to Speicher's Hornet within ten minutes of weight off wheels. Several of his HARM BIT codes failures indicated general function fail, target of opportunity mode fail, self-protect mode fail, HARM mode degradation, HARM CLC No Go, CLC fail and the ALR 67/HARM to RWR interface fail. The McDonnell Douglas team was unable to determine exactly which HARM station or stations were declared failed from the information on the memory unit. They also couldn't tell which one might have been damaged.

At 2:31:15.05, about fifty-five minutes into the flight, BIT Code 114, his signal data computer (SDC), recorded its first failure of the flight. The SDC controls the four main electronic displays in the cockpit: the HUD, the right and left digital display indicators (DDIs) and the lower-middle navigation (NAV) display. The second failure came twenty-two minutes later and was recorded at 2:53:30.65. These failures were believed to have been caused during one of three in-flight refueling events that took place before Speicher's run on the target.

The BIT code failures seemed more than normal to Bob Stumpf. "He does appear to [have been] having a bad day with the jet," he said. "We train to function with multiple degrades and it appears Spike decided he could accomplish his mission with what he had, just as I decided I could make it with the lesser amount of fuel I had." He pointed to the fact that on that night they all had considerable motivation to get their HARM missiles on the mark. Strikers [air force F-117s] were coming in below and depended on the Hornets' HARMs to shut down Iraqi missile batteries. "Those are the tough decisions that pilots have to make in the combat environment," said Stumpf.

From data taken off his DSU, Speicher received several advisories during the flight that notified him of the status of his autopilot engagement. His last one indicated that autopilot was selected at 3:38:56.55, roughly two hours and three minutes into the mission. "It doesn't surprise me that Spike was on autopilot," said Stumpf. "We were on a very benign profile and the autopilot does a great job of keeping on this sort of profile." It permits the pilot to focus on other flying aspects besides navigation. "I'm sure we were all on autopilot for much of the flight."

Scott Speicher disengaged autopilot at 3:49:42.75. He'd been at 28,160 feet traveling 364 knots. Seventeen seconds later something slammed into his Hornet so hard that it experienced abrupt power loss. Information taken five seconds prior to the last recorded frame on the DSU indicates that Speicher dropped to 27,872 feet. His airspeed had increased four knots. He was dropping into his target run. This slight nose-down input by the pilot ten seconds before loss of power is the only anomaly on the tape.

Mike Buran's Naval Safety Center analysis was not submitted to DPMO deputy director Liotta and CILHI army major W. L.

Ray until February 15, a month after Liotta drew the presumptive conclusion for Senator Smith that the ICRC had found nothing to indicate Speicher survived his shoot-down. Naval Aviation Depot Jacksonville engineers concluded that the Hornet's engines crashed with very little to no rotation. Both were in good condition and that wouldn't have been the case had they been turning on impact. This coupled with post-crash witness marks on engine components led Buran and depot engineers to the qualified assumption that both engines were no longer getting fuel and had shut down in flight. There were no entrance or exit wounds to either engine to indicate battle damage. Evidence pointed instead to a proximity detonation under the cockpit area of the aircraft. Whatever had damaged Scott Speicher's jet cut the fuel flow to the engines.

Analysis of the wing and centerline drop tanks that had been located by the ICRC team north of the main wreckage with the pylons still attached were analyzed and documented. This gave investigators another piece of the story. The pylons were torn from the fuselage, which indicated to them that Speicher's Hornet was put under excessive aerodynamic forces over a short period of time, perhaps two to three seconds, as the Hornet's altitude and approximated airspeed increased dramatically to 540 knots or .92 Mach. Charles Sapp, McDonnell Douglas' unit manager of flight load limits, estimated that the maximum G-load and sideslip in those few seconds caused the tanks to leave the airframe with their pylons still attached. He put the G-load at six Gs with sixty degrees of sideslip. But by the time his Hornet slipped into this falling leaf configuration, Speicher was no longer with the jet. He'd already punched out.

Buran's engineering investigation reported that the rocket motors that blast the canopy away from the aircraft left even burn marks on the frame. "The pilot had to have initiated the jettison," wrote Buran in his final report. There are only two ways for the canopy to jettison in an F/A-18 Hornet: the pilot pulling either of the two jettison release handles, one on the left side of the canopy or the one located between his legs. From the canopy alone it was impossible to tell which one Speicher pulled. What they did know was that he'd ejected successfully.

Buran hypothesized that the Hornet's engines shut down from an impact to the port side of the aircraft. This is the same side the DSU and recovered cockpit indicators were located. The throttle configuration on the F/A-18 is designed in such a way that if the throttle's cable is pulled forward, the aircraft loses power. If an explosion, perhaps in addition to airframe damage, resulted in the throttle system being displaced forward enough, it could have caused the engines to shut down.

There was something else that Buran's report told the Pentagon that it didn't want to hear: the pilot was not incapacitated by the missile's initial impact. One of his investigating engineers wrote: "This pilot was over enemy territory, in extremis situation and sitting in the middle of a hot cockpit fire. Logic dictates that the only way the pilot is getting rid of his canopy is by ejecting." When he consulted with flight surgeons and aviation life support system (ALSS) experts regarding pilot survivability under those circumstances, they assured Buran that Speicher had an 85 to 90 percent chance of surviving the flash heat and fire and the aerodynamic forces of the initial impact. Collene Swavely, a physical scientist in the protective clothing division at the Naval Air Warfare Center, Warminster, Pennsylvania, told Buran that three- to four-second exposure to temperatures of 650 degrees Fahrenheit would result in second-degree burns on exposed areas of skin. If Speicher had been burned just prior to ejection, it might have been to the back of his neck and any other areas left unprotected by his flight gear, including the face if his visor was up and his hands, if he wasn't wearing his flight gloves. Swavely's study proved that a ten- to twelve-second exposure to temperatures in excess of 700 degrees Fahrenheit would have been necessary to burn a pilot through his survival vest, anti-G suit, Nomex flight suit and cotton underwear. The interior canopy bubble of Scott's jet was exposed to only a few seconds of 400- to 500-degree heat. But this differed significantly from Dr. Holland's report, which suggested the cockpit was exposed to a short-lived fire "possibly reaching 650°-700° F." Holland, a forensic anthropologist, was estimating something outside his field of expertise. Engineers and physical scientists working with Speicher's wreckage knew better.

Trenholm's report picked up with Speicher's ejection from the Hornet. He concluded the canopy's distance from the primary wreckage site indicated that when the ejection handle was pulled, it separated as it should have. That said, he moved on to more pressing matters. Top of the list was the mysterious flight suit handed to them in desert just weeks before. He placed a call to Spock Anderson, who was out of the navy and working for McDonnell Douglas. He wanted to ask Anderson if he'd authorized his pilots to wear their name tags on the mission. Anderson said he'd think about it and get back to him. "But when someone says this and doesn't get your phone number to call you back," said Trenholm, "you aren't likely to get an answer."

The Sunliners wore red name tags, usually stitched with their call signs. Speicher's read "Spike." Trenholm knew it was important he figure out if the Iraqis cut off the left breast Velcro for the Spike name tag or if the Bedouins had just removed all the flight suit's usable Velcro and metal fasteners for practical use. Anderson hadn't answered the question: did he or didn't he tell his pilots to remove all patches from their flight suits before combat missions. He assumed Anderson's negative interest was an admission that he hadn't. Trenholm never got an answer to his question during the active part of the investigation. The real answer didn't come until much later. And it came from Tony Albano, Speicher's *Saratoga* roommate and best friend.

"We sanitized our flight suits," said Albano. "We didn't wear our name tags. Perhaps he [Trenholm] was thinking of the tag on the inside back collar that we used to write our names and 'last four' for the ship's laundry. But we didn't have any name tags or patches on our flight suits that night or any other mission during the war." The "last four" to which Albano referred were the last four digits of a pilot's social security number. If the Iraqis had Speicher's flight suit for any length of time, they knew exactly who they had: Scott Speicher. "The laundry label would've had Scott's last name on it."

Trenholm took the flight suit around to various bureaus and agencies for testing. He was not alone in his suspicions about the flight suit's origin. In his comprehensive report, Dr. Holland addressed the flight suit "found" by the Bedouin boy with the word "found" in quotes. He didn't believe the Iraqis' story either. Trenholm sent the flight suit over to the Body Mounted Systems Branch of the Naval Air Warfare Center in Warminster, Pennsylvania. They determined it was a CWU-27P flight suit in a size 38 Long. But the leg inseam was based on an approximate measurement. That part of the fabric of the flight suit was missing. There was no size tag nor manufacturer information inside the collar of the suit (this would also include the laundry information for the garment). Branch investigators estimated that the wearer of the suit had a 30.5-inch inseam. Speicher's anthropomorphic data was further estimated, given what they had in front of them, 71 inches tall and 168 pounds. But that wasn't right. The DIA POW/MIA database and the DUSTWUN sheet filled out for him by Spock Anderson recorded his height as 71.7 inches (5 feet 11 inches) and his weight as 154 pounds. They said he wore a 38 Long flight suit. Maybe, maybe not. Military aviators like to wear their flight suits slightly larger than their actual size to provide greater mobility. But after going to available reference materials and drawing photographic comparisons, the idea that the flight suit was in fact Speicher's began to add up for Trenholm. The suit, for him, "started quacking like a duck. I basically, for the most part, said that it was 'probable' it was his flight suit. [Now] I'm ninety-nine percent sure, just not a hundred percent sure. Personally, you know, you have a professional opinion and a personal opinion, right? My professional opinion is that most probably it's his. My personal opinion? Yeah, it's his. That's just the way I have to look at things."

The flight suit was and continues to be a pivotal piece of forensic evidence in the Scott Speicher case. But it also has a convoluted chain of custody to match the mystery of its being "found" by a Bedouin boy. Less than a month after American members of the ICRC team returned stateside, on January 9, 1996, Deputy Assistant Secretary of Defense for POW/MIA Affairs James W. Wold sent a letter to FBI director Louis Freeh asking the Bureau to analyze a flight suit "recently discovered near a desert crash site." "The flight suit is presently being evaluated to determine if it belonged to the aviator involved in the loss incident," said the letter. "In particular we are interested in any evidence of body fluids or foreign material remaining on the flight suit that may be used for DNA analysis and identification at a later date." The request further asked that "DNA testing is not desired at this time. The flight suit has already been examined by military crash investigation experts for heat damage and other crash-related evidence."

FBI special agent Joe Errera was told only that the loss incident in question "is receiving high-level DoD, State and NSC attention." Nothing else. Wold wanted results back by February 6. Due to the its strict custody requirements, the flight suit was submitted to the FBI by Bruce Trenholm and he was the only person other than Commander Mark D. Jensen, a navy helicopter pilot working for Wold, authorized to receive the flight suit once the FBI was finished testing it. Trenholm delivered the flight suit in a bag to the FBI laboratory in Washington, D.C., ten days later, on January 19.

The FBI's lab issued preliminary findings on January 31. Technicians found brown Caucasian body hairs, which they determined were insufficient for comparison purposes, meaning DNA. Dark, reddish-brown dog hair was removed from the flight suit. Blue and brown carpet fibers were also found and preserved on glass microscope slides for future comparison. "A preliminary chemical test for the possible evidence of blood was positive on stains found on the flight suit," according to the FBI lab report, but strangely, it refused to confirm whether the stain was actually blood. It only suggested "possible evidence of" but not the actual presence of blood on the flight suit. The FBI lab tested three dark splotches on the flight suit, each about an eighth of an inch in diameter. There was also a moderate presence of dark brown stains from the left arm cuff to the Velcro closure. Both Velcro closures on the sleeves were intact. Samples of stains on the crotch and armpit were taken for possible DNA analysis. None were done. Dr. Holland wrote in a report dated March 19, 1996, that "FBI chemical tests of the flight suit were positive for possible blood residues." But that's not exactly true. The FBI report never conclusively identifies the stains as blood. The FBI did find a small amount of sand and whitish plant debris.

Samples of all were placed in envelopes to be kept with the flight suit until it was retrieved by either Trenholm or Jensen.

An independent fingerprint examination of the flight suit, performed by the FBI, wasn't put in the file as of February 6, nor any time thereafter. And while it wasn't explained in detail, the FBI did run a serology workup and limited DNA testing for the lab's edification. Those results weren't entered into the file. Bureau examiners further agreed not to talk about their findings interagency and, obviously, in public. But it is known that they did agree on whatever the results of these tests showed.

When the Bureau submitted its results to Wold, its report stated that the flight suit, aside from the tests performed, belonged to either "an unknown suspect, unnamed victim or a missing person." They'd been given nothing to go on and, quite frankly, had the FBI lab been provided DNA for comparison, there might actually have been more answers. Their report described the flight suit in their custody as "olive green, very worn, heavily soiled with multiple pockets with zipper closures, a few snaps, and no inside labels." Lab technicians noticed that it was hard to tell the top of the suit from the bottom. Entire portions of it were missing. "Completely torn and shredded" were the descriptives they used. But there were still several Velcro areas sewn to the suit for squadron patches in addition to the cuffs, which they'd already noted in the report. The FBI examiner noted that the laundry tag Albano had said had Scott's name, which had been partly cut and only small parts of it were actually readable. What remained was badly faded but they were able to read portions of it that told them it was a United States Air Force summer issue flight suit. They photographed the flight suit for their records. The FBI's examination of the flight suit was inexplicably ordered discontinued on February 7 and a facsimile of its lab results sent to Trenholm at China Lake shortly thereafter.

The next day, February 8, Commander Jensen, Wold's assistant, signed out the flight suit, specimens and all test results at the FBI and took the specimens to the DNA Identification Laboratory at the Armed Forces Institute of Pathology (AFIP) in Rockville, Maryland. Jensen's was the last name officially recorded on the flight suit chain of custody log. The AFIP examined a small Ziploc bag containing stained green material; two portions of the left arm cuff, which had moderate stains that looked like dried blood; a crotch cutting and an armpit cutting. The specimens were analyzed using short tandem repeat (STR) analysis, but nothing conclusive is recorded in the report. This report, absent conclusive analyses, is signed off by two DNA analysts, Richard E. Wilson and Jeanne M. Willard; Dr. Mitchell M. Holland, branch chief of the AFIP DNA Laboratory, and Dr. Victor M. Weedn, the same DNA expert who five years earlier had run tests on DS1-256, the remains the Iraqis claimed was a pilot named "Mickel."

While the flight suit made its rounds of East Coast laboratories, Trenholm sent five small fragments of Scott Speicher's canopy bubble to Marlowe V. Moncur at Pilkington Aerospace on February 2. Moncur returned the samples five days later with a report that indicated the stretch acrylic that once made up Scott's canopy bubble had undergone "shrinkback," a process in which the thickness increases and in-plane dimensions decrease. "Surface shrinkback forces caused the fissuring and thickness increase evident in all the samples," she wrote. Based on the degree of damage to the samples, Moncur estimated that the canopy surfaces reached temperatures of 400° to 500° F, perhaps higher, while the core temperature remained below the minimum shrinkback temperature of 230° F. In other words, the canopy was exposed to intense heat that lasted only seconds. This was an assessment that gave Trenholm a better idea of the flash fire's intensity and duration. Although he was getting a pretty good picture of Speicher's last seconds in the Hornet, key elements were still missing.

Trenholm's report included an overview of F/A-18 ejection history. Investigators working Speicher's case had that history committed to memory. The first ejection from a U.S. Navy F/A-18 fleet squadron jet occurred on July 17, 1985. By the time Trenholm started looking hard at previous history there'd been fifty-eight aircrew ejections from fifty-two aircraft. Of the fifty-eight aircrew who'd ejected, forty-one were over land and seventeen over water. Six died. The six fatalities were due to three pilots initiating ejection out of the safe envelope to do so; one pilot's parachute melted during descent due to direct contact with his exploding aircraft; one pilot was not connected to his parachute; and one aircraft was struck. In the latter incident the pilot ejected and was wrapped in the ejection seat due to a freak asymmetrical drogue deployment. In no instance had a parachute been packed incorrectly. Of the forty-one ejections over land, about 70 percent received injuries, both major and minor, caused by shock loads that occurred during the parachute opening and, to some degree, in the descent or landing.

Based on the condition of parachute materials recovered in the Iraqi desert and review of past F/A-18 mishaps, Trenholm accepted or rejected parachute scenarios or ruled them "probable." "The parachute was a variable," he said later, "but not a factor." "We recognized that the parachute packed in Speicher's ejection seat was responsible for more injuries in the fleet than any other so we gave it proper attention in the report." He was referring to the GQ 1000 Aeroconical parachute. He rejected the possibility that the aircraft canopy failed to separate from the aircraft. Based on wreckage analysis, it was clear the pilot, Scott Speicher, initiated the ejection sequence. Trenholm further rejected the idea that the ejection system failed to function. The condition of the aircraft canopy and all ALSS items recovered on the site was inconsistent with an aircraft impact. The pilot couldn't have been in the aircraft when it struck the desert floor for the ICRC team to have found the items they did in the condition they were if Speicher had ridden the Hornet all the way down. If the ejection system had failed to depart the aircraft prior to impact, he explained, ALSS equipment packed with the seat is almost completely destroyed either as the result of extreme heat and/or impact with the ground or water.

From what was found in the debris field at Scott Speicher's crash site, investigators determined that Speicher's GQ 1000 Aeroconical opened during parachute descent. Though they couldn't say with 100 percent certainty if Speicher opened his parachute or the GQ 1000 deployed on its own, "it can be safely assumed it was opened based on the pieces of life raft found," said the report. The life raft, located in the seat pan of the ejection seat, normally disintegrates during a successful ejection. Strangely, the GQ 1000 was one piece of equipment that hadn't been recommended for overland ejection per NATOPS Flight Manual A1-F18AC-NFM-000. The GQ 1000 was a holdover of the blue water navy, to days when its aviators performed most of their duties at sea, not flying over land targets in Southwest and, later, Central Asia.

Based on Scott Speicher's quick exit from a hot cockpit, Trenholm included expected probable injuries and incapacitation from shock and, perhaps, a hard landing. Warren Ingram, assigned to the Emergency Egress and Crashworthy Systems Division at Naval Air Warfare Center China Lake performed a descent-rate analysis using a suspended weight of 218 pounds, consistent with the pilot's body weight and all his aviation life support equipment. He matched them to the meteorological conditions of the crash site on January 17, 1991. On the day Scott Speicher was shot down a frontal system brought very low temperatures and cloud cover with bases raised to eight thousand feet and ceilings from twenty to twenty-five thousand feet. Winds whipped from the south-southwest between six and twenty knots, increasing at higher elevations to over one hundred knots aloft. There was patchy fog in west central Iraq, and blowing sand and suspended dust reduced visibility to thirty-two hundred meters during the afternoon along the Saudi Arabia-Iraq border.

Ingram's analysis showed a minimum total velocity rate of descent of twenty-six feet per second and a maximum of thirty-three feet per second. The calculated rate of descent for Scott Speicher in his parachute might have been enough to inflict injury on landing. Injuries could have been anything from a bloody nose or a bitten tongue to compound fractures. But there was no indication of massive blood loss nor compound fractures from analysis of the flight suit.

Just before Bruce Trenholm issued his final report on the flight suit, Tony Albano got a message during a training flight that Trenholm was trying to track him down. Albano was executive officer of Training Squadron Nineteen (VT-19) in Meridian, Mississippi. Another squadron mate, Commander Mark Fox, was commanding officer of the Sunliners. Trenholm wanted to talk to him, too. They agreed to meet Trenholm at Cecil Field. Prior to the interview Trenholm asked that Albano and Fox bring squadron patches and that any photographs of Scott Speicher in his flight suit that they might have be sent to him for inclusion in his investigation file. They sent four pictures of Scott to Trenholm.

During their meeting at Cecil Field, Trenholm told Albano and Fox that he'd been on the ICRC mission to the Iraqi desert. He explained how the team was handed the flight suit. He wanted to know if Albano could look at it and see if he thought it was Speicher's. He told them about the Bedouin boy the Iraqis said "found" it, and that most of the Red Cross team figured the Iraqis planted it. He told them that the legs were slit up the back in a way that an emergency worker or doctor might cut a suit off someone who was facedown. He told them he'd estimated Speicher's height at 71 inches, his weight at 168 pounds and his flight suit size at 38 Long. Then Trenholm reached into a brown paper grocery bag and pulled out the suit.

The last time Albano had seen that flight suit, Speicher was wearing it and they were slapping hands, wishing each other luck on their first wartime mission. Now here it was. "He just pulled it out of the bag like it was nothing," said Albano. "We'd been talking and then there was the flight suit." Albano saw that the suit was worn and tattered. Pockets were missing and the patches gone. He knew that pilots removed those patches to sanitize the flight suit before combat missions. He also noticed something else: scorch marks. "The material of the flight suit won't scorch [flight suits have a chemical retardant that prevents them from burning; the material flakes away]. But there were scorch marks on the shoulders. They were too symmetrical for normal burn marks." Albano also noticed what he didn't see: no charring and little blood. He looked at Trenholm. "I'm positive that's his flight suit," he said. Then Fox hopped into his car, went to his house and grabbed his old flight suit. A circular patch of Velcro fastener on Speicher's right arm matched Fox's "Sunliners-Anytime-Anyplace" patch. An oval of Velcro on the left arm lined up perfectly with a patch their squadron gave out to those who earned it that read "F/A-18 Hornet 1000 Hours." Trenholm then told Speicher's squadron mates about the condition of the jet, and the canopy and the parachute straps and life support gear. Five years after that awful night, there seemed to be fewer answers than hoped. And the same old question. "Oh God," Albano thought. "Well, what happened to him?"

Albano reiterated that all the patches on their flight suits had been removed prior to combat missions, including the name tag over the left breast pocket. Trenholm disagreed. He maintained that the name tag had been left on Speicher's flight suit and that Spock Anderson gave permission to wear them. "That is not true," said Albano. "Nobody wore any squadron identification, including the name tag. That's fabrication. There were standing orders to every aviator in the fleet to take all that off their flight suits on a mission."

This was January or February 1996, Albano remembered. Trenholm's final report determined that the flight suit recovered in the Iraqi desert was "most likely worn by VFA-81 naval pilot LCDR M. S. Speicher." But there was no way to tell whether Scott Speicher wore the name tag that night. Odds are he didn't.

Bob Stumpf got a telephone call not long after the ICRC mission returned from Iraq. The caller said, "Hey, I saw his flight suit. They found a canopy." Stumpf thought, "Holy shit." Then he learned that there had been an option to go in and examine the wreckage covertly and apparently it hadn't happened. "That just blew me away. We have a contract with our soldiers, it's black and white, 'You go down, we're going to come get you. It doesn't matter if it takes a while. We're not going to forget you.'" But that's not what Stumpf saw happen with Scott Speicher. The evidence pointed to just the opposite. "Basically, what we said was, 'Screw you, Speicher. We're not going to honor our commitment to you. You gave your life for your country and we don't care.'" The canopy was not with the wreckage, which indicated an ejection. The flight suit was in pretty fair shape, not soaked in blood, so all the clues pointed to Scott Speicher walking away from the ejection. What happened to Speicher, in Stumpf's opinion, "should be unheard of. You can't do this job without some high level of patriotism and trust. It has to go both ways. The Pentagon just lost its teeth. Where is the spirit, the military spirit and tradition we've had for two hundred years? Where is it?"

Trenholm collaborated with other investigators to find answers. Physical evidence gathered at the crash site was analyzed and laid up against other bits and pieces of pilot gear. A picture started to form. They had located several pieces of Speicher's anti-G suit. The anti-G suit is made of a fire-resistant aramid cloth outer shell that houses a polyurethane bladder. The outer shell has waist and leg slide fasteners, adjustment lacing areas with lacing covers, and leg pockets that also have slide fasteners. The bladder system is constructed of polyurethane-coated nylon cloth and covers the pilot's abdomen, thighs and calves. The life support material recovered in the vicinity of his Hornet wreckage was consistent with portions of the CSU-15/P anti-G suit issued to navy aircrew. The six fragments found by investigators included the hose, a waist slide fastener, adjacent material to the slide fastener and two pieces of spacer and reinforcement material roughly thirteen inches and three inches in length, respectively. Though the upper arms of Speicher's flight suit showed signs of heat exposure, there was no evidence that the anti-G suit material was exposed to the flash fire that took place seconds before Speicher ejected from the jet.

One of the most encouraging finds among the debris of his Hornet was an SJU-5A ejection seat upper leg garter. The upper leg garter, connected to the pilot when seated in the aircraft and worn approximately three inches above the knee, is unique to the F/A-18 aircraft. Its purpose is to make sure the pilot's legs are pulled back when he ejects, thus enhancing the ejection seat's stability and preventing the pilot's legs from flailing during ejection. The garter was found in two pieces with about three inches missing. Like the anti-G fragments, the garter hadn't been exposed to heat.

By the time Trenholm was ready to issue his final report on Speicher's aviation life-support equipment it was February 26. His opening statement was double-speak. His area of expertise, by his own admission, is parachutes. He was specifically a parachute mishap investigator and mishap investigation support team leader at the time the Speicher case crossed his desk. He'd investigated some 350 aircraft mishaps, but none as lengthy as Speicher's. He'd become buried in information from the start. But he didn't follow the picture it drew of the pilot who'd now been missing for five years. This was a big deal. And it required follow through and evidentiary protocol that didn't happen with the flight suit. But it also didn't happen with the cockpit canopy analysis or the bits and pieces of gear strewn over the desert floor. In the end, a parachute investigator put a parachute investigator's spin on a missing person's case that required so much more.

From the pieces of life support equipment found in the search, Trenholm concluded, "Speicher ejected from the aircraft." But what else? Though the F/A-18 Hornet has a 85 to 90 percent survival rate on ejection, and no significant amount of blood or body tissue was on any of the equipment recovered, he still insisted that "the pilot may have been injured [or] incapacitated, perhaps fatally, due to trauma associated with ejection, parachute deployment or ground impact." Where was the proof? There wasn't enough left in the desert to know. Speicher's flight helmet, personal gear and parachute were never recovered. Yet during the investigation recall that Trenholm had said clearly: "The parachute was a variable, but not a factor."

J. Alan Liotta informed Secretary Perry on February 16, 1996, that there wasn't anything in the desert to prove Speicher was alive, almost two weeks ahead of investigators' final reports arriving in the Pentagon. He had nothing on which to base the statement he'd made to Perry. "When it came to Speicher," said Commander Chip Beck, "Liotta was simply not up to the task of conducting a challenging and competent investigation against the Iraqis about the topic of a potentially live and covertly held American." Beck, the CIA station chief and naval intelligence officer, was then working at DPMO. He remembered the time Liotta went into the field to oversee the crash site investigation in December 1995. "I had known Liotta for some years previously when he was a low-level and unexceptional analyst at CIA," said Beck.

Liotta didn't actually step into Iraq. Some news agencies, he observed, omitted that important detail. No, Liotta sat in a Land Rover on the Jordanian-Iraqi border long enough for the battery to die. When Liotta got back to DPMO's office in Crystal City he gathered the staff in a small conference room to go over the team's "findings." "After telling us of the ejection seat and lack of forensic evidence, Liotta, amazingly to me, concluded to the staff that 'We found no evidence that Lieutenant Commander Speicher survived the crash,'" said Beck. The silence from those around the table was both deafening and telling, he observed later. After a few seconds he challenged Liotta, saying out loud, "Excuse me, Alan, but you didn't find any evidence that he died either. You basically didn't find any evidence to support a conclusion of any type, so the investigation has to continue." The others in the room seemed surprised by his statement. He got a glare from Liotta, but no rebuttal, no response whatsoever. He also had no evidence from the team in Iraq and since he'd actually never set foot on the crash site, hadn't seen anything remotely resembling evidence. All Liotta had was hearsay and his own conclusion to pass to Perry. Scott Speicher's life hinged on the presumptive statement of a man unprepared and unwilling to do what it might take to save him.

What was going on in the Pentagon wasn't the only spin being put on the Speicher case. Baghdad had an agenda of its own to sell to the media. The Iraqi Air Force had sent two of its mishap investigators and its top general to the crash site as part of the ICRC team. General Khaldoun Khattab directed his men to pitch a large, heated tent for his use across the steppe from the ICRC's makeshift camp. Behind the general's tent sat two Russian-made Mi-8 Hip helicopters. The Iraqis used the Hip for Khattab's transportation but also to observe the ICRC's work from above. Trenholm was invited to Khattab's tent for coffee. "[We were] eating dates or something," he recalled. "He leans over, grabs my arm and says, 'The woolufs eat him.'" Not understanding, Trenholm asked Khattab to repeat what he'd said. "He was trying to say, 'The wolves ate him.' This was all too contrived and I almost didn't understand what he said at all." If Trenholm thought it was contrived, what did the media think?

Khattab repeated his wolf statement for them shortly after. Chip Beck knew Khattab was lying. But did the press?

"I was probably the only DPMO officer who had spent three or more years in North African and Middle East deserts and had seen what desert wolves do to bodies," said Beck. "First of all, they are more like big, mangy coyotes than the timber wolves we know, and they don't consume the bodies and bones in a way that would totally obliterate a pilot's remains." Beck had seen the bodies of fishermen washed up on the Sahara coastline after they'd been "played with" by desert wolves. "They can be pretty effective at spreading the remains around an area, but they are sloppy eaters and leave enough behind for a recovery team to find a fairly substantial amount of remains, certainly enough for DNA and forensic identification. The wolves would not likely eat the skull or the teeth, for instance, even if they broke [the skull] open for the soft tissue." Beck found whole skulls in the desert in areas where he personally witnessed wolves eating bodies. "I approached these 'wolves' unarmed to see what they were up to with the fishermen's bodies and they ran off. I never felt threatened at all."

But the Sahara coastline wasn't the desert plain between Iraq and Saudi Arabia, where the Arab wolf is one of the most impressive predators in the Middle East. Also called the gray wolf, it can grow up to six-and-a-half feet long and stands as much as three-and-a-half feet high. The Arab wolf weighs up to 120 pounds. It has powerful jaws and can sprint up to forty miles per hour. This is the desert version of the timber wolf. Packs of Arab wolves hunt strategically, organizing themselves into packs and communicating messages through different howl tones. They've been in Iraq for centuries. Though they've typically kept to devouring the Bedouins' cattle, sheep and goats, it is only in recent years, long after Speicher went missing in this Iraqi wasteland, that Arab wolves became highly aggressive toward humans. They are hungry. With the Bedouins now protecting their herds with tall fencing, their food source has dramatically declined. They now attack humans with increasing abandon. "They have tremendous qualities. They appear during the day and don't fear bullets and challenge even men holding rifles," said Mohammed Abu Reesha, a resident of Samawah.[1]

Still, the Iraqis had blatantly lied to the Americans, figuring they'd know nothing about wolves' nature, habitat and prey just then. Khattab told Trenholm a fable. The Qur'an tells the story of Joseph, whose brothers wanted to kill him to curry the favor of their father. The Bible tells a similar story, but the Qur'an's tale is what Khattab was thinking about as he wove his fantastic lie for Trenholm's benefit. The Qur'an's Joseph is thrown down a well. But his brothers tell their father wolves ate him. "They showed him the shirt with blood on it. [The father] said: 'It is not so, you have made up the story.'" Joseph was picked up by a caravan that had come to use the well. "'What luck,' said the man [in the caravan]; 'here is a boy,' and they hid him as an item of merchandise, worthless for a few paltry dirham." The story rung awfully familiar. But why did Khattab lie? The deception begged many questions that weren't asked and answered by the ICRC team then nor by anyone else later. But metaphorically, at least, Scott Speicher had much in common with Qur'anic Joseph, a boy whose father rejected news of his son's death, who held the bloody shirt in his hands and still didn't believe his brothers' deception, and, finally, got away from his killers through the obligatory kindness of nomadic Bedouins.

"I think we can conclude," said Beck, "that they were hiding knowledge of what really happened to Speicher." Of course they'd spun a lie to do it, pandering to the press with a fantastic tale of wolves devouring dead bodies. Khattab killed two birds with one yarn: he'd scare off tribesmen from the area with the wolf story and make the Americans think there was nothing left of their pilot. This doesn't fit, of course, the biggest fabrication of all, told to American Marines nearly thirteen years later, that yet another Bedouin boy had witnessed the burial of Scott Speicher. By then Speicher would have died a thousand deaths, from being blown to bits in his Hornet, dropped too hard by his parachute to being eaten by wolves. But none of what was found in the barren desert of Iraq in December 1995 supported any of this.

Khattab's fairytale was a prescient metaphor for the deception and lone-wolf agendas that followed the ICRC-sponsored crash investigation. Buran admitted that he, like each man on the team, was there with his own set of orders. Each had their own agenda. But the biggest one, by far, was Liotta's. He wanted to find Speicher's body under the jet. "What a way to go, what a way to send off a mission that could have gathered so much more," said Bob Dussault. The JCS and DPMO had all the information they could've wanted to keep the case open. But their agenda, their objectives, conflicted at best, got in the way. Chip Beck explained that he and Norman D. Kass, chairman of the Joint Commission Support Directorate (JCSD), spent eight hours in closed-door testimony answering questions from Congressman Bob Dornan's subcommittee on prisoners of war.

It was October 1996. DPMO had already demonstrated lackluster results in resolving the fate of thousands of unrepatriated prisoners from wars of the twentieth century. "We believed that in the case of Vietnam, in particular," said Beck, "and to a certain extent the cold war, Korea, World War II and World War I as well, this failure was intentionally contrived by longtime analysts, many of who had been in DPMO [and its previous iterations] for twenty-five to thirty years, to cover up the inaccuracy of their initial statements on live Americans." Now they had at least one publicly charged case from the Persian Gulf War to resolve. If they couldn't make it go away, the door might swing wide open for less known KIA-BNR and MIA cases from the Persian Gulf War that had yet to be discovered by the press or contested by their families.

Chip Beck was right. Liotta wasn't up to the task on Speicher's case. But nothing in his background would have suggested to his superiors that he was capable of leading the investigation either. He'd never served in the military. He had never been in the clandestine service of the CIA. He wasn't an investigator. He had no experience with original research nor firsthand collection. Beck had been all that Liotta was not: CIA case officer, chief of station, Naval Criminal Investigative Service (NCIS) agent, and naval intelligence officer. Beck had also done something else: he'd worked with Kass as a special POW investigator from November 1995 through October 1996. Liotta was so opposed to Kass' special initiative to flesh out the truth of what had happened to unrepatriated prisoners of war held for decades by Soviet and Soviet Bloc intelligence services "that he actually became part of an integral DPMO effort to sabotage and end our investigations along this path," Beck said later.

DPMO's actions, Liotta's in particular, stalled the Speicher investigation before it had a chance to gain momentum. "[Speicher] may just be the last, or most recent, in a long line of ghosts who did not die when we wanted them to be dead." Those who wanted him, who wanted all of them, to be dead became a disquieting backdrop to the Speicher investigation. No one knew (not always) who the "they" were nor how the manipulation might affect evidence, witnesses and testimony. But they were there. And each had their own reasons for never wanting a live American pilot to walk out of Iraq.

Particulars of the Speicher investigation just got worse. When Bob Dussault requested the flight suit in the spring of 1996 for independent testing, Liotta's office told him it was lost. Dussault and JSSA director colonel Chapman were shocked that the flight suit couldn't be located. Liotta pointed the finger at the FBI. He said they'd "misplaced the suit." "We received a letter from DPMO stating that it had been sent to the FBI and got lost either at the FBI or in transit back to DPMO," said Dussault later. But all Dussault knew then was that it could not be found. This was odd. That flight suit was the key piece of evidence in the case of a missing navy pilot. How could it be lost? How could it be misplaced? But Liotta hadn't told JSSA the truth. Commander Jensen, who worked for Liotta's boss, James Wold, was the last person to sign the flight suit out of FBI custody on February 8, 1996. He'd taken the suit to the AFIP in Rockville, Maryland, then back to Wold's office. "At some point," said Trenholm, "the flight suit gets back to me. I had it for over a year. But around Christmas 1997, I decided to send it by mail to the CILHI. They say they never got it." Trenholm kept the flight suit out of chain of custody in a paper grocery bag under his desk. He broke custody again by sending it via regular U.S. Mail without tracking and signature requirement by the receiver. But was the flight suit really "lost" or was that a cover story to keep a key piece of evidence from being further examined just then?

Shortly after that Christmas, Trenholm got a call from "somebody in the Pentagon" who wanted the flight suit again. "But I had to tell him, 'Sorry, buddy, no can do.'" That's when he explained that he'd tucked the flight suit, specimens and test results into a simple mailing envelope and dropped them in the closest mail drop during the holiday mail rush. Nobody, he said, told him that there was anything particularly important about the flight suit since Speicher had been declared KIA-BNR. Speicher's status change was admittedly confusing. He was retroactively made an MIA from May 23, 1991, to September 30, 1996, then switched back the next day to what he'd been: KIA-BNR. "He's dead, so what's the big deal about the flight suit?" he said later. But the chain of custody nightmare, exemplified by the flight suit, also smacked of people who couldn't get their story straight. "Somebody has it and they consider it terribly sensitive to mention who, either because it reveals too much that they do not want others to know," said Dussault, "or because they mishandled it and did not do the proper testing of all the evidence available. That would make them look dumb if that came out."

By the end of December 1997, whether the flight suit was lost or someone had it secreted away, it was unavailable for further testing. With it went important test results, DNA samples, including specifics of the Caucasian body hair, reddish-brown canine hair and carpet fibers, fingerprint analysis and forensic reports, all of which stood to play a crucial role in Scott Speicher's status: dead or alive. Nearly two years later, in July 1999, DPMO told the Senate Select Committee on Intelligence (SSCI) that the flight suit and ALSS equipment that were worn by Scott Speicher the night he was shot down had been cut off the pilot and that their condition suggested the pilot was severely injured or dead when it was done. Yet another report told them that the flight suit was in tatters, with portions of the legs missing altogether. But other reports attached to the flight suit and ALSS equipment state just the opposite. There was no way to figure this out with the flight suit missing. And there was no way to get a look at photographs of the flight suit because the Pentagon claimed one of two problems when asked to produce them: they were classified or they were lost. Which was it? It couldn't be both.

Like everything to do with Scott Speicher's case, there's always a bottom line. In this case the bottom line belongs to the flight suit handed over to the ICRC in the Iraqi desert: it "disappeared" within two weeks of Senators Smith and Grams' pressing DPMO for answers. In this respect, the flight suit seemed to follow the path of the ejection seat's and cockpit section's disappearing act. Still, to those who tried to use the flight suit to suggest Speicher had died, they'd not made their case. They'd also not done their homework, followed forensic protocol or maintained chain of custody for a critical piece of evidence. The flight suit's "loss" was just a fragment of the overwhelming denial, deceit and deception that would ensue in this case.

Endnotes

1. Halawa, Hassan and Borzou Daragahi, "Iraq wolves are big, bad and unafraid," *Seattle Time*s, March 20, 2008.

Chapter 9

Denial, Deceit and Deception

Defense Secretary William Perry said Scott Speicher's crash site yielded nothing that said he was alive. But this didn't keep navy secretary John H. Dalton from modifying the presumptive finding of death from May 23, 1991, to September 30, 1996. For that period of time Dalton made Speicher an MIA retroactive to the day after he'd been placed in the KIA-BNR status. He was also promoted to full commander on the basis of his time in grade during the period in which he was now declared MIA. But Dalton didn't leave Speicher in an MIA status.

After reaching an agreement with Joanne Speicher-Harris, the navy reaffirmed Scott's KIA-BNR status as of October 1, 1996. Joanne was given Speicher's unpaid pay and allowances for the period in which he was retroactively declared an MIA. This came to $330,858. His back pay and allowances was in addition to Scott's $150,000 Servicemembers' Group Life Insurance (SGLI) and a $50,000 special death gratuity she'd been paid in 1991. Though she was no longer, by law, Scott Speicher's primary next-of-kin, Joanne was the mother of his children and the Navy Department made the decision, after discussion with her, that she should get the money. Scott's adoptive parents were dead and his sister, Sheryl Speicher Long, wasn't in contact at that time with Joanne and Buddy Harris. Was it legal? No. Was there precedent to guide the navy in its decision? Yes. But this wasn't a black-and-white issue. There were moral and ethical considerations that transcended legal guidelines. There was the "right thing to do" and barring anyone arguing against it, Perry and Dalton made the decision to honor Scott Speicher's former wife with the payments due her and their children.

Certainly, one case should have clearly stood out to Perry and Dalton: Charles E. Shelton[1]. Air force captain Charles E. Shelton was promoted to the rank of colonel during his captivity. He was in a POW status for twenty-nine years from his date of loss and remained the only service member in that status who was never arbitrarily declared dead by the United States government until October 4, 1994, after his children petitioned the air force to change his status to KIA-BNR. This was exactly four years to the day after Shelton's wife's death. Secretary Perry signed off on it. This didn't prove Colonel Shelton was dead. This was death by a piece of paper. But Shelton's case demonstrates that absolute proof of life doesn't always get the missing man home, most especially when the Pentagon abdicates its obligation to do everything in its power to bring home one of its own.

Around 11 a.m. on April 29, 1965, his thirty-third birthday, Captain Shelton's RF-101C Voodoo aircraft left Udorn Air Base, Thailand, as the lead plane in a flight of two aircraft on a photo reconnaissance mission over northern Laos. His wingman, in the second aircraft, was Captain Richard L. Bilheimer. Shelton was on his second tour of duty in Southeast Asia. Based in Okinawa, he was on a thirty-day rotation to Udorn and set to return to his home base in Japan that night to celebrate his birthday with his wife, the former Dorothy Marian Vollman, and the couple's five children. Bad weather aborted his attempt to get a photograph of the first target so he and Bilheimer moved on to the second, located near Sam Neua, less than fifty miles from the Lao-North Vietnam border and less than one hundred miles from China's Yunan Province.

Sam Neua was home to the communist Pathet Lao headquarters, with command facilities, training centers, communication equipment and personnel quartered in a maze of mountain and river caves. Shelton and Bilheimer descended to 3,000 feet above ground level as they neared the target. Shelton was lining up for his first photo at 11:59 a.m. when fire erupted down the centerline of his jet. Shelton asked Bilheimer if he'd been hit.

"Roger. You are on fire," Bilheimer told him.

The canopy flew off Shelton's aircraft. Bilheimer reported Shelton ejected and parachuted to the ground. All of this was true. A few hours later two rescue aircraft spotted Shelton and his parachute on a tree-covered ridge line. They talked to him by radio and told him a SAR helicopter would be picking him up in a half-hour. Shelton told them he was in good shape and used his radio to direct SAR to his location.

Back in Okinawa Shelton's wing commander told Marian that her husband had been shot down, that he was alright and evading capture, and that he should be picked up by midnight her time. Before he'd left Okinawa for Udorn, Charles Shelton told Marian about the family's finances, advised her on what kind of car and house to buy, and he told her he loved her. He tried to put her mind at ease. Death was always the greatest threat, but Laos was supposed to be a "safe" flight. Neither of them had heard of any Americans captured in Southeast Asia. But it was early yet.

SAR helicopters tried to pick up Shelton but bad weather closed in and they backed off. After the sun went down Shelton pulled his parachute from a tree, buried it and hid from approaching Pathet Lao troops sent out to find him. With a shroud of low cloud cover and darkness closing in, it was impossible for rescue crews to see Shelton. But radio contact with him indicated he was still okay and evading the Pathet Lao. SAR was suspended until first light on April 30. But persistent inclement weather conditions again put off a SAR for Shelton. When the weather finally broke on May 2, it was too late. Shelton wasn't where they'd last seen him. The search was called off three days later and Shelton was listed as missing in action believed captured. Officially, he was missing in action-captured, a status later affixed to Scott Speicher.

The search for Shelton involved 148 aircraft missions and 360 flight hours. This didn't include missions flown by Air America, the CIA's air arm. Shelton evaded the Pathet Lao for three days before he was captured by two platoons of their militia. A villager reported his capture and Shelton's status was changed to prisoner of war. From witness statements and intelligence reports, lots of them, Shelton was an uncooperative prisoner from the start. He tried to escape many times. Reports received by American intelligence from villagers, informants, Pathet Lao defectors and refugees were summarized and tucked in Shelton's casualty file. Documents in his file tell the story: from his well known escapes, constant resistance and rescue attempts to Shelton killing three of his interrogators. There is also something else in the file that wasn't released publicly. There was a search team sent into Laos to look for Shelton, inserted on his last known coordinate by Air America in 1966, long after Shelton went down. The air force intelligence report explained that among the men dropped into the search area was Captain Richard Bilheimer, Shelton's wingman. This was unprecedented – to put a pilot on the ground looking for another pilot. But they needed Bilheimer to show them where Shelton was last seen. Shelton was nowhere in sight. When word leaked out that Bilheimer had been on the mission, the air force claimed to have no record of his participation.

But there was more. Recall the CIA's involvement with Scott Speicher after the Falcon Hunter came across the wreckage of his downed Hornet. No one could believe that the CIA would be party to leaving an American pilot in the Iraqi desert, but they had a lot of practice doing just that long before Speicher ever came into play. Both State Department and CIA reports show that there were at least four teams dispatched to the Sam Neua area to hunt for Shelton after he was a known prisoner of war. At least one of these planned attempts was vetoed, according to retired air force general Richard Secord, who reported that he planned a 1967 rescue attempt to get Shelton and another air force officer imprisoned with him, Captain David L. Hrdlicka, but his CIA superiors said no. Instead they went with an alternative plan that failed.

Various sources further report that Ernie Meis, a retired photo reconnaissance pilot, stated that he'd taken aerial photographs of a prison cave in August 1968 for yet another planned Shelton rescue mission. He was briefed that Shelton was being held there in a shallow pit with bars on top of it, a special holding pen designed just for Shelton because he'd tried to escape so many times. Meis was told a guard stood over Shelton with a hand grenade while others nearby fixed bayonets to their rifles to poke at him to keep him awake. Then Meis was informed of the rescue attempt. He flew the mission and took ground fire, but got the pictures the CIA and Special Forces needed to make their plans. He didn't know when a rescue might take place. But in 1983 a former CIA agent told him about it. The operation was code named Duck Soup. An exact date of the mission is classified, but sources say it was 1971 and it was to include the rescue of Shelton and Hrdlicka. After being moved between Laos and Vietnam, and later Russia, Shelton was returned to northern Laos. By then it was well known that Washington had started negotiating with Hanoi for its prisoners of war. But there were no negotiations with the Pathet Lao who held hundreds of American aviators and Special Forces prisoners. The CIA sponsored a small team of Hmong tribesmen to get inside the Sam Neua prison complex and lead Shelton and Hrdlicka out.

No one would publicly know anything about the CIA-supported Hmong mission had Rosemary Conway, a CIA operative captured in Laos in 1975, not broken confidentiality and talked about it. She was expelled from Laos shortly after capture and returned to Chicago, where she started working with Hmong refugees coming to the United States to escape persecution by the Pathet Lao. A year later, in 1976, two of them told her about the CIA and Special Forces mission that had entered Sam Neua to rescue Shelton and Hrdlicka with the help of Hmong tribesmen, who'd successfully gotten entry to the prison holding facilities. Duck Soup got them out and Shelton and Hrdlicka stayed free for ten days before being returned to their captors. No one knows exactly why. But it has been suggested that they were returned either to gather further intelligence about the communist Pathet Lao headquarters where they'd been held, to protect their rescuers' cover or that the party was attacked and Shelton and Hrdlicka were recaptured.

In yet another version of events, it was reported that their rescuers, who'd posed as communists, showed off their American "prisoners," a ruse that worked until they came up on a village where a North Vietnamese Army (NVA) company had camped. The NVA commander told them it was strict policy to turn over American prisoners to them and the rescue team decided the risk to their cover was too great and gave Shelton and Hrdlicka back to the North Vietnamese. It doesn't really matter how it happened. Shelton and Hrdlicka went back to prison. Another CIA mission had failed. When asked about Duck Soup later, the American ambassador to Laos, William H. Sullivan, said that while the operation "rang a bell in his mind" he couldn't "remember what it was." But then he added, and multiple sources now report, that he believed it had something to do with the rescue of a prisoner of war who was returned to his captors because of the death of one of his liberators.

The truncated version of the Shelton story is this: Marian Shelton knew nothing of any of these events except that her husband was still alive and rescue attempts had been made. She was told not to speak of her husband's shoot-down. The American embassy in Vientiane, Laos, cabled Washington with warnings to be ready to spin the story or keep silent about the shoot-down altogether. Laos was still "denied" territory. Someone would have to think of a credible reason why an American military jet was over Lao airspace. Then came the May 13, 1967 photo in the *Vietnam Courier* that bore the caption, "An American airman captured in Laos." That clipped newspaper photo is in Shelton's casualty file. The DIA blacked out his face, but the photo inserted in Shelton's file, the timing of its release in the *Courier*, all pointed to the man in the picture being Charles Shelton. Defense Department records further indicate that Shelton's picture appeared in a Soviet newspaper and he was named in a broadcast taped recording. It wasn't until after the war that Marian Shelton started to receive more information. She realized then that her husband was still alive and had been left behind. This part of the story – how the wife and the facts were treated – should ring familiar by now. The DIA told her on April 9, 1982, that it knew where Colonel Shelton was being held.

The United States didn't formally recognize the Lao communist regime and it refused to negotiate with the Pathet Lao for Americans the Lao publicly stated they held. Thus, Charles Shelton and scores of American service members were never released. Former DIA chief lieutenant general Eugene F. Tighe said that Vietnam, not Laos, holds the key to these missing Americans. "It's naïve to call Laos an independent nation," he said, because of Vietnam's military presence and influence over Vientiane. After Marian Shelton's death on October 4, 1990, Colonel Shelton's monthly active duty pay and allowances continued going to the Shelton family estate until his children put an end to it four years later. Colonel Charles Shelton's case was prequel to what lay ahead for Speicher. But mostly the public has forgotten Shelton and the emotions he stirred as America's only POW for twenty-nine years.

What happened to Colonel Shelton and all the other men and women who didn't come home from the Vietnam Conflict wasn't the only prequel to a tragic outcome in the Speicher case. More recently the April 17, 2011 *Salt Lake City Deseret News* documented the agonizing story of U.S. Army first lieutenant Jack J. Saunders, who went missing in action during the Korean Conflict. "Of all the horrific things that happen in war," concluded the *Deseret News*' Carma Wadley, "'missing in action' may be one of the hardest to bear, enveloping both tragedy and uncertainty. A few of those listed as MIA come back alive; many never come back at all." Saunders, who'd served with the Fifth Army in World War II, signed up for the army reserves after the war to get money to go to college. He was recalled to active duty when the Korean Conflict broke out. By the summer of 1950 Saunders was assigned to B Battery 15th Field Artillery Battalion, where he was a spotter, a job that often involved flying in small aircraft over enemy lines. Just before he was scheduled to come home in the spring of 1951, on February 13, his unit was overrun by Chinese forces near Hoengsong. Fighting was heavy and at the end of it all Saunders was unaccounted for.

More than seven months later, on September 27, 1951, letters from Major General William E. Bergin, adjutant general of the army, were delivered to LaRelle, Saunders' wife, and to his parents, Mr. and Mrs. John K. Saunders in Ogden, Utah. Bergin's letter summed up what the army knew. Since he went missing in action on February 13, First Lieutenant Saunders hadn't been located. "The Department of the Army is mindful," wrote Bergin, "of the anguish you have so long endured and you may rest assured that, without any further request on your part, you will be advised promptly if any additional information concerning your loved one is received." He ended the letter with an expression of his heartfelt sympathy and his hope that "the fortitude which has sustained you in the past will continue through this distressing period of uncertainty."[2] Though his letter guaranteed Saunders' family regular updates on his status, this is not what happened. Families with men missing in action were asked to contact the army if they heard from any soldiers who might have information on their loved ones. They were even supplied, observed Wadley, with instructions on how to write letters to prisoners of war in the hope that they might make it to the MIA.

LaRelle Saunders wrote Bergin on October 17, 1951, to let him know she'd spoken to Glen A. Rigby, who had gone MIA on February 12, the day before her husband, and who was a prisoner of the Chinese. Rigby was released and made his way back to United Nations lines. Rigby was lucky. He got out and came home alive. The fate of thousands of other prisoners of war, among them Americans, hung in the balance. China controlled the prisoner of war camps in North Korea in 1951. Information coming out of these camps from those who got home was incredibly important. "He informed me that he had been in a prison camp with my husband and he saw him the last time during the latter part of April [1951], LaRelle wrote to Bergin. "He mentioned that my husband is going as a P.F.C. [private first class] instead of an officer."

LaRelle Saunders' hopes must have been sorely dampened by the response she received from Major General Kenneth B. Bush, who thanked her for the information but cautioned: "Unofficial information has been received in numerous cases which indicates that personnel officially reported missing in action are prisoners. However," he added, "as the opposing forces [China, North Korea] are not observing the provisions of the Geneva Convention by reporting prisoners through the International Red Cross, the official status in such cases cannot be changed until the report that they are prisoners is confirmed."[3] If it didn't break her spirit, it broke her heart. The cover of the December 17, 1951 *Newsweek* showed two

American prisoners of war starring dolefully at the camera; one of them was Jack Saunders. This was a propaganda shot, one of several that the Chinese released to show the world their growing collection of American, Republic of Korea and United Nations forces prisoners of war. The magazine reported that "ignoring the Geneva Convention, the Reds have never reported the names or numbers of the prisoners they hold, let alone permitted the International Red Cross to inspect their POW camps or transmit food and medicines. But," the article continued, "a Red newsman's remark last week that 'you can expect less than half the missing to turn up prisoners,' jibed with General [Matthew Bunker] Ridgway's guess that, of the 10,988 missing Americans, 6,000 were atrocity victims. How the surviving U.S. POWs are treated is tipped off by the dreary faces in these dreary Red propaganda photos."

By this time the U.S. Army *thought* Saunders must be dead, one of the thousands of atrocity victims Ridgway predicted would not be coming home. The date of death assigned to Jack Saunders was April 30, 1951, but he wasn't moved from missing status to presumed dead until 1953. At war's end the armistice called for the return of all prisoners of war and all sick, wounded and dead soldiers, sailors and airmen. The United States got back some but not all of the men it knew were prisoners of war and otherwise missing in action.

Between 1991 and 1994 the North Koreans turned over to the United Nations 208 boxes of remains it alleged were American service members. Two of the thirty-one boxes turned over in 1993 contained the remains of Saunders; investigators found as many as seven men's remains commingled in some boxes. Saunders remains weren't conclusively identified until September 15, 2010, seventeen years after they were returned. Out of the 208 boxes, only thirty-five service members' remains have been positively identified. Saunders was identified using DNA samples from his sister Helen and a nephew and a dental match to his antemortem service record. Investigators also used information obtained from other prisoners of war, eyewitness accounts and information provided by the North Koreans when they turned over the boxes, all in an attempt to determine if it was really Saunders. Larry Greer, director of public affairs for the Department of Defense's POW/Missing Personnel Office (DPMO), told media that they didn't have a complete body "but we have enough." If there were "enough" of Jack Saunders, how, when and where did he die? *Thinking* versus *knowing* beyond a reasonable doubt when someone died take on entirely different meaning in a POW/MIA case. Saunders, in this respect, is no different from Shelton or Speicher. If Washington knew that Saunders and thousands of other American prisoners of war and missing in action were still alive after the armistice was signed on July 27, 1953, why did it not pursue repatriation of the nation's soldiers, sailors and airmen? In truth nothing was done and men like Jack Saunders had their files stamped "presumed dead" that year. This was a "paper" death, not a real one. Back to Speicher.

Scott Speicher's story would probably have ended for good on October 1, 1996, but suddenly new information started trickling out of Iraq. The Pentagon assigned a navy officer to keep Buddy Harris apprised of changes in Speicher's case. It seemed like every week or two Harris would get a call about a rumored Speicher sighting. A Canadian was in an Iraqi camp and acquired a Colt 1911 .45-caliber single-action handgun that Iraqis claimed they took from an American pilot. No, Harris told investigators, Speicher didn't carry that gun. But intelligence officers checked it out anyway and found out Harris was right. Then they came across another gun, a Beretta .45-caliber automatic that was also supposed to have belonged to Speicher. That handgun was traced to the British occupation of Iraq after World War I.

Then there was a Belgian Browning Hi-Power, a single-action nine-millimeter that Speicher purportedly bought before deployment; he'd flown into Oceana Naval Air Station and bought the gun from a Virginia Beach, Virginia gun dealer. The dealer confirmed he sold him the gun; he was positive, yes, it was Speicher who'd bought it. Speicher's initial loss had been reported in the *Virginian-Pilot* newspaper – he saw it. Ten years later, the *Pilot* published the six-part feature series on the Speicher case titled "Dead or Alive?" and it all came rushing back. The Hi-Power is similar to the Colt 1911 .45-caliber single-action. The holster for the Hi-Power and 1911 are interchangeable. Speicher was adamant, said the dealer, that he wanted to carry the Belgian Browning Hi-Power into combat. He'd done his homework, he explained. This was the sidearm carried by the British SAS and a number of other specialty services worldwide. Iraqi ruler Saddam Hussein often carried a Belgian Browning Hi-Power, as did many Iraqi military officers.

When asked about the Hi-Power later by researcher Joseph Frusci, Tony Albano said he was sure Speicher carried the standard issue .38-caliber revolver just as he did. They manned up together. Albano should know. So why did investigators look so hard at .45-caliber handguns if they knew he carried a .38 revolver? Did his searchers actually know what sidearm Speicher was carrying that night? Had they asked to make sure? Was the serial number checked against the carrier's gun locker records? This is assuming it was the .38-caliber revolver issued from the *Saratoga* gun locker. Back then a navy pilot could bring a personal sidearm on board ship and, if he so desired, that was the weapon he'd take into combat.

In another story an Iraqi doctor was said to have examined Speicher. Another man said he'd seen Speicher's name on a file when he was moving records to hide them from UN weapons inspectors. Many of these leads were dead ends. But were they? Other tantalizing information was impossible to run down. Saddam was still in power. Much of what was discovered while he was seated in Baghdad would have to wait until the day he wasn't. With every story Buddy and Joanne's anguish for Scott grew worse. Meghan and Michael, Scott and Joanne's children, were nine and seven. Buddy and Joanne had two children of their own. When they didn't know what to do, Buddy and Joanne would ask themselves a question: "If Scott walked in [the door] today, could we lay it on the line, say 'This is what we did' and feel comfortable telling him we'd done everything possible to keep our family normal and get him out?"

Back on Capitol Hill Senator Bob Smith was beginning to wonder whether what he'd been told after the ICRC mission was true. He had been assured by DPMO that there wasn't any evidence to support the conclusion Speicher survived his F/A-18 crash. But Smith had sources inside the Pentagon saying otherwise. There's more to it than you're being told, they said. Smith wanted to believe DPMO, but the more he thought about it the less certain he became. At first Speicher's Hornet was blown to bits in midair. Then they found it nearly intact in the desert. At first they said they'd sent a search team in to look for Speicher. Then it turned out they didn't. There were glaring inconsistencies.

Admiral Mike Boorda, chief of naval operations, got an overview of the Speicher case on May 14, 1996, after his staff determined Scott survived the ejection and he'd made it to the ground below. "We felt very confident," said Harris, "that he was alive on the ground. We went to Boorda and told him." He's never forgotten Boorda's reaction when staff from Harris' office told him what they knew about Speicher from evidence gathered in the Iraqi desert. Harris wasn't allowed to attend the briefing. But senior staff told him Boorda was completely shocked by the news. "They said his jaw just hit the desk. He couldn't believe it." Boorda listened to what they said, thanked the staff and asked a couple of minor questions: You sure? You positive? They explained everything Boorda asked. "His staff knew he was going through tough times, so they didn't want to push it," said Harris.

The next day Boorda wrote two suicide notes. The following day, May 16, he committed suicide in the side yard of his navy yard residence. "I think [the briefing] was one of the nails in his coffin," Harris explained. "Boorda had so much on his plate at the time." Boorda's tenure as chief of naval operations was mired in controversy. He'd been caught up in the issue of women in combat, women attrited from the navy's flight training program that became a persistent media investigation that discovered he wasn't allowed to wear Vietnam Conflict decorations with the "V" for valor. But he also faced the unrelenting hostility of the majority of his flag officers, men who believed he'd betrayed the navy by allying himself with the Clinton administration's demands to reform the service's officer corps in the wake of the Tailhook scandal. None of these controversial topics were good for the navy, observed Harris. "I think when they went in and told him about Scott, it was the final blow."

Then it happened. Senator Rod Grams' staff read something in an early December 1997 *New York Times* that floored them. The *Times'* Tim Weiner cobbled together enough Pentagon documents and firsthand military sources to construct a timeline of the Speicher investigation. He looked at how it was handled, who'd found what and the conclusions they'd drawn from available information. Among other things the story reported that after the Qataris found the crash site, the Pentagon tasked a spy satellite to take a look. The satellite image "detected a manmade symbol in the area of the ejection seat," a ground-to-air signal, the kind a pilot is trained to put down to attract collection platforms' attention. DPMO claimed the symbol didn't match Speicher's assigned symbol, but that turned out to be a gross distortion of fact. Grams' staff called him in Africa. Then they called Senator Smith. Armed with misleading correspondence that caught DPMO in an outrageous lie, Grams issued a press release stating Congress had been purposefully misled.

Days later Senator Smith fired off two letters. The first, dated December 10, was addressed to Assistant Secretary of Defense for International Security Affairs Franklin D. Kramer, whose office oversaw the ICRC mission for the United States. Smith told him he was extremely troubled about the article, especially considering what he had been told about Speicher's chances of survival. He asked for a meeting with Pentagon and DPMO staff: "Especially in view of a briefing I received on this case by Alan Liotta from DPMO on January 17, 1996, where I was told that there were no indications that Commander Speicher might have survived his loss incident." Smith instructed Kramer, Fred Smith and Alan Liotta to meet with him on Monday, December 15, to discuss both the intelligence and the DoD policy applied to the Speicher case. "I would also request," he wrote Kramer, "that you bring the documentation referenced in the *New York Times* article, including the document referencing the detection of 'a manmade symbol in the area of the ejection seat.'" The second letter, cosigned by Rod Grams, was addressed to Alabama Republican senator Richard C. Shelby, chairman of the Senate Select Committee on Intelligence (SSCI). Smith and Grams asked the SSCI to open an inquiry into all intelligence information gathered in the Speicher case. "The enclosed article published in the *New York Times* this past Sunday raises serious questions as to whether both of us may have been misled by the [Clinton] administration," they wrote Shelby.

Shelby took it from there. He contacted CIA director George J. Tenet and asked for computer files, documents, memos, raw reports, and operational messages, basically anything and everything Tenet had on Speicher. He asked Tenet to explain which of the nation's intelligence agencies considered itself responsible for the investigation.

Bob Smith then called Grams to join the meeting with Kramer, Fred Smith and Liotta scheduled for December 15. A few days earlier Grams issued a hard-hitting statement on the Speicher case that struck hard at the actions of the Pentagon and Clinton administration. "An American pilot is missing. I have directly questioned the administration about his fate, and frankly, their answers don't square with the facts. In light of this apparent misinformation, it is the Senate's obligation to step in and discover the truth." Bob Smith entered the December 15 meeting angry. He wanted answers. What he got was appeasement.

What the senators didn't know was that it appears Kramer, Fred Smith and Liotta had conspired before the appointment on how they'd get the senators off their backs. And they clearly believed they'd succeeded. On the afternoon of the same day they'd met Fred Smith sent an e-mail to Kramer and copied Liotta at 5:57 p.m. "It started out rather testy," he wrote, "but after responding to several of [Senator] Smith's questions, he became more relaxed and we had a civil discussion. Grams was concerned about a letter to him from Jim Wold [then deputy assistant secretary of defense for POW/MIA Affairs] earlier this year. Grams claims the letter was misleading."

Fred Smith said he looked at the letter Grams received from Wold and agreed. The March 3, 1997 Wold letter, copied to the Navy Casualty Office and the secretary of the navy, was misleading, from start to finish. Wold wrote: "Mr. Daly [Richard Daly, Grams' Minnesota constituent] first asks if there is any evidence that Commander Speicher survived the crash. At present we do not have any evidence that he survived the loss incident. Our specialists," he continued, "have investigated the probable crash site and Commander Speicher's F/A-18. Evidence from this site is undergoing analysis and will be released when the investigation is complete and Commander Speicher's family has been fully informed." But this "investigation," at least the part concerned with the ICRC mission two years before, had already been determined. He had to be dead. What was it Liotta told Perry in February? Evidence was "insufficient to determine the fate of the pilot." It wasn't likely a coincidence that the flight suit went missing just weeks later after the *New York Times* piece made public the denial, deceit and deception peddled to Congress and the American public by the Pentagon and DPMO. Before the end of December the most tangible piece of forensic evidence recovered in the Iraqi desert was gone. "Lost" was the word Liotta used. But was it really?

Daly's query about the manmade ground-to-air signal got a curious reply. "Mr. Daly's final question is whether pilot distress symbols were found near the crash site," wrote Wold to Grams. "Again, we do not possess any evidence that evasion codes assigned to Commander Speicher were located near his crash site." Weeks later, on April 26, Wold wrote: "Our investigation of this incident has found no symbols that correlate to civilian or military distress symbols or evasion codes." But the majority of the hour-and-a-half December 15 meeting was spent talking about the manmade symbol in the vicinity of Speicher's downed Hornet and the fact that the navy declared Speicher KIA-BNR so quickly. "On the latter," wrote Fred Smith, "I assured [Senator] Smith that the navy's designation of the case has no bearing on how we prosecute it. It is an active case."

Bob Smith seemed reasonably satisfied. But Fred Smith didn't think Bob Smith was the real threat. He was "handled" in the meeting. "The problem," Fred Smith wrote to Kramer, "is his staffers. These guys will probably be spurred on by what they heard today and continue to press the issue in some form, possibly a hearing at a later date." Senator Smith had been outmaneuvered by a glib-tongued master. Fred Smith calmed him with facile answers. It didn't matter if he was telling the truth. He was answering questions and putting the senator at ease. Bob Smith's anger subsided as the meeting moved along. After Fred Smith sensed the meeting was on firm footing, he offered to meet Senator Smith for breakfast. "[Senator] Smith was pleased to hear that," he wrote later. Then he added this under the header "Footnote": "The first and last thing [Senator] Smith wanted to talk to me about was baseball. He still remembers the fact that you [referring to Kramer] and I are Dodger fans."

Liotta answered the following morning. When he e-mailed Fred Smith at 11:01 A.M. he told him that the night before CILHI sent him a map of the area the ICRC team searched and the site of the symbol. Liotta told Fred Smith that the symbol was "well within the area." "In fact," said Liotta, "NIMA says the symbol is about nine hundred meters [less than a kilometer or a click] away, but the team searched five clicks out. I still think you should call Smith and Grams, but insist on talking to the members, not staffers." But the Iraqis hadn't let the ICRC team search the area of the ground-to-air signal. NIMA hadn't evaluated the image. JSSA had done that.

Liotta continued to argue whether the letter Wold sent to Grams was misleading. "By the by, I still disagree with you that our letter was misleading. If you look at the original constituent letter, how that was sent to us by Grams, and the facts surrounding the case (including the classification of the imagery and the analysis), our response was factual and accurate. Could it have been more robust?" he asked. "Possibly, although we then would have been treading dangerously close to disclosing classified information. Should we have called to brief Grams? In hindsight, yes. But given the way the request was received from his office, we had no indication of any particular interest in this case. We'll be more sensitive next time." Liotta had already skewed the findings of the ICRC investigation. He'd dismissed JSSA's certification of the ground-to-air signal. The significance of the latter would only come out later when Tim Connolly was told of JSSA's insistence that the ground-to-air signal was Speicher's. Exclusion of that information from discussion in 1994 of whether to go covertly or use the diplomatic option had disastrous consequences. "Well, that's one-eighty out from what was said then," said Connolly. "Knowing about the manmade symbol would've made a huge difference. The diplomatic option would've been taken totally off the table." But Liotta had kept that information from the meeting. No one from DPMO said a word.

Almost four years after Connolly's Kuwaiti secret police colonel was brought to DPMO's attention, Liotta finally requested analysis of his information. He said he saw an American pilot in a hospital in An Nasiriyah, where he was also a patient. David M. Rosenau sent an e-mail to Gregory K. S. Man and copied Gary C. Sydow, Lieutenants Kevin Wilson and Robert T. Pasquerella, James R. Caswell, Melvin E. Richmond Jr. and Jo Anne Travis, all staffers with different offices of the Department of Defense. The e-mail was dated February 18, 1998. Liotta's staff offered recipients a one-page evaluation of the sighting. They said the colonel's information didn't marry up to any known American loss incident.

The only possible loss it could have been, they insisted, was a British GR-1 Tornado crew shot down January 19, 1991. Flight Lieutenants Robert Stewart and David Waddington were injured during their ejection. Both were treated for those injuries before being transported to Baghdad. The British crew's shoot-down didn't dovetail perfectly with what the colonel said. As hard as they tried, Liotta's staff couldn't get it to fit. Colonel Abdullah Al Jairan stated that he'd seen the American pilot about fifteen days before he reported the sighting to Connolly on March 4, 1991. This didn't match up to the Tornado loss. But that didn't matter to Liotta's staff. They accused the colonel of "reporting hearsay information as firsthand." They'd never interviewed him. They'd never met him. Yet they were ready to marginalize his information without further investigation. After he returned to Kuwait, Colonel Al Jairan disappeared. He's not been relocated since he spoke to Connolly.

An Nasiriyah is nearly 230 miles southeast of Speicher's crash site. Based on known Iraqi POW handling procedures, DPMO further concluded that Speicher wouldn't have been taken to An Nasiriyah. "All Allied pilots shot down and captured west of Baghdad," they said, "were transported along the East-West Highway directly to Baghdad where they remained until release." They assumed Speicher had been captured the day he was shot down. They also assumed that Speicher was the only pilot who might have had ejection injuries. Could it have been a pilot who later died of injuries? Was it a pilot whose remains were returned to American control? Could it have been a pilot never returned at all?

No one ever got the chance to put missing aviators' pictures in front of the Kuwaiti colonel for identification. There's no question that letting the colonel get a look at a photo array would have helped CENTCOM know whether the Iraqis were holding back prisoners. And it just might have gotten another man home. Four years later it was too late for DPMO to pursue Colonel Abdullah Al Jairan's sighting of the man he'd seen languishing in an An Nasiriyah hospital bed. Instead DPMO chose to debunk old information that no one could rebut. The colonel was nowhere to be found. "The Kuwaiti intelligence officer [he was secret police] did not see LCDR Speicher," their report concluded.

Senator Shelby wrote to CIA Director Tenet again in March 1998. He wanted Tenet to produce a report that consolidated everything they knew about Speicher from the CIA, DIA, NIMA, ONI, National Security Agency (NSA), and the JCS. He wanted everything. Kevin Wilson wrote an e-mail to Bob Pasquerella on March 10. The message was originally classified secret, but it pertained to his review of material responsive to Shelby's request. Wilson told Pasquerella that Liotta "liked the overall package. Couple of things. He wants to be more specific on areas of interest. Please look," he wrote, "at the three items and try to be more definitive on the area." The first item: "LCDR Speicher is suspected of being shot down by an air-to-air missile fired from an Iraqi aircraft or by a surface-to-air missile fired from an unidentified antiaircraft battery. Provide any records that relate to the shoot down of Coalition aircraft on 17 January 1991." The second item was completely redacted. The third statement asked for details of Iraqi forces on the site of Scott Speicher's location after he was on the ground. This item is presumptive and not based on any known fact from that night. "Air Defense and/or Republican Guard units were most likely active in the area of LCDR Speicher's loss location. Identify and make available for interview any individuals from Air Defense or Republican Guard units in the area at the time of the loss that may have information pertaining to this incident or LCDR Speicher's fate."

Speicher wasn't shot down by a surface-to-air missile. This had been well established before Wilson wrote his e-mail to Pasquerella. Harris' call to the CIA years prior had already cleared this up. Carlos Johnson corroborated this finding of an air-to-air shootdown, thus definitely eliminating the SAM as the shot that took down Speicher's Hornet. So had film from airborne surveillance platforms that caught the air-to-air engagement on infrared tape and A-6E Intruder crewmen wearing night vision goggles. None of them caught a SAM rising up to take down Speicher's jet. When the ICRC team examined the actual wreckage of his F/A-18 they concluded, too, that it was an air-to-air missile that had taken down the plane.

Despite the evidence that a SAM hadn't taken down Speicher, the Pentagon continued to beat the drum. Two months after the first e-mail from Wilson to Pasquerella, Pasquerella replied to Wilson on May 11, 1998. The e-mail, originally classified secret, copied Gregory Man and Gary Sydow. He wanted all of them to know that "in an effort to identify the cause of LCDR Speicher's shoot down, I recommend reviewing the imagery within a 25 NM [nautical mile] radius of the crash site located in 1994 at 33°01'114N 042°15'28E (UTM 38S KB 43810 56910)." Pasquerella said "the most likely scenario is that LCDR Speicher was shot down by an AAM launched from a MiG-25 Foxbat; however, it is also possible he was shot down by an SA-6 SAM fired from an unidentified location." The latter statement was as wrong as it had been on January 18, 1991, when Carlos Johnson told Speicher's chain of command how he was shot down.

After what he'd read in the *New York Times* Senator Smith wasn't about to let the issue drop. There hadn't been anything in the *Times* article he'd not seen before. But the mainstream media had caught on to the story and he couldn't ignore the possibility that an intelligence failure and a cabal of mistakes, missteps and presumptive findings had conspired to leave one of America's best and brightest fighter pilots behind in the desert of Iraq. The family had been misled and lied to from day one. Smith had been given the runaround by Pentagon staff and several federal agencies. "Members of the intelligence community had been misled and it's all pretty outrageous," declared Smith later. "The fact of the matter is there's a great amount of evidence and testimony that Mr. Speicher could have survived the impact, may well have survived it and been taken to prison." From the information he'd seen Smith knew for sure that Speicher hadn't been killed when his Hornet impacted the desert floor. But there was more information, much more, to come.

It started with an Iraqi man who'd defected in 1999. He had a story, one that was hard to believe and that many tried to discredit as the purported mystery of Scott Speicher's disappearance unraveled. They called him "the driver." He'd been asked by Baghdad to proceed to a town outside the capital – in the Bedouin tribal area – to pick up a American prisoner. He told investigators he'd picked up the man, who wore a flight suit and had no significant injuries other than a small amount of dried blood on his uniform. The driver took the pilot directly to Baghdad and turned him over to military authorities.

When DIA got the driver for interrogation, they showed him many photos, some were of American service members who'd been held by the Iraqis during the war – the ones who'd been repatriated – and some were suspected KIA and MIA. They showed him photos of some who'd never been in Desert Storm. A photo of Scott Speicher was mixed in each time. The driver quickly pointed out Speicher as the pilot he'd shuttled to Baghdad. He never hesitated. He was not confused. They asked him if Speicher was picked up from "locals" who'd roughed him up four to six weeks after his shoot-down. He said no. He'd picked up Speicher *years*, not weeks, later. When DIA tried to trick him, he could not be tricked. He picked the right photo each time.

DPMO received the driver's debrief report. None of what the driver said could be misinterpreted. The DIA had provided an expert linguist to make sure that didn't happen. But DPMO continued, no matter what the driver had said, to say Speicher was long dead.

For weeks investigators grilled the driver. He passed one lie detector test after another They continued to interrogate him through 2000, just to be sure. He never wavered. Maybe he was looking for money? They gave him a greed test: There's another missing American, they told him, whose family is offering a big reward – $10,000 in American dollars – if the pilot he saw was short in stature with blond hair. Are you sure he wasn't real short with blond hair? Maybe you saw a man who looked a little different? But the defector stuck to his story. The agents determined he was probably telling the truth.

But DIA and DPMO persisted; they tried to twist the driver's words. The driver had been emphatic that he'd picked up Speicher years, not weeks, after he was shot down. "If Scott were recovered from the Bedouins in early '91," wrote Bob Dussault on April 11, 2002, only six weeks or so after the conflict, and the rest of the driver's story about the killing of the Bedouins for protecting Scott were also factual, then why didn't word come out from sources who interacted with the Bedouins in the area and reported on the crash site, took photos, and said the Bedouins had Scott two years later in '94-'95?"

"I think the timing of six weeks after the conflict," Dussault continued, "is being claimed by some in the community in order to create doubts about the very strong intelligence case that the navy and the CIA have from their clearly very credible sources, which developed via two independent chains of events. What's the chance of that happening?"

"A lot of things like that went on early because anything that was found of a positive nature was kind of shoved aside, disbelieved, because he's dead," said Harris. He described the mentality of investigators: "We just want information on the fact that he's dead." Finally, around 1997, maybe 1998, that attitude began to change somewhat because of the volumes of information coming in that there was a reasonable chance Scott Speicher had survived. "All of it started stacking up," Harris said, "started moving in a different direction. We'd get information from various sources. I had some friends that I'd met from the Pentagon and who were still working on the case." They'd call him and say, "You need to look up this, you need to look up that. Something's going on here." Harris called the Pentagon each time and ask for the information. But he usually ended up going to Washington for a face-to-face meeting. The first question out of the mouths of those sitting across the table from him would inevitably be "Well, how do you know about this?" He'd reply, "It's what I heard, so what's going on?"

Harris met navy secretary Richard B. Danzig as often as he could. "He took it seriously and he wanted to get it solved." Danzig, said Harris, got pushback from Clinton administration politicians who didn't want to touch the case. "They didn't want the State Department involved," Harris explained. "They mainly used the argument that if they changed his status it would kill him, that as soon as the Iraqis saw that he was an MIA now, they'd know the U.S. was coming after him. They'd be scared and kill him."

Navy information showed that nine of ten pilots who'd ejected from F/A-18 Hornets survive. And the Iraqis had quickly tried to find and capture every pilot who was shot down during the war, usually with success. But if Speicher was taken to Baghdad, as the driver claimed, what happened next? Could he still be alive? Would Saddam Hussein, knowing the U.S. government was quick to declare him dead in 1991, keep a pilot incommunicado indefinitely? Why wouldn't he use his prisoner as leverage against sanctions, the United States' no-fly zone, UN weapons inspections? Investigators didn't have any answers, not just then. But they did have historical insight. Iraq released an Iranian pilot from prison in April 1998. Hossein Lashgari's plane was shot down over southern Iraq at the start of the Iran-Iraq War. He was captured on September 18, 1980, and held as a prisoner of war for more than seventeen years. "Baghdad and other Arab nations," Harris said, "but Saddam in particular, have a real tendency to hang on to people. They like souvenirs.

Saddam Hussein *really* loves souvenirs." Saddam's jails were filled with Iranians he'd taken into custody between 1980 and 1988, and the 605 Kuwaitis Saddam abducted from their country when he occupied it from late 1990 into early 1991. He never gave the Kuwaitis back. "An American pilot would just be a huge boon to him," said Harris.

Senator Bob Smith, with the driver's story in hand, spent much of 1999 and 2000 pushing navy officials to change Speicher's killed in action status. He thought Speicher should be missing in action. Smith and Grams wrote a letter to Danzig on March 19, 1999, asking that the secretary of the navy exercise his authority under Title 37 U.S. Code, Section 555(a) and 556(d) to reconsider and change or modify the "finding of death" determination made by Boorda on May 22, 1991, with respect to Lieutenant Commander Speicher. They told Danzig that Scott Speicher wasn't covered by the Missing Persons Act, Title 10, U.S. Code, Sections 1501-1510, amended, because he was still listed as KIA-BNR, thus making action under Title 37 the most appropriate course of action.

The March 19 letter to Danzig reviewed Congress' entire history with the Speicher case from 1996 forward. "The results of the crash site investigation," wrote Smith and Grams, "were briefed to Congress in the winter and spring of 1996. In December 1997, we were further briefed on this matter by the principal deputy assistant secretary of defense for international security affairs, Frederick Smith, in response to concerns generated by the attached *New York Times* story." While Congress was being briefed the Department of Defense had written off Speicher. This happened not once, but many times over. Secretary of Defense Perry determined on February 16, 1996, that evidence gathered at the crash site was "insufficient" to know what happened to Speicher based on what he was hearing from Fred Smith's office. Not knowing what was going on at the Pentagon, Congress continued to investigate on its own. In February 1998 Congress got a classified follow-up briefing provided to the SSCI by DPMO. That September, pursuant to Smith and Grams' earlier inquiries, the intelligence community and the Defense Department provided the SSCI a classified chronology outlining intelligence community activities pertaining to Speicher's loss. On the basis of what they read in the briefing materials and the chronology that had been provided, Smith and Grams strongly believed the information supported their request to change Scott Speicher's status from KIA-BNR to MIA.

Smith and Grams wrote a letter the same day to President Clinton. "We are writing to express our grave concerns that you and your administration have not done more to gain an accounting from the Government of Iraq for U.S. Navy Lieutenant Commander Michael Scott Speicher." They reminded the president in the second paragraph: "Speicher is the only serviceman still unaccounted for from that conflict," which was, of course, not exactly true. But they'd not investigated far enough yet to know any different. Soon they would hear the names Cooke, Dwyer, Paul J. Weaver, Clifford Bland, Paul G. Buege, and all the rest. There were more missing than Scott Speicher.

"We understand," Smith and Grams told the president, "that requests by Department of Defense officials to have this matter further pursued with the Iraqi government through the International Committee of the Red Cross have been placed on hold by your administration for three years now 'because of the state of U.S.-Iraqi bilateral relations.' We further understand that your National Security Council may not have focused on this matter during the last several years." They implored him to act as commander in chief of the armed forces. It took President Clinton, his administration and the United States Navy nearly ten months to do anything.

Senator Smith said in 2001 that he had many reasons for what he said in the letter to the president. "There was all kinds of things left out," he said. "We were just getting it in bits and parts. When I started the process I just assumed the man was dead. And frankly, my source that I had, I didn't believe my source. I thought, 'Well, hey, the guy's killed in action. Where's all this stuff coming from?'" He couldn't believe that he'd been so blatantly misled. "We were told by DPMO personnel that there was no other information." Then he found out what DPMO was trying to hide. "We found out there was a canopy, there was a piece of the plane, there was a uniform, there was a live sighting report and on and on and on."

Kansas Republican senator Pat Roberts asked the SSCI in July 1999 to conduct an inquiry into the intelligence community's input to Washington's decision to put Speicher on the KIA list. The SSCI focused on the role and impact of intelligence and how that information interfered with the government's ability to account for Speicher. The committee came to the conclusion that the discrepancy between the available intelligence information on Speicher and the navy's determination of his fate came down to government investigators and intelligence analysts who wanted to believe and were pushing the narrative that Speicher had been killed in the early morning hours of January 17, 1991.

The committee held a closed briefing on September 15, 1999, and a closed hearing on October 28, 1999, to examine the case in secret. They heard testimony from DIA director vice admiral Thomas R. Wilson, DCI brigadier general Roderick Isler, and ONI director rear admiral Perry Michael Ratliff. The purpose of the hearing was to again review the intelligence community's input to Speicher's status as a prisoner of war, missing or killed in action. But it was also to determine how the intelligence community was organized to carry out the DCI's statutory responsibility for analytical support of POW/MIA issues and to consider recommendations for handling analysis of POW matters in the future. No one wanted any more Speichers. The SSCI concluded that information existed to suggest Speicher may have survived his aircraft being shot down, and he may at one time have been, could still be, a prisoner of war. The committee's findings prompted the establishment of a secretary of defense "tiger team," which included members of the OSD and DIA to reassess the Speicher case.

Smith and Grams made sure the Pentagon knew they were dismayed that for three years, between 1996 and 1999, the Defense Department refused to authorize further approaches to Baghdad through State. The administration was concerned that Washington's relationship with Saddam's regime didn't support it. "Nonetheless," they wrote on March 19, "our offices were informed during a briefing on March 12 that the official publicly stated position of the Department of Defense Prisoner of War/Missing Personnel Office (DPMO) with respect to whether the available evidence indicates Lt. Cmdr. Speicher perished in his aircraft incident, is 'we don't know.'" DPMO failed to perform one of its primary mandates: provide DoD participation in the conduct of negotiations with officials of foreign governments in efforts to achieve the fullest possible accounting of Americans missing as a result of military operations.

Worse yet, Smith and Grams soon uncovered the depth of the lies they'd been told. "I was told that the man was killed in action. He was classified as KIA. I was told this by sources in the intelligence community." But Senator Smith's own sources told him otherwise. "Because of that," said Smith, "I began doing my own digging with my own sources, and through a series of briefings over the years, we began to get information that in fact he should never have been classified as KIA." Finally, the SSCI asked DIA director vice admiral Tom Wilson, who agreed with Senator Smith. Wilson's challenge was to convince his own staff that they should have been looking for a live pilot since day one.

Buddy Harris didn't share the SSCI's enthusiasm for the DIA's newly-formed tiger team. They were, he said, "more skeptical than we wanted his office to be, and we didn't think they were pushing as hard as they should. A lot of agencies that should have been involved weren't." Whether Speicher was KIA-BNR or MIA didn't matter. From the time the fighting is declared over and American forces withdraw from foreign soil, responsibility for POW/MIA repatriation and remains recovery falls to the State Department, NSA, CIA and a number of additional federal agencies required to initiate a black box, more commonly called covert black ops, program to get answers. These agencies inevitably reach out to the Pentagon and associated agencies, including JSSA, for help to plan and execute the mission. Harris made the statement that "when you have a KIA-BNR, it's their choice whether they want to be involved, but if it's an MIA case, they have to be involved. They have no choice."

The State Department has an obligation to American citizens missing abroad, including imprisoned and missing service members whose status becomes known after war's end. And it has the lead role. Speicher was not the State Department's first, nor last, failure to act within the provisions of this obligation. During the Vietnam war, intelligence support for the American effort in Laos was handicapped because the administration policy, at the insistence of the State Department, excluded significant use of military intelligence assets. This was true despite strenuous efforts made by Secretary of Defense Melvin Laird to gain support for an improved POW/MIA related military intelligence effort. The 1993 Senate Select Committee on POW/MIA Affairs believed that an expanded wartime military intelligence effort in Laos might have increased significantly our ability to account for Americans never retrieved after the Paris Accords were signed. Laos was denied territory as far as the State Department was concerned. Americans weren't supposed to be there, at least not publicly. But State hamstrung military intelligence in the process.

The OSD and DIA were scheduled to publish a joint report on March 13, 2000, but were unable to agree on what the findings should be. No report was published. SSCI held an additional closed hearing on April 4. Vice Admiral Wilson testified and so did ONI acting director Paul Lowell. During this hearing Senator Pat Roberts and members of the committee reviewed the intelligence community's all-source analytical input to the secretary of the navy and Speicher's tiger team. But they also reviewed the intelligence community's responsiveness to the navy secretary's information needs on the case and sought to determine a better way for the intelligence community to support POW/MIA issues, which hadn't been addressed properly, and which was also their finding. Committee members learned, much to their dismay, that no comprehensive analytic review of all-source intelligence was produced on the fate of Scott Speicher from the time his aircraft was shot down on January 17, 1991. Intelligence coverage gapped.

The SSCI, operating under its active oversight of Speicher's case, passed the Intelligence Authorization Act, Section 304 of Senate

2507, 106th Congress (also referenced as Senate Report 106-279) dated May 4, 2000. The authorization act required the director of central intelligence to establish in the intelligence community "an analytic capability with responsibility for intelligence in support of the activities of the United States relating to prisoners of war and missing persons." The final version of this bill emphasized that the reason for the act was the inadequacy of the intelligence information provided in support of a Department of Defense decision to make a presumptive finding of death for Scott Speicher. Another SSCI closed hearing on July 25, 2000, updated members on efforts to obtain the fullest possible accounting for Speicher. By that time the committee was deeply troubled that the navy's conclusion that Speicher was killed in action during the Gulf War did not reflect the information being provided by the intelligence community. Federal regulations are clear. A presumptive finding of death is made when a survey of all available sources of information indicate, beyond doubt, that the presumption of continuation of life has been overcome. Information that Congress had in hand didn't support that conclusion.

Closed session testimony varied widely. There was the camp that wanted Speicher's status changed to MIA and there was the one that had strict instructions to do all it could to undermine the SSCI's investigation. CENTCOM commander army general Tommy R. Franks sent a navy S-3 Viking pilot on his staff in Riyadh to Washington to do just that. Commander Graig M. Hoeffer was told to do all he could to get the SSCI off the Speicher case. Franks and his predecessor, Marine Corps general Anthony C. Zinni, did very little to help Senate investigators find CENTCOM documents pertaining to Speicher. They'd provided no information about any Special Forces activity nor black operations with Speicher's name on them. Hoeffer was a "talking head." He'd been sent to muddy the investigation. But the SSCI didn't believe others' testimony blatantly intended to throw them off CENTCOM and its role in leaving Speicher behind – several times – by the very chain of command who'd sent him on his mission that night in January nearly a decade before.

The SSCI wanted documentation of Scott Speicher's whereabouts since the war, the years between 1991 and 1995 being a good start. They were looking for evidence that Speicher was with nomadic Bedouins. They were looking for the information and photographs from the Falcon Hunter. And they were looking for CIA agents' interaction with Speicher during the same time frame. To that end they asked the CIA to report to the committee by September 15, 2000.

There was nothing far-fetched about American CIA agents going into a hostile foreign country to speak to an American prisoner of war. The Shelton case was only one example. But there was also nothing that precluded them from speaking to an American pilot classified "missing in action" either. Further, there was nothing in the CIA's track record that said they were there to get the man out if he were located. They just wanted to talk to him. And they did. They talked to Speicher on at least two occasions coinciding with the Falcon Hunter's visits to the western Iraqi desert. The backstory to this CIA practice is certainly worth repeating. There is almost always abundant prequel to something we find so hard to believe. And in this case, it was never more true.

American officials have a history of highly classified clandestine visits to prisoners of war and missing in action. While examples can be resurrected as far back as World War I, one more recent will do. The December 1993 testimony of retired air force brigadier general Thomas E. Lacy made it clear that it was unpopular for anyone to talk about it. But reading his story, it isn't so difficult to accept what happened to Scott Speicher later as truth – truth no one wanted to hear and certainly today is unwilling to admit. Lacy's bona fides go to the credibility of his deposition before a Senate Select Committee on POW/MIA Affairs panel and thus bear repeating. His last assignment was commander, Field Command, Defense Nuclear Agency, Kirtland Air Force Base, New Mexico. He was responsible for the consolidated management of Department of Defense nuclear weapons testing and research, stockpile control, technical publications administration, technical analysis, weapons safety and security, and nuclear ordnance item supply systems. But Lacy was also a fighter pilot.

In August 1965 Lacy went to Southeast Asia on Project Top Dog and served as operations staff of Headquarters Seventh Air Force at Tan Son Nhut Airfield, Republic of Vietnam. In July of the following year he rotated out of Tan Son Nhut and reported to headquarters Pacific Air Forces (PACAF) at Hickam Air Force Base, Hawaii. At Hickam he worked in the office of the deputy chief of staff for plans, first as operations air officer and then as PACAF Muscle Shoals project officer. Later he'd take over as studies and analysis officer in the general planning division. Lacy went back to flying from July 1969 to July 1970 as commander of the 531st Tactical Fighter Squadron and assistant deputy commander for operations, 3rd Tactical Fighter Wing, Bien Hoa Air Base, Republic of Vietnam. This would be his last flying assignment of the war. His career air combat experience included sixty-seven combat missions in the F-86 Sabre in Korea; and eight combat missions in the F-105 Thunderchief, 227 combat missions in the F-100 Super Sabre and A-37 Dragonfly in Vietnam, and 48 combat mission in the F-17 Cobra in Cambodia.

By the time he testified before the Senate panel at the end of 1993, Lacy had been involved in prisoner of war and missing in action investigation for nearly ten years. He started, according to his testimony, in the fall of 1984 as part of a top secret program that put him face-to-face with live American prisoners of war in Laos. But the story started over twenty years before. On October 5, 1965, Lacy was at the Second Air Division in Tan Son Nhut Air Base. That day he was mission commander aboard a command and control C-130 monitoring Russian and Chinese frequencies. Then he heard that Major Dean A. Pogreba's F-105 was hit. "We directed him," said Lacy, "140 degrees to get out [to] the Gulf of Tonkin." Pogreba should've made it there between eight and ten minutes later. "Then he called and said that [he was] being shot at by a MiG. 'I've been hit. I'm bailing out.' And I'm listening to an intercept by the Chinese [who] were shooting at an aircraft that strayed across [their] border. The Chinese MiG reported him shot down well northwest of Hanoi, over the Chinese mainland itself." Lacy told them that the aircraft transmissions were recorded. This proved true. Pogreba ejected from his stricken Thunderchief. Lacy stayed in communication with him on his way down.

Then he was peppered with questions by the Senate panel.

"So our people knew that the plane went down in China?"

"Yes, sir," Lacy responded.

"Was the CIA involved in this?"

"Yes, sir," said Lacy. "After General [George B.] Simler called me back and said, 'Hey, we're in trouble because of a downed aircrew. We don't know whether the Chinese are going to come into the war or not.' He said we're going to get him out. We're going to send people in to bring him out." Simler was in Southeast Asia as director of operations for the Seventh Air Force and flew combat missions in every tactical strike aircraft assigned to the Seventh Air Force.

There were five Americans, U.S. Special Forces, said Lacy, who spoke Chinese and Vietnamese. "They were Asian Americans. They were sent in to get [Lieutenant] Colonel Pogreba [redacted] out of a prison camp in China."

"Do you know they were Asian Americans?"

"Yes, sir. I saw the people," said Lacy. "I saw the pilot. I saw three of the five live ones in January 1989."

"And they were all Special Forces?"

"Yes, sir. U.S. Army."

"At some point you hear that Pogreba has been freed from the Chinese?"

"Yes, about six weeks later. [The plan was] [redacted] we were going to bring him out of China into Vietnam. We were going to cross the northwest railroad, the Red River, bring him into Laos, to where we could get him out by other forces [redacted]."

"And you were briefing the general on this?"

"Yes. We resupplied him [Pogreba] on numerous occasions and moved him over to Haiphong, on to the coast. We sent in a helicopter, a CH-3, to pick him up. The attempt was unsuccessful."

"Are you saying they resupplied these guys in the field for *two years*?"

"Yes, sir."

"Without picking them up?"

"Yes, sir, [redacted] my involvement in it ended after about two years." He retired from the air force on November 1, 1977.

Then Lacy went to Laos. "We had a report that there were live Americans at this location [redacted]. [A witness] had seen a live American, white headed, about sixty years old, he guessed, while [the witness] was visiting his parents."

"How many prisoners in total were there?"

"Sixteen." [Though much of it is redacted, Lacy discussed going into Laos.]

"So you found the camp. Did it look like it had recently been used."

"Yes, it was not grown up with weeds. There were paths outside of the camp, footpaths. [It was] southwestern Laos. The camp name [was] Nam Ngum."

"So, you went in on December 19, 1984?"

The answer was yes.

"How long did it take you to get from the Red River to Nam Ngum?"

"Approximately three hours [by jeep]. [The] prisoner of war camp was empty." The rest was redacted.

"I left Jakarta in May 1985. Came back to the United States in July or August 1985. Ken Davenport on the White House staff [called]. He heard that I had some information on the prisoners of war [and asked if] would I [come] to Washington." Lacy went to Washington in late August 1985. "I talked to Ken Davenport and we, in turn, talked to Howard Baker, Nancy Reagan and President [Ronald W.] Reagan. We discussed the prisoners of war and the fact that I had heard that there were a lot of prisoners of war over in Laos."

Then Lacy was asked about seeing Captain Tommy Emerson Gist, who was listed MIA on May 18, 1968.

"You've seen Gist since you've been in the United States?"

"Yes, at the Veterans [Administration] hospital in Oklahoma City. As I'm aware of the situation, Captain Gist, along with 61 others, was extracted out of a prisoner of war camp at Hoa Binh [southwest of Hanoi], North Vietnam, in January [1988]. He was brought out to Nakhon Phanom, Thailand. I met Sara Gist Bernasconi, and she had remarried [in] the fall of 1987. I received a call from Sara," Lacy said. "[She had received] his ID card. This ID card is without any damage. It's intact. There's no heat. There was absolutely no way that he could have gone and burned up in the airplane. Just physically impossible." The presence of an intact military identification card spoke louder than anything else.

"You later saw Mr. Gist?"

"In the summer of 1989 [1988], in the July-August timeframe at Oklahoma City," said Lacy.

"And you saw the guy, Tommy Gist. How did you know it was Tommy Gist?

"I'd had a photograph of Tommy Gist, and birth marks on the left cheek [and I talked to him]. I told him," continued Lacy, "that Sara had been looking for him. He did not want her to see him in the condition he was in. He was in a very hallucinatory state, going in and out of consciousness. He'd had a drug problem. And he was brought back for treatment of the drug addiction. [They'd been giving him morphine and drugs for fifteen years in Vietnam.] [And he said to me 'That's right, I'm Tommy Gist.] They did have another name [on his records]: Walter Ray."

Lacy continued to tell the Senate panel about what else he'd seen. "It was 18 January 1989 [1988]," he said. "I was in Hanoi. I talked to Beverly Pogreba [who'd called Lacy] and told her yes, that I'd seen him in January 1989."

"Wait a second. You'd seen him in January 1989?" [This date was 1988.]

"Yes."

"I think we've missed something here."

"I had gone to Hanoi, inquiring of Le Duc Tho of the prisoners of war. After my meeting with the president of the United States he said he would like to determine if there were any live American prisoners of war in Southeast Asia. And I agreed to work that issue, and he, the president, agreed to reimburse me for my expenses."

"Who did you submit your vouchers to?"

"I submitted them to the president."

"You submitted them to Ronald Reagan?"

"Yes. It came out of the black budget [and] I was reimbursed, up until the fall of [redaction] [by] cash [in] an envelope." It was inferred that the date was 1989, which is not true. President Reagan was at the end of his term in the fall of 1988, which is the date to which Lacy refers. President George H.W. Bush was sworn in as the forty-first president of the United States in January 1989. Lacy's arrangement was with the Reagan White House. The first money demand from Hanoi came to the Reagan administration just after Reagan took office, and this came out in sworn testimony before the Senate Select Committee on POW/MIA Affairs from Reagan's national security advisor Richard V. Allen, who subsequently recanted. He said his memory had played tricks on him.[4] No one pressed him for the real reason for the recantation. Lacy, contrary to Allen, kept talking.

Lacy continued. "So we went to the camp at Hoa Binh, about thirty miles southwest of Hanoi. And the camp," said Lacy, "was empty."

"Did Le Duc Tho go with you?"

"Yes. And then I wanted him to go with me up to Bao Ninh, where I heard Pogreba was."

"Did you take Le Duc Tho to the second location?"

"He would not go. We went into that place [Bao Ninh, roughly thirty miles northeast of Hanoi] and that's where Pogreba and three of the five other people they'd gone in to get him out."

"Did you recognize Pogreba?"

"Yes. He was in the camp in a cell. They took us in and I saw him."

"What did he say to you?"

"That he thought that the government abandoned him there. He knew that the war was over. He had been told that his wife had remarried. And then I asked [for] him to be released and they would not release him. We went back to see Le Duc Tho."

"You are saying that you saw a live American prisoner of war and that you spoke with him, and you've identified him."

"In January of 1989 [1988]."
"In 1989 [1988]. In January?"
"Yes, sir."

Then Lacy reminded the committee panel what happens when this subject is voiced to them, to the public and to the families of missing men.

"So you got a phone call."

"This male voice says 'You will not testify before the Senate Select Armed Forces Committee on the prisoners of war and missing in action' and hung up. I've had numerous threats against my life on this subject," he told them. Lacy was not the first or last to come forward with this information whose life was threatened. But he'd spoken the truth. The Department of Defense provided Maxine Pogreba Barrell, Dean's former wife, with an intelligence report [IIR6016900892] dated July 24, 1992, that identified Pogreba [and nine others] as a prisoner of war based on data discovered in a Hanoi army museum on an optical computer disc. Barrell was unaware that the Senate Select Committee on POW/MIA Affairs had taken Lacy's deposition. Then there was the Pogreba military identification card. Like Gist's card, Pogreba's was also returned to his family in pristine condition. They'd not been told what Lacy and others knew: that he'd survived and was held prisoner of war. His aircraft, with him in it, was supposed to have exploded into a mountainside. If that were true, how could his identification card be in perfect shape?

After a July 17, 1990 *USA Today* article exposed Lacy's Pogreba story, the Air Force Office of Special Investigations (AFOSI) conducted a security review of Lacy's conduct on August 17, 1990. They were trying to find out whether Lacy had made public disclosure of classified information. He passed the security review with a bit of wordsmithing by the security officer, who used in his review "during 1988", thus when Lacy categorically stated that "such a trip has not taken place" in that time frame he was telling the truth about the date: 1988. All the dates in his Senate deposition were 1989, which was incorrect; the trips and contact with prisoners of war had, in truth, taken place in 1988. Lacy knew they'd be looking at disclosure violations after his testimony, thus it was a game of semantics. This very clever choice of words and years were recorded in his security review.

When Barrell got in touch with Lacy she learned much more about her former husband. Her heart sank. He told her he'd never given up on Dean and had made it his mission to find the "gray-haired colonel," which he said he did in 1988 traveling to Vietnam on a diplomatic passport. He'd told Dean's family that Dean was alive and well and had adjusted to solitary life in the village, which he left daily to go to work. Not long after they spoke Lacy said he'd be unable to speak with her again. He was, as he put it, "in trouble" with the U.S. government. This may have been reference to his AFOSI investigation, but he never said. Hanoi continues to deny Pogreba and the others exist. Lacy died on October 15, 2010, in Claremore, Oklahoma.

Senator Bob Smith's staff prepared a document on December 1, 1992, "U.S. POW/MIAs who may have survived in captivity," that included Dean Pogreba's story as one of its strongest cases. At the end the staff wrote that on October 5, 1965, the People's Republic of China announced that four American aircraft had intruded into Chinese airspace over Kwangsi Province on that date and one had been shot down. There was no mention of the type of aircraft involved. But Pogreba was last known to be about forty nautical miles from Kwangsi Province and was lost on that date. Two other aircraft were lost that day, but they'd crashed thirty miles from China inside North Vietnam.

What do these stories tell us about the POW/MIA issue and particularly about Scott Speicher? Admittedly, reading Lacy's testimony in the Gist case would make anyone uncomfortable. But Lacy was full of uncomfortable truths that are now part of the official testimony gathered by the Senate committee. He describes is something akin to federal witness protection for quietly repatriated prisoners of war, men presumably paid for and returned after Operation Homecoming, but brought back under the table to avoid the public finding out we really had left men behind after emphatically denying that anymore Americans were still held captive, and also the desire to keep quiet the knowledge that Washington ultimately paid reparations to get a few men home. The conditions of the deal weren't great. The men brought back wouldn't get to resume the lives they'd had before the war. They'd be forced to live with conditions that included sharp penalties for noncompliance. The worst of those conditions was the threat they'd be returned to their captors. Why do we know nothing about the program? Perhaps it because we know so little about the fate, in general, of too many of the men who have been classified as prisoners of war and missing in action. Despite what is already in this narrative, there is still more that won't be known until legislation favors disclosure. At present it does not.

So where does Tommy Gist fit in the big scheme of the POW/MIA issue? Columnist Sydney H. Schanberg found out that it was the Pentagon and the intelligence community working hand in hand with Arizona Republican senator John S. McCain, a decorated navy pilot and Vietnam prisoner of war, to keep hidden critical documents about a body of prisoners who were alive but secretly held back by Hanoi when the war ended as bargaining chips for war reparations.[5] They were never returned – well, with the exception of the few like Tommy Gist – who came back under a black program with a shallow evidentiary trail controlled from the Reagan Oval Office. All the rest are now listed, Schanberg wrote, as either dead or missing in action. "Seven successive presidents [and counting], starting with Richard Nixon, have privately endorsed this cover up and blackout on POW documents – while claiming to have directed the Pentagon and the intelligence agencies to declassify everything possible."[6]

What's going on is a shell game in which literally thousands of documents that could have been declassified long ago and provided to the families of the missing and the public have been legislated into secrecy. "John McCain," Schanberg discovered, "was a major player in this lockdown." Schanberg is referring to McCain's authorship of a bill that bears his name – Public Law 102-190, as amended, Title 50 U.S.C. 435 note (2000) – that was first enacted on December 5, 1991. The McCain Bill does not specifically direct declassification. Its "pro-release" intent does, however, imply such action to make the information available to the public. Compliance with the primary-next-of-kin's non-consent does limit the government's ability to release publicly all information containing treatment, location and condition that is declassified. On the face of it, the McCain Bill is supposed to make it easier to obtain documents that pertain POW/MIA cases. Instead, the bill is rife with bureaucratic doublespeak that has led to the release of very little documentation.

The McCain Bill has been amended regularly but it was the second revision that led directly to the gutting of the Missing Service Personnel Act, which had been strengthened in 1995 by prisoner of war advocates to include criminal penalties to read, "Any government official who knowingly and willfully withholds from the file of a missing person any information relating to the disappearance or whereabouts and status of a missing person shall be fined as provided in Title 18 or imprisoned not more than one year or both." A year later, in a closed House-Senate conference on an unrelated military bill, McCain, at the behest of the Pentagon, attached a crippling amendment to the Missing Service Personnel Act, stripping out its only enforcement clause – the criminal penalties – and reducing the obligations of commanders in the field to speedily search for missing men and to report the incidents to the Pentagon.[7] The media didn't challenge him. Even when there were facts about prisoners of war in plain sight, Schanberg observed, journalists continued to turn a blind eye. Speicher had now become one of the affected – the missing man of the moment whose own government and military apparatus now had no legal obligation to hurry up a rescue. Not that one was planned.

The CIA hadn't come back with information yet. The agency wasn't in any rush to stir the pot on the Speicher case. But Smith and Grams hadn't just asked for Tenet's report. They also wanted answers and more action from navy secretary Richard Danzig. They strongly encouraged Danzig to change Scott Speicher's status back to MIA, "a status that more accurately reflects the available evidence and provides presumptive 'benefit of the doubt' to Lt. Cmdr. Speicher. We owe nothing less to Lt. Cmdr. Speicher and his family." The navy had earlier announced that while it wasn't reviewing Speicher's case, it remained an open issue. The navy later appeared to have been swayed by the evidence. But it wasn't completely sold and certainly not enough to change his status to MIA.

Danzig came under increasing pressure from Smith and Grams to change the status. The longer he delayed, the pressure got worse. He, like many others, had one major concern with the status change: maybe the Iraqis would think the United States was going to come after Speicher. If Speicher were alive, it might get him killed. "Give me a good argument," he said to Buddy Harris, why Speicher should be an MIA. Harris had thought about this before and he gave Danzig an analogy. "I look at him like a guy with either cancer or a brain tumor," he replied. "We can keep you living in a hospital, and you'd be drugged up most of the time and have to stay in this hospital. Or we can do surgery, and it could kill you or it may set you free to live your own life. And after ten years, personally, I'll take the surgery." Danzig gave it some thought and agreed with Harris. He took the case to President Clinton. It was still risky and also embarrassing. The administration would be admitting that Speicher had been wrongly classified for a decade.

With Smith and Grams' effort to have Scott Speicher declared an MIA, Buddy and Joanne Harris were put in an awkward position. If there was the slightest chance Scott could still be alive, shouldn't they get behind the senators' plan and ask for Scott to be declared an MIA? They asked themselves that question again: If Scott walked in the door today, would they be able to say that they'd done everything they could? The answer had changed. Even though the media crush could ruin the normalcy they'd tried to carve out for themselves and the children, they thought it might also put pressure on the government to change his status and try harder to find him. The greater concern, however, seemed to be what the Speicher children might think of them for not doing something to help their father. "I don't want these kids coming up to me, at any time, and saying, 'Why didn't you do this?'" said Harris, of Meghan and Michael Scott Speicher-Harris.

Danzig was swayed. He started the process to make Commander Scott Speicher an MIA. The status would be retroactive to cover the period from October 1, 1996, to April 30, 2001. Joanne Speicher-Harris would thus receive his unpaid pay and allowances totaling $292,747. But beginning May 1, 2001, she would also start receiving Scott Speicher's monthly pay of $6,313 per month, which was based at that time on a commander's pay scale. That figure did not include the commander's allowances and career incentive pay, which pushed the payment closer to $8,000 a month. Any day now, they thought, the call would come and they'd be told Speicher's status would be officially changed to missing in action. President Clinton had signed off. It was early January 2001, ten years since Speicher's F/A-18 was shot down over Iraq, nearly as long since the navy declared him killed in action. What was about to happen would make history. No American service member, from any war, had ever been taken off the KIA list and switched back to MIA. They had to prepare Meghan and Michael for what might happen. They were worried that this would upset their lives again. "The worst thing that's going to happen," Buddy told them, "is that somebody is going to come back into your lives who loves you more than anything else. Having more than one person love you can't be bad."

Endnotes

1. Information on Colonel Charles Shelton's case was compiled from original U.S. government agency sources, documents, author interviews and published sources, including a series of articles in the *Riverside Press-Enterprise*, a California daily, by David Hendrix. Further information was available via the Homecoming II Project, October 15, 1990. Colonel Shelton's case is illustrative of what happens later in the Speicher case.

2. Wadley, Carma, "Coming home: decades after going MIA during Korean War, a Utah soldier will finally be laid to rest," *Salt Lake City Deseret News*, April 17, 2011.

3. Wadley, Ibid.

4. Schanberg, Sydney H., "Senator goes missing: where are the soldiers? The MIA-POW issue the press never asks McCain about," *Village Voice*, June 7, 2005.

5. Ibid.

6. Ibid.

7. Schanberg, Sydney H., "McCain and the POW Cover-Up: the 'war hero' candidate buried information about POWs left behind in Vietnam," *The American Conservative*, July 1, 2010.

Chapter 10

Missing In Action

Akram Jasim Al Duri had to have known that the American officials who'd come over to his office in the Algerian embassy were there about Scott Speicher. He'd seen the news. As head of the Iraqi Interest Section, he anticipated the State Department officials' next move would be coming his way. During their January 10, 2001 meeting he was presented with a demarche by the Americans. They wanted Iraq to account for Commander Michael Scott Speicher, which State Department spokesman Philip T. Reeker iterated in his morning press conference the next day. "They are obligated to do [this] under international law," he said, or the Geneva Convention. Al Duri received the communication but was not authorized by Baghdad to reply. It was forwarded to officials in Iraq to do that, which came as no surprise to Washington. "We don't have a response from Baghdad. And a similar message is being delivered to Iraq through their representatives in New York and also in Geneva," Reeker reported. The official in New York was Said Hasan Al Musawi, Iraq's permanent representative to the United Nations. In Geneva Saddam's United Nations representative was Muhammad Al Duri. None of them was surprised to receive the communication concerning Scott Speicher.

"The simple point is," said Reeker, "that we believe that the Iraqis hold additional information that could help resolve the case of Commander Speicher, and they are obligated to provide that information to the United States." Delivery of the demarche, a diplomatic note, wasn't done often between the United States and Iraq, Reeker explained. Ongoing low-intensity conflict and a no-fly zone over southern Iraq produced animosity between Washington and Baghdad that put them on less than speaking terms. "We don't have particularly close relations with Iraq, as you are well aware," he continued. "Our decision to demarche them on this issue was entirely driven by the humanitarian need that we see to resolve the case of Commander Speicher." The White House and Pentagon gave similar briefings the same day, explaining the importance of the diplomatic note from their point of view.

During a scheduled private security briefing with the Joint Chiefs of Staff, newly elected President-elect George W. Bush was joined by Vice President-elect Dick Cheney and soon-to-be Secretary of State Colin Powell. They heard troubling news about Iraq. But they also heard the information about an impending status change for Scott Speicher later that day. Before George W. Bush took office, he knew all about Speicher. Cheney and Powell arguably knew more. Why did the Clinton administration wait so long to change Speicher's status when Senators Smith and Grams petitioned for his MIA designation in 1999?

After word of Scott Speicher's status change to MIA was leaked by the State Department, reporters surrounded the Harris home in Orange Park, Florida, but Joanne and Buddy had packed up the family and left town for a week. The navy announced Speicher's status change on January 11, 2001, in a four-paragraph statement. But it was President Clinton's verbal misstep that got the media whipped into a frenzy. "We have some information that leads us to believe he might be alive," he said. "And we hope and pray that he is. But we have already begun working to try to determine whether, in fact, he's alive, if he is, where he is and how we can get him out."

Alive? What did the government know? Had Clinton, ten days before leaving office, gone too far? Hours later, he tried to temper his earlier statement. "Well, I don't want to say more than we have. All I want to say is we have evidence," said the president, "which convinced me that we can't ensure that he perished. I don't want to hold out false hope, but I thought it was wrong to continue to classify him as killed in action when he might not have been."

The next day the story was front page news across the country. Speicher's squadron mate Barry Hull and Senator Bob Smith appeared on CBS' *The Early Show*. The show's anchor, Jane Clayson, asked Smith why the U.S. government waited seven years from the time Speicher's jet was found to try to locate the pilot. Smith said he couldn't understand. Up until 1998 he'd been misled. He promised to deal later with those who'd steered Congress awry. There's not one shred of evidence, Smith said, that shows where, when, how or even if Speicher died. "This pilot, if he's alive, has been there for ten years with nobody looking for him. And that's just plain outrageous."

Hull began by saying hello to his old squadron mates. "And, Spike, if you're out there, we're thinking of you, buddy," he said. The anchor asked him if he really thought Speicher could be alive after ten years. He didn't think so, he said, but he couldn't be sure. "I believe I read somewhere where the North Vietnamese held French prisoners for twenty years. So it has happened before. And there's no assurance that he's dead." He went on to say that the question haunted him, his Sunliner squadron mates and Speicher's friends for a decade. It confounded them more as the years passed. "This is a situation where the pieces of the puzzle don't fit and no one knows exactly what happened to him. And for all we know," said Hull, "he is still alive. And that makes this tragedy so much worse."

At a Pentagon press briefing six days later, on January 16, Kenneth H. Bacon, assistant secretary of defense for public affairs, reminded reporters that Speicher's status change didn't mean the Defense Department was admitting it knew he was alive. Bacon told them the Iraqis said they didn't have records on missing pilots. "But some of their statements have been somewhat disingenuous because they only go back to 1995, when we, as you know, sent representatives in with the International Committee of the Red Cross to look at the crash site. So we have asked the Iraqis to provide whatever information they have about what happened between 1991, when the plane was shot down, and 1995, certainly, and thereafter, if they have information." The interesting issue, Bacon told reporters, was what happened right after the crash. The Iraqis were being asked to produce the impossible. They didn't get Speicher just then.

Speicher's change to MIA also meant he was now covered under U.S. Code Title 10, Chapter 76, known widely as the Missing

Persons Act. He had rights, including the right to a lawyer. Section 1503(f)(1) states this clearly. "The Secretary appointing a board to conduct an inquiry under this section shall appoint counsel to represent each person covered by the inquiry or, in a case covered by subsection (b), one counsel to represent all persons covered by the inquiry." The navy secretary was obligated by law to appoint legal counsel, a judge advocate general (JAG) attorney, for Scott Speicher. He didn't do it. Not just then.

Buddy and Joanne Harris got Jacksonville attorney Cindy Laquidara to represent them. But she didn't meet the definition of "missing person's counsel" as intended under Title 10, Section 1503(f)(1). She represented the missing man's family and other interested parties as described in the code. Section 1503(f)(3)(A) states that the missing person's legal counsel should have access to all facts and evidence considered by a board of inquiry in the case for which the counsel is appointed. Speicher's own counsel, eventually appointed, was to ensure all appropriate information concerning the case had been collected, logged, filed and safeguarded. Scott Speicher, had he been assigned a JAG lawyer early on, would have had an attorney with the qualification to hold a permanent top secret clearance. He needed someone who could daily access information on his behalf. Much of what appears in Speicher's files within the Navy Department and numerous intelligence agencies has some level of classification attached. A good portion of it reaches the threshold of special compartmentalized information and special access requiring a code word.

Jeff Manor's prediction that primary next-of-kin problems would have a ripple effect on Speicher's case came true again when it was time to make decisions over the hold, block or release of classified information. While U.S. Code states that a primary next-of-kin can request a hold on the release of classified information or block declassification of information for the public file to protect their own privacy, Scott Speicher didn't have a legal primary next-of-kin to make those decisions. To infer that the family wanted information to remain classified to protect their privacy and the sanctity of the ongoing investigation wasn't legally valid and stretched the spirit of intent of classification. Arguably, Joanne Speicher-Harris was no longer Scott's primary next-of-kin after her marriage on July 4, 1992, to Buddy Harris. She would thus have not been able to legally parse what information was released or not by any agency or department of the U.S. government. The U.S. Navy didn't realize the mistake until Buddy Harris told Admiral Arthur the truth. He'd married Scott Speicher's wife. But even knowing all this didn't seem to correct the problem. Senator John S. McCain wrote Defense Secretary William S. Cohen on January 9, 1998, to find out how the Speicher case had and was being handled, and to get a briefing on the status of the case as soon as possible. He also urged Cohen to make public all information pertaining to the Speicher case at the earliest possible time. Cohen's reply on February 13 informed McCain that it was the Speicher family's wish that information not be released to the public to protect their privacy. McCain got a classified, closed-door briefing.

But there was something else equally troubling about Speicher's case: abuse of classification to hide mistakes and missteps, ones that had no impact on national security. A good example of misuse of classification: flight suit photographs. CBS' *60 Minutes II* obtained them for its national broadcast in April 2000. But when they were requested again on December 19, 2001, and January 8, 2002, DPMO refused to release them. They'd already *been* released. In response to the 2001 and 2002 FOIA requests, DPMO responded thusly: "J. Alan Liotta, deputy director of Defense Prisoner of War/Missing Personnel Office (DPMO), an initial denial authority, has denied in their entirety the photographs responsive to the 'flight suit' portion of your request, the release of which would circumvent the DPMO Congressionally mandated mission to account for U.S. personnel missing as a result of this Nation's conflicts. Accordingly," the letter read, "the denied photographs are withheld pursuant to 5 U.S. Code, 552(b)(2)(High) governing Freedom of Information Act [FOIA]." This second category of information spelled out by "exemption two" pertains to internal matters of a more substantive nature, the disclosure of which would risk the circumvention of a statute or agency regulation, and is a clause that has generated considerable controversy over the years. Liotta was using what is more commonly called a "High 2" to stop disclosure of the photographs. But this was already moot since they'd been shown to millions of *60 Minutes II*'s viewers in April 2000 and CBS was free to continue to use these photographs at any time in the future. There was absolutely nothing about these photos that should have led to Liotta hiding behind a "High 2" clause.

DPMO has continued to hide behind classification, which is a blatant violation of federal law. In *Crooker* v. *ATF* the Federal Court of Appeals for the District of Columbia Circuit fashioned a two-part test for determining which sensitive materials are exempt from mandatory disclosure under the "High 2." This test requires both (1) that a requested document be "predominantly internal" to an agency and (2) that its disclosure "significantly risks circumvention of agency regulations or statutes." The flight suit photos do neither. First, they'd already been released for public view on national television and were no longer "predominantly internal" to the DPMO. Second, release of the photos posed no significant risk to its agency regulations or statute. When the Navy Department's FOIA policy branch chief, Doris M. Lama, requested the flight suit photos be released to her, suddenly DPMO couldn't find them. Were they now just as lost as the flight suit? It appears so.

American Journal producer Lynn Keller had an earlier experience with the DPMO two-step on Speicher's file. She submitted a FOIA to the Pentagon for all records relating to Scott Speicher on December 19, 1995, just three days after the ICRC team pulled out of Iraq. Her request was specific. She wanted live sighting reports, evidence of his escape and evasion code on the ground, any records pertaining to his aircraft ejection, his survival and capture. After Anthony H. Passarella, the Pentagon's director of the Freedom of Information and Security Review, denied her request, she wrote him a letter dated February 26, 1996. "In your letter, you say 'DPMO advised that it is involved in the ongoing investigation pertaining to Lieutenant Commander Michael Speicher, of which the Office of the Joint Task Force-Full Accounting (JTF-FA), has lead. However, DPMO further advised that it has no records pertaining to Lieutenant Commander Speicher. I am not clear on one thing. If the DPMO is involved in the Speicher investigation, then how is it possible that it has no records?" Good question.

Federal law is clear on another count, too. Whenever any U.S. intelligence agency or other element of the government finds or receives information that might be related to a missing person, the information is required to be promptly sent to the office of the service secretary. In Speicher's case the secretary of the navy was to receive copies of all intelligence information, regardless of the originating agency or department, so that proper determination could be made regarding his status. Speicher's investigation was handicapped by the lack of shared information within the Pentagon, DIA, CIA, and NSA. None wanted to share what they had with the other unless compelled by Congress to do so. Even then, it is highly unlikely they parted with *everything* they had on Scott Speicher.

After Speicher's status was changed to MIA on January 11, 2001, Senator Smith wrote to National Security Advisor Condoleezza Rice to inform her that he had "serious concerns that elements of the U.S. government have misled the Congress on this tragic case." A month later he wrote to Democrat Florida senator Bob Graham, chairman of the SSCI, and Richard Shelby, SSCI vice chairman, to ask them to formally investigate the intelligence community's performance on the Speicher case and the inspector general's glowing review of the intelligence agencies' performance. He questioned the ability of the inspector general to conduct an independent investigation given the intelligence community's blatantly poor track record regarding Scott Speicher, not the least of which included its overall failure of imagination.

The intelligence community didn't appreciate the possibilities: the who, what, when, where and how that help put the pieces of the puzzle together. Quoting Crow's Law, Reginald V. Jones, head of scientific intelligence for the British Air Staff during World War II, said, "Do not think what you want to think until you know what you ought to know." The U.S. intelligence community didn't know enough about Scott Speicher the man, the pilot, the evader, the survivor. And they didn't know how to get him back either. "As a general rule," wrote Richard J. Heuer Jr., "we are often on the side of being too wedded to our established view and too quick to reject information that does not fit these views, than on the side of being too quick to reverse our beliefs. Thus most of us do well to be more open to evidence and ideas that are at variance with our preconceptions." Heuer, retired former chief of methodology for the CIA, published this assessment in a collection of his articles under the title *Psychology of Intelligence Analysis* in 1999 for the agency's Center for the Study of Intelligence. Given the Pentagon's and intelligence community's lackluster performance on the Speicher case and the myriad of POW/MIA cases sitting on their respective doorsteps, it was obvious few had heeded Heuer's advice.

The SSCI agreed to formally investigate the intelligence community's work on the Speicher case in May 2001. A few months later, on September 11, several of the agencies already under the microscope for their failure of imagination on his case were called into question for a lapse that none appeared to have seen coming: multiple Al Qaeda attacks on the American homeland. Did they share information? How good were they at analyzing data? Could they oversee and critique their own work? The answer to all was no. If Speicher hadn't already proved that fact, 9/11 did.

Just after Speicher's status shifted back to MIA, on February 7, 2001, Senator Pat Roberts was seated in an SSCI hearing to review worldwide threats to U.S. national security. Part of the briefing was set aside for Scott Speicher. After listening to what was said he summoned CIA director Tenet, DIA director vice admiral Wilson and Thomas Singer, acting assistant secretary of state, to answer pressing questions that troubled him. He wanted to know what, if any, progress had been made to resolve Speicher's fate. "Lieutenant Commander Michael Speicher, KIA in 1991, MIA in 2001. President Clinton said the following, as of last month, when he indicated that the commander might still be alive: 'We've already begun working to try to determine whether, in fact, he's alive, if he is, where he is and how we can get him out,' the president said, 'because since he was a uniformed service person he's clearly entitled to be released, and we're going to do everything we can to get him out.'" Senators Shelby, Smith and Roberts told Tenet, Wilson and Singer that they felt they'd lost one of their own. He was left behind, they said. "We think the system failed, and we're trying to fix it," said Roberts. This could be done partly by setting up intelligence analysts to cover prisoners of war and missing in action. "We passed that in the authorization bill," Roberts iterated. "We hope that there's been a big change, and I need to know the progress you've made in establishing this capability in regard to status, budget and the breadth of activities."

Roberts asked two questions. To what extent has the new capability drawn on the resources of the DIA? "I want to thank Admiral Wilson," he said, "for his excellent work in this respect. I want to make sure that Admiral Wilson's right arm knows what your left arm is doing or vice versa." He also wanted to know if the intelligence agencies were cooperating. One Senate staffer said that while they had done a fairly good job, he took exception to the circuitous route it took them to get there. "If somebody smacks you in the face and says get going, and you do a good job after that, you are commended for doing a good job. But you don't get a check in the box that says 'initiative.'"

Two months before, the Pentagon and DIA's inspector generals gave the intelligence community glowing marks for their work on the Speicher case. "I don't agree" with the assessment, said Roberts. "I think it's noteworthy, all right, but it's not the same connotation that was in that report. Were the factors that contributed to this allegedly high-level work in place in the early and mid-1990s, when most of the effort now regarded as incomplete, and that's the nicest way I can put it, in regard to the Speicher case, were they considered in that inspector generals' report?"

"I don't know, sir," replied Tenet. "I'll have to check for you. I don't know. Do you know?" he asked, leaning over to consult with Singer.

"Did the inspector general look back as far as we had records dealing with the issue?" asked Singer. "But I... it was an independent investigation..." His voice trailed off.

"From '91 up to '96, were those factors considered, Tom?" Roberts asked Singer.

"As far as I know they were, sir," said Singer.

"How on earth could anybody reach the conclusion that they were noteworthy and excellent? That's beyond me," Roberts shot back.

During a separate interview in May 2001, several months after the SSCI hearing, Wilson himself would concede that while he'd set up the tiger team to aggressively investigate Speicher's case within the DIA, interagency cooperation "doesn't seem to have been effective yet."

Baghdad reacted angrily to the demarche it'd been served on Scott Speicher. Reuters reported on February 11, 2001, Iraq had renewed its accusations that United Nations weapons inspectors were looking for a missing U.S. Navy pilot shot down during the Persian Gulf War. They weren't there to find weapons of mass destruction. No, said Baghdad, they were after Speicher. The report originally appeared in the Iraqi weekly newspaper *Nasirriya*, which referred to a period of time well after the war when UNSCOM teams visited Iraq until they were expelled at the end of 1998. "I was informed by former UN weapons inspector Scott Ritter," said Hussam Mohammed Amin, head of the Iraqi National Monitoring Directorate, "that a team of UN weapons inspectors was looking for the body of the American pilot." Armed with what Ritter told him, Amin publicly accused the team of looking for the downed pilot in an area where there were no military sites and no inhabitants. Amin was telling the truth. There was nothing in the vicinity of Scott Speicher's crash site but desolate, barren desert and the occasional passage of nomadic Bedouins.

UNSCOM had been in Iraq since April 1991 to monitor WMD as part of the Gulf War cease-fire agreement. But Saddam didn't like it. From day one Iraq's top leadership did everything possible to deny access to facilities and records, and to preclude searches, even in remote parts of the country. When asked about Speicher in late 2001 the Iraqi Foreign Ministry repeated the same story that Amin publicly reported in Reuters, that one of the commission's missile inspection teams, UNSCOM 24, surveyed and inspected

Iraq's western area from December 17 to 19, 1991. "The team's chief, Scott Ritter," the ministry reported, "admitted later that he had been asked by the U.S. administration to search for the body of an American pilot." At least the Iraqis stayed with the same story. Ritter, on the hand, did not. He publicly denied having ever spoken to the Iraqis about looking for the remains of anyone. But it was because of his statements that the Iraqis got particularly agitated during UNSCOM 215's 1998 attempts to access Abu Ghraib, Iraq's largest and most notorious prison located on the outskirts of Baghdad. Abu Ghraib had more than fifteen thousand inmates. After UNSCOM 215's failed tries to get into this prison, UNSCOM teams were forced out of Iraq for good.

The infamous showdown at Abu Ghraib pitted German Army Medical Service lieutenant colonel Dr. Gabriele Kraatz-Wadsack, UNSCOM 215 lead investigator, and her team against a group of Iraqi record keepers who didn't want them finding evidence of Baghdad's live human experimentation using biological and chemical agents that the Iraqis were known to have conducted between 1994 and 1995. Three years later, with an UNSCOM team impatiently waiting at the prison gates, they'd gone into deception mode. Most records were removed ahead of the visit. Other records were hidden away in rooms elsewhere in the prison. Kraatz-Wadsack, a biologist, knew enough Arabic to know what she'd be looking for in their files. "She did not anticipate finding any forensic evidence," wrote Tom Marigold and Jeff Goldberg in their 1999 *Plague Wars*, "but the Iraqis are paper crazy when it comes to bureaucracy, so she marched straight to the prison's administrative offices to demand prison records for 1994-5." Predictably, they weren't there. She saw records from 1992 and 1993. Everything else was gone.

An Iraqi defector who'd escaped Iraq in 1998 later told American authorities that he'd kept prisoner records for the Iraqi government. He'd shuffle the records from one location to the next to stay ahead of UNSCOM teams like Kraatz-Wadsack's, trying to keep western officials, but most especially the Americans, from getting a look at them. Yet at least one UNSCOM inspector did get a quick look at a file with Speicher's name on it. It was a medical record that showed an Iraqi physician had given Speicher checkups in 1997 and 1998. When investigators later found and interrogated the doctor, who'd also defected, he couldn't remember the place where he'd treated Speicher.

But one fact is abundantly clear: American intelligence knew exactly who treated Scott Speicher down to their names and medical specialties. They'd been alerted to this information and recorded it in IIR 7 739 0393 03, a classified document with an unclassified subject line that detailed Iraqi physicians who'd treated Scott Speicher in Saddam's custody. Defector reports corroborate Speicher's medical treatment. These were men lucky enough to escape with Saddam's dirty secret. Whatever ailment Speicher had, Saddam made sure he got the appropriate treatment. He was trying to keep his prize alive. This much was already known from men who'd made their way to freedom.

Iraq's openly hostile resistance to Kraatz-Wadsack's team exposed only part of the pressure put on Baghdad by the United Nations Security Council. She'd come close, even if she didn't know it just then, to exposing Speicher's captivity. Iraq's heightened awareness of the Speicher case, intensified by the State Department's demarche, made it clear that the issue wasn't going to die away. Asked about Speicher, the answer was always the same: he's dead. But they weren't offering any substantive proof of his death either.

United Nations Resolution 124, enacted December 17, 1999, made it clear what the world community expected from Baghdad: "The repatriation and return of all Kuwaiti and third country nationals or their remains, present in Iraq on or after August 2, 1990 ... have not yet been fully carried out by Iraq." The resolution further created the United Nations Monitoring, Verification and Inspection Commission (UNMOVIC). Under its mandate, Iraq was instructed to provide UNMOVIC inspectors unrestricted and unimpeded access to any and all areas, facilities, equipment, records and means of transport to fulfill their mission. They also had the right to interview all officials and persons of interest under the authority of the Iraqi government. The UN Security Council further directed Baghdad to provide all necessary cooperation to the ICRC and called upon Iraq to resume its participation in the Tripartite Commission. Iraq said no. The eight-nation Tripartite Commission, chaired by the ICRC, was set up to locate and secure the release of any remaining prisoners of war who might still be in Iraq after the cease-fire.

Kuwait was initially missing, best count, 628 of its citizens. This figure was later pared down to 605 unresolved missing persons cases. Saudi Arabia claimed another seventeen missing persons. The United States claimed one: Scott Speicher. But Iraq admitted to only 126 Kuwaiti detainees and even then didn't provide enough information to Kuwait to determine their fate. Three Kuwaiti cases were closed after 1995 and only after Iraq and Kuwait agreed to bilateral meetings every other month on the Iraq-Kuwait border, attended by American, British, French and Saudi observers. This set-up didn't last. Iraq stopped coming to the meetings after Operation Desert Fox in December 1998. Just after Resolution 1248 passed, retired Russian diplomat Yuli Vorontsov was put in charge of sorting out the issue of missing Kuwaiti prisoners and illegally seized property. But he was never permitted into Iraq.

As it turned out the ICRC had been doing its part all along. Three meetings held in Geneva in 1998 established baseline objectives and protocols to account for any remaining missing persons inside Iraq. With or without a United Nations resolution, the ICRC was already hard at work doing just that. Nine meetings were eventually held in the Iraq-Kuwait demilitarized zone (DMZ), and from inside Iraq and Kuwait the ICRC monitored the treatment of detained persons from the Gulf War and the conditions under which they'd been kept. They visited detainees in Kuwait with no diplomatic protection, stateless persons and Jordanians, Sudanese, Yemenites and Palestinians without travel documents. They visited seventy-eight foreign nationals held in Iraq's Abu Ghraib detention center. This number dropped to sixty-four by 2000, a dramatic drop from the 353 foreign nationals they'd seen in 1994.

Despite glaring setbacks, the ICRC was also responsible for the repatriation in February and March 1998 of two Kuwaitis and two Saudis illegally detained in Iraq. They crossed the border at Safwan to freedom under the protection of ICRC officials. But if there was any doubt beyond the release of two Kuwaitis and what they must have conveyed of their countrymen left behind in Iraq, it should be resolved by the numbers that follow: 10,744 Red Cross messages were sent by Kuwaitis to their family member in an Iraqi prison; 9,189 replies were delivered from the prisoner to his family back in Kuwait. These numbers declined from 8,565 to 6,855, respectively, as deaths, executions and moves erased men and women from Abu Ghraib's register. But still there was no mention of Scott Speicher.

The United States Congress passed concurrent resolutions in the House and Senate to insist Iraq account for missing prisoners who'd remained in Iraq after the war. The Senate's resolution that passed July 19, 2000, was punctuated with words like "immediately" and "fullest possible accounting." Senators were trying to send a message at home, sespecially in Washington, and abroad. They wanted Baghdad to know they'd read and heard eyewitness reports from released prisoners of war who'd told them missing Kuwaitis had been seen and contacted in Iraqi prisons. Yes, they'd been seen in Abu Ghraib. They'd also been seen at other prisons and holding facilities in and with proximity to Baghdad. But importantly the Senate demanded that Baghdad immediately provide the fullest possible accounting for Scott Speicher in compliance with UN Security Council Resolution 686 and other applicable international law.

Four days later, on July 23, the House followed suit. The language of the House resolution originally focused almost completely on missing men and women from Kuwait and nine other Arab countries. "There are 605 Kuwaiti MIAs," said California congressman Dana Rohrabacher, "many of whom are civilians, and they have been held for over ten years now. To put this in proportion for the people of the United States," he explained, "this would be the equivalent of an enemy of the United States holding two hundred thousand Americans for a period of ten years. Think of what the suffering among our people and the emotional upheaval in our country would be if two hundred thousand Americans were being held by an enemy of the United States." The original draft of House

Resolution 275 didn't include Speicher. His name was omitted even though it'd been proposed by Florida Democratic congressman Robert Wexler. Just a week before the resolution came to a vote Rohrabacher amended it. "Michael Speicher, a patriotic young American who volunteered to serve his country, has not been well served by his country," he said. "During visits to Kuwait in 1998 and again in 1999, I asked intelligence officials at the American embassy about Lieutenant Commander Speicher. They told me that there is a legitimate reason for concern about whether he survived his crash and was taken prisoner."

From what he'd learned in Kuwait, Rohrabacher crafted a convincing preamble to the House resolution that made it clear Speicher had been declared dead by the United States Navy "without the conduct of an adequate search and rescue operation, however subsequent information obtained after the Persian Gulf conflict by United States officials has raised the possibility that Lieutenant Commander Speicher survived and was captured by Iraqi forces."

With a full-blown congressional inquiry underway on Speicher, the DIA made a second attempt at staffing a POW/MIA office. The DIA POW/MIA Office was stood up on September 15, 2001. Congress hadn't forgotten DIA's lackluster past performance. But despite this, DIA was again given a central, two-pronged role in U.S. efforts to account for its prisoners of war and missing in action: first, investigating and analyzing reports of living sightings and evidence that American prisoners still held in foreign lands, and second, providing the benefit of its conclusions about the fate of missing servicemen to the Department of Defense for action.

The 1993 Senate Select Committee on POW/MIA Affairs didn't think highly of DIA's performance in either capacity. Critics charged then that DIA was plagued by lack of resources, guilty of overclassification, defensive toward criticism, handicapped by poor coordination and communication with the remainder of the intelligence community, and slow to follow up on live sightings and foreign-generated intelligence reports. They'd also faulted DIA's analytical process and referred to it as a "mindset to debunk" live sighting reports. Committee members openly expressed their concern and disappointment that from time to time, with increasing frequency through the early 1990s, individuals within the agency were evasive, unresponsive, disturbingly incorrect and incredibly cavalier, often diminishing the work of those who'd performed professionally under extraordinarily difficult circumstances. So what would make DIA capable of performing better in 2001? No one was quite sure. Congress was careful to focus DIA's effort on current operational prisoner of war and missing in action cases. The reestablished DIA POW/MIA Office's first case was Speicher.

Senator Pat Roberts wrote to Defense Secretary Donald H. Rumsfeld on February 14, 2002, that a recent U.S. intelligence community assessment of the Speicher case indicated that "Commander Speicher probably survived the loss of his aircraft, and if he survived, he almost certainly was captured by the Iraqis." Roberts didn't indicate when he believed the capture occurred. "This strongly suggests," he told Rumsfeld, "the more appropriate designator or status of POW. I believe the status of POW sends a symbolic message not only to the Iraqis, but to other adversaries, current and future – and most importantly – to the men and women of the U.S. armed forces and the American people." Roberts' proposed change to POW drew strong comment. Commander Chip Beck, we are reminded, made the argument "a POW is a POW, not an MIA. This is true even if the enemy knows that the person is a POW but our side does not. As long as one party, in this case the 'holding party,' knows that the person is alive and captive, then he is a POW." Even if a POW dies in captivity, he does not become an MIA, said Beck. But there were those in the Pentagon, he explained, who'd argue that all POWs and MIAs are MIAs, which is not the case. "This lack of distinction serves the enemy's interest not ours," he observed. "It requires us to only track down those men and women who were killed in the conduct of battle, not kidnapped by the forces they confronted." Roberts pushed for POW status for Speicher because its accountability threshold is considerably higher.

Chapter 11

An American in the Basement

Charles A. Forrest was just about to conclude his Tehran meeting with members of the Supreme Council for Islamic Revolution in Iraq (SCIRI) when one of its key participants asked him to look at a report about a captured American pilot. He found the report unsettling. "There's a certain voodoo to keeping an American in the basement," he said in early 2002. "And why? It looks like it's been incredibly successful to [Hussein]. You can't believe that his doing this hasn't had some impact on U.S. policy with Iraq."

Forrest knew what he was talking about and he'd learned what Saddam Hussein was like and what he was capable of doing. His INDICT organization was established in late 1998 to lobby for the creation of an ad hoc international criminal tribunal to try Saddam's regime, at least his top tier leadership, for war crimes and crimes against humanity, including genocide and torture. His fall 2001 meeting in Tehran was one of several he'd had with SCIRI, a group committed to deposing Saddam. They didn't have to wait long. The United States invaded Iraq less than two years later and got rid of Saddam for them.

The report in Forrest's hand had been made by an Iraqi who'd left Iraq via Tehran and contacted SCIRI members there. He'd then left for Beirut, Lebanon, where several thousand Iraqis now live. These expatriates emigrated for different reasons, some political, some economic and others for strictly personal security reasons. Many have stories to tell that defy the imagination. A number of them have borne witness to the horrors of Saddam's Iraq in the *Al-Hayat* newspaper. "We receive a lot of Iraqis," said *Al-Hayat* reporter Hazem Al Amin, "because they believe the newspaper reaches many in the Arab world."

The man who'd contacted SCIRI was a former prisoner in Iraq. Hussam Al Mousawi was twenty-six years old when he told his story in the May 4, 2001 *Al-Hayat*. He'd been arrested with his whole family in 1991 by the Iraqi secret police in the city of Hillah, located in the Karbala governate. His father had been executed earlier, in 1986, and all Mousawi could think about after his arrest was his own date with an executioner. During his first period of incarceration, he told Amin that two of his brothers were executed like their father. "I had only one brother who'd remained alive, and I later discovered that he was in prison like I was," he said. "He had been put in the same prison where I was." During his ten years in prison, Mousawi was moved around, spending time in three different facilities, the first two for one month each and the rest of his imprisonment in the third, which he realized at some point was in the vicinity of Baghdad. He believed it to be Abu Ghraib. "In the third prison I was put in a cell on the fourth level underneath the ground level of the building. This was a big prison consisting of three buildings."

Saddam had several large prisons that had underground cell blocks. An Iraqi defector, who'd been a sergeant in the all-volunteer Fedayeen Saddam, worked at one of these secret sites outside Baghdad. "They were kept," he said, "in an underground cell. They were rarely let out, usually once for a very brief time every three or four months, and only when the camp was empty."[1] One of those sites was Salman Pak, just on the outskirts of Baghdad. Salman Pak was disguised aboveground with date palm trees. Only an air vent was visible on the surface. Searchers would otherwise never know that there was a vast prison complex underground. Like all of Saddam's prisons, this one was an overcrowded nightmare: little food, abominable sanitary and living conditions, and almost constant torture of some kind.

Mousawi's cell was four meters long and three meters wide. When he entered it eighteen prisoners were already crammed into the cell. "But this figure sometimes went up to as high as forty prisoners," he said. "For every prisoner or person arrested, the initial period of imprisonment, with its interrogations, was one of the hardest phases of prison life. But in Iraqi prisons, torture is used all during a person's period of imprisonment." During his interrogations, Mousawi's interrogators and guards scarred him for life. "Today I am a young man," he said, "but I have no sexual sensations. During my interrogations they destroyed that area of my body with electrical instruments of torture. And, as you can see, my jaw was broken and put back together the wrong way. This is because the interrogator kicked my jaw with his foot until it fell apart. These disfigurements on my hand are because I was burned with cigarette butts and because pincers with electricity were used on me during interrogations."

Mousawi thought if he didn't anger the security service they'd be less likely to single him out. But one day in 1997 a security service officer came to Mousawi's cell door and asked for him by name. His prison uniform was filthy and he smelled. "A disgusting smell emanated from my body because of the putridness and humidity," he explained, "and I had had scabies and whole areas of my skin had been worn away." The man cleaned him up, gave him new clothes and told Mousawi that he'd be allowed to pass out food to other prisoners. But he'd always be escorted by prison security. He was now a "feeder" on the foreigner's floor. These were men who weren't Iraqis. They were Kuwaitis, Palestinians and four western foreigners, one of them an American pilot. "There was also another one," he said, "whose nationality I did not know. He'd gone insane."

Foreign prisoners got bigger portions of food. Most were in solitary confinement cells. One day while passing out food, the guard with Mousawi announced that an intelligence inspection committee had made a surprise visit. He abruptly shoved Mousawi into a nearby cell and secured the door. The cell belonged to the American pilot. "[He] was the only one there, and it appears that he had learned to speak a little Arabic. He said to me: 'You are a temporary prisoner. They often set free those whom they choose for the job of distributing food.'" The American pilot told him he'd been taken prisoner after his airplane was shot down during the Gulf War. He asked Mousawi if he could get a message to his command after they freed him. "I refused even to talk to him," Mousawi confessed, "and I remained silent until the cell door was opened again. The officer took me out of the cell and inspected me carefully. He asked me if this American had talked to me about anything, and I said that he hadn't. I did this not out of concern for him," he iterated, "but rather out of fear that they would have suspicions about me." This was a brief encounter with the American pilot. But Mousawi was still afraid. He wanted to get out of the prison. This was 1997 and he'd been there for nearly six years already.

The following year Mousawi noticed perceptible changes on the foreigners' floor. The prison routine changed dramatically. Officers and soldiers who'd worked there tried to smuggle documents, photographs and information about Kuwaiti prisoners back to Kuwait and Saddam's security forces caught them at the border, where they were immediately executed. From that time forward, an electric gate was built at the entrance to the foreigners' floor, and the prisoners were forced to wear masks before feeders entered their cells. A Kuwaiti prisoner who'd refused to do this was dragged from his cell by a security officer and taken to an open gallery area. He was beaten over the head until he died. Not all attempts to smuggle information failed. Iraqi intelligence sold a photograph taken in 1996 of a high ranking Kuwaiti official in his prison cell for $200,000.

As a food distributor Mousawi's collateral duty was cleaning rooms, including interrogation suites, where he often found inmates' bodies, blood, human tissue and partial remains. "One could look at the body," said Mousawi, "and tell how the person was killed. Some of them had been given injections, after which their bodies shriveled up. Others had been tortured so much by the interrogators that they had been accidentally killed by them. Still others had died out of fear and had had heart failure."

He got a second chance to be with the American pilot in the same room. "He was afflicted with extreme exhaustion and was very sick," said Mousawi, "and this led to a doctor visiting him and giving him a vaccine. The doctor, an officer, ordered me to stay with him for about two hours." During that time the American again asked Mousawi if he would pass a message to his command if they set him free. "He repeated to me words, which, if I recited them and they were heard, would prove his identity." Mousawi conveyed this part of his encounter with the American pilot to the CIA. That record is classified.

Another year passed and Qusay Saddam Hussein, Saddam's younger son, took personal charge of the prison in which Mousawi and the American pilot were held. New jailers were brought in. Then the executions started. Men were executed for no crime. A young man who'd read a newspaper that stated they were in a general security prison in the Baghdad General Security Directorate was crudely hung – just because he'd read where he and all the others were being held. The prison's chief interrogator opened Mousawi's door so he'd not miss the boy's hanging. "His neck seemed very long," he said later. "The skin and flesh," he told Amin, "had been torn away, and only the bones were connected to the body. And before he was hanged, they'd cut out his tongue. The interrogating officer made sure that we knew this additional fact. He went and stood up the chair and opened the mouth of the hanged person so that we could see that his tongue had been cut out." Not long after Mousawi was called to the man's office. He'd been pardoned by Saddam and was being released.

Many months after Hazem Al Amin's article appeared in *Al-Huyat,* he was contacted in September by the American embassy in Beirut. They wanted to know if Mousawi would talk to them. "We asked him," said Amin, "and he agreed on the condition that we be present at the meeting. We went with him to the meeting, which took place at the Phoenicia Hotel." The American military attaché entered the lobby with three CIA agents. "They asked to talk to him alone, without us," Amin said. "They went up with him to a room in the hotel. When he agreed to this, we excused ourselves to leave and since then we lost contact with him [Mousawi]." Mousawi's lengthy session with the CIA was recorded on videotape. He gave them Speicher's authenticator information, the unique identifier used by American airmen and known only to the individual and his chain of command. He told them, too, about a badly burned American pilot, a man whose family didn't know it should be missing him. He'd told the agents the truth. But Mousawi hasn't been seen nor heard from since his meeting with the CIA at the Phoenicia.

Saddam Hussein compartmentalized information about Scott Speicher. He guarded it closely. Only his sons, Uday and Qusay, and a handful of his top advisors and cabinet officers knew anything about him. Some knew only that Saddam had Speicher, not where. Saddam never shared Speicher's location with his sons-in-law Lieutenant General Hussein Kamel Hassan Al Majid and Colonel Saddam Kamel Al Majid, who defected to Amman on August 7, 1995. Jordan initially granted the brothers asylum. Soon after, the brothers began to assist UNSCOM and its chairman, Rolf Ekéus, and the International Atomic Energy Agency (IAEA) inspection teams assigned to look for weapons of mass destruction in Iraq. Hussein Kamel confirmed what weapons inspectors had been able to ascertain shortly before his defection, that Iraq had operated a biological warfare program prior to the Gulf War, providing locations for large amounts of undeclared technical documentation. The defection appears to have had a psychological impact in Baghdad due to uncertainty over what Hussein Kamel might reveal: soon afterwards, inspectors were invited to revisit weapons sites and new documents were turned over for examination. Later, in their January 25, 1999 report to the UN Security Council, UNSCOM observed that the history of Iraq's weapons inspections "must be divided into two parts, separated by the events following the departure from Iraq, in August 1995, of Lt. Gen. Hussein Kamel."

The Kamels were debriefed by the CIA and British MI6. As Saddam's former defense minister and minister of industries and military industrialization, Hussein Kamel, once a rising star in Baghdad, was ready to talk to the Americans and British about what he knew. So was his brother. When the CIA asked Hussein Kamel about Speicher, he told them he didn't know where he was. He knew nothing. But he was lying. Hussein Kamel didn't know Speicher's precise whereabouts but he certainly knew all about him. His denial was a deception. "It wouldn't surprise him if he had Scott," said Buddy Harris of Hussein Kamel's reply when asked if he thought Saddam could keep an American pilot and no one would know it. "It wouldn't surprise him if he [Hussein Kamel] didn't know about it because Saddam is like a stolen art dealer." The stolen art can't be shared with the world, just the inner circle. "He can't tell anybody," said Harris of Saddam, "because they'd gain so much power just by going down and looking at it. And that's just how he [Hussein Kamel] described Saddam Hussein. That's just the kind of guy he is." Not quite.

After UNSCOM, IAEA, the CIA and British MI6 were done with the Kamel brothers, so was Jordan. On February 19, 1996, the day before Hussein Kamel returned home to Baghdad, a visitor to his house in Amman asked if he was sure it was safe to go back. "No, I am not sure. But after the way I have been treated here, I prefer to return."[2] He and his brother couldn't stay in Jordan. That much was clear. King Hussein bin Talal didn't want Saddam's sons-in-law taking up permanent residence in Jordan. After Saddam assured the Kamels they'd been forgiven, they packed up their belongings and returned to Baghdad with their wives. But Saddam hadn't really forgiven them. He forced his daughters to divorce them and the Kamels were quickly declared traitors. When they refused to turn themselves in to Saddam's security forces, members of their extended family stormed the safe house where they'd taken refuge. After a thirteen-minute firefight both were dead. They'd shamed their clan. This was an honor killing. But it was orchestrated and encouraged by Saddam. The Kamels' deaths were payback for knowing too much and talking to the Americans.

Charles Forrest said later that he believed Speicher's problems had dragged on so long, more than a decade when he last spoke of the issue with this writer, because the United States thinks that a diplomatic approach will ultimately work in a missing person's case. It doesn't always. Saddam clung to Speicher with unmatched determination while he was in power. Diplomacy means nothing to dictators whose primary means of controlling people is extreme violence. While Washington tried polite diplomacy with Baghdad, corpses were stacked up like cordwood all over Iraq. Saddam truly hated the United States. "It is hatred intensified by a tribal culture of the blood feud, one that he has embraced since Mr. Bush's father defeated him on the field of battle," wrote Richard Perle, former assistant secretary of defense, in a December 28, 2001 *New York*

Times op-ed. Saddam didn't need the world to know he had Scott Speicher. He got his joy out of knowing he'd gotten away with it. From the captor's point of view, why kill someone who provides daily pleasure? While this is repulsive to the West, it wasn't to Saddam. Maybe one day he'd let Speicher go if he could barter him in trade for something of higher value. He was capable. But others wouldn't agree. "[I] am confident," observed Chip Beck, "that Saddam [was] ruthless, clever and vengeful enough to maintain a live American pilot in secrecy if he had the opportunity – and the pilot – to do so."

There was another side of Saddam that was rarely seen. He was a devout Muslim who took many of his public prompts from the Qur'an, still others from the Christian Bible. How can someone with his long history of sadism be the same man? He was. Chris Toensing, editor of *Middle East Report* and director of the Middle East Research and Information Project (MERIP), said in early 2002, about a year before Saddam was deposed, that Americans really didn't want to understand Saddam and they didn't want to understand Arab culture either. "Americans can be obtuse and disparaging of the [Arab] culture," he said. "They don't want to know it. They don't want to understand it. It's easier to dismiss it as beneath our own, as violent and devoid of morality."

Saddam saw himself as a great Iraqi leader. He would be the one, he thought, to resurrect the glory days of Nebuchadnezzar's Babylon Empire. And it really only mattered what he thought. General Wafic Al Samarrai, who'd headed Iraqi military intelligence, commented [in broken English], "He's much fond of going into history. Perhaps, when you go to Babel, where there are these ruins, of Nebuchadnezzar, there's this building with a little inscription saying, 'This was rebuilt, reconstructed during the days of Saddam.' He's very much fond of going into history as a great leader."[3] Saddam had a lot in common with Nebuchadnezzar. Hundreds of Babylonian Jews were held by Nebuchadnezzar as prisoners for years, most until they died a natural death.

"Memorials to Saddam are legion," said Dr. Phebe A. Marr, retired senior fellow at the National Defense University Institute for National Strategic Studies. "As far as Babylon is concerned, he [had] completely renovated the hanging garden and the ancient remains of Babylon, 'restoring' them to what they were, with his name stamped on all the bricks." He wanted to be remembered in the same sentence with Nebuchadnezzar and Hammurabi, whose names and seals had been affixed to bricks in Babylon. Saddam went further. He recorded on clay or bricks his own history of events and placed them under archival corners of prominent buildings. This was something also done in ancient times. Corners of ancient buildings had a space below the foundation stone, a place where the king made sure that his histories and archives would be preserved, equivalent to a time capsule. Saddam removed the contents of many of Iraq's ancient archival corners and had them on display in his museums.

Saddam built the six hundred-room palace Nebuchadnezzar in the heart of Babylon, Iraq's ancient capital. Before Operation Desert Storm he ordered a huge statue of himself erected over the restored gates of Babylon. Nebuchadnezzar had done the same, which is documented in Daniel 3:1-7. During Saddam's Babylon restoration archaeologists discovered a plaque on the right-hand side of the ancient city gate, placed there by Nebuchadnezzar to proclaim his greatness. Saddam was inspired by it. He ordered stonemasons to place another plaque on the left-hand side of the gate to glorify his own greatness. Bricks in this location were cast with the phrase "Babylon is rising again." Saddam didn't permit tokenism to creep into Babylon's restoration. He wanted Nebuchadnezzar's Babylon reproduced to ancient specifications, including the palace throne room.

But all was not as it seemed in Babylon. Russian and Chinese technicians lived and worked there. Western intelligence suspected the Chinese were stringing the Nebuchadnezzar palace with a sophisticated and far-advanced fiber optic network that would give Saddam a deadlier integrated air defense (IAD) system. He knew the United States wouldn't attack a religious, archaeological or historic site. He knew that President George H.W. Bush's January 15, 1991 National Security Directive ordered American forces to "reduce collateral damage incidents to military attacks, taking special precautions to minimize civilian casualties and damage to nonmilitary economic infrastructure, energy-related facilities, and religious sites." After Desert Storm, Saddam used Bush's directive to his advantage. His weapons systems, munitions, new technologies he'd bought from Russia and China, and perhaps his prize prisoners would've been kept in places the Bush directive declared off-limits to attack. No one knew just then where Speicher might have been moved. But they weren't looking hard either.

British MI6 gave some startling information on Speicher to the CIA and DIA in the fall of 2001. An MI6 source recently returned from Baghdad reported what American intelligence suspected all along: only a handful of Saddam's closest associates were allowed to get near Speicher. This included his sons, Uday and Qusay, Tahir Jalil Habbush al-Tikriti, the chief of Saddam's mukhabarat, the Iraqi Intelligence Service (IIS), Hani Abd Latif Tilfa al-Tikriti, chief of Iraq's Special Security Organization (SSO), and Izzat Ibrahim Al Duri, Saddam's number two and now funder of Sunni insurgents inside post-Saddam Iraq. Saddam constructed a protection detail for Speicher. Appointed out of his Special Security Organization, this group of four, and never more than five, handpicked men was headed by Sa'iq Al Sharoub. Sharoub and his men were with Speicher from the time he was taken prisoner and would have remained with Speicher until he was killed between the United States' invasion of Iraq in March 2003 and before the end of 2005. After Sharoub took over day-to-day control of him Scott Speicher was rarely mentioned by his American name again.

Habbush hid all of Saddam's dirty laundry. He hid Speicher. The mukhabarat's principal command and control complex was in Baghdad. It was from this headquarters that the plot to kill former President George H.W. Bush was planned. The attempt was carried out in Kuwait during Bush's April 1993 visit. It was from his Baghdad headquarters that Habbush gave Speicher an Arabic name to conceal his identity from western and American intelligence services and the Israeli Mossad[4]. No one would ever see the name "Michael Scott Speicher" on a prison registry. All they'd see was another Arabic name. Among Saddam's insiders and Speicher's guards, he also earned an Arabic nickname. This name reminded them of his chief jailer, Sharoub, whose nose was big like a crow's beak. They called him "The Crow's Pilot." The mukhabarat kept most of its prisoners at Abu Ghraib, the largest and most important prison under its control. Thus Hussam Mousawi's story of the American pilot at Abu Ghraib now didn't seem so impossible. MI6 told American intelligence where Speicher was held. He'd been moved around, of course, but he wasn't beyond detection by foreign intelligence inside Iraq. Later, it was clear that MI6 also had a picture of him in captivity, passed to MI6 by a source inside Saddam's regime. Speicher had facial scars and walked with a limp they said.

The CIA and DIA sat on MI6's information for months before it was leaked on Capitol Hill to the Washington media. There were enough debunkers involved in Speicher's case to stop new information before it saw the light of day. This mindset was enough, said Bob Dussault, to prevent "ninety-nine percent of all chances of a successful recovery from being planned or executed" because their image or credibility or political position might be negatively affected by a mission that ended in a missing man coming home who was supposed to be dead. "They are political beings," he said, "who are not focused on the operator [in this case Speicher], but totally unable or unwilling to give the operator the benefit of the doubt." It was the first week of March 2002 before news that Speicher was being held in Baghdad was picked up by national media. But the news spread rapidly across the country. He was once again front page news. Then on March 8, 2002, the ICRC sent Baghdad another message about Scott Speicher. Again Red Cross officials tried to get Saddam to give him up. He didn't.

Then came word that in January 2002 Dutch intelligence made contact with an Iraqi defector who'd also shared information about an American pilot. This defector said that Speicher was moved to a military facility after the events of 9/11, a temporary move to "protect" him, Saddam's prize prisoner, from being "damaged." The American media briefly picked up on the story. State Department spokesman Richard Boucher, blitzed by press queries, issued a simple statement during his regular briefing on March 11, 2002. He said an American delegation led by Ambassador to Kuwait Richard Jones had underscored that Iraq continued "to shirk its responsibility to answer the many unresolved questions about Commander Speicher's fate." But State's response was just talk. Words wouldn't get Speicher back.

Still frustrated he wasn't getting answers on Speicher, SSCI chairman senator Pat Roberts convened a special session of the committee on March 20, 2002. The SSCI's members shared Roberts' belief that the Pentagon's stonewalling and claims that none of the intelligence on Speicher could possibly be true were hampering progress in the case. They were right. The Pentagon, CIA and DIA, if they'd not already lied outright were lying by omission. Roberts called CIA director George Tenet and DIA director vice admiral Tom Wilson to testify again. Roberts wanted the truth. "Given all the information in your possession," he asked them, "is Scott Speicher alive today? Tell us all now," he said.

There was silence. Tenet and Wilson paused. Roberts waited.

"Yes, he is," they replied.

This was one of the most important admissions in the case's history, but the public would know nothing of it had it not been leaked from closed session by an attendee with a conscience.

Retired ambassador Frances D. Cook attended a March 26 seminar on Iraq hosted by the Washington Institute for Near East Policy that featured Amatzia Baram. "[Baram] reads all Iraqi newspapers every day," said Cook, "has tons of informants and has spent a lifetime's scholarship on the subject. He also had clear evidence that Saddam read everything that [Baram] wrote up to the time he was deposed." Baram's lecture, "Iraq: Post Saddam," was prescient. After his talk was over, Cook spoke to Baram about Scott Speicher. "As a lot of folks were crowding around, I only got to ask if he thought Speicher could still be alive," she said later. "It would be very like Saddam," said Baram just then, "to keep an American all these years and not tell anyone about it. Very, very like Saddam." He said the United States needed to send someone to Baghdad to officially discuss Speicher. But he warned that Washington couldn't expect anything but propagandist rhetoric in return.

Saddam believed that the United States left Speicher behind. Thus he had the right to keep him, just because of that abandonment. Baghdad's November 6, 2001 response to the author and *Virginian-Pilot* writer Lon Wagner certainly reflected this belief. "After almost another five years' silence," wrote Dr. Fahmi El Qaisy, Iraq's minister of legal affairs, "U.S. President Clinton raised on January 12, 2001, once again and on a large scale, the issue of the pilot, Speicher. Accordingly," he continued, "the status of the pilot, Speicher, has been changed from killed in the operations into a missing person. The United States headed for the first time to the Tripartite Committee and asked to present a fact-finding file for the pilot ten years after his death." This wasn't true.

The United States was represented at both Tripartite Commissions held in 1991 and 1993. Information about Scott Speicher was requested from Baghdad both times. The Iraqi government replied in 1993 that it had no idea what had happened to Speicher. Just then that was true. But they were quick learners. By the time the United States went into Iraq in March 2003, Saddam knew everything about Scott Speicher. He'd had his American in the basement for close to nine years.

President George W. Bush addressed the UN on September 12, 2002, to call its members to action against Iraq for a long list of transgressions. He reminded them of 1991's UN Resolutions 686 and 687 that demanded Baghdad repatriate all prisoners of war from Kuwait and other nations. "Iraq's regime agreed," said Bush. "It broke its promise. Last year the secretary general's high-level coordinator for this issue reported that Kuwaiti, Saudi, Indian, Syrian, Lebanese, Iranian, Egyptian, Bahraini and Omani nationals remain unaccounted for – more than 600 people. One American pilot is among them." Speicher hadn't made President Bush's top ten list in the Iraq War Resolution, formerly the Authorization for Use of Military Force Against Iraq Resolution of 2002, Public Law 107-243,[5] enacted on October 16 of that year. The condition of Speicher's return was actually far down on Saddam's to-do list to avoid armed confrontation with the United States and its growing list of Coalition allies.

Bush's insistence that Iraq account for Speicher fell under Title 22 U.S. Code, Chapter 23, Section 1732, Release of Citizens Imprisoned by Foreign Governments. This part of the code states that whenever it is made known to the president that any citizen of the United States has been unjustly deprived of his liberty by or under the authority of any foreign government, "it shall be the duty of the President forthwith to demand of that government the reasons of such imprisonment; and if it appears to be wrongful and in violation of the rights of American citizenship, the President shall forthwith demand the release of such citizen, and if the release so demanded is unreasonably delayed or refused, the President shall use such means, not amounting to acts of war and not otherwise prohibited by law, as he may think necessary and proper to obtain or effectuate the release; and all the facts and proceedings relative thereto shall as soon as practicable be communicated by the President to Congress." But in this case it can be argued that invocation of Speicher's long-known captivity status was emotive.

The president's words sounded like a step in the right direction. But they still weren't enough. The United States hasn't demanded changes to the most important document of all: the one that covers cease-fire agreements with the nation's enemies. A clause authorizing military action into enemy territory post-conflict to recover prisoners of war and missing in action who've not been turned over at the peace table has yet to be added to the United States' postwar cease-fire agreements. Add the clause and lives can and will be saved.

Navy secretary Gordon R. England had reclassified Speicher missing-captured on October 11, 2002. He also promoted him to navy captain. Missing-captured denotes a service member who has been seized as the result of action by an unfriendly military or paramilitary force in a foreign country. Under terms of the 1949 Geneva Convention England's reclassification of Speicher as missing-captured was the equivalent of prisoner of war. About two weeks later, on October 30, President Bush signed into law the Persian Gulf War POW/MIA Accountability Act of 2001 [U.S. Senate 1339]. Attached to Senate 1339 was an asylum program to encourage any Middle Eastern national, including his family, who returns a live American prisoner of war from the Persian Gulf War. This amendment to the Bring Them Home Alive Act of 2000, also called the Speicher Bill, was an important step forward. "It's not only for Scott," said Senator Pat Roberts on January 6, 2003. "It's for every person who wears the uniform." Roberts was still trying to meet with Iraq's UN representative, Mohammed Al Duri, to discuss Speicher's repatriation when he spoke about the passage of Senate 1339. He'd written to Saddam to encourage the meeting with Al Duri. Al Duri indicated then that he'd asked Saddam's compliance to effect Speicher's humanitarian release. But nothing came of it.

"There are signs of an American POW in Iraq," Roberts said after returning from a congressional visit to the Middle East. A few days later, during a January 10 appearance on CNN's *Wolf Blitzer Live*, he said "I can't tell you what it's like if you look at one mistake after another. We did actually leave somebody behind." We'd left behind more than one. But Roberts didn't say it. He couldn't. His SSCI was still investigating and Speicher's case of survival was so strong. The public didn't need to know just then about the possibility of more Americans left behind from the Persian Gulf War. America didn't need another Vietnam. But it had one. Speicher was not the only American who was missing from Operation Desert Storm.

Gulf War servicemen weren't informed that Iraq wasn't the only enemy who might capture and keep them prisoner. This was most especially true of men who went down in southern Iraq and near Iraq's disputed border and territorial waters with Iran. No one told the families of unaccounted-for Gulf War airmen, whose files were marked with a presumptive finding of death because their bodies were not recovered, about "the axis." This was the tripartite agreement between Iran, Iraq and Syria formalized after the Persian Gulf War. The House Republican Research Committee's Task Force on Terrorism and Unconventional Warfare published a paper about it on August 10, 1992, more than a year-and-a-half after the war ended. The pact had everything to do with Iran's planning for a major war in the Middle East with Iran leading a powerful bloc of Muslim states against Israel. America's presence in Kuwait during the first Persian Gulf War and its push into southern Iraq in January 1991 was the canary in the coal mine for Tehran; it was the defining moment of a short-lived war with long-term consequences. Iran advanced its war planning against the United States. Tehran didn't have a choice. The United States didn't go home after it drove Iraq out of Kuwait.

Postwar escalation of hostilities between Washington and Baghdad pushed Tehran to tighten its grip over a strategic alliance that stretched from the Mediterranean to Iran. The axis was just part of a much larger Islamic bloc that was being consolidated by Tehran which also includes Sudan and the Muslim countries of Central and South Asia, among them Afghanistan and Pakistan. This bloc remains central to Tehran, which has been making plans for nearly two decades to wage major war in the region and has built its strategic plans around the assumption that war is inevitable. The primary objective of this war is to evict the United States from the Muslim world, especially the Persian Gulf region, and to "liberate" Jerusalem from the Jews.

Syria shares Iran's political strategic view and believes, too, that war is imminent. Damascus long ago concluded that there could be no compromise between Israel and Syria because their respective positions are too far apart to be reconciled. To Damascus, the peace process is meaningless; peace talk does nothing for the stability of an already unstable region. Any proffer of peace is viewed as a strategic façade engineered by Washington to expand and consolidate its position in the Middle East. Thus Damascus remains convinced that drastic action, including war with Israel, is required to break repeated diplomatic deadlocks and reverse decades old American influence in the region.

Iraq's crisis with the United States post-Desert Storm centered on UN weapons inspections, all of which did nothing more than strengthen Baghdad's relationship with Tehran and Damascus. The alliance became stronger in many respects. To prove its loyalty to its axis partners, Baghdad had a longer road to travel; it was the least trusted member of the pact. If Saddam was such a distrusted ally, why support him? Why partner with him? The reason is quite simple. Iraq's geographical location is the link between Iran and Syria. Iraq is the crucial element in Tehran's design – then and now. Immediately before, during and after Desert Storm Baghdad was being transformed into a loyal and active participant in the Iran-led bloc. The sense of urgency felt by Iran and Syria over Iraq's connection to the axis was best reflected in the decision Tehran and Damascus made to accept Saddam remaining in power. To ensure that Iraq's ability to contribute to a war against Israel remained intact, Tehran and Damascus gave aid to Saddam to make sure he survived the UN embargo, could subvert sanctions and rebuild Iraq's military power. But they also explored ways to ultimately replace Saddam with a leader more to their liking, an observation made clear in the House Republican task force report first published in the fall of 1992.

Saddam was completely aware of Tehran's thinking and responded with a strategy of his own. He was certainly eager to prove his loyalty to Tehran and the partnership. Saddam didn't hide the fact that he'd willingly participate in a war with Israel. But on the other hand he also demonstrated his resolve to stay in power by actively purging perceived traitors in his military, where his most dangerous challenges came from Syrian Ba'athists, and by suppressing Shi'as to deprive Tehran of popular support against Iraq's Ba'athist minority. But ultimately this convoluted process of power posturing and the pursuit of seemingly contradictory goals couldn't stand up to Tehran's dominant influence. The ramifications of Saddam's fall is symptomatic of a Middle East sliding rapidly toward a war instigated by Tehran.

The origins of the alliance between Tehran, Baghdad and Damascus, and its central role in a major war with Israel, are not new. Observers in the years since Desert Storm document this concept as the cornerstone of Grand Ayatollah Ruhollah Musavi Khomeini's plan for an Islamic Revolution that would both secure and export that revolution only if Iran constituted the core of a regional bloc. Former Iranian president Abol Hassan Bani Sadr said that Khomeini was thinking about "an 'Islamic belt in the Middle East,' a group of Shi'ite countries under his heel that would include Iran, Iraq, Syria and Lebanon."

While it was impossible for Iran to achieve this bloc while at war with Iraq, once the war was over former enemies faced a common enemy: the United States. Iraq faced the United States in Desert Storm; Iran watched. But Tehran also did more than watch; it got its hands dirty. Khomeini's axis was infused by Iraq's war with the United States. When Saddam called for an all-Islamic jihad against the Great Satan, for the destruction of Israel and the restoration of a Khomeini-style traditional Islamic rule over the holy shrines of Jerusalem, Mecca and Medina in the spring of 1990, he was expanding his great war to an Islamic war against the United States. How could Tehran and Damascus ignore the chance to join in? They didn't.

Baghdad reached a strategic agreement with Tehran, then also in direct contact with Damascus, in the summer of 1990. By mid-June 1990 Barzan Ibrahim Al Hassan al-Tikriti, Saddam's half-brother and Iraq's ambassador to Switzerland, personally negotiated the cooperation and coordination of terrorist and procurement of operations in Europe with Cyrus Nasseri, special representative of Ayatollah Ali Akbar Hashemi Rafsanjani, then Iran's president. During negotiations Tehran insisted that support and assistance for crucial elements of the Iraqi war effort had to address the strategic posture in the region in which Iran and Syria were to be given a greater role and power. The result of these deliberations was codified in a formal secret pact signed by Iran and Iraq on July 28, 1990. Then, on August 15, Baghdad recognized and handed to Tehran a so-called strategic victory in the already concluded Iran-Iraq War: Iraq's agreement with Iran let Tehran provide Baghdad with vital support without becoming directly involved in a Gulf conflict. This "grand design" was backed completely by Rafsanjani and Hafez Al Assad, then president of Syria.

But on the eve of the Persian Gulf War Iran pulled out of the deal because Tehran didn't think that Baghdad could deliver strategic gains, despite the fact that Iraq had, just then, the fourth largest army in the world and its air force and air defense system were only exceeded in sophistication by the United States and Russia. Mostly, Tehran just didn't trust Saddam's intentions. As the war unfolded, Rafsanjani and Assad saw no reason why a Tikriti Sunni, Saddam, might succeed at leading and dominating an Islamic jihad. They viewed him as a failure waiting to happen.

Tehran made the decision not to support Saddam's war with the United States the first time, largely because Iraq failed to pull off a surprise attack against the American-led Coalition in December 1990 and also due to Iraq's later adoption of a passive strategy. Tehran and Damascus didn't believe Baghdad could carry out the joint world-wide terrorist campaign and thus ordered their terrorist networks not to support Iraq. But this didn't mean they weren't in Iraq and watching and acting with impunity. Iran stayed out of the conflict, at least on the surface. Tehran convinced Baghdad to deploy to Iran many of Iraq's strategic reserves, including its aircraft, tanks and artillery, weapons that were later used by the Iranians. Saddam sent his frontline MiGs to Iran, too. These are the same MiGs that American air force F-15s chased down trying to flee over the Iraq-Iran border. For its part, Syria went so far as to send a token force to Saudi Arabia to cover its own position.

Despite Iran and Syria's actions to counter an untrustworthy Saddam, Iraq stayed loyal to the pact. By early 1991 Saddam believed so much in this strategy that his only viable option, noted observers of his decision-making process, was to absorb the United States' first strike and stay on the defensive. Baghdad gambled that a combination of America's threat to Shi'ite holy shrines in Najaf and Karbala, and a call for Shi'a-dominated jihad would be too enticing for Tehran and Damascus to avoid and thus he'd get their support against the United States in an all-out war. Tehran thought about it. In January 1991 there were high-level meetings to debate the possibility of reversing policy and joining with Iraq in the war against the United States. But Tehran ultimately decided to stay on its own course, one which kept them focused on an alliance it controlled.

Iran opted to avoid direct participation in the Persian Gulf War but stepped up intelligence collection, including taking and accepting prisoners from Operation Desert Storm. They'd be valuable sources of information then and useful later when Iran eventually confronted the United States on its own terms. Better for Tehran if the United States didn't know they had them either. American prisoners in Iranian custody became men without a country. They'd been declared legally dead and no one would ever know what had really happened to them. They joined Iran's "United Nations" of prisoners, men and women who found their way into Iranian jails, some for more than thirty years and others as recent as 2010. There are Americans, Brits, Canadians, Aussies, French, high-value Israeli military prisoners, and thousands of others, many of them from Southwest and Central Asia. Some were diplomats and members of ruling families, others were humanitarian aid and religious workers, journalists, businessmen; some were just tourists who wandered too close to the wrong border. But those of particular concern in the West were soldiers, sailors and airmen who'd been captured by Iranian forces over a protracted period of time, others traded or sent to them by Baghdad for safekeeping – a rainy day – and to keep them beyond the reach of western and Israeli intelligence trying to find them. Human trafficking of prisoners of war is practiced with impunity between Iran, Iraq and Syria, Pakistan, Afghanistan, Russia and the former Soviet republics, China and America's old enemies in Southeast Asia, including Vietnam, Laos and Cambodia, and not to forget the United States' East Asian enemy North Korea.

The Islamic Revolutionary Guard Corps (IRGC) Qods Force, the Iranian special operations and intelligence group responsible for covert operations outside of Iran, continue to work largely unimpeded and often little noticed inside Iraq, just as they did during the Persian Gulf War. There are approximately five thousand men assigned to the Qods Force unconventional warfare mission; this is the equivalent of one Special Forces division, plus additional smaller formations, and these forces are given special priority in terms of training and equipment. In addition, the IRGC has a special Qods

Force that plays a major role in giving Iran the ability to conduct unconventional warfare overseas using various foreign terrorist organizations as proxies.[6] But the IRGC, with or without the use of its Qods Force, has also developed tactics that in most respects form a layered or "mosaic" defense with the army and air forces, where the IRGC kept up constant pressure on any advancing U.S. forces inside Iraq, especially after the start of Operation Iraqi Freedom.

The IRGC has developed and used special stay behind units or "cells" that would include some 1,800 to 3,000 teams of three to four soldiers whose main mission was, and is, to attack American lines of supply and communication, strike at elements in rear areas, and conduct ambushes of combat troops. This includes sending units forward into countries like Iraq and Afghanistan to attack U.S. forces there, or encourage local forces to do so, and sending teams to raid or infiltrate the southern Gulf States friendly to the United States.[7] The Qods Force has thus long maintained significant presence in Iraq's Shi'a territory and among Iraq's Shi'a militias.

The Qods have shaped present day operations in Iraq from past experience. General David H. Petraeus, then commander of Multi-National Forces-Iraq (MNF-I), stressed the growing role of the Qods Force and IRGC in his congressional testimony back in April 2007, when he explained that American forces found Qods operatives in Iraq and seized computers that indicted Iran's special operations component for some of the war's most serious transgressions. Seized computers contained hard drives with highly classified Iranian special operations plans, including a twenty-two-page "how-to" manual detailing plans, approval process and conduct of an attack that led to the deaths of five American soldiers in Karbala. He said that the IRGC Qods Force had provided "substantial funding, training on Iranian soil, advanced explosive munitions and technologies as well as run-of-the-mill arms and ammunition, in some cases advice and in some cases even a degree of direction. Our sense," Petraeus continued, "is that these records were kept so that they could be handed in to whoever it is that is financing them ... And, again, there's not [a] question ... that Iranian financing is taking place through the Qods Force of the Iranian [Revolutionary] Guard Corps."[8]

The incident at Karbala to which General Petraeus referred was the direct result of sophisticated, well planned and well rehearsed Qods Force deception operation that took place on January 20, 2007, at the provincial joint coordination center (PJCC) against a small U.S. Army civil affairs unit embedded with Iraqi security forces and civilian leaders from the surrounding area. About five o'clock in the afternoon local time, between five and seven black GMC SUVs approached an Iraqi security forces checkpoint. The vehicles were filled with twelve men wearing American desert camouflage and Iraqi uniforms. All had the requisite equipment and identification to show the checkpoint guards. No one thought twice about the vehicles. They'd seen them enough times as part of American diplomatic convoys and, certainly, security personnel drove them, too, so when the vehicles' occupants flashed American military identification cards and spoke in perfect English no one saw a problem. They were certain the men in the vehicles were American and called ahead to the PJCC, where the Americans were in a meeting to discuss safety measures for Shi'as attending Ashura. But the men in the SUVs weren't Americans. They were on a mission and knew exactly who they wanted and where they were.

They moved past Iraqi police in the compound and right through the PJCC building for the army civil affairs team. The Americans never saw what was coming. They'd never gotten word that the unexpected "American" convoy was fast approaching. Once in the compound the men inside the SUVs split into two groups, going into the building from the front and back. A grenade thrown into the first floor common area killed one soldier and wounded three others. Outside the civil affairs team's vehicles were destroyed and two American soldiers pulled from one of them were transferred to the attackers' SUVs. Inside two more Americans were captured and also put in the SUVs. Qods Force operatives subsequently executed the four Americans.

There are several important takeaways from the Karbala incident that pointed to a well oiled Qods Force operation: the American uniforms and equipment were genuine; the attackers spoke English without the accent of native Iraqi speakers; their appearance, one of them was described as having blonde hair; and the "American" identification cards they'd shown the checkpoint guard were real enough for them to gain entry. They looked, acted and sounded like American soldiers.

The IRGC and Qods Force had considerable experience operating in Iraq, Kuwait, Saudi Arabia and the rest of the southern Gulf states prior to the Persian Gulf War. From Desert Shield forward the IRGC exercised well-executed covert and deception operations in the capture of American servicemen, especially downed airmen, from redresses of corpses burned beyond recognition to seeding crash sites with human artifacts and remains that couldn't be identified except by association with a crash site or debris field. By the time American mortuary services personnel recovered some remains, it had been weeks since the aircraft loss. Remains were in poor condition and to transport them back to the mortuary at Dover Air Force Base body parts were soaked in formaldehyde, a process that made DNA identification and further forensics analysis impossible.

No one questioned why a U.S. Navy Hornet off the USS *Theodore Roosevelt* (CVN-71) never turned up in the shallow waters of the Persian Gulf; it should've but it didn't. Why? No one questioned how a Marine Corps aviator's intact harness with his name in perfectly readable condition was strapped to a charred torso. No one questioned the identification of partial remains recovered from the shallows of Maridin Island around the wreckage of a U.S. Air Force AC-130; not at first. Everyone assumed they knew the story associated with each incident. Families took information provided by their loved one's branch of service as truth. They assumed wrong. They'd not been told the full story.

Washington knew about the pact between Iraq, Iran and Syria; it knew that the United States' military presence in the Persian Gulf and Red Sea had Tehran on the brink of going to war, and it knew that encroaching on Iranian air space and over its disputed territory could strike the match that lit a broader regional conflict. But Washington also knew something else: that going all the way to Baghdad and deposing Saddam would also draw Iran and Syria into the fight. Tehran and Damascus weren't ready for Saddam to go, not just then. The Bush administration hedged its bet and said no to Baghdad. The U.S.-led Coalition stopped with the liberation of Kuwait. 'Ihis was a fateful decision that left missing American and Coalition servicemen in jeopardy of never being recovered.

Tehran's posture during the Persian Gulf War was passive-aggressive. Iran continued to focus on consolidation of its strategic axis, also its major reason for half-heartedly supporting southern Iraq's Shi'a uprising in the spring of 1991, despite the close relationship between Iraq's Shi'a elite and Tehran's mullahs, many of whom were quartered in Najaf and Karbala during the shah's reign.

By mid-1991, all of the Middle East's main powers were rethinking their regional strategic posture. The Islamic bloc dominated by Tehran and Damascus was clearly emerging as the dominant power in the region, a powerful alliance made stronger after it was enjoined to former Soviet Central Asian republics Afghanistan and Pakistan. This gave the Islamic bloc unprecedented power in the Near East. But as far as the Arab world was concerned, wrote congressional experts later, this bloc wasn't very different from the alliance Saddam advocated on the eve of, and during, the first phase of the Persian Gulf War. Thus Baghdad could have linked up to the Islamic bloc ostensibly without Saddam's losing face. By the end of 1991 the Islamic bloc was the key to Iraq's ability to survive UN-imposed sanctions. Saddam had, in fact, as early as the spring of that year, recognized Tehran as the region's dominant power.

Saddam's dealings with Tehran and its new bloc were the outcome of a profound change in Baghdad's reading of the region's strategic position. Baghdad realized that UN sanctions weren't going away, thus it pursued ad-hoc arrangements aimed at overcoming short-term problems to its long-term position and commitments in the region. Iran and Syria made good partners and were especially crucial to Iraq's long-term importation of military assistance that kept Saddam in power. They could also take that power away by withdrawing tactical support. When it was ready, Iran let the United States do the heavy lifting, when we removed Saddam from power in the spring of 2003, and Iraq of decades of Sunni Ba'athist rule.

Post-Persian Gulf War Iraq's use of Iran and Syria as ports of entry for all forms of imports banned by sanctions was Baghdad's best bet. There was no western oversight in these countries and both were overtly hostile to the United States but otherwise cooperative with all other international governing bodies. In its pursuit of this option, Baghdad was fully aware of the cost to its strategic position in the axis. But Iraq also got help from the Sudan, which negotiated Baghdad's postwar deal with Tehran. During the war Sudan had been one of Iraq's closest allies and, in fact, had dispatched a large Iraqi expeditionary force for the seizure of Islam's holy shrines at Hejaz, including Mecca and Medina, and the blocking of the Red Sea. Sudan's support followed the coming to power in 1991 of Hassan Al Turabi and the Muslim Brotherhood. Turabi transformed Sudan into an Islamic republic that shifted its allegiance to Tehran. Thus the first meaningful contacts between Iran and Iraq had been revived in Khartoum in April 1991. Iranian officials discussed issues concerning cross-border trade with Iraqi intelligence officials concealed among representatives of an Iraqi trade union delegation then participating in a Khartoum conference. In these discussions Sa'ad Abd Al Majid Al Faisal al-Tikriti, a Ba'ath Party regional command chairman in Salah al Din Province north of Baghdad, emerged as a major figure in the Sudan-Iran-Iraq negotiations. A longtime associate of Turabi, Sa'ad was also involved in clandestine financing operations for the Egyptian Islamist networks via Sudan.

Tripartite discussions between Iraq, Iran and Sudan dragged on inconclusively through the summer of 1991, according to congressional reports published at that time. Tehran insisted that Baghdad recognize the "new" strategic reality in the region before any agreement could be reached. At the same time Iran slowly withdrew its behind-the-scenes support for Shi'a and Kurdish uprisings that had sprung up in southern and northern Iraq to demonstrate its good faith to Saddam. The turning point in these negotiations came when a high-level Baghdad delegation arrived in Tehran for the October 19-22, 1991 Iranian-hosted terrorist conference. The Iraqi delegation's presence was largely symbolic; it was Saddam's attempt to placate Tehran. But it didn't really go far enough. Iranian leadership still didn't trust Baghdad and left no doubt about it by giving quarter to Saddam's sworn enemy, the Supreme Council for Islamic Revolution in Iraq (SCIRI).

While Iraqi officials tried to mend fences with their Iranian counterparts, Sudan was putting the finishing touches on its final transformation to an Iranian fiefdom; this was finished by mid-December 1991 during a visit to Khartoum by a large Iranian delegation led by Rafsanjani and 157 other senior Iranian officials, including Ali Akbar Velayati, foreign minister; Akbar Torkan, first head of Iran's Ministry of Defense and Armed Forces Logistics; Hojatoleslam Ali Fallahian, head of Iranian intelligence; Mohsen Reza'i Mirgha'ed, head of the Islamic Revolutionary Guard Corps (IRGC); Zulradr, IRGC chief of staff; Gholam Reza Foruzesh, minister of Construction Jihad; Abdul Hussein Vahaji, minister of Commerce, and Masoud Roghani Zanjani, head of the Iranian budget office. Turabi and General Omar Al Bashir successfully brokered a strategic realignment between Tehran and Baghdad during this visit.

The first indication of a fundamental change in Iran's position came on December 24, 1991, when Tehran demanded that the new axis should include both Iran and Iraq if it was to truly represent the interests of the region's nations. Tehran was aware that problems would continue to haunt the alliance as long as Saddam stayed in power – and said so. But, Tehran argued, when comparing the threat of American presence and the ramifications of a regional power vacuum, it was still preferable to have strong regional security organization free of external influence, even if it meant putting up with Saddam in the short-term. On December 29, 1991, Lieutenant General Ayad Futayyih Khalifa Al Rawi, Iraq's Qods Force chief of staff, arrived in Khartoum to negotiate the transfer of several Iraqi military assets in Sudan to the Sudanese and Iranian forces in return for an Iranian role in lifting the blockade against Iraq. Sudanese major general Muhammad Abdallah Uwaydah, speaking later of Ayad's visit, observed that "the need to lift the economic blockade against steadfast Iraqi people and their army" as one of the primary issues discussed in Khartoum.

Soon after the Khartoum summit Iran announced its support of twenty-five Iraqi military advisors stationed in the Juba area of southern Sudan. The arrival of these advisors brought the total number of Iraqi military advisors in Sudan to about 100. These Iraqi experts worked within a force dominated by Iranian IRGC, also called the Pasdaran, and Afghan mujahideen who'd come to "fight the infidels and purify Sudan." In the final phases of the Sudanese offensive against the Sudan People's Liberation Army (SPLA), Iraqi pilots flew against the rebels in support of Taburi's Iranian-led offensive.

In early 1992, in return for consolidating its strategic hegemony over Sudan, Tehran agreed in principle to supply Iraq with weapons, and to serve as a port of entry for weapons bought in the former Union of Soviet Socialist Republics (USSR), the People's Republic of China (PRC), and the Democratic People's Republic of Korea (DPRK), as well as industrialized goods and food. Iran and Syria further agreed to serve as the major outlets for Iraq's oil. Baghdad, in return, guaranteed uninterrupted land and air space for weapons and other equipment moving between Iran and Syria. Thus, if North Korean SCUD derivatives purchased for Syria were being shipped to Iran, they'd be moved to Syria through northern Iraq. Similar arrangements existed for the large number of tanks and self-propelled artillery Syria bought with Iranian funds in Russia and eastern Europe.

The most visible part of the Iran-Iraq pact was the improvement in Iraq's relationship with Syria. In the second half of December 1991, while negotiations were still going on in Khartoum, Saddam sent Hafez Al Assad a message with Barzan Ibrahim Al Hasan al-Tikriti, Saddam's uterine half-brother and a leader within the IIS, in which he proposed several layers of cooperation against their common enemies. He encouraged and praised Assad's strong position in negotiations with Israel. Barzan explicitly conveyed to Assad, that Syria should lead the Arab world's confrontation with Israel. Soon thereafter the Iraqi trade minister met with his Syrian counterparts to institutionalize the rapidly growing trade between their two countries.

Meetings followed in Cairo between the Iraqi oil minister and Syria's oil and minerals minister. Cross-border trade began in December 1991. Within the first month Iraq exported to Syria oil products in exchange for consumer goods, largely clothing, and processed food from Lebanon and Syria. By early 1992 these commercial activities were formalized further with the opening of the Al Walid and Abu Kamal border crossing posts. A few months later, in the spring of that year, goods from Lebanon and Syria were clearly reaching Iraqi markets, a fact that hadn't been missed by western observers. Thus in March 1992 both Tehran and Damascus articulated their new position on Iraq. "The situation is currently completely different than the situation during the Gulf War," *Al-Hayat* reported. "Kuwait was liberated, and therefore there is no justification for the use of force against Iraq."

President Assad accepted assurances from Tariq Aziz that Iraq wouldn't challenge Syria's position in the Arab world. By mid-March the *Tehran Times* blasted the UN embargo as serving only the interests of the United States. "The continuing imposition of sanctions against Iraq can only be said to be due to the resulting failure of the US-led policy to deal effectively with Saddam Hussein." Tehran added that under current conditions, Saddam remained relatively stable, facing no danger of being toppled by UN sanctions. Tehran further iterated that the only reason for keeping sanctions on Iraq was President George H.W. Bush's desire to rack up a foreign policy win during an election year. Since the sanctions were helping Washington, Iran's interest shifted to money laundering, acquisition of military hardware and technology, and international terrorism in Europe.[9] Iran's diversified clandestine activities in western Europe were largely resolved and common modes of operation had been worked out in meetings that spring.

The next meeting of the axis took place in mid-May 1992 and it was then that its participants took the pact one step farther, completing the draft text of the new Iran-Iraq Strategic Treaty and each of its equally important sub-agreements. The Iraqi delegation included Ali Hassan Abd Al Majid al-Tikriti, Iraq's defense minister; Qusay Hussein; Barzan, and Sa'dun Hammadi, formerly Iraqi prime minister and a prominent Shi'a. The Iranian delegation was headed by Hussein Bahramani, a close friend of Uday Hussein. The talks only went so far, largely due to Iran's extensive demands. A series of follow-up meetings were set to work out Tehran's demands of Baghdad. Khartoum sent officials to Baghdad, in the interim, to pressure Saddam to agree to Tehran's proposals. Iran and Iraq did come to agreement on other issues of mutual interest that would be discussed at a smaller summit and within several committees in Khartoum. To improve the secrecy of these clandestine negotiations, it was agreed that most of their ongoing discussions between high level participants would take place in Khartoum as if via the sovereign protection ensured by an embassy.[10]

After Bashir and Assad agreed on Syria's new policy toward Iraq, Sudanese chief of staff general Abd Ali Rahman Ali traveled to Baghdad, also in mid-May, to finalize the conditions of the new "heroic pan Arab posture" that was codified between Iraq and its neighbors. The Sudanese military delegation then continued to Tehran, bringing with them Iraqi responses to sub clauses of the pact. General Ali met with Rafsanjani to talk about Iraq. The expansion of the IRGC presence in the Sudan was also discussed at this meeting.

By the middle of May 1992 Iran and Iraq were already, in effect, implementing and formally on the verge of signing, a major strategic treaty that picked up where their pre-Gulf War agreement left off. They added specific arrangements to counter the implied "new world order" in the Persian Gulf. With assurances from Tehran and Damascus, Baghdad was convinced that no matter what Washington threatened, there might be additional tactical military strikes, but no all-out war by the United States and its allies. Baghdad's treaty with Tehran and Damascus gave Saddam an opportunity to rebuild Iraq's economy and military with active support from Iran and Syria as part of an anti-American axis. The most important part of the deal for Baghdad was its procurement of military hardware from the China and North Korea delivered through Iran. This arrangement put sophisticated weapon systems, including the F-7 fighter and anti-ship cruise missile, at the top of Saddam's wish list.

A comprehensive, well defined anti-American strategy had been articulated by members of the axis by mid-June. All parties agreed that there could be no compromise with the United States. Tehran's *Jahan-i Islam* told its followers that Washington's policy "is actually aimed at annihilating the [Islamic] Revolution and gradually dissolving the Iranian system." This is just one example of the media message promulgated to the Muslim world. Confronted with such a threat from the United States, Tehran concluded Iranians "are not prepared to retreat even an inch in their anti-Zionist positions and in their support for Muslims and the deprived. They will do their best to fight against the mischief, machinations, and plundering of the hegemonistic U.S. government."

The pact between Iran and Iraq was refined and clarified in the months ahead. During a late June 1992 meeting in Baghdad Ali Khorram, special envoy of Iran's foreign minister, Ali Akbar Velayati, carried special letters from Iranian leaders to their Iraqi colleagues that expressed Tehran's "desire to promote bilateral relations" with Saddam's regime. Iranian support for Iraq "removing the dust of the Atlantic-Zionist aggression" and "their great achievements in the field of reconstruction" punctuated Tehran's communication to Baghdad. But Tehran also wanted something else: it wanted to resolve outstanding issues concerning Iraqi prisoners of war from the Iran-Iraq War.

Syria was already fully committed to an anti-American strategy and said so. Damascus considered the inevitable struggle in the region to be an integral part of a global assault by the United States on the Third World. In late June the authoritative *Al-Ba'ath* newspaper pointed out: "World War III began with the Malta Summit and has not yet ended. Civil, ethnic, and border wars are the bullets of World War III, which will not end before every U.S. ministry becomes a ministry of the whole world." Damascus made it clear enough that "it is not in the U.S. interest for the wars raging in several parts of the world to come to an end because U.S. control requires continuing tension. This is what makes the United States not serious about solving the Middle East crisis." Damascus thus concluded that there was no escape from active participation in a war against the United States.

"In order not to lose the right and the future we have to give priority to our pan-Arab issues, prove to the world that we are a nation whose stage of division is over, and that we will not be the victim of the new world and the division caused by the Third [World] War, which began with the Malta Summit and whose chapters have not ended yet," *Al-Ba'ath* reiterated, invoking, once again, mention of the Malta Summit, a meeting that took place between U.S. President George H. W. Bush and Soviet leader Mikhail Gorbachev between December 2-3, 1989, just weeks after the fall of the Berlin Wall. Its main purpose was to provide the two superpowers with the chance to discuss what many dubbed the "new world order" that quickly took shape in Europe with the lifting of the Iron Curtain. The Malta Summit was viewed by the world as the most significant meeting of its kind since 1945 and signaled the end of the cold war. For Damascus a strategic axis dominated by Iran and Syria, and the entire Islamic bloc, remains its primary instrument for waging World War III.

Iran's new regional strategy and posture was best reflected in its analysis of the Persian Gulf War and its aftermath. Tehran's *Abrar* newspaper defined the Gulf War as an "expansionist attack by American armed forces" on Iraq. Tehran concluded that despite all the West's sanctions and subversion attempts since the war, Saddam's regime proved its ability to survive. *Abrar* repeated Tehran's commitment to regional collective security with Iran as the local hegemonic power and then suggested that Iraq be a major part of such a regional arrangement provided the principles of Saddam's regime can be changed, though not the regime itself. If Iraq could make these changes "in view of its considerable potential capability, ... [it] can also complement this chain of regional cooperation." Later, in early July 1992, the conservative *Jomhuri-ye Islami* warned against the dismemberment of Iraq by any ethnic group and stated that such efforts "should not be tolerated" by Tehran. Tehran pointed out that "Iraq is not the personal fiefdom of Saddam or his Ba'athist regime," and thus strategic realities mustn't be predicated on the quality of the particular regime in Baghdad. "Iran condemns and will not accept any efforts to Balkanize Iraq," *Jomhuri-ye Isla-*

mi iterated, and cautioned that "hatred of Saddam and his Ba'athist regime is certainly not a justification to endorse the disintegration of the Islamic land of Iraq." Tehran's resolute position was being hailed in Iranian media at the very time Saudi Arabia and Kuwait were openly contemplating the advisability of the dismemberment of Iraq along ethnic lines as the only viable way to topple Saddam and reduce Iraq's military threat.

Baghdad's new-found confidence was clear enough to the West after Barzan's two-part article was published in *Al-Jumhuriyah*. Iraq's claim to Kuwait was revived as part of Iraq's long-term regional arrangement based on "redrawing the political map of the Arabian Peninsula. The current GCC [Gulf Cooperation Council] must accept this change," Barzan wrote, "if it wants to last and survive." He explained that "it will be difficult for Kuwait to preserve its [territorial] integrity in the future because that would necessitate keeping Iraq in a weakened state." Iraq, he argued, was already rapidly rebuilding its military strength, and was thus ready to facilitate and defend the "reintegration of Kuwait into Iraq" because "Iraq will never forget that Kuwait is part of its territory." Barzan stressed that Iran was no longer a threat to Iraq. "Differences with Iran will be solved, and another war with Iran is not impossible," he wrote. He also anticipated that the Arab-Israeli conflict would soon be solved once and for all. Iraq believed that major strategic changes would come in the aftermath of the "expansion" of the GCC to include greater "unified" Syria and Jordan in the organization.

Final negotiations of the strategic agreement between Iran, Iraq and Syria came in early July 1992 in Khartoum, a gathering that took place in the shadow of the anniversary of Bashir's coup. Iran's delegation was headed by nuclear physicist Dr. Hassan Ghafuri Fard, vice president and minister of sports, but whose unspoken and most important title was senior intelligence official. He was accompanied to Khartoum by Muhammad Kazem Khonsari, secretary general of the Horn of Africa and Middle East Department of the Iranian Foreign Ministry. Tehran made it clear that Khonsari was in Khartoum to conduct bilateral talks. Ghafuri's role wasn't discussed. But it wasn't to talk strategic agreement. Baghdad sent

Deputy President Taha Yassin Ramadan and State Minister for Foreign Affairs Muhammad Sa'id Al Sahhaf, both traveling on special instructions from Saddam. The Syrian delegation was led by Deputy Premier Muhammad Zuhayr Mashariqah and Labor and Social Affairs Minister Ali Khalil. Mashariqah and Khalil arrived in Khartoum to talk about "Arab solidarity to confront threats against the Arab nation" with their hosts and Iranian and Iraqi delegates.

Iran wasted no time outlining the new regional reality. Within days of the Khartoum summit, *Jahan-i Islam* published a series of articles defining Iran's comprehensive strategy. Tehran considered the ongoing Iraqi crisis, embodied by the world's reaction to the UN's attempt to enter Saddam's agriculture ministry, as a catalyst for a wider confrontation in the region. Tehran was further troubled by the potential exploitation of Iraq's Kurdish problem to dismember the country. Iran was clearly committed to an orderly and measured consolidation of the strategic axis before it was possible to successfully confront the United States and Israel. Tehran wasn't interested in premature regional engagement over Washington's policy vis-à-vis Iraq. No, Tehran was more patient than that and it might take years to mass Iranian forces in and around Iraq to make its hegemonic ambitions come true.

Still, Tehran was worried Saddam might set off another round of explosive attacks by the United States. *Jahan-i Islam* pointed out that public opinion of Saddam in the West was such that "his annihilation can be considered as a humanitarian success for anyone who can achieve it. Bush wants this achievement for himself to maintain his position and credibility among the American public and to defeat his opponent in the presidential elections."

Tehran contended that the United States might go to any extreme to ensure the reelection of President Bush, even if it destroyed the Middle East in the process. Tehran's strategy for dealing with this problem was twofold: preserve the best interests of the Muslim world and confront the American threat. The former included the reality that deposing Saddam, under any circumstances, would be perceived as a great achievement by Washington. Thus it was in Tehran's interest to support Saddam publicly, until it saw a good chance of getting rid of Saddam and installing new leadership in Baghdad. *Jahan-i Islam* concluded, "Invariably, Iran's stance will be of special significance. Defending its strategic principles, Iran should also act in such a way as to avoid strengthening the West's position."

Baghdad publicly appeased the Iranians by going along with Tehran's hegemonic ambition. During his speech on the Ba'ath Revolution anniversary, Saddam declared Iraq's commitment to, and support for, Tehran's regional policies and strategy. Most of Saddam's speech was devoted to his regime's achievements and commitment to pan Arab causes. But it included several very deviations from past pronouncements. Most important was Saddam's discussion of foreign, meaning United States and Western, intervention in the Middle East, in which Saddam attributed the Iran-Iraq War to foreign conspiracies not unlike the conspiracy against Iraq during the Persian Gulf War and following crisis. "Part of the foreigners' role in the confrontation with Iran in the second Al Qadisiyah and in the foreigners' aggression against us in the Mother of Battles," said Saddam, were aimed at enabling the West to reestablish control over the region and its oil resources.

Saddam's speech also included another key element: his analysis of the situation in the region and the Third World. Baghdad's position was virtually identical to the strategic analysis that drove Tehran's quest for an Islamic bloc and the strategic axis. Saddam explained that after the collapse of the Soviet Union, the Third World faced new threats. "Third World nations and their supporters," he said, "must strive to get their act together and grapple with the dangers facing them and all of humanity. This is in order for these nations to safeguard human and national rights. Those who are interested among the Arabs ought not to limit themselves," he cautioned, "to a halfhearted defense in the face of treason, trickery and foreign ambitions. They must be bolder, franker and more energetic and committed to a unified position and collective action."

Echoing Tehran's policies, Saddam warned that under current global conditions "a lopsidedly powerful United States would be tempted to aspire to domination of the world. In order for the United States to gain control for longer, controlling Middle East oil and directing the politics of the region are crucial to the promotion of its aspirations." He believed, as did Tehran, that the United States was determined to occupy the states of the Arabian Peninsula "since they own most of the oil in the region." A few days later the Ba'ath Party newspaper *Al-Thawarah* urged Arabs "to escalate their jihad and wage battles of honor to liberate the nation's territories and free its resources and will of all usurpist and covetous enemies and also of all traitors who are abandoning Arab rights to foreigners and causing weakness, surrender, and treason to prevail." *Al-Thawarah* identified the Houses of Al Saud and Al Sabah as the arch enemies of the Arab world and urged the peoples of Saudi Arabia and Kuwait to topple them. In still another article *Al-Thawarah* stressed that the Middle East was entering a new era of confrontation with the United States and, ultimately, of great victories for Islam.

Al-Thawarah further explained that the crisis that followed the first Gulf war "closed a chapter in the Arab political life" that had included recognition of the central role of the conservative regimes of the Arabian Peninsula, and opened a new era characterized by a combative alliance to further the cause of jihad. Although the newspaper didn't mention Iran and the axis specifically, it hinted heavily at Baghdad's shift of loyalty to Tehran.

Baghdad used UNSCOM inspectors' attempt to enter its agriculture ministry to create an international crisis, an opportunity for Saddam to demonstrate to Tehran his defiance of the United States and the West but, importantly, Saddam's willingness to take risks in pursuit of the axis' confrontational policy toward the United States. "The agriculture ministry farce left Saddam in place stronger than he'd been since the Gulf War," according to congressional findings that included the observation of a Baghdad diplomat. Saddam made full use of his renewed power to further the axis' strategic objectives. Thus it was little wonder that Baghdad called the agriculture ministry incident a "stupendous victory" against the United States. Iraq's assertiveness grew beyond this "victory" and on the second anniversary of the invasion of Kuwait, Baghdad media was saturated with stories that Iraq would soon return to and annex the emirate again. "It will happen again, inshallah," was the headline in the Baghdad *Babil* below a large color photograph of Saddam praying in October 1990 on the Kuwait City waterfront.

"It goes without saying that Kuwait is part of Iraq," *Al-Jumhuriyah* told its readers. "In the end Kuwait will return to its rightful owners. How and when? History has the answer." Radio Baghdad broadcast Prime Minister Muhammad Hamza Al Zubaydi hailing August 2, 1990, as "an immortal day, if not the dearest and most glorious day, in the psyche of the Iraqis." He was confident Iraq would one day rule Kuwait. "The return of Kuwait, a usurped territory, to the motherland, Iraq, epitomized the Iraqis' firm national will, apart from allowing one of their dreams to come true." Kuwait was, Zubaydi explained, Iraq's nineteenth province. Beyond printed press and radio, the Iraqi military boasted its highest strategic priority was reoccupation of Kuwait. "Today Iraq is the ferocious rival, the opposite pole of the United States," wrote Abdul Jabbar Mohsin, Saddam's press secretary, in *Al Qadisiyah*, the organ of Iraq's defense ministry. "Iraq's enemies," he said, "are bewildered. They do not know how to confront Iraq." But others worried that Saddam's overconfidence might lead to what it eventually, did: disastrous choices.

Saddam took his cues from Tehran. The strategic objectives articulated by the axis were precisely defined by Grand Ayatollah Ruhollah Musavi Khomeini, head of the 1979 Iranian Revolution and the country's first Supreme Leader, a role he filled for a decade. Khomeini outlined the strategic axis in January 1980 when he presented his perception of the state of the world. "We are at war against infidels," he said. "I ask all Islamic nations, all Muslims, all Islamic armies and all heads of Islamic states to join the holy war. There are many enemies [who will] be killed or destroyed. Jihad must triumph." He identified how the Islamic bloc would liberate Jerusalem in a summer 1982 sermon in which he said that it was "our belief" that "Muslims should unite and defeat America. They should know that they can do this, and they have many possibilities," he said. "America and the West's lifeline depends [on] this region's oil." He then spoke about the annihilation of Israel that he would reiterate publicly many times.

Iranian Supreme Leader Ayatollah Ali Hussein Khamene'i, Khomeini's successor, delivered a sermon on July 29, 1992, in which he indicated that Tehran accepted Saddam's explanation of the real guilty party in the Iran-Iraq War. He explained: "During eight years of imposed war the enemy was openly fighting us. In appearance it was Iraq, but behind Iraq was the United States, NATO and all the reactionaries." Khamene'i's sermon was a warning to Tehran and to the entire Muslim world that they were on the verge of a fateful confrontation between Islam and the West, a confrontation that could result in the expansion of the Muslim world by force of arms.

"Today, in the world of Islam," Khamene'i said during his now-famous sermon, "we are duty-bound to prepare the Islamic people, the Muslim world, and our own people to the highest degree possible. They must be aware, must recognize the enemy, must know their duties. Today, considering the formation of Islamic rule and hoisting the banner of Islam, an unprecedented event in the history of Islam since its early days, the Muslims have this capability. We have no right," he concluded, "to make a mistake recognizing its enemy today, in recognizing the direction of the onslaught." If nothing was done, he warned, "the Islamic society is in danger." He pointed in the direction of the preferable solution, urging his audience to "learn from the early days of Islam," when Muhammad and the first Caliphs led their armies to occupy an Islamic empire. He said Iran was comparable, evidenced by its recent experience, to lead the Islamic bloc to victory. "Our nation is the first nation, which, relying on the Qur'an and through the slogans of [the] Qur'an and Islam, was able to defeat the United States and the world of arrogance." Khamene'i said: "We ask Allah to guide us in our difficult struggle in his path that we may be able to recognize and understand our duties and responsibilities and continue to advance the paths of the prophets and imams and the [Islamic] revolution."

Further agreements only strengthened the alliance between Iran, Iraq and Syria. The August 5-8, 1992 Higher Syrian-Iranian Joint Committee sought to strengthen relations with Baghdad, thus leaving no question that they would come to Saddam's aid if conditions deteriorated in Iraq. The Iranian delegation, headed by

Vice President Hassan Ebrahim Habibi, and the Syrian delegation, chaired by Vice President Abd Al Halim Khaddam, met with President Assad. The summit covered Tehran and Damascus' cooperation politically, economically and commercially, and also included exchange of important regional developments; Iraq was the focus of their discussion. They also had meetings and joint sessions with the leaders of Hezbollah, the Syrian-backed Lebanese Popular Front for the Liberation of Palestine-General Command (PFLP-GC), and other terrorist organizations. Habibi later described the outcome of these talks as "good and positive."

At the end of Iran and Syria's August summit, it was clear that both of them shared equal concern over Israel. *Al-Ba'ath* praised Tehran's commitment to "liberating Jerusalem from the destruction of the Zionist usurper." But *Al-Ba'ath* wasn't done; it stressed the importance of "the firm, joint struggle being waged by Syria and Iran against Zionist ambitions and expansionist schemes in the region." Syrian-Iranian relations had made great strides toward mutual trust and respect, *Al-Ba'ath* reported. Syria's national newspaper, *Al-Thawra,* echoed *Al-Ba'ath* but called the peace process futile and warned its readers that war was only a matter of "when" not "if." *Al-Thawra* repeated Syria's commitment to "a comprehensive solution" that by Arab definition, observed the August 10 congressional report, would amount to the destruction of Israel.

All of this has everything to do with America's missing in the Middle East; it always has. Khomeini wasn't preaching anything new. Saddam wasn't threatening anything that hadn't been heard before. The West had heard Islam's call to war many times over. But history has a way of repeating itself to those who've ignored it. Thomas Jefferson would have been the first to agree that none of what happened before and after the Persian Gulf War was unforeseen. The United States couldn't get back the lion's share of its sailors and Marines over two hundred years ago and it fought two wars against the North African regencies trying to do so. Jefferson was ambassador to France when he made his first attempts to win the freedom of Americans captured by Arabs and imprisoned in squalid jails and slave camps. Jefferson's dim view of paying tribute and ransom to the Barbary pirates who'd captured and enslaved Americans grew stronger as his experience with the issue deepened. He strongly believed that continued tribute payments to Barbary pirates would only invite further attacks and kidnappings, not stop them.

His reasons were twofold: an Islamic crusade, also called a jihad, that he'd come to understand through his study of the Muslim religion, and money. In early spring 1786, Jefferson joined John Adams, America's ambassador to Great Britain, in London to negotiate with Tripoli's envoy, Ambassador Sidi Haji Abdul Rahman Adja, for the release of the crews of two American naval vessels who'd been taken captive in July 1785. When they asked why Tripolitan pirates made war on nations that had done them no harm, the Tripolitan ambassador replied that it was in their Qur'an that all nations that had not acknowledged the Prophet Mohammed were sinners. It was thus the right and duty of the faithful to plunder and enslave, and that every Muslim who was slain in this warfare went to paradise.

During America's salad days in the Mediterranean, we didn't understand the major division of orthodox Islam and it didn't know that the Barbary States of Algeria, Libya, Morocco, and Tunisia, as they are called today, formed the Maghreb, an area demarcating Islam's lands west of Egypt. The North African regencies formed Islam's back door to the Christian Levant. Muslim warriors secured and held their position in North Africa beginning in the seventh century, quickly establishing the two major divisions of orthodox Islam: Dar Al Islam, the House of Submission, and Dar Al Harb, the House of War. The former, even in modern times, covers all lands and people who practice their Islamic faith freely; the latter refers to the relationship between an Islamic state and its non-Islamic neighbors and the duty of all Muslims to bring nonbelievers under the cloak of Islam. The Dar Al Harb remains the vehicle for converting non Islamic nations and territories to Dar Al Islam. Prisoners of war were offered, as they are today, a choice: convert to Islam and live peaceably and quietly under a Muslim identity, or remain in prison, a slave to a Muslim master.

Jefferson rightly perceived that their piracy was not only a religious holy war on Christians, but also any infidel of any nation who strayed into the Mediterranean. He also understood another fact, one that persists today: militant Islam's *profiteering* from prisoners of war. Men enslaved by Islamic masters worked to make them wealthier. Much like today, prisoners of the Barbary states were forced to work in agriculture, mining and construction. Most of them would die of disease, starvation, accidents and execution. Few made it to "old age" as captives of Islam.

At the end of their meeting in London, the Tripolitan ambassador reiterated that the Barbary States considered themselves at war with the United States and the price to end it was at least 30,000 guineas, about $3.5 million today. It was clear to Jefferson that there would be no end to the Barbary pirates' demands. But he also knew that the United States had no money to mount a navy; the original thirteen states having resisted the levy of taxes to build a fleet. Though Adams continued to advocate paying off the Barbary States, he had clearly underestimated the cost. The ambassador's demand amounted to one-tenth of the United States' annual budget at that time. In the years to come, the regencies would demand as much as twenty percent of the United States' annual budget in tribute and ransom. Jefferson was right; the cost was growing and there was no way to stop it unless the United States was willing to fight to get its prisoners back. But would it?

Jefferson argued that paying the ransom would only lead to future demands, perhaps demands the country would never be able to meet. He knew that America couldn't pay for the problem to go away. They'd always come back for more money. Jefferson's July 11, 1786 letter to Adams read thusly, "I acknolege [*sic*] I very early thought it would be best to effect a peace thro' the medium of war." Paying tribute, he wrote, would not only invite more demands, but even if a coalition proved workable, the only solution was a strong navy that could carry the fight to the pirates, thus into the bay of Tripoli. Jefferson's August 18, 1786 letter to James Monroe clarified his point further when he observed that the Barbary States "must see the rod," and that perhaps one of them must be struck with it to carry home the point that the United States would deal a swift blow to pirates quartering American hostages. "Every national citizen must wish to see an effective instrument of coercion, and should fear to see it on any other element than the water," he wrote to Monroe. "A naval force can never endanger our liberties, nor occasion bloodshed; a land force would do both."

Jefferson was sorely disappointed in the response to his letters. "From what I learn from the temper of my countrymen and their tenaciousness of their money," Jefferson observed in a December 26, 1786 letter to the president of Yale College, Ezra Stiles, "It will be more easy to raise ships and men to fight these pirates into reason, than money to bribe them." Jefferson's words stirred debate, but at the end of the day his countrymen were more interested in making money than decisively vanquishing the nation's first unconventional enemy. John Adams spoke for the national majority when he wrote that it was more prudent to pay the pirates two hundred thousand pounds sterling than jeopardize making one million pounds sterling in annual trade. The fight for American prisoners of war was a catalyst of the situation today in the Middle East and it is a problem, unresolved in Jefferson's time, that has spun out of control. Thus the slaveholder mentality that plagued the United States' experience with the Arab world in Jefferson's time has been renewed – some might observe for the worse – when it was again employed by Iran, Iraq and Syria in modern times.

America's latest experience, starting with its second invasion of Iraq in March 2003, was certainly defined by centuries' old history and not-too-distant conflicts in the region. The March 5, 2004 *Stratfor Weekly* suggested that Iraqi Shi'a didn't rise up against the United States, at first, for two reasons: they didn't want to do anything that might result in a Sunni government following Saddam in Iraq, and, most importantly, the Iranians who'd helped organize and define the Iraqi Shi'a community had their own strategic interests. Tehran wanted Iraq either neutralized or turned into a protectorate of Iran. Though Iraq had historically been Iran's enemy, a view most often forwarded by Western analysts, this has not always been the case. Both were a part of the early Muslim empire. Both were a part of ancient Mesopotamia and the great Persian and Greek empires that preceded Islam. Both perceived the United States and Western incursion in the Middle East as the greatest threat to their respective sovereignty and to Islam. They had a common enemy. The "American problem" in Iraq afforded Iran the chance it needed to redefine the geopolitical status of Iraq, thus fulfilling Tehran's fundamental hegemonic interest. Certainly, the Iranians were more concerned with pursuing their national interest than their ideological and religious principles over what to do about their Shi'a brothers and sisters in Iraq.

The Shi'a had few choices. They could side with the Sunnis and try to drive the United States and its allies out of Iraq or they could side with the United States against the Sunnis and kill two birds with one stone. The choice wasn't that difficult. From a broader perspective, Iran helped make that choice. Much of what happened in early 2003 was about timing. Tehran was ultimately ready to shed Saddam as a member of the pact. The world was just as weary of Saddam. United Nations special rapporteur Max van der Stoel described Saddam's regime as one of the most despotic and totalitarian regimes the world has witnessed since the close of World War II.[11] The Iraqi government was despised for its long record of mistreatment, torture, disappearances and killings of prisoners crammed into Iraq's notoriously putrid and barbaric prison system. Baghdad was known, too, for the forced exile and withdrawing the citizenship of men and women of letters, intellect and science who stood to challenge the regime's "Saddam-think."

By the spring of 2003, arguably Iran had enough of its military manpower, equipment and intelligence juxtaposed inside Iraq to follow, and even get ahead of, the American military invasion. After the decision was made to get rid of Saddam, Iran was ready for the Americans to depose him. Iran's focus turned to undermining the United States' presence after Saddam was gone to include the introduction and employment of sophisticated improvised explosive devices (IEDs), small arms and use of Qods team attacks on American and Coalition troops. This wasn't difficult either. The Iranians' presence was transparent. From personnel to weaponry employed against American and Coalition troops, it was clear they were operating with impunity in most, if not all, of the country.

The only threat to Tehran's strategic plan came during the five-year period from 2003 to 2008, when the Sunni insurgency challenged Iraq's political stability and threatened to put an end to Iran's hegemony if it succeeded. But the United States beat back Al Qaeda in Iraq and cut the flow of funding from Ba'athists in exile – at least that was the plan. Tehran's insurance policy was its tether to the majority of Shi'a politicians who'd assume power in post-Saddam Iraq; some had held posts in Iran, living there in exile until Saddam was gone. Some still held those positions after assuming leadership of Iraq. These were the men who'd ensure that Tehran had its "protectorate." This gave Iran its fait accompli: the United States and its allies did the heavy lifting and suppressed the Sunni insurgency and Tehran got tacit control of the country. Caught in the middle was Scott Speicher. What would happen to him?

Endnotes

1. Hedges, Chris, "Iraqi defectors tell of Kuwaitis in secret jail in Baghdad," *New York Times*, November 12, 2001.

2. Cockburn, Patrick, "Vengeance is family affair for Saddam," *Independent*, February 26, 1996.

3. PBS *Frontline interview* first broadcast and published on January 20, 1996.

4. The Mossad – which literally means "the Institute" – is short for HaMossad leModi'in uleTafkidim Meyu'adim, is the national intelligence agency of Israel.

5. House Joint Resolution 114 is a joint resolution passed by the United States Congress on October 16, 2002, as Public Law 107-243, 116 Statute 1498, authorizing the Iraq war.

6. Cordesman, Anthony H., "Iran's Revolutionary Guards, the Al Quds Force, and other intelligence and paramilitary forces," rough working draft, Center for Strategic and International Studies, Washington, D.C., August 16, 2007.

7. Connell, Michael, "The influence of the Iraq crisis on Iranian warfighting doctrine and strategy," CNA Corporation, Alexandria, Virginia, April 2007; *Kayhan*, Iranian daily newspaper, February 20, 2007.

8. Gertz, Bill, "US general calls Al Qaeda 'Public Enemy No. 1' in Iraq," *Washington Times*, April 27, 2007.

9. U.S. House of Representatives Task Force on Terrorism and Unconventional Warfare House Republican Research Committee. "Tehran, Baghdad and Damascus: the new Axis pact," August 10, 1992.

10. Ibid.

11. Coalition for Justice in Iraq, "Latest censorship news: another voice silenced, May 8, 2000. http://www.oneworld.org/index_oc/news/iraq080500.html

Chapter 12

A Find in the Desert

There wasn't much to look at in 2009 when searchers arrived with heavy equipment to excavate for what they believed to be Speicher's body. The surface of the Iraqi desert throughout Anbar Province resembles the surface of Mars, mostly bits of rock and, unlike Mars, an occasional small clump of vegetation. Nothing remarkable. Nothing to indicate from the surface that searchers would make a find in the desert. After all, there were no obvious disturbances to the ground, no grave markers, no rock piles for a grave site – nothing concrete to go on, just a few bits of scrap from the jet that had pancaked on the desert floor eighteen years before.

When the 150 Marines from Task Force Personnel Recovery, Multi-National Force-West (MNF-W) began arriving at the site on July 22 to search for human remains, they got their first glimpse of this hot, inhospitable dig site. By the time they were done five days later, the Marines had excavated the equivalent of four football fields with backhoes and bulldozers to the depth four feet, but found only a few skeletal fragments. Then began a rapid-fire effort to inform the public that these were the mortal remains of Scott Speicher, and close the case. What happened after these bits and pieces of human bone were retrieved had little to do with his best interest or the American people's understanding of how we have still failed, in truth, to account for a man whose death took place many years after his navy jet went down over Iraq.

The task force had come to this site in the desert on the word of an unnamed Iraqi citizen. Without any landmark, the team had arrived, churned up enough bone to make an identification and the Department of Defense, without hesitation, quickly made it known to the media that the partial remains just recovered in the desert were definitely those of Scott Speicher, located in "a shallow unmarked grave" in Anbar Province on July 28, 2009, two-and-a-half miles from where the Defense Department now indicated his downed F/A-18 Hornet had impacted – 19.13 miles south of 33°0 1'12.5849"N, 042°15'00.0175"E – remnants of which have largely disappeared from the desert landscape save pieces of scrap metal of no use to the Bedouins passing through the site. The area where the remains were found was roughly 62 miles west of Ramadi (33°26' 26"N 043°16'30"E), which is situated about 70 miles west of Baghdad. Thus, Speicher's partial remains were supposedly located approximately 130 miles on a direct line west of Iraq's capital and far north on a different longitudinal axis from the crash site, which was documented by the ICRC team as 33°00'114"N 042°15'28E, 125 miles *south*west of Baghdad or 18.6 miles to the south of a major east-west highway in a desert region with no substantial natural landmarks.

According to the MNF-Iraq CJ3 Personnel Recovery Division (PRD) Sensitive Site Exploitation (SSE) for Human Remains Report dated August 1, 2009, bottom line up front (BLUF) summary, the Marines located portions of a human skull and the Atlas (C1) vertebra and three Thoracic vertebrae. The Atlas is the superior (first) cervical vertebra of the spine that supports the globe of the head; the three Thoracic vertebrae are found in the middle segment of the vertebral column, located between the cervical and lumber vertebrae. The BLUF summary states: "Using Speicher's dental records, we were able to preliminarily identify the human remains as those of CAPT Speicher." The skull, Atlas and Thoracic vertebrae were found at 33°02'07.7241"N, 042°17'35.4492"E. No other human remains were recovered, according to the same report, during the SSEs and these remains were transferred to the Office of the Armed Forces Medical Examiner at Dover Air Force Base. The distance between where the Department of Defense now tried to put the original crash site and the location of these partial remains is 4.365 kilometers or 2.712 miles.

When the ICRC team's original crash coordinates and the remains recovery site are compared, the distance would be 3.320 kilometers or 2.063 miles between one and the other. The calculation of distance between the ICRC original crash coordinates for Speicher's F/A-18 Hornet and the coordinate exploited by the Marines is 1.484 kilometers or .922 miles – almost a mile off-target from where the jet was first located on the desert floor on January 17, 1991.

"We were originally briefed," wrote Buddy Harris to Secretary of the Navy Raymond E. Mabus on September 4, 2009, "and it was given to the press, that the remains were found about 1,200 meters [.745 miles] from the crash site." On later summations the distance was determined to be 2,000 meters [1.24 miles] from the crash site. But this distance would be further if using the original ICRC crash coordinates, thus pushing the distance out a bit farther than the figure provided to Speicher's family. When calculating the distance between the MNF-W dig sites, there is a significant difference in geographical points on a map. The bottom line, not to muddy the point, is that Harris further challenged the distance finding. "I used the maps supplied as evidence, and asked if they were accurate. I was told they absolutely were, and then indicated that the maps show CAPT Speicher's remains being found over 4,000 meters [2.48 miles – about 2.5 miles] from the crash site." This, Harris pointed out, was a very important difference, especially when the MNF-Iraq CJ3 PRD report tried to call Speicher's exit from his stricken Hornet a "sympathetic" ejection. A sympathetic ejection is completely implausible in the Speicher case. This theory was created, Harris wrote, because a Bedouin informant first said the body was buried within 200 meters [.124 miles] of the crash site. "Of course he also said that they had to wait for the fire to go out, and yet it was determined years ago that there was no fire on the ground. The flat spin," noted Harris, "actually snuffed out any remnants of fire on impact, and the fuel drop tanks were lost on initial contact with the air-to-air missile and fell elsewhere."

Back to the purported Iraqi national who provided the information that this was the remains of Scott Speicher. This unnamed

Iraqi stated, according to the August 1, 2009 PRD SSE report that "he watched his brother inter the forearm and hand and portions of a 'blonde' scalp in the vicinity of the crash site in January 1991." This is the same Bedouin who claimed that the forearm was covered with the leather from a jacket still attached. Scott Speicher was not dressed in any leather flying gear that night. Further, the stateside forensics team subsequently stated that were this story true, the flight suit would certainly show indications of a missing limb or other major trauma – it did not. The "blonde scalp" descriptive was also inaccurate. Speicher had dark brown hair, and the forensics team later found no impact damage to the skull pieces. When the second Bedouin was brought in, he was still over 2,000 meters [1.24 miles] off from where Scott Speicher's partial remains were eventually recovered.

The Bedouin story was a lie of convenience – a Taqqya – the Muslim requirement to lie to infidels for the betterment of Islam and the protection of other Muslims. The American public just might believe that a Bedouin could find his way back to a specific spot in a desert, a location without any remarkable landmark and no sign it was ever a crash site. But a story like that can only hold up so long. Sooner than later someone would demand to know where the recovered remains were before they were hastily buried for the Marines to find. Sooner than later the question would be asked who put them there? When had they done it? And why just then? Most important of all: If this wasn't the original burial site, where was the rest of the body?

Nothing in the PRD SSE BLUF nor subsequent documentation fit what was already known about the crash site from original imagery and prior site exploitation. In 1991 there was a jet canopy and ejection seat located some distance from the downed Hornet. The canopy was a mile or more away – definite ejection. The desert didn't cover the remains the PRD SSE located – people did. Partial remains? An ejected body would have been intact, not in pieces. But since it is known that the ejection seat was photographed, documented and retrieved, and the jet's avionics package recovered shortly after Speicher's shoot-down, a discussion of body parts purportedly buried and miraculously "found" eighteen years later cannot be taken as truth.

The prequel to the PRD SSE visit indicates that on July 19 all coordination with the military working dog (MWD) teams had been completed. Dog food, desert dog booties, air-conditioned kennels, desert goggles and dog respirators were planned for the SSE. The following day, July 20, two CH-46 helicopters took a II Marine Air Wing (MAW) explosive ordnance disposal (EOD) expert and two members of the MAW hazardous materials (HAZMAT) team, all from the Marine base at Al Asad, to the crash site, which this group of Marine Wing Support Squadron (MWSS) personnel identify as 33°01'08.6977", 042°15'28.3790" on July 20; this set of coordinates is roughly a half-mile from the crash site coordinates reported in the PRD SSE BLUF. The distance is 0.737 kilometers or .458 miles. Recall that if this was the original crash site, even in the condition located and documented in 1995 and barring what is now known to have been documented in 1991, Speicher's Hornet smacked the desert floor in a compact area, the direct result of a flat spin that put the jet upright and in a tight debris field. So, why the guessing game played by EOD and HAZMAT? The MWSS Marines were there, according to the report, to survey a possible landing zone (LZ) for their helicopters while the rest of the team examined the "crash site" for possible unexploded ordnance and possible burial sites.

A member of the MWSS team ascertained that there were no depleted uranium armor-piercing rounds but they did discover 20-millimeter rounds of high explosive incendiary (HEI). This discovery reduced the HAZMAT threat. The site was extensively littered with carbon fibers that were also identified by HAZMAT and would require the MWSS recovery crews to don masks while recovering aircraft parts. Everything about Speicher's combat load was already documented, including the ICRC team's mapping and photographing of the ordnance it buried before departing the area on December 16, 1995. This begged the question as to why the EOD and HAZMAT team would be looking for depleted uranium armor-piercing rounds in their initial search. Speicher's mission profile didn't indicate he was seeking armored targets. The other point that should be obvious is that had there been depleted uranium around Speicher's jet, it would have been documented when the crash site was exploited ten times prior to the recovery of Speicher's remains, especially in 1991, 1995 and 2004. But it wasn't there.

An experienced global SERE expert with operator perspective and skills knowledgeable of PRD SSE and still active in the field, commented extensively on the MNF-I CJ3 PRD field report. He has ground experience in all global regions – deserts, jungles, mountains, oceans, arctic and mixed. He knows the ins and outs of survival without thinking; survival has been his life-long career since the mid 1960s. He knows the Speicher story. This expert's November 15, 2011 commentary offered valuable insight into the MNF-W effort, including what the Marine team would eventually recover. He also commented on what they didn't find. But what struck him most, from the beginning of the task force mission, was its orchestration. There were human remains dog teams and indelicate heavy equipment being convoyed to two dig sites. Barely into the report he was incredulous. There seemed to be a dog-and-pony show creeping toward Speicher's crash area with everything present but the pony. "The dog is there – where is the pony?"

The morning of July 23, at half past eight local time, the MWSS team reported that "any suspicious mounds are identified as possible gravesites. These are spotted as having stones piled on top to create a sort of burial mound." But this is not what these are. The Bedouin people make and use these mounds of stones as ground navigation aids – road signs – to help guide them in featureless areas, because the location of water and grazing for their animal herds are critical to their survival. Twenty minutes later, the MWSS team "recovers a portion of canopy and a ring from what they assume to be Speicher's leg binder." There are two potential "binders" here – two entirely different meanings – offered without explanation. First, it could be part of the kneeboard binder that would not have been at the crash site after ejection (it would still be attached to the pilot). Second, it could mean the leg binder – actually a garter or restraint to pull the pilot's legs against the seat to prevent leg amputation by the instrument panel on ejection and this, too, would not have been at the crash site after ejection. In his evaluation of this part of the report, the personnel recovery expert wrote that the individual who crafted the MNF-I CJ3 PRD field summary "is not an ejection seat aviator." But this prompted a lengthier comment:

"This mission was FUBAR at the planning stage," he wrote. "Whoever planned this expedition...has no desert field knowledge or experience. And July in a hot desert area – all kinds of heavy equipment and numerous personnel, all expected to dig, sift dirt, [and] hike around looking for clues/evidence but no environmentally controlled tent for a rest or break area out of the heat [photos with the report do not indicate the team had proper cover] – would have required a generator – why not a refrigerator, too?" The worst by far was the heavy equipment present on the site to "excavate." "Heavy equipment destroys evidence – [you] never see an archaeologist or CSI [crime scene investigator] with a D7 CAT," he emphasized in bold. "The dogs' abilities on [an almost] 20-year-old-site under such extreme [conditions] are minimal. This safari is a recipe for heat injury – sun/heat stroke – if they did a proper job. I doubt it," he continued. "The environment was too extreme. After 20 minutes working, workers would have been spent."

The expert is correct about the weather. Summer is hot and dry throughout Iraq and the desert is the hottest part of the country. Diurnal temperature spreads are the widest of the year in summer because the air is so dry it cannot retain heat after sunset. With the exception of Iraq's mountain ranges, mean highs throughout the rest of the country are 102° to 110°F – that's 39° to 43°C – all summer. Extreme highs are 115° to 125°F (46° to 52°C). The average temperatures in Iraq range from higher than 48°C which is equivalent to 120°F in July and August to below freezing in January. The summer months are marked by two wind phenomena: the southern and southeasterly sharqi, a dry, dusty wind with occasional gusts to 50 miles an hour, occurs from April to early June and again from late September through November; the shamal, a steady wind from the north and northwest, prevails from mid-June to mid-September. Very dry air that accompanies the shamal permits intensive heating of the land surface but also provides some cooling effect. Dust storms accompany these winds and may rise to a height of several thousand feet, causing hazardous flying conditions and closing airports for brief periods.

The MNF-I CJ3 PRD report timeline indicates the MWSS team dug throughout the day, including peak daytime hours. In fact, on July 23, at noon local time, it was recorded that heat forced all working crews to halt with the exception of the heavy equipment (HE-bulldozers and backhoes) because those vehicles were air-conditioned. At 1:25 p.m. local time, the MWD handlers reported difficulty keeping their dogs cool in the intense heat – it was noted that the temperature was at 120°F and higher. "There is no ice to cool the dogs' water and the AC [air conditioned] kennels produce little cool air to reduce the dogs' body temperature," stated the report.

At 3 p.m. on July 23, with one F/A-18 pilot from the II MAW present, the team recovered an inert AIM-7M Sparrow missile. "The TD [target designator] had been crudely removed." The "recovery" of the AIM-7M Sparrow at this location did not jive with the ICRC team having accounted for, recorded and photographed all but one HARM from Speicher's combat load, all of his combat load, including Sparrow missiles, was buried together in the desert by the ICRC. It was all in the ICRC team report, including photographs. Of note, two hours after this "discovery" Marine Corps brigadier general John E. Wissler, deputy commanding general of MNF-W, and his staff arrived at Dig Site 1. At that time the team requested a source to positively identify the interment site – that is, if they found one.

After dark fell, sometime between half past nine and half past ten, "suspicious mounds" in the vicinity of 33°01'07.8495"N, 042° 14'49.8779"E were excavated using a backhoe. The human remains team inspected holes and excavated areas of Dig Site 1. No human remains were detected. But in the process, remarked the personnel recovery expert who went over their report, the team "destroyed a Bedouin road sign. The result – locals are aggravated with [the Americans]. Imagine how we would feel if a foreigner tore down or altered all of our road signs on an intersection of two to three interstate highways. If [these mounds] had been local graves it might have been worse." As it turns out, it was much worse – local graves were crudely dug up – in the search for Speicher. But we weren't supposed to know about it and neither were the Iraqi people.

According to an Iraq Survey Group report from May 2-3, 2004, recently released and highly redacted by the DIA, those remains dug up earlier and sent back to Washington for examination at Dover mortuary turned out to be that of a 25- to 30-year-old woman who'd been buried there for 25 to 50 years, because American investigators didn't have a forensic anthropologist on scene who could tell the difference between male and female skeletal remains or recognize Iraqi burial custom.

The "suspicious mounds" hunt would not stop there – more digging ensued. In fact, on July 24, after another full day of digging with heavy equipment, the team continued after dark using a thermal imagery product provided to them by the DIA to dig six more holes, all described as possible gravesites for Scott Speicher. No human remains were found.

Dig Site 2 was explored the following day. This site was located at 33°02'08.9587"N, 042°17'31.0184"E – a full 4.605 kilometers or 2.861 miles from Dig Site 1. At 8 A.M. on July 25 MWSS personnel used orange safety cones to mark sites that they believed pertained to Speicher's personal gear recovered and documented in earlier reports: the flight suit handed over to the ICRC team at 33°02'14. 9843"N, 042°17'23.0111"E (this is full 3.047 kilometers or 1.893 miles from the ICRC's crash site coordinates); the life raft located at 33°02'14.0003", 042°17'35.9893" (this is 3.353 kilometers or 2.083 miles from the ICRC's crash site coordinates); a flare picked up at 33°02'25.9985", 042°17'22.0184" (3.108 kilometers or 1.931 miles from the ICRC documented crash site); and fragments of Speicher's G-suit found at 33°02'07.8443", 042°17'32.0159" (this, based on the ICRC crash site data, is 3.243 kilometers or 2.015 miles from the jet). "This establishes the theory that there may have been a sympathetic ejection during the crash throwing CAPT Speicher 2 KM from the crash site and having him drug by high winds [across the desert floor]," according to the author of the MNF-I CJ3 PRD report. "As the parachute canopy is full of air from the winds it drags CAPT Speicher's remains towards a grassy patch leaving a trail of personal items. In the vicinity are obvious signs of Bedouin encampments such as: metal pots for cooking, empty rice bags, bones of slaughtered herd animals, clothing debris and automotive parts." Speculation about Speicher being dragged across the desert in his parachute is creative but completely false.

Details from the ICRC's report published in early 1996 are worth repeating and would have been helpful to the Marine PRD team lead. Recall based on wreckage analysis, it was clear that Speicher, initiated the ejection sequence. Parachute expert Bruce Trenholm further rejected the idea that the ejection system failed to function. The condition of the aircraft canopy and all ALSS items recovered on the site was inconsistent with an aircraft impact. The pilot couldn't have been in the aircraft when it struck the desert floor.

Revisiting the weather and wind issue is instructive. On the day Scott Speicher was shot down a frontal system brought very low temperatures and cloud cover with bases raised to eight thousand feet and ceilings from twenty to twenty-five thousand feet. Winds whipped from the south-southwest between six and twenty knots, increasing at higher elevations to over one hundred knots aloft but unremarkable at the desert floor. There was patchy fog in west central Iraq, and blowing sand and suspended dust reduced visibility to thirty-two hundred meters (1.988 miles) along the Saudi Arabia-Iraq border.

To the personnel recovery expert who reviewed the MWSS work, the sympathetic ejection theory was "BS – the ejection system won't throw… the seat two kilometers (1.24 miles) after impact." The expert is correct about the ejection seat. The canopy came down just under two miles from the jet and was found propped up on desert floor .38 miles from the jet – considerably under the half-mile mark – dragged there by Bedouins who used it as a travel marker in the desert. Had Speicher been dragged across the desert floor in his parachute, he noted: "The body's skid marks

– that far – would have been visible on initial imagery. The Nylon/Nomex is very tough – and in layers: parachute harness, survival vest, G-suit, flight jacket, and then [the] flight suit." Had he been dragged that distance, the flight suit would have been shredded, he added, from the waist down due to the aforementioned gear worn over the flight suit above the thighs. "There would have been damaged boots found. Where is the helmet? Drug helmets are really scratched and broken. Where is the torn-up harness and the hardware?" None of what was found showed any sign of having been abraded by dragging across the desert floor.

At 8:05 A.M. local time the MWSS recovers a piece of the G-suit below the surface at 33°02'06.7875"N, 042°17'34.1677"E (based on the ICRC crash coordinates this is 3.291 kilometers or 2.045 miles from that location and .061 kilometers or .038 miles from the section of G-suit recovered by the ICRC team). Of this find, the MNF-I CJ3 PRD report concludes that for it to be deposited subsurface "his remains must be close by."

"This is an unsupportable statement," concluded the expert. "Somebody buried it – no relation to [a] body."

Thirty minutes after the G-suit fragment was found, a female Koch fitting was recovered subsurface at 33°02'06.7875"N, 042°1 7'34.1677"E – the same location as the G-suit fragment. Koch fittings come in male and female or upper and lower, not left and right as suggested in the MNF-I CJ3 PRD document. The female Koch fitting attaches to the parachute riser and the male Koch fitting to the pilot's torso harness. The female fittings are slightly different in design so the aviator's fingers can access them in the opposite direction. The MNF-I CJ3 PRD concludes of the female Koch fitting: "It is in good condition lending more relevance to the theory that Speicher's remains were dragged by high winds. Easily identifiable on the Koch fitting are the patent and serial numbers on the front side and "-110-10303-7 D0082881R (R stands for right) on the backside." There were no high winds at ground level at the time Speicher went down. In a photograph a female Koch fitting is missing its mate. There are two buckles, two parts each to this piece of hardware. Where is the male part? If you don't have it, observed the personnel recovery expert, no drag occurred – the parachute collapsed as it should on release. "High winds and dragging for two kilometers would have scratched up the hardware real bad – it is not. The fitting was cut off the riser strap."

At 9:35 a.m. Baghdad time of July 25, MWSS personnel reported that they had recovered from the surface a portion of the main lift web of the parachute riser at 33°02'07.0048"N, 042°1 7'36.7043"E (3.345 kilometers or 2.079 miles from the ICRC documented crash site and only .060 kilometers or .037 miles from the G-suit fragment and female Koch fitting – they are located in the same spot). The lift webs are the front portion of the harness from the shoulder to the leg strap junction and includes the risers if there are no riser releases. The Marines' report describes "white in color webbing with metal buckle and five white nylon cords that were cut horizontally. The bottom portion of the webbing was cut horizontally. This is a possible indicator that Bedouins cut Speicher's remains out of his parachute harness to recover the parachute silk and other portions for scrap. These last three pieces of evidence present at Dig Site 2 as most likely being the site of CAPT Speicher's remains." The facts do not support this speculation. The white strap is sun bleached. The strap isn't abraded at all. What was found can be interpreted the other way: Speicher did as he was trained in SERE school. "Could be," offered the personnel recovery expert, "he walked back to [the jet] to look for anything salvageable. A lost [or inoperable] radio explains why items were buried near the wreckage." But he also took it further, noting that survivors are taught to remove long straps and 550 paracord – parachute cord – and other parts to take with them to support survival, in the case of the cord, for example, a line to reach the bottom of deep wells, build shelter, and in the case of canopy and seat pan material, shade shelter, camouflage, sleeping protection, water filter, and improvise clothing. Unwanted material is buried – shallow – including the harness, G-suit, helmet, anything at all the pilot determines unnecessary. "Hide or bury – SOP [standard operating procedure] since World War II."

Recall that information gleaned from Speicher's jet indicated that five seconds prior to the last recorded frame on the DSU he'd dropped to 27,872 feet. His airspeed had increased four knots. He was dropping into his target run. This slight nose-down input by the pilot ten seconds before loss of power – the disabling blast from the air-to-air missile – is the only anomaly on the tape. What happens in the seconds after this is unknown – the DSU stopped recording. But it was determined from this information and additional input from parachute expert Bruce Trenholm, that Speicher ejected at approximately 12,000 to 14,000 feet, and would have come down about 2,000 to 3,000 meters – between 1.24 and 1.86 miles – northeast of the crash site using prevailing winds at the time of his ejection and initial location of the canopy.

Speicher would then have done what the personnel recovery expert suggested (and artifact at the crash site supports) that he moved away from the crash site, and unless he could have determined a direction of escape or was evading under duress, to a place he could keep the crash site in view for extraction purposes. "As it turns out," Harris wrote Mabus, "this is exactly how everything was found. The facts indicate a normal ejection, not sympathetic." When Harris questioned the sympathetic ejection theory, at first he was told an ejection seat expert would be called in to make a determination. But that never happened.

Another factor that should have been considered by the MNF-I CJ3 PRD reporter: A good Bedouin is poor and likely to turn in equipment for reward or trade it in the closest black-market souk. "The only common sense explanation for burying," the personnel recovery expert noted, "is the evader did it or the locals were helping him and did it. Islam calls for helping strangers in trouble. They may have done it to help hide him."

A used and crushed navy signal flare was found less than an hour later at 33°02'02.5013"N, 042°17'31.1005"E (this is 3.201 kilometers or 1.989 miles – almost two miles – from the ICRC crash site coordinates for Speicher's Hornet). The key word in this descriptive is used. A Bedouin wouldn't know how to employ a flare. "It's not easy if you haven't been trained how to use it," according to the expert. "Without a radio, GTAS [ground-to-air signal], a flare/smoke/mirror are an evader's only alternatives to signal." And as for the "crushed" condition of the expended flare, perhaps, he suggested, someone drove over it with a D7 CAT or another piece of heavy equipment. The presence of an expended navy signal flare supports Speicher's normal ejection from the aircraft. Who else would have expended that flare and others found at the site? Speicher would have been the only person on the site with any reason, any impetus to expend that flare and others located in the area to signal the crash site. By noon, of note, the heat index at the Marines' two dig sites had reached over 130°F.

The significance of finding the surface part of the seat pan collocated with the flare was lost on the MWSS personnel who picked up and recorded the artifact at 2:43 p.m. Baghdad time. The seat pan is part of the ejection system and indicates that there was, indeed, an ejection by the pilot from the aircraft.

Between roughly 6:30 p.m. and 7 p.m. a cadaver dog team swept the area of Dig Site 2 but the dog only indicated something on the plow of the backhoe. No dog would have been effective in that environment. The surface heat on metal objects would have been 160°F or better. Diesel fumes hung heavy in the air. There was fresh subsurface dirt from heavy equipment pulling up the desert floor. Importantly, it was an 18-year-old site. Worse for the dogs, their sinuses would be dried out.

Back at Dig Site 1 the author of the MNF-I CJ3 PRD report was called over to take a look at a piece of bone found by a Marine on the surface in the vicinity of 33°01'13.3634"N, 042°15'36.8648"E (this is 1.280 kilometers or .795 miles from ICRC-documented crash site); he thought it was part of a human forearm. But the cadaver dog didn't react to the bone, which was bleached white on one side and, after closer inspection, seemed to belong to an animal. This discovery led to some confusion in reporting because the original source who had drawn the Marines to the site had purportedly told them he'd found an arm or wrist bone. Earlier in the day a Marine had located what he thought was a finger bone. The time and place this finger bone was found isn't documented but the report places it near Dig Site 1. Incredibly, there was no forensic anthropologist and no medical doctor on hand to make a determination as to whether the bone belonged to a human or an animal.

The following morning, on July 28, at 8:30 a.m., another piece of evidence was uncovered that also indicated an ejection: the SKU3-A survival kit release handle from the pilot's equipment. The serial number for this devise is NSN No. 30941ASSY102D550-3. This is the quick release for the seat pan and is a positive indicator that this was a pilot initiated ejection. Nearby this find at 33°02'03 .6033"N, 042°17'38.5039"E and 33°02'04.1855", 042°17'38.4090" the Marines raking sand piles discovered a series of bones alongside a green vegetative area "possibly used by the Bedouins." The MNF-I CJ3 PRD report identified the area as one previously used by Bedouins to slaughter small herd animals. The bones appeared too small to be human. The bones were collected. Speicher's Hornet had come down proximal to a Bedouin encampment and herd area. There should have been no speculation here. The Bedouin people make steady use of the herd area where Speicher's jet originally pancaked on the desert floor.

At 5:42 a.m. on the morning of July 28, the Marines recovered a human skull subsurface at 33°02'07.7241"N, 042°17'35.4492"E. The skull was decayed with no flesh or hair present. The task force's combat camera was summoned to document the find. The skull was cracked and in neat portion with the upper teeth intact. The parts fit together to identify the teeth in order. A surgeon who had arrived on scene carrying Speicher's nineteen-year-old antemortem dental records tentatively identified the remains as belonging to Scott Speicher. But his dental work wouldn't have been difficult to confirm if it was him. When Speicher was fifteen years old he busted out his two front teeth in a sledding accident. Both of his upper central incisors were crowned and he had four amalgam fillings. The surgeon saw that the upper jaw was intact and that the two front teeth had been capped. Further inspection, within a half-hour of the skull's discovery, documented not only the two capped teeth in the upper center but two fillings – one right and one left – all of which matched Speicher's dental x-rays. This left no doubt that the team had found Speicher's skull. "The teeth were healthy and intact" observed the surgeon. Two additional portions of the skull temporal lobes were further identified.

Shortly after the discovery of Speicher's skull, the task force transmitted a message back to Wissler at MNF-W headquarters using the code word "treasure" to indicate what they'd found. Speicher's skull was recovered about twelve inches below the surface after a D7 CAT pushed the soil and a Marine picked through the uncovered mound of soil. The area had been swept the prior day by a human remains team but they'd found nothing. The Marines continued to dig in the area of the skull recovery. Flatbeds with sifters arrived on the site from Dig Site 1 (which had already been closed down) to continue the search for human remains. The Atlas and Thoracic vertebrae were subsequently recovered. The Atlas bone was in excellent condition.

A single sifter load had given up a portion of an olive green flight suit and the Atlas. Searchers identified the cloth as part of a flight suit because of "the label portion located on the back neck in white fabric and black English lettering. The label has several English letters readable." This is the portion of the flight suit that would have the size, manufacturer, serial number and washing instructions. Recall that prior analysis of the flight suit turned over to the ICRC team had no size tag nor manufacturer information inside the collar of the suit – all identifying labels had been cut out. The discovery of this label proximal to the skull is suspect.

There was no mention – at least in the PRD SSE report – of manmade artifacts in the gravesite other than the flight suit label. With no remnants of metal fasteners and zippers from clothing, it becomes clear that this wasn't Scott Speicher's original burial site. The remains recovered by the Marines had been moved at least twice, according to Buddy Harris in an interview with Joe Frusci, and that is confirmed by the full forensics report available to Harris and signed off by the secretary of the navy. The MNF-W PRD task force was digging a salted site, with just enough of Speicher's skull, most importantly his distinctive dental work, to make a positive identification. Given what was already known about Speicher's last moments in the jet, the ejection and where he would have landed, what did it mean?

The day after, the search for Speicher's remains came to an end. On July 30, the task force convoy pulled out of Dig Site 2 for the last time and returned to their base at Al Asad. MNF-W Task Force Personnel Recovery immediately turned over Speicher's remains to the Al Asad Mortuary Affairs Collection Point (MACP) for transport home. From there the remains were sent to Dover Port Mortuary at Dover Air Force Base, Delaware, where an Armed Forces Institute of Pathology (AFIP) Office of the Armed Forces Medical Examiner (AFME) recorded that he had positively identified the remains as belonging to Speicher. The date was August 1. AFIP's DNA laboratory in Rockville, Maryland, then radiographically confirmed the bits and pieces as Speicher's on August 2 using comparison DNA from the remains to reference samples provided by his children.

Taking DNA samples from Speicher's children – and make no mistake, these are his children – is not a failsafe match. In an April 17, 2011 *Salt Lake City Deseret News* article Larry Greer, director of public affairs for the Department of Defense's POW/Missing Personnel Office, tells us why: "We rarely get a clear-cut identification right off." Samples, according to Greer, must be taken from certain relatives; the necessary identifiers are not passed down, thus offspring do not qualify.

Who is eligible? For a missing male service member it is his biological maternal grandmother, mother, the mother's sister and brother and children by the mother's sister but not her brother to include the missing man's female and male cousins and then only the children of the female cousin (the missing man's second cousins). The list also includes a missing man's biological brother and sister, but only the children of the sister to include a niece and nephew but then only the children of the niece (the missing man's great nieces and nephews). The most important aspect of mtDNA is that it is an extremely stable genome. Scientists estimate that mutational changes in mtDNA will occur only once in every forty to sixty generations, so as long as family relationships can be established, mtDNA enables forensic scientists to go back generations in a family tree to observe these maternal relationships.

Greer further spelled out the general scope of criteria used to arrive at an identification: mitochondrial DNA (mtDNA), dental records, eyewitness accounts and recovered artifacts and all of them, taken together, have to add up. Clearly, since Speicher's remains were found in a seeded site, not all of Greer's criteria for identification could be satisfied. More questions are raised than answered, by the discovery of Scott Speicher's limited skeletal remains nearly two-and-half miles from the site where his Hornet went down in the early hours of January 17, 1991. But the use of DNA testing to confirm identity poses the question – again – when and where Scott Speicher's sample was acquired for comparison. Armed Forces DNA Identification Laboratory (AFDIL) analysts had the bones but where did they get a testable, reliable sample of his DNA?

DNA – deoxyribonucleic acid – earlier referenced with regard to Dr. Victor Weedn's earliest application of the science in the Speicher case, is a catch-all for any number of nuclear and mtDNA tests. The DNA match on Speicher was more difficult because he was adopted and the Defense Department never pursued his biological parents nor his mother's biological relatives for reference samples. Thus proof-positive identification using nuclear DNA provided by biological parents and mtDNA from a biological mother or close female blood relative of the mother wasn't possible. In April 2005 the Department of Justice (DOJ) published a guide for families, a "what they should know" about the advantages and limitations of DNA in identifying human remains. In it, the DOJ stressed that mtDNA is inherited only from the mother. Fathers never pass on mtDNA to their children; however, mtDNA typically is not as powerful for making identifications as nuclear DNA. This means that in some instances two unrelated people may have similar mtDNA. Because of the way it is inherited, only maternal relatives, such as a brother, sister, and mother, can be used for mtDNA testing. Comparing the mtDNA profile of unidentified remains with the profile of a potential maternal relative can be an important technique in missing persons investigations.

Even if investigators had Speicher's biological mother's DNA, and they did not, mtDNA has limitations. The Department of Defense's AFIP has stated that nuclear DNA (nucDNA) testing is most commonly used now in forensic labs around the world to pinpoint a specific identity. But the drawback is that it can be used mostly only on high quality samples, thus other appropriate DNA references by which to confirm the identity are necessary, such as samples from immediate family and a blood reference sample from the person to be identified, in this case Scott Speicher. There wasn't a high quality blood reference sample for Scott unless it was taken from him while he was in the desert with the Bedouin tribesmen and used to confirm his identity for the State Department – this would have taken place in the 1993 to 1994 time frame – gathered by the Falcon Hunter on one of his trips into the desert as instructed by his ONI handler.

The only immediate blood relatives examiners could go to for a DNA comparison sample were Michael Speicher-Harris and Meghan Speicher-Harris. The Speichers' children's DNA had been used by Dr. Victor Weedn in the spring of 1991 to eliminate Speicher as the source of the pound-and-a-half of flesh turned over by the Iraqis as a pilot named "Mickel." Without a DNA reference sample for Speicher, recall that it was only possible to exclude DS1-256 as those of the children's father. To establish paternity, investigators needed a good DNA reference sample from Scott Speicher. Like a good crime scene investigation there would have to be samples from the crime scene evidence and a suspect, extraction of DNA from the evidence and the suspect, and analysis of it for the presence of a set of specific DNA regions that are also referred to as markers to get a match.

Mitochondrial DNA points only to maternal lineage, but it is easier to extract from severely degraded bone and tooth samples, and these reference samples can be from any maternal relative, regardless of the generation. There were no biological maternal relatives to provide mtDNA for Scott Speicher. MtDNA would have been especially helpful in identifying Speicher's remains had his biological mother or a close maternal blood relative been located.

A July 2002 special report to the National Institute of Justice explains that some older, perhaps degraded biological samples that lack nucleated cellular material such as hair, bones and teeth that can't be analyzed by other means, often including short random repeat (STR) and restriction fragment length polymorphism (RFLP) benefit from mtDNA testing. Recall that Speicher's only known DNA sample was extracted from hair found on his shipboard electric razor and deodorant bar. The DNA sequence Dr. Weedn got from both was very poor, so much so that it was barely enough to confirm his finding that the pound-and-a-half of flesh the Iraqis tried to pass off as Speicher in March 1991 wasn't him, a finding weighted heavily by comparison of the Speicher children's DNA against DS1-256 that rendered the degraded sample from Speicher's shipboard items inconsequential in his final report. There was no match analysis available between this degraded, very poor hair sample and Speicher's children. Speicher's sample was unusable.

Certainly this very poor hair sample that wasn't useful then wouldn't be useful today. When employing DNA testing hair will inevitably degrade as a consequence of the testing process, so it is beneficial to get a conclusive result the first time. Weedn couldn't get that back in the spring of 1991. Thus if Speicher were a missing person-turned-homicide case like that of the murdered two-year-old Florida girl Caylee Anthony – and in nearly all respects his case is – the absence of a DNA reference sample of Speicher and the condition of the original sample, absence of chain of custody of items from which that sample was drawn and storage method of the evidence from 1991 would not hold up in an actual trial. It is crucial to make certain that you have the hair of the proper individual for testing as it is so easy for hair of one individual to become commingled with another if they live in close quarters.

Speicher lived in close quarters in a two-man room aboard ship. He shared a sink in that room with Tony Albano. He showered in a shared officers' shower/bathroom down the passageway from where he slept. Where and how did he store the razor and the soap bar? When his personal effects were boxed and forwarded to

Weedn how was each item packaged for shipment? Who selected and handled each item placed in the box? Did the box sit on a pallet in extreme heat/extreme cold waiting for shipment? Was a DNA reference sample taken from everyone who handled Speicher's personal effects prior to Weedn's request for items that might contain Speicher's DNA?

Not only were the personal effects Weedn received from Speicher's stateroom useless but it can be argued that the items had also been contaminated prior to receipt in the lab and that barring no one in his squadron aboard the *Saratoga* being notified right away that these personal effects might be of high value in the future identification of his remains, they'd otherwise been comingled in a box and stored away until the ship was due to arrive back in Jacksonville. When the items were eventually requested, they had sat in improper storage for several weeks. It is not just the type of sample collected that is important, but also other variables that impact the usable result, including poor storage conditions, from damp environment to extreme heat and cold; poor sample handling to include possible contamination with other DNA, dirt, the container in which they are stored, to the absence of enough DNA present on a hairbrush, soap bar, razor, toothbrush or piece of clothing to get the DNA profile of the person of interest.

The forensic scientists at AFDIL use the latest DNA typing methods to provide for the identification of remains or other biological evidence. For current casualties, nuclear DNA (nucDNA) provides a tool for positive identification, when other forensic techniques, such as a fingerprint or dental comparison is not possible. Unfortunately, according to AFDIL's published information, nucDNA is not a viable tool in older remains due to many environmental factors that cause the nucDNA to degrade. These factors include ultraviolet light from the sun, heat, and moisture. For older remains, recovered from the battlefields of Korea, the cold war, World War II, and Southeast Asia (SEA), mtDNA has proved to be a useful investigative tool that adds additional detail towards identification, although it is not able to provide proof positive identification without further case history and dental and fingerprint matching. Scott Speicher's case was unique in nearly every respect from the DNA perspective.

There are only two copies of nucDNA per human cell, except for red blood cells, which have no nucleus. Half of the nucDNA component comes from the biological mother while the other half comes from the biological father. On the other hand, there are hundreds to thousands of copies of mtDNA per cell. Thus, mtDNA analysis is more successful on degraded remains because the amount of mtDNA found in cells and required for analysis lasts a much longer period of time. It is possible that mtDNA stays viable in bones and teeth up to thousands of years if the environmental conditions are favorable.

In looking at nucDNA, a child is a biological copy of the mother's and father's because of the inherited nuclear DNA and is thus significantly different from mtDNA for testing purposes. One limiting factor of mtDNA is that some DNA sequences are observed more frequently than others. In some of the more common mtDNA sequences, four to six percent of the population can have the same sequence even though they are not known to be maternally related to each other. As a result, mtDNA cannot be used by itself for positive identification and must be coupled with other forensic information to help establish the identity of an individual. Regardless, it is an extremely valuable forensic tool in support of the identification process.

"DNA identification [of persons] can be quite effective if used intelligently," observed Daniel Drell of the U.S. Department of Energy (DOE) Human Genome Project. Forensic laboratories occasionally use mtDNA comparison to identify human remains, and especially to identify older unidentified skeletal remains because the greater number of copies of mtDNA per cell increases the chance of obtaining a useful sample, and because a match with a living blood relative is possible even if numerous maternal generations separate the two. Although unlike nuclear DNA mtDNA is not specific to one individual, it can be used in combination with other evidence such as anthropological and circumstantial, to establish a basis for the assumption that remains belong to a particular individual. This wasn't the case with Speicher. Speicher's purported remains weren't particularly "old" either but they'd also been badly disposed of and transported – again – at least twice before they'd been seeded at the site at which they were "found," thus these facts should have impaired or slowed down future analysis of what was left of him, not speeded it up.

Forensic scientists assumed on the basis of circumstantial evidence and juxtaposition of the remains to the general region of the crash site that they had the partial remains of Scott Speicher. Dr. Julie Heinig's October 1, 2007 article for the DNA Diagnostic Center indicated that forensic DNA evidence is rarely pristine; in fact, analysis is often difficult because of partial DNA profiles, sample degradation, and male/female DNA mixtures. "In the past five years, there has been an increase in the use of STR loci by forensic laboratories, especially in cases where using conventional autosomal STRs has achieved limited success," she wrote. "An individual's genetic information, which includes autosomal DNA (atDNA) markers such as the 13 Combined DNA Index System (CODIS) core STR loci, is inherited from both biological parents. Everyone receives exactly half of his or her genetic markers from each parent.

Because of the unique combination of the mother's and father's DNA, genetic information is different for each child (except identical twins). The Y chromosome DNA markers, however, are conserved and passed down paternally from a father to all of his male offspring without changing (except when mutations occur)." Performing the Y-STRs test from Michael Speicher-Harris' DNA sample, AFIP might quickly come to the conclusion that the remains were those of his father. Y-STRs are short tandem repeats found on the male-specific Y chromosome in the nuclear DNA and the result of comparison of father and son markers can indicate relatedness between two men, though not the exact degree of the relationship. The coding genes, mostly found on the short arm of the Y chromosome, are vital to male sex determination, spermatogenesis and other male related functions. The Y-STRs are polymorphic among unrelated males and are inherited through the paternal line with few changes from one generation to the next. "Unlike autosomal

STRs, a Y-STR profile cannot uniquely identify an individual," Heinig cautioned. Effective use of this reverse parentage test would still require a DNA reference sample from the missing person to prove parentage before the child's DNA could be used to prove the remains were those of his father.

Speicher was adopted and there was no DNA reference sample for him. Had the AFIP located his biological family, it could have constructed a DNA profile from a sampling of that biological next-of-kin and compared it to the profile obtained from his children. This is not the best way to arrive at a DNA profile for a missing person. But lacking better options available to a forensic investigator, it can be done.

The Department of Defense didn't investigate how Speicher's remains got to the location where they were interred in a shallow pit for the MNF-W personnel recovery team to find. There appeared little interest in pursuing the original burial site and the rest of the body – they hadn't found the original crime scene. The Defense Department's purported identification of his remains using a DNA and dental match did not determine exactly when, where and how he died. Determination of all that would take weeks, if not months. But this is not what happened. None of the when, where and how questions were answered for the public when the announcement was made that the long hunt for Speicher had sadly come back to the place where it all began, in the same piece of desert where his plane had gone down eighteen years earlier. This was the story fabricated for public consumption; it was not what the evidence told investigators and forensic scientists behind the scenes and away from public scrutiny.

Before they got started with their examination, Buddy Harris publicly stated that he'd met for a week with a ten-member forensics panel made up of the DoD's current go-to civilian and military forensic team, a group comprised largely of men and women known for their work within the AFIP, AFME, and AFDIL in Rockville, Maryland. Judging from the actual timeline, there wasn't a week from the time of the remains' arrival stateside and actual remains examination to the publication of the final forensics report. The remains were received for analysis on August 1 and the forensics report was generated on August 6 – a five-day window – and the first day was taken up by the remains' arrival for examination and the last by publication of the report. The use of DoD-only personnel made the team's findings and reporting easier to control and lessened the likelihood that a member of the team would convey findings to the media. The August 6, 2009 200-page forensics report generated by the Joint Pathology Center (JPC) on Scott Speicher's remains was subsequently released by Secretary of the Navy Mabus under cover of a memorandum dated November 12, 2009; most of it is classified. A death certificate for Scott Speicher was issued on August 7, 2009, followed by an amended autopsy examination report dated a week later, on August 14, that provided the cause of death as homicide by undetermined means.

There are several points that need to be gone over. According to the Centers for Disease Control (CDC) homicide is defined as a death resulting from the use of physical force or power, threatened or actual, against another person, group, or community when a preponderance of evidence indicates that the use of force was intentional. Two special scenarios that the National Center for Health Statistics (NCHS) regards as homicides are included in the National Violent Death Reporting System (NVDRS) definition: 1) arson with no intent to injure a person and 2) a stabbing with intent unspecified. This category excludes vehicular homicide without intent to injure, unintentional firearm deaths, combat deaths or acts of war, and deaths of unborn fetuses. The term "undetermined intent" or "undetermined means" is used when a death results from the use of force or power against oneself or another person for which the evidence indicating one manner of death is no more compelling than evidence indicating another. This category includes coroner/medical examiner rulings such as "accident or suicide," "undetermined," "jumped or fell," and self-inflicted injuries when records give no evidence or opinions in favor of either unintentional or intentional injury. Speicher was homicide by undetermined means because the Office of the Armed Forces Medical Examiner wasn't provided enough information – no backstory and one could argue not enough of Speicher's body – to make a more specific determination of cause of death.

The finding of homicide by undetermined means is the same cause and manner of death that Orange County, Florida chief medical examiner Dr. Jan C. Garavaglia found in the Caylee Anthony case. The Anthony case has brought the public closer to the importance of forensic findings in criminal prosecution. To wit it is also perspective in the Speicher case. In the Anthony case, Caylee's nearly complete disarticulated skeletonized remains were conclusively identified by nuclear DNA comparison done by the FBI DNA laboratory at Quantico, Virginia; the sample was taken from Caylee's right tibia. But with Caylee there was ample source material for a reference sample. In Speicher's case his fragmented skeletonized remains led the armed forces medical examiner to the same determination that Garavaglia reached in the death of Caylee Anthony: it was homicide.

The armed forces medical examiner had considerably far less remains with which to work to arrive at manner of death. There were anthropological considerations in the Speicher case of greater importance. Yet another observation that begs mention is the time it took to arrive at and publish a finding in the Anthony case: twelve days from the initial receipt and separation of items by Garavaglia's office on the evening of December 11, 2008, to publication of the coroner's 36-page report on December 23, a document that includes all pertinent examination, toxicology and findings might lead us to wonder how the Joint Pathology Center could produce a 200-page report in under five days.

Death by homicide means that another human being killed Scott Speicher; it is not a catch-all classification for killed in action on a military medical examiner's report. A homicide ruling also does not imply criminality or intent; courts are left to make that determination. But circumstance can also provide the medical examiner some guidance in how to initially classify the manner of death. Given the preponderance of evidence that led to Speicher's missing-captured status, if a captor killed him, that would be a homicide.

A medical examiner will further label the homicide by manner of death but in a case like Speicher's or Anthony's in which an autopsy or subsequent investigation fails to provide conclusive evidence supporting a specific manner in which the individual was murdered the option is to rule the homicide "by undetermined means." Other kinds of deaths such as suicide, accidental or natural causes can also be ruled undetermined. Speicher's small amount of remains revealed no visible flesh and it was impossible for the medical examiner to gauge the type of trauma to the remaining bone fragments. Absent more of the body on his table, the armed forces medical examiner could not determine the manner of homicide that brought Scott Speicher's life to an end.

On January 17, 2011, on the twentieth anniversary of Scott Speicher being shot down, Buddy Harris appeared on Florida's First Coast News to do an interview with anchor Jeannie Blaylock. In his lap was a copy of the August 6 forensics report. Marines, he told Blaylock, recovered part of Speicher's skull, the pieces of which Harris told Blaylock had been largely reconstructed, as well as seven vertebrae and four rib fragments. In lawyer and professor Ronald F. Becker's *Criminal Investigation* (Jones and Bartlett, 2008) he makes the point that the skull is the first part of the skeleton to decompose but if recovered it is also the Holy Grail for the medical examiner. If enough of the skull can be found to reconstruct large sections, which it was in Speicher's case,it can be very useful in determination of cause of death. While Speicher's recovered skull bones are described as "decayed," the condition of the skull sections and teeth were also described as "excellent" from the examiner's point of view. Further, information extrapolated from Speicher's vertebrae and other bone fragments – what was left – told a story about what wasn't found. The question of where the rest of the body might be can't be ignored.

The collection plan for Speicher's remains included the use of heavy equipment. The presence of heavy equipment and heavy vehicle traffic over the site was less than desirable in a remains collection effort in which the context and integrity of the site under, near and around where they were located was just as significant to resolving Speicher's fate as the skull, vertebrae and rib fragments that were found. Damage to important skeletal remains and human artifacts at the scene no doubt occurred. Becker iterates that if recovery personnel do not handle remains appropriately[1] after skeletal remains are found inadvertent damage can occur to bones in transport. The bones must all be packaged in separate bags. Not all skull bones and fragments should be in one bag. Not all vertebrae should be comingled in another. Robert B. Pickering and David Bachman's *The Use of Forensic Anthropology* (CRC Press, 2009) makes the case that the presence of the forensic anthropologist increases the chance of finding many bones from the skeletal remains that might be present in the dig site but are otherwise missed by the untrained collector. Marines stepping through Dig Site 1 and Dig Site 2 picked up bones they couldn't identify as human or animal. The presence of a forensic anthropologist is especially important if the remains are scattered or clumsily disinterred by heavy equipment. The forensic anthropologist would have been a great asset to document the environment in which the remains were found.[2]

The Speicher forensics report indicates that Speicher couldn't have been killed on January 17, 1991, after he was shot down about fifty miles from an Iraqi chemical weapons plant far west of Baghdad. New testing on Speicher's dental remains, said Harris, proved it. New advances in forensic odontology can be used to determine the age at time of death and also the sex of victims whose remains are mutilated beyond recognition. From this perspective it was highly likely time of death could be established for Scott Speicher using these methods – if that's what was used – and barring a copy of the complete forensic report there is no way to know with one hundred percent certainty that this is how the AFDIL forensic odontologist arrived at his determination. According to research published jointly by scientists Kanar Alkass, Bruce A. Buchholz, Susumu Ohtani, Toshiharu Yamamoto, Henrik Druid, and Kirsty L. Spalding in the May 1, 2010 *Molecular & Cellular Proteomics,*[3] they observed that in disasters that claim many victims as well as unsolved homicide cases, looking at victims' teeth to determine how old they were at the time of death is now being used to help identify them.

Alkass, et al. note that traditional morphological methods used by anthropologists to determine age are often imprecise, whereas chemical analysis of tooth dentin, such as aspartic acid racemization, has shown reproducible and more precise results. Lawrence Livermore National Laboratory researcher Bruce Buchholz and his colleagues from the Department of Forensic Medicine and the Department of Cell and Molecular Biology, Medical Nobel Institute, Karolinska Institute in Stockholm, Sweden, and the Institute for Frontier Oral Science and Department of Human Biology, Kanagawa Dental College, Yokosuka, Kanagawa, Japan, have been looking at victims' teeth using radiocarbon testing to determine how old they were at time of death, work that was also spotlighted in the May 21, 2010 Homeland Security Newswire and a Lawrence Livermore May 19, 2010 news release.

Buchholz has used Lawrence Livermore's Center for Accelerator Mass Spectrometry to determine that the radioactive carbon-14 (C14) produced by above-ground nuclear testing in the 1950s and 1960s remains in the dental enamel, the hardest substance in the body. Above-ground testing of nuclear weapons during the cold war between 1955 and 1963 caused a surge in global levels of carbon-14, or radiocarbon, which has been carefully documented over time; it is also naturally produced by cosmic ray interactions with air and is present at low levels in the atmosphere, food and all living things. What Buchholz calls "the bomb curve" forms a chronometer of the past 60 years. Thus, scientists like Buchholz can relate the extensive atmospheric record for carbon-14 to when the tooth was formed and calculate the age of the tooth and its owner. "We show," Buchholz observed, "how combining these two methods also can assist in estimating the date of death of an unidentified victim. This strategy can be of significant assistance in forensic casework involving identification of dead victims."[4] The radiocarbon analysis showed that dating the teeth with the carbon-14 method would estimate the birth date within one year.

"The tooth doesn't change much after death," wrote Buchholz in a May 2, 2011 e-mail. "It doesn't change much while alive either. The enamel is really a mineral; it is not live tissue. It does not incorporate any new material after it is formed. The dentin is more like bone. It has both mineral and live components." Alone, the carbon-14 properties of the tooth, he cautioned, can't tell us whether a service member died in the 1960s or 1980s. More information would be needed. "The C14 is used to determine date of birth," he iterated. "The aspartic acid racemization may work. The slow conversion of aspartic acid [amino acid] from L-form to D-form occurs over time and we used it to estimate age at death." Proteins are composed of folded strands of twenty different smaller subunits called amino acids, all of which, with the one exception of glycine, come in two different configurations: the levorotary (L-form) on the left and the dextrorotary (D-form) on the right. These two forms are called enantiomers, chirals or stereoisomers, which basically means that they have the same molecular and structural formula but cannot be superimposed on each other no matter how they are oriented in space. The majority of all living things use only the L-form but as soon as a living thing dies the L-amino acids spontaneously begin the conversion to the D-form; this is the process Buchholz refers to as racemization.

"The L-form to D-form conversion is temperature dependent and the mouth is significantly warmer than the ground in most places. By measuring the ratio of D-form to L-form you can estimate how long a person was alive," Buchholz continued. "Combining this information with a date of birth, you can get an estimate of age at death. There are caveats of course. In a hot climate, the temperature of the soil may be close to body temperature. If a body has been burned, the intense heat of the fire renders the technique unusable." Speicher wasn't burned; he hadn't died in crash of his Hornet. "The C14 can be skewed by mineral exchange in the soil," Buchholz observed, "but the process is quite slow and depends on the alkalinity of the soil. Traditional archaeology uses bone collagen to date bones rather than enamel due to the possibility of mineral exchange of hundreds to thousands of years in the ground. Bone collagen is a lifetime average of C14 and not useful in this context [of determining the age of a human being at time of death]."

Harris further indicated that the forensics report included the findings of new DNA tests on Speicher's flight suit, which the forensics report now states was found "mostly intact" in 1995. Bob Dussault observed what he'd always believed would have been done – and absent available State Department vetting of this – to verify who they had in the desert back in the 1993/4 time frame was taking a sample of Speicher's DNA then. "To me," he remarked, "it just seemed the logical test of absolute proof barring all else." The other opportunity to verify identity would have been later, Dussault iterated, "if we had one of those sources, like the guy who disappeared out of the hotel in Lebanon [in the custody of the CIA]." It is highly unlikely, he noted, that DNA analysis of the flight suit or the examination of the teeth is how the armed services medical examiner and forensic team arrived at identification. "I think those make plausible stories for public consumption but were useless from a scientific standpoint."

Recall that the flight suit made the rounds of East Coast laboratories for testing in early 1996. "Mostly intact" is not the finding of the FBI laboratory analysis of the flight suit conducted in January 1996, which concluded that large pieces of it were missing altogether. To reiterate the FBI's original findings: Lab technicians noticed that it was hard to tell the top of the suit from the bottom. Entire portions of it were missing. "Completely torn and shredded" were the descriptives they used and photographs of the suit prove the assertion. Recall that "a preliminary chemical test for the possible evidence of blood was positive on stains found on the flight suit," according to the FBI lab report, yet the Bureau couldn't confirm if the stain was actually blood because it did not have permission from the DoD just then to conduct the additional testing to certify that finding. Thusly, the FBI only suggested "possible evidence of" but not the actual presence of blood on the flight suit. The FBI lab tested three dark splotches on the flight suit, each about an eighth of an inch in diameter.

The Bureau also found, again, a moderate presence of dark brown stains from the left arm cuff to the Velcro closure.

Both Velcro closures on the flight suit's sleeves were intact. Samples of stains on the crotch and armpit were taken for possible DNA analysis. None of these tests were done by the Bureau; it bears repeating that flight suit specimens were examined at the DNA Identification Laboratory at the Armed Forces Institute of Pathology (AFIP) in Rockville, Maryland (the same facility today known as the AFDIL). The AFIP looked at a small Ziploc bag containing stained green material; two portions of the left arm cuff, which had moderate stains that looked like dried blood; a crotch cutting and an armpit cutting. The specimens were analyzed using short tandem repeat (STR) analysis, but nothing conclusive is recorded in the unredacted lab report. This report, absent conclusive analyses, is signed by two DNA analysts: Richard E. Wilson and Jeanne M. Willard, as well as Dr. Mitchell M. Holland, branch chief of the AFIP DNA Laboratory and Dr. Victor M. Weedn, the same DNA expert who five years earlier had run tests on DS1-256, the remains the Iraqis claimed was a pilot named "Mickel."

Despite conclusions published in both the FBI report and testing done by the DNA laboratory at the AFIP, CILHI chief anthropologist Dr. Thomas D. Holland wrote in a report dated March 19, 1996, that "FBI chemical tests of the flight suit were positive for possible blood residues." The flight suit, marred by broken chain of custody and a story that it was at some point "lost" only to later miraculously reappear, was tested again after Speicher's partial remains were reported recovered from the Iraqi desert. New DNA tests included as part of the August 6, 2009 forensics report reveal that there was "no blood" on the flight suit. Regardless of whether testing was done in 1996 or 2009, DNA testing then and now could have readily spotted the presence of blood on the flight suit. Of interest, Dr. Thomas Holland, involved in the earliest testing of the flight suit, is today the scientific director and forensic anthropologist to the Joint POW/MIA Accounting Command (JPAC), gaining command of the CILHI, and was still engaged in the investigation that produced the latest forensics report.

The Speicher flight suit resurrected for testing after the remains were located in the summer of 2009 had not been handled and stored properly since it was obtained by investigators in December 1995. Depending on who we are to believe regarding the whereabouts of the flight suit – Bruce Trenholm or Buddy Harris – it is clear that chain of custody was broken and broken so badly that contamination of the flight suit, wherever it was kept during this period of time compromised the use of it as evidence. A U.S. Department of Justice National Institute of Justice (NIJ) special report published in July 2002 observed that because of the particularly sensitive nature of DNA technology, the potential contamination of evidence "should be carefully considered."

The NIJ report tells us why contamination of evidence – just as Ronald Becker suggests – can kill a case or introduce reasonable doubt, especially in a criminal trial: Technologies used to analyze evidence prior to the forensic application of DNA were not always sensitive to contaminants. Evidence in older cases, including Speicher's, may have been collected in ways that lacked appropriate contamination or cross-contamination safeguards, which can make the DNA results less useful or even misleading. In these cases, clarifying results by identifying the contributor of an additional profile can determine whether the DNA results should be used. When a mixture is detected, a careful reconstruction of the evidence collection, storage, and analysis process must be undertaken. Applied to the Speicher case, DNA profiles would have been required from on-scene personnel who first handled the flight suit, including DIA and DPMO staff who eventually came in contact with it, outside experts like Trenholm and Speicher's squadron mates Albano and Fox brought in to identify it, and evidence technicians and laboratory scientists who had access to the evidence for comparison and who would soon publish the results of their analyses. In these instances, proper chain of custody reconstruction is critical. But the chain of custody log and forensic reports attached to Speicher's flight suit, if we take Trenholm at his word, were lost in the mail. If we are to take Buddy Harris at his word, this otherwise critical piece of evidence in the Speicher case was handed back to Speicher's family and has thus been subject to unknown handling practices and storage contamination for an equally unrecorded period of time. For all of these reasons in addition to questions about DNA sampling discussed in Chapter 6 and questionable origin of the flight suit and the condition thereof first raised in Chapter 8, it cannot be the flight suit that yielded usable DNA – not in 1996 and not in 2009.

On a protracted investigation, often a cold case, according to the NIJ special report, when collecting unsolved case evidence, ideally from a storage facility, an investigator is still likely to find any number of packaging disasters. Evidence might be stored in heavy duty plastic bags, stapled shut as an old form of sealing. Multiple items might be sealed in one plastic bag or even unpackaged in large, open cardboard boxes. Unprotected microscope slides from medical facilities and laboratories could also be recovered when going through cases like Scott Speicher's that have drawn out over two decades.

NIJ advises that no attempt should be made by a new investigator or case officer to separate and repackage evidence. The condition and position that the evidence has been stored in could provide valuable clues to the forensic scientist for testability of the evidence. Only when evidence is found unpackaged should a new investigator properly package and label the item(s) to minimize the possibility of contamination from that point forward. When Scott Speicher went missing in action in January 1991 and no body was recovered at the end of the first Gulf War, the investigation of what happened to him bears close resemblance to the criminal investigation in a civilian missing person's case. Thus it is critically important that any evidence items were handled minimally and only by individuals wearing disposable gloves.

We know from Trenholm's account of storing the flight suit in a paper bag under his desk to looking at remains recovery operation photographs from July 2009 that none of this handling procedure took place. As always, the NIJ report further recommends, it is also very important that all actions taken as a result of opening, evaluating, packaging or repackaging evidence are documented thoroughly in the case folder. As with all criminal investigations, including the case of Scott Speicher, chain of custody issues are critical to maintaining the integrity of the evidence. In all cases, the ultimate ability to use DNA evidence will hinge on the ability to prove that the chain of custody was maintained and never broken.

To put what was found in the Iraqi desert in July 2009 in context, very little of Scott Speicher's skeletal remains were found. There are 206 bones in the human body. The human skull has twenty-eight bones, including eight cranial, fourteen facial, and six ear bones. There is the horseshoe-shaped hyoid bone of the neck that is the only bone that does not articulate – connect to a joint – to another bone. We have thirty-three vertebrae, including twenty-four articulating and nine fused, in the spinal column; we don't have roughly twenty-six of Speicher's, just the Atlas and the three Thoracic – and fragments. Humans have twenty-four rib bones plus the sternum, also called the breastbone; the shoulder girdle consisting of two clavicles, the most frequently fractured bones in the body, and two scapulae.

Speicher's forensic team reported only four rib fragments, not intact rib bones. Also missing were the pelvic bones, three fused bones called the coxal bone or the Os Coxae, and thirty bones in each of the arms and legs totaling 120 bones. Also absent were a few partial bones, ranging from eight to eighteen in number that are related to human joints. Generally, it can be assumed that the site was seeded with the skull and jawbone section to give American authorities a dental and DNA match. Whoever had done it wanted to be certain that the hunt for Scott Speicher was over once and for all. The condition of the remains might suggest to forensic scientists probable cause of death and, if not cause of death, certainly how those remains had been disposed. The degradation of the small amount of recovered remains suggests that American investigators should be searching for the original burial site.

Bones speak volumes. A total forensic examination of Speicher's remains should have started with tests of microfibers and microbes and soils on and around the bones, and if the remains were washed before burial. Forensic scientists could then compare soils, particulates and pollens and other discoveries from the site and on the bones with global regions where those soils, pollens and other like trace are present. The proof of where Scott Speicher was buried prior to where he was found is in the form of those micro trace particles picked up and carried in the bones. But this would also be a process made easier had the MNF-W personnel recovery team not employed backhoes and bulldozers to turn up the desert floor, and used indelicate hand-digging tools that included shovels and iron rakes to turn up the soil and sand, even after the first remains were exposed. Compare the collection effort by the ICRC in 1995 to the MNF-W in 2009.

While some Marines wore desert military issue padded palm work gloves, this type of glove and any other military issue work glove worn by recovery team participants is contaminated by the wearer's DNA, work environment and two dig sites; some wore no gloves at all. The only way to avoid cross contamination of forensic evidence, including the skeletal remains MNF-W recovered in July 2009, was to adhere to crime scene consultant and training instructor Dick Warrington's cautionary to "put on gloves [preferably Nitrile gloves free of powder and latex, layered if needed], use gloves, change gloves. Do that every time you touch a piece of evidence. Likewise, use disposable tweezers, scalpels, etc. Change these each time they are used as well."[5] But the recovery team that dug up the desert was largely comprised of Marines without forensic training who'd been drawn to the site by an unnamed Bedouin who purportedly told MNF-W that he was eleven years old in 1991 and, though he didn't have direct knowledge of where Speicher was buried, he could lead them to Bedouins who did. The information was secondhand, at best, suspect, and it was wrong. Photographs from the MNF-W recovery mission indicate that the area where the remains were buried had no discernible landmark near the gravesite. Absent a Bedouin standing over a fresh dug grave, there would be no way to know where a body was buried, especially one reportedly left there almost twenty years before. Thus the Marines' "big dig."

The method used to dig for Speicher's remains obliterated the context of the site. More than two years[6] before Speicher's remains were returned, Bob Dussault reiterated the importance of proper handling and analysis of the remains of service members recovered throughout the world, and given the attention paid to those found in Vietnam, he addressed the troubling practice of salting original crash sites – or close approximations of the same – with the remains of the lost. "We have the capability to prove that our men were buried elsewhere and partial remains seeded where they are found." These locations can be far removed from the seeded burial site, including another country, suggesting that the individual could have been buried elsewhere for a particular length of time before being disinterred for salting at a site previously associated with the body. Thus burial could stretch across a broad spectrum of global regions dependent on the relationship between the original captor and other nations interested in the prisoner.

Finding the original Speicher burial site – even the secondary site and beyond – is facilitated by the study of microtrace particles picked up and carried on the bones. "But no one is checking this trail and recording [the] stories the bones can tell," Dussault opined, "They don't want to know where our men died, how they died and when they died." Did Speicher die in 2003? 2004? 2005? Where did he die? How did he die? These are questions that need an answer. Certainly, it would BE telling if Speicher's partial remains convinced Washington to search harder for the rest of his body, a body that would tell us he was held and kept alive long after Baghdad disavowed knowledge of him. John Noble's story tells us that this disavowal by the enemy isn't anything new; however, Washington's collective memory of such stories is, at best, short-lived.

Buddy Harris saw the complacency of the armed forces medical examiner firsthand. "When it was determined that the medical examiner supplying the autopsy report was taking everything the Bedouin said as gospel in writing his assumptions," Harris told Mabus, he questioned whether the forensics matched the Bedouin story. Then the dental anthropologist determined that it would be impossible for Scott Speicher to have been buried within three days of death, and it was then that Harris and the rest of the forensics team knew something was wrong. "When I read the OAFME [Office of the Armed Forces Medical Examiner] [report] of the Chief

Forensic Anthropologist and Chief Deputy Medical Examiner for Special Investigation Dr. [William C.] Rodriguez [III], he stated the remains are consistent with a lengthy postmortem interval of approximately 18 years," he continued. "Since this would eliminate the possibility of anything but a short period of captivity," Harris asked Rodriguez – hypothetically – if Speicher had been flying during Operation Iraqi Freedom in 2003 and shot down, would the remains just recovered in Iraqi desert and identified as belonging to Speicher, be consistent with those that spent just six years in that environment? Rodriguez answered yes. The room went very quiet.

Then Harris asked Rodriguez the minimum time these remains were probably in this environment. Though difficult to tell not knowing how much time Speicher had spent above ground versus below – alive and then dead – and coupled with the fact the forensics team concurred that it was clear to them that the remains were buried at least twice, Rodriguez's best guess was four-and-a-half to eighteen years given the team had no backstory to go with the remains they were tasked to analyze. When asked why he put the eighteen years in his report, Rodriguez stated that he was asked if these remains were consistent with eighteen years in that environment, and the answer to that ambiguously worded question is yes.

From Speicher's highly redacted forensics and autopsy reports, and Buddy Harris' November 27, 2009 statements to Joe Frusci regarding when Speicher expired, and coupled with nearly twenty years of intelligence reporting and information gathering, it appeared blood last flowed through Scott Speicher approximately four-and-a-half to five years prior to the recovery of his remains in July 2009, thus narrowing the time of death to after the United States invasion of Iraq in March 2003 and sometime before the end of 2005. This approximation could have been best made using a radiocarbon test of his dental remains; there is no way of knowing if this was the means by which a forensic anthropologist arrived at the date when Scott Speicher was last alive. But like Rodriguez, the forensic team hadn't been provided much prequel on which to base their findings. If the backstory and the forensic finding are considered together, Scott Speicher was about 47 years old at time of death. Can these approximations be narrowed further? Possibly.

There is no method, without the rest of his body, that can establish Speicher's precise moment of death. Investigators have only been able to come up with a window of time in which the death might have happened and then, as forensics expert Becker has explained[7] that time frame can be reduced, as already suggested, whenever and however a victim's points of contact prior to death can be established. Since Speicher's remains were moved at least twice prior to being salted proximal to the crash site, investigators had already begun to draw some conclusion as to where the rest of his remains are interred.

The American public may never get to see the actual forensics report. A Freedom of Information Act (FOIA) request for a copy of it dated January 18, 2011, and submitted to the Department of the Navy FOIA Office was denied in a letter dated February 25. Robin Patterson, Department of the Navy Public Affairs/FOIA Policy Branch chief, wrote: "In an effort to assist you, we contacted the Office of the Secretary of the Navy, Naval Criminal Investigative Service and the Navy Bureau of Medicine and Surgery, the offices within the Navy that would most likely have cognizance of the records you are seeking [the 200-page forensics report]. After these offices conducted diligent searches in accordance with the Department of the Navy's FOIA regulations (32 CFR §701.8(a)(1)), they have been unable to locate any records responsive to your request."

Though dated February 25, the denial letter wasn't mailed until April 1, the day a second call was placed to Patterson's office to find out whether her office intended to respond. Clarice Julka, a navy FOIA specialist, offered to send it immediately via e-mail; this was already many weeks after her office's response letter was written and signed off by Patterson. A paper copy of the letter arrived the following week; it was postmarked April 1. The letter suggested the denial could be appealed to the Department of the Navy Office of the Judge Advocate General (JAG); this was submitted and mailed on April 1 and received by JAG on April 7, 2011. The following day a form letter was sent out. The appeal was assigned a case number and an uncertain response date. Claiming small staff and the size and complexity of other claims, the JAG office wrote "we are unable to provide an estimated completion date at this time." But on May 5 the JAG office telephoned an update: they'd recovered a memo that referenced the report but not the report itself. The JAG officer assigned to the appeal asked if this writer knew how to get in touch with "Commander Harris" to have him replicate his copy of the forensics report to satisfy the appeal request. There were two witnesses to the phone call, taken during a meeting in the presence of a retired navy captain and a retired navy commander, both former navy medical corps. The most important question, and a point that was clearly made during this conversation: Is the secretary of the navy in the habit of signing off on major findings his office cannot locate?

Buddy Harris is a retired United States Navy officer with a paper trail leading back to his Navy Bureau of Personnel (BUPERS) file and whose wife, Scott's former spouse and the Speicher children, received Speicher's monthly pay and allowances for years after his status was changed to missing in action-captured. The United States government would have to have Harris' contact information to mail a monthly retirement check, make notification of change in retiree benefits and send out a myriad of new information and meeting invitations pertaining to Scott Speicher. Harris has been the family's primary point of contact since the search for Speicher began. By his own account and documentation entered into Speicher's case file, Harris has been present at Speicher's repeated status review boards, had constant contact with the Office of the Secretary of the Navy, DIA and DPMO and the JAG headquarter office on the Washington Navy Yard. A good telephone number and e-mail for Harris would most certainly come up in any of the aforementioned agencies' points of contact files on the Speicher case, or a call to Cindy Laquidara, general counsel of the Office of the General Counsel for the city of Jacksonville, Florida, and the attorney whose name is most publicly associated with the Speicher case, can readily locate Harris.

Buddy Harris carried a copy of the August 6, 2009 200-page forensics report into the First Coast News interview under the cover of the November 12 SECNAV memo, aware or not of an ongoing effort to quash the report's existence and bury critical evidence in Scott Speicher's case. He told Blaylock that "the report dates back to November 12, 2009, but was basically 'glossed over' by the media." In truth, the report dates to August 6, less than a week after Scott Speicher's purported remains became available for examination by the Office of the Armed Forces Medical Examiner at Dover, Delaware. Secondly, the report wasn't made available by name, date, title and the agency that generated it; the media couldn't ask for or know about a document that was never intended to see the light of day.

After the JAG headquarters located reports to satisfy the January 18, 2011 FOIA for this and other relevant documents, the JAG corrected the date on the forensics report to August 6 and the cover memo as November 12. Harris' First Coast News interview has been widely circulated on Internet and social media sites. Thusly, there is no question that the document and others like it exist and that it was released by Secretary of the Navy Mabus by direction as stated on the November 12 memo. Each of the offices queried by Office of Navy FOIA in its "diligent search" for the document already had intimate knowledge of it, including the Navy JAG office on the Washington Navy Yard. The Judge Advocate General of the Navy is the principal advisor to the Secretary of the Navy and the Chief of Naval Operations on legal matters pertaining to the navy.

Speicher had a JAG lawyer assigned to represent him from 2002, and all status changes and communication with Speicher's family were and still are a legal matter of utmost importance to the Office of the Secretary of the Navy, thus it is difficult to believe that the secretary's office wouldn't know anything about Scott Speicher's forensics and autopsy reports and would further claim no knowledge of two memos, one dated September 4, 2009, that was sent to the SECNAV regarding the dispensation of Speicher's remains and the other the SECNAV-generated document dated November 12.

The Judge Advocate General's May 25, 2011 letter in response to the April 1 appeal of the January 18, 2011 FOIA request to the Department of the Navy FOIA Office for the forensic report and all releasable correspondence, reports and message traffic dating from June to November 2009 regarding the recovery of Captain Speicher's remains, is telling. The JAG office identified the forensic report generated by the Joint Pathology Center (JPC) dated August 6, 2009, a 200-page report pulled together just five days after Speicher's remains were returned to the United States; both aforementioned memos; the August 14, 2009 amended autopsy report and Speicher's death certificate held by the Armed Forces Institute of Pathology (AFIP) Office of the Medical Examiner (OME), all of which are responsive to the original FOIA request.

"Although CNO cannot release these documents because they are not the release authority," states the G.E. Lattin, deputy assistant judge advocate general, General Litigation Division, acting, "I am recommending your request back to CNO for the purpose of referring these documents to the appropriate agency where they will determine if the information can be released." But page two of the letter would appear to countermand all of what Lattin stated on page one. The only verbiage at the top of page two read thusly: "As the Secretary of the Navy's designee, I am responsible for this final denial of your appeal. You may seek judicial review of this decision." The letter is signed below by Lattin.

It was less than a week between arrival of Speicher's remains for examination and generation of the final report. Given the nature of the testing required to achieve absolute certainty that these were Speicher's remains, the end product (a 200-page forensics report) was more the product of foregone conclusion than sure science and forensic investigation. What did all of them know before Speicher's purported remains were located in the Iraqi desert? More importantly, when did they know it? They clearly knew enough to fill up a 200-page document. Staffing, reviewing and editing a document of this length, breadth and importance would have taken a minimum of 30 to 60 days. Not counting the day Speicher's remains arrived for examination, this leaves four days to do the impossible and the day following that to publish the report.

The JAG's letter dated May 25 was mailed June 7 and received the following day; the day that this letter was mailed, the Armed Forces Institute of Pathology Office of the Medical Examiner had already vetted the FOIA request for Speicher's death certificate and autopsy report and crafted a letter regarding dispensation of the same. "Under the FOIA, Exemption 6 protects information about individuals in 'personnel and medical files and similar files' when the disclosure of such information 'would constitute a clearly unwarranted invasion of personal privacy.' With this exemption in mind, and lacking any consent from Capt. Speicher's next-of-kin for release of the above cited documents, the portion of your FOIA request forwarded to our office is denied," according to the OME letter received June 11. But here's the problem with the OME invoking Exemption 6:

"In order to determine whether Exemption 6 protects against disclosure, the OME would have to have engaged in the following two lines of inquiry: first, determine whether the information at issue is contained in a personnel, medical or 'similar' file covered by Exemption 6[8] (which the OME did do); but then it universally applied the second part of the test without determining if the disclosure 'would constitute a clearly unwarranted invasion of personal privacy' by balancing the privacy interest that would be compromised by disclosure against any public interest in the requested information." When engaging in this analysis, it is important to remember that the Court of Appeals for the District of Columbia Circuit has declared that "under Exemption 6, the presumption in favor of disclosure is as strong as can be found anywhere in the Act. Additionally, it is important to keep in mind that Exemption 6 cannot be invoked to withhold from a requester information pertaining only to himself."[9]

To warrant protection under Exemption 6, information must first meet its threshold requirement; in other words, it must fall within the category of "personnel and medical files and 'similar' files," yet, even if it were to qualify under this header that does not indicate the information cannot be released. Once it has been established that information meets the threshold requirement of Exemption 6, the focus of the inquiry, according to guidance provided by the Department of Justice, turns to whether disclosure of the records at issue "would constitute a clearly unwarranted invasion of personal privacy." This requires a balancing of the public's right to disclosure against the individual's right to privacy – once determined to be dead, Scott Speicher no longer has privacy rights.

But a further wrinkle is that Speicher's death occurred in a foreign country. First, it must be ascertained whether a protectible privacy interest exists that would be threatened by disclosure.[10] If no privacy interest is found, further analysis is unnecessary and the information at issue must be disclosed. If there is a public interest in disclosure that outweighs the privacy interest, the information should be disclosed; if the opposite is found to be the case, the information should be withheld.[11] To wit, the invocation of Exemption 6 has been argued in federal courts and the Supreme Court most often with regard to whether the release of such information would imply that the subject of the release had done something criminal or unprofessional in nature, or the release of such information might do damage to the reputation of someone else in the individual's family. This is not the case with Speicher nor Speicher's family with regard to documentation responsive to the January 18, 2011 FOIA request.

Invocation of next-of-kin privacy doesn't hold credence under Exemption 6 in this case. Speicher's next-of-kin was, until his children turned eighteen, designated, right or wrong, by the Department of Defense to be his former wife Joanne Speicher-Harris and her husband, Albert "Buddy" Harris. During this time and since, as recently as Harris' January 17, 2011 First Coast News interview, the Speicher-Harris clan have invited the media into Speicher's case and this can be cited in the hundreds of articles written, including the six-part *Virginian-Pilot* series "Dead or Alive?" to which Harris contributed lengthy interviews and that was published ahead of the book about Speicher's case, *No One Left Behind*. There have been additional and often lengthy public interviews provided to the media by Speicher-Harris attorney and Jacksonville general counsel Cindy Laquidara. Now, when the public's best interest – and those of men and women still missing – would be best served by knowing the government's approximation of Speicher's date and cause of death, the AFIP OME retreated to Exemption 6 to avoid release, thus pausing behind the tenets of the court's finding in NARA v. Favish, 541 United States 157, 171 (2004).[12]

The application of survivor privacy interest is largely applied, and was initially argued, with regard to criminal cases. In *Reporters Committee* the Court found a "strong privacy interest" in the nondisclosure of records of a private citizen's criminal history, "even where the information may have been at one time public." The Supreme Court has also held that information need not necessarily be what might be considered "intimate" or "embarrassing" to a living person to qualify for Exemption 6 protection. The privacy interests cognizable under the FOIA that pertain to a living person exist in such identifying information as a person's name, address, phone number, date of birth, criminal history, medical history and social security number. Though initially it must be determined "whether disclosure of the files 'would compromise a substantial, as opposed to de minimis, privacy interest,' because 'if no significant privacy interest is implicated'... FOIA demands disclosure."[13]

The Court of Appeals for the District of Columbia Circuit has explained that, in the FOIA context, when assessing the weight of a protectable privacy interest, "[a] substantial privacy interest is anything greater than a de minimis privacy interest." According to the Court, when a substantial privacy interest is found, the inquiry under the privacy exemptions is not finished, it is only advanced to address the question whether the public interest in disclosure outweighs the individual privacy concerns. Thus, as the District of Columbia Circuit has held, "a privacy interest may be substantial – more than de minimis – and yet be insufficient to overcome the public interest in disclosure."[14]

The District of Columbia Circuit has also emphasized the practical analytical point that under the FOIA's privacy-protection exemptions, "[t]he threat to privacy . . . need not be patent or obvious to be relevant." At the same time, courts have found that the threat to privacy must be real rather than speculative. In National Association of Retired Federal Employees [hereinafter NARFE] v. Horner, the District of Columbia Circuit explained that the "relevant point" of its prior holding in Arieff v. United States Department of the Navy was that "mere speculation" of an invasion of privacy "is not itself part of the invasion of privacy contemplated by Exemption 6."

In a request for Speicher's autopsy and death certificate, while the AFIP OME can attempt to block the release of both documents, this is the "mere speculation" of invasion of privacy as defined by Arieff v. United States Department of the Navy 712 Federal 2d 1462, 1467-68 (District of Columbia Circuit 1983) (finding that Exemption 6 did not apply when there was only a "mere possibility" that the medical condition of a particular individual would be disclosed by releasing a list of pharmaceuticals supplied to a congressional doctor (quoting Rose, 425 United States at 380 n.19)) and thus not the intended application of Exemption 6. Further, the NARFE court went on to explain that "[f]or the Exemption 6 balance to be implicated, there must, of course, be a causal relationship between the disclosure and the threatened invasion of privacy." In some instances, the disclosure of information might involve no invasion of privacy because, fundamentally, the information is of such a nature that no expectation of privacy exists.[15]

According to Department of Justice guidance, living federal employees involved in law enforcement, as well as military personnel and Internal Revenue Service employees, do possess, by virtue of the nature of their work, protectable privacy interests in their identities and work addresses. In light of this privacy interest, the Department of Defense now regularly withholds personally identifying information about all military and civilian employees with respect to whom disclosure would "raise security or privacy concerns." But this is not the case for Speicher, who has been determined to be deceased. Or has he? From Navy FOIA, JAG to AFIP OME the reaction to a FOIA for postmortem Speicher documentation can best be characterized as a classic runaround over a case in which the government has repeatedly claimed with absolute certainty: "Scott is dead." If he is, and the proof is properly documented, there should be no problem releasing the official record to anyone. But if the Department of Defense and those who promulgated the reports requested on the FOIA have constructed their conclusions on shaky, perhaps uncertain, ground, that would explain the runaround.

The exercise of the Privacy Act is weak in this case. But it was the only choice at the AFIP OME's disposal. Classifying something to avoid embarrassment or that reveals a government failure or mistake is a violation of classification procedure and it happens more than the public is made aware. Due to media attention, the Department of Defense, in particular, has been caught hiding missteps and mistakes too often in recent memory and thus the AFIP OME stayed away from trying to use denial because the information was "classified" and instead invoked the Privacy Act. Speicher's postmortem information is not classified nor is it covered under the Privacy Act.

So where was Scott Speicher when he died? The photograph of Speicher that is used on the cover of this narrative was provided by an intelligence source in the Washington, D.C. beltway. Information about the photograph dates it to 2003/4. The source obtained the picture with a cellular telephone camera from a computer screen in an office where the source worked. What troubled the source about the photograph was the left eye, dark and looking down. The source suggested "a detached retina," perhaps from "... beatings or a stroke." The left side of the face sags. There is a pronounced scar above the right eye. Curiously, Speicher is clean-shaven with a military haircut but clearly older. Reluctant to pinpoint the picture's origin, the source deflected, at first stating that it must have come from an open Web site. When pushed, they admitted that's not where the picture was obtained. "It was not long after viewing the picture again there that it disappeared from the [site]. In fact, the whole site disappeared," recalled the source. "Interesting. Of course, some of the [people] there work for various three-letter agencies, ... including DIA and CIA."

"'Age-enhanced' photos don't include such enhancements as new scars and eye damage," conceded the source, moving closer to the truth about the picture. When pressed, the response was this: "News organizations would have gotten their pictures of him from the friends and family, the Pentagon...So somebody's taking a secret to the grave with them, I guess, if nobody will admit to it [the photograph] ... which makes me think it was a 'leak' of some sort, even more. Scared to admit it," the source continued, "for one reason or another." The picture was provided by the source in 2010. But as the source reiterated – no one wants to own up to it.

"I doubt anyone would admit that it's a picture of him alive," added the source. "If they denied [him] the homecoming he deserved then, and he died within a couple years of being found [the source pinpoints his recovery around Labor Day, September 2003], then concerned parties would likely believe they could continue the charade/farce/cover up that he died when he was shot down – despite the high survivability of the Martin-Baker ejection seats, and everything else." The source further noted – using vague terms – that his health was so bad that he wasn't expected to live much longer, and iterated that since his wife was long remarried and his children grown... that [he] was "probably... already heartbroken about having been declared dead so fast and his wife remarrying. Considering the effect of eight or so years of imprisonment with torture by Saddam, Uday and Qusay [and others], it isn't hard to imagine how screwed up his body and how poor his health might have been. He might also have lived longer after rescue," the source continued, "than they expected him to, which makes the denied homecoming celebration even more bitter."

When the Mossad witnessed Speicher's move prior to American forces entering Iraq on March 19, 2003, it signaled a series of moves that purportedly took Speicher northeast in the country, according to the intelligence source, who suggested that transport was provided by the Fedayeen Saddam, a group established in 1995 by Uday Hussein who recruited typically young men fiercely and fanatically loyal to the regime, to carry out guerrilla warfare and special assignments. The Fedayeen, dressed in civilian clothing, moved about the country doing the regime's bidding, including infiltration of the Republican Guard and Special Republican Guard to ferret out potential traitors and nonbelievers. According to the Council on Foreign Relations, in addition to organizing smuggling and other illegal efforts along Iraq's borders, "the group [was] thought to be directly responsible for some of the regime's most brutal acts. It [was] widely reported to operate a death squad that [conducted] extra-judicial executions."[16]

The source suggested that Speicher – at some point – made it as far north as As Sulaymaniyah Province within Iraqi Kurdistan in the custody of his captors. As Sulaymaniyah's capital is the city of Sulaymaniyah, which is ringed by the Azmar Range, Goizja Range and the Qaiwan Range to the northeast, Baranan Mountain in the south and the Tasluje Hills in the west. As Sulaymaniyah Province borders the Iranian provinces of West Azerbaijan, Kurdistan and Kermanshah, and includes the tripoint border with modern Turkey. Near the end of thc war in Iraq, Uday and Qusay Hussein fled together to Syria, according to media reports, and were later expelled by Damascus and returned to northern Iraq. Despite this turn of fate, the Hussein brothers' discovery in the north in Mosul surprised American intelligence, largely due to the population's hostility toward them that began with the regime's purging of the Kurds to control the region. Uday and Qusay Hussein were killed on July 22, 2003, when Task Force 20, assisted by soldiers from the U.S. Army's 101st Airborne Division, surrounded and assaulted the Mosul house in which they were hiding. For them, their father and Scott Speicher, the last exposure they would share in Iraq orbited in the northern and northeastern part of the country.

Back to the question of when and where Speicher died and why it matters, especially if we are to believe a 200-page forensics report could be generated in less than a week. If we are to believe the source – and this source's information must be part of the conversation regarding Scott Speicher's fate – there are hard questions that must be asked and answered. First and foremost, is it possible he was secured to an overseas safe house? The answer to that question is, absolutely. Agencies such as the CIA maintain a wide variety of properties around the world not attributable to the agency, prepositioned assets that can be commandeered under certain circumstances. The CIA spied on Osama bin Laden from a safe house in Abbottabad, Pakistan, much to the chagrin of the Pakistani government.

The troubling lack of transparency with the forensics report would indicate that the real deception lies in when Speicher died and when most of the forensics report was actually generated – far in advance – most believe, before it was inked by the OFME and presented to the media on August 6, 2009. Another question is, who provided the clean shave and military haircut? Who tended to Scott Speicher before his actual death?

These are questions that deserve an answer and when it comes, it needs to be the truth without the deception and cover up that's cloaked this case for more than 20 years.

"I would not be at all surprised," added the source, "if he died elsewhere, was buried, then exhumed a few years later to extract some 'fragmentary evidence' like jawbone, teeth, whatever they 'found' in Iraq, and that it was then buried in a country [Iraq] where the U.S. has great freedom of action and authority." Why? "All to backstop an official cover story – perhaps to cover people's asses, if you will. After Saddam and many others are dead or captured and we're close to leaving, why continue the fiction? Because others who were involved in some way and might be culpable are at risk of discovery and possible prosecution."

Note that Speicher has a little "smile" in the picture and is staring straight into the camera, just as he was trained to do in his SERE training so there would be proof of life whether he survived the experience or not. If he was kept in a safe house before his death how did he really die and by whose hand? "I prefer not to say exactly why," said the source. "That picture is the only 'hard' evidence I have seen that indicates Scott must have been rescued. You know how sensitive and deniable SCI [special compartmentalized information] is... It occurred to me that he would only be denied a homecoming, that is, a public repatriation, if he was not expected to live long due to health consequences of being Saddam's prisoner." The same source put his death in mid-February 2005, right after Valentine's Day. Whether this is the case or not is a question that does require an answer.

"I think some people could use reminding," cautioned the source, "that 1) there is no statute of limitations for charges relating to murder [and] 2) the truth does come out eventually."

Endnotes

1. Becker, Ronald F. *Criminal Investigation*. Third edition. Sudbury, Massachusetts: Jones and Bartlett, 2008, p. 236.

2. Pickering, Robert B. and David Bachman. *The Use of Forensic Anthropology.* Boca Raton, Florida: CRC Press, 2009, p. 173.

3. Alkass, Kanar et al., "Age estimation in forensic sciences: application of combined aspartic acid racemization and radiocarbon analysis," *Molecular & Cellular Proteomics*, May 1, 2010. Available online at http://www.mcponline.org

4. "Identifying disaster victims: looking at teeth to determine victims' age at time of death," *Homeland Security Newswire*, May 21, 2010, available online at http://homelandsecuritynewswire.com/identifying-disaster-victims-looking-teeth-determine-victims-age-time-death and "Putting Teeth Into forensic science," *Lawrence Livermore National Laboratory Public Affairs* available online https://www.llnl.gov/news/newsreleases/2010/NR-10-05-07.html

5. Warrington, Dick, "Put on gloves, use gloves, change gloves," *Forensic Magazine*, published online June 25, 2010 http://www.forensicmag.com/tip/put-gloves-use-gloves-change-gloves

6. Bob Dussault e-mail correspondence, May 14, 2007.

7. Becker, p. 239.

8. 5 U.S.C. § 552(b)(6), (7)(C) (2006), amended by OPEN Government Act of 2007, Pub. Law No. 110-175, 121 Statute 2524; see also Presidential Memorandum for Heads of Executive Departments and Agencies Concerning the Freedom of Information Act, 74 Federal Regulation 4683 (January 21, 2009) (emphasizing that the Freedom of Information Act reflects a "profound national commitment to ensuring an open Government" and directing agencies to "adopt a presumption in favor of disclosure"); according to Attorney General Eric Holder's Memorandum for Heads of Executive Departments and Agencies Concerning the Freedom of Information Act (March 19, 2009), available at http://www.usdoj.gov/ag/foia-memo-march2009.pdf; FOIA Post, "OIP Guidance: President Obama's FOIA Memorandum and Attorney General Holder's FOIA Guidelines – Creating a New Era of Open Government" (posted April 17, 2009).

9. Department of Justice Guide to the Freedom of Information Act Exemption 6, available at http://www.justice.gov/oip/foia_guide07/exemption6.pdf

10. Multi AG Media LLC, 515 Federal 3rd at 1229 ("The balancing analysis for FOIA Exemption 6 requires that we first determine whether disclosure of the files 'would compromise a substantial, as opposed to de minimis, privacy inter-

est[.]'" (quoting National Association of Retired Federal Employees v. Horner, 879 F.2d 873, 874, District of Columbia Circuit 1989)).

11. Associated Press v. DoD, 554 Federal 3rd 274, 291 (2nd Circuit 2009) ("Only where a privacy interest is implicated does the public interest for which the information will serve become relevant and require a balancing of the competing interests." (quoting FLRA v. VA, 958 Federal 2nd 503, 509 (2nd Circuit 1992))); see also NARA v. Favish, 541 United States 157, 171 (2004) ("The term 'unwarranted' requires us to balance the family's privacy interest against the public interest in disclosure."). Further interpretation offered in Department of Justice Guide to the Freedom of Information Act Exemption 6.

12. 541 United States 157, 165-70 (2004) ([T]he concept of personal privacy . . . "is not some limited or 'cramped notion' of that idea.") (Exemption 7(C)); see also FOIA Post, "Supreme Court Rules for 'Survivor Privacy' in Favish" (posted April 9, 2004) (highlighting breadth of privacy protection principles in Supreme Court's decision). Note that the AFIP OME did not cite Exemption 7.

13. Multi Ag Media LLC v. USDA, 515 Federal 3rd 1224, 1229 (District of Columbia Circuit 2008) (quoting NARFE, 879 Federal 2nd at 874); see, for example, Consumers' Checkbook Center for the Study of Servs. v. HHS, 554 Federal 3rd 1046, 1050 (District of Columbia Circuit 2009) ("[W]e must determine whether 'disclosure would compromise a substantial, as opposed to a de minimis, privacy interest.'" (quoting NARFE, 879 Federal 2nd at 874)); Associated Press v. DoD, 554 F.3d 274, 285 (2nd Circuit 2009) ("Thus, 'once a more than de minimis privacy interest is implicated the competing interests at stake must be balanced in order to decide whether disclosure is permitted under FOIA.'" (quoting FLRA v. VA, 958 Federal 2nd 503, 510 (2nd Circuit 1992))).

14. Multi AG Media LLC 515 Federal 3rd 1230 (quoting National Association of Home Builders v. Norton, 309 Federal 3rd 26, 35 (District of Columbia Circuit 2002)); see, for example, Consumers' Checkbook, 554 Federal 3rd at 1050 ("If a substantial privacy interest is at stake, then we must balance the privacy interest in nondisclosure against the public interest."); Associated Press v. DOJ, 549 Federal 3rd at 66 ("Notwithstanding a document's private nature, FOIA may nevertheless require disclosure if the requester can show that revelation of the contents of the requested document would serve the public interest."); Scales v. EOUSA, 594 Federal Supplement 2nd 87, 90 (District Court District of Columbia 2009) ("Given the significant individual privacy interest, disclosure of 7(C) material is warranted only when the individual's interest in privacy is outweighed by the public's interest in disclosure.") (Exemption 7(C)).

15. People for the American Way Foundation, 503 Federal Supplement 2nd at 306 ("Disclosing the mere identity of individuals who voluntarily submitted comments regarding the Lincoln video does not raise the kind of privacy concerns protected by Exemption 6."); Fuller v. CIA, No. 04-253, 2007 WL 666586, at 4 (District Court of District of Columbia February 28, 2007) (finding that information reflecting only professional and business judgments and relationships "cannot fairly be characterized as personal information that exemption (b)(6) was meant to protect"); Alliance for the Wild Rockies v. Department of the Interior, 53 Federal Supplement 2nd 32, 37 (District Court of District of Columbia 1999) (finding that commenters to proposed rulemaking could have no expec-

tation of privacy when agency made clear that their identities would not be concealed).

16. Council on Foreign Relations Backgrounder, "What is the Fedayeen Saddam?" http://www.cfr.org/iraq/iraq-fedayeen-saddam/p7698

Chapter 13

The Cover-Up of The Cover-Up

Despite the Pentagon's strong inclination to close Speicher's case, it is important to the family, to military operators and to many in Congress to know the truth about what happened to him. They'd like to know where his remains were originally buried and why only partial remains, most of them fragments, were deposited where they were found. Where is the rest of him? We may never get that answer. "Buddy is right about one thing," wrote Joe Frusci on November 28, 2009, during a follow-up interview with Harris, "they are just trying to cleanse themselves of this, tie it in a nice bow, and put it to rest."

The Pentagon doesn't appear anxious to say when, where and how he died, classifying much of the forensics report to conceal what really happened to him, including the results of classified DNA and forensics testing on his recovered remains. "I am aware of an effort underway," wrote Harris to navy secretary Mabus, in his lengthy letter of September 4, 2009, "to ascertain that CAPT Speicher died in the crash, so even though some mistakes were made, he was dead anyway, so no harm, no foul. I have no intention of rehashing the mistakes made that night [the night Scott Speicher got shot down]." In retrospect, perhaps Harris should have rehashed the "issues in the flying of it" to wit he invariably makes mention when forced to challenge the government investigation into Speicher's missing status.

Rather than come forward with the truth in the Speicher case, the DIA and DPMO got the DIA POW/MIA analytic cell chief, Thomas Brown, to provide the Associated Press with an "exclusive" on November 28, 2009, the same day that Frusci conveyed Harris' umbrage with the way the Pentagon was moving swiftly to tie

Scott's case in "a nice bow" and make it go away, and before any media knew of or had a chance to FOIA the forensics report and read what parts of it weren't classified. The "facts" as Brown tried to convey them in an article[1] by Pamela Hess titled "Saddam was telling the truth in missing Gulf War pilot [case]," were misleading because he and the DIA and DPMO knew that the press would never go back and really look up the mountain of paperwork that would have proven his response to Hess was riddled with inconsistencies and wrong information. Brown's first statement, that Speicher's bones lay twelve inches deep in the Iraqi sand where "a group of Iraqis had led an American search team in 1995" is highly misleading and just as inaccurate. He also left out entirely the presence of an Iraq Survey Group team on the site after the U.S. invasion in March 2003 that went to the original crash site, unearthed what it thought were his remains, and sent them to Dover Air Force Base mortuary for testing; those remains did not belong to Scott Speicher.

We now know that the remains left for the MNF-W to recover had been moved at least twice before being hastily buried, again, twelve inches below the desert surface and far removed from Speicher's original wreckage. Brown's statement about the remains is tainted with innuendo and that is not what a government agency should be engaged in, most especially when the DIA and DPMO have used it to mislead the American public and hide the truth.

Iraq had already set the precedent seeding a crash site in the case of Saudi pilot colonel Mohammed Nazerah. The vernacular used by the Iraqis when they referenced Nazerah is the same that they used for Speicher; it was only after rumors of Nazerah's capture and captivity circulated in early 2000 that a joint ICRC – Saudi team was permitted to search Nazerah's crash site and retrieve remains. There had been reports in the Saudi media that Nazerah was last seen in an Iraqi jail and that there was photographic proof that he was still alive.

In summary, Baghdad patently rejected the existence of evidence that Nazerah was still alive and in their custody and put off the ICRC – Saudi team's entry to investigate the site in the spring of 2000. Saddam relented many months later, that October, and permitted the joint ICRC – Saudi team to the crash site if it worked alongside their Iraqi counterparts, perhaps a lesson learned by the Iraqis after the ICRC team that explored the Speicher crash site five years earlier. There were only small pieces of human bone collected – it was all that remained of Nazerah's body – but it was still enough to get a positive identification at a Geneva DNA laboratory. "After verifying the laboratory data, the [Saudi] Ministry of Aviation and Defense is now certain that the aforementioned pilot was martyred,"[2] a ministry official said in a statement carried by the official Saudi Press Agency.

Perhaps most relevant to Speicher's case was the observation shared by all forensic examiners who dug the Nazerah crash site: the Saudi pilot's remains had been placed where they were found only recently. This is the same pilot that Baghdad stated was shot down on February 13, 1991, and his body buried by an Iraqi officer in a minefield – an officer Baghdad also stated would come forward and identify the gravesite for the ICRC-Saudi team. The wreckage of Nazerah's plane was located about one kilometer (.62 miles) away.

Back to Brown. He was far from done with innuendo and sleight of hand. Hess reported that the search for Speicher was frustrated by two wars, "mysteriously switched remains, Iraqi duplicity and a final tip from a young nomad in Anbar Province." First, there were no "mysteriously switched remains" or "Iraqi duplicity" involved. Despite what Carlos Johnson said about no Iraqi aircraft firing on an American jet on January 17, 1991, and despite information and imagery in the U.S. Air Force's possession, Brown told Hess Speicher was shot down by a MiG-25. "The search was soon complicated by the Iraqi discovery," Brown stated, "of a different crash site – of a downed air force A-10 fighter. The Iraqis brought the unidentified American A-10 pilot's remains to a Basrah hospital for safekeeping, labeling him 'Mickel' for a clumsy translation of what might have been the pilot's belt buckle, manufactured by McDonnell Douglas."

First of all, the A-10 is a ground-attack aircraft manufactured by Fairchild Republic, not McDonnell Douglas, making it highly unlikely any Warthog driver would be wearing a McDonnell Douglas belt buckle; he would be wearing a flight suit, so where might he be "wearing" a belt buckle? The same could be said of Speicher, who even though his aircraft, the F/A-18 Hornet was manufactured by McDonnell Douglas, would have no reason to be wearing a belt buckle at the time of his loss; he was wearing a standard navy issue flight suit underneath a pressure suit, his MA-2 torso harness and SV-2 survival vest, not his shipboard wash khaki shirt and pants that require a belt buckle. Under close examination of a navy harness and vest of the same period, and to further dispel Brown's off-the-wall belt buckle statement, the torso harness has no "McDonnell Douglas" on the Koch fittings and buckle; the same is also true of the survival vest straps and buckles.

"The Iraqis are not as dumb as DIA would like us to think," Dussault stated more recently. "The Iraqis [knew and know] McDonnell Douglas as one of the biggest and well known companies in the military industrial complex. The Iraqis probably even own or have captured [over time] hundreds of products made by this company. They know this company real well."

We already knew that on March 20, 1991, the Iraqis turned over to the ICRC remains they claimed belonged to a "U.S. pilot by the name of Mickel." They even supplied a death certificate along with these remains, which amounted to a pound-and-a-half of desiccated flesh, not four, as Brown would have the public believe from his November 2009 statement to the AP. The remains arrived at Dover Air Force Base, Delaware, on March 23, 1991, and shortly thereafter were assigned a case number: DS1-256. Dr. Victor Weedn excluded the remains as those of Speicher and observed the person to whom the remains did belong had dark olive skin, typical of someone from the Middle East.

Remains with dark olive skin were also not those of air force first lieutenant Patrick Olson, a fair-skinned, red-haired OA-10 pilot lost on February 27, 1991, in Operation Desert Storm. Olson was on a combat mission in Saudi Arabia in which he was directing other warplanes toward Iraqi tanks. He had a call from army troops who believed Iraqi tanks were about to pull an end run on their position. They needed immediate close air support. Olson put his Warthog into a nearly vertical dive as he banked sharply to aim at the Iraqi armor. Gunfire erupted around him and hit his aircraft. The damage was serious. Olson tried to land the aircraft at King Khalid Military City Forward Operating Location (KKMC FOL) and was just inches from putting it down on a sand airfield when the aircraft cartwheeled; he did not have time to eject. There was little left of the aircraft.

The remains didn't belong to Warthog pilot captain Stephen Richard Phillis either, shot down in combat on February 15, 1991. Phillis was hit by ground fire approximately sixty miles northwest of Kuwait City while attacking Republican Guard targets. He was believed to have been engaged by an SA-13 Gopher, a surface-to-air missile. Though Phillis was declared missing in action for several weeks, his wreckage was found when a United States Army squad stumbled onto a piece of it and determined that he had gone down with the aircraft and had not tried to eject; no one is certain why he did not get out of the A-10 before it impacted the ground. But his remains also had nothing to do with the pound-and-a-half of flesh turned over by the Iraqis. His skin tone and genetic characteristics wouldn't have been a match either. Olson and Phillis were the only recorded A-10 pilots to die during Desert Storm. One A-10 that crashed was a wheels up, hard stick landing and the pilot didn't die nor was he captured. Thus it stands to reason that the A-10 wreckage to which Brown refers are one of the three aircraft shot down in which the pilots involved were subsequently captured. These pilots were Lieutenant Colonel Jeffrey Fox, Lieutenant James Sweet, and Captain Richard Dale Storr. All were returned in early March 1991.

Brown would have the public believe that Baghdad made a hasty gamble in the return of the pound-and-a-half of flesh. There was no "hasty gamble" involved. The Iraqis were providing the United States exactly what it wanted: a set of remains that Washington could say belonged to Scott Speicher. The Iraqis had no interest in whether those remains were ever proved to be Speicher's. Baghdad's only interest was to: look like it was trying to help. "Keep in mind," observed Dussault, "if there were ever a problem later, the Iraqis could always claim they had no way of knowing for sure whose remains they had because they did not have a DNA sequence to match against [the remains they provided] for proof of Speicher's remains or anybody else's. Nor did they have a DNA lab to conduct such DNA analysis reliably." This was also in the time frame that the Iraqis had no idea where Speicher was, because Cheney had already declared him dead, that he was even alive. Thus, why would Saddam and his intelligence service be concerned about finding him? The Iraqis believed Speicher was dead.. This is also the reason it was possible for Speicher to evade with the help of a Bedouin family group, and survive for a longer than anyone expected. No one was looking for him. Saddam wouldn't get Speicher for nearly four years. But the manner in which Brown presented the "mysteriously switched remains" was designed to make the public focus on it and imply Saddam knew better and was intentionally trying to confuse the West; he wasn't, not then.

The Iraqis were never, as Brown told Hess, "duplicitous" about the remains. They'd given the United States what it wanted: a small bit of flesh from a body that was located at "botched" coordinates the DIA had provided. While the Iraqis may have believed DIA was wrong about Speicher's shoot-down location, they didn't care. Baghdad could just as easily have made the assumption that DIA was confused and/or being duplicitous with them. There could not have been an Iraqi "switch of remains" as DIA claimed happened. Saddam did not have Speicher's remains at that time since he, too, believed he was dead. We know from a combination of forensic reporting and information reported up to four-and-a-half to six years prior to the time Speicher's partial remains were recovered in the desert that he was alive until some time between the spring of 2003 and before the end of 2005.

Brown told the AP that the "Iraqis had already identified [Speicher's] crash site but had failed to come forward out of fear they would be accused of covering it up [the location of the crash site]." Brown further stated that in 1993 the Iraqis took the Qatari bustard hunters to the site to get the Qataris to come forward as the ones who "stumbled" on the wreckage. In saying this, Brown would be claiming an Iraqi intelligence success and a DIA failure to locate the wreckage ahead of Baghdad. This is not how the crash site was located. Baghdad had no idea where it was at that time and neither did DIA – or did it? DIA claimed it did not know where Speicher's crash site was until the Falcon Hunter provided photographs and coordinates to his ONI case officer, who later passed that information to DIA. At that point, in 1993, DIA and DPMO were still convinced that Speicher went down with his Hornet and could not have survived.

After the ICRC team confirmed that Speicher's remains weren't in, or under or in proximity to his jet in 1995, DIA and DPMO still weren't convinced. "I do not consider it a true statement," observed Dussault, "that the Iraqis led the falcon hunters to the aircraft. The falcon hunters had been going into that area every hunting season; they also knew the Bedouin tribes and nomads in the area. The hunters clearly had been to Speicher's aircraft even before 1993. The roaming Bedouins and the falcon hunters were already conversing about the site and Speicher before this time frame." So had a navy intelligence/CIA clandestine officer who rode up on the smoldering wreckage while the war was still being fought. The covert officer was a deliberate visitor to the site.

Brown further states that a piece of the wreckage turned over by the Falcon Hunter matched Speicher's Hornet; actually, it didn't but investigators hadn't realized it yet. The maintenance log for Speicher's Hornet had been taken off the *Saratoga* by the original evaluation team on board *LaSalle* and was not available to them. The serial numbers on the wreckage retrieved by the Falcon Hunter came back to a Hornet flown in the Persian Gulf War, identified as Bureau Number 163470. The last man to fly that jet was Michael Scott Speicher. Or so they thought. Again, the navy assigns each of its aircraft a specific, unique bureau number (BuNo). Scott Speicher was lost in AA403 Bureau No. 163484, which was stricken from the inventory on January 17, 1991. Bureau No. 163470, the aircraft number recorded on Speicher's incident reports after the Falcon Hunter's December 1993 retrieval, is wrong. He had picked up a part cribbed from another Hornet and used to make a repair on

Speicher's jet. But from the time he found this piece, report after report included the wrong bureau number for Speicher's aircraft until the error was discovered and the record corrected.

Again, Brown's statement is misleading. Brown went to some length to describe the wrong loss coordinate for Speicher's Hornet as a "data glitch" rather than an outright mistake by DIA and DPMO, and, of course, something far worse by those who'd recorded the wrong coordinates on his original loss reports the night he was shot down. He characterized the Iraqis as "puzzled" because they knew an American F/A-18 had been shot down west of Baghdad but followed the wrong U.S. coordinates and searched for Speicher's plane in the south, finding nothing. The Iraqis weren't the ones who were puzzled; it was DIA and DPMO who claimed that distinction. The only reason the Iraqis knew that an F/A-18 had been lost on January 17, 1991, was because Secretary of Defense Cheney told them so on day one of the war. Further, Cheney also told them Speicher was killed in action.

Brown infers that Speicher's flight suit, the one handed to the ICRC team's Bruce Trenholm, was half-buried when it was pointed out to investigators by a Bedouin boy. From investigator's reports and interviews, we know that this is patently false. The flight suit was handed over to investigators and not retrieved from the ground nor laid over a rock. No one knows where the Iraqis first located this flight suit. Clearly, the possibility of more than one flight suit was raised by statements made by one ICRC investigator corroborated by additional U.S. government agency personnel and Buddy Harris. The flight suit recovered in the desert and subsequently photographed and documented by the FBI, shown to Speicher's squadron mates Fox and Albano, and then purportedly later "lost" after Bruce Trenholm mailed it to CILHI, cannot be the one that Buddy Harris claims to have in his possession today if Trenholm was being truthful about it being lost in the mail. Thus, there are two flight suits only if the first flight suit is really "lost" and not merely locked away by DPMO to keep any other government agency or interested party from examining it.

"I was told by Angela Santana [who ran the freescottspeicher.com Web site before it was taken down] that Buddy claimed to her that he had the flight suit. Was [supposed] to be a secret," wrote Speicher's childhood friend Jeff Paussa on January 22, 2011. "That was '05 give or take a year, from what she told him. [The flight suit was] shredded for sure yet no whole piece [was] totally missing." But he also observed that the same intelligence apparatus that initially demanded chain of custody of the flight suit as critical evidence in a missing person's case is also the group that claimed to have lost the suit. "Fact is," Paussa continued, "that if they [the government] don't have it and if Buddy has one, then he has it. If the government still has theirs then Buddy can't have one. In other words if they are [both] claiming to still have the one that had been on Scott in Iraq, one or the other is lying."

The gamesmanship going on with the flight suit alone is enough to give anyone pause. The question could easily be asked as to why such a critical piece of forensic evidence in a case that had already become so controversial was returned to a civilian, in this case, Harris, and legal chain of custody permanently severed. Harris told Frusci that he had it. The flight suit, handed over like an Easter egg surprise for the ICRC team in December 1995, was already contaminated by the circumstance in which it was produced for investigators. Without question, as Paussa has suggested, there are two flight suits involved in this case. But since the original flight suit first examined by the FBI would appear to be unavailable for further examination and the one in Harris' possession is just as tainted and outside investigators' chain of custody, we may never know what the flight suit recovered in 1995 might have told us.

Hess wrote that U.S. officials were "blinded by the myopia that tainted prewar intelligence – the American conviction that Hussein's government lied about everything. As it turned out, the Iraqis lied, but sometimes they told the truth."

The DIA and DPMO and others in the intelligence community failed in the Speicher case; they failed in the collection and follow-on analyses that would have led them directly to Speicher as an evader and Speicher as a prisoner who was moved routinely and who tried to his last breath to tell us where he was. They were blinded to reporting that pointed to Saddam as the captor. They never really understood what was going on. They were too slow figuring out what happened to Scott Speicher before and after he was in Saddam's custody.

"For more than a decade," Hess wrote, "speculation swirled that the 33-year-old Speicher, a lieutenant commander when he went missing, had been captured alive." That was disproved, Brown observed, by the team that found and confirmed his remains. This Brown statement is complete fabrication and took advantage of the fact that the reporter and the American public had yet to learn what was in the forensics report. Brown's statement was further obfuscation of the truth by the DIA and DPMO and, in a word, a lie to excuse their massive intelligence failure in Speicher's case. "DIA is again pushing a lie to the public and also is not providing the operators the benefit of the doubt they deserve," observed Bob Dussault after reading the Hess article. "Let the bones speak." Brown would have the public believe Speicher wasn't captured or tortured. "He needs to swear under oath," continued Dussault, "this is something he knows [to be fact] with evidence and is neither speculation nor his personal belief." Brown can't. The forensic report has declared Speicher's death "homicide by undetermined means." What Brown told Hess is conjecture that can't be supported. "See if you can get the three-star general in charge of DIA to write that down [what Brown said] and sign it. You will not get this."

Buddy Harris was so certain that Scott would come home in the months before the American invasion of Iraq in March 2003 because he was privy and party to the back channel negotiation between Iraq's United Nations representative Mohammed Al Duri and U.S. Department of State for Scott's repatriation. When asked about Speicher, Al Duri spoke in the hypothetical to avoid implicating the regime. If Baghdad had him, what would the United States give to get him back? But then the Bush adminstration's campaign to invade Iraq reached fever pitch. In the weeks just prior to the decision to invade, Al Duri abruptly broke off the negotiation.

Suddenly he "didn't know who Scott Speicher was and never heard of him."

Al Duri left the United States for Baghdad just after disavowing any knowledge of the man he'd been talking about for weeks. During the negotiation, with Baghdad's prize prisoner in jeopardy of being discovered, Uday Hussein moved Speicher multiple times[3]; one of those moves was spotted clearly by the Israeli Mossad a couple of weeks prior to the 2003 invasion. How did Washington know this? American intelligence was listening and watching once the negotiation started, anticipating that Al Duri would go back to Saddam and Uday Hussein for direction; he did. After that, the chase for Scott Speicher was on. Further, it is also known that during his imprisonment in Iraq, Speicher was kept in approximately twelve different prisons and dozens of temporary holding facilities and safe houses. Speicher was kept at Hakmiyah Prison the longest.[4]

From the start of the U.S. invasion of Iraq in March 2003, American Special Forces under the auspices of the 75th Exploitation Task Force, later the Iraq Survey Group (ISG), and a joint team of CIA and DIA operatives continued to look for Scott Speicher. But the task force was faced with the uphill challenge of getting Speicher back from a regime that stood steadfast in its belief that it hadn't lost the first war with the United States in 1991 and that Speicher was the ultimate trophy of Baghdad's victory. Major General Keith Dayton's ISG brought together a unique blend of collection, analytic, and force maneuver assets to conduct both the ongoing WMD investigation and manage the growing terrorism threat posed by Al Qaeda in Iraq; these were the ISG's primary tasks. Secondary was to look for Speicher. Experts in the functional areas of Iraqi WMD's came from the CIA, DIA, Department of Energy (DoE), State, DoD, as well as United Kingdom and Australia; this expansive group gathered and analyzed data to develop a picture of Iraq's WMD program and plan further collection. Several participants were former United Nations inspectors with long experience in Iraq. Inclusion of DoE on the WMD hunt was expected. But DoE also formed a private intelligence group that focused on Speicher and through this group's collective effort sources were cultivated and important information gleaned and analyzed.

"Indeed, in the security-conscious world of Saddam, it would be surprising to find explicit direction related to sensitive topics like WMD. This would especially be the case for programs of presidential interest or direction. It is important to understand what one should expect to see and what one should not expect to see," observed Charles A. Duelfer, special advisor to the DCI on Iraq's WMD. Scott Speicher's name could have readily followed "WMD" on the list of "sensitive topics" to which Duelfer referred. Speicher was, in fact, a shining example of the regime's denial and deception operations. Related to this, Duelfer noted, was a further important factor that greatly affects how evidence is perceived: Key regime figures, whether it was the WMD issue that Duelfer reported to the DCI – or Scott Speicher – had a much better understanding of how the West viewed their programs than the other way around. Consider, he reported, how many Western technocrats studied in Baghdad vice how many key Iraqi WMD figures studied in the West; many, if not most of the Iraqis studying abroad learned to speak English fluently and they learned, too, important lessons about the way the West perceived them.

Further, many years of UNSCOM weapons inspections taught their Iraqi WMD counterparts how they looked for and analyzed Baghdad's program. Certainly this informed Baghdad how to elude UNSCOM inspection. Likewise, Washington's steady entreaties for Scott Speicher, queries that started with the request to visit the site of his crashed Hornet, told them all they needed to know about what the Clinton administration wanted and, more importantly, that the pilot in question was Scott Speicher, the man whose face was plastered across newspapers around the world after his loss. After that, it wasn't so hard for Saddam to catch up to Speicher and those who'd helped him. Baghdad reacted to news that Washington wanted in to the crash site with an investigation of its own, one that proved successful.

Two interactions in the 1990s, pointed out by Duelfer, may be illustrative of just how fast Baghdad learned to anticipate and compensate for repeated American and United Nations "intrusions" in Iraq. An Iraqi minister in 1994 asked, "Why do you Americans always attack buildings?" Iraq had been subjected to several bombing attacks and the question seemed simple on the surface, but it revealed something more about American assumptions, especially those made by intelligence analysts who'd looked at overhead imagery and identified buildings that looked like they might have some function. Digital imagery is often used for targeting weapons such as cruise missiles. Implicit in this process is an assumption that destroying a building will destroy the capability. Discussions and observations of the Iraqis showed that they reacted to this understanding of the American process by effectively dissolving the images we were focusing on. They disassociated capability from the buildings we were able to image. To wit, they would simply take key equipment and move it out of buildings and disperse it in ways that we could not resolve into our targeting and intelligence operating system. This was shrewd but obvious, Duelfer would later say. It affected the data we were examining.

A second example of just how fast Iraq learned to read UNSCOM inspectors was in the concealment of material they might want to see. Prior chapters have discussed this, most notably Lieutenant Colonel Dr. Gabriele Kraatz-Wadsack's showdown with the Iraqis at Abu Ghraib. The inspectors assumed that only Saddam would give instructions on sensitive matters such as WMD, thus inspectors investigated government departments directly connected to the Iraqi presidency such as the Diwan, the Special Security Organization, the Special Republican Guard, and any organ of the government with direct reporting to Saddam and his sons, Uday and Qusay. Saddam's presidential office was made up of two sections: the presidential secretary and the presidency office, the "Diwan" to which Duelfer referred in his final report to the DCI. The Diwan was an administrative presidential bureau with no policymaking authority. Formed in July 1979 the Diwan researched and studied issues requested at the highest level by Saddam, the council of ministers, the economic affairs committee and the Revolutionary Command Council.

In effect, the inspectors were modeling an organization chart that branched out from Saddam. These organs became high priority targets for the UN inspectors. This was perfectly logical from their perspective. But one effect of this investigation was to teach the Iraqis how we investigated and what we looked for. And like the previous case where Iraq reacted by dissolving the image that we looked for, it should be expected that Iraq would avoid using entities that would show up on organization charts or that would follow the types of order we had earlier tried to picture. Scott Speicher was off the grid. We weren't supposed to "see" him though he was certainly there. Just as it had done since the 1990s to successive teams of UNSCOM inspectors, Baghdad scrambled the signatures with which we might locate and reacquire Speicher.

From one information capture, it was clear that within a year of being in the country, the task force conducted searches in dozens of locations – the number most often mentioned exceeded 60 sites – with some indication that Speicher had been there or might have been present at some time just prior to their arrival. For every local who told them Speicher was there, another was telling his captors they were coming. Speicher's searchers also found, disturbingly, medical debris that indicated to them he was not well.

But in most of these places, Speicher's searchers found the markings accompanied by dates that have since made headlines back home: the initials MSS carved in a cell wall at Hakmiyah Prison in central Baghdad and that same summer the discovery of the same MSS initials and a date – 9-15-94 – scratched into an I-beam in an old maintenance shack on Al Sahra Airfield near Tikrit. Similar MSS markings, said Brown, had been found all over Iraq; he is correct about this. But Brown's statement also left out all mention of Speicher's ground-to-air signals discussed earlier in this narrative, signs that would have taken him considerable time and effort to craft for overhead collection platforms.

The FBI cut down the I-beam with Speicher's initials and sent it back to the United States, specifically the Smithsonian Institution, for testing. Brown told the Associated Press reporter that the I-beam was written in an ink reserved for Iraqi religious groups and that an American prisoner wouldn't have been likely to have access to it. Given where this was written, on a ceiling I-beam out of line of sight, in English alphabet, not Arabic script, it would seem far more logical to assume that he used the most readily available ink in the camp – possibly the only ink available for miles – that which belonged to a Bedouin tribal elder who saw to the religious requirements of his clan. "How can DIA determine that the markings MSS and 9-15-94 were false leads based on the DIA mindset that claims Speicher could not have gotten his hands on a special ink reserved for religious groups," wrote Dussault. "As far as I know, and totally consistent with religious peoples around the world, especially in tough and threatening times, the probabilities are much higher of a POW obtaining assistance from a religious person, regardless of the faith, than from any other group the POW could come in contact with. To admit that such a sacred ink exists," he continued, "is proof enough that religious people exist in Iraq. Thus, it is likely that Speicher could have come across someone who cared enough about him to provide him with ink, ink that might be the only kind available to him."

Taking this one step further, there is a pattern to Speicher's dozens of markers, by date and location, that fall into two categories: pre- and post-capture. Brown would have us believe that these initial marks, by his own admission found all over the country, were unable to be tied to Speicher by the DIA POW/MIA analytic cell. They would appear to have missed the Bedouin migration pattern entirely, a pattern followed by the Bedouin family group with which Speicher traveled for just over three years. The I-beam marker was made by Speicher after his location and capture by Saddam's IIS. After that capture, it is clear that the location of his markers shifted to Saddam's official and makeshift jails, bunkers and safe houses. Speicher provided a date at each location he could, even at the risk of his jailers plastering and painting over them. Speicher's trail of markers in English alphabet, often left with an associated date and sometimes a symbol, were heartfelt and comforting graffiti for a man who was never going to get home again and he knew it.

The DIA does not want the American public to know any further details about the I-beam. But the U.S. Army Reserves staff sergeant who found Speicher's initials on the beam was concerned enough that his discovery wasn't being seriously pursued by Brown and his DIA analytic cell that he sent this information to Danny Belcher, executive director of Task Force Omega of Kentucky, on February 2, 2005. Belcher redacted the staff sergeant's personal information from the document he was sent, hopeful it might protect the soldier from repercussions associated with sharing a document that the DIA would not have wanted revealed to the public. But pertinent details of the staff sergeant's service, unit and the question-and-answer he completed for DIA's Tom Brown were published by Belcher on his Web site; Brown would have no problem identifying this soldier, who was sent into Iraq in March 2003 and remained in-country until February 2004. Attached to the document were photographs of the I-beam, the building and the compound in which they were found along with the soldier's e-mail correspondence with Brown. "I am concerned that this was not investigated properly," the soldier wrote Belcher. At that time, the I-beam's discovery hadn't been made public like Speicher's initials in Hakmiyah Prison. The staff sergeant's concern came to light after a question-and-answer with DIA's Brown:

"I need to ask some questions," Brown wrote to the staff sergeant. "First, this is not a JAG [Judge Advocate General] manual investigation. There are NO UCMJ [Uniform Code of Military Justice] issues involved here. Sir, you have my word on this."

Then Brown introduced himself to the staff sergeant. "I am the Intelligence Community lead analyst on the Speicher issue. I am not too recently retired USMC MSgt (E-8) 98G (Korean) [cryptologic linguist] equivalent, and used to teach the 98G (Korean) course at Goodfellow AFB, Texas, and I feel extremely fortunate that a fellow SNCO [senior noncommissioned officer] found the initials. I am also grateful that a SNCO had enough situational awareness of political events and issues important to the Commander, CENTCOM, the SECDEF and the President of the United States that he was able to recognize the initials as being potentially very important to his country and reported the find ASAP. [Name redacted], you bring great credit to your chain of command, your Unit, and the United States Army. Well done."

"Since I am back at Washington," Brown wrote, "I do not have a clear view of what's on the ground. As you can probably surmise, more questions are raised than answered when a discovery such as this occurs. Some of the questions," he told the staff sergeant, will seem redundant, but please bear with us (me), I've got a lot of dogs pulling my chains on this one [Speicher]."

The staff sergeant replied to Brown that he was very happy that someone "is asking the 'hard' questions. I was afraid that this discovery was going to slip through the cracks. Believe me that UCMJ issues and a JAG investigation are the last thing on my mind. I know that reporting what I discovered was the right thing to do, and if it assists in the investigation of Commander Speicher or can help bring some closure to the Speicher family, then the year away from my family will have been worth it." He didn't have anything to gain and sought no recognition for reporting the discovery. "My only motivation," he told Brown, "is to help bring a fellow warrior home to his family." He then answered the thirteen questions Brown asked of him.

Brown's first question asked if the staff sergeant believed it was U.S. Marines who first occupied this facility, a complex of buildings that was at some undetermined point after the army's arrival renamed Forward Operating Base Speicher and later Contingency Operating Base Speicher. The base is located 105 miles north of Baghdad and just under 7 miles west of the Tigris River. According to a prior e-mail exchange between Brown and the staff sergeant, Brown believed that the Marines were not the first to occupy the base. "As far as you are concerned, is the 64th CSG [Combat Support Group] the only unit to occupy the facility where the MSS initials were found?"

"In the latter stages of the ground war I believe," replied the staff sergeant, "that the Marines may have done a recon through Al Sahra Air Base (Camp Speicher) and cleared the buildings, and may have occupied it for a very short period of time. I do not believe that the Marines ever occupied the buildings we occupied due to the fact that there was no 'American paraphernalia.'" He was referring to items such as empty MRE (meals ready to eat) and MRE packs.

"There was evidence that the buildings may have been occupied by local nationals that were acting in a 'caretaker' status." (i.e. a live goldfish bowl in one of the offices). I believe that Al Sahra Air Base was in an inactive status for quite some time. To the best of my knowledge my unit, the 345th RAOC [Rear Area Operations Center], and the 64th CSG were the only units to ever occupy these particular buildings."

Then Brown asked the question that had already made the Marines balk. He said that it was speculated that the initials might have been a prank since the base was called Camp Speicher. "Can you answer," wrote Brown, "as honestly as possible, your opinions on these initials possibly being a prank?" He asked that the staff sergeant not take this question personally or as an "approach" against any of the soldiers under him. "I have already addressed HQ USMC on this question and they took immediate umbrage that a Marine would do such a thing; however, they assured me they would look into it fully." He offered his apologies "up front."

"There is no need to apologize," came the staff sergeant's reply, "and I do not take this question personally or as an attack on my integrity." But he also made it clear that he did not believe that the initials on the I-beam were a prank perpetuated by Marines or soldiers.

Still, asked Brown, how did the camp get its name? The staff sergeant told him he didn't know exactly how Al Sahra Airfield came to be known as Camp Speicher. He could only speculate that it was due to the fact that Speicher's F/A-18 Hornet went down somewhere near the base. "This question," he told Brown, "is probably better directed to the 4th ID [Infantry Division] officials."

"Please explain, in detail," asked Brown, "the events leading up to the finding of the initials. For example, what was the plan of the day, what were your orders, instructions, how did you happen to be in the vicinity of the carport, etc., as much detail as possible."

"At the time I discovered the initials on the beam I was escorting local national (Kurdish) construction workers," the staff sergeant replied. He had met them that morning at the main gate and escorted the men through the search area and identification checkpoint at the entrance to Camp Speicher. The Kurds had been contracted to enclose the carport where the initials were found, throwing up walls on three sides to convert it to a work area for the motor pool.

"At approximately 1200 hours we broke for lunch. [Name redacted] and myself were sitting with the workers eating lunch, and I noticed the initials. It did not register with me at first, and then it just hit me a few minutes later. I pointed this out to [name redacted] and at that time it was decided to report it to the 64th CSG S-2 [Intelligence]."

From ground photographs Brown and the DIA POW/MIA analytic cell had obtained from the base, they observed that the staff sergeant's unit had written bay numbers on the forward I-beams of the carport. He wanted to know how the initials MSS compared to the writing on the forward I-beams.

"In my opinion," replied the staff sergeant, "there is no comparison. The bay numbers that were written on the forward I-beams are very bold and dark and have not faded. The initials on the rear I-beam appeared faded and weathered. Although I am not a handwriting analyst, in my opinion they do not appear similar."

Then Brown asked him, citing a previous inquiry and knowing that the 64th CSG was using the building as a headquarters for command and control and classrooms if, as a SNCO, could the classrooms be used to hold prisoners of war or a prisoner. "In other words, if you caught an HVT [high value target] in Tikrit, could you hold him securely in the classrooms at this facility?"

"The 64th CSG along with my unit, the 345th RAOC, is/was using this building for their headquarters, offices and sleeping quarters. There are a few rooms in this building that could possibly be used to hold a POW for a short period of time," the staff sergeant replied. The other building, he told Brown, the one used as a sleeping quarters next door could also possibly have been used to hold a prisoner of war; it had decorative wrought-iron grates over the windows.

But there was another building just around the corner and across from the stadium in Camp Speicher occupied by the staff sergeant's unit that he believed might have been a detention facility. "This building had metal doors and bars on the windows. This building is only about 200 meters [655 feet] from the buildings that we occupied."

Brown asked, in his opinion or knowledge, did the staff sergeant have any idea how the Iraqis used this building. Was it a private residence? Was there any evidence to suggest members of the regime used the building?

"To the best of my knowledge, the buildings that we occupied were part of the Iraqi Air Academy," the staff sergeant answered back. "There was a lot of training material scattered throughout the buildings [such as] films, manuals, papers and logbooks. Some of the training material was in English and dealt with flight dynamics, aircraft recognition and air traffic control operations. There were also many pictures of Saddam Hussein and books printed in Arabic that appeared to be printed text of speeches that he had given. So the answer to the last part of your question is yes, former regime members could have used the building." He'd told Brown all he could about the building. Then he suggested Brown interview Iraqi nationals living in Al Seccor, a village less than six-tenths of a mile from the main gate at Camp Speicher. Al Seccor was built to house men and women and their families who worked at the airfield. Perhaps they'd know more.

Brown pressed. He wanted to know if there was any association of the building occupied by the sergeant's unit and the Iraqi Air Academy next door? Or the hospital across the street?

"The building appeared to possibly be the headquarters of the Iraqi Air Academy. I do not know, nor do I believe, that this building was associated with the hospital across the street," he replied. "However, if Commander Speicher's plane was shot down near Al Sahra Air Base, and he was injured in any way, he could have been treated at the hospital." There was no indication of this. But the staff sergeant didn't know it just then.

"When did the 64th CSG arrive at Camp Speicher?" asked Brown.

"The 345th RAOC and the 64th CSG arrived at Camp Speicher on or about 21 Apr 03," the sergeant told him. "Upon arrival at Camp Speicher the buildings were immediately occupied."

Then Brown wanted to know when the 64th CSG and 345th RAOC were due to rotate out of Iraq and who might replace them. Both left Iraq in early February 2004. There was no replacement planned for the 345th RAOC. The 64th CSG was replaced by the 167th CSG; he didn't know when the group might arrive in Iraq.

Repeating an earlier question, Brown wanted to know when the first troops arrived at Camp Speicher; the staff sergeant directed him back to his earlier response. When he asked again when Camp Speicher was established and when it was named, Brown stated that it would be "nice if we could identify who named it and why."

"When we first arrived at Al Sahra Air Base, it was known as FLB [Forward Logistics Base] Sycamore." But he still didn't know when the name was changed to Camp Speicher. He again told Brown to check with the 4th Infantry Division chain of command. Brown was ready to dismiss Speicher's initials and date on the I-beam as a prank until the soldiers and Marines who'd occupied the base patently denied it. Only then did he, the analytic cell and "the dogs" pulling Brown's chain realize that this wasn't the tact to use to dismiss the staff sergeant's find.

Then came the results of the Smithsonian's ink analysis. Surely no one would believe a prisoner of war used a holy man's ink to scratch his initials and date on the shack's I-beam. At least they hoped not.

The DIA would also have the American public believe that the prison wall section bearing Speicher's initials was dismantled by the FBI and sent, like the I-beam, back to the United States for testing. When DPMO's representatives, including Adrian Cronauer, the agency's spokesman, were asked about the wall section in Hakmiyah Prison cell 46 at a June 27, 2003 National Alliance of

Families question and answer session, the alliance membership was told that the wall section was already in the United States undergoing that testing. The June 27 exchange between the alliance and DPMO was tape recorded and later transcribed for the organization's July 12, 2003 newsletter *Bits 'N' Pieces*; it went thusly:

"My question is to you, Mr. Cronauer. Where is the piece from the jail cell. Do we have this back in the United States and are we testing it [pause] and have we tested the jail cell to find out any more information?"

There is muffled discussion heard on the tape until DPMO assistant director Jack Kull cut him off: "I can answer that." Cronauer tells him to go ahead.

"Yes, the answer to the question is [pause] yes, we have that portion of the wall, yes it is in the United States and yes, it is being examined by a forensic laboratory."

"And how long will that take?" asked the alliance member.

"I can't tell you that," said Kull. "I can tell you that it has been here for about the last three weeks."

"So we will have some answers very shortly then [pause] it won't take years, since they have that piece?" asked the alliance member.

"Well that...the...I can't give you a specific time, in terms of how long it will take them to run all of the different tests that they can run," Kull replied. "There is a limited amount of information that we can get from that piece of wall. We can find out, perhaps, how long ago his initials were put in the wall. Unless there is a blood or some sort of DNA sample near the initials, we cannot necessarily say who put those initials in the wall. But a whole series of tests is being conducted right now and like I said, I don't have a time frame for when those...Let me just say this. That particular bit of evidence is not under the control right now of the Defense Prisoner of War/Missing Personnel Office [DPMO]. There are entities in country, in Iraq right now, who are looking [75th Exploitation Task Force and CIA]...who are gathering evidence for war crimes prosecution. So other elements of the government are looking at this. If Speicher was in fact captured and was alive for a period of time after the downing, and he was killed, then this is potentially evidence to charge those involved in the former Iraq regime with. So that evidence is on that side of the house right now, not just the U.S. Army, CILHI, the [Defense Department's] central identification lab [in Hawaii]."

"We're kind of on a time limit here, so I wanted to know," said the alliance member, "What's being done with the rest of the jail cell. Have they made any .... I mean just because they have this one piece of block, there could be something in that jail cell ... and is it top priority?"

"Yes, of course .... The jail cell ...." said Kull.

"But it won't take a long time if it's a top priority, on the front burner?" asked the alliance member, pressing.

"It has already been done," Kull told the member. "The jail cell has already been done. There is a considerable amount of effort, ongoing, in Iraq at this time. Every single known detention facility, jail cell ..."

Florida senator Bill Nelson was just as skeptical of DPMO's statement about the prison wall writing as the membership of the National Alliance of Families who'd heard it. He was photographed on July 7, 2003 – two weeks *after* Kull's claim that the wall section was already in the United States – examining undisturbed Hakmiyah cell 46 and the section of wall with Speicher's initials, MSS, along with a smaller H, and another set of initials, MJM, surrounded by a circle carved into the wall. The MJM was interpreted by those who'd known the pilot best as Scott's expression of his family – wife Joanne and children Meghan and Michael Jr. Nelson took rubbings of Speicher's initials and also a smaller letter H collocated with the second S on the wall, and displayed them for the media. This event and photographs posted on the senator's Website directly contradict information presented by DPMO representatives weeks earlier at National Alliance of Families forum.

To clarify, the only collection that took place inside cell 46 was material for DNA testing, including a hair. According to Gretchen Hitchner, Nelson's press secretary, "the cell is intact." When challenged about the cell being intact and not in the United States for testing, DPMO replied "That particular bit of evidence is not under the control right now of the Defense Prisoner of War/Missing Personnel Office." But this raises the troubling possibility of an agency in the search for Speicher misleading another.[5]

Further, Buddy Harris publicly stated on January 17, 2011, that he had found the initials MSS written on Speicher's military paperwork, filled out before Scott left for Iraq. Next to his initials MSS, Speicher wrote that the paper on which he wrote it should be saved because those letters might be important some day; they were. Jim Stafford, Scott Speicher's high school friend and president of the now defunct Friends Working to Free Scott Speicher, had known him for thirty years. "I've seen his handwriting. The M, the S, those were Scott's. There is no doubt in my mind he was in that [Hakmiyah] cell.[6] Stafford was on hand for a national vigil held for Speicher in January 2004 in the nation's capital. Many of Speicher's childhood friends attended the event, including Jeff Paussa, who had known him for forty years and traveled from Kansas City, Missouri, to be there. "He was remarkably funny and very smart," he said. "The gang of us who were friends remember he never brought books home and always got straight As."[7]

But DPMO's disavowal of the MSS initials wasn't the worst of it. In his September 3, 2003 *Insight* column, Timothy W. Maier wrote about a secret two-page Pentagon report that was leaked to the *Washington Times* a month earlier. The report suggested Speicher died when his Hornet was shot down. Nelson took the report's content as a message for him to back off his crusade to find out what happened to Speicher. Infuriated, Maier reported, Nelson slammed the pessimistic *Times* story, claiming it was full of faulty information, such as labeling the Iraqi defector who'd seen Speicher alive a liar.[8]

When Nelson confronted the Pentagon about the secret two-page report, he was surprised to find there was no such document. With a bit more digging, Nelson's staff learned that the document was dated June 23, 2003, and had been written by the DIA, which had repeatedly up to that point debunked stories that American service members had been left behind in Vietnam and were just then working double-overtime to do the same to Speicher. "There's nothing new in the report," Nelson, a member of the Senate Armed Services Committee and the one who'd pushed successfully for Speicher's promotion to navy captain, opined.

What he read was nonetheless disturbing. The DIA report falsely stated that information that Speicher survived the crash was primarily based on the word of an Iraqi defector assigned the identification number 2314, even though Nelson insisted – and this is true – there were more witnesses, more intelligence information and more evidence – like Speicher's flight suit – that support the backstory of Speicher's survival. Add the initials MSS that Nelson had seen for himself at Hakmiyah Prison, which the DIA report didn't address, and Nelson's observation that "Somebody is leaking disinformation that is incorrect," makes the release of the secret two-page report more odious. "He didn't die in the crash," said Nelson. "I truly believe that someone is trying to kill the Speicher investigation."[9]

What about defector 2314? "None of the information provided by 2314 has proven accurate," stated the two-page DIA report. The DIA claimed it had witnesses who disputed 2314's account, witnesses who they said had called 2314 a "born liar." The DIA's "witnesses were two medical doctors, 2314's supervisor and a psychiatrist, who'd earlier indicated to American investigators that they'd confirm 2314's story yet after undergoing extensive interrogation by American intelligence officers, both men changed their story and denied any knowledge of seeing Speicher in 1998. Oddly, the DIA report did mention that an Iraqi prisoner reported to Marines that he heard two prison guards discussing the "U.S. pilot." Recall, too, the Kraatz-Wadsack incident at Abu Ghraib and the intelligence information report that pertained to doctors who'd treated Speicher – hardly the only such report to come out of post-Saddam Iraq.

It's interesting that Nelson brought up the issue of the flight suit. Curious to know whether the flight suit Trenholm purportedly "lost" really was lost the National Alliance of Families went to a confidential source knowledgeable of the issue and he told them that he'd heard "a month or so ago [prior to publication of the September 3, 2003 *Insight* article] that when the flight suit was being transferred between agencies, they lost it. Have heard nothing since," he continued, "so I suspect it remains missing. I think someone in the government needs to stand up and tell what really happened with it."[10]

Back to the discovered initials, Brown's admission about the Speicher markings being found all over the country was a surprise. They were, indeed, found all over Iraq. But then his analytic cell moved to discredit them all. The problem with doing so is twofold. First, since DIA took the position it can't tie the MSS markings to Speicher, it now has to explain how dozens of these markings show up all over Iraq in English lettering, not Arabic script, before American forces entered the country. Second, the Special Forces members involved and those who were there to analyze sections of the prison wall and cut down the I-beam as evidence became first-hand witnesses to every significant find in the Speicher case after the United States' 2003 invasion.

Not all of Speicher's searchers were silenced about what they saw; it was disturbing to see this evidence and to know that Speicher had repeatedly left his marker everywhere he went, hope fading each time no one came to his rescue. Equally disturbing, however, is Brown's DIA report dated June 23, 2003, in which the agency goes on record that the ISG "has searched every known location associated with Speicher. Other than at Hakmiyah Prison, where U.S. forces found the initials 'MSS' carved in a cell wall, no significant evidence of his [Speicher's] status has been discovered." Thus, Brown's November 28, 2009 admission of there being Speicher markings all over Iraq contrasts sharply with his analytic cell's reporting six years earlier, statements that now appear to have been less than truthful. Brown can't claim he was new to the investigation when he made his most recent admission and then claim ignorance of what was reported in 2003; he told Pamela Hess he'd personally worked the Speicher investigation for 15 years.

The only "tangled" web being woven about Speicher is the information that Brown tried to sell the American public and used the Associated Press to do it. This was the same misdirectional tactic the Defense Department and intelligence services, most especially the DIA, admittedly perpetuated with the *New York Times'* Tim Weiner in 1997. Brown's information is contradicted not only by scientific findings but reliable intelligence collected and vetted prior to location of Speicher's remains; many of these reports have already been included in prior chapters. This much is clear: Speicher didn't die on January 17, 1991. There were no Bedouins who buried his body after his Hornet crashed. The magnesium from the tires on Speicher's Hornet smoldered for days after it pancaked on the desert floor. Investigators later stated that the local population stayed away from the debris field that rung the Hornet because of the ordnance on the ground. They didn't bury him after he parachuted to the desert floor. There was no Bedouin boy who witnessed any burial. There wasn't any burial. Just as there hadn't been a Bedouin boy who'd found the flight suit turned over to the ICRC team in December 1995. That was a staged event. Speicher's remains discovered in twelve inches of turned up sand was just what the personnel recovery expert called it – a dog-and-pony show.

Scott Speicher didn't die until after the U.S.-led invasion of Iraq that started on March 20, 2003. He was very much alive up to that point. Mossad reported a sighting of Speicher being moved two weeks prior to this date. He was being moved to northeast Baghdad. This was his last reported sighting. Buddy Harris was so certain, at the time, that U.S. Special Forces would recover him alive that he and Joanne believed Scott could walk through the door any day. They were confident he'd be recovered by the Special Forces team that had trained for weeks to go get him.

There was ample evidence that Speicher was alive at the time the United States invaded Iraq, reliable information and documentation provided in scores of classified intelligence documents and communications to the Pentagon and the intelligence community, and from witness statements that could not be disproved. The Iraq Survey Group (ISG), a large team put together to collect and analyze intelligence in Iraq after Saddam was deposed in March 2003, contained a cell devoted to solving Speicher's fate and other missing in action cases. The Speicher cell was comprised of fifteen personnel at the DIA in Washington in addition to ancillary support from the CIA, NIMA, and six additional field personnel working in Iraq; the Washington cell was run by Colonel Greg Eanes, formerly the CSAR coordinator in Riyadh when Speicher went missing.

Asked to comment on the speculation about Speicher's interaction with the Bedouins, ISG investigators who'd gone out to interview Bedouin tribesmen in mid-January 2004 confirmed my timeline of Speicher's interaction with the Bedouins. "They can come up with all the theories they want to," said the ISG team lead who conducted the Bedouin interviews. "Amy's information as far as the Bedouins taking him initially is correct. I've verified that myself, although I've never spoken to Amy [about the Bedouin involvement with Scott Speicher]. Either that or we ran across the same incorrect sources, which I doubt."[11] That wasn't all. There was concurrence with the Bedouin timeline at CIA, Office of Naval Intelligence (ONI), JCS, and among several senior directors and analysts at JSSA, even though initially CIA wasn't part of the ONI and JCS effort. Everything gathered was consistent. "There were no contradictions or opposite/competing views," said Bob Dussault. The exception, not unexpected, was DIA and the DPMO.

The effort to recover Speicher started with the DoD with the ONI source – the Falcon Hunter – who had located him with the Bedouin family group that had protected him since he was shot down. The Falcon Hunter reported Speicher alive to his ONI handler. The Joint Chiefs of Staff, JSSA and ONI worked the case from there. "We learned later," recalled Dussault later, "that the CIA had a different, independent source who said the exact same thing: Scott was being held by Bedouins and they were prepared to turn him over to the U.S. to get him out of their area as soon as it could be effected. JCS told me," he continued, "months later that the same CIA source came in again to reiterate that the Bedouins wanted to turn him over immediately and did not want to keep and protect him any longer since the longer they kept him the more danger everyone was in of being caught by Saddam's forces and being killed for helping an American."[12]

Dussault recollected that it was almost a year between the first CIA notification to the JCS and the second. Subsequent to the second notice – in the 1994/5 time frame – the chairman of the Joint Chiefs of Staff general John M. Shalikashvili summoned his staff and told those present that there was little DoD could do about the Speicher case, even if he was alive and with the Bedouin family group because the conflict that put him there was over and military people couldn't go back and get him. Shalikashvili told them everything had to be worked through the State Department and CIA. This was the December 23, 1994 Pentagon meeting now best remembered for Shalikashvili's "old bones" comment. The meeting left many people upset. "This chairman's declaration also ended all the preparations that were being planned and exercised by the JSOC [Joint Special Operations Command] and Delta Force to develop a mission to extract Scott as soon as a turnover point was identified and an extraction mission could be approved by a Presidential Finding," Dussault remembered.

The time frame in which Speicher died can be narrowed by intelligence reporting that came through the Iraq Survey Group (ISG), which had employed the Special Forces team set out to find him. The Speicher team exhausted all in-country leads regarding the fate of Captain Speicher and departed the Iraq Survey Office (ISO) in May 2004; we know from the forensics report that the last time blood could have flowed through the remains recovered in the Iraqi desert dated Speicher being last alive four-and-a-half to six years prior to this discovery. No new leads were developed after the team's departure. All data previously collected with regard to the status of Captain Speicher was sent to Thomas Brown's DIA cell.

Credible information conveyed by Fares Fayeq Al Ayadhi on May 23, 2008, indicated that his father, Fayeq Mohammad Ali Al Ayadhi, pen name Fayeq Abdul Jaleel, was among the 605 Kuwaiti men and women kidnapped by Iraq in the fall of 1990. Fayeq Mohammad Ali Al Ayadhi was one of the most well known poets in the Arab world and the best known of the Kuwaitis kidnapped by Iraq. "He lived the rest of his life [after the kidnapping] as human collateral, Hussein's political trump card used to negotiate with the U.S.

and Kuwait governments," Fares Al Ayadhi wrote. Fayeq's remains were recovered in Iraq in June 2006; he'd been redressed in the same clothes he was wearing the day he was kidnapped. He'd been shot between the eyes. When the mass grave was opened, it reeked of bodies that had only been in the ground a short period of time, some, like his father, no more than three years. They'd certainly not been interred for a dozen years. The redress is a significant detail.

DNA testing of Fayeq's remains determined that he'd been alive for more than twelve years in captivity before he was executed in 2003, as the United States invaded Iraq a second time. The redress was a weak attempt to disguise this fact. DNA evidence showed that at least one hundred and fifty Kuwaiti prisoners of war, including Fares' father, and, Fares has documented, Scott Speicher, were still alive when the Americans entered Iraq. Fares knows his father was alive; he has one last letter his father dated and wrote to Fares just immediately prior to his execution, delivered to him by a former Iraqi intelligence officer who had been so moved by his father's poetry that he risked his life to convey the message. Fares has this letter.

A captured IIS document contains the actual orders from Qusay Hussein directing the Republican Guard to take Kuwaiti prisoners, held for over twelve years, and use them as human shields at strategic locations around Baghdad. From the Iraqi presidential office, special office of the secretary, on the execution of Saddam's orders and according to the decision of the March 4, 2003 Revolutionary Command Council, a total of 448 [of the original 605] captured Kuwaitis "who are located at the Al Nida Al Agher Prison and the Intelligence/General Center and Kazema Prison in Al Kazema, to make them human shields at all locations that are expected to be attacked by the American aggressors. Put them," stated the document, "in communication locations and essential ministries, radio and television, Military Industrial Commissions, and all other locations expected to be attacked by the criminal Anglo-American aggressors." Transporting them would be left to the Iraqi Intelligence Services Directorate and Republican Guard chief of staff. All of this would be accomplished under the direct supervision of the

Special Security Organization (SSO)/Organization Security. The one-page order is signed by Qusay Hussein, supervisor of the Republican Guard Secretariat, and dated March 14, 2003. Just days before Qusay signed the document Speicher was moved to northeast Baghdad.

The CIA held a meeting in Fares Al Ayadhi's Kuwait home with an aide to Qusay Hussein and Kuwaiti intelligence to release all prisoners of war held by Iraq. The deal for their repatriation was ultimately struck, wrote Fares, in [early] 1995 between Lieutenant General Hussein Kamel Hassan Al Majid, Saddam's son-in-law, the CIA and Kuwait. Baghdad wanted $950 million, wrote Fares, but a family feud between jealous brothers, Uday and Qusay Hussein, ended the deal. He has a copy of the agreement document; this was the "ransom note" that answers the question most often asked: why did Baghdad not use them for bargaining purposes. Saddam's sons did just that. Later, Fares said, Saddam killed Hussein Kamel because he knew too much about the deal. Saddam believed Hussein Kamel told western intelligence all about the American and Kuwaiti prisoners in his custody. But Hussein Kamel had known much more. He died, at least in part, because Scott Speicher was alive in Saddam's custody. He and his brother, Colonel Saddam Kamel Al Majid, were liabilities Saddam and his sons couldn't afford.

While the Iraqis tacitly admitted they held Kuwaiti prisoners of war, they could never be quite so obvious about Speicher. The Kuwait National Committee for Missing and Prisoners of War (NCMPA) compiled dossiers after the Persian Gulf War, which documented the existence of the 605 prisoners. These were filed with the United Nations, the International Committee of the Red Cross, and the Arab League, and all had been made available to international governments and the media. The dossiers provide irrefutable evidence that Iraq held these Kuwaiti men and women as prisoners. Included in the files are eyewitness reports from released POWs who had seen Kuwaiti prisoners and had close contact with them in the Iraqi prison system.

Far worse and more damning are official Iraqi documents, like Qusay Hussein's March 14, 2003 order, chronicling in detail the arrest, imprisonment and transferring of unaccounted-for Kuwaitis in significant number, from one detention center to another. Saddam's subsequent capture and execution didn't help the Kuwaiti government get answers. There are 369 Kuwaitis unaccounted for and at least some of them may still be alive in Syrian and Iranian prisons, sent there as part of Baghdad's pact with its stronger partners in Damascus and Tehran. Fares told this writer that DNA testing on Speicher's remains would reveal that he lived longer, much longer, like his father and was killed after the American-led invasion. He knew this already to be true before Speicher's remains were ever tested.

So why hide the circumstances of Scott Speicher's death? There are two parties to this last deception in the Speicher case: Baghdad and Washington. The Iraqis, even now, don't want the United States to know that he was ever in Saddam's custody. This would require they share all the particulars of his imprisonment and possibly his death. All of this information was contained in meticulously kept IIS folders that Saddam shipped off to his old ally Russia before Baghdad's fall. American intelligence captured the inventory of the boxes, but not the boxes themselves. They were long gone. There were eighteen of them in all, sent on a Russian convoy out of Iraq in March 2003. But the Iraqis had other records that were found. These records provided proof of life.

Back home in the United States, Washington didn't want the American public to know anything of Scott Speicher's imprisonment and his subsequent death. No politician, Pentagon official or intelligence agency chief wanted to admit the mistakes, missteps and debunking that got Speicher killed. No one wanted to tell the thousands of men and women of the United States military and their families that Scott Speicher was the captive of a madman for over eight years and that we couldn't get him back soon enough to save his life. No one wanted to utter the words that Speicher had been left behind so many times the Pentagon lost count. How would the Pentagon explain the cover-up of the cover-up that started with Scott Speicher's shoot-down on January 17, 1991. One lie required another and another until the truth was nearly impossible to figure out. None of it helped Scott Speicher.

When Speicher's fifth status review board was appointed on June 13, 2005, and convened two weeks later, Speicher was likely already dead. Seated on the board were Rear Admiral Joseph F. Kilkenny, the ranking officer and thereby the board's president, and Captains David C. Taylor, Patrick Driscoll, and David F. Hayes, a navy lawyer assigned as legal advisor to the board, and Lieutenant Commander Nadeem Ahmad, assistant legal advisor to the proceeding. Speicher's legal counsel, Captain Michael E. McGregor, was there, too. So was Buddy Harris.

While this board had the findings of Speicher's initial status review board convened in May 1991, the three secretarial determinations made in 1996, 2001, and 2002, the intelligence community interim report on Speicher's case published for March 2005, and the March 1996 search and recovery report of the Speicher crash site, various other memorandum from other navy and Defense Department agencies, most of it classified at the secret level, it wanted more. The chief of the Intelligence Community POW/MIA Analytic Cell, quartered at DIA, again, Thomas Brown, and two members of the cell staff were present to explain national level intelligence efforts on Speicher's behalf and specifically their 2005 Intelligence Community Interim Report findings, conclusions that bore little resemblance to what Brown later told the media. The intelligence community briefings were provided at secret level. By the time this board convened its members had much to talk about, almost all of it subsequently classified. They called back Brown and another member of the cell to answer additional questions. Then they made a new request for additional information regarding the shoot-down of Speicher's Hornet, which was provided and attached to the record of proceedings; this document is also classified. The head of the Office of Naval Intelligence Air Warfare Branch gave them a brief on the shoot-down event. This would seem to tell us only one thing: how Scott Speicher was shot down still mattered.

After reviewing information made available to them, Speicher's status review board concluded that Speicher's Hornet had been taken down by an air-to-air missile launched by an Iraqi aircraft; that Captain Speicher "likely" ejected from the aircraft and "may have been" captured by Iraqi forces; and that there was "no credible evidence" to suggest he was dead. Clearly the evidence shown to them did not include the nighttime infrared imagery and many, many additional pieces of critical intelligence that would have removed uncertain language like "likely" and "may have been" from their findings. The board concluded that Baghdad knew more than it had produced to date about what happened to him. They recommended that Speicher be continued in the status/category of missing-captured. Secretary of the Navy Gordon England later signed off.

Of note, the board also wanted Brown and his analytic cell to resolve their unanswered questions. Fast forward to Brown's November 28, 2009 Associated Press interview. Rather than come forward with the full backstory of Speicher's case, Brown gave an interview to an Associated Press reporter that became a very public attempt to debunk the forward progress of Speicher's case from start to finish. This included an unnamed senior Defense Department official who told the *Washington Times*' Rowan Scarborough on July 22, 2004, that "What I have heard [Major General Keith Dayton] say is there is no evidence he was ever in captivity." Dayton was the former chief of the Iraq Survey Group.

There were strong indicators in the fall of 2008 that Speicher's file was going to be closed; something was wrong. Navy secretary Donald C. Winter was pushing too hard to put an end to Scott Speicher's case, at least on paper, and declare him officially dead. What did he know that Speicher's family didn't? Winter needed lead time to head off Speicher's status review board, set to convene in January 2009 to determine if his status should remain what it had been since January 2002: missing-captured. Evidence collected and testimony from investigators, analysts and the pleas of his family convinced the board that Speicher should stay missing-captured. But Winter didn't agree. He must have been taken aback when he saw the board's finding. Rather than react quickly to the board's recommendation, he waited. He took it slow. First he declared that

Speicher's status should be bumped back to MIA. When the family balked, he said no. He'd be MIA. By then Speicher's family, friends, colleagues and supporters must have wondered why the change. Winter didn't. He, like so many other Pentagon insiders and intelligence agency chiefs intimate with Speicher's file, already knew he was gone.

Timing was the only consideration after they'd all agreed on how to handle the Speicher family and the fallout from the public announcement that Speicher's remains were "found" in the Iraqi desert. The Bedouin boy cover story wasn't the best, but it worked. The public, they thought, had never bought into the idea that Speicher could've still been alive all that time anyway, so why not drag out the Bedouin boy story one more time? Winter had also employed faulty logic in his change of Speicher's status. He wrote on March 10, 2009 that his review of the board proceedings and "the compelling evidence" presented by the intelligence community caused him great concern about the reliability of the board's recommendation, given its members' failure to employ a logical analytic process to their evaluation of the evidence in the intelligence assessment.

"The board's recommendation is premised on the conclusion that Captain Speicher was alive upon landing in Iraq after ejecting from his aircraft. They base this on a statistical analysis of F/A-18 ejections; however that analysis was based solely on peacetime ejections, and not the combat environment in which this ejection occurred. They also chose to ignore the lack of any parachute sighting, emergency beacon transmission or survival radio transmissions," Winter concluded.

First, the ejection occurred at night at 3:35 A.M. Baghdad time on a pitch black night and the parachute is not made to be seen. Thus, no parachute sighting was possible. Second, the emergency beacon – the ELT – had been disconnected in all the *Saratoga*'s ejection seat aircraft, including, of course, VFA-81 F/A-18 Hornets, a fact thoroughly vetted by the ICRC team that visited the crash site in December 1995. Further, the disconnection of the ELTs was confirmed and documents signed by the squadron's former maintenance officer, Commander Steven R. Minnis and the Sunliners' commanding officer, Commander Michael T. Anderson; both men are now retired. The fact that the ELT disconnect is even an issue at this or any other juncture of the Speicher case harkens back to the fact the maintenance log for the squadron – including, of course, AA403 – were removed from VFA-81 and the air wing to the *LaSalle*; this log book and the ordnance log for the Sunliners were now gone. The best testament to those log books being gone is the preponderance of questions that couldn't be readily resolved had the books been available to the board regarding the ELTs being disabled.

No, the log books were now nowhere to be found. Third, if Speicher's brand new AN/PRC-112 survival radio, issued just hours before launch, was lost when he ejected, he wouldn't have been able to communicate by that device. Additionally, the AN/PRC-112 was found to have an over eighty-percent fail rate the first night – the batteries on these radios shorted out. Since Speicher had the AN/PRC-112 securely strapped to his leg – recall that it didn't fit securely in the vest pocket – it might have been damaged as he came to the desert floor.

Certainly, it is easy enough to understand what happened and why the radio may have not been in good enough condition to communicate by voice. But what about those clicks heard on the guard channel that corresponded to a pilot survival radio? As it turned out, they could not have come from any other aircraft lost in the first two air strikes over Iraq but Scott Speicher. Then there is the troubling refusal of senior officers with firsthand, intimate knowledge of what took place in that night to publicly divulge what they know, the kind of men who hope the facts are uncovered by other means, and they never have to offer up what they know. Such was the case with a senior officer who took part in the assemblage on board the Red Sea command ship *LaSalle* immediately after Speicher went down. He has indicated that Speicher had both the AN/PRC-112 and the AN/PRC-90 survival radios in his possession when he went down – the AN/PRC-112 strapped to his leg – and the AN/PRC-90 in the vest pocket, where it fit. The same officer has also indicated that Speicher attempted to communicate with the AN/PRC-90 radio, not the brand new AN/PRC-112, and "it was a distress call, we just chose to do nothing."

The bottom line is that Winter's point of argument was highly flawed. But he and the DIA and DPMO that had fed him the information for his finding letter had only one objective in mind: they wanted Scott Speicher's file marked "case closed." Winter wrote, "Given the current state of U.S. presence and access to the territory of Iraq, and the discrediting of all intelligence sources who previously claimed to have seen Captain Speicher in captivity, there is currently no credible evidence that Captain Speicher is 'captured.' For Captain Speicher to be in captivity today one would have to accept a massive conspiracy of silence and perfectly executed deception that has lasted for over 18 years and that continues today." Winter left out the most important two words he should have used in his final statement on the Speicher case: "intelligence failure." The only "discrediting" of sources who had seen Speicher in captivity was done by the agencies that had already rated the same sources credible after passing multiple lie detector and greed tests but who later decided, since the agency involved couldn't get any forward traction with the information provided, it should discredit the source to hide another failure. No one could ask the source directly either because the source, no matter which one it was, could no longer be located. In each case the last contact the source had before he "disappeared" was a member of a U.S. intelligence agency.

What happened in the Speicher case can hardly be called a "perfectly executed deception," especially when those involved in it broke their silence and provide the backstory that make this and other narratives like it possible. There was no "conspiracy of silence" in this case; just outright denial, deceit and deception, none of which was flawlessly executed. The fact is, the same senior officer who was on *LaSalle* indicated that there were 11 other cases "similar to Speicher's" [men who went missing but whose captivity status was being kept from their families and the American public] out there and these were just the ones he had been privy to while still on active duty.

In a letter from Buddy Harris to Secretary of the Navy Raymond E. Mabus dated September 4, 2009 – just a few weeks after Scott Speicher's partial remains were found in the Iraqi desert – Harris noted that he and the entire board were surprised that any of what Winter used as the basis to challenge Speicher's status was even mentioned by the briefers. Addressing the wartime versus peacetime ejection analysis, Harris stated that there was no "analysis." "It was merely the unsubstantiated conjecture of a briefer [who] knew nothing of ejections and combined all aircraft into one category, and to aviators, his findings made absolutely no sense." All of the issues raised by Tom Brown's Intelligence Community POW/MIA Analytic Cell in front of the board had been completely resolved years before, "but for some reason the briefers decided it needed to be brought into question again, and Secretary Winter used it as overwhelming evidence in status determination."

When Harris later asked one of Brown's briefers why he brought up the ELT issue with Secretary Winter, he stated that they [Intelligence Community POW/MIA Analytic Cell] were still resolving it, and that he found that the squadron allowed each pilot to choose whether or not to disconnect the ELT, and they were sorting out what Scott Speicher chose. This is a false assumption by the briefer. The decision to disconnect the ELTs in the *Saratoga*'s aircraft was an air wing decision and it was a function of each squadron's maintenance department to send a technician out to disable the emergency beacon in each jet. No squadron permits – not then and not now – an individual pilot to make that decision. To further clarify, it is also a time-consuming process to make this happen. The information proffered to Harris by the briefer was just another insight into the debunking mindset that tainted Speicher's entire case. "I was flabbergasted," wrote Harris to Mabus, "that this was even being considered, but unfortunately, it didn't stop there ... but the swaying and distortion of facts to arrive at an agreeable conclusion is not acceptable, and does a tremendous disservice to CAPT Speicher."

Just as regrettably, no one told the Speicher family about all that could go wrong. They'd not been told the depressing backstory of

America's prior failures to account for live American prisoners of war and missing in action. Without context everything seemed to be happening just to them. They got help from an attorney. So had many POW/MIA families. Some have had the same attorney working for them for more than a decade. What happened to Speicher and what was happening to his family was history repeating itself. Daniel Warren Gray would've told them what he told his bosses at DPMO on April 21, 2004, the day he sent them his resignation letter. He'd tell Speicher's family that the Pentagon and DPMO had failed to act on behalf of known live prisoners of war and missing in action. Like Colonel Millard Peck before him, Gray observed that military personnel working the POW/MIA issue had been marginalized and hamstrung. They had no say. He listed some of DPMO's glaring transgressions. He laid them out off the top of his head, still struggling with his disappointment that no one had come home on his watch. He started with no response to reports of live Americans in Southeast Asia; the 185 report; American prisoners of war moved from Laos to Vietnam; the Schederov report about Hrdlicka; why he believed the Lao have not and never will cooperate on the POW/MIA issue; Lao possession of a file cabinet containing POW information that DPMO never requested be turned over; never talking to Lao doctors in Beijing who'd worked previously with American prisoners of war in northeast Laos; DPMO's attitude towards Stony Beach; Gray's knowledge of and position on the Deferred and No Further Pursuit cases that choked DPMO's file cabinets, and he ended with his position on the Speicher case. Gray never intended for the American public to read his "good-bye note." A DPMO colleague released it without his knowledge, compelled to do so by what Gray tried to convey to the leadership of his agency, those who'd made his job difficult, if not impossible, to do. He was not alone in his characterization of POW/MIA issues addressed in his interoffice correspondence. His colleague wouldn't have released it if he didn't share Gray's view.

The man who'd written this resignation letter, DPMO intelligence research officer Daniel Warren Gray, spent nineteen years, eight months as a Department of Defense civilian, serving as the

Lao-Cambodian team chief; an intelligence analyst; chief of the POW team during Desert Storm in 1991; chief of DPMO's current operations division, and intelligence collection manager. His collection team controlled human (HUMINT), signal (SIGINT) and imagery (IMINT) intelligence in support of the POW issue for years. He was chosen as collection manager for the DIA POW/MIA analytic cell in late 2001, and returned to DPMO on February 2, 2002. He remembered this date for one reason. When he returned to DPMO, Chief of Staff Joe Harvey told him he was denied access to work Southeast Asia POW/MIA case files.

Before he became a civilian, Gray had a career in the U.S. Army. He was chief of the Site Development Office, Joint Casualty Resolution Center, Nakhon Phanom, Thailand, in 1973-74 as an army major. For most of his military career he'd been a counterintelligence officer. As a civilian he'd become a threat to the people who'd employed him: DIA and DPMO. He knew when, where, how and why information was being covered up. He also knew who'd done it. But worse yet, he knew that men had been left behind in the custody of captors to die a slow, often painful, death.

American service members and citizens have been spotted since the end of the war in Vietnam by United Nations high commissioners and United States and foreign nonprofit and religious aid workers and United States Agency for International Development (USAID) officers, including USAID's Disaster Assistance Response Team (DART), in remote Vietnamese and Lao tribal areas, Burma, Cambodia and North Korea. Most have been held in some form of captivity since they were taken during the war. Others, left in villages, have been forced to make new lives for themselves. They have native wives and children, even grandchildren, now. They have menial jobs. None are called by their American names. They are "eagle whites" with native names. All are watched carefully by Hanoi, even the ones moved between Cambodia, Laos, Burma, China, North Korea and Russia. They are worked hard and they have no papers, no identification and no way out of where they've been left for decades. Those in captivity, even older men, are bought and sold for little money by warlords and provincial governments, who employ them in fields, to clear and build roads, and mine coal. Many will die of disease, exposure, accident, execution or old age. Most of these American service members who've been left behind were once the best and brightest this country could send to war. They were U.S. Air Force, Navy, Marine Corps and Army aviators, Special Forces and CIA. They were all left behind.

The number of men left behind from America's wars of the twentieth century is so staggering that the Pentagon was quick to bury statistics from the Persian Gulf War lest the public think it had another Vietnam on its hands. When the SSCI chose to publicly acknowledge its Speicher investigation, there were still more Gulf War cases they didn't talk about, cases just as compelling. When Speicher's case broke publicly in 1997, it was couched as a singular story of loss and mystery. No one who picked up their *New York Times* and read Tim Weiner's story thought it was much more than that – a straight-forward case of missteps and mistakes that left a U.S. Navy pilot in the Iraqi desert. How sadly they are mistaken. Already there were stronger cases from the past that could have predicted the course of Speicher's case from its ugly beginning to tragic end. From those cases it isn't so hard to understand that Speicher's predicament was history repeating itself. Only then is it possible to see that the intelligence available in his case should have been believed from the start rather than debated and debunked for years. No one was also willing to step up to the plate for him. But then no one had done anything for missing men in the past, either.

The "185 report," Gray referred to concerns the 185 American prisoners of war and missing in action held in Southeast Asia after Operation Homecoming in 1973 who'd been specifically reported as left behind. This document was deemed to be so important and possibly credible that the collection representative was directed to pursue it and conduct follow-ups immediately. When this information became known, Jimmy Carter had just won the White House. Nothing happened. Not then, not later. No action was taken on this report again in 1998 when the Joint Commission Support Directorate (JCSD), the same group responsible for the gulag study and finding that American servicemen and citizens were imprisoned in the former Soviet Union, requested the collection representative provide access to the 185 report. Gray later said that the collection representative told him that she had no idea what report they were talking about and thus couldn't provide it to them for further investigation. "Personnel from the JCSD threatened to initiate an Inspector General investigation into the lost report. Suddenly," said Gray, "the lost report was 'found.'"[13] By late 1998 JCSD tried to pursue the 185 report but it went nowhere. They didn't have the funding to investigate all the leads attached to the report.

Details of the 185 have never been taken to any country in Southeast Asia to demand an explanation. Disturbingly, Gray said, "the same collection representative [who] received the report in 1993, [who] lost the report in 1998 and who would have been responsible for any follow-up since its receipt, remains in place and the report remains unresolved."

"Now you're getting to appreciate all the reasons none of the over 400 American POWs in Laos, declared there by the chief of the Laotian military on public television at the end of the war," observed Bob Dussault on April 12, 2002, "never have seen their homeland!" There were even more in North Vietnam. The more time that passes "all become less and less attractive for return."

The enormity of the Speicher cover up would make anyone question how it could have been pulled off for so many years with any number of points at which the truth could be discovered. You have read here about POW/MIA cases similar to that of Scott Speicher, but what you don't know, because of the classification of the material up to now, *is the ability* of Washington – and the White House – *to hide* these crimes against military men like Speicher under the collective nose of the American public. That unthinkable, coordinated effort, crafted to insulate the U.S. government against recrimination and embarrassment, was cloaked in one lie after another to prevent the truth from coming out when Speicher needed real help. In the big scheme of things, Speicher became just one more case that proved easier to isolate and cover up, most especially for those who knew the classified information in his case file and how to make it go away. Could it be worse? The answer to this question is no. Not for Speicher. Could it be worse on a bigger scale? Of course it could.

Speicher's case punctuates a long history of hiding truth under the cover of classification to avoid it getting in the way of a grander objective, perhaps a bigger problem. Examples of this pattern of behavior continue to come out with further declassification of National Archives records. Most recently, documents released on September 10, 2012, and seen in advance by the Associated Press, lend weight to the belief that suppression within the highest levels of the U.S. government helped cover up Soviet guilt in the killing of some 22,000 Polish officers and other prisoners in the Katyn forest and other locations in 1940.[14]

Here's the short version of the Katyn story past and present – the one you need to know to appreciate the enormity of the crime, the cover-up that followed and techniques used then that have most certainly carried forward to the present. Bear with the narrative – it does lay the foundation for the classification of Speicher's file to cover up the chronology and action that led directly to his death. So does the Korean Conflict backstory that briefly follows it. Take note of the language used by the captor in each case and the response from Washington. From this instructive description of events it will become readily apparent that having an American in the basement is a generational affair to the United States' enemies. There are many Speichers out there. Just how many are alive today from World War II, Korea, Vietnam and the cold war is unknown, but the existence of these men – and some women – has been known since they went missing. Nothing was done to bring them home. Luck was with men like John Noble but so many others would never know freedom again.

The American POWs at Katyn sent secret coded messages to Washington with news of a Soviet atrocity, observed historians who first reviewed the newly released documents. In 1943 they saw rows of corpses in an advanced state of decay in the Katyn forest, on the western edge of Russia. What they saw was clear proof that the killers could not have been the Nazis who had only recently occupied the area. Testimony about the infamous massacre of Polish officers might have lessened confusion over the tragic fate that befell Poland under the Soviets, some scholars believe. Instead, this testimony mysteriously vanished into the heart of American power. The long-held suspicion has been that President Franklin Delano Roosevelt didn't want to anger Josef Stalin, an ally whom the Americans were counting on to defeat Germany and Japan. The evidence is among about 1,000 pages of newly declassified documents that the United States National Archives released and is putting online.

The most dramatic revelation thus far, according to the Associated Press, was evidence of the secret codes sent by two American POWs – army captain Donald B. Stewart and colonel John H. Van Vliet Jr. – information historians were unaware of, and which they explained added to evidence that the Roosevelt administration knew of the Soviet atrocity at Katyn relatively early on. The newly declassified pages make it possible to flesh out what Washington knew and when it knew it.

Though today's historians may not have known about the information just declassified and held in the National Archives, the congressional committee that investigated the Katyn forest mass murder did. Just like most of the evidence uncovered in the Speicher case by senators and congressmen, information in the Katyn forest massacre was heard, handled and buried. Much was known and much would subsequently be learned of the fate of the Poles who perished at Katyn.

Historians had long assumed that the grounds of a People's Commissariat for Internal Affairs (NKVD) rest and recreation facility at Smolensk, Russia, had been both an execution and burial site for nearly a fifth of the Polish military officers and enlisted men captured by the Soviets. But post-cold war revelations paint a different picture of events, suggesting that the victims were shot in the basement of the NKVD headquarters at Smolensk and at an abattoir in the same city, observed Benjamin Fischer, while also leaving open the possibility that some of the men had been executed in the forest itself.

While the Soviets began covering up the truth of what happened at Katyn in April 1943, destroying physical evidence, documents and erasing all mention of Katyn from their maps and official reference works, Democratic representative Ray J. Madden's House Select Committee, which held its first public hearing in Washington, D.C., on October 11, 1951, determined that certain reports and files concerning the Katyn massacre had likewise disappeared or were suppressed by departments of the United States government. In the course of the hearings held by this committee through July 2, 1952, testimony was taken from a total of 81 witnesses; 183 exhibits were studied and made part of the record; and more than 100 depositions were taken from witnesses who could not appear at the hearings. Committee staff further questioned more than 200 individuals who offered to appear as witnesses but whose information was mostly corroborative.

Records and documents assembled from the U.S. Departments of State and War provided Madden's committee a clearer picture of the important part the Katyn massacre played in shaping the future of postwar Europe. Secrets documents gathered by the committee revealed, too, that as early as the summer of 1942 American authorities considered the Polish army extremely vital to the Allied war effort against Adolph Hitler and Italian dictator Benito Mussolini. Documents introduced to the House Select Committee described efforts made to rebuild the Polish army on Russian soil as quickly as possible.

American authorities learned as early as 1942 of Poland's desperate efforts to locate the country's missing officers, men needed to lead the new Polish army. These same documents noted that when high-level Polish officials failed to obtain an adequate reply from the Soviets regarding the whereabouts of their missing officers, American emissaries intervened. In every instance, however, American officials were given the same reply: The Soviets had no knowledge of their whereabouts. United States ambassador to Moscow admiral William Harrison Standley advised the State Department on September 10, 1942, that Soviet officials were opposed to United States intervention in Russo-Polish problems. This attitude was stated to Admiral Standley by Politburo member and foreign affairs commissar Molotov when Standley inquired about the missing officers. Despite Soviet denials, throughout 1942 and 1943 – until the mass graves were discovered at Katyn – the United States government continued to aid the Poles. But the record also shows the total lack of cooperation by the Russians.

When the Russians finally broke diplomatic relations with Poland on April 26, 1943, following Poland's request for the International Committee of the Red Cross (ICRC) investigation of the Katyn massacre, Ambassador Standley warned the State Department that Russia had been seeking a pretext to break with Poland for some time. He emphasized that the Soviets were plotting to create a pro-communist satellite Polish government that would take over Poland after the war. He warned that Russia was planning to create, in fact, an entire wall of Soviet satellite governments in eastern Europe, which would, in turn, jeopardize lasting peace on the continent. Madden's committee concluded that it was apparent American authorities knew of the growing tension between the Soviets and Poles during the 1942 to 1943 period – and they also knew about the hopeless search for the Polish officers – but at the time, "all of these factors were brushed aside, on the theory that pressing the search would irritate Soviet Russia and thus hinder the prosecution of the war to a successful conclusion."

The Katyn investigation conducted by Madden's committee revealed that many individuals throughout the State Department, U.S. Army Intelligence (G-2), Office of War Information (OWI) and Federal Communications Commission (FCC), and a host of other government agencies, failed to properly evaluate the material being received from American sources overseas. In many instances, this information was deliberately withheld from public knowledge. There was a definite lack of coordination on intelligence matters between U.S. Army intelligence and the State Department, at least as far as the missing Polish officers and the Katyn massacre was concerned.

Former American ambassador Averell Harriman and former undersecretary of state Sumner Welles were asked by the House Select Committee to explain why the United States acquiesced so frequently to outrageous Soviet demands. Both stated that the underlying consideration throughout World War II was military necessity. While they agreed that American foreign policy called for a free postwar Poland to assure stability in Europe, they also concurred that a combat ready Polish army to fight in the Allies' Near East campaign was urgently needed. Harriman and Welles further insisted that during the war the paramount concern of the Roosevelt administration was the maintenance of the United States' alliance with the Soviet Union. As key witnesses before the committee, both men maintained that the Allies feared Russia might make a separate peace with the Germans.

American emissaries who reported the status of conditions concerning the Soviets were either bypassed or disregarded if their views were critical of the Soviets. When a number of the them made anti-Soviet observations, President Roosevelt dispatched his personal representative to Moscow to confer directly with Stalin. This fact was corroborated by the testimony of Ambassador Standley, who told the Madden committee that when he warned against Russia's postwar plans for forming a pro-Soviet bloc of nations around the Soviet Union in 1943, President Roosevelt sent Wendell Wilkie to Moscow. Standley was not provided details of Wilkie's meeting with Stalin.

Harriman and Welles, testifying before the committee, conceded in effect that Washington had taken a gamble on Russia's pledge to work harmoniously with western democracies after the war. The White House lost the bet. Harriman argued that agreements concluded at Tehran and Yalta would have assured lasting peace had Moscow kept its word. He insisted, too, that territorial concessions made at the Big Three conferences were predicated on the military reality that the Soviets were actually physically in control of these territories. Thus, to have resisted Soviet demands or attempted to drive them out by force would have meant prolonging the war. Harriman further testified that concessions made to the Soviets at Yalta were made at a time when the American Joint Chiefs of Staff insisted on getting the Soviets into the war with Japan at any cost. While Harriman confessed that he personally "was full of distrust of the Soviets at the time," he absolved the Roosevelt administration's actions, declaring that the Soviets breached the terms of Yalta and that the communist government that emerged in postwar Poland was not representative of its people.

Madden's committee clearly believed that the United States and Great Britain's tragic concessions, largely made at Yalta, wouldn't have happened at all had the Polish officer corps and the lion's share of Poland's intelligentsia not been murdered at Katyn in the spring of 1943. Under solid leadership, a Polish army might well have reversed early setbacks experienced by the Allies in the war. The Kremlin's hand would not have been as strong at Yalta, and many of the concessions attributed to military necessity would have been obviated. This contention was borne out by a portion of the telegram sent to the State Department on June 2, 1942, by Anthony Joseph Drexel Biddle Jr., American ambassador assigned to the Polish government-in-exile in London. "The absence of these officers," stated Biddle, "is the principal reason for the shortage of officers in the Polish forces in Russia ... The possible death of these men," he continued, "most of whom have superior education, would be a severe blow to the Polish national life."

President Roosevelt was clearly concerned about the tenuous relationship between the Soviets and Poles. When Stalin informed the President of his decision to break off diplomatic relations with the Poles following their demand for an ICRC investigation of Katyn, Roosevelt sent a personal message urging Stalin to reconsider this action. The tone of Roosevelt's message demonstrated his desire, above all, to retain cordial relations with the Soviets. When again, in 1944, former ambassador George Howard Earle, who served as a special emissary for President Roosevelt in the Balkans, tried to convince the President that the Soviets were guilty of the Katyn massacre, Roosevelt dismissed it and sent Earle to American Samoa for the duration of the war. Later testifying before Madden's committee, Earle explained that he had predicated his statement to President Roosevelt on secret documents and photographs of Katyn clearly establishing Soviet guilt. When shown this material, Earle quoted the President as replying, "George, this is entirely German propaganda and a German plot. I am absolutely convinced the Russians did not do this."

To Madden's committee, it was readily apparent that the President and the State Department ignored numerous documents from ambassadors Standley, Biddle, and John Gilbert Winant, America's emissary to Great Britain during World War II, who reported information that strongly pointed to Soviet perfidy. The House Select Committee's report made it clear that President Roosevelt's dealings with the Soviets throughout the war were predicated on a strong desire for mutual cooperation with Russia in the war effort, a desire founded on the belief that Soviet Russia was sincere in its promise to honor the terms negotiated at Big Three conferences. "It is equally obvious," concluded the committee, "that this desire completely overshadowed the dictates of justice and equity to our loyal but weaker ally, Poland."

So what did Washington know?

Americans had witnessed events at Katyn after the massacre. On May 22, 1945, an American infantry officer, Colonel Van Vliet, arrived in Washington, D.C. from Europe and promptly reported to Major General Clayton Bissell, army chief of staff in charge of intelligence (G-2), to record his observations at Katyn. Van Vliet's testimony, along with that of Captain Stewart, was among the most important testimony by independent witnesses who had visited Katyn shortly after the German announcement of the Polish officers' mass graves. Van Vliet and Stewart were captured by the Germans in North Africa and taken to Germany as prisoners of war. They visited Katyn, along with two British officers, compelled by the Nazis to do so, in May 1943. It was apparent to Van Vliet that the Nazis had hoped to bolster the credibility of their charges that the Soviets had massacred the Poles by taking the colonel, Captain Stewart, and two British officers to the gravesite.

Neither Van Vliet nor Stewart would concur with the Nazis that the murders were the work of the Soviets, at least not while in captivity. But as soon as he returned to the United States, Van Vliet went directly to the G-2 to make his report. He was unequivocally convinced the Soviets had killed the Poles, and so, by then, was

Captain Stewart. "The decision I reached, I can never forget," Stewart later told Madden's committee, "My decision was that those [Polish] men were killed by the Russians while they were prisoners of the Russians."

General Bissell promptly classified Van Vliet's dictated report top secret and Van Vliet was ordered to never speak of what he saw again. This report was made in a single, original manuscript without copies. General Bissell then ordered Colonel Van Vliet to maintain absolute secrecy concerning his observations of and conclusions about Katyn. This top secret document had disappeared from army intelligence files by the time Madden's committee went to find it as part of its investigation. The search for the Van Vliet report had been one of the most important tasks of the committee. An independent investigation conducted by the U.S. Army Inspector General in 1950 concluded the report had been "compromised" and that there was nothing to indicate it had ever left army intelligence headquarters. This finding was in response to General Bissell's allegation that he "believed" he had forwarded Van Vliet's top secret report to the Department of State, but there was no record of such a transmittal from G-2 to State.

Appearing before Madden's committee on two different occasions, General Bissell steadfastly maintained his belief that he had forwarded the document to the Department of State on May 25, 1945, introducing into evidence a letter he had written to assistant secretary of state Julius Cecil Holmes on that date, inquiring if the State Department had any record of another Van Vliet document, an interrogation by a Swiss protecting-power official shortly after Van Vliet had been at Katyn. Bissell's May 25 letter bore no notation that an enclosure was attached. No receipt record for this top secret report was ever located, thus there was no way to prove the document was actually received by State.

General Bissell subsequently introduced into evidence another letter he wrote on August 21, 1945, to Frederick B. Lyon, Holmes' assistant at State. In this letter, Bissell included a report by a British officer who had also been taken to Katyn by the Nazis. The general concluded his August 21 letter: "This report substantiates in effect the statement of Col. John H. Van Vliet Jr., forwarded to General Holmes on the 25th day of May 1945." In his testimony before the House Select Committee, Bissell contended that this particular phrase from his August 21 letter substantiated his earlier claim that he'd sent the Van Vliet report to the State Department.

Holmes, sent to London as minister to the American embassy from 1948 to 1954, and Lyon, both testified before the committee. Under oath, Holmes and Lyon disavowed any knowledge of having ever received the Van Vliet report from Bissell. They also stated that if they had discussed this report with Bissell, they would have remembered it because of the political significance of it at that time. The committee thus concluded that Bissell was mistaken in his claim that he might have forwarded the Van Vliet report to State. The committee also found that the Van Vliet report was either removed or purposely destroyed by army intelligence. General Bissell himself admitted to the committee that if the Van Vliet report had been publicized in 1945, when Yalta agreements for creating a United Nations organization were being carried out in San Francisco, Soviet Russia might never have taken a seat in the organization.

Justifying his designation of the Van Vliet report as top secret, Bissell stated he was merely carrying out the spirit of the Yalta agreement. He admitted the report was explosive and came at a time when the United States was still trying to get commitment from the Soviets to enter the war against Japan. General Bissell clearly contradicted his own theory when he told the committee that the Van Vliet report could not have been sent to the secretary of the army "because it had nothing to do with the prosecution of the war at that time." The committee expressed dismay that the assistant chief of staff of army intelligence was considering the political significance of the Van Vliet document and had failed to treat it objectively from a strictly military intelligence standpoint.

In the opinion of the committee, it was the duty and obligation of General Bissell to process the Van Vliet document with care so that it reached the State Department for evaluation and action. Bissell testified, "I saw in it [Van Vliet's report] great possibilities of embarrassment; so I classified it the way I have told you, and I think I had no alternative." More amazing to the committee was the testimony of three high-ranking American army officers assigned to Bissell's intelligence command. Testifying in executive session, all three agreed there was a pool of "pro-Soviet civilian employees and some military in army intelligence who found explanations for almost everything that the Soviet Union did." These same witnesses told of tremendous efforts exerted by this group to suppress anti-Soviet reports. The committee also heard testimony that top-ranking army officers who'd been too critical of the Soviets were bypassed for promotion and specific mention was made that assignment to army intelligence for these men was out of the question. They might talk. Worse than that they might testify before a committee like Madden's what they found out about the effort to hide material unfavorable to the Soviet Union. The overuse of classification to hide Soviet guilt at Katyn – still one of the greatest crimes in modern history – wouldn't become fully known for decades to follow.

Certainly, there was no question that army intelligence knew the military potential of the Polish army that was being organized in Russia in early 1941. Madden's committee later heard testimony from those who'd worked most closely with the Poles prior to Katyn and knew of the fate of the officer corps and intelligentsia massacred there. Word of the incident was first reported to an American army colonel named Henry I. Szymanski when he was assistant United States military attaché in Cairo. In March 1942 Colonel Szymanski was sent to join the Poles as the American liaison officer. Szymanski told the House Select Committee that he never carried out his mission in Russia because the Soviets refused his visa. Szymanski's specific assignment was to ascertain what had happened to the Polish officers in Russia, largely because the United States considered these Polish officers critical to the Allied war effort. Szymanski was recalled in November 1942 to give a full account of Soviet obstruction to the creation of a much-needed Polish army. Evidence unearthed by the committee revealed that Szymanski's highly critical reports of Soviet Russia were buried in the basement of army intelligence, and subsequently moved to the "dead file" of that department.

A compliant media helped the Katyn deception. The Office of War Information (OWI) and the Federal Communications Commission (FCC) each had a palpable role in the cover up of the Katyn massacre. When the Nazis, on April 13, 1943, announced to the world the finding of mass graves of the Polish officers and intelligentsia at Katyn and openly accused the Soviets, the Allies were stunned by the action and called it propaganda. Elmer Davis, a news commentator who at that time headed the Office of War Information, an agency established by Executive Order, told the House Select Committee he reported directly to President Roosevelt. Under further questioning, he admitted frequent conferences with the State Department and other government agencies; however, testifying before the committee, when faced with his own broadcast of May 3, 1943, in which he accused the Nazis of using the Katyn massacre as propaganda, Davis admitted under congressional questioning that the broadcast was made on his own initiative. His admission demonstrated the failure to coordinate between government agencies.

An April 22, 1943 State Department memorandum, read into the record, stated, in part, "on the basis of the various conflicting contentions [concerning Katyn] of all parties concerned, it would appear to be advisable to refrain from taking any definite stand in regard to this question." Davis bore responsibility for having accepted the Soviet propaganda version of the Katyn massacre without full investigation and corroborative information. But a basic fact check by Davis necessitated a forthcoming army intelligence and State Department and that wasn't going to happen. The OWI and FCC did engage in activities beyond the scope of their responsibilities, and this overstepping included silencing radio commentators, which first came to light in August 1943 when the House committee investigating the National Communications Commission (NCC) discovered what they had done. This cross-decking [collusion] of government agencies to complete the cover up would set precedent that continues to present.

OWI and FCC staff were used to silence Polish radio commentators in Detroit and Buffalo, who broadcast in foreign languages over the airwaves about the mass graves of Polish officers at Katyn just after the announcement of the discovery was made; they reported facts indicating that the Soviets might be guilty of the massacre. In May 1943 a member of the FCC staff suggested to a member of the OWI staff that the only way to prevent these comments was to contact the Wartime Foreign Language Radio Control Committee. This committee consisted of station owners and managers who were endeavoring to cooperate with the OWI and FCC during the war years. Accordingly, a meeting was arranged in New York with two members of the committee. There, an OWI staff member specifically requested that the Detroit Polish radio commentator restrict his comments to straight news items concerning Katyn, and only those put out by the standard wire services. The fact that a member of the FCC staff attended this meeting was significant because the FCC member was in New York to discuss the renewal of the radio license of one of these industry members. Further, the owner of the Detroit radio station was contacted and requested to restrict his Polish commentator's on-air reporting, and this was done. By applying indirect pressure on the station owner, these staff members accomplished their task, namely, keeping the full facts of the Katyn massacre story from the American people.

Office of Censorship officials subsequently testified and supported the conclusion of the committee that the OWI and FCC officials had overstepped the bounds of their official government responsibilities on Katyn. Testimony offered before Madden's committee proved that the Voice of America, successor of the OWI, had failed to fully utilize available information concerning the Katyn massacre until the creation of the House Select Committee in 1951. The committee was thus not impressed with statements that publication of facts concerning the Katyn massacre, prior to 1951, would lead to an ill-fated uprising in Poland. Neither was it convinced by OWI officials' statements that, had Polish-Americans heard or read about the Katyn massacre in 1943, it would have resulted in their lessened participation in the Allied war effort.

The White House maintained its silence on the Katyn massacre for decades. The cover-up of the truth cost many Americans their lives, including men like Scott Speicher. The case set a precedent and a pattern of behavior that gave America's enemies the road map to take down service members and get away with it. When America protected the Russians in the matter of Katyn forest, the White House showed the Kremlin that it didn't value human life and the truth anymore than it did.

The December 1952 conclusions of the House committee that studied the Katyn massacre found striking similarity between it and events taking place in Korea. "For 2 years the Soviets disavowed any knowledge of the vanished Polish officers and deceived the Polish government [-in-exile] in its search for these men," concluded the House Select Committee. "Today," the report concluded, "the Communists are similarly prolonging the Korean peace talks because they cannot account for the 8,000 American soldiers reported by General [Matthew Bunker] Ridgway 'killed as war crimes victims.' There are many indications that Katyn was a blueprint for Korea." The White House's handling of the Katyn forest massacre was blueprint for far more than Korea.

When Sumner Welles was asked by a member of Madden's committee if a firmer attitude toward the Soviets during the war would have helped avoid some of the trials and travails of postwar problems with North Korea, Welles replied:

> It is a very difficult thing to answer in the light of hindsight. As I look at it today, I think you are entirely correct. As we looked at it then, of course, the success of the war effort was the major effort; and I must remind the committee that the one overshadowing fear on the part of our military authorities at that time was a separate peace on the part of the Soviet Government with Germany.

Records unequivocally indicate that the Katyn massacre undermined Polish-Soviet relations throughout World War II, but also continue, in the present, to do the same. Katyn, as Madden's report observed, was a means to an end. The Soviets had plotted to take over Poland as early as 1939. The massacre of the lion's share of Poland's military officers and intelligentsia was designed to eliminate intellectual leadership that might have blocked Russia's ambitions for complete communization of Poland. Poland was one step of Josef Stalin's greater plan to communize Europe and, eventually, the entire world, including the United States. The United States had been warned repeatedly of Soviet Russia's designs on Poland and the rest of Europe. Whatever the justification might have been, the House Select Committee was convinced the United States' relations with the Soviets put us in the tragic position of winning the war but losing the peace. The price was steep, including scores of American service members and civilians whose lives were bartered away to the Soviets for the same reasons the United States let Soviet Russia off the hook for the Katyn massacre.

President Roosevelt, who Harriman told the committee "set our foreign policy," was the final authority on all foreign policy decisions. The President, according to Harriman, thought that Russia would disintegrate immediately after the end of the war. When warned by his advisors that Russia would become a great menace, Roosevelt silenced them. Roosevelt committed the United States to agreements with the Russians in spite of the fact, as Harriman told the committee, "a series of misdeeds by the Russians, from our standpoint, beginning with the Joachim von Ribbentrop treaty, that it [revelation of Katyn massacre] would have contributed, I think, to further distrust of the Soviets." Roosevelt's misjudgment that Moscow would honor its treaties and agreements, in spite of the factual record of the Kremlin's past broken promises, has proven to be the major error of the United States' foreign policy during the twelve-year Roosevelt administration. Republican congressman Timothy Patrick Sheehan, of Illinois, a member of Madden's committee, told fellow members of the House that the Katyn massacre "was but a small part of the giant error made in our foreign policy program. If our Government," he observed, "would have disclosed the truth about Katyn and the sellout of Poland, it would have had to disclose more truths about the perfidy of Russia."

The Katyn forest massacre involved a total of approximately 15,000 Polish prisoners of war, of whom 8,300 to 8,400 were determined to be officers, contrary to Nazi and Soviet accounts that erred in calling all of the victims "officers." The prisoners of war, most of who had been called up as reservists before the invasion of Poland, included one prince; eleven admirals; two generals; seven chaplains; three landowners; 24 colonels; 17 naval captains; 29 lieutenant colonels; 258 majors; 654 captains; 200 pilots; 3,420 noncommissioned officers; 85 privates; 43 government officials; 20 university professors; 300 physicians, though that number could have been as high as 800; several hundred lawyers, architects, chemists, engineers, businessmen, and teachers, and at least 100 writers and journalists – the cream of Poland's intelligentsia and nearly half the Polish officer corps, all part of Stalin's long-range plan to prevent the resurgence of ethnic, nationalist Poles who might resist the Soviet Union's future invasion and subjugation of their country. Also killed were 700 to 900 Polish Jews, including the chief rabbi of the Polish army, Major Baruch Steinberg.

According to the Associated Press, Washington's silence remained a source of deep frustration for many Polish-Americans for decades following World War II. One of them is eighty-one-year-old Franciszek Herzog, a Connecticut man whose father and uncle died in the Katyn forest. After Mikhail Gorbachev's 1990 admission of Soviet culpability in the massacre, Herzog was hoping that Washington would be just as open. He was sadly mistaken. Herzog made three attempts to get an apology from President George H. W. Bush. "It will not resurrect the men," he wrote to Bush. "But will give moral satisfaction to the widows and orphans of the victims." The reply Herzog got in 1992 was not from Bush but the State Department. The letter didn't satisfy him. The Associated Press got a copy of his letter and the government's response released through the George H.W. Bush Presidential Library. The letter, dated August 12, 1992, and signed by Thomas Gerth, then deputy director of the Office of East European Affairs, shows that the government continued to state it had no irrefutable evidence until Gorbachev's admission. "The U.S. government," according to the letter, "never accepted the Soviet government's claim that it was not responsible for the massacre. However, at the time of the Congressional hearings in 1951-1952, the U.S. did not possess the facts that could clearly refute the Soviets' allegations that these crimes were committed by the Third Reich. These facts, as you know, were not revealed until 1990, when the Russians officially apologized to Poland." This was a lie. It had plenty.

"There's a big difference between not knowing and not wanting to know," said Herzog. "I believe the U.S. government didn't want to know because it was inconvenient to them." He was only partly right. The White House, in its silence, effectively became a coconspirator in the deaths of Poland's officer corps and intelligentsia. The American government aided and abetted the Kremlin's – and subsequently America's future enemies' – bad behavior. The Poles paid a high price. An eyewitness to the exhumation of their bodies later provided his report in 1955 to the House Select Committee on Communist Aggression:

> A typical feature of the bodies exhumed from this grave [No. 5] was the fact of the hands of all of them being tied behind their backs with a white cord tied in a double knot. Their greatcoats were tied round their heads. These greatcoats were tied with the same kind of cord at the neck level and sometimes a second knot had been made over the head of the victim. At the neck there was a simple knot and the rest of the cord was passed down the back, wound round the tied hands and then tied again at the neck. In this way the hands of the victims were pulled up to the height of the shoulder blades. Victims tied up in this way were unable to give any resistance because every move of the hands tightened the noose around the neck thereby throttling them. They were besides, unable to make any sound on account of the greatcoats over their heads ... such a way of tying up the victims before execution was inflicting especially refined torture before death.

This was the fate of the Poles killed at Katyn. But there were also thousands of American and Allied prisoners of war and missing in action – unaccounted for – at the end of World War II whose cases will not be resolved until Washington declassifies the intelligence that documents the fate of each man. How many Americans in the basement were there at the end of that war? The answer – thousands.

At the end of World War II on October 31, 1945, the War Department's statistical branch documented 6,595 prisoners who'd not been returned to American military control. In a cable sent by army lieutenant colonel L.L. Ballard Jr. dated December 31, 1945, there were still 5,414 men's names still on that list with a current status of "prisoners of war." The War Department's figures had come down but were already being underreported should anyone outside the military find out. The Soviet Union was literally returning American prisoners of war and missing in action one at a time. The Russians waited for the American military to ask for the man by name – just as the Iraqis did at the end of the Gulf War – and if it didn't they had another prisoner for life. In the three-month-period between October and December 1945 the Russians returned just 435 men but that still didn't explain the other 646 men moved from prisoner of war status to make up the difference between 6,595 to 5,414 names on Ballard's roster. Another statistic to keep in mind is that just one thousand total American prisoners of war were repatriated in the last six months of 1945 – a number much larger than Ballard would ever keep in an official log of the missing.

The real explanation of the 646 names on Ballard's list could only be this: the War Department had issued a presumptive finding of death (PFOD) for these men. The number of American servicemen in this category of known prisoners of war not returned in June 1945 was, in fact, closer to the 20,000 first calculated by General Albert W. Kenner, Supreme Allied Commander general Dwight Eisenhower's headquarters surgeon general, in his May 30, 1945 memorandum with the subject heading "Displaced Persons, Allied Ex-PW and German PW." In this memorandum, Kenner documented detailed numbers of Allied ex-prisoners of war and displaced persons (DP) reported captive in territory occupied by the Soviet army. The 20,000 in his report did not include missing in action, only known prisoners of war. Kenner knew, as did Eisenhower, that by the end of October, the War Department was likely able to make legal presumed findings of death in the majority of these cases, leaving the number of "prisoners not returned to military control" not 12,500 but 6,595. The figure of 11,753 declared dead under the category "other missing in action," on Ballard's roster actually represented presumed findings of death as authorized by U.S. Public Law 490. These presumed findings of death were derived from both prisoners of war and missing in action on Ballard's list, decreasing the numbers in those categories and increasing the number in the declared dead category.

As the result of these findings, Lieutenant Colonel Ballard felt obligated to explain to the director of the Relief to Prisoners of War of the Red Cross, Maurice Fate, that for "statistical purposes" the numbers of prisoner of war (current status) and missing in action (current status) were "still large." Ballard explained further to the Red Cross that "these casualties cannot be moved to other categories" until each man can be found, legally, to be dead. This finding of death occurs, he pointed out, after an "investigation to date leaves little logical doubt that a given man is permanently lost."

The most striking aspect of these documents is the revelation that the War Department's chief of the Strength Accounting and Statistical Office's main function was to resolve each outstanding case by determining – as soon as enough time elapsed to make it legally possible – that each man is "permanently lost," and thus dead. The focus of the War Department's efforts wasn't in the direction the American public might have thought; that is, to make a thorough effort to determine the fate of each man. Given the obvious and observed policy of the Soviet government to hold citizens and soldiers from Western countries, known even then to American officials from the president of the United States on down the military chain of command, Lieutenant Colonel Ballard's efforts should have been to determine where the Soviets were holding these men, and not to "await a legal determination of death under [Public Law] 490, which may take up to next September."

The ability to wave the wand of presumptive finding of death was first used at the end of World War I and by the end of World War II was used with increasing abandon to declare missing American soldiers, sailors and airmen administratively dead. In truth, thousands of American personnel who were known prisoners of the Germans at the end of 1945 – documented and witnessed by repatriated prisoners of war – weren't repatriated after the eastern territory in which the Nazis had held them was liberated by the advancing Red Army. Most of these men would be quickly labeled "legally dead." They and hundreds of thousands of Europeans captured and kidnapped during the war vanished into the Soviet gulag system.

The Soviet Union had a plan. The rationale of the plan to hold American and Allied servicemen and civilians was motivated by complex and repugnant reasons that Moscow would turn into school house lessons for its allies and satellite states in the postwar environment. These were lessons that Damascus, Baghdad, Tehran and those to the east in Beijing, Hanoi, and Pyongyang would perfect by the late twentieth century. In the memoirs of former secretary of state James F. Byrnes, there is an illuminating conversation captured in writing between Byrnes and Molotov, Soviet commissar of foreign affairs. In late September 1945, several weeks after Japan's surrender in Tokyo Bay, Byrnes wrote Molotov, who came to see him in London, following specific instructions from the Kremlin to do so.

"Molotov wanted to complain of the way in which the surrender terms [with Japan] were being carried out," wrote Byrnes. "He complained particularly about the way the Japanese army was being demobilized. It was dangerous, Molotov iterated, to merely disarm the Japanese and send them home; they should be held as prisoners of war. The United States should do what the Red Army was doing with the Japanese it had taken in Manchuria – make them work – he said. No one can say with absolute accuracy just how many Japanese prisoners have been taken to the Soviet Union, he told Byrnes, but "in mid 1947 the best guess was that approximately 500,000 [of them] were still there."

The problem of accounting for prisoners of war and missing in action was complicated by Soviet prisoner policy and deception operations in the postwar period. In Eastern Europe, as well as the Far East, the Red Army guarded millions of prisoners – human capital – that the Soviet government viewed as slave labor. These people were not only American, Allied and Axis prisoners of war but hundreds of thousands of displaced Western and Eastern European citizens and, largely forgotten, Japanese civilians, all of who desperately wanted to flee Red Army-held territory. Nationalities of smaller countries in Western Europe, including the Dutch, Belgians, Finns and Swedes, as well as former Nazi-occupied nations such as France tragically had little military, political and diplomatic clout with the Soviet government to secure repatriation of their citizens at the end of the war. The result was even more tragic. Tens of thousands of Dutch and Belgians, and hundreds of French were never repatriated by the Soviets. The French, in particular, bore the brunt of the Soviet "make them work" policy.

Nearly a month after Eisenhower's June 19, 1945 cable declaring "only small numbers of U.S. prisoners of war still remain in Russian hands" and that these men "no doubt are scattered singly and in small groups as no information is available of any large numbers in specific camps," Eisenhower sent another cable marked secret priority to the head of the American military mission to the Soviet Union, Major General John R. Deane, in Moscow. This June 25, 1945 cable fleshed out circumstances that continue to shock the public today. "[There is the] possibility that several hundred American prisoners of war liberated from Stalag Luft 1, Barth [Germany], are now confined by the Russian army in the Rostock area pending identification as Americans as reported by an American who recently returned from such confinement."

Staff Sergeant Anthony Sherg was one of one thousand air force commissioned and noncommissioned officers who left Stalag Luft 1 immediately prior to the Red Army's assumption of control in Barth after which Sherg and the others were to get air transport from Wismar. Sherg belonged to a group of ten men arrested by Russian soldiers and held in jails in Bad Dorberan, and then on to Rostock.

Ten more Americans soon joined them there. The Russians continued to pick up groups of American servicemen from Stalag Luft 1 and bring them to Rostock as the round-up point. According to the cable: "Russian authorities demanded identification papers, which no prisoner possessed, and refused to consider dog tags proof of the Americans' status." The Americans were well fed and quartered but they weren't going anywhere. Berg began to think they'd never be turned over, and after twenty-five days in Russian custody, he escaped and made his way to the British line. There were hundreds of Americans who didn't escape Soviet captivity.

The fact is that anyone bold enough to get away from Soviet forces was lucky. German recordkeeping indicated that before the Red Army "liberated" Stalag Luft 1 on May 1, 1945, there were roughly 8,939 Allied airmen – 7, 588 American and 1,351 Royal Air Force – imprisoned there. Stalag Luft 1 was just one of Germany's many prisoner of war camps. Quietly, Washington believed Moscow could answer for at least 60,000 missing Americans[15], but even this figure was conservative. Figures reported by the War Department for public consumption proved astonishingly low.

The United States gave up more than strategic position to the Soviet Union at the end of the World War II; it is believed that tens of thousands of servicemen were taken into Soviet custody as the Red Army liberated German prisoner of war camps and most did not come home. Estimates for Americans left behind in the aftermath of the war in the Far East were not included in this number and no one knows, with any precision, how many men that might be. Reports located decades later in Moscow archives make it clear that information from the tightly-controlled Soviet state news and propaganda machine, coupled with what was made available to American and Russian researchers between 1991 and 2004, didn't provide details of their fate. Documents shown to American investigators by Russian state archivists were reviewed carefully before being handed over. In the end these reports were snapshots, controlled glimpses into the fate of tens of thousands of Americans and millions of Westerners collected by the Soviet Union at war's end.

The Soviet Union made ruthless demands on its allies and exacted a heavy price from its enemies at the end of World War II, but never more than when it came to picking and choosing who they'd keep and who they'd return. There are at least five reasons why the Soviets swallowed up the Allies' prisoners of war, missing in action and citizens from nearly every nation in western Europe. First, there is the issue of economic concessions that the Kremlin demanded and what interpreter Red Army major Vasilli Vershenko called "credits." Vershenko explained that Russians and Americans had agreed to a pact that called for the Russians to receive "credits" for each American prisoner of war returned and that repatriation of American prisoners of war was thus "a complex logistical matter."

In truth the cumulative number of unaccounted-for American servicemen from the European theater was far higher than Washington was going to publicly admit. Eisenhower was left hamstrung by backdoor deals made between Roosevelt and Stalin. In the Pacific, General Douglas A. MacArthur was less conciliatory to the Russians. He wanted answers and he wanted his people back. But the pushback from Washington left him little room to repatriate men who'd never see home again.

The second point went back to what Molotov described as "dangerous" – to merely disarm an adversary (or in the case of the United States, an ally who could potentially be a future adversary) and it was imperative they be "made to work."

Third, the Soviet Union believed it their right to use former prisoners of war and kidnapped persons as slave labor to rebuild their industrial base.

Fourth, as a related British cable indicated, there was a compelling need for the Allies to satisfy Moscow's "inclination to blackmail us into dealing with Warsaw authorities" and for other political reasons. In other words, the Russians took Allied servicemen and civilians as hostages.

Lastly, in holding onto Allied servicemen and civilians Moscow was ensuring that Russia's military and displaced civilian population were forcibly repatriated to the Soviet Union, including east European citizens who didn't want to return to their home countries then under Soviet control. The western Allies were resistant to forcible repatriation. Eisenhower's staff had received details from American and British liaison officers that Soviet troops sent back to Russia faced a grim fate. But they never understood the scope.

Soviet soldiers, sailors, airmen and displaced persons who were captured by the Germans and recovered by American and British forces were often found wearing German work camp uniforms. Soviets captured by the Germans were given the option of starving to death or joining labor battalions. Most joined German labor battalions. Once repatriated to the Soviet Union, they were sent immediately to slave labor camps. Soviets sent to slave labor camps were the lucky ones; the others were shot shortly after turnover. Thus former Soviet military and civilian prisoners of war left in Allied control were extremely reluctant to be repatriated. The description that follows, reported in a January 28, 1946 memorandum scripted by Parker W. Burnham in Munich, was the result of Allied soldiers' attempt to repatriate 399 former Russian soldiers by train to the Soviet Union.

> All of these men refused to entrain. They begged to be shot. They resisted entrainment by taking off their clothes and refusing to leave their quarters. It was necessary to use tear gas and some force to drive them out. Tear gas forced them out of the building into the snow where those who had cut themselves fell exhausted and bleeding in the snow. Nine men hanged themselves and one had stabbed himself to death and one other who had stabbed himself subsequently died; while 20 others are in the hospital for self inflicted wounds. The entrainment was finally effected of 368 men who were sent off accompanied by a Russian liaison officer on a train carrying American guards. Six men escaped en route. A number of men in the group claimed they were not Russians.

Russian practices were just as coldblooded in the Pacific.

Washington was deeply aware of the plight of American servicemen taken to the Soviet Union. The American embassy in Moscow received a message, for example, on December 10, 1945, that made it clear that as of the previous August 30, the Russians were holding approximately forty-five former American prisoners of war, including two officers – one captain and one lieutenant – and forty-three enlisted men at Rada, near Tambov in the Stalingrad area. This single report was one of many indicating that Moscow had lied that it knew nothing of Americans in its prisons, camps and hospitals. A week after the embassy received this report, the Office of Strategic Services (OSS), precursor to the CIA, received intelligence from Tambov collected from a former Polish prisoner captured by the Russians in 1944. In April 1945 the Polish informant was moved to Tambov with what he described as "several score [of] Americans" as well as British detainees. The Pole told U.S. authorities that the Americans and British prisoners at Tambov were insistent that he notify Allied authorities of their plight.

As the cold war between the United States and Soviet Union deepened in the years immediately following World War II, Secretary of State George C. Marshall decided in June 1947 that not even those who had collaborated with the Nazis should be repatriated to Soviet bloc nations against their will. Marshall declared that involuntary repatriation was contrary to America's long history of offering political asylum, thus the practice of forcible repatriation would no longer be honored. Marshall's decision to end forcible repatriation would complicate, if not kill, efforts by Washington to secure the release of tens of thousands of U.S. servicemen and roughly 2,000 American civilians who remained in Soviet custody, many already pressed into hard labor in the Russian gulag.

The scope of the issue that flowered after World War II is almost beyond comprehension. Creative measures to secure the release of Americans from the Soviet Union proved futile. American ambassador to the Soviet Union Walter Bedell Smith suggested to General Lucius D. Clay, the American military governor of Germany, that the general might try trading Russians convicted of criminal offenses in the American zone for American servicemen and civilians held by the Soviet Union. The Truman administration considered Smith's suggestion briefly, but shied away from sending anyone back to Russia unless it was "voluntarily." Smith's plan was flawed from the start. The Soviet Union held the upper hand in the negotiation. When Clay's deputy, Major General George Hays, informed the Soviet military administrator in Germany that he would not give back anymore Russian prisoners, guilty or not of crimes, until discussions were held regarding Americans detained in the Soviet Union, Soviet lieutenant general Mikhail Dratvin shot back that all persons in Russia claimed by the U.S. as citizens were not United States nationals or had already been sent out of the country. Dratvin then demanded that all Soviet prisoners in Germany be released immediately to Moscow. By the end of 1948, the American embassy in Moscow gave up trying to get back the lion's share of American citizens in the Soviet Union.

Secretary of State Byrnes' reply to Robert Murphy, the American military advisor in Germany, would be repeated again years later when questions about the Yalta agreement's repatriation policy came up at the confirmation hearing of Charles Eustis Bohlen as ambassador to the Soviet Union in the spring of 1953.

Bohlen was asked by Senator Homer Ferguson:

"How do you account for the fact that we did not sense what was going on and refuse to carry out an agreement that not only enslaved these people but took their lives?"

Bohlen replied:

"The purpose of it ... was that there were 60,000 American prisoners ... under the control of the Red Army, and the purpose was to get those prisoners back."

The discourse over American prisoners of war and missing in action who'd yet to come home from World War II continued for decades after the war was declared over. Madden's committee had in mind the large number of American unaccounted-for and in Soviet custody when it considered the Katyn massacre and the predicament in which Washington found itself after the cease-fire in Korea. The Second World War was both prequel and sequel – we weren't supposed to forget the hundreds of men of the American Expeditionary Force who'd been missing for decades, they'd been snatched in Bolshevik Russia during the undeclared incursion there at the end of World War I. But we did forget about them and we paid a steep price for that absentmindedness less than three decades later. The House Select Committee had every reason to be worried. Even today the question should be asked: If everything being put out by the U.S. government about America's World War II unaccounted-for were true, why is the information still largely classified?

The Department of Defense moved swiftly to control public knowledge of what happened to the unaccounted-for American servicemen in the wake of the Korean Conflict. While the entire affair was a political inconvenience to Washington, the conclusion of a report with the title "Recovery of Unrepatriated Prisoners of War" concluded that "such as they are, our current efforts in the political field, plus the 'stand-by' alternatives developed by the military, represent the full range of possible additional efforts to recover personnel now in custody of foreign powers. On one hand, we are bound at present by the President's 'peaceful means' decree. The military courses of action apparently cannot be taken unilaterally, and we are possessed of some rather 'reluctant' allies in this respect. The problem becomes a philosophical one. If we are 'at war,' cold, hot or otherwise, casualties and losses must be expected and perhaps we must learn to live with this type of thing."

The individual who crafted the "Recovery of Unrepatriated Prisoners of War" was James J. Kelleher. He didn't have "to live with this type of thing" in a Soviet or Chinese prison as an American prisoner of war. But his report made one particularly prescient point: "If we are in for fifty years of peripheral 'firefights' we may be forced to adopt a rather cynical attitude on this [prisoner of war business] for political course of action something like [Marine Corps] General [Graves B.] Erskine outlined which would (1) instill in the soldier a much more effective 'don't get captured' attitude, and (2) we should also push to get the military commander more discretionary authority to retaliate, fast and hard against these Communist tactics."

Official U.S. government documents make it clear: nearly one thousand American prisoners of war, and an undetermined number of some 8,000 American missing in action, were still held captive after the Korean Conflict cease-fire prisoner exchange called Operation Big Switch. None were not repatriated later either. Three days after the start of Big Switch, the August 8, 1953 *New York Times* reported that General James A. Van Fleet, retired commander of the United States Eighth Army in Korea, estimated that a large percentage of the 8,000 American soldiers listed as missing in Korea were alive. A report by the United Nations Combined Command for Reconnaissance Activity, Korea, five days into Operation Big Switch, was more pointed: "Figures show that the total number of MIAs, *plus known captives, less* [emphasis added] those to be U.S. repatriated, leaves a balance of 8,000 unaccounted for." The report mentioned numerous reports of United Nations prisoners of war being transferred to Manchuria, and China, and the Soviet Union from the beginning of hostilities in Korea. Specifically, the report documented "many prisoners of war transferred have been technicians and factory workers. Other prisoners of war transferred had a knowledge of Cantonese and are reportedly used for propaganda purposes."

The number of known unrepatriated American prisoners of war from the Korean Conflict was cited by Hugh M. Milton II, assistant secretary of the United States Army, in a January 16, 1954 memorandum. Milton's report came four months after the end of Big Switch. Section 3, Part B of Milton's memorandum was the most important; it was titled "The Unaccounted-for Americans Believed to be Still Held Illegally by the Communists" and it was classified secret. "There are approximately 954 United States personnel falling into this group," read the report. "What the Department of the Army and other interested agencies [are] doing about their recovery falls into two parts. First," Milton wrote, "the direct efforts of the UNC [United Nations Command] Military Armistice Commission to obtain an accurate accounting, and second, efforts by the G2 [intelligence] of the army, both overt and covert, to locate, identify, and recover these individuals. G2 is making an intensive effort through its information collection system worldwide, to obtain information on these people and has a plan for clandestine action to obtain the recovery of one or more to establish the case positively that prisoners are still being held by the Communists." Milton's biggest problem was that the latter obtained no results. The direct efforts of the United Nations commission was held in abeyance pending further study of the problem by the State Department.

During Operation Big Switch, some repatriates, according to Milton's report, stated that they had been informed by the communists that they "were holding 'some' U.S. flyers as 'political prisoners' rather than as prisoners of war and that *these people would have to be 'negotiated for' through political or diplomatic channels* [emphasis added]. Due to the fact that we did not recognize the red regime in China, no political negotiations were instituted, although [the] State [Department] did have some exploratory discussions with the British in an attempt to get at the problem." The situation went idle until late November 1954 when Peking radio announced that 13 of these "political prisoners" had been sentenced for "spying." This announcement caused a public uproar and a demand from the American public, congressional leadership and veterans' organizations calling for their immediate release.

Worse yet was Milton's second point. "A further complicating factor in the situation," he concluded, "is that to continue to carry these personnel in a missing status is costing over one million dollars annually. It may become necessary at some future date to drop them from our records as 'missing and presumed dead.'" The Department of Defense did, indeed, "drop them" from its missing in action roll and moved them over to "presumed dead." In an April 29, 1954 memorandum to Major General Robert N. Young, assistant chief of staff and G1 of the United States Army, Milton reported that the Defense Department's steady progress in dropping Korean Conflict prisoners of war from the Pentagon's records was being executed under provisions of Public Law 490.

"After careful review of each case and interrogation of returning prisoners of war, [the Department of the Army] has placed 618 soldiers, known to have been in enemy hands and unaccounted for by the communist forces" into five categories. Public law permitted the army to reach a presumptive finding of death – administratively determined with no proof of actual death – in 313 of the cases in Milton's purview. Another 275 were classified "reported dead" on the slim authority of returning prisoners. Another 21 were listed as "dishonorable discharge." Just four were "under investigation, prognosis undecided" (missing in action over one year). Of the total under cover of the April 29 memorandum, only two were listed as "returned to military control."

Milton's original 954 unaccounted-for had been whittled down to 618 through a series of presumptive findings of death of Americans "unaccounted for but believed to be still held illegally by the communists." Operation Big Switch ended on September 6, 1953, leaving more questions and concerns about American servicemen left behind that wouldn't be answered in time to save most of them. According to the "Interim Report of U.S. Casualties" prepared by the Office of the Secretary of Defense, as of December 31, 1953, the total number of American soldiers still listed as missing in action from the Korean Conflict was 13,325 but without explanation the next day – the first day of a new year – the number of missing in action was reported as 2,953 with the number of dead or presumed dead upped to 5,140. Of the total number, only 5,131 missing in action were reported repatriated and 101 were listed as "current captured."

There are several observations of indoctrination and interrogation techniques exercised over prisoners of war held by Soviet, Chinese and North Korean communists. What they did, how they did it and how they got away – and continue to get away with it – continues to shape the slave holder mentality of Russian-trained surrogates worldwide. The North Korean system most closely resembles China's general timetable for interrogation and extraction of a confession in a manner that was quite different from the Russian system. The Chinese and North Koreans immediately attempted to produce long lasting behavioral and attitudinal change in the prisoner of war. Indoctrination played a particularly important role for the Chinese and North Koreans. This was a strategy that relied less on the brutal and often prolonged isolation used by the Russians.

Instead, they emphasized group interaction rather than solitary confinement – at least in the beginning. Prisoners were confined to cells that could hold six to eight men, a tactic that emphasized public self-criticism and group criticism for indoctrination and the use of diary writing as distinct from verbal discussion. This kept the prisoner busy providing his captors with his "autobiography." Chinese as well as North Korean interrogators were generally less experienced and less knowledgeable about Americans and Europeans than the Russians.

In Wilfred Olaf Reiners' *Soviet Indoctrination of German War Prisoners,* published in the spring of 1959, the author pointed out that there were certain fundamental differences between American prisoners of war held in Korea versus European prisoners of war, especially Germans, interned in the Soviet Union. The overwhelming majority of American prisoners of war had no basic discord with their government or American political and social institutions. By comparison, there were, among the Europeans, distinct groups opposed to their political regime at home, or at least to certain aspects of their home country's rule. But European belligerents were locked in a life-and-death struggle during World War II, while the war waged on the Korean peninsula remained a regional conflict. This implied major differences in the waging of war and the treatment of prisoners of war. Further, an American serviceman who collaborated with the enemy knew he had to accept full responsibility for this action after repatriation, whereas the European was not necessarily faced with that problem. Ultimately the vast number of prisoners of war held by the Soviet Union precluded the kind of intensive indoctrination that American soldiers received from the Chinese during the Korean Conflict.

The Soviets structured their indoctrination program for prisoners of war with two basic objectives in mind: prisoners of war used as propaganda instruments and, later, as political pawns, even if their home country didn't know – at least at first – that the Russians had them. The Red Army's propaganda division used individual prisoners of war for the production and dissemination of propaganda leaflets and radio broadcasts. Prisoners were most often persuaded to participate in propaganda almost immediately after capture and prior to being sent to permanent prison camps. Others were put through an anti-Fascist school, then assigned to psychological warfare duties. Such propaganda activities were aimed at both military and civilian populations and were designed to reduce fighting spirit and the will to resist. Another objective of Soviet prisoner of war indoctrination was the creation inside the Soviet Union of a group of anti-Nazi Germans, friendly to the communist Russia, who could either be the nucleus of a future German government or could exert influence on a possible coup d'état. After the war, many of these indoctrinated Germans were transferred to the Soviet sector of occupied Germany to fill key positions in the new government bureaucracy.

Certainly, Washington, from the White House to the Defense Department, knew what was going on. A Foreign Service dispatch signed by American consul general Julian F. Harrington and dated March 23, 1954, was sent from the U.S. diplomatic post in Hong Kong to the State Department in Washington. The dispatch addressed in detail hundreds of American prisoners of war captured on the Korean peninsula who were documented en route to Siberia. According to a Turkish refugee from Manchuria, several hundred American prisoners of war were being transferred via Chinese trains to Russian trains at Manchouli near the border of Manchuria and Siberia; they were seen in late 1951 and again in the spring of 1952 by an informant and the informant's Russian acquaintance. The informant was interrogated on two occasions by the assistant air liaison officer and the consulate general, who agreed that the information was likely true. "In a railway restaurant [the source] closely observed three POWs who were under guard and conversing in English. POWs wore sleeve insignia which indicated POWs were Air Force noncommissioned officers. Source states that there were a great number of negroes among POW shipments and also states that at no time were any POWs observed returning from Siberia." Washington wanted more information. They got it.

When the source was asked about the nationality of the guards accompanying the American prisoners of war, the answer was clear.

"On [the] Chinese side POWs [were] accompanied by Chinese guards. POWs passed through [a] gate bisecting [a] platform to [a] Russian train manned and operated by Russians. Russian trainmen wore dark blue or black tunic with silver colored shoulder boards. [The] source says this [is the] regular train uniform but he knows the trainmen are military wearing regular train uniforms." Asked specifically to further describe the three Americans inside the train restaurant, he told the air liaison officer that they were 30 to 35 years old; he stuck to his original description. They were air force noncommissioned officers. The insignia on their sleeves indicated the men were staff sergeants and several inches above the rate was a propeller, but not all three had the propeller. Trainloads of American prisoners of war made this trip through Manchouli into Siberia. They were never seen again.

Based on the Hong Kong report and other information in the possession of Secretary of State John Foster Dulles, Dulles sent a message to Ambassador Charles E. Bohlen in Moscow on April 19, 1954, that read thusly: "This report corroborates previous indications United Nations Command prisoners of war might have been shipped to Siberia during Korean hostilities."

Nearly four decades after the cease-fire that ended fighting on the Korean peninsula, Task Force Russia (TFR) was organized in the summer of 1992 under the auspices of the United States Army to support the American side of the United States-Russian Joint Commission on prisoners of war and missing in action from World War II, Korea and the cold war. There were two elements in the task force, the analysis and administration division in Washington and the research, interview and liaison group in Moscow. One year in, Task Force Russia was put under the Office of the Assistant Secretary of Defense for POW/MIA Affairs, and the Washington branch was renamed the Joint Commission Support Branch (JCSB). The task force was making progress until the Moscow operation was suspended by Russian president Vladimir Putin.

Arguably the most important paper published by the Washington group was the famous 77-page report originally marked for internal use only. Included in the document are subjective evaluations, opinions, and recommendations regarding American prisoners of war and missing in action that "may impact future United States foreign policy decisions." At the time the report was leaked, it had not been "finalized" for public release. The document's executive summary concluded the following:

"United States Korean War prisoners of war were transferred to the Soviet Union and never repatriated."

"This transfer was a highly secret MGB [Ministerstvo Gosudarstvennoy Bezopasnosti – a primary Soviet security organ] program approved by the inner circle of the Stalinist dictatorship."

"The rationale for taking selected prisoners to the USSR was to exploit and counter [the] United States' aircraft technologies; to use them for general intelligence purposes, and it is possible that Stalin, given his positive experience with Axis prisoners of war, viewed [American] prisoners of war as potentially lucrative hostages."

"The range of eyewitness testimony as to the presence of American Korean War prisoners of war in the gulag is so broad and convincing that we cannot dismiss it."

"The Soviet 64th Fighter Aviation Corps which supported the North Korean and Chinese forces in the Korean War had an important intelligence collection mission that included the collection, selection and interrogation of prisoners of war."

"A [Soviet] general staff-based analytical group was assigned to the Far East Military District and conducted extensive interrogations of United States and other United Nations prisoners of war in Khabarovsk. This was confirmed by a distinguished retired Soviet army officer, Colonel Gavril [Ivanovich] Korotkov, who participated in this operation. No prisoners were repatriated who related such an experience."

"Prisoners were moved by various modes of transportation. Large shipments moved through Manchouli and Pos'yet."

"Khabarovsk was the hub of a major interrogation operation directed against United Nations prisoners of war from Korea. Khabarovsk was also a temporary holding and transshipment point for [American] prisoners of war. The MGB controlled these prisoners, but the GRU [Glavnoye Razvedovatel'noye Upravlenie – the Soviet's primary military intelligence organization] was allowed to interrogate them."

"Irkutsk and Novosibirsk were transshipment points, but the Komi Autonomous Soviet Socialist Republic (ASSR) and Perm Oblast were the final destinations of many prisoners of war. Other camps where American prisoners of war were held were the Bashkir ASSR, the Kemerovo and Archangelsk Oblasts, and the Komi-Permyatskiy and Taymyskiy National Okrugs."

"Prisoner of war transfers also included thousands of South Koreans, a fact confirmed by the Soviet general officer, Khan San Kho, who served as the deputy chief of the North Korean MVD [Ministry of Internal Security]."

Korotkov observed that American prisoners of war were kept under the control of the MGB. Military interrogators were generally given only a few hours with the Americans, although they sometimes had up to a few days, depending on the nature and perceived value of the information or source. While the prisoners were at Khabarovsk, the MGB controlled them when they were not being interrogated. Once the process was finished, the prisoners were returned to the control of the MGB, thus Korotkov told American investigators that he had no direct knowledge of the fate of these personnel. Although Korotkov did not know the exact number, he felt that the number of Americans processed through Khabarovsk was "in the hundreds."

None of these developments should have come as a surprise to Washington, not in the 1950s and certainly not when the Joint Commission Support Branch crafted the 77-page report. The CIA published an information report dated July 15, 1952, "Location of Certain Soviet Transit Camps for Prisoners of War from Korea," and an article by Zygmunt Nagorski Jr., in the May 1953 *Esquire*, "Unreported G.I.s in Siberia," had already blown the lid off the issue of Americans left behind in the Soviet Union. Russia had, by far, the largest number of Americans in the basement of any nation in the world and it still does. In addition to the Manchouli transit point, other routes for prisoners transferred to the Soviet

Union were identified by Nagorski, who got his information from two sources inside the MVD and an employee of the Trans-Siberian Railroad. They told him about the prisoner transit point across the North Korean-Soviet border at Pos'yet and the transfers made between November 1951 and April 1952 when ice closed the Pacific coast and the Tatar Straits. Prisoners of war were taken from Pos'yet through Chita by rail to Molotov near Perm. The dates of this operation coincide exactly with the dates for the transfer of prisoners in the Hong Kong report. Another route was by sea when the ice receded.

The 77-page report also referenced something else: it included the joint commission's research into a Soviet MVD one-thousand-page study, published in 1950, that documented the exploitation of foreign prisoners of war. This top secret document, "About Spies, Operative Work with POWs and Internees Taken Prisoner During the Great Patriotic War of the Soviet People, 1941-1945," was, according to Dr. Paul M. Cole in his work on the Soviet's Sharaskha system, a summary that "assesses the methods and results of programs used to exploit foreign prisoners of war on Soviet territory." As part of this exploitation program, Soviet security agencies heavily recruited agents among the country's prisoner of war population who would be activated on their eventual return to their respective homeland. The mission of turncoat prisoners of war – the advantage to the Russians – was to employ them to exact critically important political and economic concessions inside their home country and in postwar Germany and Japan, where new governance meant new leadership.

The Soviet Union had on hand a vast, well practiced, efficiently operating and profitable system for the collection, incarceration and exploitation of prisoners of war by mid 1950. Moscow's foreign prisoner program grew more sophisticated with the outbreak of war in Korea. Soviet state policy toward exploitation of prisoners of war was blatantly contained in the minutes of a September 19, 1952 meeting between Stalin and Chinese foreign minister Chou En-Lai in which Stalin recommended that communists hold back at least twenty percent of United Nations prisoners of war as hostages. This was one of the documents handed over to Ambassador Malcolm Toon, head of the American side of the U.S.-Russian Joint Commission for POW/MIAs, in November 1992 during his Moscow visit.

"Concerning the proposal that both sides temporarily withhold twenty percent of the prisoners of war and that they return all the remaining prisoners of war – the Soviet delegation will not touch this proposal," Stalin told Chou En-Lai, "... it remains in reserve for Mao Tse-tung." From these meeting minutes, the joint commission concluded that large numbers of United Nations prisoners of war, the overwhelming number of whom were soldiers of the Republic of Korea Army (ROKA), were already being secreted away in camps throughout the Soviet Union, a conclusion that was not without documented support.

The essence of the meeting between Stalin and Chou En-Lai was corroborated by that retired senior Soviet officer, Khan San Kho, who had been seconded to the North Korean People's Army, promoted to the rank of lieutenant general, and who was posted as the deputy chief of the North Korean MVD. Khan San Kho stated in November 1992 that he assisted in the transfer of thousands of South Korean prisoners of war into 300 to 400 camps in the Soviet Union, most in the taiga. The taiga is the forested area of Russia and the West Siberian plains below the tundra line that also includes most of the territory east of the Yenisey River and some in Central Asia as well. Khan's testimony demonstrated for the joint commission that the prisoner of war division of the gulag was operating efficiently during the Korean Conflict, absorbing large numbers of United Nations prisoners of war.

Although Khan admitted only to what he knew about the fate of ROKA prisoners of war, his interview strongly suggested the high probability that other United Nations prisoners of war, including Americans, had also been secreted away in the Russian gulag system. Khan's information is corroborated by intelligence, interviews and information discovered by Nagorski and others decades earlier.

Recall, too, the role played by Soviet army colonel Korotkov, who'd served from July 1950 to mid 1954 as part of a general staff-based analytical group. Korotkov reported directly to Marshal Rodion Malinovskiy, then commander in chief, Far East Military District, on developments in tactical and technical intelligence gained from the ongoing war in Korea. Korotkov's political section was responsible for reporting on political information, the morale and psychological well-being of American units engaged in Korea, all information used immediately to support communist propaganda activities and possibly Moscow's refinement of operational and contingency plans. During his August 1992 interview with the joint commission, Korotkov told American investigators that Soviet military specialists had been approved to interrogate U.S. prisoners of war. There were two stages to this process, he told them.

Korotkov explained – in detail – that interrogation of American prisoners of war started in North Korea. "These were conducted at the front," he said, "immediately after prisoners of war had been transferred into North Korea-based Soviet forces. Initial contact focused on gaining operational and tactical intelligence such as order of battle." The second stage was transfer to the Soviet Union. Korotkov wasn't aware of exactly who selected out particular American prisoners of war for transfer to Russia for further interrogation. He wasn't certain what criteria had been used to pick them but he did tell American investigators that it most likely hinged on the prisoner's experience, such as the seniority of field grade officers and above. Two separate groups handled these military interrogations: the Glavnoye Razvedovatel'noye Upravlenie (GRU)-subordinated intelligence group that was interested in detailed tactical and technical intelligence, and the main political directorate-subordinated group, which was interested in political intelligence.

So what happened when the State Department queried the Russians about Korean Conflict prisoners of war? The answer it got back from Moscow would reverberate for decades. A May 12, 1954 Soviet communiqué doused cold water on Washington's hopes to find out more about missing men who'd fought in Korea. "The United States assertion... that American prisoners of war who participated in military actions in Korea [and] have allegedly been transferred to the Soviet Union and at the present time are being kept under Soviet guard is devoid of any foundation whatsoever and is clearly far-fetched," replied an agitated Soviet ministry of foreign affairs, "since there are not and have not been any such persons in the Soviet Union." The Soviet response did two things that would happen repeatedly in the back-and-forth with Moscow and its surrogate states over prisoners of war and men who'd simply gone missing. First, the Kremlin refused to characterize the men as "prisoners of war." Second, it refused to acknowledge their American citizenship. Both of these tactics were later used by Baghdad in the Speicher case.

From the Soviet point of view their patent denial was accurate. From the United States' point of view it was a lie. But Washington ignored Moscow's repeated tutorial – the lessons learned – when it came to the Russians' cache of missing Americans: "We don't recognize the citizenship of American prisoners of war." The Russians still don't and proof of this was promulgated in an April 15, 1991 State Department press advisory in which Washington again requested the Russians "provide us with any additional information on any other U.S. citizens who may have been detained as a result of World War II, the Korean Conflict or the Vietnam War," a request that repeated the mistake of asking for information only about "American" citizens and not "persons" detained in those wars. The State Department repeated the same mistake it had made thirty-seven years before.

The State Department's April 15, 1991 press advisory included the usual verbiage that it was only pursuing Moscow on this matter "in the interest of following every credible lead in providing families of U.S. service members with information about their loved ones." This was another mistake. Referring to the men as "U.S. service members" didn't impress the Russians. They didn't, after all, know anything about "Americans" and certainly not "service members." The third mistake was the advisory's specific request for information about two American aircraft shot down in the early 1950s. The mistake wasn't that State asked about them but that it didn't take the opportunity to ask the Russians any specific questions about unrepatriated prisoners of war from World War II through Vietnam.

Had the State Department provided the Russians with a far more comprehensive and appropriately phrased request the response might have been different. The sincerity of the State Department's declared intention to follow "every credible lead in providing families of U.S. service members with information about their loved ones" meant nothing to Moscow. A January 28, 1990 memorandum from Michael Oksenberg, an American authority on China, to Zbigniew Brzezinski, national security advisor under President Jimmy Carter, exhibited the cynicism and "mindset to debunk" toward unrepatriated prisoners of war that was just as present then as it had been before and remains today. Oksenberg wrote that a letter from Brzezinski was an important step "to indicate that you take recent refugee reports of sightings of live Americans 'seriously.' This is simply good politics; DIA [Defense Intelligence Agency] and State are playing this game, and you should not be the whistleblower. The idea is to say," he advised Brzezinski, "that the President [Carter] is determined to pursue any lead concerning possible live MIAs." To Oksenberg, unrepatriated prisoners of war equated to a well crafted political shell game.

The Executive Branch's disinformation tactics against concerned mothers and fathers, wives and missing men's children, extended out from the White House to include United States senators and congressmen. An illustrative case was found in a December 21, 1953 correspondence sent to Secretary of State John Foster Dulles from Senate Majority Leader Lyndon Baines Johnson regarding a constituent letter Johnson received from Paul Bath of Marshall, Texas, who wrote to him soon after reading a *U.S. News and World Report* December 18, 1953 article "Where are 944 missing GIs?"

Dulles' first reaction was to call Johnson and dispose of the matter by telephone; however, since Bath requested a written reply, Thruston Ballard Morton, assistant secretary of state for congressional relations, was asked to take care of it. Morton drafted and redrafted the letter to Bath four times. But this was only because he was unwilling to provide content that might actually inform Johnson's constituent and he was at odds with a persistent foreign service officer who felt otherwise. Morton shot down the first three drafts until the final letter to Bath was void of all substance. In fact the third draft was so disagreeable to Morton that he typed out two sentences and attached it to the draft and crossed out all other sentences that addressed State's performance on the prisoner of war and missing in action issue. Copies of Morton's four drafts still exist, and they demonstrate just how the State Department artfully acted to mislead Johnson, the future thirty-sixth president of the United States, and then the most powerful member of the Senate.

Morton's final letter to Johnson referencing the letter from Paul Bath read, in part, that he was enclosing copies of a statement that addressed efforts being made "to secure the return of American prisoners of war who *might* [emphasis added] still be in communist custody," which Morton believed would be of assistance to Johnson in his reply to Bath. Morton told Johnson that "it continues to be our [State's] determined purpose to obtain the return of all personnel in communist custody and we will do everything possible to accomplish this objective." He then informed the senator that "with regard to questions as to whether there are military personnel or other United Nations citizens in the custody of the Soviet government, a few of the prisoners of war of other nationalities recently released by the Soviet government have made reports alleging that American citizens are imprisoned in the Soviet Union. All of these reports," he told Johnson, "are being investigated by this Department with the cooperation of other agencies of the government."

Morton's ultimate deception was in the last paragraph.

> You are probably aware that representations which the United States government recently made to the Soviet government resulted in the release in Berlin on December 29 of Homer H. Cox and Leland Towers, two Americans reported by returning [German] prisoner of war as being in Soviet custody. The Department will investigate, as it has done in the past, every report indicating that American citizens are held in the custody of foreign governments.

Recall that Cox and Towers, who played such an important role in the John Noble case, were the same men now referenced in Morton's letter to Johnson. Particularly noteworthy, Morton's final letter was, in stark contrast to his three rejected drafts, lacking the specific and accurate information that would have better informed and warned Johnson of what lay ahead in the unfolding Noble story.

The State Department couldn't get beyond the word "might." But Morton couldn't come to the truth. Three prior drafts of the letter he ultimately sent to Johnson prove that this is fact. Here, too, State took credit for what was going to happen – the release of two Americans – and for investigating "every report indicating that American citizens are held in the custody of foreign governments," but on the other hand State was dismissing any possibility that they were ever there. State's version of the truth was a slippery slope. Aside from claiming the good-news story that it was fighting to get Americans out of the clutches of the Soviet Union, State fibbed, knowing full well that the Soviets had them withering away in prisons and gulags – all without any intention of ever going to get them. The State Department knew that North Korea hadn't returned nearly one thousand prisoners of war as well as an undetermined number of the 8,000 missing in action who had actually been captured alive, held and transferred out of North Korea to Russian and Chinese prisons.

As is always the case with the Russians and Chinese, the real story continues to be a slow rollout. Communist China released a Canadian squadron leader thirteen months after the last United Nations prisoner of war was repatriated by communist forces and three months after Operation Big Switch ended. The American public shouldn't be so surprised when it comes to the improbable and the unthinkable when it concerns their countrymen taken by foreign governments and asymmetrical forces. China quietly repatriated two American prisoners of war in 1973 who'd been captured during the Korean Conflict when Beijing also returned pilot Philip Smith, shot down over the Gulf of Tonkin during the Vietnam Conflict. Smith was held in a Chinese jail in solitary confinement for seven years. During his interrogation sessions the Korean Conflict prisoners of war were paraded in front of him – just to remind him they'd been there for more than two decades and so could he – to encourage his cooperation. Smith later stated that the Chinese told him: "They wouldn't release me, and would hold me like they'd done to these other guys until I recanted." These men, unknown to the American public by name, were held for more than twenty years.

At the end of Operation Big Switch, the United States government did, indeed, leave American prisoners of war behind, men held until the day they died of old age, injury or execution in the custody of Russian, Chinese and North Korean captors. Whether any of these men are alive today is tragically unclear, and an absolute failure of the code that no one is left behind. The fate of more than 8,000 men listed as missing in action is further unclear because they were administratively declared "presumed dead" by their own government and no one was investigating nor was anyone in Washington trying to get them back. No rebuttal was ever made to General Van Fleet, who stated in the fall of 1953 his belief that a large percentage of the 8,000 Americans soldiers listed as missing in Korea were alive and in enemy custody. "A large percentage" implies "into thousands" of American service members who were never repatriated by communist forces at the end of the Korean conflict. Still, there were more revelations to come.

Seven years after Operation Big Switch, there was a foreign service dispatch to the State Department headquarters that contained the names of two American Korean Conflict prisoners of war working in a Soviet phosphorus mine. This cable, dated September 8, 1960, was "sanitized" by the U.S. government and the names of the men, originally included in the communiqué, were redacted. The names were blacked out by State to purportedly protect the abandoned men's privacy rights but history tells us that they probably wouldn't have cared much about privacy rights if it meant they might come home. It was an absurdity to have blacked out the names for this reason, particularly after both soldiers were left alive to die as slave labor. But it could still be worse.

A Soviet gulag was bad. But the real horror came when American Korean Conflict prisoners of war were selected as laboratory specimens for North Korean military drug testing. After they were injected with the drug, observed and documented, the American servicemen were executed. A U.S. report made public on June 20, 1996, but dated April 27, 1992, stated that American air force intelligence first learned of the alleged program in September 1990 while debriefing an unidentified U.S. intelligence source on Soviet techniques in interrogating prisoners of war. "During the Korean War a Soviet and a Czech drug testing program utilized American and other United Nations prisoners of war as laboratory specimens. At the conclusion of the testing program a number of American prisoners of war were executed. The individuals," the report continued, "were executed to preclude public exposure of the information."

The primary objective of the Soviet drug experimentation program, included in the report, was "to develop methods of modifying human behavior and destroying psychological resistance." The report, made public by California Republican congressman Bob Dornan at a House hearing on Korean Conflict prisoner of war and missing in action issues, also had a note attached from Lieutenant General James R. Clapper Jr., then director of the Pentagon's Defense Intelligence Agency (DIA). Clapper wrote that his agency had extensively investigated the information provided by the source, who remained unidentified to the public. "Information uncovered by DIA indicates that up to 'several dozen' unwilling participants in this program may have been executed upon its conclusion in North Korea." The publicly released report didn't reveal what kinds of drugs were used on the American prisoners but Clapper's note suggested that discovery of the experiments may not have been shared by American intelligence with members of Congress.

Clapper further wrote that while intelligence reports concerning American prisoners of war were normally distributed to the State Department, other government agencies and congressional panels, he'd only shared the one that pertained to drug testing with the top two officials of the Department of Defense because he was concerned that "the attached intelligence report could seriously impact ongoing foreign policy activities of the United States government." Clapper's latter statement wasn't any different from those who'd been in his position before nor from men who'd come after him. Clapper described the source of the information as reliable. "The source," Clapper wrote, "was well placed in that he personally saw progress reports on the work in North Korea that were forwarded to top leadership in the Czech Central Committee and Ministry of Defense," thus suggesting that the source was a Czech. "He remains," he continued, "a very sensitive source who has provided reliable information to the U.S. intelligence community for many years." Men just like Clapper's source were deeply embedded in Speicher's case and are protected for the importance of their position and the value of their information.

If this could happen to thousands of American soldiers, sailors and airmen in every war and incursion of the twentieth century, what would stop the White House, the Pentagon and compliant media from hiding the fate of one Gulf War pilot decades later? The answer is – very little. The backstory on this issue, cases similar to, or virtually identical to his own, assured Speicher's fate. This was a fate that sprung from precedence of prior agreement, practice and the path of least resistance. The State Department and Central Intelligence Agency were guilty of all of the aforementioned, and of being party to the cover-up of Speicher's predicament and his death. The Pentagon, DIA, DPMO and Speicher's navy chain of command were guilty of the same but mostly they killed him, slowly and surely, when they left him to die in the Iraqi desert, covered up the evidence that he was alive and wanted to be rescued, and then kept silent that he was captured and still wanted to come home.

The consensus – and sometimes the argument – among those who insist that Scott Speicher was successfully recovered and died in the control of Americans and not the enemy, is that he was in poor physical and mental condition and for that reason was unable to be reunited with his family. Each source said that Speicher's overwhelming health problems were so great that he died "not long" after this return. A source did mention that "he'd [Speicher] been near death at least once." Speicher's rescue and evaluation at an American facility would be a good news story only if those who controlled and quartered him didn't care if Scott Speicher lived to tell his side of the story to the outside world. But that was not the case. His American controllers – Defense Department leadership – wanted the truth about what really happened quashed. Revealed, it would do the OSD, DIA and DPMO too much damage. Their credibility would be destroyed. If a classified rescue is to be part of the conversation in Speicher's case, so must the possibility he would never have been reintroduced to his former life. In this respect, he would have shared the fate of Tommy Gist and those like him about whom Lieutenant General Lacy testified before open and closed sessions of the Senate Select Committee on POW/MIA Affairs.

Most who had much to offer regarding Speicher's rescue had in common the proclivity to speak in the third person to avoid implication of their direct involvement and knowledge. Certainly, explaining Speicher's existence to the American public would be difficult after DIA and DPMO had spent so much effort trying to prove he'd died and was buried under his jet. They also didn't need Scott Speicher recovering to the point that he'd make contact with the outside world, able to tell his side of an ordeal that would have differed dramatically from the one that DIA and DPMO had already sold to the American public. Go back to the shoot-down and imagine Speicher starting from the beginning of what had happened to him. A downed pilot's story is going to be raw and real and no one would be able to question it. Those who'd left him there to die could be expected to pay the consequence of having left him behind. They might even go to jail. So could those who'd concocted the story of his demise and aided and abetted the cover-up of the cover-up.

Returning to the photograph on the cover of this book and in these pages there are aspects of it that look like it was made for some official purpose, perhaps to help locate him or perhaps as part of documentation of Speicher after he had been in American custody for a period of time. None would confirm more than they had to about the photo and where it came from but a member of an intelligence group working on Speicher's case through DIA stated that it wasn't one that the source had seen nor had the group ever specifically used. The image shocked the source whose discomfort level discussing it was palpable.

Having been shown a prior photograph of Speicher – one taken while he was in enemy custody – during a September 28, 2008 meeting with a source, it is clear that Speicher had been an Iraqi prisoner. But in the photograph included here he's not in enemy custody. The subject who so closely guarded Speicher's captivity photo and who was subject to an interview conducted in two parts for over six hours wouldn't allow it out of his control. Though he'd traveled from out of state to the meeting, the source had frequently traveled in and out of the United States, including Southwest, Central and Southeast Asia. According to this source, it was valuable to him and was secured "in a safe place." When pressed, it was made abundantly clear that safe place was "out of the country." He exhibited tradecraft. He'd taken precautions to keep anyone from getting information about the location by cropping the photo to Speicher's face and upper body even though he repeatedly stated that it was taken at Iraq's Hakmiyah Prison. The photo was taken long after Speicher had been taken into Saddam's custody and it showed. Speicher's hair, including a moustache, had touches of gray. There was no smile – not even a little smile – in that picture. He stared back at the camera with a lifeless expression. The "blank" look was disturbing. He was beaten down and haggard and clearly in disbelief that he was still a prisoner. The comparison to the later photo is thus a dramatic one.

The source's photograph wasn't the only one of Speicher in captivity. There were others. After I returned from London in May 2001 the CIA believed that while in Britain I had obtained copies of Speicher's captivity photos purportedly in the possession of British intelligence at Whitehall. I didn't. When a CIA officer tracked down a mutual acquaintance it wasn't to question the existence of the pictures; it was to ask if I intended to publish them in *No One Left Behind*. They already knew about the photographs. But that wasn't the end of it. There was a point where the pictures began to take on a life of their own. They were tangible and out there. Thus it was no surprise that a real one or the source of one would eventually find me.

Looking at Speicher's face in the photo shown on the cover and page 549, it is filled out again and not the gaunt appearance of someone who'd been held in a series of Iraqi prisons, safe houses, spider holes and government buildings to avoid detection. He looks like he's had some rehabilitation. There's that slight smile. Take note that his nose is severely deviated, which it is not in the captivity photograph that I saw. Some would suggest that it was better that he expired in an American facility and not under enemy control. The sources concur that this facility was in Hawaii. They'd also argue that it is inconceivable that there'd be a 200-page forensics report[16] in hand on August 6, 2009 – one that if read without redaction might document Speicher's condition prior to and after his death – because it was already written and required just the right scenario in the desert to put an end to Scott Speicher's story. Thus, too, the all-government team – no outside contractors – were brought in to put the case to bed.

Why take the partial remains back to the Iraqi desert? The story had to fit what DIA and DPMO had always contended happened to Speicher: he died on January 17, 1991, and was buried under his jet. This is the scenario that had been repetitively fed to the media and thus to the American public, and neither would be likely to question the location of Speicher's remains if they were said to have been located at his crash site. Additionally, it would look a lot like what the Iraqis had done to seed the remains of Saudi pilot colonel Mohammed Nazerah at his crash site. Juxtaposing the remains proximal to Speicher's crash site would be easier for the ICRC, international watchdog groups and to any savvy reporter who might question this new "discovery," especially after prior digs in and around the Speicher crash site produced nothing. But recall that they didn't exactly pinpoint the precise location of the crash site for the reburial of these partial remains – it wasn't, in fact, close – and they didn't count on Buddy Harris informing the media that the remains had been moved *at least twice* – a fact documented in the forensics report – before being deposited where they were found.

Endnotes

1. Hess, Pamela, "Saddam was telling truth in missing Gulf War pilot," Associated Press, November 28, 2009. http://www.huffingtonpost.com/2009/11/29/saddam-was-telling-truth-_n_373004.html

2. Gulfnews.com, "DNA tests prove identity of Saudi pilot," September 1, 2001. http://gulfnews.com/news/gulf/uae/general/dna-tests-prove-identity-of-saudi-pilot-1.423991

3. Joseph Frusci telephone interview with Buddy Harris, August 18, 2008.

4. Frusci interview with Harris, Ibid.

5. National Alliance of Families, *Bits 'N' Pieces*, July 12, 2003.

6. Jontz, Sandra, "Friends hold D.C. vigil for downed pilot," *Stars and Stripes*, January 19, 2004.

7. Ibid.

8. Maier, Timothy W. "Secret report adds to mystery," *Insight*, September 3, 2003.

9. Ibid.

10. National Alliance of Families, *Bits 'N' Pieces*, September 12, 2003.

11. DoE contractor e-mail communication with Iraq Survey Group team lead, March 23, 2004.

12. Bob Dussault e-mail correspondence dated August 26, 2012.

13. Gray interview published online by *All POW-MIA InterNetwork*, February 18, 2005.

14. Gera, Vanessa and Randy Herschaft, "AP exclusive: memos show US hushed up Soviet crime," Associated Press, September 10, 2012. http://www.npr.org/templates/story/story.php?storyId=160883505

15. There are more than 73,000 men unaccounted for from World War II.

16. When Minnesota POW/MIA activist Richard Daly received a response to his December 19, 2012 FOIA for Speicher's forensic reports on file with the Armed Forces Medical Examiner System (ARMES) at Dover Air Force Base, Delaware, he got a curious response, one quite different than the claim to this author and including a prior Judge Advocate General investigation that no such document existed in their system. The ARMES FOIA officer Paul R. Stone replied to Daly on January 4, 2013, that while the request documents are government reports – thus admitting here that they exist – "that fact does not affect the release exemption or the HIPPA [*sic*] [Health Insurance Portability and Accountability Act (HIPAA)] privacy protections cited in my December 7, 2012 letter to you. Indeed, that exemption and the privacy protections in place exist precisely because these are government documents." Of the actual forensic reports themselves, Stone stated that there were just two on file. "One is the anthropological report and [the] other is the autopsy report. Both reports are three pages in length each." Stone hoped that this would satisfy Daly's request – it didn't. The HIPAA

privacy protection is applied to those who are treated medically before death and thus treatment information for that individual would remain private. Invoking HIPAA on the Speicher forensic report is more than curious and could well indicate that the sources were correct – that Speicher was repatriated secretly, treated and died in American custody and, to wit, that it might also include Iraqi records of treatment seized with the fall of the Saddam Hussein regime. The bulk of the 200-page forensic report, a document made public vis-à-vis the Buddy Harris January 17, 2011 interview, would include forensic and further sensitive documents already released and discussed herein and more. The fact that Daly got a completely different answer from Stone than me indicates a classic attempt to compartmentalize and selectively release information per requester, hoping that none of them have contact with one another and might compare what they have received from the same government agency, department or source. At the time of this writing there are moves to have the HIPAA cover reduced to two years after death.

Chapter 14

Requiem for a Fighter Pilot

Everything about Scott Speicher comes down to choices and the importance of accountability that has shamefully trailed the nation's POW/MIA issue since its founding. Over the years since Speicher went missing in Iraq there were bad choices made. The worst thing anyone could have done, they did. Most did absolutely nothing. They forgot that a man's life was sacred. They forgot that one life mattered more than a career, more than admitting a mistake was made. Scott Speicher is dead because of it. Those who did this to him will have to live with their choices. Well-meaning politicians learned enough about Speicher to make headlines at his expense. Then they let him go. American intelligence had a failure of imagination. Then they let him go. The press grew tired of chasing a ghost. Then they dropped the story. Following Speicher's trail was just too much work. The public was apathetic. If he wasn't headline news, they weren't interested. When he was, they didn't understand the story. There wasn't a national outcry to go get Speicher. He wasn't at the top of anyone's priority list. Should he have been? Absolutely.

That we lost our moral compass with the Speicher case is no surprise. America's founding fathers knew that morality would face its greatest challenge in this country, where we started with so much enthusiasm for truth and honesty, when faced with the temptations of self-interest and greed. Morality is inextricably tied to our nation's government. But would it last? James Madison wrote that "to suppose that any form of government will secure liberty or happiness without any virtue in the people is a chimerical idea." Certainly this includes respect for the equal rights of every citizen. Rightful government necessarily reflects this proper relationship in its policies and in its dealings with its own citizens and with other nations. Truth and honesty are intimate elements of morality. Thomas Jefferson wrote John Adams in 1823 that "truth being as cheap as error, it is as well to rectify [an error of fact] for our own satisfaction." One mistake left uncorrected would surely lead to one false consequence after another, he'd told Adams in a letter four years earlier.

Thomas Jefferson told us who we'd become. He also told who we should be. In the text of his first inaugural address in 1801, he said: "the essential principles of our government ... form the bright constellation which has gone before us and guided our steps through an age of revolution and reformation. The wisdom of our sages and blood of our heroes have been devoted to their attainment," he said. "They should be the creed of our political faith, the text of [our] civic instruction, the touchstone by which to try the services of those we trust; and should we wander from them in moments of error or of alarm, let us hasten to retrace our steps and to regain the road which alone leads to peace, liberty and safety." We never regained the moral high ground in time to save Scott Speicher. Career self-interest, failure of imagination, and money all played a role in Speicher's demise. These were all predicted long ago. Long before Speicher was born there were thousands of American servicemen who'd faced the same fate. Men who'd become prisoners of war and men who were missing in action. Some knew exactly what fate they'd been dealt. Some knew exactly where men had been taken. But no one did anything then, either, to go get them. Speicher became another name added to a growing list of fighting men who'd been left behind by his country.

There were men who thought he was still alive. But too many of them didn't act on it. This is true, even today, of those who were important to his investigation, men and women who represented the Pentagon and intelligence agencies, including CIA, DIA, NSA and ONI who forsook Speicher to save a security clearance and a career. There were those who worried if they told what they knew – if they tried to help Scott Speicher – that once they'd left government and military service that security clearance wouldn't travel with them to the private sector, where some continue to have lucrative contracts with the Pentagon and intelligence agencies for which they once worked. They'd be ostracized for doing right by him. Examples of this are blatant in the Speicher case. These individuals, without question, lost their moral compass long ago. Scott Speicher's blood is on their hands, not only for the wanton betrayal when he was shot down, but the catastrophic intelligence failure that cloaked his case from day one. The legion that lined up against Speicher embraced a cover-up that made the military a fraudulent and criminal activity – a party to the cabal of officers and "men in clothes" who signed Speicher's death warrant shortly after his shoot down on January 17, 1991. Military officers – active duty and retired – need to be confronted and held accountable for their decisions and their actions. Civilian and military intelligence officers and personnel who were involved in the case – current and retired – need to be confronted and held accountable for their actions. Government appointed and elected officials – active and retired – need to be confronted and held responsible for their role in the death of Scott Speicher.

And what of Buddy Harris. The drawback for Buddy Harris being granted limited-scope top secret clearance during the course of the Speicher investigation is obvious: he was only shown what the Pentagon and intelligence agencies wanted him to see, when they wanted him to see it. After Admiral Arthur took him off the case, Harris' ability to access special compartmentalized information (SCI) on his own was gone. Despite his best effort, there was much more to Speicher's entire case that he was never going to be told by the navy. Once an intelligence agency compartmentalizes information, it can effectively wall it off on a need-to-know basis within its own organization and between other intelligence agencies, even if that other agency has a vested interest in the case. This is what happened with information pertaining to Scott Speicher.

The bottom line here is that no one was ever intended to find out what really happened to Scott Speicher. That senior officer who participated in the decision on the *LaSalle* was willing to bet money on it. He also stated that the family was "paid off" and was purposefully being fed wrong information – a concerted effort to confuse and discredit that has certainly followed the Speicher case. Researcher Joe Frusci concurred after he dug into the case, gathered information and interviewed participants in the investigation, including Buddy Harris and Tony Albano. "One thing I do agree with," Frusci wrote later, "is that Buddy and the family are not telling the right information. Whether they are being lied to or know the truth, but just do not say, Buddy did not tell me all he could."[1] Frusci observed that Harris initially stated the remains dated to four-and-a-half years, "then it was six [years], now [it is] somewhere around five years."[2] Certainly, it is not on the basis of what Harris alone has publicly stated and provided to Frusci during his interviews regarding the partial remains that it is possible to narrow Speicher's time of death. There was corroboration and, ultimately, a photograph provided, that narrowed that time frame further. Thus corroboration and correlation were critical and – in truth – strengthen Harris' statement of "four-and-a-half years" regarding the condition of the remains and the date blood would have last flowed through Scott Speicher's body.

Much of the most valuable intelligence information on his case from the time Speicher was shot down through the time he was "discovered" still alive in the desert in 1994 – a surprise only to those who'd left him to die in the desert three years before – was gathered up from all participatory departments and agencies thus making the ubiquitous "we don't know anything" or "we have nothing" easier to say with a straight face when confronted with a specific question regarding Scott Speicher from his family, Congress or the media. Much of the most valuable information and communication that was in the Speicher file has been pushed to the black, a special access program (SAP) with a code word; some of it has been purposefully erased – all to hide what happened to Scott Speicher from the time he was shot down, to the when, where and how he died. But such a broad effort ultimately falls apart when participants, wrought with guilt and still able to perceive the difference between right and wrong, can't keep the secret that's eaten away at them – for some – more than twenty years. The apologies come first, followed by the truth. Are they scared? Yes. Are they still afraid of retribution? Absolutely. They've broken the cycle of lies and cover-up. Those who've told the truth know that there is no going back once they've talked. They also know that there are more who know what happened, but who will never be courageous enough to talk. But what concerns them most are those who know the truth and still fight so hard to keep it from ever being told to the American public. There's much at stake for those who've come forward and it was not a matter each didn't think about for a long time before they decided to tell what they knew. The guilt they feel is palpable; it is in their voices and it is in the words they've written.

Certainly, there are men and women who should be respected for what they did to speak for and act on behalf of Scott Speicher when they were in a position to do so. Vice Admiral Charles W. "Willy" Moore Jr., then NAVCENT and Fifth Fleet commander and later deputy chief of naval operations for readiness and logistics, said he believed Speicher was still alive when he wrote of him on November 18, 2001. He'd known Speicher very well. Moore was Speicher's weapons training flight instructor in the A-7 Corsair II back in 1981-82. "He is one of the finest young men I have ever served with," Moore observed, "and I have never had the feeling that he is gone [just then]. I often fantasize about how joyous it would be if he were to find his way out of there." He'd worked closely on Speicher's case as Joint Staff J33 (Current Operations). "So I have a keen interest in his whereabouts and welfare," Moore continued. He had seen all the highly classified intelligence on Speicher during his back-to-back Joint Staff tours of duty from 1993 to 1999.

"There are several others, general officers, staff officers, survival instructors and mission planners, who were also involved and knew some of the amazing and shocking events related to this case," said Bob Dussault on January 11, 2002. "I think the evidence the government has to deal with [could have been] responded to in two ways. Look at it, giving [Speicher] the benefit of the doubt: assume he is alive until this is proved otherwise or give the info no credibility and believe Speicher is dead and didn't survive until he walks in the room." He stressed the need for action. "At this stage of the game for me," said Dussault, "I must do the right thing for the person and the right thing for the nation. It is the principle of liberty in its simplest form. We must do it for Scott and all our military personnel or we don't do right by any." It's too late to save Scott Speicher but not the rest. "Leaving a single operator forgotten or totally on their own, when they have been taught to expect allegiance, love and recovery efforts by their own country is wrong."

Barry Hull, Scott's squadron mate, said it's an obligation that is part of the deal from day one. "When I hang my ass out and I go across the border, if I get shot down or something happens to me, I absolutely know, there is no question in my mind, that those snakeaters are coming to get me. Those guys are going to do whatever they have to do to get me." If he had been in Scott Speicher's position, he said he would've thought, "If they in their minds know I'm dead, well, they're probably not going to come get me now. [But] if it's three or four years later and they find out something different," said Hull, "they better get their ass over there. And we had an opportunity to do it and we made a conscious decision not to."

Hull will live with what happened that night over the Iraqi desert for the rest of his life. He thinks often of what he might have done differently to prevent Scott's loss. There's a twinge of guilt that he's never shaken. Of all of Scott Speicher's squadron mates, he's also taken his loss the hardest. "There is not another navy pilot," he said in the fall of 2001, "that if you get five guys together somebody's not going to say something bad about him. Somebody's going to criticize everybody. That's the nature of the job and the mentality, except with Speicher. He was just a great guy all around and it sounds so phony to say that, but it's actually true in this situation. He was probably the best pilot in the squadron because he was just a naturally good pilot."

Everyone who knew him and some who didn't, in their own way, have missed Scott Speicher. "I almost went down to Arlington today," said squadron mate Craig Bertolett as the eleventh anniversary of Scott's disappearance fast approached. He'd done it enough times in the past. "My wife and I invariably reflect on where we were and what we were doing and remember Spike on the evening of January 17." For others, it cuts to the heart of the code they live by and – have ingrained in their hearts.

There is an unspoken obligation in the U.S. military chain of command that they will leave no one behind enemy lines without making every reasonable effort to recover that service member. Among America's elite Special Forces, this guarantee is codified and its message is simple. This code applies in peace and war. "The warriors believed they had a responsibility," said Admiral Stanley Arthur. "You lose one of your own, you go back and find him." Thus the irony of Secretary of Defense William S. Cohen's farewell address at Fort Myer, Virginia, on January 17, 2001, ten years to the day after Scott Speicher was lost over Iraq, was hard to miss. He repeated General William Tecumseh Sherman's words to Ulysses S. Grant. Sherman said to his old friend, "I always knew that if I was in trouble you'd come for me if alive." Chairman of the Joint Chiefs of Staff general Henry H. Shelton had given Cohen a fountain pen with Sherman's words engraved on it. "Mr. Chairman," he said. "I always knew that if I were ever in trouble, that you would always be there for me as you've been for all the men and women who wear our uniform. You are a warrior and you carry the warrior's code not only on your sleeve, but in your soul." No one was there for Scott Speicher and he wore the uniform of his country. Where were the warriors when he needed them? By then they knew he was alive. Where was the warrior's code that said leave no man behind?

Vietnam POW vice admiral James B. Stockdale wrote: "In the end the prisoner learns he can't be hurt and he can't be had as long as he tells the truth and clings to that forgiving hand of the brothers who are becoming his country [his fellow prisoners], his family… What does it all come down to? It does not come down to coping or supplication or hatred or strength beyond the grasp of any normal person. It comes down to comradeship, and it comes down to pride, dignity, an enduring sense of self-worth and to that enigmatic mixture of conscience and egoism called personal honor."[3] Certainty for most of the men who knew what had happened to Scott Speicher, men who also knew where he was and what he'd been put through, was when he walked up to you and touched your face and said, "I'm alive." They'd never admit anything short of this as proof he was alive and wanted to come home. But Scott Speicher beat the odds for years. He left markers on the ground for overhead imagery. He left his initials and dates where he'd been on walls, ceilings and objects that might be found by ground searchers. He left his initials, dates and evader code on the walls of Iraqi prisons, holding facilities and safe houses. He did everything he could to fulfill his promise to come home to Joanne and his children. He'd told her before he left on deployment that he'd be back. "I guarantee it."

Still, he didn't make it home. Scott Speicher embraced and lived the Code of Conduct that, in six brief articles, addresses those situations and decision areas that, to some degree, all military personnel could encounter. This is the code that Speicher continued to employ, to think about and to honor while he was absent from his family, his friends and his countrymen. It includes basic information useful to American prisoners of war in their efforts to survive honorably while resisting their captor's efforts to exploit them to the advantage of the enemy's cause. Such survival and resistance requires varying degrees of knowledge of the meaning of the six articles of the Code of Conduct (CoC). These are the same powerfully worded guiding principles imbued in Admiral Stockdale and that were key to his survival as the senior ranking prisoner of war of the Vietnam conflict. These were the articles that Speicher carried forward into his own bid to survive and come home to his wife and children and they bear repeating, because they mattered to him, just as they should matter to his senior government and military leadership, and to his immediate chain of command who failed to uphold their end of the Code.

Here they are:

Article I:

I am an American, fighting in the forces which guard my country and our way of life. I am prepared to give my life in their defense.

Article I applies to all members of the U.S. military at all times. A member of the armed forces has a duty to support U.S. interests and oppose U.S. enemies regardless of the circumstances, whether located in a combat environment or in captivity. Past experience of captured Americans reveals that honorable survival in captivity requires that a service member possess a high degree of dedication and motivation. Maintaining these qualities requires knowledge of and a strong belief in the following: the advantages of American democratic institutions and concepts; love of and faith in the United States and a conviction that the U.S. cause is just; and faith in and loyalty to fellow prisoners of war. Possessing the dedication and motivation such beliefs and trust foster enables prisoners of war to survive long and stressful periods of captivity, and return to their country and families honorably with self-esteem intact.

Article II:

I will never surrender of my own free will. If in command, I will never surrender the members of my command while they still have the means to resist.

Members of the armed forces may never surrender voluntarily. Even when isolated and no longer able to inflict casualties on the enemy or otherwise defend themselves, it is their duty to evade capture and rejoin the nearest friendly force.

Surrender is the willful act of members of the armed forces turning themselves over to enemy forces when not required by utmost necessity or extremity. Surrender is always dishonorable and never allowed. When there is no chance for meaningful resistance, evasion is impossible, and further fighting would lead to their death with no significant loss to the enemy, members of armed forces should view themselves as "captured" against their will versus a circumstance that is seen as voluntarily "surrendering." They must remember that the capture was dictated by the futility of the situation and overwhelming enemy strengths. In this case, capture is not dishonorable.

The responsibility and authority of a commander never extends to the surrender of command, even if isolated, cut off, or surrounded, while the unit has a reasonable power to resist, break out, or evade to rejoin friendly forces.

Members of the armed forces should understand that when they are cut off, shot down, or otherwise isolated in enemy-controlled territory, they must make every effort to avoid capture – a course of action Scott Speicher took in the Iraqi desert – and that the courses of action available include concealment until recovered by friendly rescue forces [the Bedouins], evasive travel to a friendly or neutral territory, and evasive travel to other pre-briefed areas.

But the service member must also understand that capture does not constitute a dishonorable act if the service member has exhausted all reasonable means of avoiding it and the only alternative is death or serious bodily injury. Scott Speicher understood perfectly and demonstrated that he was capable of staying alive using survival skills while evading, the procedures and techniques of rescue by search and recovery forces, and the procedures for properly using specified evasion destinations.

Article III:

If I am captured I will continue to resist by all means available. I will make every effort to escape and to aid others to escape. I will accept neither parole nor special favors from the enemy.

The misfortune of capture does not lessen the duty of a member of the armed forces to continue resisting enemy exploitation by all means available. Contrary to the Geneva Conventions, enemies whom U.S. forces have engaged since 1949 have regarded the prisoner of war compound as an extension of the battlefield. The prisoner of war must be prepared for this fact.

The enemy has used a variety of tactics to exploit prisoners of war for propaganda purposes or to obtain military information in disregard of the Geneva Conventions. The CoC requires resistance to captor exploitation efforts. In the past, enemies of the United States have used physical and mental harassment, general mistreatment, torture, medical neglect, and political indoctrination against prisoners of war and this continues to be true in the present, including those American service members who hold the status "missing in action."

The enemy has tried to tempt prisoners of war to accept special favors or privileges not given to other prisoners of war in return for statements or information desired by the enemy or for a pledge by the prisoner of war not to attempt escape. Prisoners of war must not seek special privileges or accept special favors at the expense of fellow prisoners of war.

The Geneva Conventions recognize that the regulations of a prisoners country may impose the duty to escape and that prisoners of war may attempt to escape. Under the guidance and supervision of the senior military person and POW organization, POWs must be prepared to take advantage of escape opportunities whenever they arise. In communal detention, the welfare of the POWs who remain behind must be considered. A POW must "think escape," must try to escape if able to do so, and must assist others to escape.

The Geneva Conventions authorize the release of prisoners of war on parole only to the extent authorized by the prisoner of war's country and prohibit compelling a prisoner of war to accept parole. Parole agreements are promises a prisoner of war gives the captor to fulfill stated conditions, such as not to bear arms or not to escape, in consideration of special privileges, such as release from captivity or lessened restraint. The United States does not authorize any military service member to sign or enter into any such parole agreement.

There are several aspects of Article III that service members should understand, including that captivity is a situation involving continuous control by a captor who may attempt to use the prisoner of war as a source of military information, for political purposes, and as a potential subject for political indoctrination. The service member must be familiar with the rights and obligations of both the prisoner of war and the captor under the Geneva Conventions and be aware of the increased significance of resistance should the captor refuse to abide by the provisions of the Geneva Conventions. Be aware that the resistance the Code of Conduct is so focused on captor exploitation efforts because such efforts violate the Geneva Conventions. Thus resistance beyond that identified above subjects the prisoner of war to possible punishment by the captor for order and discipline violations. Certain actions by the prisoner of war can be prosecuted as criminal offenses against the detaining power.

Members of America's armed forces need to be intimately familiar with, and prepared for, the fact that certain countries have reservations to Article 85 of the 1949 Geneva Convention – the Third Geneva Convention – relative to the treatment of prisoners of war. Article 85 offers protection to a prisoner of war convicted of a crime based on facts occurring before capture. Further, the service member should understand that captors from countries that have expressed a reservation to Article 85 often threaten to use their reservation as a basis for adjudging all members of opposing armed forces as "war criminals." As a result, prisoners of war may find themselves accused of being "war criminals" simply because they waged war against these countries before capture. The U.S. government and most other countries do not recognize the validity of this argument.

Ultimately, service members need to know that successful escape by a prisoner of war can compel the enemy to divert forces that might otherwise be fighting, and thus provides the United States valuable information about the enemy and other prisoners of war in captivity, and serves as a positive example to all members of the armed forces. For all captured individuals, an early escape attempt takes advantage of the fact that the initial captors are usually not trained guards, that the security system is relatively lax, and that the prisoner of war is not yet in a debilitated physical condition.

Article IV:

If I become a prisoner of war, I will keep faith with my fellow prisoners. I will give no information or take part in any action which might be harmful to my comrades. If I am senior, I will take command. If not, I will obey the lawful orders of those appointed over me and will back them up in every way.

Officers and noncommissioned officers shall continue to carry out their responsibilities and exercise their authority in captivity. Informing, or any other action detrimental to a fellow prisoner or war, is despicable and is expressly forbidden. Prisoners of war especially must avoid helping the enemy to identify fellow prisoners of war who may have knowledge of, value to the enemy, and who may be made to suffer coercive interrogation. Strong leadership is essential to discipline. Without discipline, camp organization, resistance, and even survival may be impossible. Personal hygiene, camp sanitation, and care of the sick and wounded are critical.

Wherever located – be it a prison or encampment – prisoners of war should organize in a military manner under the senior military POW eligible for command. The senior prisoner of war – officer or enlisted – in the prisoner of war camp or among a group of prisoners of war shall assume command according to rank without regard to military service. The senior prisoner of war cannot evade that responsibility and accountability. When taking command, the senior prisoner of war shall inform the other prisoners of war and shall designate the chain of command.

If the senior prisoner of war is incapacitated, or is otherwise unable to act for any reason, the next senior prisoner of war shall assume command. Every effort shall be made to inform all prisoners of war in the camp – or the group – of the members of the chain of command who shall represent them in dealing with enemy authorities. The responsibility of subordinates to obey the lawful orders of ranking American military personnel remains unchanged in captivity.

United States government and military policy on prisoner of war camp organization requires that the senior military prisoner of war assume command. The Geneva Convention on prisoners of war provides additional guidance to the effect that in prisoner of war camps containing only enlisted personnel, a prisoners' representative shall be elected. Prisoners of war should understand that such an elected representative is regarded by U.S. policy as only a spokesperson for the senior prisoner of war. The prisoners' representative does not have command, unless the prisoners of war elect the senior prisoner of war to be the prisoners' representative. The senior prisoner of war shall assume and retain actual command, covertly if necessary.

Maintaining communications is one of the most important ways that prisoners of war aid one another. Communication breaks down the barriers of isolation that an enemy may attempt to construct and helps strengthen a prisoner of war's will to resist. Each prisoner of war, immediately upon capture, shall try to make contact with fellow prisoners of war by any means available and, thereafter, shall continue to communicate and participate vigorously as part of the prisoner of war organization.

As with other provisions of the Code of Conduct, common sense and the conditions in the prisoner of war camp should determine the way in which the senior prisoner of war and the other prisoners of war structure their organization and carry out their responsibilities. American military personnel should recognize that leadership and obedience to those in command are essential to the discipline required to effect successful organization against captor exploitation. In captivity situations involving two or more prisoners of war, the senior ranking prisoner of war assumes command; all others should obey the orders and abide by the decisions of the senior prisoner of war regardless of differences in military service affiliations. Failure to do so will result in the weakening of organization, a lowering of resistance, and, after repatriation, may result in legal proceedings under the Uniform Code of Military Justice (UCMJ).

Understand that faith, trust, and individual group loyalties have great value in establishing and maintaining an effective prisoner of war organization. Understand that a prisoner of war who voluntarily informs or collaborates with the captor is disloyal to the United States and fellow prisoners of war and, after repatriation, is subject to disciplinary action under the UCMJ for such actions.

Article V:

When questioned, a prisoner of war is required by the Geneva Conventions and the Code of Conduct, and is permitted by the UCMJ, to give name, rank, service number, and date of birth. Under the Geneva Conventions, the enemy has no right to try to force a prisoner of war to provide any additional information. But it is unrealistic to expect a prisoner of war to remain confined for years reciting only name, rank, service number, and date of birth. There are many prisoner of war camp situations in which certain types of conversation with the enemy are permitted. For example, a prisoner of war is allowed, but not required by the Code of Conduct, the UCMJ, or the Geneva Conventions, to fill out a Geneva Conventions "capture card," to write letters home, and to communicate with captors on matters of camp administration and health and welfare.

The senior prisoner of war is required to represent fellow prisoners of war in matters of camp administration, health, welfare, and grievances. The cautionary is this: prisoners of war must constantly bear in mind that the enemy has often viewed them as valuable sources of military information and propaganda that they can use to further their war effort. Accordingly, each prisoner of war must exercise great caution when completing a "capture card," when engaging in authorized communication with the captor, and when writing letters. A prisoner of war must resist, avoid, or evade, even when physically and mentally coerced, all enemy efforts to secure statements or actions that may further the enemy's cause.

Examples of statements or actions prisoners of war should resist include giving oral or written confessions; making propaganda recordings and broadcast appeals to other prisoners of war to comply with improper captor demands; appealing for U.S. surrender or parole; engaging in self-criticisms; and providing oral or written statements or communications on behalf of the enemy or harmful to the United States, its allies, the armed forces, or other prisoners of war. Captors have used prisoners of war answers to questions of a personal nature, questionnaires, or personal history to create improper statements such as those listed above.

A POW should recognize the enemy might use any confession or statement as part of a false accusation that the captive is a war criminal rather than a prisoner of war. Moreover, certain countries have made reservations to the Geneva Conventions in which they assert that a war criminal conviction has the effect of depriving the convicted individual of prisoner of war status. These countries may assert that the POW is removed from protection and the right to repatriation is thus revoked until the individual serves a prison sentence.

If a prisoner of war finds that, under intense coercion, he unwillingly or accidentally discloses unauthorized information, the service member should attempt to recover and resist with a fresh line of mental defense. Prisoner of war experience has shown that although enemy interrogation sessions may be harsh and cruel, it is usually possible to resist, if there is a will to resist. The best way for a prisoner of war to keep faith with the United States, fellow prisoners of war, and oneself is to provide the enemy with as little information as possible.

Article VI:

I will never forget that I am an American, fighting for freedom, responsible for my actions, and dedicated to the principles which made my country free. I will trust in my God and in the United States of America.

A member of the armed forces remains responsible for personal actions at all times. Article VI is designed to assist members of the armed forces to fulfill their responsibilities and survive captivity with honor. The Code of Conduct does not conflict with the UCMJ, which continues to apply to each military member during captivity or other hostile detention. Failure to adhere to the Code of Conduct may subject service members to applicable disposition under the UCMJ.

When repatriated, prisoners of war can expect their actions to be subject to review, both as to circumstances of capture and as to conduct during detention. The purpose of such review is to recognize meritorious performance and, if necessary, investigate any allegations of misconduct. Such reviews are conducted with due regard for the rights of the individual and consideration for the conditions of captivity.

A member of the armed forces who is captured has a continuing obligation to resist all attempts at indoctrination and remain loyal to the United States. The life of a prisoner of war may be very hard. Prisoners of war who stand firm and united against enemy pressures aid one another immeasurably in surviving the ordeal. Failure to follow the guidance of the Code of Conduct may result in subsequent disposition under the UCMJ. Every member of the armed forces of the United States may be held legally accountable for personal actions while detained.

As prescribed in federal law, it is the responsibility of the U.S. government and his military chain of command to take care of both the prisoner of war and dependents and that pay and allowances, eligibility and procedures for promotion, and benefits for dependents continue while the prisoner of war is detained even if the enemy does not report the service member as being a prisoner of war and his or her status reflects missing in action. Thus it is important for all members of the U.S. armed forces to have their personal affairs and family matters – pay, powers of attorney, wills, debt payments, and children's education – kept current through discussion, counseling and filing legal documents before being exposed to risk of capture.

So why does the American armed forces maintain this Code of Conduct – one written so strongly in the language of prisoner of war as a legal status – if there is no longer a prisoner of war designation according to Department of Defense Directive 1300.18? Ask just about any member of the U.S. armed forces about the Code of Conduct and they know at least a little bit about it – if not a lot – depending on their service and what job they do. The Code is a guide that, if followed, can help the service member stay focused on the principles spelled out in each article. But it is also a two-way street that must be honored by the highest level of the U.S. government from the president of the United States as commander in chief to the missing man's chain of command. Scott Speicher is a case in point. The failure to honor the Code after his shoot-down and to do what was necessary and right to go get him was a failure of leadership but also a crime. They who were responsible for and made the conscious decision that no one was ever going to know what happened to Scott Speicher are party to the Code of Conduct and subject to the articles spelled out for members of the armed forces. No code works without being mutually supported. But it goes off the rails when it is put aside to hide a wrong.

The spirit of the Code continues once the prisoner of war comes home. What should an American prisoner of war do if he returns home and knows that another prisoner of war was last seen alive and had been taken, removed suddenly from the group, and didn't make it home? The answer is obviously to report the man's last known status when the repatriated prisoner of war returns home. This was done successfully by Vietnam POW returnees who had such information. The fact is, this was the number one topic on each Operation Homecoming debriefers' checklist. Hundreds of stories and names were recovered in these sessions and reports gathered about men who were seen and heard from but who abruptly disappeared and never made it back. There were other stories, too, about men who never showed up in North Vietnamese prisons but should have. These scenarios aren't unique to the Vietnam Conflict. These stories continue today.

What happens when the returnee finds out that his country does nothing with the information he's provided about a man who didn't make it home? What is the point of the Code of Conduct if the United States does little to find and recover the service member it left behind? How should a returnee respond? How does the repatriated prisoner of war continue to live by the Code and have honor after the war is done knowing that someone just like him is still there? Does he continue to keep faith with his countryman? To continue to pursue and help him? The spirit of the Code lives until right is done for all. The government fails to achieve honor and fails to live up to the Code if it doesn't go after the men it leaves behind. Taking the easy road isn't the way to achieve honor. Honor comes at a price and it comes because someone chooses to do the right thing. Keeping faith goes both ways and that's where Scott Speicher didn't get the support he needed.

The Code the military person is supposed to follow in wartime is also a Code for his country to follow at all times – until all missing are brought home, dead or alive. This is what the Code truly means about having faith in your fellow military member when the worst happens – as it did for Scott Speicher – and it includes never giving up on those who are missing and may have been secreted away to imprisonment in another country, one far from where he was originally captured.

If soldiers live by the Code, they also don't do the math when it comes down to getting back one of their own – alive or dead. Certainly, it's no coincidence that the most elite U.S. forces – the U.S. Army Rangers, the U.S. Navy SEALs and the U.S. Marine Corps – have their own code when it comes to leaving no man behind. Maybe they know a thing or two about what it means to honor their own and bring him home to his family one. Perhaps they just know what they'd want if they were ever in the same jam. "Maybe they know something the bookkeepers like [Secretary of Defense] Robert McNamara [in Vietnam], so brilliant with numbers, never did," observed a commentary in the March 8, 2002 *Wall Street Journal*. "That if an officer wants his men to take his talk of brotherhood seriously, he'd better show them that he takes it seriously himself. And he's not willing to risk lives to collect his dead, where does he draw the line? With a man he thinks is probably already dead? With a wounded one who likely won't live yet is holding up the others? With one who might die?"

When air force fighter pilot captain Scott O'Grady was shot down on June 2, 1995, by a Bosnian Serb SA-6, he ejected from his stricken F-16C Falcon over hostile territory. This became known in some circles as the Mrkonjić Grad incident. But to O'Grady, who'd been patrolling the no-fly zone, doing his job, it was life or death. He evaded capture for six days and was rescued on June 8 by U.S. Marines of the 3rd Battalion 8th Marines, 24th Marine Expeditionary Unit based on the USS *Kearsarge* (LHD-3). The lives of more than four dozen people were put at risk to rescue one pilot.

The *Wall Street Journal* mentioned what happened, albeit briefly, when it observed "the terrible beauty underscored by the return home"...of the body of Aviation Boatswain's Mate, Handler, First Class (ABH1) (SEAL) Neil Roberts and the six other American soldiers who'd given their lives trying to recover his body from near where he'd died, atop Takur Ghar mountain, Afghanistan. For the U.S. side, the battle proved the deadliest entanglement of Operation Anaconda, an effort early in the war in Afghanistan to rout Taliban forces from the Shahi-Kot Valley and Arma Mountains.

"Although I sacrificed personal freedom and many other things, I got just as much as I gave," he wrote his wife in an "open in the event of my death" letter. My time in the Teams [SEAL teams] was special," Neil Roberts, just 32, wrote. Trying to assuage what he knew would be her grief, he told her, "For all the times I was cold, wet, tired, sore, scared, hungry and angry, I had a blast."

To his last action, Petty Officer First Class Roberts was true to his SEAL ethos and to the unconditional commitment he made to the navy when he enlisted. His moment of truth came when he was utterly alone, surrounded by a ruthless enemy deep in hostile territory and undoubtedly knew there was no chance of escape or rescue. Never forget that it is sailors just like Petty Officer Roberts and his brother SEAL team members who continue to serve today.

"All the times spent in the company of my teammates was when I felt the closest to the men I had the privilege to work with," Roberts wrote in the letter to his wife. "I loved being a SEAL. If I died doing something for the Teams, then I died doing what made me happy. Very few people have the luxury of that."

No commander, we are often reminded, can promise to bring all his men back alive but he can give them his word that no one will be left behind. Joe Galloway, the war reporter who chronicled the landmark 1965 Battle of Ia Drang, the first major battle between regulars of the United States Army and regulars of the People's Army of Vietnam of North Vietnam (PAVN/NVA) during the Vietnam Conflict, and who later coauthored the critically acclaimed 1992 book *We Were Soldiers Once... and Young* with Lieutenant General Harold G. "Hal" Moore, would observe later that perhaps there are two parts to this Code: "Anyone can see what it costs. But maybe you have to be a soldier to understand what it's worth."[4]

Endnotes

1. Joe Frusci e-mail correspondence dated July 1, 2010.

2. Ibid.

3. This was the dedication Admiral Stockdale wrote for the SSC on POW/MIA Affairs' January 13, 1993 report.

4. *Wall Street Journal*, "They were soldiers," March 8, 2002.

Afterword

Those who knew I was writing this story hoped that I would get to tell it in full. They hoped that all the information and experience that they'd shared with me and that I had researched, dug up, resurrected, vetted and lived would end up in these pages. Lawrence R. Gardella, another man left *alive* to die by the United States in another time and place in American history, a man whose true story of survival, escape and redemption inspired this afterword to the Speicher story, wrote to his audience at the end of his book *Sing a Song to Jenny Next*[1], that he didn't have all the answers. Not all the questions you have after reading the long overdue ending to Scott Speicher's story can be answered either.

Gardella's words left a powerful, lasting impression on me. He cautioned what I will echo here. But for some of your questions, if I gave the answer, it would endanger the lives of prisoners of war and missing in action still out there, waiting to come home. These are the individuals to whom I owe my faith, loyalty and devotion. I owe as much to those, like me, who have never broken faith with the warfighter. From them I learned my craft. From them I know that I am not alone in trying to put the pieces together. But answers come at a price. In writing this book I hope you begin to understand that cost. I hope you will know, once and for all, that we have asked more than the full measure of devotion of Scott Speicher and all the men and women like him, those who came before and those sure to follow.

When I first took an oath to my country, now a quarter-century ago, I also made a promise to myself to be honest and true to the men and women with whom I served. They are my family. I had no idea when I started down this road that this promise would evolve to a sacred trust with the many missing Americans left behind on the field of battle. Do I break this promise by telling Scott's story? Do I break it by telling the collective story of America's prisoners of war and missing in action? No. The government that sent them to fight on foreign soil and left them behind did that long ago. But in the shadow of broken promises I found good people, professionals whose life's work, like mine, is committed to bringing them home.

I cannot tell you what the outcome will be for all the unaccounted-for men and women – military and civilian – I have come to know through their files, photographs, families and friends. I can tell you that there are men, our countrymen, who know where they are, how they are and why they are still held captive. These are America's dirty secrets. Secrets are easier to keep with support from determined enemies, acquiescent media and an apathetic public. Only God knows the rest, the stories of those whose mortal bodies have given way, their souls taken rest in faraway lands. There is not a day that passes that I do not think about one, if not all, the men whose lives touched mine and whose stories stand beside Scott Speicher's in this narrative.

There is something else, something you should all know: secrets that end up costing a man his life are the hardest to keep. The guilt and the pain that comes from it are indescribable to those forced to live with the burden of what they know. When I interviewed, spoke to and provided counsel to those who tried to help Scott Speicher, men and women who provided valuable information, context and eyewitness testimony, I always thanked them on Scott's behalf. To more than one of them this expression of thanks was gut wrenching. "If I were Scott I wouldn't thank any of us who stood by and did nothing," said a member of the evaluation team that convened immediately after his shoot down. This was the same group of military officers and "men in clothes" that began the cover-up that sealed Scott Speicher's fate. "This thing cost a good man years of suffering and eventually his life, and it cost a wife her husband and children their father; there is no thank you or forgiveness for such a thing." Pausing, he continued: "My motives aren't pure, at best I'm trying to extinguish my own guilt; what's done cannot be undone... I never spoke a word to anyone until ... the guilt caught up with me and it was far too late. I will never be able to make up for the decision I made to forget and move along. I just try to honor him [Scott Speicher] by being a good father, grandfather, husband, friend and countryman. Thank you so much for taking up this fight for those of us who wouldn't."

When I think about what could have been for Scott Speicher, I come back to the hopeful comment Carlos Johnson made. "America has some great Americans in it. But it just doesn't realize it yet." In death as in life, Scott Speicher *is* a great American. He was supported by some great Americans, men and women who never broke faith with him and tried desperately to get him home. "The naval service and the nation must 'keep the promise' with those brave individuals who dedicate themselves to 'duty, honor, country,'" said Craig Bertolett. "Only by doing so will we be worthy of future selfless service."

Endnotes

1. Gardella, Lawrence. *Sing a Song to Jenny Next*. New York: Dutton, 1981.

Author's Note

Scott Speicher's story has been a twenty-year journey. Certainly, there was the constant reminder of the man himself – the one who wanted to come home – and at the end there was the vacant, painful sense of loss that he couldn't be saved. If I never write another book, the work that went into the pursuit and telling of his story will have been enough. Scott Speicher matters and because he is alive in these pages, he is forever part of the conversation. What happened to him should never be allowed to happen again.

Throughout this narrative you have read about the role of the Falcon Hunter and that of additional unnamed – though well-described sources – who informed and supported the telling of Scott Speicher's story. Those who asked for confidentiality and those who must have it to keep them safe were and are deserving of this protection. While it is always preferable to be able to use the name of the source, there are circumstances that warrant honoring anonymity. A case in point is the Falcon Hunter. Exposing him by name could possibly cause him – and his family – harm. More than that, it is my ethical obligation to withhold the identity of a living covert CIA or intelligence source.

The Falcon Hunter's name and significant role and position of influence in his home country of Qatar, and also Saudi Arabia, most of Southwest Asia, and the United States is known to me. The Falcon Hunter's role as a critical informant and operator reference Scott's case was confirmed by at least six persons closely associated with and who had direct knowledge of his activity. Not providing his identity or those of similarly important informants in no way diminishes the case made on Scott's behalf. Information provided by these sources has been corroborated and confidentiality – and their trust in me to keep it – is intact.

Glossary

A	
AA-6 Acrid/R-40	Russian-made long-range air-to-air missile
ADS	Air defense system
AFIP	Armed Forces Institute of Pathology
AFOSI	Air Force Office of Special Investigations
AIM-7M	Sparrow missile
AIM-9M-2, -4	Sidewinder missile
ALSS	Aviation life support system
AMHS	Automated message handling system
AMRAAM	Advanced medium range air-to-air missile
AMSC	Senior chief aviation structural mechanic
AOCS	Aviation Officers' Candidate School
AOR	Area of responsibility
APC	Armored personnel carrier
ARCENT	Army Central Command
ASSR	Autonomous Soviet Socialist Republic
ATO	Air tasking order
AWACS	Airborne warning and control system
AWOL	Absent without leave
B	
BIT	built-in test
BLUF	bottom line up front
BuNo	U.S. Navy aircraft bureau number
BUPERS	Bureau of Naval Personnel
BVR	beyond visual range
C	
CACO	casualty assistance calls officer
CAG	carrier air wing commander
CAP	combat air patrol
CDC	Centers for Disease Control
CDR	U.S. Navy commander
CENTAF	Central Command Air Force Commander
CENTCOM	U.S. Central Command
CI	counterintelligence
CIA	Central Intelligence Agency
CILHI	U.S. Army Central Identification Laboratory in Hawaii
CLC	command launch computer
CNN	Cable News Network

CNO	Chief of Naval Operations
COMINT	communications intelligence
COMLATWING	commander light attack wing
CSAR	combat search and rescue
CSG	combat support group
CTAPS	Contingency Tactical Action Planning System
CTF	combined task force
CTG	combined task group
CVIC	carrier intelligence center
CVW	carrier air wing

D

DCAG	deputy carrier air wing commander
DCI	Director of Central Intelligence
DIOR	Directorate for Information Operations and Reports
DDI	Director of Defense Intelligence; duty director of intelligence; digital display indicator
DFC	Distinguished Flying Cross
DIA	Defense Intelligence Agency
DL	deputy lieutenant; a British county official
DMZ	demilitarized zone
DNA	deoxyribonucleic acid
DoD	Department of Defense
DoD POW/MIA Office	Department of Defense Prisoner of War/Missing in Action Office
DPMO	Defense Prisoner of War/Missing Personnel Office
DSO	Distinguished Service Order
DSU	data storage unit
DUSTWUN	Duty Status Whereabouts Unknown

E

E & E	escape and evasion
EID	electronic identification
ELINT	electronic intelligence
ELT	electronic transponder

F

FAA	Federal Aviation Administration
FBI	Federal Bureau of Investigation
FOD	foreign object debris
FOIA	Freedom of Information Act
FSU	Florida State University

G

G2	U.S. Army military intelligence
G5	U.S. Army civil affairs
GCC	Gulf Cooperation Council
GRU	Glavnoye Razvedovatel'noye Upravlenie

GTAS	ground-to-air signal
H	
HARM	high-speed anti-radiation missile
HAZMAT	hazardous material
HEI	high explosive incendiary
HET	heavy equipment transport
HF	high frequency
HUD	head-up display
HUMINT	human intelligence
HVD	high-value definition
I	
IADS	integrated air defense system
ICRC	International Committee of the Red Cross
ID	infantry division
IFF	identify friend or foe
IFV	Infantry fighting vehicle
IIR	intelligence information report
INC	Iraqi National Congress
INDICT	A London-based human rights organization
IPB	intelligence preparation of the battlefield
IQAF	Iraqi Air Force
IRNA	Islamic Republic News Agency
ISG	Iraq Survey Group
ISO	Iraq Survey Office
J	
J2	intelligence directorate of a joint staff
J3	operations directorate of a joint staff
JAG	Judge Advocate General
JCS	Joint Chiefs of Staff
JCSD	Joint Commission Support Directorate
JCS/JSOC	Joint Chiefs of Staff/Joint Special Operations Command
JFACC	Joint Force Air Component Commander
JMAO	Joint Mortuary Affairs Office
JPC	Joint Pathology Center
JPRA	Joint Personnel Recovery Agency
JRCC	Joint Rescue Coordination Center
JSI-3	Chief Asia division for counterintelligence
J-STARS	Joint surveillance and target attack radar system
JSOC	Joint Special Operations Command
JSOTF	Joint Special Operations Task Force
JSSA	Joint Services Survival, Evasion, Resistance, and Escape (SERE) Agency
JTF-SWA	Joint Task Force-Southwest Asia
JTIDS	Joint Tactical Information Distribution System

K	
KBE	Knight Commander of the Order of the British Empire
KCB	Knight Commander of the Order of the Bath
KFIA	King Fahd International Airport
KIA	killed ın action
KIA-BNR	killed in action, body not recovered
KKMC FOL	King Khalid Military City Forward Operating Location
KTO	Kuwait theater of operations
L	
LSO	landing signal officer
Lt. Col.	U.S. Air Force lieutenant colonel
Lt. Comdr./LCDR	U.S. Navy lieutenant commander
LCOL	U.S. Army lieutenant colonel
LtCOL	U.S. Marine Corps lieutenant colonel
LT	U.S. Navy lieutenant
LZ	landing zone
M	
MAW	Marine Air Wing
MACP	Mortuary Affairs Collection Point
MC	Military Cross
MERIP	Middle East Research and Information Project
MGB	Ministerstvo Gosudarstvennoy Bezopasnosti; Soviet Ministry of Security
MAJ	U.S. Air Force, Army or Marine Corps major
MIA	missing in action
MNF-W	Multi-National Force-West
MSP	maintenance status panel
mtDNA	mitochondrial DNA
MVD	Ministerstvo Vnutrennikh Del; Soviet Ministry of Internal Affairs
MWSS	Marine Wing Support Squadron
N	
NATOPS	Naval Air Training and Operating Procedures Standardization Program
NAV	navigation display
NAVCENT	U.S. Naval Forces Central Command
NVDRS	National Violent Death Reporting System
NAVSAFECEN	U.S. Naval Safety Center
NAWC	U.S. Naval Air Warfare Center
NAWCWD	U.S. Naval Air Warfare Center Weapons Division
NBC	nuclear, biological and chemical
NCA	National Command Authority
NCHS	National Center for Health Statistics
NIMA	National Imagery and Mapping Agency

NKVD	Narodnyy Komissariat Vnutrennikh Del; People's Commissariat for Internal Affairs
NPIC	National Photographic Interpretation Center
NRCC	U.S. Naval Forces Central Command Rescue Coordination Center
NSA	National Security Agency
NSC	National Security Council
NSWC	Naval Strike Warfare Center
NTCSA	Navy Tactical Command Systems Afloat
nucDNA	nuclear DNA
NVGs	night vision goggles

O

O-5	U.S. Navy commander; U.S. Air Force, Army, Marine Corps lieutenant colonel
O-6	U.S. Navy captain; U.S. Air Force, Army, Marine Corps colonel
OIA	Office of Imagery Analysis
ONI	Office of Naval Intelligence
OSD	Office of the Secretary of Defense

P

PACAF	Pacific Air Forces
PCR	polymerase chain reaction
PID	positive identification
PIREPS	pilot reports
PJCC	provincial joint coordination center
PKIA	probable killed in action
POW	prisoner of war
POW/MIA	Department of Defense Special Office for Prisoners of War and Missing in Action
PRC	People's Republic of China
PRD	Personnel Recovery Division
PSYOP	psychological operations

R

RAOC	rear area operations center
RHAW	radar homing and warning
RIO	radar intercept officer
ROE	rules of engagement
ROI	Republic of Iraq
ROKA	Republic of Korea Army
ROM	read-only memory
RWR	radar warning receiver

S

SA-6 Gainful	two stage, solid-fuel, low-altitude SAM
SAM	surface-to-air missile

SAS	British Special Air Service
SCIF	special compartmentalized information facility
SCIRI	Supreme Council for Islamic Revolution in Iraq
SCUD	short-range ballistic missile
SDC	signal data computer
SEAD	suppression of enemy air defenses
SECDEF	Secretary of Defense
SECNAV	Secretary of the Navy
SERE	Survival, Evasion, Resistance, and Escape
SIGINT	signals intelligence
SITREP	situational report
SNCO	senior noncommissioned officer
SNORT	Supersonic Naval Ordnance Research Track
SOCCENT	Special Operations Component, U.S. Central Command
SOCCENT J2	Special Operations Component, U.S. Central Command Intelligence
SOCCENT J3	Special Operations Component, U.S. Central Command Operations
SPC	U.S. Army specialist
SPEAR	Strike Projection Evaluation and Anti-Air Warfare Research
SPECWAR	special warfare
SPINS	special instructions
SSCI	U.S. Senate Select Committee on Intelligence
SSE	sensitive site exploitation

T

TADIL-A	Tactical Digital Information Link-Airborne
TD	target designator
TDD	target detecting device
TFR	Task Force Russia
TFW	U.S. Air Force Tactical Fighter Wing
TOO	target of opportunity
TOT	time on target

U

UHF	ultra-high frequency
UMCJ	Uniform Code of Military Justice
UN	United Nations
UNMOVIC	United Nations Monitoring, Verification and Inspection Commission
UNSC	United Nations Security Council
UNSCOM	United Nations Special Commission
USAR	U.S. Army Reserve
USSR	Union of Soviet Socialist Republics

V

VA	U.S. Navy attack squadron

VAW	U.S. Navy carrier airborne early warning squadron
VF	U.S. Navy fighter squadron
VFA	U.S. Navy strike fighter squadron
VMFA	U.S. Marine Corps strike fighter squadron
VT	U.S. Navy training squadron
VX	U.S. Navy experimental squadron
VX	V-series human-made chemical warfare agent classified as a nerve agent; more toxic than sarin gas

W

WHS	Washington Headquarters Services

Select Bibliography

Primary Sources

Acting Assistant Chief of Staff (G-2). Memorandum. "Alleged confinement of American officers and soldiers in Russian prisons," November 12, 1930.

Acting U.S. Secretary of State. Telegram Number 3936, April 20, 1945. The telegram was to Lord Halifax.

—. Telegram Number 3923, April 20, 1945. To Lord Halifax.

Allied Supreme Command U.S. Chief of Staff General George C. Marshall Order WARX-58751, March 26, 1945. This order was issued to the U.S. Military Mission Moscow and other European commands.

Central Intelligence Agency. Cable Number CILO-00167-75. "The responsibility of the Democratic Republic of Vietnam Intelligence and Security services in the exploitation of American prisoners of war," 17 November 1975.

Commander, Naval Safety Center. Memorandum. "DPMO/CILHI Aircraft Mishap Investigation F/A-18C BUNO 163470," February 15, 1996. To Casualty Identification Laboratory Hawaii (CILHI) and DPMO.

Congressional Record. Transcripts related to the Congressional assent to the use of force in Iraq, October 9, 2002 (Senate), pages S10205-S10208. Available from the *Congressional Record Online* via Government Printing Office DOCID:cr09oc02-79.

Congressional Research Service. Memorandum. "Published Cold War shoot down incidents involving U.S. military aircraft resulting in U.S. casualties," July 1992.

Department of Defense. "Personnel recovery strategic communication guidance," January 30, 2008.

—. "Department of Defense strategy to recover and account for missing personnel," October 16, 2006.

Deputy Secretary of Defense. Memorandum. "Implementation of the Personnel Recovery Strategic Communication Guidance," March 4, 2008.

Donald R. Heath, deputy to Robert Daniel Murphy. Memorandum. "Overland exchange of ex-prisoners of war and displaced persons liberated all Allied Expeditionary Force and the Red Army," June 1, 1945. The communiqué was to the U.S. secretary of state.

Headquarters Communication Zone European Theater of Operations U.S. Army Paris, France (Major General J. E. Hull) Order, April 20, 1945. The order was sent to the commanding general of the Mediterranean theater of operations.

Iraq Survey Group (ISG). Statement for the Record. Brigadier General Joseph J. McMenamin, commander, ISG, October 2004.

Joint Commission Support Branch (Research and Analysis Division). Working papers. "The transfer of U.S. Korean War POWs to the Soviet Union," August 26, 1993.

Joint Commission Support Directorate, Defense POW/Missing Personnel Office, "The Gulag Study," Fifth Edition, February 11, 2005.

Joint ICRC-Iraqi recovery team anthropologist. Memorandum. "Search and Recovery Report, 41/CIL/96, An F/A-18 Aircraft Crash Site in the Vicinity of Tulul ad al-Dulaym, Wadi Thumayl, Republic of Iraq, 10-15 December 1995," March 19, 1996. To Commander, Casualty Identification Laboratory Hawaii (CILHI).

Letter from U.S. government to Mr. Huckleberry, evaluating the affidavit taken by the U.S. Justice Department, November 8, 1930.

Letter in files of Committee to Acting Secretary of State Frank L. Polk from the U.S. Secretary of War, dated May 12, 1919, acknowledging receipt of April 28, 1919, letter regarding negotiations with Bolshevik government in Russia for the exchange of Allied prisoners, which also referred to Cable Number 230 from the military attaché in Archangel, Russia.

Major General John R. Deane. Letter to Lieutenant General K. D. Golubev, Red Army, Soviet assistant administrator for repatriation, June 20, 1945. Deane was commanding general, U.S. Military Mission Moscow.

Major General R. W. Barker. Memorandum. "Report on conference with Russian officials relative to repatriation of prisoners of war and displaced persons," May 23, 1945.

Military Attaché Archangel Telegram Number 2045-297, February 4, 1919. The telegram was sent to military intelligence.

Multi-National Force-Iraq (MNF-I) CJ3 Personnel Recovery Division (PRD) PRD SSE for Human Remains, August 1, 2009. Subject: Captain (USN) Michael Scott Speicher, (PR-05-516) SSE for Human Remains in MNF-W, 22-29 July 2009.

Naval Air Warfare Center (NAWC) Weapons Division, China Lake. Report. "Investigation of aviation life support system equipment recovered near F/A-18 BUNO 163470, crash site in the western region of Iraq," February 26, 1996. To Casualty Identification Laboratory Hawaii (CILHI) and DPMO.

NOAA Satellite and Information Service/National Climatic Data Center (NCDC). Climate of Iraq. http://www.ncdc.noaa.gov/oa/climate/afghan/iraq-narrative.html

Office of Strategic Services (OSS). Report Number EES/18645/1/22, marked "U.S.S.R.-General."

Office of Strategic Services-Central Intelligence Group (OSS-CIG). Secret Report Number 49584. "U.S.S.R. POW and internee camp near Tambov, April-May 1945.

Office of the Assistant Secretary of Defense, International Security Affairs. Memorandum. "Task Force Russia Operational Priorities," September 10, 1992.

Office of the Secretary, U.S. Department of the Navy. Memorandum for the Record. "Captain Michael Scott Speicher," October 11, 2002.

Office of U.S. Congressman Randy Forbes. Press Release. "Forbes calls search for Lt. Comdr. Speicher, Gulf War's only MIA," March 14, 2002.

Office of U.S. Senator Ben Nighthorse Campbell. Press Release. "Bush signs Campbell's POW/MIA bill into law," October 30, 2002.

Office of U.S. Senator Bill Nelson. Press Release. "Pentagon completes first report on missing Navy pilot," March 28, 2003.

Office of U.S. Senator Bob Smith. Press Release. "Smith to support President's Iraq resolution," October 3, 2002.

Office of U.S. Senator Pat Roberts. Press Release. "Pentagon accepts Senator Roberts' plea to change status of missing Gulf War pilot," October 11, 2002.

—. Press Release. "Senator Roberts requests meeting with Iraq on fate of missing Gulf War pilot," January 6, 2003.

—. Press Release. "Republican members of intelligence committee officially elect Senator Roberts as chairman," January 7, 2003.

Office of White House Press Secretary. Transcript of Press Conference. Briefer, Scott McClellan, May 15, 2003.

Premier Josef V. Stalin Personal and Secret Cable, March 22, 1945. Stalin's cable was sent to President Franklin Delano Roosevelt.

President Franklin Delano Roosevelt Cable, March 18, 1945. The cable was sent to Soviet Marshal Josef V. Stalin.

SHAEF Main (Tedder) Cable Number S-94080, June 29, 1945. The cable was to AGWAR.

SHAEF Main SCARF (Eisenhower) Secret Routine Cable Number S-91662, June 19, 1945. The cable was sent to U.S. Military Mission Moscow.

SHAEF Mission France Secret Routine Cable Number MF-14427, May 30, 1945. The cable was sent to SHAEF Forward.

Treaty of Algiers, June 30 and July 3, 1815. Available at http://www.yale.edu/lawweb/avalon/diplomacy/barbary/bar1815t.htm The treaty was signed between the United States of America and His Highness Omar Bashaw, Dey of Algiers, also known as Umar Ben Muhammad.

U.S. Air Force 6004th Air Intelligence Service Squadron. Air Intelligence Information Report (declassified June 5, 1997). "USAF personnel possibly alive in Communist captivity," October 19, 1955.

U.S. Ambassador W. Averell Harriman Urgent Top Secret Cable, March 8, 1945. The cable was a personal message sent to President Franklin Delano Roosevelt.

U.S. Ambassador W. Averell Harriman Cable Number PH-1449, March 14, 1945. The cable was sent to U.S. Secretary of State Edward R. Stettinius Jr.

U.S. Army 9th Army Cable Number KX-21617, May 17, 1945. The cable was sent from the Ninth Army's commanding general to the commanding general SHAEF Forward.

U.S. Department of Defense. Memorandum for Correspondents Number 144-M, June 26, 1995.

U.S. Department of Defense. News Briefing. Reporter questions Speicher case, January 16, 2001.

—. News Briefing. Enemy prisoners of war briefing and interview, April 7, 2003.

U.S. Department of State. Memorandum. "An upcoming meeting with Soviet Foreign Affairs Commissar Molotov," April 19, 1945. The memorandum was sent to the U.S. secretary of state and contained a list of nine points with a brief description of U.S. policy on each point.

U.S. Department of State. International Information Programs. "Iraq must respond to questions about missing pilot," March 25, 2002.

U.S. Department of the Navy Bureau of Medicine and Surgery, Mortuary Affairs Branch. Memorandum. "DNA testing of Desert Storm remains – DS1-256," May 6, 1991.

U.S. House of Representatives Subcommittee on Military Personnel of the House National Security Committee. Statement of Jan Sejna. Washington, D.C.: U.S. House of Representatives, September 17, 1996.

—. Statement of Colonel Phillip Corso (retired), September 17, 1996.

U.S. House of Representatives Task Force on Terrorism and Unconventional Warfare House Republican Research Committee. "Tehran, Baghdad and Damascus: the new Axis pact," August 10, 1992.

U.S. Military Mission Moscow Cable Number M-24784, June 25, 1945. The cable was sent from Gammell and Deane to SHAEF Main for Eisenhower.

U.S. Military Mission Moscow Cable Number S-89942, May 31, 1945. The cable was sent "for Deane" from SHAEF Main signed SCARF (Eisenhower).

U.S. Naval Flight Surgeon's Manual: Third Edition 1991: Chapter 22: Emergency Escape from Aircraft. http://www.vnh.org/FSManual/22/02EscapeSystems.html

U.S. Secretary of State John Foster Dulles. Secret Memorandum (declassified July 30, 1991). "Americans detained in the Soviet Union," July 18, 1955. The memorandum was sent to Chairman of the Presidium of the Supreme Soviet (President of the Soviet Union) Nikita Khrushchev.

U.S. Secretary of War. Annual Report. Washington, D.C.: Office of the Chief of Military History, 1919.

U.S. Senate Armed Services Committee. Statement for the Record. Vice Admiral Thomas R. Wilson, director, Defense Intelligence Agency, "Global threats and challenge through 2015, March 8, 2001.

U.S. Senate Committee on Foreign Relations Republican Staff. *An Examination of U.S. Policy Toward POW/MIAs*. Washington, D.C.: U.S. Senate, May 23, 1991.

U.S. Senate Committee on Judiciary. *Communist treatment of prisoners of war: a historical survey*. Washington, D.C.: U.S. Government Printing Office, 1972.

U.S. Senate Committee Report 5-10. On February 1, 1973, President Richard Nixon sent a secret letter to Vietnamese prime minister Pham Van Dong promising $4.5 billion in postwar reconstruction aid. After Vietnam released the verifiable 591 POWs in a much-publicized ceremony, the money was not rendered. This report expressed the belief that the Vietnamese kept several hundred other POWs after Operation Homecoming as "collateral" – they were needed to insure that the United States would fulfill its promise for postwar aid.

U.S. Senate Concurrent Resolution 124. Lieutenant Commander Michael Scott Speicher, U.S. Navy: Persian Gulf War's First Casualty. 106th Congress, 2nd Session, July 19, 2000, and amendments.

U.S. Senate Select Committee on Intelligence. Committee Press Release. Reports Intelligence Authorization Act for Fiscal Year 2001. Washington, D.C.: U.S. Senate, May 4, 2000.

U.S. Senate Select Committee on Intelligence. Hearing Transcript. Current and Projected National Security Threats to the United States. Washington, D.C.: U.S. Senate, February 2, 2000.

U.S. Senate Select Committee on POW/MIA Affairs. Committee Report. Washington, D.C.: U.S. Senate, January 13, 1993.

U.S. War Department Cable Number 1272 (Military Intelligence). "Russian prisoners arriving in France from Germany," December 17, 1918.

U.S. War Department Cable Number 2045-221 (Military Intelligence), November 26, 1919.

U.S. War Department Telegram Number 221, April 14, 1919. The telegram was from Archangel to Military Intelligence.

Secondary Sources

Adams, Henry. *History of the United States of America during the Administrations of Thomas Jefferson*. New York: Library of America, 1986.

Anton, Frank. *Why Didn't You Get Me Out? A POW's Nightmare in Vietnam*. New York: St. Martin's Paperbacks, 1997.

Barnes, Scott. *BOHICA: A True Account of One Man's Battle to Expose the Most Heinous Cover-up of the Vietnam Saga*. Canton, Ohio: BOHICA Corporation, 1987.

Becker, Ronald F. *Criminal Investigation*. Third edition. Sudbury, Massachusetts: Jones and Bartlett, 2008.

Byrnes, James F. *Speaking Frankly*. New York: Harper & Brothers Publishers, 1947.

Cawthorne, Nigel. *The Bamboo Cage: The True Story of American POWs in Vietnam*. New York: S.P.I. Books, 1994.

Cole, Paul M. *POW/MIA Issues*. Volume I (Korean War). Santa Monica, California: RAND Corporation, 1994. Cole's three-part study was commissioned by the Office of the Secretary of Defense and the Joint Staff (Contract Number MDA903-90-C-0004).

—. *POW/MIA Issues*. Volume 2 (World War II and the early Cold War). Santa Monica, California: RAND Corporation, 1994. This volume covers early Task Force Russia (TFR) research in the former Soviet Union.

—. *POW/MIA Issues*. Volume 3 (Appendixes). Santa Monica, California: RAND Corporation, 1994.

—. *The Sharaskha System: The Link Between Specialized Soviet Prison Camps and American POW/MIAs in Korea*? (Draft) Santa Monica, California: RAND Corporation, 1993.

—. *World War II, Korean War – Early Cold War MIA-POW Issues*. (Draft) Santa Monica, California: RAND Corporation, April 1993.

Commager, Henry Steele, ed. *Documents of American History*. New York Appleton-Century-Crofts, 1973.

Copp, DeWitt S. *Incident at Boris Gleb: The Tragedy of Newcomb Mott*. New York: Doubleday & Company, 1968.

Denton, Jeremiah A. Jr. *When Hell Was in Session*. Mobile, Alabama: Traditional Press, 1982.

Gardella, Lawrence. *Sing a Song to Jenny Next*. New York: Dutton, 1981.

Hendon, William M. and Elizabeth Stewart. An Enormous Crime: The Definitive Account of American POWs Abandoned in Southeast Asia. New York: Thomas Dunne Books by St. Martin's Press, 2007.

Herrington, Stuart A. *Peace with Honor? An American Reports on Vietnam 1973-1975*. Novato, California: Presidio Press, 1983.

Hoover, Herbert. *Herbert Hoover: An American Epic*. Volume III (Hoover Institution on War, Revolution and Peace). Chicago: Henry Regnery Company, 1961.

Jensen-Stevenson, Monika and William Stevenson. *Kiss the Boys Goodbye: How the United States Betrayed Its Own POWs in Vietnam*. New York: Dutton, 1990.

Jones, Reginald V. *The Wizard War: British Scientific Intelligence, 1939–1945*. New York: Cowan, McCann & Geoghegan, 1978.

Kennan, George. *Russia and the West Under Lenin and Stalin*. Boston: Little and Brown and Company, 1960.

Kimmerle, Erin H. and Jose Pablo Baraybar. *Skeletal Trauma: Identification of Injuries Resulting from Human Rights Abuse and Armed Conflict*. Boca Raton, London and New York: CRC Press, 2008.

Mann, Edward C., III. *Thunder and Lightning: Desert Storm and the Airpower Debates*. Maxwell Air Force Base, Alabama: Air University Press, 1995.

Moore, Joel R., Harry H. Mead and Lewis E. Johns. *The History of the American Expedition Fighting the Bolsheviki Campaigning in North Russia 1918-1919*. Detroit, Michigan: Polar Bear Publishing Company, 1920.

Nimmo, William F. *Behind a Curtain of Silence: Japanese in Soviet Custody, 1945-1956*. New York: Greenwood Press, 1988.

Noble, John H. *I Was A Slave in Russia*. New York: The Devin-Adair Company, 1958.

Patti, Archimedes L. A. *Why Viet Nam? A Prelude to America's Albatross*. Berkeley, California: University of California Press, 1980.

Pickering, Robert B. and David Bachman. *The Use of Forensic Anthropology*. Boca Raton, Florida: CRC Press, 2009.

Rhodes, Benjamin D. *The Anglo-American Winter War with Russia, 1918-1919: A Diplomatic and Military Tragicomedy*. New York: Greenwood Press, 1988.

Ryan, Chris. *The One That Got Away*. London: Brassey's, 1998.

Santoli, Al. *To Bear Any Burden*. London: Abacus by Sphere Books, 1988.

Schemmer, Benjamin F. *The Raid: The Son Tay Prison Rescue Mission*. New York: Ballantine Books, 2002.

Solzhenitsyn, Aleksandr I. *The Gulag Archipelago 1918-1956: An Experiment in Literary Investigation V-VII*. New York: Harper & Row, Publishers, 1976.

White, William Lindsay. *The Captives of Korea: An Unofficial White Paper on the Treatment of War Prisoners*. New York: Charles Scribner's Sons, 1957.

Yarsinske, Amy Waters. *No One Left Behind: The Lt. Comdr. Michael Scott Speicher Story*. New York: Dutton/NAL, 2002, 2003.

Articles, Oral Histories, Pamphlets, Papers, Reports and Speeches

Afrol News. "Systematic maltreatments revealed in Saharawi camps," September 23, 2007.

Alkass, Kanar et al., "Age estimation in forensic sciences: application of combined aspartic acid racemization and radiocarbon analysis," *Molecular & Cellular Proteomics*, May 1, 2010. http://www.mcponline.org

Allison, Wes, "The lost American," *St. Petersburg Times State*, March 28, 2004.

Amirov, Valeri, "A front far away from the motherland," *Na Strazhe* (Moscow), June 30, 1992.

Amnesty International. Report. "Overview of Morocco, Western Sahara," no date.

Arizona Daily Star. "POWs used in Soviet drug tests, June 21, 1996.

Associated Press. "Ex-Soviets receive list of U.S. missing," January 4, 1992.

—. "Iraqi defectors return to Baghdad," February 20, 1996.

—. "Korean War POWs in Siberia," May 4, 1996.

—. "Navy releases Boorda report; two notes written by admiral are withheld," November 2, 1996.

—. "China returns remains of 10 WWII airmen," January 18, 1997.

—. "Author says evidence is that pilot is alive, prisoner in Iraq," July 14, 2002.

—. "Text of Bush's speech to U.N. on Iraq," September 12, 2002.

—. "Navy changes status of missing pilot," October 11, 2002.

—. "Asylum offered to any Iraqi who delivers American Gulf War POW," October 30, 2002.

—. "Senators press Saddam on Gulf War pilot," January 6, 2003.

—. "Text of the Senate War Resolution," March 20, 2003.

—. "Report: British troops find makeshift morgue in Southern Iraq," April 5, 2003.

—. "Missing '91 pilot's initials found in Baghdad prison," April 23, 2003.

—. "Ex-Iraqi officials key to missing pilot," April 24, 2003.

—. "Investigators yet to prove Speicher was in Iraqi prison cell," August 7, 2003.

—. "Navy board recommends intensified search for pilot missing since 1991," July 13, 2005.

BBC News. "Remains of Saudi pilot found," October 25, 2000. http://news.bbc.co.uk/2/hi/middle_east/990449.stm

BBC Breakfast with Frost. Interview. General Sir Peter de la Billière, commander, Desert Storm British troops and professor Paul Rogers, Bradford University, March 30, 2003.

Beck, William G., "POW definition compared to MIA," POW/MIA E-mail Network, August 20, 1998.

Bennett, Brian, "Notes from Saddam in custody," *Time*, December 14, 2003.

Bezlyudnyy, Sergey Ivanovich, "I taught Saddam's aces to fly," *Komsomolskaya Pravda*, February 23, 1991, in JPRS Report – Soviet Union, JPRS-UMA-91-014, June 5, 1991.

Bohlen, Celestine, "Advice of Stalin: Hold Korean War POWs," *New York Times*, September 25, 1992.

—. "Russians give U.S. more POW documents," *New York Times*, September 5, 1993.

Bostom, Andrew G., "Treatment of POWs," *FrontPageMagazine.com*, March 28, 2003.

Brett, Forrest, "Scott Speicher: once, twice, three times betrayed," *Jacksonville Vibe*, Volume 1, Issue 7, October 2003.

Brooke, James, "Korean War U.S. POWs in Soviet jails," *New York Times*, July 19, 1996.

—. "Decades later, tales of Americans in Soviet jails," *New York Times*, July 19, 1996.

Brownlee, Phillip, "Saddam could be key to finding MIA pilot, Roberts says," *Wichita Eagle*, April 27, 2003.

Bull, Leona C., "Can we get Speicher back?" *Journal of Aerospace and Defense Industry News*, July 22, 2002.

Burns, John F., "Hussein and mobs virtually empty Iraq's prisons," *New York Times*, October 21, 2002.

Burns, Robert, "Memoir reports GIs held in gulags in '50s," Associated Press, February 27, 2000.

—. "Navy considering changing missing pilot's status to MIA-captured," Associated Press, August 14, 2002.

—. "Put missing pilot back on radar, Navy says," Associated Press, July 8, 2005.

Capshaw, Ron, "Evidence suggests Saddam still holds American pilot," *Richmond Times-Dispatch*, July 21, 2002.

Carpenter, P. Mason. Thesis. "Joint operations in the Gulf War: an Allison analysis." School of Advanced Air Power Studies, Air University, Maxwell Air Force Base, June 1994.

Carroll, Diane, "Today's POWs recall those captured in Persian Gulf War," *Kansas City Star*, March 27, 2003.

Casey, Kathryn, "The wings of love," *Ladies' Home Journal*, June 1991.

Centner, Christopher M. "Ignorance is risk: the big lesson from Desert Storm air base attacks," *Airpower Journal*, Volume 6, Number 4, Winter 1992. http://www.airpower.maxwell.af.mil/airchronicles/apj/centner.html

Chol, Kim Myong, "US-DPRK: Time for real non-aggression," *Asia Times*, November 7, 2003.

CNN.com. "Security tight ahead of India-Pakistan summit," July 12, 2001. Available at http://archives.cnn.com/2001/WORLD/asiapcf/south/07/12/ind.pak.summit/index.html

—. "Pentagon considers classifying Gulf War pilot as POW," March 16, 2002.

—. "Is Speicher still alive?" CNN American Morning with Paula Zahn, July 15, 2002. Transcript of Interview.

—. "Senators press Iraq on Gulf War pilot," January 6, 2003.

—. "Report suggests missing pilot alive in Iraq," January 10, 2003.

—. CNN Wolf Blitzer Reports, January 10, 2003. Transcript.

—. CNN Live with Daryn Kagan, April 17, 2003. Transcript of Interview.

Coalition for Justice in Iraq, "Latest censorship news: another voice silenced, May 8, 2000. http://www.oneworld.org/index_oc/news/iraq080500.html

Cockburn, Patrick, "Vengeance is family affair for Saddam," *Independent*, February 26, 1996.

Connell, Michael, "The influence of the Iraq crisis on Iranian warfighting doctrine and strategy," CNA Corporation, Alexandria, Virginia, April 2007.

Coon, Charlie, "EUCOM troops aid airlift of Moroccan ex-POWs," *Stars and Stripes* (European edition), August 20, 2005.

Cordesman, Anthony H., "Desert Fox: key official US and British statements and press conferences," Center for Strategic and International Studies (CSIS) Middle East Studies Program, Washington, D.C., January 31, 1998.

—. "Iraqi military forces ten years after the Gulf War," Center for Strategic and International Studies (CSIS), Washington, D.C., August 2000.

—. Rough working draft. "Iran's Revolutionary Guards, the Al Quds Force, and other intelligence and paramilitary forces," Center for Strategic and International Studies (CSIS), Washington, D.C., August 16, 2007.

Cordner, Stephen, and Helen McKelvie, "Developing standards in international forensic work to identify missing persons," IRRC December 2002, Volume 84, Number 848.

Cotterell, Bill, "Reports show Speicher still alive in Iraq, says Nelson," *Tallahassee Democrat*, April 1, 2003.

Council on Foreign Relations. Backgrounder. "What is the Fedayeen Saddam?" http://www.cfr.org/iraq/iraq-fedayeen-saddam/p7698

Craig, Jeremy, "Ex-POWs fear troops' fate," *Augusta Chronicle*, March 27, 2003.

C-SPAN.org. "No One Left Behind," Barnes and Noble Booksellers, Jacksonville, Florida, July 2002.

Culpeper Star-Exponent. "Left behind," July 22, 2002. Editorial.

Davis, Rachel, "Nelson attacks 'negative leaks' on pilot's fate," *Florida Times-Union*, August 14, 2003.

DeCamp, David, "Crenshaw seeks information on Speicher," *Florida Times-Union*, July 31, 2003.

Dudney, Robert S., "Weighing the evidence on POWs," *Air Force Magazine*, July 1993.

Eisman, Dale, "Iraq offers new talks on missing Navy pilot," *Virginian-Pilot*, April 11, 2002.

—. "Senate demands updates on missing Gulf War pilot," *Virginian-Pilot*, June 27, 2002.

Ensley, Gerald, "Friends on mission to return lost pilot," *Tallahassee Democrat*, September 30, 2002.

Faleh, Waiel, "Mob kills Saddam's defector sons-in-law after they return home," February 24, 1996. http://www.detnews.com/menu/stories/37272.htm

—. "Iraq releases details of search at crash site for missing U.S. pilot," Associated Press, January 15, 2001.

Faramarzi, Scheherezade, "Iraqi military defector plans to return home," Associated Press, February 19, 1996. http://www.newstimes.com/archive96/feb1996/ing.htm

Foreign Press Foundation. "Grossman in Moscow in Iraq talks; 'saving pilot Speicher... ?'," September 29, 2002.

FOXNews.com. "Pentagon may reclassify status of missing Gulf War pilot," August 14, 2002.

—. "Missing Gulf War pilot reclassified as 'missing-captured'," October 11, 2002.

—. The Big Story Weekend with Rita Cosby, March 29, 2003. Media Release.

—. The Big Story with Rita Crosby, March 29, 2003. Transcript of Interview.

—. "U.S. military urgently searching for POWs in Iraq," April 11, 2003.

FOX30 WAWS Jacksonville. "Senator Nelson: Speicher may have been seen alive," March 28, 2003.

Francis, Ryan, "Missing in action," *Jacksonville Magazine*, Volume 18, Number 10, November 2002.

Frey, Jennifer, "Dead or alive? Pilot, husband and father may be in Iraq," *Washington Post*, April 20, 2003.

Galnor, Matt, "Candlelight vigil marks day Speicher went down," *Florida Times-Union*, January 18, 2004.

Gera, Vanessa and Randy Herschaft, "AP exclusive: memos show US hushed up Soviet crime," Associated Press, September 10, 2012. http://www.npr.org/templates/story/story.php?storyId=160883505

Gertz, Bill, "Pentagon asks Iraq about U.S. pilot," *Washington Times*, March 13, 2002.

—. "New reports say Iraq holding U.S. pilot," *Washington Times*, January 10, 2003.

—. "U.S. maintains search for missing 1991 aviator," *Washington Times*, June 25, 2002.

—. "FBI lab probes initials of pilot," *Washington Times*, March 2, 2004.

—. "US general calls Al Qaeda 'Public Enemy No. 1' in Iraq," *Washington Times*, April 27, 2007.

Gertz, Bill and Rowan Scarborough, "Speicher update," *Washington Times*, July 5, 2002.

—. "Inside the Ring – DIA says Speicher alive," *Washington Times*, February 14, 2003.

—. "Team to search for pilot lost since first Gulf War," *Washington Times*, March 22, 2003.

—. "Army bid to locate pilot turns up empty," *Washington Times*, April 21, 2003.

—. "Progress reported in search for Speicher," *Washington Times*, April 25, 2003.

Gibbons, Timothy J., "Speicher's remains found 18 years after crash in Iraq," Jacksonville.com, August 3, 2009. http://jacksonville.com/news/metro/2009-08-03/story/speichers_remains_found_18_years_after_crash_in_iraq

—. "Speicher family still has questions," Jacksonville.com, August 4, 2009. http://jacksonville.com/news/metro/2009-08-04/story/speicher_family_still_has_questions

Gilmore, Gerry J., "Wolfowitz: Iraq knows more about missing U.S. airman," Armed Forces Press Service, January 24, 2003.

Goldich, Robert L., "POWs and MIAs: Status and Accounting Issues," Issue Brief for Congress, Congressional Research Service, Library of Congress, March 12, 2003.

Goldstein, David, "Book asserts that Navy pilot downed in Gulf War is a prisoner in Iraq," *Kansas City Star*, June 26, 2002.

—. "Evidence prompts Navy to change status of Gulf War pilot to 'missing-captured,'" *Kansas City Star*, October 12, 2002.

—. "Senator from Kansas seeks meeting with Iraq on Gulf War pilot," *Kansas City Star*, January 7, 2003.

—. "Special teams look for former KC man shot down in '91 war," *Kansas City Star*, April 9, 2003.

—. "U.S. teams continue hunt for missing pilot from KC," *Kansas City Star*, April 24, 2003.

—. "U.S. will use reward, posters in effort to find downed pilot," *Kansas City Star*, May 29, 2003.

—. "Wanted: Alive," *Kansas City Star*, May 30, 2003.

—. "Report questions Gulf War pilot's fate," *Kansas City Star*, July 17, 2003.

—. "Press Hussein on Speicher case, senator says," *Kansas City Star*, December 16, 2003.

Gordon, Craig, "New status on downed pilot – Navy: No evidence American shot down during Gulf War is dead," *Newsday*, October 12, 2002.

Gotshall, Rich, "Listen to war stories," *Indianapolis Star*, August 11, 2002.

Gulfnews.com. "DNA tests prove identity of Saudi pilot," September 1, 2001. http://gulfnews.com/news/gulf/uac/general/dna-tests-prove-identity-of-saudi-pilot-1.423991

Halawa, Hassan and Borzou Daragahi, "Iraq wolves are big, bad and unafraid," *The Seattle Times*, March 20, 2008.

Halloran, Richard, "Washington talk; U.S. considers the once unthinkable on Korea," *New York Times*, July 13, 1989.

Haynes, Judith, "Missing pilot case subject of book," *Daily Press*, November 3, 2002.

—. "Foreign relations speaker at fall conference," *Virginia Legionnaire*, December 2002.

Heart of Illinois POW/MIA Association. Chapter magazine, May-June 2003.

Hedden, Heather, "Arabic names," *The Indexer*, Volume 25, Number 3, April 2007.

Hedges, Chris, "Iraqi defectors tell of Kuwaitis in secret jail in Baghdad," *New York Times*, November 12, 2001.

Hendren, John, "U.S. wants information from Iraq before talks on missing Navy pilot," *Los Angeles Times*, July 11, 2002.

Hess, Pamela, "Saddam was telling truth in missing Gulf War pilot," Associated Press, November 28, 2009. http://www.huffingtonpost.com/2009/11/29/saddam-was-telling-truth-_n_373004.html

Hiro, Dilip, "Flying the Iraqi skies," *The Nation*, March 15, 1999. http//past.thenation.com/issue/990315/0315hiro.shtml

Homeland Security Newswire. "Identifying disaster victims: looking at teeth to determine victims' age at time of death," May 21, 2010. http://homelandsecuritynewswire.com/identifying-disaster-victims-looking-teeth-determine-victims-age-time-death

INC News Center. "Iraqi defectors tell of Kuwaitis in secret jail in Iraq," November 12, 2001. http://209.50.252.70/p_en/news/archives/00000264.htm

Intel Watch. "Inside the Pentagon - opportunity lost," Volume 19, Number 25, June 19, 2003.

Jelinek, Pauline, "Fate of U.S. pilot in Iraq still unknown," *Kansas City Star*, August 8, 2003.

Jontz, Sandra, "Friends hold D.C. vigil for downed pilot," *Stars and Stripes*, January 19, 2004.

Keenan, Marney Rich, "Story that almost mirrors 'Cast Away' is eerily real," *Detroit News*, March 30, 2002.

Kelley, Matt, "Navy changes status of missing Gulf War pilot to missing-captured," Associated Press, October 11, 2002.

Kerr, Jessie-Lynne, "Attorney wants to quiz Iraqis on Speicher," *Florida Times-Union*, March 4, 2004.

Kiam, Matthew, "Status is…for navy fighter pilots; an air-to-air kill," *New York Times*, November 15, 1998.

Kinsolving, Les, "McClellan queried on Speicher status," *WorldNetDaily.com*, May 15, 2003.

Kopp, Carlo, "Desert Storm – the electronic battle," *Australian Aviation*, June/July/August 1993. http://www.saunalahti.fi/~fta/storm-01.htm

Kornblut, Anne E. and Robert Schlesinger, "U.S. revisits Gulf War pilot's case," *Boston Globe*, November 11, 2002.

Kumar, Palash, "Families of missing Indian 'POWs' head to Pakistan," Reuters, June 1, 2007.

Las Vegas Review-Journal. "Missing pilot," March 13, 2002. Editorial.

Laurant, Darrell, "Author attempts to bring soldier back from 'dead'," *Lynchburg News and Daily Advance*, April 10, 2003.

Lawrence Livermore National Laboratory Public Affairs. "Putting teeth into forensic science," https://www.llnl.gov/news/newsreleases/2010/NR-10-05-07.html

Lehmert, Amanda, "Cape-based soldiers train to survive capture by enemy," *Cape Cod Times*, March 28, 2003.

LeBoutillier, John, "An American Gulf War pilot is alive in Baghdad, part 4," *The Idler* (www.the-idler.com), March 29, 2002.

—. "Two Scotts," NewsMax.com, April 25, 2003.

—. "Speicher, Saddam and WMD: Together?" NewsMax.com, June 3, 2003.

Lewis, Mark F., "Could he still be alive?" *Tampa Tribune*, July 21, 2002.

Life. "MIA: 25 compelling cases from Vietnam," November 1987.

London Daily Telegraph. "Beating Saddam will be no cakewalk," March 22, 2002.

—.U.S. hardliners want answers from Iraq on Gulf War pilot," August 18, 2002.

Lumpkin, John J., "Saddam denies having prohibited weapons," *Kansas City Star*, December 15, 2003.

—. "Investigators may have found clue from Gulf War U.S. pilot," *Virginian-Pilot*, April 24, 2003.

Lytle, Tamara, "Bush warns of 'unique' threat," *Orlando Sentinel*, October 8, 2002.

MacKenzie, Ross, "Random walk: Coulter, SpecOps, Speicher, Mainliners, Sacagawea, etc.," *Richmond Times-Dispatch*, September 19, 2002.

Mahnaimi, Uzi and Michael Smith, "Britons kidnapped in Iraq are 'held by Iran,'" Timesonline.com, April 27, 2008. http://www.timesonline.co.uk/tol/news/world/iraq/article3822830.ece

Maier, Timothy W., "Forgotten flier," *Insight Magazine*, May 27, 2002.

—. "Scott Speicher left in Iraq to save face?" WorldNetDaily.com, May 14, 2003.

—. "'Secret' report adds to mystery," *Insight Magazine*, September 3, 2003.

Mandeville, Laure, "Russia's ambiguities complicate the game with Teheran," *Le Figaro*, September 25, 2007.

McCaslin, John, "Inside the Beltway – Remembering Scott," *Washington Times*, January 13, 2004.

McDowell, Patrick, "Freed U.S. POWs say were treated roughly," *Washington Post*, April 13, 2003.

McElhatton, Jim, "Secret files missing at National Archives," *Washington Times*, May 1, 2012.

McGirk, Jan, "Royal falconers in search of bustards clash with tribesmen," *The Independent*, November 17, 2003.

McKinzie, Richard D. and Theodore A. Wilson. Oral history interview with W. Averell Harriman, Washington, D.C., 1971. Interview provided by the Harry S. Truman Library Institute for National and Security Studies. Available via http://www.trumanlibrary.org/oralhist/harriman.htm

Miami-Herald. "Book describes errors, bureaucratic bungling," October 27, 2002.

Michel, Christopher, "Leave no one behind: Are we doing enough to free Captain Scott Speicher," *Military.com*, November 4, 2002.

Miller, Mark Crispin, "Death of a fighter pilot," *New York Times*, September 15, 1992.

MSNBC and NBC News. "Clues to U.S. pilot reportedly found," http://www.msnbc.com, July 11, 2003.

Musawi, Nabil, "The plan for liberation," Guardian Unlimited, December 18, 1998. http://www.guardian.co.uk/Iraq/Story/0,2763,210012,00.html

Nadler, Gerald, "U.S. says Iraq is stonewalling on fate of pilot from Gulf War," Associated Press, August 22, 2002.

National Alliance of Families. *Bits 'N' Pieces*, July 12, 2003.

—. September 12, 2003.

National Gulf War Resource Center. "Search for pilot given priority," March 20, 2002.

NBC News. "U.S. mulls POW status for pilot lost in Iraq," August 15, 2002.

Nelan, Bruce W., "Lost prisoners of war: 'Sold down the river'? *Time*, September 30, 1996.

New York Times. "Captives release repeatedly sought," April 18, 1921.

—. "The other Russians," January 5, 1954.

—. "Vietnam rejects POW document," September 10, 1993.

—. "World news briefs; North Korea denies holding U.S. prisoners," June 30, 1996.

—. "Navy still thinks Gulf War pilot captured," March 2, 2004.

News4Jax.com. "Author: Evidence shows pilot is alive, prisoner in Iraq," July 14, 2002.

—. "Newspaper: Scott Speicher sighted in Baghdad," March 24, 2003.

O'Kane, Maggie, "All our inquiries pointed to Iran's sole role in the abductions," *The Guardian*, December 31, 2009. http://www.guardian.co.uk/world/2009/dec/31/guardian-films-irans-role-abductions

OrlandoSentinel.com. "Serving in death," August 4, 2009. Editorial. http://www.orlandosentinel.com/news/opinion/orl-edped-speicher-legacy-080309080409aug04,0,715008.story

Otterman, Sharon. Backgrounder. "Iraq: the role of tribes," Council on Foreign Relations, November 14, 2003.

Otto, Steve, "Remembering another loss and wondering," *Tampa Tribune*, October 16, 2002.

Phucas, Keith, "Special operations veteran: Worst ahead," *Philadelphia Times Herald*, April 6, 2003.

—. "Experts speculate about Iraqi president's fate," *Philadelphia Times Herald*, April 14, 2003.

Pinkham, Paul, "Speicher case draws new focus, passion," *Florida Times-Union*, April 28, 2002.

—. "Speicher case draws notice from Jackson camp," *Florida Times-Union*, June 20, 2002.

—. "Don't give up on Speicher, expert says," *Florida Times-Union*, August 2, 2002.

—. "Move could elicit data on Speicher," *Florida Times-Union*, August 15, 2002.

—. "Speicher Bill offers incentive to help POWs," *Florida Times-Union*, October 31, 2002.

—. "Lawyer, Iraqis talk of Speicher," *Florida Times-Union*, December 5, 2002.

—. "New strategies aimed at finding missing pilot," *Florida Times-Union*, December 6, 2002.

—. "Speicher case plan hinted," *Florida Times-Union*, December 7, 2002.

—. "Senator Nelson to head to Middle East on Speicher mission," *Florida Times-Union*, January 17, 2003.

—. "Hair in Iraqi jail not Speicher's," *Florida Times-Union*, August 9, 2003.

Pinkham, Paul and Rachel Davis, "Speicher book sparks disputes," *Florida Times-Union*, July 17, 2002.

Pollack, Andrew, "DNA evidence can be fabricated, scientists show," *New York Times*, August 18, 2009.

Price, Joyce Howard, "U.S. search intensifies for pilot in 1991 war," *Washington Times*, April 21, 2003.

Reuters. "Jordan rebuffs Iraqi effort to regain defectors," August 11, 1995.

—. "DNA tests prove identity of Saudi pilot," September 1, 2001. http://gulfnews.com/news/gulf/uae/general/dna-tests-prove-identity-of-saudi-pilot-1.423991

—. "U.S. lists pilot as missing/captured in Iraq," October 11, 2002.

—. "Missing U.S. pilot's initials said seen in Iraq jail," April 23, 2003.

Richards, David R., "Downed Desert Storm pilot was left behind by military," *Indianapolis Star* (www.Indystar.com), August 17, 2002.

Risen, James, "U.S. officers to search for pilot from 1991 war," *New York Times*, April 7, 2003.

Rodriguez, Alex, "Secrecy stalls search for Cold War MIAs," *New York Times*, October 3, 2007.

Rosenberg, Carol, "Dead or alive? New cause for hope for navy pilot highlights a painful Gulf War legacy," *Miami Herald*, October 27, 2002.

Sadik, A., and D. Zampini, "Tretij Den' (i posledujuschie...)"["The Third Day (and beyond...)""] *Aviacija i vremja (Aviation and Time)* No. 6 (2005).

Scarborough, Rowan, "Senator asks navy for report on pilot," *Washington Times*, July 17, 2003.

Schanberg, Sydney H., "Senator goes missing: where are the soldiers? The MIA-POW issue the press never asks McCain about," *Village Voice*, June 7, 2005.

Schippert, Steve, "Qods Force, Karbala and the language of war: U.S. soldiers executed after Karbala abduction: Chizari's revenge and Suleimani's test?" ThreatsWatch.org, January 29, 2007. http://analysis.threatswatch.org/2007/01/qods-force-karbala-and-the-lan/

Sciolino, Elaine, "Aide resigns in dispute about Vietnam MIAs," *New York Times*, May 22, 1991. http://www.nytimes.com/1991/05/22/world/aide-resigns-in-dispute-about-vietnam-s-mia-s.html

Shaw, Gwyneth K., "Saddam denies knowing of missing Navy pilot," *Orlando Sentinel*, December 16, 2003.

Shelley, David, "Leave no one behind? Don't bet on it," *Jacksonville Daily News*, September 1, 2002.

Shenon, Philip, "Pentagon analyst insists North Korea is still holding POWs," *New York Times*, June 21, 1996.

Sherwell, Philip, "For the desert's forgotten prisoners of war, home is a mirage," *The Age*, February 15, 2001. http://www.theage.com.au/

Shirk, Charlene, "Inside the Speicher mystery," First Coast News, Jacksonville, Florida, February 6, 2004. http://www.firstcoastnews.com

Shultz, John, "Friends fear for safety of Navy pilot missing since '91 conflict," *Kansas City Star*, March 20, 2003.

Smith, Michael, "Friendly fire threat to Gulf troops," *London Daily Telegraph*, January 6, 2003.

Smith, Wes, "Gulf War pilot listed as 'captured,'" *Orlando Sentinel*, October 12, 2002.

—. "Evidence grows that pilot lives, family says," *Orlando Sentinel*, July 14, 2002.

—. "U.S. forces hunt for pilot from '91 war," *Orlando Sentinel*, March 29, 2003.

Smolowe, Jill, "Prisoners of war: Iraq's horror picture show," *Time.com*, February 4, 1991.

Spangler, Jessica C., Jodi A. Irwin, et al., "The intersection of genetic identity: the application of multiple marker systems to establish identity 50 years after death," 17th International Symposium on Human Identification, sponsored by Promega Corporation, Nashville, Tennessee, October 9-12, 2006.

Spanogle, Robert W., "'No One Left Behind' – Legionnaires must help solve the mystery of navy lt. comdr. Scott Speicher, *American Legion Dispatch*, Volume 12, Issue 3, September 27, 2002.

Stafford, Margaret, "Cheney talks about Iraq at congressional fund-raiser," *Topeka Capital-Journal*, September 23, 2002.

Stanglin, Douglas and Peter Cary, "Korea: An old war's dark new secrets," *U.S. News & World Report*, September 23, 1996.

Sullivan, Ellen, "If these bones could speak: identifying skeletal remains," *UAB Magazine*, Volume 18, Number 4, Fall 1998. http://main.uab.edu/show.asp?durki=45647

Sun-News of the Northland. "Little thoughts on eternal wisdom," October 9, 2002.

Suprynowicz, Vin, "Is missing Gulf War pilot Michael Scott Speicher alive?" *Federal Observer*, Volume 2, Number 241, August 30, 2002.

—. "A ruthless transformation," *Las Vegas Review-Journal*, July 21, 2002.

Taipei Times. "'Forgotten' POWs focus of Korean talks," August 24, 2005.

Taft, William Howard, et al. *UMCA Service with Fighting Men*. New York: Associated Press, 1922.

Taylor, Kate, "Saddam amnesty sparks Baghdad protest," Slate.com, October 23, 2002.

Tersigni, Maria Teresa A., "Frozen human bone: a microscopic investigation," *Journal of Forensic Science*, January 2007, Volume 52, Number 1.

Theodoulou, Michael, "Critics spotlight Iraq's secret prisons," *Christian Science Monitor*," November 4, 2002.

Thomas, Gordon, "Snatching top gun – Michael Scott Speicher from his twelve year incarceration as Saddam's prisoner," *Globe-Intel*, April 4, 2003.

Thomas, Judy, "The disappearance of Scott Speicher; fate of downed pilot still clouded in mystery," *Kansas City Star*, January 27, 2001.

Thompson, Elizabeth M., "War prisoner repatriation," Editorial Research Report Number 21, Washington, D.C., December 3, 1952.

Thompson, Mark, "Pentagon: we don't call them POWs anymore," *Time U.S.*, May 17, 2012. http://nation.time.com/2012/05/17/pentagon-we-dont-call-them-pows-anymore/

Tillman, Barrett, "What happened to Harley Hall," *The Hook*, Summer 1999. http://tailhook.org/HallSu99.htm

Tsoi, Nathan, "Behind the lines: No One Left Behind," www.militarylifestyle.com, September 19, 2002.

Usborne, David, "Iraq accused of hiding truth about missing U.S. pilot," *Independent* of United Kingdom, August 23, 2002.

Valley Morning Star. "MIA pilot's shadow lingers over Iraq," October 29, 2002. Editorial.

Ventimiglia, Jack "Miles", "No one left behind? What about Speicher?" *Sun-News of Northland*, September 25, 2002.

—. "Speicher status changes: now presumed captured," *Sun-News of Northland*, October 16, 2002.

Voice of America. "Bring Them Home Alive Act," September 3, 2002. Transcript of Interview.

Wadley, Carma, "Coming home: decades after going MIA during Korean War, a Utah soldier will finally be laid to rest," *Salt Lake City Deseret News*, April 17, 2011.

Wainwright, Loudon, "When Johnny comes marching home again – or doesn't," *Life*, November 10, 1972.

Wall Street Journal. "They were soldiers," March 8, 2002.

Warrington, Dick, "Put on gloves, use gloves, change gloves," Forensic Magazine, published online June 25, 2010 http://www.forensicmag.com/tip/put-gloves-use-gloves-change-gloves

Washington Times. "Navy pilot in Iraq?," October 16, 2002. Editorial.

—. "DNA doesn't match missing Gulf War pilot's," August 9, 2003.

Weiner, Tim, "U.S. at least breaks the ice with North Korea on MIAs," *New York Times*, January 15, 1996.

—. "Naïveté at the CIA: Every nation's just another U.S., *New York Times*, June 7, 1998.

Wolf, Jim, "U.S. lists pilot as missing/captured in Iraq," Reuters, October 11, 2002.

Word, Ron, "Author claims pilot shot down in Iraq could be prisoner," *St. Louis Post-Dispatch*, September 29, 2002.

—. "U.S. resumes search for missing Florida pilot," *Miami Herald*, January 12, 2004.

—. "Speicher mystery remains priority in Iraq – Searchers return to his crash site in hunt for clues," *Florida Times-Union*, January 12, 2004.

—. "Crews return to Iraqi desert to search for Navy pilot," *Virginian-Pilot*, January 12, 2004.

—. "Further tests on body of navy pilot from Gulf War," *Gaea Times*, August 3, 2009. http://news.gaeatimes.com/navy-awaiting-dna-results-on-body-identified-as-gulf-wars-first-casualty-129525/

WVEC-TV. "POW rescue expert believes U.S. in good position to rescue personnel," March 24, 2003.

—. "Hostage taking is generally ineffective, expert says," April 13, 2004.

Yaphe, Judith S., "Tribalism in Iraq, the old and new," *Middle East Policy*, June 1, 2000.

Yarsinske, Amy Waters and Lon Wagner, "Dead or Alive?" *Virginian-Pilot*, December 30, 2001-January 4, 2002. Six-part feature, front page:

—. "A pilot is lost," *Virginian-Pilot*, December 30, 2001.

—. "Speicher declared dead," *Virginian-Pilot*, December 31, 2001.

—. "New evidence emerges," *Virginian-Pilot*, January 1, 2002.

—. "The search begins," *Virginian-Pilot*, January 2, 2002.

—. "Rumors raise questions," *Virginian-Pilot*, January 3, 2002.

—. "Is he alive?" *Virginian-Pilot*, January 4, 2002.

Zaloga, Steven J., "The Russian in MiG Alley," *Air Force Magazine*, Volume 74, Number 2, February 1991.

ABOVE – Scott Speicher (right) was five or six years old when this picture was taken, recalled his childhood friend Kenny Boschert (left). Courtesy of Ken S. Boschert.

BELOW – Scott Speicher is shown here in his Nathan Bedford Forrest High School yearbook. Speicher graduated from the Jacksonville, Florida high school in 1975. Photograph by Steve Earley/*Virginian-Pilot*.

This photograph of the Sunliner officers was taken in the winter of 1990 on the deck of the USS *Saratoga* (CV-60); a squadron F/A-18 is the backdrop. Included in the picture (front row, left to right) Tony "Bano" Albano, Mark "MRT" Fox, Bill "Maggot" McKee, Michael "Spock" Anderson, Scott "Spike" Speicher, Steve "Ammo" Minnis, (standing, left to right) are Donald Bodin, James Newcom, Marc Scaccia, Eduardo Callao, James Ellis, Michael Meyers, Nicholas "Mongo" Mongillo, Christopher Adams, Thomas Hoffman, Barry "Skull" Hull, Robert King, Douglas "Coop" Cooper, Craig "Bert" Bertolett, Conrad "Banker" Caldwell, Philip "Chauncey" Gardner, Robert Wildermuth, Christopher Colon, and David Harrod. Photograph courtesy of Craig R. Bertolett.

LEFT – Sunliner officers had a "cheesy mustache contest" during the deployment. Participants, shown here, included (sitting/kneeling, left to right) Conrad "Banker" Caldwell, David Harrod and Eduardo Callao, and (standing, left to right) Craig "Bert" Bertolett, Michael Meyers, Christopher Adams, Donald Bodin, Marc Scaccia, Barry "Skull" Hull, and Scott "Spike" Speicher. The picture was taken in September 1990. Photograph courtesy of Craig R. Bertolett.

RIGHT – Commander Mike "Spock" Anderson, the Sunliners' commanding officer, and Commander Bill "Maggot" McKee, the Sunliners' executive officer, were photographed on the deck of the *Saratoga* on March 11, 1991, after Operation Desert Storm was officially over, and during the ship's Suez transit. Photograph by and courtesy of Craig R. Bertolett.

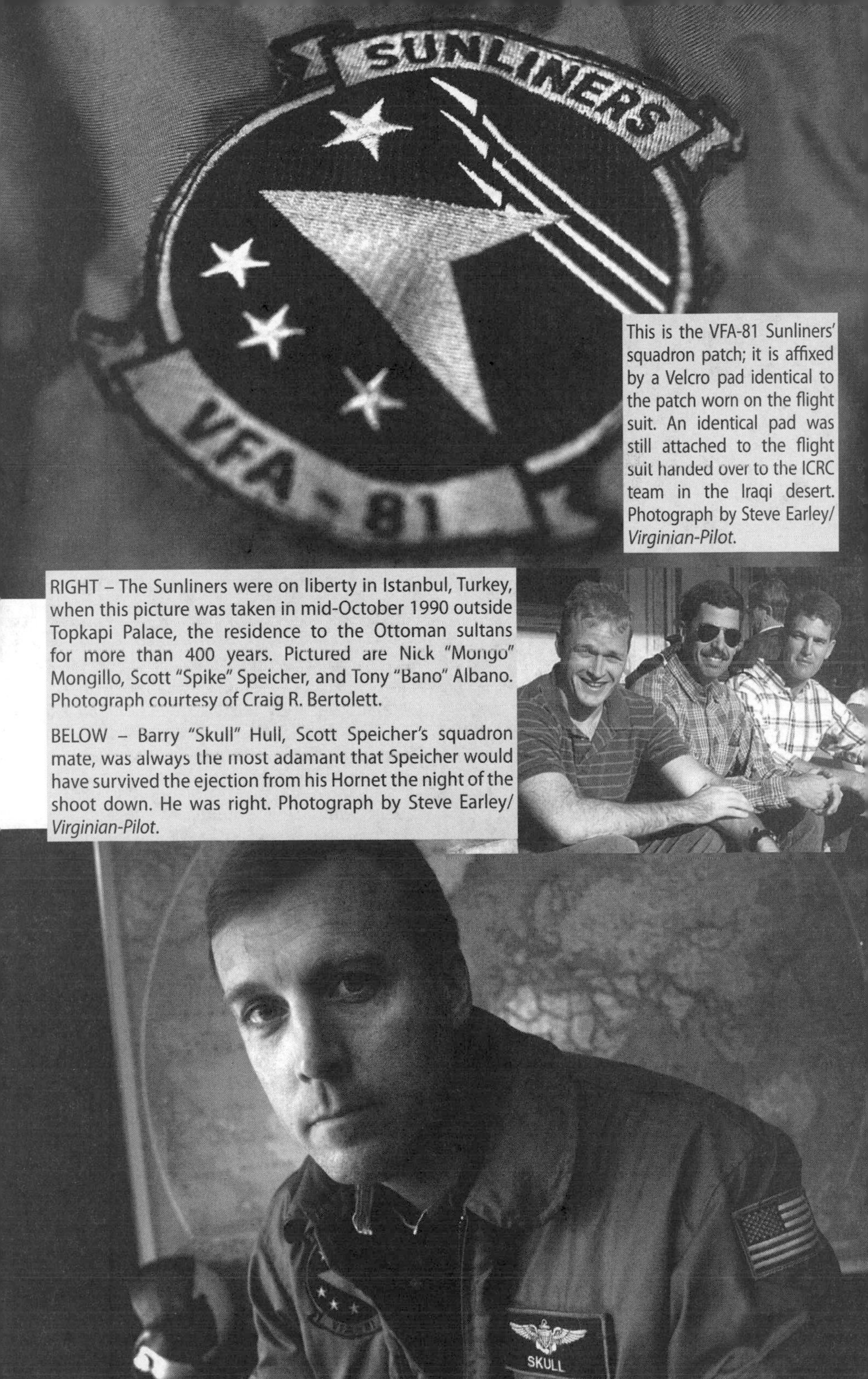

This is the VFA-81 Sunliners' squadron patch; it is affixed by a Velcro pad identical to the patch worn on the flight suit. An identical pad was still attached to the flight suit handed over to the ICRC team in the Iraqi desert. Photograph by Steve Earley/ *Virginian-Pilot*.

RIGHT – The Sunliners were on liberty in Istanbul, Turkey, when this picture was taken in mid-October 1990 outside Topkapi Palace, the residence to the Ottoman sultans for more than 400 years. Pictured are Nick "Mongo" Mongillo, Scott "Spike" Speicher, and Tony "Bano" Albano. Photograph courtesy of Craig R. Bertolett.

BELOW – Barry "Skull" Hull, Scott Speicher's squadron mate, was always the most adamant that Speicher would have survived the ejection from his Hornet the night of the shoot down. He was right. Photograph by Steve Earley/ *Virginian-Pilot*.

ABOVE – This was the Sunliners' lineup for the first airstrike of Operation Desert Storm. Changes were subsequently made to what aircraft each pilot flew on the mission. Speicher flew AA403. Photograph by Steve Earley/Virginian-Pilot.

LEFT – Tim Connolly, who worked on Speicher's case from inside the Pentagon, was never satisfied with the official version of what happened; he probed deeper. Photograph by Steve Earley/ Virginian-Pilot.

BELOW – Members of the ICRC Promise Kept team sift carefully through the remains of Speicher's F/A-18C Hornet "to find his remains" or evidence of what happened to him. They are wearing face masks to shield them from Boron fibers contained in the jet's wreckage. A flight suit was handed over to the team near this site. Photograph courtesy of the Department of Defense.

ABOVE – Pieces of wreckage were on the desert floor and easily recognizable, including the jet's 20-millimeter cannon, foreground, that was mounted in the nose of the jet. Photograph courtesy of the Department of Defense.

BELOW LEFT – The ICRC Promise Kept team found Speicher's canopy after it had been stood on end, near a rise in the terrain. The Bedouins had put it there as a landmark. Photograph courtesy of the Department of Defense.

BELOW RIGHT – The starboard engine of Speicher's Hornet was photographed by investigator Mike Buran. Photograph courtesy of the Department of Defense.

60119055 - S-BG-WP

Q1 CH

60119055 S BG WP

Q1

JJE

ABOVE – Shown here is the flight suit handed over to the ICRC Promise Kept team and evaluated by the FBI. Photograph courtesy of the FBI.

LEFT – This is the left arm cuff of the flight suit. The Bureau found a moderate presence of dark brown stains from the cuff to the Velcro closure. Photograph courtesy of the FBI.

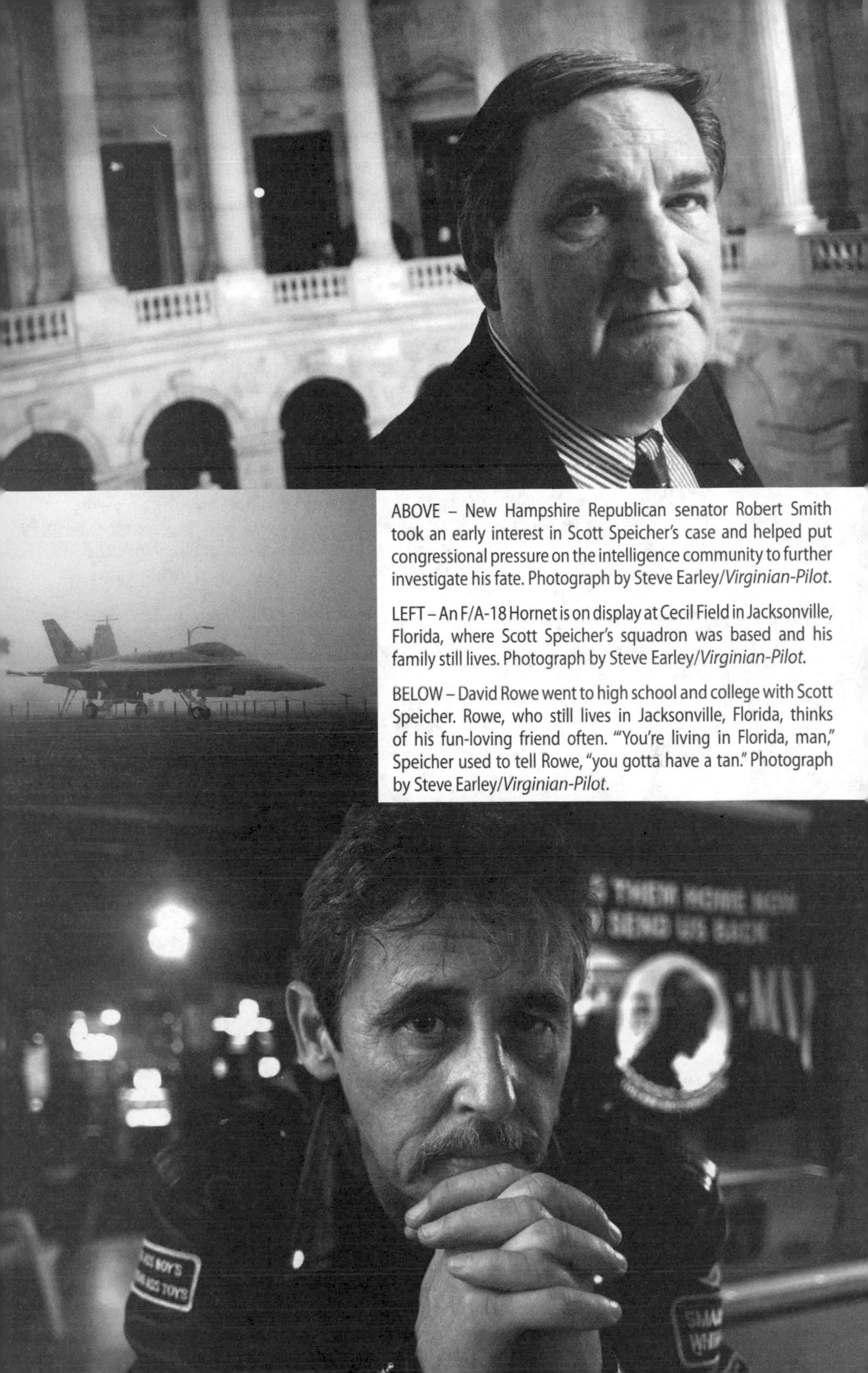

ABOVE – New Hampshire Republican senator Robert Smith took an early interest in Scott Speicher's case and helped put congressional pressure on the intelligence community to further investigate his fate. Photograph by Steve Earley/*Virginian-Pilot*.

LEFT – An F/A-18 Hornet is on display at Cecil Field in Jacksonville, Florida, where Scott Speicher's squadron was based and his family still lives. Photograph by Steve Earley/*Virginian-Pilot*.

BELOW – David Rowe went to high school and college with Scott Speicher. Rowe, who still lives in Jacksonville, Florida, thinks of his fun-loving friend often. "'You're living in Florida, man,' Speicher used to tell Rowe, "you gotta have a tan." Photograph by Steve Earley/*Virginian-Pilot*.

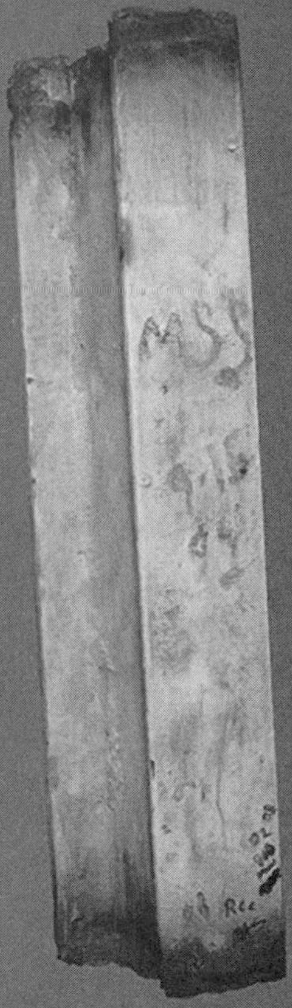

ABOVE – Florida senator Bill Nelson was just as incredulous by DPMO's statement about the prison wall writing as the membership of the National Alliance of Families who'd heard it. He was photographed on July 7, 2003 – two weeks after Kull's claim that the wall section was already in the United States – examining undisturbed Hakmiyah cell 46 and the section of wall with Speicher's initials, MSS, along with a smaller H, and another set of initials, MJM, surrounded by a circle carved into the wall. The MJM was interpreted by those who'd known the pilot best as Scott's expression of his family – wife Joanne and children Meghan and Michael Jr. Nelson took rubbings of Speicher's initials and also a smaller letter H collocated with the second S on the wall, and displayed them for the media. This event and photographs posted on the senator's Web site directly contradict information presented by DPMO representatives weeks earlier at the National Alliance of Families forum.

LEFT – The initials MSS and the date – 9-15-94 – were scratched into an I-beam in an old maintenance shack on Al Sahra Airfield near Tikrit. The airfield was later named Camp Speicher. The find was reported by an army staff sergeant. The FBI cut it down and sent it back to the Smithsonian for testing. Photograph courtesy of the Defense Intelligence Agency.

BELOW – Closeup of the I-beam. Photograph courtesy of the Defense Intelligence Agency.

ABOVE – At Scott Speicher's high school in Jacksonville, Florida, he's prominently recognized and remembered on an Operation Desert Storm honor roll. Photograph by Steve Earley/*Virginian-Pilot*.

BELOW – When this photograph was provided by a confidential source, it was clear that it was Scott Speicher and it was clear that it was taken just before his death. The source's photograph wasn't the only one of Speicher in captivity.

ABOVE – U.S. Marines from Task Force Personnel Recovery, Multi-National Force-West conduct recovery efforts in the vicinity of Scott Speicher's crash site in Anbar Province, Iraq, on July 23, 2009. Photograph courtesy of the United States Marine Corps.

BELOW – Speicher's partial remains were recovered by Marines from Task Force Personnel Recovery, Multi-National Force-West in Anbar province, Iraq, on July 28, 2009. Photograph courtesy of the United States Marine Corps.

ABOVE – Marines from Task Force Personnel Recovery, Multi-National Force-West were photographed here on July 28, 2009, the same day portions of Speicher's skull and jawbone were recovered by the search team. Photograph courtesy of the United States Marine Corps.

BELOW – Scott Speicher's family members stand by as his remains arrive at Naval Air Station Jacksonville on August 13, 2009. Albert "Buddy" Harris is second from left; Joanne Speicher-Harris is standing right of Harris. Scott Speicher's two children, Meghan and Michael Jr., are standing fifth and sixth from the left. Courtesy of Chief Mass Communications Specialist Anthony C. Casullo/Official United States Navy Photograph.

ABOVE – Visitors pay their respects to Scott Speicher at All Saints Chapel at Naval Station Jacksonville in Jacksonville, Florida, on August 13, 2009. Courtesy of Chief Mass Communications Specialist Anthony C. Casullo/Official United States Navy Photograph.

BELOW – A navy honor guard from Naval Air Station Jacksonville carries the remains of Scott Speicher in front of All Saints Chapel at Naval Station Jacksonville on August 14, 2009, in Jacksonville, Florida. Courtesy of Chief Mass Communications Specialist Anthony C. Casullo/Official United States Navy Photograph.

ABOVE – Mourners line the route of the funeral procession bearing Scott Speicher's remains as it passes in front of Lakeshore Methodist Church in Jacksonville, Florida, on August 14, 2009. Speicher taught Sunday school at the church. Speicher's remains were interred at Jacksonville Memory Gardens in Orange Park, Florida. Courtesy of Chief Mass Communications Specialist Anthony C. Casullo/Official United States Navy Photograph.

BELOW – Scott Speicher's centograph at Arlington National Cemetery was removed after his partial remains were recovered in Anbar Province, Iraq, on July 28, 2009. Photograph by Steve Earley/Virginian-Pilot.

Index

A

B

C

D

E

F

G

H

I

J

K

L

M

N

O

P

Q

R

S

T

U

V